P9-CRI-141

THE FUNDAMENTALS

THE FUNDAMENTALS

The Famous Sourcebook Of Foundational Biblical Truths

- Edited by R. A. Torrey and Others
- Updated by Charles L. Feinberg and Others
- Biographical Introductions
  by Warren W. Wiersbe

KREGEL PUBLICATIONS
Grand Rapids, Michigan 49501

The Fundamentals: The Famous Sourcebook of Foundational Biblical Truths; edited by R. A. Torrey; updated by Charles L. Feinberg; biographical introductions by Warren W. Wiersbe. © 1958, 1990 by Biola University. Published by Kregel Publications, a division of Kregel, Inc., P. O. Box 2607, Grand Rapids, MI 49501. All rights reserved. First Kregel Publications edition: 1958.

Library of Congress Cataloging in Publication Data

The Fundamentals: the famous sourcebook of foundational
   biblical truths / edited by R. A. Torrey; updated by
   Charles L. Feinberg; biographical introductions by
   Warren W. Wiersbe.
      p.   cm.

   Updated edition of: *Fundamentals for Today*. 1958.
   1. Fundamentalism. 2. Theology, Doctrinal. I. Torrey,
R. A. (Reuben Archer), 1856-1928. II. Feinberg, Charles
Lee. III. Wiersbe, Warren W. IV. Fundamentals for today.

BT82.2.F87   1990   230'.046—dc20   90-30214
                                                       CIP
ISBN   0-8254-2633-2

      5 6 7 8 9 Printing/Year 95 94 93 92 91

Contents

6 *Contents*

Preface

In 1909 God moved two Christian laymen, Lyman and Milton Stewart, to underwrite the expenses of issuing a series of twelve volumes that would set forth the fundamentals of the Christian faith. With a desire to combat the inroads of liberalism, these were sent free to ministers of the gospel, missionaries, Sunday school superintendents, and others engaged in aggressive Christian work throughout the English speaking world.

The oversight of the selection of articles to be included in *The Fundamentals* was given to a special committee of men who were known to be sound in the faith. Leadership of this committee included such stalwarts as A. C. Dixon and R. A. Torrey.

Later, in 1917, under the sponsorship of the Bible Institute of Los Angeles (now Biola University), a four-volume edition was issued which included all but a few of the original articles.

To celebrate its Jubilee Year in 1958, the Bible Institute, in cooperation with Kregel Publications, sponsored the release of a new edition of *The Fundamentals*. Under the general oversight of Dr. Charles L. Feinberg, a committee of professors from Talbot Theological Seminary selected the most theologically and culturally relevant articles from the original *Fundamentals*, and carefully updated them for the contemporary reader. This collection was published as *The Fundamentals for Today* and went through several printings.

Recognizing that this classic collection of foundational biblical truths is as relevant as when first published, Kregel Publications now releases this new, one-volume edition of the 1958 collection for which Dr. Warren W. Wiersbe has graciously provided Biographical Introductions and a helpful Foreword.

It is the prayer of all involved that the Author of the Truth supported in these *Fundamentals*—the Lord God Himself—may through these writings bless and edify His people everywhere.

THE PUBLISHERS

Foreword

Edited by A. C. Dixon, who was later assisted by Louis Meyer and R. A. Torrey, the twelve volumes comprising *The Fundamentals* were published from 1910 to 1915 and sent free to pastors, missionaries, and other Christian workers. Financed by wealthy California oil magnates, the brothers Lyman and Milton Stewart, three million individual volumes were distributed in the English-speaking world.

At that time in history, Fundamentalism was becoming a force to reckon with, thanks to effective preachers, popular Bible conferences and publications that taught "the fundamentals" and also exposed the growing apostasy of that day. The *Scofield Reference Bible* was published in 1909 and became the standard text for Bible students of the dispensational school. It was a time of growth and challenge.

From May 25 to June 1, 1919, six thousand people met in Philadelphia at "The World Conference on Christian Fundamentals." W. H. Griffith Thomas chaired the Resolutions Committee, and among the fifteen well-known speakers on the program were W. B. Riley, R. A. Torrey, Lewis Sperry Chafer, James M. Gray and William L. Pettingill. Delegates came from 42 states and most of the Canadian provinces, as well as seven foreign countries.

Said W. B. Riley in his first address, "The future will look back to the World Conference on Christian Fundamentals . . . as an event of more historical moment than the nailing up, at Wittenberg, of Martin Luther's ninety-five theses. The hour has struck for the rise of a new Protestantism."

In this day of fragmented fellowships and diluted doctrines, the church must discover again the broad base which the "Fundamentalist Fathers" built and from which they ministered. Our modern pluralistic society makes it easy for us to become so tolerant that we almost cease to have convictions, or so intolerant that we think our special group is the sole custodian of truth. It is good to have *The Fundamentals* back in print again, and I trust that the new generation of Bible students will get acquainted with this galaxy of great leaders and learn from them the essentials of doctrine and practice.

WARREN W. WIERSBE

CANON DYSON HAGUE (1857-1935) was ordained in 1883 after studying the arts and divinity at the University of Toronto. He served as curate at St. James' Cathedral in Toronto and as rector of St. Paul's in Brockville, Ontario, and St. Paul's in Halifax, Nova Scotia. From 1897 to 1901, Hague taught apologetics, liturgics, and homiletics at Wycliffe College in Toronto. His writings include several books on Anglican liturgy.

1

The History of the Higher Criticism

By Canon Dyson Hague, M.A.
RECTOR OF THE MEMORIAL CHURCH, LONDON, ONTARIO
LECTURER IN LITURGICS AND ECCLESIOLOGY,
WYCLIFFE COLLEGE, TORONTO, CANADA

Revised by Charles L. Feinberg, Th.D., Ph.D.

What is the meaning of the term "Higher Criticism"? At the outset it must be explained that the word "higher" is an academic term, used in this connection in a purely special or technical sense. It is used in contrast to "Lower Criticism." Higher criticism means nothing more than the study of the literary structure of the various books of the Bible. Such study is indispensable to ascertain the author, date, circumstances, and purpose of a writing.

Why Is Higher Criticism Identified with Unbelief?

It must be stated that there is a higher criticism which is reverent in tone and scholarly in work. But the work of the higher critic has not always been pursued in a reverent spirit nor in the spirit of scientific and Christian scholarship. In the first place, the leaders of this movement based their theories largely on their own subjective conclusions. They have based their conclusions largely on the very dubious basis of the author's style and supposed literary qualifications. Style is an unsafe basis for the determination of a literary work. Because a man is a philological expert does not insure that he is able to understand the integrity or credibility of a passage of Scripture any more than the beauty or spirit of it. The qualification for the perception of Biblical truth is spiritual insight.

In the second place, higher critical theories have been in the hands of those who go far in the realm of the conjectural. It was Newton who warned that no regard whatever should be paid to the mere conjectures or hypotheses of thinkers. Thirdly, the dominant men of the movement were men with a strong bias against the supernatural. Some of the men who have been the most distinguished in the higher critical movement have been men who have no faith in the God of the Bible, and no faith in either the necessity or the possibility of a personal supernatural revelation. It is not our position that all higher critics were or are anti-supernaturalists, but the dominant figures have been and are. Sadly enough, the higher criticism has become identified with a system of criticism which is based on hypotheses and suppositions which have for their object the repudiation of the traditional theory, and has investigated the origins, forms, styles, and contents, apparently not to confirm the authenticity and credibility and reliability of the Scriptures, but to discredit in most cases their genuineness, to discover discrepancies, and throw doubt on their authority.

The Origin of the Movement

Who were the men whose views have moulded the thinking of the leading writers of the higher critical school today? Three stages in this development are discernible: (1) The French-Dutch; (2) the German; and (3) the British-American. The views which are now accepted as axiomatic seem to have been first hinted at by Carlstadt in 1521. The higher criticism may really be said to have originated with Spinoza, the rationalist Dutch philosopher. In 1670 he came out boldly and impugned the traditional date and Mosaic authorship of the Pentateuch, ascribing the Pentateuch to Ezra or some other late compiler. In 1753 a French physician, Jean Astruc, reputedly a free-thinker of profligate character, set forth for the first time the Jehovistic and Elohistic divisive hypothesis, and opened a new era. He claimed that the use of the two names, Jehovah and Elohim, showed the Book of Genesis was composed of different documents. Astruc may be called the father of the documentary theories. He asserted there are traces of no less than ten or twelve different memoirs in the Book of Genesis. He denied its divine authority, and considered the book to be marred by useless repetitions, disorder, and contradiction.

Eichhorn published in 1780 his work on Old Testament introduction. He further developed the documentary theory of Astruc, and was followed by Vater and later by Hartmann. They ultimately made the Pentateuch a heap of fragments, joined together by an editor or redactor. In 1806 De Wette propounded the view that the Book of Deuteronomy was written in the age of Josiah (II Kings 22:8). Before long Vatke had unreservedly declared the post-Mosaic and post-prophetic origin of the first four books of the Bible. In succession came Bleek, Ewald, Hupfeld, Graf, Kuenen, and Wellhausen with their respective views on the non-Mosaic authorship of the Pentateuch.

After the German stage of criticism came the British-American. Davidson, Robertson Smith, G. A. Smith, Driver, and Briggs followed the trail blazed by the German rationalistic writers. The list is admittedly a very partial one, but these are prominent names in connection with the movement.

The Views of the Critics

Three things can certainly be asserted of nearly all, if not all, of the leaders. They denied the validity of miracle and any miraculous narrative. Miracles were considered legendary or mythical. They denied the reality of prophecy. Prophecy was called conjectures or coincidences, if not imposture. They denied the reality of revelation; they were avowed unbelievers of the supernatural. The religion of the Old Testament was simply a human religion. The formative forces of the higher critical movement, then, were rationalistic forces. Unbelief was the antecedent, not the consequent, of their criticism.

The Crucial Point

According to the faith of the universal Church, the Pentateuch is one consistent, coherent, authentic, and genuine composition, inspired by God, written by Moses some fourteen centuries before Christ. It is, moreover, a portion of the Bible that is of paramount importance, for it is the basic substratum of the whole revelation of God and the introductory section of the Word of God, bearing His authority and given by inspiration through His servant Moses. That is the faith of the Church.

The Critics' Theory

According to the higher critics the Pentateuch consists of four completely diverse documents. They are (1) the Jehovist, (2) the Elohist, (3) the Deuteronomist, and (4) the Priestly Code documents, generally designated as J, E, D, P. These different works were composed at various periods of time from the ninth to the fifth centuries. These documents represent different traditions of the Hebrews, and are at variance in most important matters. They were surely not compiled and written by Moses. In the editorial process no limit apparently is assigned to the work of the redactors. Higher critics conclude that the documents contain three kinds of material: the probably true, the certainly doubtful, and the positively spurious.

A Discredited Old Testament

Not only is the Pentateuch discredited, but the rest of the Old Testament is dealt with in a similar manner. The Psalms are not from the time of David, but from the Maccabean age. Isaiah was written by a number of authors. Daniel was a purely pseudonymous work, written in the second century B.C. in the time of Antiochus Epiphanes.

A Discredited Bible

There can be no doubt that Christ and His apostles accepted the whole of the Old Testament as inspired in every part, from the first chapter of Genesis to the last chapter of Malachi. All was implicitly believed to be the very Word of God himself. And ever since their day the view of the universal Christian Church has been that the Bible is the Word of God. The Bible, according to the critics, can no longer be viewed in this light. It is not the Word in the old sense of that term. It simply *contains* the Word of God, and in many of its parts it is just as uncertain as any other human book. It is not even reliable history. Its records of ordinary history are full of falsifications and blunders.

A Revolutionary Theory

The higher criticism has been in the hands of men who disavow belief in God and Jesus Christ, therefore their theory is truly a revolutionary one. It is a theory of inspiration that completely overthrows the accepted ideas of the Bible and its unquestioned standard of authority and truth. For whatever this so-called divine element is, it appears to be quite consistent with defective argument, incorrect interpretation, if not what the average man would call forgery or falsification. To accept it the Christian will have to readjust completely his ideas of honor and honesty, of falsehood and misrepresentation. Men used to think that forgery was a crime, and falsification a sin. Men used to think that inaccuracy would affect reliability and that proven inconsistencies would imperil credibility. Now it appears that all these may exist, and yet, marvelous to say, faith is not to be destroyed, but placed on a firmer foundation.

If Not Moses, Who?

If Moses did not write the books of Moses, who did? If there were three or four, or six, or nine authorized writers, why not fourteen, or sixteen, or nineteen? And what of the indeterminate number of redactors? Whence came their authority? Moses we know, and Samuel we know, and Daniel we know, but ye anonymous and pseudonymous, who are ye? The Pentateuch with Mosaic authorship, as Scriptural, divinely accredited, is upheld by tradition and scholarship, and appeals to reason. But a mutilated scrapbook of anonymous compilations, with its pre- and post-exilic redactors and redactions, is confusion worse confounded.

No Final Authority

Another serious result of the higher criticism is that it threatens the Christian system of doctrine and the whole fabric of systematic theology. Previously any text from any part of the Bible was accepted as a proof-text for the establishment of any truth of Christian teaching, and a statement from the Bible was considered an end of controversy. But now the higher critics think they have changed all that. They claim that the science of criticism has dispossessed the science of systematic theology.

Not Obscurantists

There are, however, two questions that must be faced by every student of the Bible. The first is this: Is not refusal of the higher critical system mere opposition to light and progress and the position of ignorant alarmists and obscurantists? The desire to receive all the light that the most fearless search for truth by the highest scholarship can yield, is the desire of every believer in the Bible. No really healthy Christian mind can advocate obscurantism. But it is the duty of every Christian to test all things, and to hold fast that which is good. The most ordinary Bible reader is learned enough to know that the investigation of the Book, that claims to be supernatural, by those who are the avowed enemies of all that is supernatural, and the study of subjects that can be understood only by men of humble and contrite heart, by men who are admittedly irreverent in spirit, must certainly be received with caution.

The Scholarship Argument

The second question is also serious: Are we not bound to receive these views when they are advanced, not by rationalists, but by Christians, and not by ordinary Christians, but by men of superior and unchallengeable scholarship? There is a widespread idea especially among younger men that the critics must be followed, because their scholarship settles the questions. This is a great mistake. No expert scholarship can settle questions that require a humble heart, a believing mind, and a reverent spirit, as well as a knowledge of Hebrew and philology; and no scholarship can be relied upon as expert which is manifestly characterized by a biased judgment, a curious lack of knowledge of human nature, and a still more curious deference to the views of men with a prejudice against the supernatural.

There is also a widespread idea among younger men that because scholars are experts in Hebrew that, therefore, their deductions as experts in language must be received. This, too, is a mistake. No scholar in the world ever has or ever will be able to tell the dates of each and every book in the Bible by the style of the Hebrew. And all the scholarship is not on one side. It is not true that the only people who oppose the higher critical views are the ignorant, the prejudiced, and the illiterate. Has rationalism its scholars? So has the orthodox position. And they are not one whit behind those who espouse the modern viewpoint. Shall we stand with the enemies of Scripture truth or with Christ in his view of the Old Testament?

We desire to stand with Christ and his Church. If we have any prejudice, we would rather be prejudiced against rationalism. If we have any bias, it must be against a teaching which unsteadies heart and unsettles faith. Even at the expense of being thought behind the times, we prefer to stand with our Lord and Savior Jesus Christ in receiving the Scriptures as the Word of God, without objection and without a doubt. A little learning, and a little listening to rationalistic theorizers and sympathizers may incline us to uncertainty; but deeper study and deeper research will incline us, as it inclined other scholars, to the profoundest conviction of the authority and authenticity of the Holy Scriptures, and to cry, "Thy word is pure; therefore thy servant loveth it."

GEORGE FREDERICK WRIGHT (1838-1921) graduated from Oberlin Theological Seminary in 1862 and pastored in Bakersfield, VT (1861-1872) and Andover, MA (1872-1881) before returning to Oberlin to teach (1881-1907). Keenly interested in geology and the relationship between science and religion, Wright pioneered an apologetic that was unique in his day. He edited *Bibliotheca Sacra* and published, among others: *The Logic of Christian Evidences* (1880), *Studies in Science and Religion* (1882), *The Divine Authority of the Bible* (1884), a biography of Charles Finney (1891), and his autobiography (1916).

ANDREW C. ROBINSON Ballineen, County Cork, Ireland. (Additional biographical information unavailable).

2

The Authorship of the Pentateuch

"The Mosaic Authorship of the Pentateuch"
By Professor George F. Wright, D.D., LL.D.
Oberlin College, Oberlin, Ohio

"Three Peculiarities of the Pentateuch Incompatible With
the Graf-Wellhausen Theories of Its Composition"
By Andrew C. Robinson, M.A.
Ballineen, County Cork, Ireland

Revised by Charles L. Feinberg, Th.D., Ph.D.

For about a century an influential school of critics has deluged the world with articles and volumes, attempting to prove that the Pentateuch did not originate during the time of Moses, and that most of the laws attributed to him did not come into existence until several centuries after his death, and many of them not till the time of Ezekiel. By these critics the partriarchs are relegated to the realm of myth or dim legend, and the history of the Pentateuch generally is discredited.

I. The Burden of Proof

In approaching the subject it is in place to consider the burden of proof. The Mosaic authorship of the Pentateuch has until very recent times been accepted without question by both Jews and Christians. Such acceptance, coming to us in unbroken line from the earliest times of which we have any information, gives it the support of what is called general consent, which, while perhaps not absolutely conclusive, compels those who would discredit it, to produce incontrovertible opposing evidence. But the evidence which the critics produce in this case is wholly circumstantial, consisting of inferences from a literary analysis of the documents, and from the application of a discredited evolutionary theory concerning the development of human institutions.

II.   FAILURE OF THE ARGUMENT FROM LITERARY ANALYSIS

(a)   *Evidence of Textual Criticism*

It is an instructive commentary on the scholarly pretensions of this whole school of critics that, without adequate examination of the facts, they have based their analysis of the Pentateuch upon the text which is found in our ordinary Hebrew Bibles. While students of the New Testament have expended an immense amount of effort in the comparison of manuscripts, and versions, and quotations to determine the original text, these Old Testament critics have done little in that direction.   This is certainly a most unscholarly proceeding, yet it is admitted to be the fact by higher critics of note.   Now the fact is that while the current Hebrew text, known as the Masoretic, was not established until about the seventh century A.D., we have abundant material with which to compare it, and to carry us back to that current a thousand years nearer the time of the original composition of the books.   There are the Greek translation of the Old Testament known as the Septuagint, the Samaritan Pentateuch, other Greek versions, Syriac renderings, and the Latin Vulgate of Jerome. All this material furnishes ample ground for correcting in minor particulars the current Hebrew text; and this can be done on well established scientific principles which largely eliminate conjectural emendations.

On bringing the light of this evidence to bear upon the subject some remarkable results are brought out, the most important of which relate to the very foundation on which the theories concerning the fragmentary character of the Pentateuch are based.   The most prominent clue to the documentary division is derived from the supposed use by different writers of the two names, Jehovah and Elohim, to designate the deity.   Now the original critical division into documents was made on the supposition that several hundred years after Moses there arose two schools of writers, one of which in Judah used the name Jehovah when speaking of God, and the other in the northern kingdom, Elohim.   So the critics came to designate one set of passages as belonging to the J document and the other to the E document.   These, they supposed, had been cut up and pieced together by a later editor, so as to make the existing continuous narrative.   But when, as frequently occurred, one of these words is found in passages where it is thought the other name should have been used, it is supposed, wholly on theoretical grounds, that a mistake had been made by the editor or redactor, and so with no further ceremony the objection is arbitrarily removed without consulting the direct textual evidence.

These facts, which are now amply verified, utterly destroy the value of the clue which the higher critics have all along ostentatiously put forward to justify their division of the Pentateuch into conflicting E and J documents, and this the critics themselves are now compelled to admit. The answer they give is that the analysis is correct, even if the clue which led to it be false. On further examination in the light of present knowledge, legitimate criticism removes a large number of the alleged difficulties which are put forward by higher critics, and renders of no value many of the supposed clues to the various documents.

(b) *Delusions of Literary Analysis*

But even on the assumption of the practical inerrancy of the Masoretic text the arguments against Mosaic authorship of the Pentateuch drawn from the literary analysis, are seen to be the result of misdirected scholarship, and to be utterly fallacious. The long lists of words adduced as characteristic of the writers to whom the various parts of the Pentateuch are assigned, are readily seen to be occasioned by the different objects aimed at in the portions from which the lists are made. The absurdity of the claims of the higher critics to having established the existence of different documents in the Pentateuch by a literary analysis has been shown by a variety of examples. Professor C. M. Mead, the most influential of the American revisers of the translation of the Old Testament, in order to show the fallacy of their procedure, took the Epistle to the Romans, and arbitrarily divided it into three parts, according as the words "Christ Jesus," "Jesus,'" or "God" were used; and then by analysis showed that the lists of peculiar words characteristic of these three passages were even more remarkable than those drawn up by the destructive critics of the Pentateuch from the leading fragments into which they had divided it. The argument from literary analysis after the methods of these critics would prove the composite character of the Epistle to the Romans, as fully as that of the critics would prove the composite character of the Pentateuch.

III. Misunderstanding Legal Forms and the Sacrificial System

Another source of fallacious reasoning into which the critics have fallen arises from a misunderstanding of the sacrificial system of the Mosaic law. The critics assert that there was no central sanctuary in Palestine until several centuries after its occupation under Joshua, and that at a later period all sacrifices by the people were forbidden except at the central place when offered by the priests, unless it was where there had been a special theophany. But these statements show an entire misunderstanding of the facts. In interpreting Joshua 18:1, Judges 18:31, and I Samuel 2:24, the critics make a most humiliating mistake in repeatedly substituting "sanctuaries" for "altars," assuming that, since there was a plurality of altars in the time of the judges, there was by so much a plurality of sanctuaries. They have completely misunderstood the permission given in Exodus 20:24. The whole place referred to (so ASV) is Palestine, the Holy Land. Sacrifices such as the patriarchs had offered were always permitted to laymen, provided they used only an altar of earth or unhewn stones free from adornments characteristic of heathen altars. But altars of earth, having no connection with a temple of any sort, are not houses of God, and will not become such on being called sanctuaries by critics several thousand years after they have fallen out of use.

But besides the lay sacrifices which were continued from patriarchal times and guarded against perversion, there were other classes of offerings (Num. 28) established by statute. A failure to distinguish clearly between classes of sacrifices has led the critic into endless confusion, and error has arisen from their inability to understand legal terms and principles. The Pentateuch is not mere literature, but it contains a legal code. It is a product of statesmanship consisting of three distinct elements which have always been recognized by lawgivers; namely, the civil, the moral, and the ceremonial. All these strata of the law were naturally and necessarily in existence at the same time.

In putting them as successive strata, with the ceremonial law last, the critics have made an egregious and misleading blunder.

IV. THE POSITIVE EVIDENCE

The Mosaic authorship of the Pentateuch is supported, among other facts, by the following weighty considerations. (1) The Mosaic era was a literary epoch in the world's history when such writings were common. In view of the codes of laws that antedated Moses' day, it would have been strange if such a leader had not produced a code of laws. (2) The Pentateuch so correctly reflects the conditions in Egypt at the period assigned to it, that it is difficult to believe that it was a literary product of a later age. (3) Its representation of life in the wilderness is so accurate, and so many of its laws are adapted only to that life, that it is incredible that literary men a thousand years later should have imagined it. (4) The laws themselves bear unmistakable marks of adaptation to the stage of national development to which they are ascribed. (5) The little use that is made of the sanctions of a future life is evidence of an early date, and of a peculiar divine effort to guard the Israelites against the contamination of Egyptian ideas on the subject. (6) The subordination of the miraculous elements in the Pentateuch to the critical junctures in the nation's development is such as could be obtained only in genuine history. (7) The whole representation conforms to the true law of historical development. Nations do not rise by virtue of inherent resident forces, but through the struggles of great leaders enlightened directly from on high or by contact with others who have already been enlightened.

The defender of the Mosaic authorship of the Pentateuch has no occasion to quail in the presence of the critics who deny that authorship and discredit its history. He may boldly challenge their scholarship, deny their conclusions, resent their arrogance, and hold on to his confidence in the well authenticated historical evidence which sufficed for those who first accepted it.

Finally, there are three, among other, very remarkable peculiarities in the Pentateuch which are incompatible with modern theories of its composition. The first is the absence of the name Jerusalem from the Pentateuch. On the traditional view the absence presents no difficulty; the fact that Bethel, Hebron, and other shrines are named, while Jerusalem is not, would merely mean that at these other shrines the patriarchs had built their altars, while at Jerusalem they had not. But from the modern view, which holds that the Pentateuch was in great part composed to glorify the priesthood in Jerusalem, and that the Book of Deuteronomy in particular was produced to establish Jerusalem as the central and only acceptable shrine for the worship of Israel, the omission seems very strange indeed. The conclusion is inescapable: at the time the Pentateuch was written, Jerusalem with all her sacred glories had not yet entered into the life of Israel.

The second remarkable peculiarity is the absence of any mention of sacred song from the Pentateuch. A strange omission this would be, if the Priestly Code, which defines the duties of the Levites, had been composed in post-exilic times, when Levite singers and songs of praise formed leading features in the ritual.

The third remarkable peculiarity is the absence of the divine title "Lord of Hosts" from the Pentateuch. Before the time of Samuel the title is never used; after his time it is used some 281 times. Why is it missing from the Pentateuch? It is an unmistakable mark that the Pentateuch could not have been composed in the way asserted by criticism. It would have been a literary impossibility for such a number of writers, extending over hundreds of years, to have one and all, never by accident, slipped into the use of this divine title for Jehovah, "Lord of Hosts," so much in vogue during those centuries. The reason is obvious: the Pentateuch was written before any of these features came into use.

DAVID HEAGLE Emeritus, Stuttgart, Germany. (Additional biographical information unavailable).

3

The Bible and Modern Criticism

By David Heagle, D.D.
EMERITUS, STUTTGART, GERMANY
Translated from the original German by F. Bettex, D.D.,

Abridged and emended by James H. Christian, Th.D.

How does the Bible prove itself to be a divinely inspired, heaven-given book, a communication from a Father to His children, and thus a revelation?

First, by the fact that, as does no other sacred book in the world, it condemns man and all his works. It does not praise either his wisdom, his reason, his art, or any progress that he has made; but it represents him as being in the sight of God, a miserable sinner, incapable of doing anything good, and deserving only death and endless perdition. Truly, a book which is able thus to speak, and in consequence causes millions of men, troubled in conscience, to prostrate themselves in the dust, crying, "God be merciful to me a sinner," must contain more than mere ordinary truth.

Secondly, the Bible exalts itself far above all merely human books by its announcement of the great incomprehensible mystery that, "God so loved the world that He gave His only begotten Son; that whosoever believeth in Him should not perish, but have everlasting life" (John 3:16). Where is there a god among all the heathen nations, be he Osiris, Brahma, Baal, Jupiter or Odin, that would have promised those people that, by taking upon himself the sin of the world and suffering its punishment, he would thus become a savior and redeemer to them?

Thirdly, the Bible sets the seal of its divine origin upon itself by means of the prophecies. Very appropriately does God inquire, through the prophet Isaiah, "Who, as I, shall call, and shall declare it, and set it in order for Me since I established the ancient people? and the things that are coming and shall come to pass, let them declare" (Ch. 44:7). Or says again, "I am God, declaring the end from the beginning, and from ancient times, things not yet done, saying, My counsel shall stand, and I will do all My pleasure; calling a ravenous bird from the east, and the man of My counsel from a far country. Yea, I have spoken, I will also bring it to pass; I have purposed, I will also do it" (Ch. 46:10, 11). Or, addressing Pharaoh, "Where are thy wise men, and let them tell thee, and let them know what the Lord of Hosts hath purposed upon Egypt" (Ch. 19:12). Again we say, where is there a god, or gods, a founder of religion, such as Confucius, Buddha, or Mohammed, who could, with such certainty, have predicted the future of even his own people? Or where is there a statesman who in these times can foretell what will be the condition of things in Europe one hundred or even ten years from now? Nevertheless the prophecies of Moses and his threatened judgments upon the Israelites have been literally fulfilled. Literally also have been fulfilled (although who at the time would have believed it?) the prophecies respecting the destruction of those great ancient cities, Babylon, Nineveh, and Memphis. Moreover, in a literal way has been fulfilled what the prophets David and Isaiah foresaw concerning the last sufferings of Christ—His death on the cross, His drinking of vinegar, and the casting of lots for His garments. There are also other prophecies which will still be most literally fulfilled, such as the promises made to Israel, the final judgment, and the end of the world. "For," as Habakkuk says, "the vision is yet for an appointed time, and will not lie. Though it tarry, wait for it; it will surely come" (Ch. 2:3).

Fourthly, the Bible has demonstrated its peculiar power by its influence with the martyrs. Think of the hundreds of thousands who, at different times and among different peoples, have sacrificed their all, their wives, their children, all their possessions, and finally life itself, on account of this book. Think of how they have, on the rack and at the stake, confessed the truth of the Bible, and borne testimony to its power.

Lastly, the Bible shows itself every day to be a divinely given book by its beneficent influence among all kinds of people. It converts to a better life the ignorant and the learned, the beggar on the street and the king upon his throne, yonder poor woman dwelling in an attic, the greatest poet and the profoundest thinker, civilized persons and uncultured savages. Despite all the scoffing and derision of its enemies, it has been translated into hundreds of languages, and has been preached by thousands of missionaries to millions of people. It makes the proud humble and the dissolute virtuous; it consoles the unfortunate, and teaches man how to live patiently and die triumphantly. No other book or collection of books accomplishes for man the exceeding great benefits accomplished by this book of truth.

Modern Criticism and Its Rationalistic Method

In these times there has appeared a criticism which, constantly growing bolder in its attacks upon this sacred book, now decrees, with all self-assurance and confidence, that it is simply a human production. Besides other faults found with it, it is declared to be full of errors, many of its books to be spurious, written by unknown men at later dates than those assigned, etc., etc. The fundamental principle upon which this verdict is based is, as Renan expressed it, reason is capable of judging all things, but is itself judged by nothing. However, a purely rational revelation would certainly be a contradiction of terms; besides, it would be wholly superfluous. But when reason undertakes to speak of things entirely supernatural, invisible and eternal, it talks as a blind man does about colors, discoursing of things concerning which it neither knows nor can know anything; and thus it makes itself ridiculous. It has not ascended up to heaven, neither has it descended into the deep; and, therefore, a purely rational religion is no religion at all.

Incompetency of Reason for Spiritual Truth

Reason alone has never inspired men with great sublime conceptions of spiritual truth, whether in the way of discovery or invention; but usually it has at first rejected and ridiculed such matters. Just so it is with these rationalistic critics, who have no appreciation or understanding of that high and sublime in God's

Word. They understand neither the majesty of Isaiah, the pathos of David's repentance, the audacity of Moses' prayers, the philosophic depth of Ecclesiastes, nor the wisdom of Solomon which "uttereth her voice in the streets." Ambitious priests, according to them, at a later date than is commonly assigned, compiled all those books to which we have alluded; also they wrote the Sinaitic law, and invented the whole story of Moses' life.

No Agreement Among the Critics

Do these critics then, to ask the least of them, agree with one another? Far from it. To be sure, they unanimously deny the inspiration of the Bible, the divinity of Christ and of the Holy Spirit, the fall of man and the forgiveness of sins through Christ; also prophecy and miracles, the resurrection of the dead, the final judgment, heaven, and hell. But when it comes to their pretendedly sure results, not any two of them affirm the same things, and their numerous publications create a flood of disputable, self-contradictory and naturally destructive hypotheses.

What Are the Fruits of This Criticism?

In the classroom it ensnares, in lecture halls it makes great pretences, for mere popular lectures it is still serviceable; but when the thunders of God's power break in upon the soul, when despair at the loss of all one has loved takes possession of the mind, when remembrance of a miserable lost life or of past misdeeds is felt and realized, when one is on a sickbed and death approaches, and the soul, appreciating that it is now on the brink of eternity, calls for a Savior—just at this time when its help is most needed, this modern religion utterly fails.

But suppose all the teachings of this criticism were true, what would it avail us? It would put us in a sad condition indeed. For then, sitting beside ruined temples and broken-down altars, with no joy as respects the hereafter, no hope of everlasting life, no God to help us, no forgiveness of sins, feeling miserable, all desolate in our hearts and chaotic in our minds, we should be utterly unable either to know or believe anything more. Can such a view of Christianity be true? No! If this modern criticism were true, then away with all so-called Christianity, which only deceives us with idle tales! Away with a religion which has nothing to offer us but the commonplace teachings of morality! Away with faith! Away with hope! Let us eat and drink, for tomorrow we die!

Conclusion

Let us then, by repudiating this modern criticism, show our condemnation of it. What does it offer us? Nothing. What does it take away? Everything. Do we have any use for it? No! It neither helps us in life nor comforts us in death; it will not judge us in the world to come. For our Biblical faith we do not need either the encomiums of men, nor the approbation of a few poor sinners. We will not attempt to improve the Scriptures and adapt them to our liking, but we will believe them. We will not criticize them, but we will ourselves be directed by them. We will not exercise authority over them, but we will obey them. We will trust him who is the way, the truth, and the life. His Word shall make us free.

"Lord, to whom shall we go? Thou hast the words of eternal life. And we believe and are sure that Thou art that Christ, the Son of the living God" (John 6:68, 69). "And he answered, Behold, I come quickly: hold that fast which thou hast; that no man take thy crown" (Rev. 3:11).

JAMES ORR (1844-1913) graduated from Glasgow University in his native Scotland. Between 1874 and 1891, he was a parish minister at East Bank United Presbyterian Church in Hawick. He left the pastorate to teach church history at the United Presbyterian Theological College in Glasgow until 1901, when he became professor of apologetics and dogmatics at Glasgow (later called Trinity) College. Orr enjoyed studying the progress of church doctrine, which he saw as following a divine logic. His major works included *The Christian View of God and the World* (1893, republished in 1989 by Kregel Publications) and *The Progress of Dogma* (1897).

4

Holy Scripture and Modern Negations

By Professor James Orr, D.D.
UNITED FREE CHURCH COLLEGE, GLASGOW, SCOTLAND

Abridged and emended by James H. Christian, Th.D.

Is there today in the midst of criticism and unsettlement a tenable doctrine of Holy Scripture for the Christian Church and for the world; and if there is, what is that doctrine? That is unquestionably a very pressing question at the present time. "Is there a book which we can regard as the repository of a true revelation of God and an infallible guide in the way of life, and as to our duties to God and man?" is a question of immense importance to us all. One hundred years ago, the question hardly needed to be asked among Christian people. It was universally conceded, taken for granted, that there is such a book, the book which we call the Bible. Here, it was believed, is a volume which is an inspired record of the whole will of God for man's salvation; accept as true and inspired the teaching of that book, follow its guidance, and you cannot stumble, you cannot err in attaining the supreme end of existence, in finding salvation, in grasping the prize of a glorious immortality.

Now a change has come. There is no disguising the fact that we live in an age when, even within the Church, there is much uneasy and distrustful feeling about the Holy Scriptures — a hesitancy to lean upon them as an authority and to use them as the weapons of precision they once were; with a corresponding anxiety to find some surer basis in external church authority, or with others, in Christ himself, or again in a Christian consciousness, as it is named — a surer basis for Christian belief and life. Sometimes the idea is taken up that the thought of an authority external to ourselves must be wholly given up; that only that can be accepted which carries its authority within itself by the appeal it makes to reason or to our spiritual being, and therein lies the judge for us of what is true and what is false.

The idea of the authority of Scripture is a conception which lies in the Scriptures themselves. This belief in the Holy Scripture was accepted and acted upon by the Church of Christ from the first. The Bible itself claims to be an authoritative Book, and an infallible guide to the true knowledge of God and of the way of salvation. This view is implied in every reference made to it, so far as it then existed, by Christ and his Apostles. That the New Testament, the work of the Apostles and of apostolic men, does not stand on a lower level of inspiration and authority than the Old Testament, is, I think, hardly worth arguing. In that sense, as a body of writings of divine authority, the books of the Old and New Testament were accepted by the Apostles and by the Church of the post-apostolic age.

Take the writings of any of the early Church fathers, and you will find their words saturated with references to Scripture. You will find the Scriptures treated in precisely the same way as they are used in the biblical literature of today; namely, as the ultimate authority on the matters of which they speak.

By all means, let criticism have its rights. Let purely literary questions about the Bible receive full and fair discussion. Let the structure of books be impartially examined. If a reverent science has light to throw on the composition or authority or age of these books, let its voice be heard. On the other hand, we are not bound to accept every wild critical theory that any critic may choose to put forward as the final word on this matter. We are compelled to look at the presuppositions on which each criticism proceeds, and to ask, How far is the criticism controlled by those presuppositions? We are bound to look at the evidence by which the theory is supported, and to ask, Is it really borne out by that evidence? When theories are put forward with every confidence as fixed results, and we find them, as we observe them, still in constant process of evolution and change, constantly becoming more complicated, more extreme, more fanciful, we are entitled to inquire, Is this the certainty that it was alleged to be? *Now that is my complaint against much of the current criticism of the Bible —* not that it is criticism, but that it starts from the wrong basis, that it proceeds by arbitrary methods, and that it arrives at results which I think are demonstrably false results.

There is certainly an immense change of attitude on the part of many who still sincerely hold faith in the supernatural revelation of God. I find it difficult to describe this tendency, for I am desirous not to describe it in any way which would do injustice to any Christian thinker, and it is attended by so many signs of an ambiguous character. Jesus is recognized by the majority of those who represent it as "the Incarnate Son of God," though with shadings off into more or less indefinite assertions even on that fundamental article, which make it sometimes doubtful where the writers exactly stand. The process of thought in regard to Scripture is easily traced. First, there is an ostentatious throwing overboard, joined with some expression of contempt, of what is called the verbal inspiration of Scripture — a very much abused term. Jesus is still spoken of as the highest revealer, and it is allowed that his words, if only we could get at them — and on the whole it is thought we can — furnish the highest rule of guidance for time and for eternity. But even criticism, we are told, must have its rights. Even in the New Testament the Gospels go into the crucible, and in the name of synoptical criticism, historical criticism, they are subject to wonderful processes, in the course of which much of the history gets melted out or is peeled off as Christian characteristics. Jesus, we are reminded, was still a man of his generation, liable to error in his human knowledge, and allowance must be made for the limitations in his conceptions and judgments. Paul is alleged to be still largely dominated by his inheritance of Rabbinical and Pharisaic ideas. He had been brought up a Pharisee, brought up with the rabbis, and when he became a Christian, he carried a great deal of that into his Christian thought, and we have to strip off that thought when we come to the study of his Epistles. He is therefore a teacher not to be followel further than our own judgment of Christian truth leads us. That gets rid of a great deal that is inconvenient about Paul's teaching.

The Old Testament and the Critics

If these things are done in the "green tree" of the New Testament, it is easy to see what will be done in the "dry tree" of the

Old. The conclusions of the more advanced school of critics are here generally accepted as once for all settled, with the result—in my judgment, at any rate—that the Old Testament is immeasurably lowered from the place it once held in our reverence. Its earlier history, down to about the age of the kings, is largely resolved into myths, legends, and fictions. It is ruled out of the category of history proper. No doubt we are told the legends are just as good as the history, and that the ideas which they convey to us are just as good, coming in the form of legends, as if they came in the form of fact.

But behold, its laws, when we come to deal with them in this manner, lack divine authority. They are the products of human minds at various ages. Its prophecies are the utterances of men who possessed indeed the Spirit of God, which is only in fuller degree what other good men, religious teachers in all countries, have possessed—not a spirit qualifying, for example, to give real predictions, or to bear authoritative messages of the truth to men. Consequently, in this whirl and confusion of theories which you will find in our magazines, encyclopedias, reviews, and books which have appeared to annihilate conservative believers, is it any wonder that many should be disquieted and unsettled, and feel as if the ground on which they have been wont to rest was giving way beneath their feet? So the question comes back with fresh urgency, "What is to be said of the place and value of Holy Scripture?"

Is There a Tenable Doctrine for the Christian Church of Today?

Let me try to indicate the lines along which I would answer the question, "Have we, or can we have, a tenable doctrine of Holy Scripture?" For a doctrine of Scripture which satisfies the needs of the Christian Church and measures up to the Bible's claims for itself it seems to me that three things are indispensably necessary. These are: first, a more positive view of the structure of the Bible than at present obtains in many circles; second, the acknowledgement of a true supernatural revelation of God in the history and religion of the Bible; third, the recognition of a true supernatural inspiration in the record of that revelation. Can we affirm these three things? Will they bear the test? I think they will.

The Structure of the Bible

First as to the structure of the Bible, there is needed a more positive idea of that structure than is at present prevalent. You take much of the criticism and you find the Bible being disintegrated in many ways, and everything like structure falling away from it. You are told, for example, that the Books of Moses are made up of many documents, which are very late in origin and cannot claim historical value. You are told that the laws they contain are also, for the most part, of tolerably late origin, and the Levitical laws especially are of post-exilian construction; they were not given by Moses; they were unknown when the Children of Israel were carried into captivity. Their temple usage perhaps is embodied in the Levitical law, but most of the contents of that Levitical law were wholly unknown. They were the invention of priests and scribes in the post-exilian period. They were put into shape, brought before the Jewish community returned from Babylon, and accepted by it as the law of life. Thus, you have the history of the Bible turned pretty much upside down, and things take on a new aspect altogether.

Must I then, in deference to criticism, accept these theories, and give up the structure which the Bible presents? Taking the Bible as it stands, I find—and without any particular critical learning you will find it—what seems to be evidence of a very definite internal structure, part fitting into part and leading on to part, making up a unity of the whole in that Bible. The Bible has undeniably a structure as it stands. It is distinguished from Koran, Buddhist, Indian scriptures, and every other kind of religious books. It is distinguished just by this fact, that it is the embodiment of a great plan or scheme or purpose of divine grace extending from the beginning of time through successive ages and dispensations down to its culmination in Jesus Christ and the Pentecostal outpourings of the Spirit. The *history* of the Bible is the history of that development of God's redemptive purpose. The *promises* of the Bible mark the stages of its progress and its hope. The *covenants* of the Bible stand before us in the order of its unfolding. You begin with Genesis, which lays the foundation and leads up to the Book of Exodus; and the Book of Exodus in turn, with its introduction to the law-giving, leads up to what follows.

Deuteronomy looks back upon the history of the rebellions and the laws given to the people, and leads up to the conquest. I need not follow the later developments, coming away down through the monarchy and the prophecy and the rest, but you find it all gathered up and fulfilled in the New Testament. The Bible, as we have it, closes in Gospel and Epistle and Apocalypse, fulfilling all the ideas of the Old Testament. There the circle completes itself with the new heaven and the new earth wherein dwelleth righteousness. Here is a structure, a connected story, a unity of purpose extending through this Book and binding all its parts together. Is that structure an illusion? Do we only, and many with us, dream that it is there? Do our eyes deceive us when we think we see it? Or has somebody of a later date invented it, and put it all, inwrought it all, in these earlier records, legends and stories, or whatever you like to call it—skillfully woven into the story until it presents there the appearance of naturalness and truth? I would like to find the mind capable of inventing it, and then the mind capable of working it into a history once they got the idea itself. But if not invented, it belongs to the reality and the substance of the history; it belongs to the facts; and therefore to the Book that records the facts. There are internal attestations in that structure of the Bible to the genuineness of its contents that protest against the efforts that are so often made to reduce it to fragments and shiver that unity and turn it upside down. "Walk about Zion . . . tell the towers thereof; mark ye well her bulwarks"; you will find there is something there which the art of man will not avail to overthrow.

"Now, that is all very well," I hear some one say, "but there are facts on the other side; there are those manifold proofs which our critical friends adduce that the Bible is really a collection of fragments and documents of much later date, and that the history is really quite a different thing from what the Bible represents it to be." However, when I turn to the evidence I do not find it to have that convincing power which our critical friends assign to them.

I am not rejecting this kind of critical theory because it goes against my prejudices or traditions; I reject it simply because it seems to me the evidence does not sustain it, and that the stronger evidence is against it. I cannot go into details; but take just the one point I have mentioned—this post-exilian origin of the Levitical law. I have stated what is said about that matter—that those laws and institutions pertaining to priests, Levites, and sacrifices that you find in the middle of the Pentateuch had really no existence, no authoritative form, and to a large extent no existence of any kind until after the Jews returned from Babylon, and then they were given out as a code of laws which the Jews accepted. But let the reader put himself in the position of that returned community, and see what the thing means. These exiles had returned from Babylon. They had been organized into a new community. They had rebuilt their temple, and then long years after that, when things had got into confusion, those two great men, Ezra and Nehemiah, came among them, and by and by Ezra produced and publicly proclaimed what he called the law of Moses, the law of God by the hand of Moses which he had brought from Babylon. A full description of what happened is given in the eighth chapter of the Book of Nehemiah. Ezra reads that law from his pulpit of wood day after day to the people, and the interpreter gives the sense. Now, mind you, most of the things in this book that he is reading to the people, had never been heard of before—never had existed, in fact; priests and Levites such as are there described had never existed. The law itself was long, complicated, and burdensome, but the marvelous thing is that the people meekly accept it all as true—meekly accept it as law, at any rate—and submit to it, and take upon themselves its burdens without a murmur of dissent.

That is a very remarkable thing to start with. But remember, further, what that community was. It was not a community with oneness of mind, but it was a community keenly divided in itself. If you read the narrative you will find that there were strong opposing factions; there were parties strongly opposed to Ezra and Nehemiah and their reforms; there were many, as you see in the Book of Malachi, who were religiously faithless in that community. But marvelous to say, they all join in accepting this new, burdensome, and hitherto unheard of law as the law of Moses, the law coming down to them from hoary antiquity. There were priests and Levites in that community who knew something about their own origin; they had genealogies and knew something about their own past. According to the new theory, these Levites were quite a new order; they had never existed at all before the time of the exile, and they had come into existence through the sentence of degradation that the prophet Ezekiel had passed upon them in the 44th chapter of his book. History is quite silent about this degradation. If anyone asks who carried out the degradation, or why was it carried out, or when was it done, and how came the priests to submit to the degradation, there is no answer to be given at all. But it came about somehow, so we are told.

So these priests and Levites are there, and they stand and listen without astonishment as they learn from Ezra how the Levites had been set apart long centuries before in the wilderness by the hand of God, and had an ample tithe provision made for their support, and cities, and what not, set apart for them to live in. People know a little about their past. These cities never had existed except on paper; but they took it all in. They are told about these cities, which they must have known had never existed as Levitical cities. They not only hear but they accept the heavy tithe burdens without a word of remonstrance, and they make a covenant with God pledging themselves to faithful obedience to all those commands. Those tithes laws, as we discover, had no actual relation to their situation at all. They were drawn up for a totally different case. They were drawn up for a state of things in which there were few priests and many Levites. The priests were only to get the tithe of a tenth, but in this restored community there were a great many priests and few Levites. The tithe laws did not apply at all, but they accepted these as laws of Moses.

And so I might go over the provisions of the Law one by one— tabernacle, priests, ritual, sacrifices, and Day of Atonement, but these things, in their post-exilian form, had never existed; they were spun out of the inventive brains of scribes; and yet the people accepted them all as the genuine handiwork of the ancient lawgiver. Was ever such a thing heard of before? Try it in any city. Try to get the people to take upon themselves a series of heavy burdens of taxation or tithes or whatever you like, on the ground that it had been handed down from the middle ages to the present time. Try to get them to believe it; try to get them to obey it, and you will find the difficulty. Is it credible to anyone who leaves books and theories in the study and takes a broad view of human nature with open eyes? I aver that for me, at any rate, it is not; and it will be a marvel to me as long as I am spared to live, how such a theory has ever gained the acceptance it has done among unquestionably able and sound-minded men. I am convinced that the structure of the Bible vindicates itself, and that these counter theories break down.

A Supernatural Revelation

I think it is an essential element in a tenable doctrine of Scripture, in fact the core of the matter, that it contains a record of a true supernatural revelation; and that is what the Bible claims to be — not a development of man's thoughts about God, and not what this man and that one came to think about God, how they came to have the ideas of a Jehovah, who was originally the storm-god of Sinai, and how they manufactured out of this the great universal God of the prophets—but a supernatural revelation of what God revealed himself in word and deed to men in history. If that claim to a supernatural revelation from God falls, the Bible falls, because it is bound up with it from beginning to end. Now, it is a must here that a great deal of our modern thought parts company with the Bible. I am quite well aware that many of our friends who accept these newer critical theories, claim to be just as firm believers in divine revelation and in Jesus Christ and all that concerns him, as I am myself. I rejoice in the fact, and I believe that they are warranted in saying that there is that in the religion of Israel which you cannot expunge, or explain on any other hypothesis but divine revelation.

But what I maintain is that this theory of the religion of the Bible which has been evolved, which has peculiarly come to be known as the critical view, had a very different origin—in men who did not believe in the supernatural revelation of God in the Bible. This school as a whole, as a widespread school, holds the fundamental position—the position which its adherents call that of the modern mind—that miracles did not happen and cannot happen. It takes the ground that they are impossible; therefore its followers have to rule everything of that kind out of the Bible record.

I have never been able to see how that position is tenable to a believer in a living personal God who really loves his creatures

and has a sincere desire to bless them. Who dares to assert that
the power and will of such a Being as we must believe God to be—
the God and Father of our Lord Jesus Christ — is exhausted in the
natural creation? Who can believe that there are no higher things
to be attained in God's providence than can be attained through the
medium of natural law? Who ventures to declare that there is in
such a Being no capability of revealing himself in words and
deeds beyond nature? If there is a dogmatism in the world, it is
that of the man who claims to limit the Author of the universe by
this finite bound. We are told sometimes that it is a far higher
thing to see God in the natural than to see him in something that
transcends the natural; a far higher thing to see God in the orderly
regular working of nature than to suppose that there has ever been
anything transcending that ordinary natural working. But the question is, Has this natural working not its limits? Is there not something that nature and natural workings cannot reach, cannot do for
men, that we need to have done for us? And are we so to bind
God that he cannot enter into communion with man in a supernatural economy of grace, an economy of revelation, an economy of
salvation? Are we to deny that he has done so? That is really
the dividing line both in Old Testament and New between the
different theories. *Revelation,* surely, all must admit if man is to
attain the clear knowledge of God that is needed; and the question
is one of fact, Has God so revealed himself? And I believe that
it is an essential part of the answer, the true doctrine of Scripture,
to say, "Yes, God has so revealed himself, and the Bible is the
record of that revelation, and that revelation shines in its light
from the beginning to the end of it." Unless there is a whole-
hearted acceptance of the fact that God has entered, in word and
deed, into human history for man's salvation, for man's renovation,
for the deliverance of this world, a revelation culminating in the
great Revealer himself—unless we accept that, we do not get the
foundation for the true doctrine of Holy Scripture.

The Inspired Book

Now, just a word in closing, on Inspiration. I do not think
that anyone will weigh the evidence of the Bible itself very carefully without saying that at least it claims to be in a peculiar and
especial manner an *inspired* book. There is hardly anyone, I think,

who will doubt that Jesus Christ treats the Old Testament in that way. Christ recognizes that it was a true divine revelation, that he was the goal of it all; he came to fulfil the law and the prophets. The Scriptures are the last word with him—*"Have ye not read?"* *"Ye do err, not knowing the Scriptures."* It is just as certain that the Apostles treated the Old Testament in that way, and that they claimed that in them and in their word was laid "the foundation on which the Church was built," Jesus Christ himself, as the substance of their testimony, being the chief corner-stone; "built upon the foundation of the Apostles and Prophets" (Ephesians 2:20; see 3:5).

The Bible's Own Test of Inspiration

What does the Bible itself give us as the test of its inspiration? What does the Bible itself name as the qualities that inspiration imparts to it? Paul speaks in Timothy of the *Sacred Writings that were able to make wise unto salvation through faith which is in Christ Jesus.* He goes on to tell us that *All Scripture is given by inspiration of God and is profitable for doctrine, for reproof, for correction, for instruction in righteousness, in order that the man of God may be perfect, thoroughly furnished unto all good works.* When you go back to the Old Testament and its praise of the Word of God you will find the qualities of inspiration are just the same. "The law of the Lord is perfect," etc. Those are the qualities which the inspired Book is alleged to sustain—qualities which only a true inspiration of God's Spirit could give; qualities beyond which we surely do not need anything more.

Does anyone doubt that the Bible possesses these qualities? Look at its structure; look at its completeness; look at it in the clearness and fullness and holiness of its teachings; look at it in its sufficiency to guide every soul that truly seeks light unto the saving knowledge of God. Take the Book as a whole, in its whole purpose, its whole spirit, its whole aim and tendency, and the whole setting of it, and ask, Is there not manifest the power which you can only trace back, as it traces back itself, to God's Holy Spirit really in the men who wrote it?

WILLIAM HENRY GRIFFITH THOMAS (1861-1924) was a co-founder of Dallas Theological Seminary. His formal theological training began at King's College in London and was continued at Oxford University, which was awarded him his B.D. in 1895. From there he moved on to St. Paul's Church, where he emphasized prayer and Bible study; his church conducted six prayer meetings a week. In 1905, Griffith Thomas became principal of Wycliffe Hall at Oxford. Thinking his ministry needed a broader scope, he moved to Canada in 1910 and became professor of Old Testament literature and exegesis at Wycliffe College in Toronto. Among his 26 books are such works as *The Prayers of St. Paul, Grace and Power, Christianity Is Christ, The Pentateuch, Genesis, Outline Studies in Matthew, Outline Studies in Luke, The Apostle Peter, The Apostle John, Studies in Colossians and Philemon,* and *The Holy Spirit,* many of which have been republished by Kregel Publications. Griffith Thomas died shortly before Dallas Seminary opened.

5

Old Testament Criticism and New Testament Christianity

By Professor W. H. Griffith Thomas, D.D.
WYCLIFFE COLLEGE, TORONTO, CANADA

Revised by Charles L. Feinberg, Th.D., Ph.D.

For some time a large number of Christians have felt compelled to object to the attitude of many scholars to the Old Testament Scriptures. Critical scholars have taught the absolute denial or only partial acceptance of the historical character of the partriarchs; the alleged unhistorical character of the records relating to the time of Moses, the unreliability of the prophets in their predictions of the future; the error of the New Testament writers in assigning historical value to the Old Testament records; and the liability to error even on the part of our Lord himself, who throughout repeatedly assumed the divine authority of the Old Testament. We do not question for an instant the right of Biblical criticism considered in itself. It is a necessity for all who use the Bible to employ their judgment on what is before them. What is called "higher" criticism is not only a legitimate, but a necessary method for all Christians, for by its use we are able to discover the facts and form of the Old Testament Scriptures. Our hesitation and objection are not intended to apply to the method, but to what is believed to be an illegitimate, unscientific, and unhistorical use of it.

1. *Is the Testimony of Nineteen Centuries of Christian History and Experience of No Account in This Question?*

For nearly eighteen centuries these modern views of the Old Testament were not heard of. Yet this is not to be accounted for by the absence of intellectual power and scholarship in the Church. Men like Origen, Jerome, Augustine, Thomas Aquinas, Erasmus, Calvin, Luther, Melancthon, to say nothing of the English Puritans and other theologians of the seventeenth century, were not intellectually weak or inert, nor were they wholly void of critical insight with reference to Holy Scripture. Yet they, and the whole Church with them, never hesitated to accept the view of the Old Testament which had come down to them, not only as a heritage from Judaism, but as endorsed by the apostles. Omitting all reference to our Lord, it is not open to question that the views of Paul, Peter and John about the Old Testament were the views of the whole Christian Church until the end of the eighteenth century. And, making every possible allowance for the lack of historical spirit and modern critical methods, are we to suppose that the whole Church for centuries never exercised its mind on such subjects as the contents, history, and authority of the Old Testament?

Furthermore, this is a matter which cannot be decided by intellectual criticism alone. Scripture appeals to conscience, heart, and will, as well as to mind; and the Christian consciousness, the accumulated spiritual experience of the Body of Christ, is not to be lightly regarded, much less set aside, unless it is proved to be unwarranted by fact. While we do not say that "what is new is not true," the lateness of these modern critical views should give us pause, before we virtually set aside the spiritual instinct of centuries of Christian experience.

2. Does Criticism Readily Agree with the Historical Position of the Jewish Nation?

The Jewish nation is a fact in history, and its record is given to us in the Old Testament. There is no contemporary literature to check the account there given, and archaeology affords us assistance on points of detail only, not for any long or continuous period. This record of Jewish history can be proved to have remained the same for many centuries. Yet much of modern criticism is compelled to reconstruct the history of the Jews on several important points. It involves, for instance, a very different idea of the character of the earliest form of Jewish religion from that seen in the Old Testament as it now stands; its views of the patriarchs are largely different from the conceptions found on the face of the Old Testament narrative; its views of Moses and David are essentially altered from what we have before us in the Old Testament.

Now, what is there in Jewish history to support all this reconstruction? Absolutely nothing. We see through the centuries the great outstanding objective fact of the Jewish nation, and the Old Testament is both the means and record of their national life. It rose with them, grew with them, and it is to the Jews alone we can look for the earliest testimony to the Old Testament canon.

In view of these facts, it must be concluded that the fundamental positions of modern Old Testament criticism are utterly incompatible with the historic growth and position of the Jewish people. Are we not right, therefore, to pause before we accept this subjective reconstruction of history? Let anyone read the writings of Wellhausen, and then ask himself whether he recognizes at all in them the story as given in the Old Testament.

3. *Are the Results of the Modern View of the Old Testament Really Established?*

It is sometimes said that modern criticism is no longer a matter of hypothesis; it has entered the domain of facts. Some of its more zealous adherents have claimed a complete victory for its postulates. But is this really so? It is interesting and disconcerting also to find these same claimants speaking of questions as still open which were supposed to be settled and closed decades ago. In the first place, is the excessive literary analysis of the Pentateuch at all probable or even possible on literary grounds? Let anyone work through a section of Genesis in a critical introduction to the Old Testament or in a critical commentary, and see whether such an involved combination of authors is at all likely, or whether, even if likely, the various authors can now be distinguished? Is not the whole method far too purely subjective to be probable and reliable?

Further, the critics are not agreed as to the number of documents, or as to the portions to be assigned to each author. Some years ago criticism was content to say that Isaiah 40-66, though not by Isaiah, was the work of one author, an unknown prophet of the exile. But later writers consider these chapters the work of two writers, and that the whole Book of Isaiah did not receive its present form until long after the return from the exile.

Then, these differences in literary analysis involve differences of interpretation and differences of date, character, and meaning of particular parts of the Old Testament. The opinion has been voiced that new work has been sufficient to upset the entire current reconstructions of Israel's religion, and the statement issues from a reliable critical source. As long as statements of fact in the Old Testament are assumed to be generally false, so long will permanent results be impossible.

4. *Is the Position of Modern Criticism Really Compatible With a Belief in the Old Testament as a Divine Revelation?*

The problem before us is not merely literary, nor only historical; it is essentially religious, and the whole matter resolves itself into one question: Is the Old Testament the record of a divine revelation? This is the ultimate problem. It is admitted by both sides to be almost impossible to minimize the differences between the traditional and the modern views of the Old Testament. They relate to different conceptions of the relation of God to the world, of the course of Israel's history, the process of revelation, and the nature of inspiration of the Scriptures. Israel's religion before the period of the great prophets was supposed to be identical with other Semitic religions, which were polytheistic. Does not the Old Testament reveal, however, the uniqueness of God's dealings with Israel from the time of Abraham to the eighth century B.C.?

.We may next take the character of the narratives of Genesis. The real question at issue is their historical character. Modern criticism regards the accounts in Genesis as largely mythical and legendary. Yet it is certain that the Jews of the later centuries accepted these patriarchs as veritable personages, and the incidents associated with them as genuine history. Paul and the other New Testament writers assuredly held the same view. If, then, they are not historical, surely the truths emphasized by prophets and apostles from the patriarchal stories are so far weakened in their supports.

Take, again, the legislation which in the Pentateuch is associated with Moses, and almost invariably introduced by the phrase, "The Lord spake unto Moses." Modern criticism regards this legislation as unknown until a thousand years after the time of Moses. Can this be accepted as satisfactory? Are we to suppose that "The Lord spake to Moses" is only a well-known literary device intended to invest the utterance with greater importance and more solemn sanction? This position, together with the generally accepted view of modern criticism about the forgery of Deuteronomy in the days of Josiah, cannot be regarded as in accord with historical fact or ethical principle.

Yet some critics strongly assert that the new views are compatible with belief in the divine authority of the Old Testament. Upon what grounds does this compatibility rest? To deny historicity, to correct dates by hundreds of years, to reverse judgments on which a nation has rested for centuries, to traverse views which have been the spiritual sustenance of millions, and then to say that all this is consistent with the Old Testament as a revelation from God, is at least puzzling, and will not afford either mental or moral satisfaction to very many. It is no mere question of how we may use the Old Testament for preaching, or how much is left for use after the critical views are accepted. But even our preaching will lack a great deal of the note of certitude. If we are to regard certain biographies as unhistorical, it will not be easy to draw lessons for conduct, and if the history is largely legendary, our deductions about God's government and providence must be essentially weakened. But the one point to be faced is the historic credibility of those parts of the Old Testament questioned by modern criticism, and the historical and religious value of the documents of the Pentateuch. It remains to be proved that modern views are in harmony with acceptance of the Old Testament as the record of a divine revelation.

5. *Is Modern Criticism Based on a Sound Philosophy Such as Christians Can Accept?*

At the basis of much modern thought is the philosophy known as idealism, which, as often interpreted, involves a theory of the universe that finds no room for supernatural interpositions of any kind. The great law of the universe, including the physical, mental, and moral realms, is said to be evolution, and though this doubtless presupposes an original Creator, it does not, on

the theory now before us, permit of any subsequent direct intervention of God during the process of development.   This general
philosophical principle applied to history has assuredly influenced,
if it has not almost moulded, a great deal of modern criticism of
the Old Testament.   It is not urged that all who accept even the
position of a moderate criticism, go the full length of the
extreme evolutionary theory; but there can be no reasonable
doubt that most of the criticism of the Old Testament is materially
affected by an evolutionary theory of all history which tends to
minimize divine intervention in the affairs of the people of Israel.
It is certainly correct to say that the presupposition of much
present-day critical reasoning is a denial of the supernatural,
and especially of the predictive element in prophecy.

As to the theory of evolution regarded as a process of uninterrupted differentiation of existences, under purely natural laws,
and without any divine intervention, it will suffice to say that it is
not proved in the sphere of natural science, while in the realms of
history and literature it is palpably false.   The records of history
and of literature reveal from time to time the great fact and factor
of personality, the reality of personal power, and this determinative
element has a peculiar way of setting at naught all idealistic theories
of a purely natural and uniform progress in history and letters.
Quite apart from instances of forceful personality as have arisen
from time to time through the centuries, there is one Personality
who has not yet been accounted for by any theory of evolution—the
Person of Jesus of Nazareth.

There are sufficient data in current Old Testament criticism to
warrant the statement that it proceeds from presuppositions
concerning the origins of history, religion, and the Bible, which
in their essence are subversive of belief in divine revelation.
And such being the case, we naturally look with grave suspicion
on results derived from so unsound a philosophical basis.

6. *Can Purely Naturalistic Premises Be Accepted Without Coming to Purely Naturalistic Conclusions?*

Graf, Kuenen, and Wellhausen are admittedly accepted as
masters by their followers, and the results of their literary
analysis of the Pentateuch have been generally regarded as con-

clusive. On the basis of this literary dissection, certain conclusions have been formed as to the character and growth of Old Testament religion, and as a result the history of the Jews is reconstructed. Now it is known that the leading critics deny the supernatural element in the Old Testament. This is the presupposition of their entire position. Will it be claimed that it does not materially affect their conclusions? And is there any safe or logical place to stop for those who accept so many of their premises? The extreme subjectivity of modern criticism is part of the logical outcome of its general position. The tendency of their views is towards a minimizing of the supernatural in the Old Testament.

Take, as one instance, the Messianic element. In spite of the universal belief of Jews and Christians in a personal Messiah, a belief derived in the first place solely from the Old Testament, and supported for Christians by the New Testament, modern criticism will not allow much clear and undoubted prediction of him. Insight into existing conditions is readily granted to the prophets, but they are not allowed to have had much foresight into future conditions connected with the Messiah. Yet Isaiah's glowing words remain, and demand a fair, full exegesis such as they do not get from many modern scholars.

If it be pointed out that many British and American higher critics have been firm believers in the divine authority of the Old Testament, and of a divine revelation contained therein, then it can be said with truth that these men, grounded in the Christian faith in days gone by, maintain their old convictions, but at the same time admit principles and methods which are logically at variance with them. There is also the danger that others, following their premises, will carry their positions to their logical conclusions.

7. *Can We Overlook the Evidence of Archaeology?*

It is well known that during the last hundred years a vast number of archaeological discoveries have been made in Egypt, Palestine, Babylonia, and Assyria. Many of these have shed remarkable light on the historical features of the Old Testament. A number of persons and periods have been illuminated by these discoveries, and are now seen with a clarity which was before impossible. It is a simple and yet striking fact that not one of these discoveries during the whole of this time has given any support to the distinctive features and principles of the higher critical position, while, on the other hand, many of them have afforded abundant confirmation of the traditional and conservative view of the Old Testament. It is necessary to mention but a few of these confirmations. Archaeology has confirmed the antiquity of writing, the historicity of the account of the campaign of the kings in Genesis 14, the puzzling story of Sarah and Hagar, the Egypt of Joseph and Moses, the historicity of Sargon and Belshazzar, and the nature of the Aramaic language of Daniel and Ezra. It has been interesting to note how a number of leading archaeologists have abandoned many of their former higher critical positions, and come out forcefully in favor of the historicity and value of the Old Testament.

8. *Are the Views of Modern Criticism Consistent with the Witness of Our Lord to the Old Testament?*

The Christian Church approaches the Old Testament mainly and predominantly from the standpoint of the resurrection of Christ. We naturally ask what our Master thought of the Old Testament, for if it comes to us with his authority and we can discover his view of it, we ought to be satisfied. In the days of our Lord's life on earth one pressing question was, "What think ye of the Christ?" Another was, "What is written in the law? How readest thou?" These questions are still being raised in one form or another, and today as of old, the great problems—two storm-centers, as they have well been called—are Christ and the Bible. The two problems really resolve themselves into one, for Christ and the Bible are inseparable. If we follow Christ, he will teach us the Bible; and if we study our Bible, it will point us to Christ. Each is called the Word of God.

He came, among other things, to bear witness to the truth (John 18:37), and it is a necessary outcome of this purpose that he should bear infallible witness. He came to reveal God and God's will, and this implies and requires special knowledge. It demands that every assertion of his be true. The divine knowledge did not, because it could not, undergo any change by the incarnation. He continued to exist in the form of God, even while he existed in the form of man (Phil. 2:6). In view of this position, we believe that we have a right to appeal to the testimony of Christ to the Old Testament. The place it occupied in his life and ministry is sufficient warrant for referring to his use of it. It is well known that, as far as the Old Testament canon is concerned, our highest authority is that of our Lord himself; and what is true of the Old Testament as a whole, is surely true of these parts to which our Lord specifically referred.

Let us be clear, however, as to what we mean in making this appeal. We do not for a moment intend to close all possible criticism of the Old Testament. There are numbers of questions untouched by anything our Lord said, and there is consequently ample scope for sober, necessary, and valuable criticism. But what we do say is, that anything in the Old Testament stated by our Lord as a fact, or implied as a fact, is, or ought to be, thereby closed for those who hold Christ to be infallible. Criticism can do anything that is not incompatible with the statements of our Lord; but where Christ has spoken, surely the matter is closed.

What, then, is our Lord's general view of the Old Testament? There is no doubt that his Old Testament was practically, if not actually, the same as ours, and that he regarded it as of divine authority, as the final court of appeal for all questions connected with it. The way in which he quotes it shows this. To the Lord Jesus the Old Testament was authoritative and final, because divine.

No one can go through the Gospels without being impressed with the deep reverence of our Lord for the Old Testament, and with his constant use of it in all matters of religious thought and life. His question, "Have ye never read?", his assertion "It is written," his testimony, "Ye search the Scriptures" (ASV), are plainly indicative of his view of the divine authority of the Old Testament as we have it. He sets his seal to its historicity and its revelation of God. He supplements, but never supplants it. He amplifies and modifies, but never nullifies it. He fulfills, but never makes void.

This general view is confirmed by his detailed references to the Old Testament. Consider his testimony to the persons and to the facts of the old covenant. There is scarcely a historical book from Genesis to II Chronicles, to which our Lord does not refer; while it is perhaps significant that his testimony includes references to every book of the Pentateuch, to Isaiah, to Jonah, to Daniel, and to miracles, the very parts most called in question today. Above all, it is surely of the deepest moment that at his temptation he should use three times as the Word of God the book (Deuteronomy) about which there has, perhaps, been the most controversy of all. Again, therefore, we say that everything to which Christ can be said, on any honest interpretation, to have referred, or which he used as a fact, is thereby sanctioned and sealed by the authority of our infallible Lord.

Nor can this position be met by the statement that Christ simply adopted the beliefs of his day without necessarily sanctioning them as correct. Of this there is not the slightest proof, but very much to the contrary. On some of the most important subjects of his day he went directly against prevailing opinion. His teaching about God, righteousness, the Messiah, tradition, the Sabbath, the Samaritans, women, divorce, John's baptism, were diametrically opposed to that of the time. And this opposition was deliberately grounded on the Old Testament, which our Lord charged them with misinterpreting. The one and only question of difference between him and the Jews as to the Old Testament was that of interpretation. Not a vestige of proof can be adduced that he and they differed at all in their general view of its historical character or divine authority. If the current Jewish views were wrong, can we think our Lord would have been silent on a matter of such importance, about a book which he cites or alludes to over four hundred times, and which he made his constant topic in teaching concerning himself? If the Jews were wrong, Jesus either knew it, or he did not. If he knew it why did he not correct them as in so many other and detailed instances? Who will dare to consider the other alternative?

Nor can this witness to the Old Testament be met by asserting that the limitation of our Lord's earthly life kept him within current views of the Old Testament which need not have been true views. This statement ignores the essential force of his personal claim to be "the Word." On more than one occasion our Lord claimed to speak from God, and that everything he said had the divine warrant. Let us notice carefully what this involves. It is sometimes said that our Lord's knowledge was limited, and that he lived here as man, not as God. Suppose this is granted for argument's sake. Very well; as man he lived in God and on God, and he claimed that everything he said and did was from God and through God. If, then, the limitations were from God, so *also were the utterances;* and, as God's warrant was claimed for every one of these, they are by so much divine and infallible (Jn. 5:19, 30; 7:13; 8:26; 12:49; 14:24; 17:8). Even though we grant to the full a theory that will compel us to accept a temporary disuse or non-use of the functions of deity in the person of our Lord, yet the words actually uttered as man are claimed to be from God, and therefore we hold them to be infallible. We rest, therefore, upon our Lord's personal claim to say all and do all by the Father, from the Father, for the Father.

There is, of course, no question of partial knowledge after the resurrection, when our Lord was manifestly free from all limitations of earthly conditions. Yet it was after his resurrection also that he set his seal to the Old Testament (Luke 24:44). We conclude that our Lord's positive statements on the subject of the Old Testament are not to be rejected without charging him with error. If on these points, on which we can test and verify him, we find that he is not reliable, what real comfort can we have in accepting his higher teaching, where verification is impossible? We believe we are on absolutely safe ground, when we say that what the Old Testament was to our Lord, it must be and shall be to us.

We may be certain that no criticism of the Old Testament will ever be accepted by the Christian Church as a whole, which does not fully and satisfactorily account for: (1) its supernatural element, (2) the enlightened spiritual experience of the saints of God in all ages, (3) the general tradition of Jewish history and the unique position of the Hebrew nation through the centuries, (4) the apostolic conception of the authority and inspiration of the Old Testament, and (5) the universal belief of the Christian Church in our Lord's infallibility as a Teacher of the truth.

WILLIAM CAVEN (1830-1904) emigrated from Scotland in 1847. In his new homeland, Canada, he graduated from Knox College in Toronto before being ordained as a Presbyterian minister in 1852. After several years of pastoral work, Caven returned to Knox in 1866 to become professor of exegetical theology. Caven was a strong advocate of church unification, and he was instrumental in forming the Presbyterian Church in Canada, which included the Church of Scotland. Other interests included missions and eschatology. His most notable writings were compiled posthumously in *Christ's Teachings Concerning the Last Things* (1908).

6

The Testimony of Christ
to the Old Testament

By *William Caven, D.D., LL.D.*
LATE PRINCIPAL OF KNOX COLLEGE, TORONTO, CANADA

Revised by Charles L. Feinberg, Th.D., Ph.D.

Both Jews and Christians receive the Old Testament as a revelation from God, while the latter regard it as standing in close and vital relationship to the New Testament. Everything connected with the Old Testament has in recent years been subjected to the closest scrutiny—the authorship of its several books, the time when they were written, their style, their historical value, their religious and ethical teachings. Apart from the veneration with which we regard the Old Testament writings on their own account, the intimate connection which they have with the New Testament necessarily gives us the deepest interest in the conclusions which may be reached by Old Testament criticism. For us the New Testament dispensation presupposes the Mosaic, and the books of the New Testament touch those of the Old at every point.

We propose to take a summary view of the testimony of our Lord to the Old Testament, as it is recorded by the evangelists. The New Testament writers themselves largely quote and refer to the Old Testament, and the views which they express regarding the old economy and its writings are in harmony with the statements of their Master; but we here confine ourselves to what is related to the Lord himself. Let us consider, first, what is contained or necessarily implied in the Lord's testimony to the Old Testament Scriptures, and secondly, to the critical value of his testimony.

I. THE LORD'S TESTIMONY TO THE OLD TESTAMENT

Our Lord's authority may be cited in favor of the Old Testament canon as accepted by the Jews in his day. He never charges them with adding to or taking from the Scriptures, or in any way tampering with the text. Had they been guilty of so great a sin, it is hardly possible that among the charges brought against them, this matter should not even be alluded to. The Lord reproaches his countrymen with ignorance of the Scriptures, and with making the law void through their traditions, but he never hints that they have foisted any book into the canon, or rejected any which deserved a place in it.

Now, the Old Testament canon of the first century is the same as our own. The evidence for this is complete, and the fact is hardly questioned. The New Testament contains, indeed, no catalogue of the Old Testament books, but the testimony of Josephus, of Melito of Sardis, or Origen, of Jerome, of the Talmud, decisively shows that the Old Testament canon, once fixed, has remained unaltered. It is certain that the Septuagint agrees with the Hebrew as to the canon, thus showing that the subject was not in dispute two centuries before Christ. Nor is the testimony of the Septuagint weakened by the fact that the Old Testament Apocrypha are added to the canonical books. The Lord, it is observed, never quotes any of the apocryphal books, nor refers to them.

No Part Assailed

If our Lord does not name the writers of the books of the Old Testament in detail, it may at least be said that no word of his calls in question the genuineness of any book, and that he distinctly assigns several parts of Scripture to the writers whose names they bear. The Law is ascribed to Moses; David's name is connected with the Psalms; the prophecies of Isaiah are attributed to Isaiah; and the prohecies of Daniel to Daniel. The references to Moses as legislator and writer are clear and numerous (Cf. Matt. 8:4; 19:8; Lk. 16:31; Mk. 7:10; Lk. 24:27, 44; Jn: 5:45-47; 7:19, 22, 23). The Psalms are quoted by our Lord more than once, but only once is a writer named. The 110th Psalm is ascribed to David; and the validity of the Lord's argument depends on its being Davidic. The reference, therefore, so far as it goes, confirms the inscriptions of the Psalms in relation to authorship. Isaiah is quoted in a number of passages (Cf. Matt 13:14, 15; Mk. 7:6; and Lk. 4:17, 18). In his great prophecy of the downfall of the Jewish commonwealth, the Lord cites Daniel 9:27 and 12:11 in Matthew 24:15.

Narratives and Records Authentic

When Christ makes reference to Old Testament narratives and records, he accepts them as authentic, as historically true. He does not give or suggest in any case a mythical or allegorical interpretation. The accounts of the creation, of the flood, the overthrow of Sodom and Gomorrah, as well as many incidents and events of later occurrence, are taken as authentic. It may, of course, be alleged that the Lord's references to the creation of man and woman, the flood, the cities of the plain, and the rest, equally serve his purpose of illustration whether he regards them as historical or not. But on weighing his words it will be seen that they lose much of their force and appropriateness unless the events alluded to had a historical character (Cf. Matt. 19:4, 5; 24:37, 39; 11:23, 24). These utterances, everyone feels, lose their weight, if there was no flood such as is described in Genesis, and if the destruction of wicked Sodom may be only a myth. Illustrations and parallels may, for certain purposes, be adduced from fictitious literature, but when the Lord would awaken the conscience of men and alarm their fears by reference to the certainty of divine judgment, he will not confirm his teaching by instances of punishment which are only fabulous. His argument that the holy and just God will do as he has done, will make bare his arm as in the days of old, is robbed, in this case, of all validity.

A view frequently urged is that, as with other nations, so with the Jews, the mythical period precedes the historical, and thus the earlier narratives of the Old Testament must be taken according to their true charcter. In later periods of the Old Testament we have records which, on the whole, are historical; but in the very earliest times we must not look for authentic history at all. We merely remark that our Lord's brief references to early Old Testament narrative would not suggest the distinction so often made between earlier and later Old Testament records on the score of trustworthiness.

The Old Testament from God

We advance to say that Christ accepts the Old Dispensation and its Scriptures as in a special sense from God; as having special, divine authority. Many who recognize no peculiar sacredness or authority in the religion of the Jews above other religions of the world, would readily admit that it is from God. But their contention is that all religions have elements of truth in them, that they all furnish media through which devout souls have fellowship with the Power which rules the universe, but that none of them should exalt its pretensions above the others, far less claim exclusive divine sanction; all of them being the product of man's spiritual nature, as molded by his history and environment, in different nations and ages.

But the utterances of Jesus Christ on this question of the divine origin of the Old Testament religion are unmistakable; and not less clear and decided is his language respecting the writing in which this religion is delivered. God is the source, in the directest sense, of both the religion and the records of it. No man can claim Christ's authority for classing Judaism with Confucianism, Hinduism, Buddhism, and Parseeism. It is abundantly evident that the Jewish faith is to our Lord the one true faith, and that the Jewish Scriptures have a place of their own, a place which cannot be shared with the sacred books of other peoples, "For salvation is of the Jews."

Almost any reference of our Lord to the Old Testament will support the statement that he regards these Scriptures as from God. He shows that Old Testament prophecy is fulfilled in himself, or he vindicates his teaching and his claims by Scripture, or he enjoins obedience to the law, or he asserts the inviolability of the law till its complete fulfilment, or he accuses a blinded and self-righteous generation of superseding and nullifying a law which they were bound to observe (cf. Matt. 5:18; 15:4; 21:13; 22:32; and Mk. 7:8). So many passages of the Old Testament are quoted or alluded to by the Lord as having received, or as awaiting fulfilment, that it is scarcely necessary to make citations of this class. These all most certainly imply the authority of Scripture; for no man, no creature, can tell what is hidden in the remote future.

We are not forgetting that the Lord fully recognizes the provisional character of the Mosaic law and of the Old Dispensation. Were the Old faultless, no place would have been found for the New. Had grace and truth come by Moses, the advent of Jesus Christ would have been unnecessary. But in all this there is nothing to modify the proposition which we are illustrating, that is, that our Lord accepts the Old Testament as from God, as stamped with divine authority, and as truly making known the divine mind and will.

God Speaks

Our Lord surely attributes to the Old Testament a far higher character than many have supposed. God speaks in it throughout. and while he will more perfectly reveal himself in his Son, not anything contained in the older revelation shall fail of its end or be convicted of error. Christ does not use the term "inspiration" in speaking of the Old Testament, but when we have adduced his words regarding the origins and authority of these writings, it will be evident that to him they are God-given in every part. It will be seen that his testimony falls not behind that of Paul (II Tim. 3:16) and Peter (II Pet. 1:21).

Words and Commands of God

In speaking of Christ as teaching that the Old Testament is from God we have referred to passages in which he says that its words and commands are those of God (Cf. Matt. 15:4 and Mk. 7:8, 9). Passages like these do more than prove that the Old Testament expresses on the whole the mind of God, and, therefore, possesses very high authority. If it can certainly be said that God spoke certain words, or that certain words and commandments are of God, we have more than a general endorsement. It needs, of course, no proof that the words quoted in the New Testament as spoken by God are not the only parts of the Old Testament which have direct divine authority. The same might evidently be said of other parts of the book. The impression left on every unprejudiced mind is that such quotations as the Lord made, are only specimens of a book in which God speaks throughout. There is surely no encouragement to attempt any analysis of Scripture into its divine and its human parts, to apportion the authorship between God and the human penman, for, as we have seen, the same words are ascribed to God and to his servant Moses. The whole is spoken by God and by Moses also. All is divine and at the same time all is human. The divine and the human are so related that separation is impossible.

Absolute Infallibility of Scripture

Attention may be called specially to three passages in which
the Lord refers to the origin and the absolute infallibility of
Scripture. They are Matthew 22: 42-45, John 10:34-36, and Matthew 5:17, 18. In the first, the reference is to Psalm 110, and our
Lord says David was completely under the Spirit's influence in
the production of the Psalm, so that the word has absolute
authority. Such is clearly the Lord's meaning, and the Pharisees
have no reply to his argument. In the second passage Christ vindicates himself from the charge of blasphemy in claiming to be the
Son of God, and that on the basis that the Old Testament Scripture
could not be broken. The authority of Scripture thus extends to
its individual terms (in this case, "gods"). If this is not verbal
inspiration, it is difficult to see what is. In the last text the Lord
in his Sermon on the Mount refers to his own relation to the
Old Testament economy and its Scriptures. No stronger words
could be employed to affirm the divine authority of every part of the
Old Testament; for the law and the prophets mean the entire Old
Testament. The question now remains, Can the words of Christ
be taken at their full meaning, or must they be discounted for some
reason or other? This question is of momentous import and will be
considerly presently.

Fulfilment of Prophecy

The inspiration of the Old Testament is clearly implied in the
many declarations of our Lord respecting the fulfillment of
prophecies contained in them. It is God's prerogative to know, and
to make known, the future. Human presage cannot go beyond
what is foreshadowed in events which have transpired, or is
wrapped up in causes which we plainly see in operation. If,
therefore, the Old Testament reveals, hundreds of years in advance,
what is coming to pass, omniscience must have directed the pen of
the writer; these Scriptures must be inspired (Cf. Matt. 26:31;
Jn. 5:46, 15:25; and Lk. 24:44-46 for such predictions). To teach
that the Old Testament contains authentic predictions is, as we
have said, to teach that it is inspired. The challenge of Isaiah is in
point (Isa. 41:23).

We thus find that our Lord recognizes the same Old Testament
canon we have, that so far as he makes reference to particular

books of the canon he ascribes them to the writers whose names they bear, that he regards the Jewish religion and its sacred books as in a special sense from God, that the writers of Scripture, in his view, spoke in the Spirit, that their words are so properly chosen that an argument may rest on the exactness of a term, that no part of Scripture shall fail of its end or be convicted of error, and that the predictions of Scripture are genuine predictions, which must all in their time receive fulfillment.

II. The Value of Christ's Testimony

It remains that we should briefly consider the value for the student of the Bible, of Christ's testimony to the Old Testament. Can we accept the utterances of Christ on these matters as having value, as of authority, in relation to biblical scholarship? Can we take them at their face value, or must they be discounted? There are two ways in which it is sought to invalidate Christ's testimony to the Old Testament.

1. *Ignorance of Jesus Alleged*

It is claimed that Jesus had no knowledge beyond that of his contemporaries as to the origin and literary characteristics of the Scriptures. The Jews believed that Moses wrote the Pentateuch, that the narratives of the Old Testament are all authentic history, and that the words of Scripture are all inspired. Christ shared the opinions of his countrymen on these topics, even when they were in error. To hold this view, it is maintained, does not detract from the Lord's qualifications for his proper work, which was religious and spiritual, not literary; for in relation to the religious value of the Old Testament and its spiritual uses and applications he may confidently be accepted as our guide. His knowledge was adequate to the delivery of doctrine, but did not necessarily extend to questions of scholarship and criticism. Of these he speaks as any other man; and to seek to arrest or direct criticism by appeal to his authority, is procedure which can only recoil on those who adopt it. This view is advanced, not only by critics who reject the deity of Christ, but by many who profess to believe that doctrine.

The doctrine of the *kenosis* is invoked to explain the imperfection of our Lord's knowledge on critical questions, as evidenced by the way in which he speaks of the Pentateuch and of various Old Testament problems. The subject of the limitation of Christ's knowledge during his earthly life is a difficult one, and its consideration is not in place here. But we may confidently affirm that the Lord's knowledge was entirely adequate to the perfect discharge of his prophetic office. To impute imperfection to him as the Teacher of the Church were indeed impious. Is it not quite clear that if the Lord's teaching be found in error, then his prophetic office is assailed? For the allegation is that, in holding fast to what he is freely allowed to have taught, we are imperiling the interests of faith. The critics whom we have in view must admit either that the points in question are of no importance, or that the Lord was imperfectly qualified for his prophetic work. Those who have reverence for the Bible will not admit either position.

2. *Theory of Accommodation*

The theory of accommodation is brought forward in explanation of those references of Christ to the Old Testament which endorse what are regarded as inaccuracies or popular errors. He spoke, it is said, regarding the Old Testament after the current opinion and belief. This belief was sometimes right and sometimes wrong; but where no interest of religion or morality was affected, where spiritual truth was not involved, he allowed himself, even where the common belief was erroneous, to speak in accord with it. The Lord is declared to have acted prudently, for no good end could have been served, it is asserted, by crossing the common opinion upon matters of little importance, and thus awakening or strengthening suspicion as to his teaching in general. As to the accommodation thus supposed to have been practiced by our Lord, we observe that if it implies, as the propriety of the term requires, a more accurate knowledge on his part than his language reveals, it becomes difficult in many instances to vindicate his perfect integrity.

Furthermore, we may say that if our Lord's statements about the authorship of parts of Scripture give a measure of countenance to opinions which are standing in the way of both genuine scholarship and of faith, it is hard to see how they can be regarded as instances of a justifiable accommodation. It seems to us that in this case you cannot vindicate the Lord's absolute truthfulness except by imputing to him a degree of ignorance which would unfit him for his office as permanent Teacher of the Church.

Two Positions Clear

Two positions may be affirmed: (1) The legislation of the Pentateuch is actually ascribed to Moses by the Lord. If this legislation is in the main long subsequent to Moses, and a good deal of it later than the exile, the Lord's language is positively misleading, and endorses an error which vitiates the entire construction of Old Testament history and the development of religion in Israel. (2) Moses is the writer of the law and it may with propriety be spoken of as his writings. The words of Jesus evidence that he regarded Moses as the writer of the books which bear his name. Less than this robs several of our Lord's statements of their point and force.

If all Scripture bears testimony to Christ, we cannot refuse to hear him when he speaks of its characteristics. It is folly, it is unutterable impiety, to decide differently from the Lord any question regarding the Bible on which we have his verdict; nor does it improve the case to say that we shall listen to him, when he speaks of spiritual truth, but shall count ourselves free when the question is one of scholarship. Alas for our scholarship when it brings us into controversy with him who is the Prophet, as he is the Priest and King of God, and by whose Spirit both prophets and apostles spoke!

Our object has been to show that the Lord regards the entire book, or collection of books, of the Old Testament, as divine, authoritative, infallible. Our Lord's testimony to the character of the Old Testament must remain unimpaired.

CANON G. OSBORNE TROOP (1854-1932) received a bachelor's degree from King's College in Windsor, Nova Scotia, in 1877. He served churches in Halifax, Nova Scotia; St. John, New Brunswick; Montreal; and Toronto between 1878 and 1920. His often published letters to local newspapers which discussed both theological and secular issues of his day.

7

The Internal Evidence of the Fourth Gospel

by Canon G. Osborne Troop, M.A.
MONTREAL, CANADA

The whole Bible is stamped with the divine "Hall-Mark"; but the Gospel according to St. John is *primus inter pares.* Through it, as through a transparency, we gaze entranced into the very holy of holies, where shines in unearthly glory "the great vision of the face of Christ." Yet man's perversity has made it the "storm center'" of New Testament criticism, doubtless for the very reason that it bears such unwavering testimony both to the deity of our Lord and Saviour, Jesus Christ, and to his perfect humanity. The Christ of the Fourth Gospel is no unhistoric, idealized vision of the later, dreaming church, but is, as it practically claims to be, the picture drawn by "the disciple whom Jesus loved,'" an eye-witness of the blood and water that flowed from his pierced side. These may appear to be mere unsupported statements, and as such will at once be dismissed by a scientific reader. Nevertheless the appeal of this article is to the instinct of the "one flock" of the "one Shepherd." "They know his voice . . . a stranger will they not follow."

1. There is one passage in this Gospel that flashes like lightning —it dazzles our eyes by its very glory. To the broken-hearted Martha the Lord Jesus says with startling suddenness, *"I am* the resurrection and the life; he that believeth on me, though he die, yet shall he live; and whosoever liveth and believeth in me, shall never die."

It is humbly but confidently submitted that these words are utterly beyond the reach of human invention. It could never have entered the heart of man to say, *"I am* the resurrection and the life." "There is a resurrection and a life," would have been a great and notable saying, but *this speaker* identifies *himself* with the resurrection and with life eternal. The words can only be born from above, and he who utters them is worthy of the utmost adoration of the surrendered soul.

In an earlier chapter John records a certain question addressed to and answered by our Lord in a manner which has no counterpart in the world's literature. "What shall we do," the eager people cry; "What shall we do that we might work the works of God?" "This is the work of God," our Lord replies, "that ye believe on him whom he hath sent" (John 6:28, 29). I venture to say that such an answer to such a question has no parallel. This is the work of God that ye accept me. I am the root of the tree which bears the only fruit pleasing to God. Our Lord states the converse of this in chapter 16, when he says that the Holy Spirit will "convict the world of sin . . . because they believe not on *me*." The root of all evil is unbelief in Christ. The condemning sin of the world lies in the rejection of the Redeemer. Here we have the root of righteousness and the root of sin in the acceptance or rejection of his wondrous personality. This is unique, and proclaims the Speaker to be "separate from sinners" though "the Lord hath laid on him the iniquity of us all." Truly,

> *He is his own best evidence,*
> *His witness is within.*

2. Pass on to the fourteenth chapter, so loved of all Christians. Listen to that voice, which is as the voice of many waters, as it sounds in the ears of the troubled disciples: "Let not your heart be troubled; ye believe in God, believe *also* in *me*. In my Father's house are many mansions: *if it were not so, I would have told you.* I go to prepare a place for you. And if I go and prepare a place for you, I will come again, and receive you unto myself; that where I am, there ye may be also."

Who is he who dares to say: "Ye believe in *God*, believe *also* in me"? He ventures thus to speak because he is the Father's Son. Man's son is man: can God's Son be anything less than God? Elsewhere in this Gospel he says: "I and the Father are one." The fourteenth chapter reveals the Lord Jesus as completely at home in the heavenly company. He speaks of his Father and of the Holy Spirit as himself being one of the utterly holy family. He knows all about his Father's house with its many mansions. He was familiar with it before the world was. Mark well, too, the exquisite touch of transparent truthfulness: "If it were not so, I would have told you." An *ear*-witness alone could have caught and preserved that touching parenthesis, and who more likely than the disciple whom Jesus loved?

As we leave this famous chapter let us not forget to note the wondrous words in verse 23: "If a man love me, he will keep my words; and my Father will love him, and we will come unto him and make our abode with him."

This saying can only be characterized as blasphemous, if it be not the true utterance of one equal with God. On the other hand, does any reasonable man seriously think that such words originated in the mind of a forger? "Every one that is of the truth heareth my voice," and surely that voice is here.

3. When we come to chapter 17 we pass indeed into the very inner chamber of the King of kings. It records the highpriestly prayer of our Lord, when he "lifted up his eyes to heaven and said, Father, the hour is come, glorify thy Son that thy Son may also glorify thee." Let any man propose to himself the awful task of forging such a prayer, and putting it into the mouth of an imaginary Christ. The brain reels at the very thought of it. It is, however, perfectly natural that St. John should record it. It must have fallen upon the ears of himself and his fellow-disciples amidst an awe-stricken silence in which they could hear the very throbbing of their listening hearts. For their very hearts were listening through their ears as the Son poured out his soul unto the Father. It is a rare privilege, and one from which most men would sensitively shrink, to listen even to a fellow-man alone with God. Yet the Lord Jesus in the midst of his disciples laid bare his very soul before his Father, as really as if he had been alone with him. He prayed with the cross and its awful death full in view, but in the prayer there is no slightest hint of failure or regret, and there is no trace of confession of sin or need of forgiveness. These are all indelible marks of genuineness. It would have been impossible for a sinful man to conceive such a prayer. But all is consistent with the character of him who "spake as never man spake," and could challenge the world to convict him of sin.

With such thoughts in mind, let us now look more closely into the words of the prayer itself.

"Father, the hour is come; glorify thy Son, that thy Son also may glorify thee: As thou hast given him power over all flesh, that he should give eternal life to as many as thou hast given him. And this is life eternal, that they might know thee, the only true God, and *Jesus Christ whom thou hast sent.*"

Here we have again the calm placing of himself on a level with the Father in connection with eternal life. And it is not out of place to recall the consistency of this utterance with that often-called "Johannine" saying recorded in St. Matthew and St. Luke: "All things are delivered unto me of my Father: and no man knoweth the Son, but the Father; neither knoweth any man the Father, save the Son, and he to whomsoever the Son willeth to reveal him."

We read also in St. John 14:6: "No man cometh unto the Father but by me." And as we reverently proceed further in the prayer we find him saying: "And now, O Father, glorify thou me with thine own self, with the glory which I had with thee *before the world was.*"

These words are natural to the Father's Son as we, know and worship him, but they are beyond the reach of an uninspired man, and who can imagine a forger inspired of the Holy Ghost? Such words would, however, be graven upon the very heart of an ear-witness such as the disciple whom Jesus loved.

We have in this prayer also the fuller revelation of the "one flock" and "one Shepherd" pictured in chapter ten: "Neither pray I for these alone, but for them also which shall believe on me through their word; that they all may be one; *as thou, Father, art in me, and I in thee, that they also may be one in us*: That *the world* may believe that thou hast sent me. And the glory which thou gavest me I have given them; that they may be one, even as we are one: I in them, and thou in me, that they may be perfected into one; and that the world may know that thou hast sent me, and *hast loved them, as thou hast loved me.*"

In these holy words there breathes a cry for such a unity as never entered into the heart of mortal man to dream of. It is no cold and formal ecclesiastical unity, such as that suggested by the curious and unhappy mistranslation of "one fold" for "one flock" in St. John 10:16. It is the living unity of the living flock with the living Shepherd of the living God. It is actually the same as the unity subsisting between the Father and the Son. And according to St. Paul in Rom. 8:19, the creation is waiting for its revelation. The one Shepherd has from the beginning had his one flock in answer to his prayer, but the world has not yet seen it, and is therefore still unconvinced that our Jesus is indeed the Sent of God. The world has seen the Catholic Church and the Roman Catholic Church but the Holy Catholic Church no eye as yet has seen but God's. For the Holy Catholic Church and the Shepherd's one flock are one and the same, and the world will not see either "till he come." The *Holy* Catholic Church is an object of faith and not of sight, and so is the one flock. In spite of all attempts at elimination and organization wheat and tares together grow, and sheep and wolves-in-sheep's-clothing are found together in the earthly pasture grounds. But when the Good Shepherd returns he will bring his beautiful flock with him, and eventually the world will see and believe. "O the depth of the riches both of the wisdom and knowledge of God! How unsearchable are his judgments, and his ways past finding out!"

The mystery of this spiritual unity lies hidden in the high-priestly prayer, but we may feel sure that no forger could ever discover it, for many of those who profess and call themselves Christians are blind to it even yet.

4. The "Christ before Pilate" of St. John is also stamped with every mark of sincerity and truth. What mere human imagination could evolve the noble words: "My kingdom is not of this world; if my kingdom were of this world, then would my servants fight, that I should not be delivered to the Jews: but now is my kingdom not from hence . . . To this end was I born, and for this cause came I into the world, that I should bear witness unto the truth. Every one that is of the truth heareth my voice"?

The whole wondrous story of the betrayal, the denial, the trial, the condemnation and crucifixion of the Lord Jesus, as given through St. John, breathes with the living sympathy of an eyewitness. The account, moreover, is as wonderful in the delicacy of its reserve as in the simplicity of its recital. It is entirely free from sensationalism and every form of exaggeration. It is calm and judicial in the highest degree. If it is written by the inspired disciple whom Jesus loved, all is natural and easily "understanded of the people"; while on any other supposition, it is fraught with difficulties that cannot be explained away. "I am not credulous enough to be an unbeliever," is a wise saying in this as in many similar connections.

5. The Gospel opens and closes with surpassing grandeur. With divine dignity it links itself with the opening words of Genesis: *"In the beginning* was the Word, and the Word was with God, and the Word was *God* . . . And the Word became flesh, and dwelt among us, and we beheld his glory, the glory as of the Only Begotten of the Father, full of grace and truth." What a life-like contrast with this sublime description is found in the introduction of John the Baptist: "There came *a man* sent from God whose name was John." In the Incarnation Christ did not become *a* man but *man.* Moreover, in this St. Paul and St. John are in entire agreement.

"There is one God," says St. Paul to Timothy; "one Mediator also between God and man — *himself man* — Christ Jesus." The reality of the divine Redeemer's human nature is beautifully manifested in the touching interview between the weary Saviour and the guilty Samaritan woman at the well; as also in his perfect human friendship with Mary and Martha and their brother Lazarus, culminating in the priceless words, "Jesus wept."

And so by the bitter way of the Cross the grandeur of the Incarnation passes into the glory of the Resurrection. The last two chapters are alive with thrilling incident. If any one wishes to form a true conception of what those brief chapters contain, let him read "Jesus and the Resurrection," by the saintly Bishop of Durham (Dr. Handley Moule) and his cup of holy joy will fill to overflowing. At the empty tomb we breathe the air of the unseen kingdom, and presently we gaze enraptured on the face of the Crucified but risen and ever-living King. Mary Magdalene, standing in her broken-hearted despair, is all unconscious of the wondrous fact that holy angels are right in front of her and standing behind her is her living Lord and Master. Slowly but surely the glad story spreads from lip to lip and heart to heart, until even the honest but stubborn Thomas is brought to his knees, crying in a burst of remorseful, adoring joy, "My Lord and my God!"

Then comes the lovely story of the fruitless all-night toil of the seven fishermen, the appearance at dawn of the Stranger on the beach, the miraculous draught of fishes, the glad cry of recognition, "It is the Lord!", the never-to-be-forgotten breakfast with the risen Saviour, and his searching interview with Peter, passing into the mystery of St. John's old age.

In all these swiftly-drawn outlines we feel ourselves instinctively in the presence of the truth. We are crowned with the Saviour's beautitude: "Blessed are they that have not seen, and yet have believed," and we are ready to yield a glad assent to the statement which closes chapter twenty: "Many other signs truly did Jesus in the presence of his disciples, which are not written in this book; but these are written that ye might believe that Jesus is the Christ, the Son of God; and that believing ye might have life in his Name."

JAMES ORR (1844-1913) graduated from Glasgow University in his native Scotland. Between 1874 and 1891, he was a parish minister at East Bank United Presbyterian Church in Hawick. He left the pastorate to teach church history at the United Presbyterian Theological College in Glasgow until 1901, when he became professor of apologetics and dogmatics at Glasgow (later called Trinity) College. Orr enjoyed studying the progress of church doctrine, which he saw as following a divine logic. His major works included *The Christian View of God and the World* (1893, republished in 1989 by Kregel Publications) and *The Progress of Dogma* (1897).

8

The Early Narratives of Genesis

By Professor James Orr, D.D.
UNITED FREE CHURCH COLLEGE, GLASGOW, SCOTLAND

Revised by Charles L. Feinberg, Th.D., Ph.D.

By the early narratives of Genesis are to be understood the first eleven chapters of the book, those which precede the time of Abraham. These chapters present peculiarities of their own, although the critical treatment applied to them is not confined to these chapters, but extends throughout the whole Book of Genesis, the Book of Exodus, and the later history with much the same result in reducing them to legend.

We may begin by looking at the matter covered by these eleven chapters, to see what they contain. First, we have the sublime introduction to the Book of Genesis, and to the whole Bible, in the creation account in Genesis 1. This chapter manifestly stands in its fit place as the preface to all that follows. Where is there anything like it in all literature? There is nothing anywhere, in Babylonian legend or anywhere else. You may ask what interest religious faith has in the doctrine of creation, in any theory or speculation on how the world came to be. The answer is that it has the very deepest interest. The interest of religion in the doctrine of creation is that this doctrine is our guarantee for the dependence of all things on God, the ground of our assurance that everything in nature and providence is at his disposal. Suppose there was anything in the universe that was not created by God, that existed independently of him, how could we be sure that that element might not thwart, defeat, destroy the fulfilment of God's purpose? The Biblical doctrine of creation forever excludes that supposition.

Following on this primary account of creation is a second narrative in a different style, from chapter 2 to 4, but closely connected with the first by the words, "In the day that the Lord God made earth and heaven."' This is sometimes spoken of as a second narrative of creation, and is often said to contradict the first. But this is a mistake. As has been pointed out before, this second narrative is not a history of creation in the sense of the first at all. It has nothing to say of the creation of either heaven or earth, of the heavenly bodies, of the general world of vegetation. It deals simply with man and God's dealings with man when first created, and everythng in the narrative is regarded and grouped from this point of view. The heart of the narrative is the story of the temptation and the fall of man. It is sometimes said that the fall is not alluded to in later Old Testament books, and therefore cannot be regarded as an essential part of revelation. It would be truer to say that the story of the fall, standing at the beginning of the Bible, furnishes the key to all that follows. What is the picture given in the whole Bible? Is it not that of a world turned aside from God, living in rebellion against him, disobedient to his calls, and resisting his grace? What is the explanation of this universal apostasy and transgression, if it is not that man has fallen from his first estate? For certainly this is not the state in which God made man, or wishes him to be. The truth is, if this story of the fall were not there at the beginning of the Bible, we would need to put it there for ourselves in order to explain the moral state of the world as the Bible pictures it to us, and as we know it to be. In chapter 4, as an appendix to these chapters, there follows the story of Cain and Abel, with brief mention of the commencement of civilization in Cain's line, and of the start of a godly line in Seth.

Returning to the style of Genesis 1, we have the genealogical line of Seth from Adam to Noah, in chapter 5. You are struck with the longevity of those patriarchal figures in the dawn of time, but not less with the constant sad refrain which ends each notice, Enoch's alone excepted, "and he died." This chapter connects directly with the creation account in Genesis 1, but presupposes equally the narrative of the fall in the intervening chapters. Critical works often assert the contrary, but some of the leading critics must admit that the story of the flood presupposes the fall narrative.

Then you come to the flood story in Genesis 6, in which two narratives are alleged to be blended. Yet criticism itself must admit that these two stories fit wonderfully into each other, and the one is incomplete without the other. If one, for instance, gives the command to Noah and his house to enter the ark, it is the other that narrates the building of the ark. What is still more striking, when you compare the Bible stories with the Babylonian account of the deluge, you find that it takes both of these so-called narratives in Genesis to make up the one complete story of the tablets. Following the flood and the covenant with Noah, the race of man spreads out again as shown in the table of nations in chapter 10. In 10:25 it is noted that in the days of Peleg the earth was divided; then in chapter 11 you have the story of the divine judgment at Babel confusing human speech, and this is followed by a new genealogy extending to Abraham.

Such is a brief survey of the material, and on the face of it, it must be admitted that this is a wonderfully well-knit piece of history of its own kind which we have before us, not in the least resembling the loose, incoherent, confused mythologies of other nations. There is nothing resembling it in any other history or religious book, and when we come to speak of the great ideas which pervade it, and give it its unity, our wonder is still increased. Critical scholars will acknowledge the great ideas, but they claim they were not there originally, but inserted later by the prophets to make the old legends religiously profitable. It is preferable by far to believe that the great ideas were there from the very first.

The truth is, a great deal depends on the method of approach to these old narratives. There is a saying, "Everything can be laid hold of by two handles," and that is true of these ancient stories. Approach them in one way and they are a bundle of fables, legends, myths, without historical basis of any kind. Then these myths can be treated in such a way that Cain is composed originally out of three distinct figures, blended together, Noah out of another three, and so on. Approach these narratives in another way and they are the oldest and most precious traditions of our race; worthy in their intrinsic merit of standing where they do at the commencement of the Word of God, and capable of maintaining their right to be there; not merely vehicles of great ideas, but presenting in their own ancient way the memory of great historic truths. The story of the fall, for example, is not a myth, but embodies the shuddering memory of an actual moral catastrophe in the beginning of our race, which brought woe and death into the world.

We come now to the question, Is there any external corroboration or confirmation of these early narratives in Genesis? The remarkable discoveries in Babylonia are well known, and throw extraordinary light on the high culture of early Babylonia. Here, long before Abraham, we find ourselves in the midst of cities, arts, books, libraries, and Abraham's own age was the flourishing period of this civilization. Instead of Israel's being a people just emerging from the dim dawn of barbarism, we find in the light of these discoveries that it was a people on whom had converged the riches of a civilization extending millenniums into the past. For us the chief interest of these discoveries is the help they give us in answering the question, How far do these narratives in Genesis embody for us the oldest traditions of our race? There are two reasons which lead us to look with some confidence to Babylonia for the answer to this question. For one thing, in early Babylonia we are already far back into the times to which many of these traditions relate; for another, the Bible itself points to Babylonia as the original area of those traditions. Eden was in the region of Babylonia, as shown by its rivers, the Euphrates and Tigris. It was in Babylonia the ark was built; and on a mountain in the vicinity of Babylonia the ark rested. It was from the plain of Shinar, in Babylonia, that the new dispersion of the race took place. To Babylonia, therefore, if anywhere, we are entitled to look for light on these ancient traditions, and we find it.

Take only one or two examples. The first is that old tenth chapter of Genesis, the table of nations. It has been acclaimed an ethnographical document of the first importance. Here we have (verses 8-10) certain statements about the origin of Babylonian civilization. We find (1) that Babylonia is one of the oldest of civilizations; (2) that the Assyrian civilization was derived from Babylonia; and (3) strangest of all, that the founders of the

Babylonian civilization were not Semites, but Hamites, descendants of Cush. Each of these statements was in contradiction to old views, and to what was currently believed about these ancient people until the discoveries taught otherwise. Yet it will not be disputed that exploration has justified the Bible on each of these points.

Glance now at the stories of creation, Paradise, and of the deluge. Some cuneiform accounts bear a remote resemblance to the story of Paradise and the fall. On the other hand, the libraries of Mesopotamia have furnished versions of the story of the deluge. The flood narrative, like the Babylonian creation story, is debased, polytheistic, and mythical with little analogy to the account in Genesis. Did the Israelites borrow their narrative from these sources? The contrast in spirit and character between the accounts would forbid any such derivation. The debased form may conceivably come from corruption of the higher, but not the reverse. The relation is one of cognateness, not of derivation. These traditions came down from a much older source, and are preserved by the Hebrews in their purer form.

Something must be said on the scientific and historical aspects of these narratives. Science is invoked to prove that the narratives of creation in Genesis 1, the story of man's origin and fall in chapters 2 and 3, the account of patriarchal longevity in chapters 5 and 11, the story of the deluge, and other matters, must all be rejected, because they are in open contradiction to the facts of modern knowledge. When science is said to contradict the Bible, what is meant by contradiction? The Bible was never given us in order to anticipate or forestall the discoveries of twentieth century science. The Bible, as every informed interpreter of Scripture has always held, takes the world as it is, and uses popular language appropriate to the common man, not the specialist. It does not follow that because the Bible does not teach modern science, we are justified in saying that it contradicts it. In these narratives of Genesis the standpoint of the author is so true, the illumination with which he is endowed so divine, his insight into the order of nature so unerring, that there is little, if anything, in his description that even yet, with our advanced knowledge, needs to be changed.

It would be well if those who speak of disagreement with science would look to the great truths embedded in these narratives which science may be called upon to confirm. There is, for example, (1) the truth that man is the last of God's created works, the crown of God's creation. Does science contradict that? (2) There is the great truth of the unity of the human race. No ancient people believed in such unity of the race, and at one time science cast doubts upon it. Does science contradict that? (3) There is the declaration that man was made in God's image. Does the science of man's nature contradict that? (4) The region of Babylonia is given as the very area of man's origin. Is this in contradiction with history? It lies outside the realm of science to contradict this.

In conclusion, it is clear that the narratives of creation, the fall, the flood, are not myths, but narratives containing the knowledge or memory of real transactions. The creation of the world was certainly not a myth, but a fact, and the representation of the different creative acts dealt likewise with facts. The language used was not that of modern science, but under divine guidance the sacred writer gives a broad, general picture which conveys a true idea of the order of the divine working in creation. Man's fall was also a tremendous fact with universal consequences in sin and death to the race. Man's origin can only be explained through an exercise of direct creative activity. The flood was an historical fact, and the preservation of Noah and his family is one of the best and most widely attested of human traditions. In these narratives in Genesis and the facts which they embody, is really laid the foundation of all else in the Bible. The unity of revelation binds them up with the Christian Gospel.

GEORGE LIVINGSTONE ROBINSON (1864-1958) put his knowledge of Old Testament to good use in his successful archaeological exploration of Palestine. His most important find was the high place of Petra. Robinson graduated in 1877 from Princeton University with a bachelor's degree, and in 1893 he graduated from Princeton Theological Seminary. His varied teaching career included stints at Knox College, Toronto; the American School of Archaeology in Jerusalem; and McCormick Theological Seminary in Chicago. His writings include *The Biblical Doctrine of Holiness, Leaders of Israel*, and *Why I Am a Christian*.

9

One Isaiah

By *Professor George L. Robinson, D.D.*
FORMERLY OF MCCORMICK THEOLOGICAL SEMINARY, CHICAGO

Revised by Charles L. Feinberg, Th.D., Ph.D.

For more than two millenniums there was no serious doubt that Isaiah the son of Amoz was the author of every part of the book that bears his name. The Christian Church was unanimous on this matter, until certain German scholars more than a century and a half ago called the unity of the book into question. The critical disintegration of the Book of Isaiah began with Koppe, who in 1780 first doubted the genuineness of chapter 50. In 1789 Doederlein suspected the whole of chapters 40-66. He was followed by Rosenmueller, who was the first to deny to Isaiah the prophecy against Babylon in chapters 13:1—14:23. Eichhorn, at the beginning of the last century, further eliminated the oracle against Tyre in chapter 23, and with Gesenius and Ewald, also denied the Isaianic origin of chapters 24-27. Gesenius also ascribed to some unknown prophet chapters 15 and 16. Rosenmueller went further, and pronounced against chapters 34 and 35. Not long afterwards (1840), Ewald questioned chapters 12 and 33. Thus by the middle of the last century some thirty-seven or thirty-eight chapters were rejected as no part of Isaiah's actual writings.

In 1879-80 the celebrated Franz Delitzsch of Leipzig, who for years had defended the genuineness of the entire book, finally yielded to the modern critical position, and in the 1889 edition of his commentary interpreted chapters 40-66, though with much hesitation, as coming from the close of the period of the Babylonian exile. About the same time (1889-90) Driver and George Adam Smith gave popular impetus to similar views in Great Britain. Since 1890 the criticism of Isaiah has been even more microscopic than before. Duhm, Stade, Guthe, Hackmann, Cornill, and Marti on the continent, and Cheyne, Whitehouse, Box, Glaze-brook, Kennett, and others in Great Britain and America, have questioned portions which hitherto were supposed to be genuine.

Even the unity of chapters 40-66, which were supposed to be the work of the Second Isaiah, has been given up. What prior to 1890 was supposed to be the unique product of some celebrated but anonymous sage who lived in Babylonia in the sixth century B.C., is now commonly divided and subdivided, and in large part distributed among various writers from Cyrus to Simon. At first it was thought sufficient to separate chapters 63-66 as a later addition to "Deutero-Isaiah's" prophecies; but more recently it has become the fashion to distinguish between chapters 40-55, which are alleged to have been written in Babylonia about 549-538 B.C., and chapters 56-66, which are claimed to have been composed about 460-445 B.C. Some carry disintegration even farther than this, especially in the case of chapters 56-66, which are subdivided into various fragments, and said to be the product of a school of writers rather than a single pen. Opinons also conflict as to the place of their composition, whether in Babylonia, Palestine, Phoenicia, or Egypt.

The present state of the Isaiah question is complex and dead-locked. No important commentaries on Isaiah have appeared since 1900. Among those who deny the integrity of the book have been Driver, G. A. Smith, Skinner, Cheyne, Duhm, Guthe, Marti, Kennett, and more recently Pfeiffer with many others. Those who have defended the unity of Isaiah have been Naegelsbach, W. H. Green, Margoliouth, Robinson, Moeller, and more recently Allis, E. J. Young, Fitch, and others.

What is the basic reason for the dissection of the book? The fundamental axiom of criticism is the dictum that a prophet always spoke out of a definite historical situation to the present needs of the people among whom he lived, and that a definite historical situation should be pointed out for each prophecy. This fundamental postulate underlies all modern criticism of Old Testament prophecy. This principle on the whole is sound, but it can easily be overworked. Certain cautions are necessary: (1) It is impossible to trace each separate section of prophecy, indepen-dently of its context, to a definite historical situation. (2) It is not necessarily the greatest event in a nation's history, or the event about which the most is known, that may actually have given birth, humanly speaking, to a particular prophecy. Israel's history is full of crises and events, any one of which may easily be claimed to furnish an appropriate, or at least a possible, background for a given prophecy. (3) The prophets usually spoke directly to the needs of their own day, but they spoke also to the generations yet to come. Isaiah commanded that his teachings be preserved for the future (8:16; 30:8; and 42:23).

When or how the Book of Isaiah was edited and brought into its present form is unknown. Jesus ben Sirach, the author of Ecclesiasticus, writing about 180 B.C., cites Isaiah as one of the notable worthies of Hebrew antiquity, in whose days, "the sun went backward and he added life to the king" (Ecclus. 48:20-25; cf. Isa. 38:4-8); and he adds, who "saw by an excellent spirit that which should come to pass at the last, and comforted them that mourned in Zion." Evidently, therefore, at the beginning of the second century B.C., at the latest, the Book of Isaiah had reached its present form, and the last twenty-seven chapters were already ascribed to the son of Amoz.

Furthermore, there is absolutely no proof that chapters 1-39, or any other considerable section of Isaiah's prophecies ever existed by themselves as an independent collection; nor is there any ground for thinking that the Messianic portions have been systematically interpolated by editors long subsequent to Isaiah's own time. The recently discovered Dead Sea Scrolls (1947) reveal no break between the former and latter portions of the Book of Isaiah.

Certain false presuppositions govern the critics in their disintegration of the Book of Isaiah. For one the conversion of the heathen (2:2-4) was beyond the horizon of an eighth century prophet; for another the picture of universal peace (11:1-9) signifies a late date; for still another the concept of universal judgment (14:26) is beyond the range of Isaiah's thought; for yet another the apocalyptic nature of chapters 24-27 fits a time after Ezekiel. Radicals deny *in toto* the existence of Messianic passages among Isaiah's own predictions. But to deny to Isaiah of the eight century all catholicity of grace, all universalism of salvation or judgment, every highly developed Messianic ideal, every rich note of promise and comfort, all sublime faith in the sacred character of Zion, as some do, is unwarrantedly to create a new Isaiah of grealy reduced proportions, a statesman of not very optimistic vein though a preacher of righteousness, and the exponent of a cold ethical religion without the warmth and glow of the messages which are actually ascribed to the prophet of the eighth century.

The basic postulates of much criticism are unsound, and broad facts must decide the unity or collective character of Isaiah's book.   To determine the exact historical background of each section is simply impossible, as the history of criticism plainly shows.   Verbal exegesis may do more harm than good.   Greater regard must be paid to the structure of the book.   When treated as an organic whole, the book is a grand masterpiece.   One great purpose dominates the author throughout, which is brought gradually to a climax in a picture of Israel's redemption and the glorification of Zion.   Failure to recognize this unity incapacitates a man to do it exegetical justice.   To regard the book as a heterogeneous mass of miscellaneous prophecies which were written at widely separated times and under varied circumstances from Isaiah's own period down to the Maccabean age, and freely interpolated throughout the intervening centuries, is to lose sight of the great historic realities and perspective of the prophet.   In short, the whole problem of how much or how little Isaiah wrote would become immensely simplified if critics would only divest themselves of a mass of unwarranted presuppositions and arbitrary restrictions which fix hard and fast what each century can think and say.

There are, moreover, arguments that corroborate a belief that there was but one Isaiah.   The circle of ideas is strikingly the same throughout.   For example, take the name of God which is almost peculiar to the Book of Isaiah, "The Holy One of Israel." This title occurs in the Book of Isaiah a total of twenty-five times, and only six times elsewhere in the Old Testament.   The presence of this divine name in all the different sections of the book (1:4; 10:20; 30:11, 12, 15; 45:11; 54:5; 60:9, 14) is of more value in identifying Isaiah as the author of all these prophecies, than if his name had been inscribed at the beginning of every chapter, for the reason that his theology is woven into the very fiber and texture of the whole book. Another concept repeated in the book is that of a "remnant" (1:9; 11:11, 12, 16; 28:5; 46:3; 65:8, 9). Another is the position held by "Zion" in the prophet's thoughts (2:3; 24:23; 30:19; 34:8; 46:13; 52:1; 60:14; 62:1, 11; 65:11, 25; 66:8). These and others stamp the book psychologically with an individuality which it is difficult to account for, if it be broken up into various sections and distributed, as some do, over the centuries.

A second argument for one Isaiah is literary style. It is remarkable that the clause, "for the mouth of Jehovah hath spoken it," should be found three times in the Book of Isaiah, and nowhere else in the Old Testament (cf. 1:20; 40:5; 58:14). Most peculiar is the tendency on the part of the author to emphatic reduplication (cf. 2:7, 8; 40:1; 43:11; 51:12; 62:10). Isaiah's style differs widely from that of every other Old Testament prophet, and is as far removed as possible from that of Ezekiel and the post-exilic prophets.

Historical references are a third argument for unity of authorship. Take, for example, the prophet's constant reference to Judah and Jerusalem in 1:7-9; 5:13; 24:19; 40:2, 9; 62:4 also to the temple and its ritual of worship and sacrifice in 1:11-15; 43:23, 24; and 66:1-3, 6, 20. As for the exile, the prophet's attitude to it throughout is that of both anticipation and realization (cf. 57:1; 3:8; and 11:11, 12).

Finally, a fourth argument for one Isaiah is the predictive element. This is the strongest proof of the unity of the book. Prediction is the very essence of prophecy. Isaiah was pre-eminently a prophet of the future. With unparalleled suddenness he repeatedly leaps from despair to hope, from threat to promise, from the actual to the ideal. Isaiah spoke to his own age, but he also addressed himself to the ages to come. His verb tenses are characteristically futures and prophetic perfects. He was exceptionally given to predicting; thus, before the Syro-Ephraimitic War (734 B.C.) he foretold the fall of Ephraim (7:8) and the spoiling of Damascus and Samaria (8:4; cf. 7:16); before the downfall of Samaria in 722 B.C., he foretold the fate of Tyre (23:15); prior to the siege of Ashdod in 711 B.C. he predicted

judgment on Moab and Kedar (16:14; 21:16); not long before
the siege of Jerusalem by Sennacherib in 701 B.C. he foretold
the failure of the invasion (29:5) and the fall of Assyria (30:17,
31; 31:8). Repeatedly he pointed to predictions which he had
already made in the earlier years of his ministry, and to the fact
that they had been fulfilled (cf. 41:21-23, 26ff.; 42:9, 23; 43:9,
12; 44:7, 8, 27, 28; 45:1-4, 11, 21; 46:10, 11; and 48:3, 5, 6-8,
14-16).

From all these numerous explicit and oft-repeated predictions
one thing is obvious, namely, that great emphasis is laid on prediction throughout the Book of Isaiah. Cyrus must be considered
as predicted from any point of view. It really makes little
difference at which end of history one stands, whether in the
eighth century B.C. or in the sixth, Cyrus is the subject of prediction to the author of chapters 40-48. Whether, indeed, he is
really predicting Cyrus in advance of all fulfilment, or whether
Cyrus to him is the fulfilment of some ancient prediction, does
not alter the fact that Cyrus was the subject of prediction on
the part of somebody. If a decision must be made as to when
Cyrus was actually predicted, it is obviously necessary to assume
that he was predicted long before his actual appearance. This is
in keeping with the test of prophecy in Deuteronomy 18:22. There
is a similar prediction in the Old Testament: King Josiah was
predicted by name more than two centuries before he came (I Kings
13:2). The very point of Isaiah's argument everywhere is that he
is predicting events which God alone is capable of foretelling and
bringing to pass; in other words, that prescience is the proof of
Jehovah's deity.

Why should men object to prediction on so large a scale?
Unless there is definiteness about any given prediction, unless it
transcends ordinary prognostication, there is no special value in
it. The only possible objection is that prediction of so minute a
character is abhorrent to reason. But the answer to such an
objection is already at hand; it may be abhorrent to reason, but
it is certainly a handmaid to faith. Faith has to do with the
future, even as prediction has to do with the future; and the Old
Testament is preeminently a book which encourages faith.

The one outstanding differentiating characteristic of Israel's religion is predictive prophecy. Only the Hebrews ever predicted the coming of the Messiah of the kingdom of God. Accordingly to predict the coming of a Cyrus as the human agent of Israel's deliverance is but the reverse side of the same prophet's picture of the divine Agent, the obedient, suffering Servant of Jehovah, who would redeem Israel from their sin. Deny to Isaiah the son of Amoz the predictions concerning Cyrus, and the prophecy is robbed of its essential character and unique perspective; emasculate these latter chapters of Isaiah of their predictive feature, and they are reduced to a mere prediction after the event, and their religious value is largely lost.

JOSEPH DAWSON WILSON (1840-1925) was one of the founders of the Reformed Episcopal Church in America (1874). From 1867 to 1874, he was rector of Calvary Church, Pittsburgh, and then served congregations in Illinois, Missouri, and British Columbia. In 1901, he joined the faculty of the Reformed Episcopal Seminary in Philadelphia. His publications included *Studies on Words From the Cross* (1884) and *Did Daniel Write Daniel?* (1896).

10

The Book of Daniel

By Professor Joseph D. Wilson, D.D.
THEOLOGICAL SEMINARY OF THE REFORMED EPISCOPAL CHURCH, PHILADELPHIA

Abridged and emended by Charles L. Feinberg, Th.D., Ph.D.

Modern objections to the Book of Daniel were started by scholars who were prejudiced against the supernatural. Daniel foretells events which have occurred in history. Therefore, these scholars argue, the alleged predictions must have been written after the events.

But the supernatural is not impossible, nor is it improbable, if sufficient reason for it exists in the purpose of God. It is not impossible, for instance, that an event so marvelous as the coming of the divine into humanity in the person of Jesus Christ should be predicted. So far from being impossible, it seems exceedingly probable; and furthermore, it seems not unreasonable that a prophet predicting a great and far distant event, like that mentioned above, should give some evidence to his contemporaries or immediate successors that he was a true prophet. Jeremiah foretold the seventy years captivity. Were his hearers warranted in believing that? Certainly. For he also foretold that all those lands would be subjected to the king of Babylon. A few years showed the latter prophecy to be true, and reasonable men believed the prediction of the seventy years exile.

Certain scholars have set forth an opinion that the Book of Daniel is a pious fraud. Others have tried to save something of the wreckage of the book, which has been the comfort and stay of suffering saints through the ages, by dwelling on its moral and religious teaching. Such apologists have done harm in fostering the idea that a fraud may be used for holy purposes, and that a forger is a proper teacher of religious truth.

These scholars find in Daniel 8, under the figure of a little horn, that Antiochus Epiphanes is predicted as persecuting the Jews. The vision is of the ram and he-goat which represent Persia and Greece, so specified by name. A notable horn of the he-goat, Alexander the Great, was broken, and in its place arose four horns, the four kingdoms into which the Greek Empire was divided. From one of these four came the little horn. That this refers primarily to Antiochus Epiphanes there is no doubt. He died about 163 B.C. The theory of the destructive critics is that some "pious and learned Jew" wrote the Book of Daniel at that time to encourage the Maccabees in their revolt against this evil king; that the book pretends to have been written in Babylon, some 370 years before, in order to pass it off as a revelation from God. This theory has been supported by numerous arguments, mostly conjectural and all without proof.

The imaginary Jew is termed "pious" because of the lofty religious ideas in the book, and "learned" because of his intimate acquaintance with the conditions and appointments of the Babylonian court four centuries before his day. But as no man, however learned, can write an extended history out of his imagination without some inaccuracies, the critics have searched diligently for mistakes. The chief of these alleged mistakes will be considered now.

We meet a difficulty at the threshold of the critical hypothesis. Daniel 9:26 foretells the destruction of Jerusalem and the temple; a calamity so frightful to the Jewish mind that the Greek translation of the Old Testament shrank from translating the Hebrew. What sort of encouragement was this? The hypothesis limps at the threshold.

Since Anthiochus Epiphanes is predicted in chapter 8, the critics try to force him into chapter 7. They attempt to identify the little horn of chapter 7 with that of chapter 8. There is no resemblance between them. The little horn of chapter 7 springs up as an eleventh horn among *ten* kings. He is diverse from the other kings. He continues until the Son of Man comes in the clouds of heaven, and the kingdom which shall never be destroyed is set up. Antiochus Epiphanes, the little horn of chapter 8, comes out of one of the *four* horns into which

Alexander's kingdom resolved itself. He was not diverse from other kings, but was like scores of other evil monarchs, and he did not continue until the Son of Man.

These differences render the attempted identification impossible, but an examination of the two sets of prophecies in their entirety shows this clearly. Chapters 2 and 7 are a prophecy of world history until the millennial kingdom. Chapters 8 and 11 refer to a crisis in Jewish history, a crisis now long past.

Chapter 2 with its dream of the colossal image tells of four world-kindoms, to be succeeded by a number of sovereignties, some strong and some weak, continuing until the God of heaven would set up a kingdom never to be destroyed. Chapter 7 with the vision of the four beasts parallels chapter 2. The same four world-empires are in view; the fourth beast which is succeeded by ten kings continues until the coming of the Son of Man, who will set up an eternal kingdom. These four world-empires were Babylon, Persia, Greece, and Rome. There have been no other world-empires since. Efforts have been made to unite the different parts of the vision, but this is impossible.

These prophecies which are illustrated in every particular by history to the present time stand in the way of the theory. The Roman Empire must be eliminated to get rid of prediction, and any help to that end has been welcomed. Some critics make the kingdom of the Seleucidae, which was one of the parts of the Greek Empire, the fourth world-kingdom, but it never was a world-kingdom. It was part of the Greek Empire, one of the four heads of the leopard. Other critics create an imaginary Median Empire between Babylon and Persia. There was no such empire. The Medo-Persian Empire was one. Cyrus the Persian conquered Babylon. History says so and excavations confirm it.

The attempt of the little horn of chapter 8, Antiochus Epiphanes, to extirpate the true faith failed. Yet it was almost successful. Daniel's prophecy encouraged the faithful few to resist the Greek and their own faithless fellow countrymen. God foresaw and forewarned. The warning was unheeded by the mass of the Jews, but fortunately there was a believing remnant and the true faith was saved from extinction.

The Seventy Weeks of Daniel 9:24-27. "Weeks" in this prophecy are not weeks of days but "sevens" or "heptads" of years. From the issuance of a commandment to restore and rebuild Jerusalem unto Messiah there would be 69 sevens, i.e., 483 years. Messiah would be cut off and have nothing, and the people and their prince would destroy Jerusalem and the temple. It came to pass in the procuratorship of Pontius Pilate. Messiah appeared; he was cut off; he had nothing of his rightful kingdom on David's throne. And before that generation passed away, the Romans destroyed the city and sanctuary, and scattered the Jewish nation, bringing to an end their political economy. Unto Messiah the Prince there were to be 483 years from the edict to rebuild Jerusalem. That decree was issued in the twentieth year of Artaxerxes Longimanus, about 445 B.C. The 483 years terminated in the time of Pontius Pilate, who governed from 26 A.D. to 36 A.D.

All this is plain enough, and if the words of Daniel had been written after the death of our Saviour and the fall of Jerusalem, no one could fail to see that the Lord Jesus Christ is indicated. But if written in the exile, this would be supernatural prediction, hence the struggles to evade somehow the implications of the passage. To find some prominent person who was "cut off" before 163 B.C. was the first requirement. The highpriest Onias, who was murdered through his rivals for office, was the most suitable person. He was in no sense the Messiah, but having been anointed he might be made to serve. He died 171 B.C. The next step was to find an edict to rebuild Jerusalem, 483 years before 171 B.C. That date was 654 B.C. during the reign of Manasseh, son of Hezekiah. No decree could be found there. But by deducting 49 years, the date was brought to 605 B.C., and since in that year Jeremiah had foretold (Jer. 25:9) the destruction of Jerusalem, perhaps this would do.

There were two objections to this view; one, that a prophecy of desolation to the city and sanctuary then in existence was not a commandment to restore and rebuild, and the other objection was that this also was a supernatural prediction, and as such, not acceptable to the critics. So recourse was had to the decree of Cyrus (Ezra 1:1-4) made in 536 B.C. But Cyrus' decree authorized, not the building of Jerusalem, but the temple. Nor is it likely that a wise king like Cyrus would have permitted a fortified city to be built in a remote corner of his empire close to his enemy, Egypt, with which the Jews had frequently plotted in previous years. The city was not restored until the twentieth year of Artaxerxes (Neh. 2:3, 8, 13). Permission to build could safely be given then, for Egypt had been conquered, and the loyalty of the Jews to Persia had been tested. Moreover, the date of Cyrus' decree does not meet the conditions. From 536 B.C. to 171 B.C. is 365 years and not 483. A "learned and pious Jew" would not have made such a blunder in arithmetic when foisting a forgery on his countrymen.

There were four decrees concerning Jerusalem issued by the Persian court. The first under Cyrus, mentioned above, the second under Darius Hystaspis (Ezra 6). The third in the seventh year of Artaxerxes (Ezra 7:12-26). All of these concern the temple. The fourth in the twentieth year of Artaxerxes was the only one to restore and rebuild a walled town.

Supposed Inaccuracies

The critical interpretations of the aforementioned prophecies are so unnatural, that they place a heavy strain on our credulity. Accordingly, attempts have been made to discredit the Book of Daniel by showing it could not have been written in Babylon, and by disclosing historical inaccuracies. The alleged inaccuracies can be shown to confirm the historical accuracy and reliability of the book.

(1) First, there may be mentioned the fact that no historian mentions Belshazzar. It was assumed that the name had been invented. Excavations have shown beyond a doubt that Belshazzar lived in Babylon.

(2) Fault is found with the title "king" which Daniel gives to Belshazzar; it is asserted that no tablets have been found dated in his reign. Since Belshazzar was co-regent with his father, his father's name would be in the dates. He was the heir to the throne, and even if not formally invested, was the virtual king in the eyes of the people.

(3) It is contended that Belshazzar was not the son of Nebuchadnezzar as is stated in Daniel 5:11. If he were the grandson through his mother, the same language would be used, and the undisturbed reign of Nabonidus, his father, is accounted for in this way.

(4) The critics have attacked Daniel's mention of the "Chaldeans" as a guild of wise men. The claim is that only four centuries after Daniel's time did the term signify a guild. Herodotus visited Babylon, and used the word in the same sense as Daniel and in no other (Herod. 1:181, 185).

(5) As to the Greek words in Daniel, relied on by Driver to prove a late date, when we find that these are the names of musical instruments, and that the Babylonians knew the Greeks in war and commerce, and realize that musical instruments carry their native names with them, this argument vanishes like the rest.

(6) It is urged that Daniel begins the captivity (1:1) in the third year of Jehoiakim, 606 B.C., whereas Jerusalem was not destroyed until 587 B.C. But Daniel dates the captivity, which was in three invasions and three deportations, from the time that he and his friends were carried away. The seventy years captivity were reckoned from the first deportation, and Daniel tells us when that was. The captivity ended in 536 B.C.

(7) The Aramaic. Some have claimed Aramaic was not spoken in Babylon; others, that the Aramaic of Babylon was different from that of Daniel. In 1906 and 1908 papyri in Aramaic from the fifth century B.C. were unearthed. They disclose Aramaic was the common language of the people, the very language which the frightened Chaldeans used when their angry king threatened them (Dan. 2:4).

Daniel was a wise and well-known man in the time of Ezekiel, else all point in the irony of Ezekiel 28:3 is lost. He was also eminent for piety and esteemed as a channel of the divine revelation (Ezekiel 14:14, 20). A striking collocation this: Noah the second father of the race, Job the Gentile, and Daniel the Jew.

Daniel is better attested than any other book of the Old Testament. Ezekiel mentions him; Zechariah appears to have read the book; and our Savior recognized Daniel as a prophet (Matt. 24:15). These are sufficient attestations.

CANON DYSON HAGUE (1857-1935) was ordained in 1883 after studying the arts and divinity at the University of Toronto. He served as curate at St. James' Cathedral in Toronto and as rector of St. Paul's in Brockville, Ontario, and St. Paul's in Halifax, Nova Scotia. From 1897 to 1901, Hague taught apologetics, liturgics, and homiletics at Wycliffe College in Toronto. His writings include several books on Anglican liturgy.

11

The Doctrinal Value of the First Chapters of Genesis

By the Rev. Dyson Hague, M.A.
VICAR OF THE CHURCH OF THE EPIPHANY; PROFESSOR OF LITURGICS,
WYCLIFFE COLLEGE, TORONTO, ONTARIO, CANADA

Revised by Gerald B. Stanton, Th.D.

I. GENESIS — THE FOUNDATION FOR ALL SCRIPTURE

The Book of Genesis is in many respects the most important book in the Bible. It is of the first importance because it answers, not exhaustively, but sufficiently, the fundamental questions of the human mind. It contains the first authoritative information given to the race concerning these questions of everlasting interest: the being of God; the origin of the universe; the creation of man; the origin of the soul; the fact of revelation; the introduction of sin; the promise of salvation; the primitive division of the human race; the out-calling of Israel and the preliminary part of God's redemptive program. In one word, in this inspired volume of beginnings, we have the satisfactory explanation of all the sin and misery and contradiction now in this world, and the reason of the scheme of redemption.

Or, let us put it another way. The Book of Genesis is the seed in which the plant of God's Word is enfolded. It is the starting point of God's gradually-unfolded plan of the ages. Genesis is the plinth of the pillar of the Divine revelation. It is the root of the tree of the inspired Scriptures. It is the source of the stream of the holy writings of the Bible. If the base of the pillar is removed, the pillar falls. If the root of the tree is cut out, the tree will wither and die. If the fountain head of the stream is cut off, the stream will dry up. The Bible as a whole is like a chain hanging upon two staples. The Book of Genesis is the one staple; the Book of Revelation is the other. Take away either staple and the chain falls in confusion. If the first chapters of Genesis are unreliable, then the revelation of the beginning of the universe, the origin of the race, and the reason for its redemption are gone. If the last chapters of Revelation are displaced, the consummation of all things is unknown. If you take away Genesis, you have lost the explanation of the first heaven, the first earth, the first Adam, and the fall. If you take away Revelation you have lost the completed truth of the new heaven, and the new earth, man redeemed, and the second Adam in Paradise regained.

Furthermore, in the first chapters of the Book of Genesis, you have the strong and sufficient foundation of the subsequent developments of the kingdom of God; the root-germ of all Anthropology, Soteriology, Christology, Satanology, to say nothing of the ancient and modern problems of the mystery and culpability of sin, the unity of the race, and God's establishment of matrimony and family life.

We assume from the start the historicity of Genesis and its Mosaic authorship. It was evidently accepted by our infallible Lord Jesus Christ as historical, as one single composition, and as the work of Moses. It was accepted by Paul, who wrote under the inspiration of the Spirit, and by the divinely appointed leaders of God's chosen people. It has validated itself to God's people throughout the ages by its realism and consistency, and by what has been finely termed its subjective truthfulness. We postulate especially the historicity of the first chapters. These are not only valuable, they are vital. They are the essence of Genesis.

The Book of Genesis is neither the work of a theorist nor of a tribal annalist. It is still less the product of some anonymous compiler or compilers in some unknowable era, of a series of myths, historic in form but unhistoric in fact. Its opening is an apocalypse, a direct revelation from the God of all truth. Whether it was given in a vision or otherwise, it is impossible to say. But it is possible, if not probable, that the same Lord God, who revealed to his servant as he was in the Spirit on the Lord's Day the apocalypse of the humanly unknown and unknowable events of man's history which will transpire when this heaven and this earth have passed away, would also have revealed to his servant, being in the Spirit, the apocalypse of the humanly unknowable and unknown events which transpired before this earth's history began. It has been asserted that the beginning and the end of things are both absolutely hidden from science. Science has to do with phenomena. It is where science must confess its impotence that revelation steps in, and, with the authority of God, reveals those things that are above it. The beginning of Genesis, therefore, is a divinely inspired narrative of the events deemed necessary by God to establish the foundations for the Divine Law in the sphere of human life, and to set forth the relation between the omnipotent Creator and the man who fell, and the race that was to be redeemed by the incarnation of his Son.

The German rationalistic idea, which has passed over into thousands of more or less orthodox Christian minds, is that these earliest chapters embody ancient traditions of the Semitic-oriental mind. Others go farther, and not only deny them to be the product of the reverent and religious mind of the Hebrew, but assert they were simply oriental legends, not born from above and of God, but born in the East, and probably in pagan Babylonia.

We would therefore postulate the following propositions:

1. The Book of Genesis has no doctrinal value if it is not authoritative.

2. The Book of Genesis is not authoritative if it is not true. For if it is not history, it is not reliable; and if it is not revelation, it is not authoritative.

3. The Book of Genesis is not true if it is not from God. For if it is not from God, it is not inspired; and if it is not inspired, it possesses to us no doctrinal value whatever.

4. The Book of Genesis is not direct from God if it is a heterogeneous compilation of mythological folklore by unknowable writers.

5. If the Book of Genesis is a legendary narrative, anonymous, indefinitely erroneous, and the persons it described the mere mythical personifications of tribal genius, it is of course not only non-authentic, because non-authenticated, but an insufficient basis for doctrine. The residuum of dubious truth, which might with varying degrees of consent be extracted therefrom, could never be accepted as a foundation for the superstructure of eternally

trustworty doctrine, for it is an axiom that that only is of doctrinal value which is God's Word. Mythical and legendary fiction, and still more, erroneous and misleading tradition, are incompatible not only with the character of the God of all truth, but with the truthfulness, trustworthiness, and absolute authority of the Word of God. We have not taken for our credentials cleverly invented myths. The primary documents, if there were such, were collated and revised and rewritten by Moses acting under the inspiration of God.

A sentence in Margoliouth's *Lines of Defence* deserves an attentive consideration today. We should have some opportunity, said the Oxford professor, of gauging the skill of those on whose faith the old-fashioned belief in the authenticity of Scripture has been abandoned (p. 293). One would perhaps prefer to put the idea in this way. Our modern Christians should have more opportunity not only of appraising the skill, but of gauging also the spiritual qualifications of a critical school that has been characterized nortoriously by an enthusiasm against the miraculous, and a precipitate adoption of any conclusion from a rationalistic source which militates against the historicity of Genesis.

Christians are conceding too much nowadays to the agnostic scientist, and the rationalistic Hebraist, and are often to blame if they allow them to go out of their specific provinces without protest. Their assumptions ought to be watched with the utmost vigilance and jealousy (cf. Gladstone, *The Impregnable Rock of Holy Scripture,* pp. 62-83).

But to resume. The Book of Genesis is the foundation on which the superstructure of the Scriptures rests. The foundation of the foundation is in the first three chapters, which form in themselves a complete monograph of revelation. And of this final substructure, the first three verses of the first chapter are the foundation.

In the first verse of Genesis, in words of supernatural grandeur, we have a revelation of God as the first cause, the Creator of the universe, the world and man. The glorious Being of God comes forth without explanation, and without apology. It is a revelation of the one, personal, living God. There is in the ancient philosophic cosmogony no trace of the idea of such a Being, still less of such a Creator, for all other systems began and ended with pantheistic, materialistic, or hylozoistic conceptions. The divine Word stands unique in declaring the absolute idea of the living God, without attempt at demonstration. The spirituality, infinity, omnipotence, sanctity of the Divine Being, all in germ lie here. Nay more. The later and more fully revealed doctrine of the unity of God in the Trinity may be said to lie here in germ also.

The fact of God in the first of Genesis is not given as a deduction of reason or a philosophic generalization. It is a revelation. It is a revelation of that primary truth which is received by the universal human mind as a truth that needs no proof, and is incapable of it, but which being received, is verified to the intelligent mind by an irresistible force, not only with ontological and cosmological, but with teleological and moral arguments. Here we have in this first verse of Genesis, not only a postulate apart from Revelation, but three great truths which have constituted the glory of our religion.

(1) The unity of God, in contradiction to all the polytheisms and dualisms of ancient and modern pagan philosophy.

(2) The personality of God, in contradiction to that pantheism whether materialistic or idealistic, which recognizes God's immanence in the world, but denies His transcendence. For in all its multitudinous developments, pantheism has this peculiarity, that it denies the personality of God, and excludes from the realm of life the need of a Mediator, a Sin-Bearer, and a personal Saviour.

(3) The omnipotence of God, in contradiction, not only to those debasing conceptions of the anthropomorphic deities of the ancient world, but to all those man-made idols which the millions of heathenism today adore. God made these stars and suns, which man in his infatuation fain would worship. Thus in contradiction to all human conceptions and human evolutions, there stands forth no mere deistic abstraction, but the one, true, living and only God. He is named by the name Elohim, the name of divine majesty, the Adorable One, our Creator and Governor; the same God who in a few verses later is revealed as Jehovah-Elohim, Jehovah being the covenant name, the God of revelation and grace, the ever-existent Lord, the God and Father of us all (Green, *Unity of Genesis*, pp. 31, 32; *Fausset's Bib. Ency.*, p. 258).

One of the theories of modernism is that the law of evolution can be traced through the Bible in the development of the idea of God. The development of the idea of God? Is there in the Scriptures any real trace of the development of the idea of God? There is an expansive and richer and fuller revelation of the attributes and dealings and ways and workings of God, but not of the idea of God. The God of Genesis 1:1 is the God of Psalm 90, of Isaiah 40:28, of Hebrews 1:1, and Revelation 4:11.

"In the beginning God created the heaven and the earth." Here in a sublime revelation is the doctrinal foundation of the creation of the universe, and the contradiction of the ancient and modern conceptions of the eternity of matter. God only is eternal.

One can well believe the story of a Japanese thinker who took up a strange book, and with great wonder read the first sentence: "In the beginning God created the heaven and the earth." It struck him that there was more philosophy of a theological character, satisfying to the mind and soul, in that one sentence than in all the sacred books of the orient.

That single sentence separates the Scriptures from the rest of human productions. The wisest philosophy of the ancients, Platonic, Aristotelian or Gnostic, never reached the point that the world was created by God in the sense of absolute creation. In no cosmogony outside of the Bible is there a record of the idea that God created the heaven and the earth, as an effort of his will, and the fiat of his eternal, self-existent Personality. *Ex nihilo nihil fit.* The highest point reached by their philosophical speculations was a kind of atomic theory; of cosmic atoms and germs and eggs possessed of some inexplicable forces of development, out of which the present cosmos was through long ages evolved. Matter was almost universally believed to have existed from eternity. The Bible teaches that the universe was not self caused, nor a mere passive evolution of his nature, nor a mere transition from one form of being to another, from non-being to being, but that it was a direct creation of the personal, living, working God who created all things out of nothing by the fiat of his will, and the instrumentality of the eternal Logos. In glorious contrast to agnostic science with its lamentable creed, "I believe that behind and above and around the phenomena of matter and force remains the unsolved mystery of the universe," the Christian holds forth his triumphant solution, "I believe that in the beginning God created the heaven and the earth" (John 1:1-3; Heb. 1:1; Col. 1: 16). The first verse of the Bible is a proof that the Book is of God.

And so with regard to the subsequent verses. Genesis is admittedly not a statement of scientific history. It is a narrative for mankind to show that this world was made by God for the habitation of man, and was gradually made fit for God's children. So in a series of successive creative developments from the formless chaos, containing in embryonic condition all elemental constituents, chemical and mechanical, air, earth, fire, and water, the sublime process is recorded according to the Genesis narrative in the following order:

1. The creation by direct divine act of matter in its gaseous, aqueous, terrestrial and mineral condition successively (Gen. 1:1-10; cf. Col. 1:16; Heb. 11:3).

2. The emergence by divine creative power of the lowest forms of sea and land life (Gen. 1:11-13).

3. The creation by direct divine act of larger forms of life, aquatic and terrestrial; the great sea monsters and gigantic reptiles, the *sheretjim* and *tanninim* (cf. Dawson, *Origin of the World,* p. 213; Gen. 1:20-21.)

4. The emergence by divine creative power of land animals of higher organization, herbivora and smaller mammals and carnivora (Gen. 1:24-25).

5. Finally, the creation of man by a direct divine act (Gen. 1:26-27). Not first, but last. The last for which the first was made, as Browning so finely puts it. Herein is the compatability of Genesis and science, for this sublime order is just the order that some of the foremost of the nineteenth and twentieth century scientists have proclaimed. It is remarkable, too, that the word for absolutely new creation is only used in connection with the introduction of life (Gen. 1:1, 2, 27). These three points where the idea of absolute creation is introduced are the three main points at which modern champions of evolution find it impossible to make their connection.

II. The Beginning of Mankind

Next we have in this sublime revelation the doctrinal foundation for the beginning of mankind. Man was created, not evolved. That is, he did not come from protoplasmic mud-mass, or sea-ooze bathybian, or by descent from fish or frog, or horse, or ape; but at once, direct, full made, did man come forth from God. When you read what some writers, professedly religious, say about man and his bestial origin, your shoulders unconsciously droop, your head hangs down, your heart feels sick. Your self-respect has received a blow. When you read Genesis, your shoulders straighten, your chest emerges. You feel proud to be that thing that is called man. Up goes your heart, and up goes your head. The Bible stands openly against the evolutionary development of man, and his gradual ascent through indefinite aeons from the animal. It does not stand against the idea of the development of the plans of the Creator in nature, or a variation of species by means of environment and processes of time. That is seen in Genesis and throughout the Bible, and in this world. But the Bible does stand plainly against that garish theory that all species, vegetable and animal, have originated through evolution from lower forms through long natural processes. The materialistic form of this theory to the Christian is most offensive. It practically substitutes an all-engendering protoplasmic cell for the only and true God. But even the theistic-supernaturalistic theory is opposed to the Bible and to science for these reasons:

1. There is no such universal law of development. On the contrary, scientific evidence is now standing for deterioration. The flora and the fauna of the latest period show no trace of improvement, and even man, proud man, from the biological and physiological standpoint has gained nothing to speak of from the dawn of history. The earliest archaeological remains of Egypt, Assyria, Babylonia, show no trace of slow emergence from barbarism. That species can be artifically improved is true, but that is not transmutation of species (Dawson, *Origin of the World,* pp. 227-277).

2. No new type has even been discovered. Science is universally proclaiming the truth of Genesis 1:11, 12, 21, 24, 25 "after his kind," "after their kind," that is, species by species. Geology with its five hundred or so species of ganoids proclaims the fact

of the non-transmutation of species. If, as they say, the strata tell the story of countless aeons, it is strange that during those countless aeons the trilobite never produced anything but a trilobite, nor has the ammonite ever produced anything but an ammonite. The elaborately artificial exceptions of modern science only confirm the rule (cf. Townsend, *Collapse of Evolution*).

3. Nor is there any trace of transmutation of species. Man develops from a single cell, and the cell of a monkey is said to be indistinguishable from that of a man. But the fact that a man cell develops into a man and the monkey cell develops into a monkey, shows there is an immeasurable difference between them. And the development from a cell into a man has nothing whatever to do with the evolution of one species into another. "To science, species are practically unchangeable units" (*Origin of the World*, p. 227). Man is the sole species of his genus, and the sole representative of his species. The abandonment of any original type is said to be soon followed by the complete extinction of the family.

4. Nor has the missing link been found. The late Robert Etheridge of the British Museum, head of the geological department, and one of the ablest of British paleontologists, has said: "In all that great museum there is not a particle of evidence of transmutation of species. Nine-tenths of the talk of evolutionists is not founded on observation, and is wholly unsupported by facts." And Professor Virchow is said to have declared with vehemence regarding evolution: "It's all nonsense. You are as far as ever you were from establishing any connection between man and the ape" (or, as more recently asserted, between man and a "common ancestor" with the ape). A great gulf is fixed between the theory of evolution and the sublime statement of Genesis 1:26, 27. These verses give man his true place in the universe as the consummation of creation. Made out of the dust of the ground, and created on the same day with the highest group of animals, man has physiological affinities with the animal creation. But he was made in the image of God, and is therefore transcendently superior to any animal. "Man is a walker, the monkey is a climber," said the great French scientist, De Quatrefages, years ago. A man does a thousand things every day that a monkey could not do if he tried ten thousand years. Man has the designing, controlling, ordering,

constructive, and governing faculties. Man has personality, understanding, will, conscience. Man is fitted for apprehending God and for worshipping God. The Genesis account of man is the only possible basis of revelation. The revelation of fatherhood; of the beautiful, the true, the good; of purity, of peace; is unthinkable to a horse, a dog, or a monkey. The most civilized simian could have no affinity with such conceptions, or of receiving them if revealed.

It is, moreover, the only rational basis for the doctrine of regeneration in opposition to the idea of the evolution of the human character, and of the great doctrine of the incarnation. Man once made in the image of God, by the regenerating power of the Holy Ghost is born again and made in the image of God the Son.

III. DOCTRINAL FOUNDATIONS IN GENESIS

Further, we have in this sublime revelation of Genesis the doctrinal foundation of: (1) The unity of the human race, (2) the fall of man, and (3) the plan of redemption.

(1) The unity of the human race. With regard to this unity, Sir William Dawson has said that the Bible knows but one Adam. Adam was not a myth, or an ethnic name. He was a veritable man, made by God; not an evolutionary development from some hairy anthropoid in some imaginary continent of Lemuria. The Bible knows but one species of man, one primitive pair. This is confirmed by the Lord Jesus Christ in Matthew 19:4. It is reaffirmed by Paul in Acts 17:26, whichever reading may be taken, and in Romans 5:12; I Corinthians 15:21, 47, 49. Nor is there any ground for supposing that the word Adam is used in a collective sense, and thus leave room for the hypotheses of the evolutionary development of a large number of human pairs. All things in both physiology and ethnology, as well as in the sciences, which bear on the subject confirm the idea of the unity of the human race.

(2) The fall of man. The foundation of all Hamartiology and Anthropology (doctrines of sin and of man) lies in the first three chapters of Genesis. It teaches us that man was originally created for conmmunion with God, and that whether his personality was dichotomistic or trichotomistic, he was entirely fitted for personal, intelligent fellowship with his Maker, and was united with him in

the bonds of love and knowledge. Every element of the Bible story recommends itself as a historic narrative. Placed in Eden by his God, with a work to do, and a trial-command, man was potentially perfect, but with the possibility of fall. Man fell by disobedience, and through the power of a supernatural deceiver called that old serpent, the devil and Satan, who from Genesis 3 to Revelation 19 appears as the implacable enemy of the human race, and the head of that fallen angel-band which abandoned through the sin of pride their first principality.

This story is incomprehensible if only a myth. The great Dutch theologian Van Oosterzee says, "The narrative presents itself plainly as history. Such an historico-fantastic clothing of a pure philosophic idea accords little with the genuine spirit of Jewish antiquity" (*Dogmatics, II*, p. 403).

Still more incomprehensible is it, if it is merely an allegory which refers fruit, serpent, woman, tree, eating, etc., to entirely different things from those mentioned in the Bible. It is history. It is treated as such by our Lord Jesus Christ, who surely would not mistake a myth for history, and by St. Paul, who hardly built Romans 5 and I Corinthians 15, on cleverly composed fables. It is the only satisfactory explanation of the corruption of the race. From Adam's time death has reigned.

This story of the fall stands, moreover, as a barrier against all Manicheism, and against that Pelagianism which declares that man is not so bad after all, and derides the doctrine of original sin which in all our Church confessions distinctly declares the possession by every one from birth of this sinful nature. The penalty and horror of sin, the corruption of our human nature, and the hopelessness of our sinful estate are things definitely set forth in the Holy Scripture, and are St. Paul's divinely inspired deductions from this fact of the incoming of sin and death through the disobedience and fall of Adam, the original head of the human race. The race is in a sinful condition (Rom. 5:12). Mankind is a solidarity. As the root of a tree lives in stem, branch, leaf and fruit; so in Adam, as Anselm says, a person made nature sinful, in his posterity nature made persons sinful. Or, as Pascal finely puts it, original sin is folly in the sight of man, but this folly is wiser than all the wisdom of man, for without it who could have said what man is. His whole condition depends upon this imperceptible point (*Thoughts,* Ch. 13, 11). This Genesis story further is the foundation of the Scripture doctrine of all human responsibility and accountability to God. A lowered anthropology always means a lowered theology, for if man was not a direct creation of God, if he was a mere indirect development, through slow and painful process, of no one knows what, or how, or why, or when, or where, the main spring of moral accountability is gone. The fatalistic conception of man's personal and moral life is the deadly gift of naturalistic evolution to our age.

(3)   The plan of redemption. With regard to our redemption, the third chapter of Genesis is the basis of all Soteriology (doctrine of salvation). If there was no fall there was no condemnation, no separation and no need of reconciliation. If there was no need of reconciliation, there was no need of redemption; and if there was no need of redemption, the Incarnation was a superfluity, and the crucifixion folly (Gal. 3:21). So closely does the apostle link the fall of Adam and the death of Christ, that without Adam's fall the science of theology is evacuated of its most salient feature, the atonement. If the first Adam was not made a living soul and fell, there was no reason for the work of the Second Man, the Lord from heaven. The rejection of the Genesis story as a myth, tends to the rejection of the Gospel of salvation. One of the chief cornerstones of the Christian doctrine is removed, if the historical reality of Adam and Eve is abandoned, for the fall will ever remain as the starting point of special revelation, of salvation by grace, and of the need of personal regeneration. In it lies the germ of the entire apostolic Gospel.

Finally, we have in Genesis 2 the doctrinal foundation of those great fundamentals, the necessity of labor and for a day of rest, the divine ordinance of matrimony, and the home life of mankind. The weekly day of rest was provided for man by his God, and is planted in the very forefront of the home. Our Lord Jesus Christ endorses the Mosaic story of the creation of Adam and Eve, refers to it as the explanation of the divine will regarding divorce, and sanctions by his infallible *imprimatur* that most momentous of ethical questions, monogamy. **Thus the great elements of life** as God intended it, the three universal factors of happy, healthy, helpful life, law, labor, love, are laid down in the beginning of God's Book.

IV. OTHER IMPORTANT ISSUES IN GENESIS

Three other remarkable features in the first chapters of Genesis deserve a brief reference.

The first is the assertion of the original unity of the language of the human race (Gen. 11:1). Max Muller, a foremost ethnologist and philologist, declares that all our languages, in spite of their diversities, must have originated in one common source (cf. Saphir, *Divine Unity*, p. 206; Dawson, *Origin of the World*, p. 286; Guinness, *Divine Programme*, p. 75).

The second is that miracle of ethnological prophecy by Noah in Genesis 9:26, 27, in which we have foretold in a sublime epitome the three great divisions of the human race, and their ultimate historic destinies. The three great divisions, Hamitic, Shemitic, and Japhetic, are the three ethnic groups into which modern science has divided the human race. The facts of history have fulfilled what was foretold in Genesis four thousand years ago. The Hamitic nations, including the Chaldean, Babylonic, and Egyptian, have been degraded, profane, and sensual. The Shemitic have been the religious with the line of the coming Messiah. The Japhetic have been the enlarging and the dominant races, including all the great world monarchies, both of the ancient and modern times, the Grecian, Roman, Gothic, Celtic, Teutonic, British and American, and by recent investigation and discovery, the races of India, China, and Japan. Thus Ham lost all empire centuries ago; Shem and his race acquired it ethically and spiritually through the Prophet, Priest and King, the Messiah; while Japheth, in world-embracing enlargement and imperial supremacy, has stood for industrial, commercial, and political dominion.

The third is the glorious promise given to Abraham, the man to whom the God of glory appeared and in whose seed, personal and incarnate, the whole world was to be blessed. Abraham's spiritual experience with God is the explanation of the monotheism of the three greatest religions in the world. He stands out in majestic proportion, as Max Muller says, as a figure, second only to One in the whole world's history. Apart from that promise the miraculous history of the Hebrew race is inexplicable. In him centers, and on him hangs, the central fact of the whole of the Old Testament, the promise of the Saviour and his glorious salvation (Gen. 12:3, 22:18; Gal. 3:8-16).

In an age, therefore, when the critics are waxing bold in claiming settledness for the assured results of their hypothetic eccentricities, Christians should wax bolder in contending earnestly for the assured results of the revelation of God as it is found in the opening chapters of Genesis.

The attempt of modernism to save the supernatural in the second part of the Bible by mythicalizing the supernatural in the first part, is as unwise as it is fatal. Instead of lowering the dominant of faith amidst the chorus of doubt, and admitting that a chapter is doubtful because some *doctrinaire* has questioned it, or a doctrine is less authentic because somebody has floated an unverifiable hypothesis, it would be better to take our stand with such men as Romanes, Lord Kelvin, Virchow, and Liebig, in their ideas of a Creative Power, and to side with Cuvier, the eminent French scientist, who said that Moses, while brought up in all the science of Egypt, was superior to his age, and has left us a cosmogony the exactitude of which verifies itself every day in a reasonable manner; with Sir William Dawson, the eminent Canadian scientist, who declared that Scripture in all its details contradicts no received result of science, but anticipates many of its discoveries; with Professor Dana, the eminent American scientist, who said, after examining the first chapters of Genesis as a geologist, "I find it to be in perfect accord with known science"; or best of all, with him who said, "Had you believed Moses, you would have believed me, for he wrote of me. But if you believe not his writings, how shall you believe my words?" (John 5:45, 46).

GEORGE FREDERICK WRIGHT (1838-1921) graduated from Oberlin Theological Seminary in 1862 and pastored in Bakersfield, VT (1861-1872) and Andover, MA (1872-1881) before returning to Oberlin College to teach (1881-1907). Keenly interested in geology and the relationship between science and religion, Wright pioneered an apologetic that was unique in his day. He edited *Bibliotheca Sacra* and published, among others: *The Logic of Christian Evidences* (1880), *Studies in Science and Religion* (1882), *The Divine Authority of the Bible* (1884), a biography of Charles Finney (1891), and his autobiography (1916).

MELVIN GROVE KYLE (1858-1933) was a Presbyterian clergyman who specialized in biblical archaeology and Egyptology. He lectured on these subjects at the Xenia Theological Seminary, which became the Pittsburgh-Xenia Theological Seminary, and served as president of that school from 1922-1930. He edited the *Bibliotheca Sacra* in 1921, and also wrote a column on archaeology for *The Sunday School Times*. In 1927, he served as moderator of the United Presbyterian Church. He published several books on biblical archaeology, including *The Deciding Voice of the Monuments in Biblical Criticism, Moses and the Monuments*, and *The Problem of the Pentateuch.*

12

The Testimony of Archaeology to the Scriptures

"The Testimony of the Monuments
to the Truth of the Scriptures"
By Professor George F. Wright, D.D., LL.D.
OBERLIN COLLEGE, OBERLIN, OHIO

"The Recent Testimony of Archaeology to the Scriptures"
By M. G. Kyle, D.D., LL.D.
PRESIDENT, PITTSBURGH-XENIA THEOLOGICAL SEMINARY

Revised by Charles L. Feinberg, Th.D, Ph.D.

All history is fragmentary. Each particular fact is the center of a great complex of circumstances. No man has intelligence enough to insert a hypothetical fact into circumstances not belonging to it, and make it fit exactly. This only infinite intelligence can do. A successful forgery, therefore, is impossible, if we have a sufficient number of the original circumstances with which to compare it. It is this principle which gives such importance to the examination of witnesses. If the witness is truthful, the more he is questioned the more accurately will his testimony be seen to accord with the framework of circumstances into which it is fitted. If false, the more will his falsehood become apparent.

Remarkable opportunities for cross-examining the Old Testament have been afforded by the uncovering of long-buried monuments in Bible lands and by the deciphering of the inscriptions on them. It is the purpose of this chapter to give the results of a sufficient portion of this examination to afford a reasonable test of the competence and honesty of the historians of the Old Testament, and of the faithfulness with which their record has been transmitted to us. The limitations of space will not permit more than a sampling of the vast evidence now available to us.

The Identification of Belshazzar

Attention is being centered first on one of the Old Testament narratives against which some of the harshest judgments of modern critics have been hurled. We refer to the statements in the Book of Daniel concerning the person and career of Belshazzar. In the fifth chapter of Daniel Belshazzar is called the son of Nebuchadnezzar, and is said to have been king of Babylon and to have been slain on the night the city was captured. Some historians have denied the historical character of Belshazzar altogether; according to others he was the son of Nabonidus, who was then king, and who is known to have been out of the city when it was taken, and to have lived some time afterwards. Here is a glaring discrepancy, a flat contradiction between profane and sacred historians. But in 1854 Sir Henry Rawlinson found, while excavating the ruins of ancient Ur, inscriptions which stated that Nabonidus (Nabunaid) associated with him on his throne his eldest son, Bel-shar-usur, and allowed him the royal title, thus making it credible that Belshazzar should have been in Babylon, as he is said to have been in the Bible, and that he should have been called king, and that he should have perished in the city while Nabonidus survived outside the realm. For a number of years Nabonidus busied himself with campaigns in the city of Tema, Arabia. That Belshazzar should have been called king while his father was still living is no more strange than that Jehoram should have been appointed by his father, Jehoshaphat, king of Judah, seven years before his father's death (II Kings 1:17; 8:16), or that Jotham should have been made king before his father, Uzziah, died of leprosy, though Uzziah is still called king in some of the references to him.

That Belshazzar should have been called son of Nebuchadnezzar is readily accounted for on the supposition that he was his grandson, and there are many things to indicate that Nabonidus married Nebuchadnezzar's daughter in order to consolidate his position as a usurper of the throne. If this view be rejected, there is the natural supposition that in the loose use of terms of relationship common in the Orient, "son" might be applied to one who was simply a successor. In the inscriptions on the monuments of Shalmaneser III, Jehu, the extirpator of the house of Omri, is called the "son of Omri." The status of Belshazzar is confirmed incidentally by the fact that Daniel is promised in 5:6 the "third" place in the kingdom, and in 5:29 is given that place, all of which implies that Belshazzar was second only. Thus, what was formerly thought to be an insuperable objection to the historical accuracy of the Book of Daniel proves to be a mark of accuracy. The coincidences are all the more remarkable for being so evidently undesigned.

The Black Obelisk of Shalmaneser

From various inscriptions we are now able to trace the movements of Shalmaneser III (858-824) through most of his career. A few years after his accession to the Assyrian throne, an important battle was waged at Karkar on the Orontes against a strong coalition of twelve kings. The "Monolith Inscription" of Shalmaneser III describes this battle. Among the kings of the coalition appears the name of "Ahab, the Israelite," an attestation to the prominence of Ahab among the rulers of his day. On a later campaign of Shalmaneser III, Jehu of Israel was compelled to pay him heavy tribute. This is recorded on the famous Black Obelisk found by Layard in 1846 in Shalmaneser's palace at Nimrod. Thus archaeology bears witness to the historicity of these Israelite kings.

The Moabite Stone

One of the most important discoveries for the Old Testament is that of the Moabite Stone, discovered at Dibon, east of the Jordan, in 1868, which was set up by King Mesha (about 850 B.C.) to commemorate his deliverance from the yoke of Omri, king of Israel. The inscription is valuable, among other things, for its witness to the plane of civilization of the Moabites at that time, and to the close similarity of their language to that of the Hebrews. On comparing the Moabite account with II Kings 3:4-27, we find an account which parallels and supplements the biblical narrative in a remarkable way.

The Expedition of Shishak

Shishak (Sheshonk of the Egyptians and the founder of the Libyan Dynasty) is the first name of an Egyptian king to be found in Scripture (I Kings 11:40). Taking advantage of the disruption of the Solomonic kingdom, Shishak invaded Jerusalem, spoiling the royal palaçe and the house of the Lord. He was also interested in Syria as well as Palestine. The record of his victories is inscribed on a wall of the great southern court of the temple of Amun at Karnak in Egypt. More than 150 names of Palestinian towns are inscribed, though about a score or more are illegible. Some of the cities mentioned, the larger ones being in Israel, are Gath, Sharuhen, Arad, Gibeon, Beth-horon, Aijalon, Taanach, Megiddo, Bethshean, Shunem, Edrei, and Mahanaim. The inscription is important, not only because it corroborates the biblical account, but also because it names the cities involved and supplements the record of the Bible.

Israel in Egypt

If we could find the names of the patriarchs in the inscriptions and could identify them with certainty with the biblical characters, the case would be materially helped. The names Jacob-el and Joseph-el are found on a monument from the time of Thutmose III, but there is nothing to connect them with the patriarchs. The chances of finding the names of the patriarchs on the inscriptions would appear to be small, for the patriarchs lived nomadic lives, and had generally little touch with the political movements of their time (except for Joseph). However, there is another way whereby the biblical narrative may be tested. If the biblical accounts reflect accurately the conditions and customs of the day, they bear the strongest possible marks of authenticity and trustworthiness. Abraham's visit to Egypt in Genesis 12:10-20 can be tested in all its five prominent features against the Egyptian background of his day, and will be found corroborated in every detail. The account of Joseph's sojourn in Egypt is linked with the problem of the Hyksos. More recent studies reveal that there were an early period of Hyksos infiltration into Egypt and a later period. These coincide with the contact Abraham had with Egypt, and the later relationship Joseph sustained to it. Whether from the angle of distinctive pottery, the contribution to the field of metallurgy, type of town defense, or the use of horses and chariots, the rule of the Hyksos in Egypt is splendidly illuminated, and forms the backdrop of Israel's contact with that land. The Joseph story may be tested against its Egyptian background on more than a dozen particulars, down to the method of embalming, and its reliability is attested at every turn. The Bible has received no greater attestation to its truthfulness from any land of antiquity, than it has enjoyed from the land of Egypt.

The Hittites

Before our twentieth century the biblical references to a Hittite people were looked at askance by the critics. In no uncertain terms it was claimed no such people as the Hittites ever existed. The biblical accounts dealing with this people were, then, nothing more than legendary. These attacks against the trustworthiness of the Scripture were completely met in 1906 when Hugo Winckler of Berlin discovered the royal library and record-office of the Hittites at their capital, Boghaz-keui in Asia Minor, about 150 miles south of the Black Sea and east of modern Ankara, Turkey. The result of the labors of a number of scholars on the Hittite inscriptions has been the emergence of a people and an empire scarcely less important than the Egyptians or Assyrians.

The Tell el-Amarna Tablets

The discovery of the clay Tell-el-Amarna Tablets in 1887 was by accident. A peasant woman was digging, to get dust to fertilize her garden, in the ruins of Tell el-Amarna in Upper Egypt, about 200 miles south of Cairo on the eastern bank of the Nile. Upon careful study by competent scholars these tablets proved to be part of the official archives of the kings Amenhotep III and Akhnaton. Amarna was the capital during the reign of the religious reformer, Akhnaton. The tablets are dated about 1400-1360 B.C., about the time of the entrance of Israel into Canaan from Egypt, according to the early dating of the Exodus, and the time immediately following it. They treat of the political affairs of the kings of Egypt and the rulers under the Egyptian kings in Babylonia, Syria, and Palestine. This was the period of great internationalism in the Near East.

From the standpoint of the Bible these letters are the most important find in Egypt. They are important politically, epigraphically, geographically, and historically. They reveal the extent and nature of diplomatic communication in that day. The political situation they portray in Palestine is one of an absence of concentrated power; rulers responsible to the Egyptian king governed the different city-states. The letters give the Canaanite version of the invasion of the land under Joshua. The tablets throw light on how extensively and continuously the art of writing was known and practiced at that early date. The language of Canaan was almost identical with Hebrew. Help has been received for the spelling of proper names of Canaanitish origin, since the scribes of Egypt had to address their letters to the various Egyptian viceroys in Palestine. The most remarkable feature about the language of the letters is that it is in the Babylonian cuneiform language, though it consists of Egyptian governors writing to Egyptian kings. Evidently, Babylonian was the international language of the day. Geographically, the letters identify a goodly number of places along the Syrian and Canaanitish coastland. As to the historical material, one estimate places it, as to amount, to about one-half of the Pentateuch.

It is sufficient to say that, while many more positive confirmations of the seemingly improbable statements of the sacred historians can be adduced, there have been no discoveries which contravene their statements. The cases already enumerated relate to such widely separated times and places, and furnish explanations so unexpected to difficulties that have been thought insuperable, that their testimony cannot be ignored or rejected. That this history should be confirmed in so many cases, and in such a remarkable manner by monuments uncovered millenniums after their erection, can be nothing else than providential. Surely, God has seen to it that the failing faith of these later days should not be left to grope in darkness. When the faith of many was waning, and many heralds of truth were tempted to speak with uncertain sound, the very stones have cried out with a voice that only the deaf could fail to hear. Both in the writing and in the preservation of the Bible we behold the handiwork of God.

(Note: A discussion of the important Dead Sea Scrolls has been purposely omitted, because it is even yet too early for a definitive evaluation of these significant finds.)

JAMES ORR (1844-1913) graduated from Glasgow University in his native Scotland. Between 1874 and 1891, he was a parish minister at East Bank United Presbyterian Church in Hawick. He left the pastorate to teach church history at the United Presbyterian Theological College in Glasgow until 1901, when he became professor of apologetics and dogmatics at Glasgow (later·called Trinity) College. Orr enjoyed studying the progress of church doctrine, which he saw as following a divine logic. His major works included *The Christian View of God and the World* (1893, republished in 1989 by Kregel Publications) and *The Progress of Dogma* (1897).

13

Science and Christian Faith

By Professor James Orr, D.D.
UNITED FREE CHURCH COLLEGE, GLASGOW, SCOTLAND

Revised by Gerald B. Stanton, Th.D.

In many quarters the belief is industriously circulated that the advance of "science," meaning by this chiefly the physical sciences — astronomy, geology, biology, and the like — has proved damaging, if not destructive, to the claims of the Bible and the truth of Christianity. Science and Christianity are pitted against each other. Their interests are held to be antagonistic. Books have been written, such as Draper's *Conflict Between Religion and Science,* White's *Warfare of Science with Theology in Christendom,* and Foster's *Finality of the Christian Religion,* to show that this warfare between science and religion has ever been going on, and can never in the nature of things cease till theology is destroyed and science holds sole sway in men's minds.

This was not the attitude of the older investigators of science. Most of these men were devout Christian men. Naville, in his book *Modern Physics,* has shown that the great discoverers in science in past times were nearly always devout men. This was true of Galileo, Kepler, Bacon, and Newton; it was true of men like Faraday, Brewster, Kelvin, and a host of others in more recent times. The late Professor Tait of Edinburgh, writing in *The International Review,* has said: "The assumed incompatibility of religion and science has been so often and confidently asserted in recent times that it has . . . come to be taken for granted by the writers of leading articles, and it is, of course, perpetually thrust before their too trusting readers. But the whole thing is a mistake, and a mistake so grave that no truly scientific man runs, in Britain, at least, the smallest risk of making it. With a few, and these very singular exceptions, the truly scientific men and true theologians of the present day have not found themselves under the necessity of quarreling." The late Professor G. J. Romanes has, in his *Thoughts on Religion,* left the testimony that one thing which largely influenced him in his return to faith was the fact that in his own university of Cambridge nearly all the men of most eminent scientific attainments were avowed Christians. "The curious thing," he says, "is that all the most illustrious names were ranged on the side of orthodoxy. Sir W. Manson, Sir George Stokes, Professors Tait, Adams, Clerk Maxwell, and Bayley — not to mention a number of lesser lights, such as Routte, Todhunter, Ferrers, etc. — were all avowed Christians" (p. 137). It may be held that things are now changed. To some extent this is perhaps true, but anyone who knows the opinions of our leading scientific men is aware that to accuse the majority of being men of unchristian or unbelieving sentiment is to utter a gross libel.

If by a conflict of science and religion is meant that grievous mistakes have often been made, and unhappy misunderstandings have arisen, on one side and the other, in the course of the progress of science — that new theories and discoveries, as in astronomy and geology, have been looked on with distrust by those who thought that the truth of the Bible was being affected by them — that in some cases the dominant church sought to stifle the advance of truth by persecution — this is not to be denied. It is an unhappy illustration of how the best of men can at times err in matters which they imperfectly understand, or where their prejudices and traditional ideas are affected. But it proves nothing against the value of the discoveries themselves, or the deeper insight into the ways of God of the men who made them, or of real contradiction between the new truth and the essential teaching of the Scriptures. On the contrary, as a minority generally perceived from the first, the supposed disharmony with the truths of the Bible was an unreal one, early giving way to better understanding on both sides, and finally opening up new vistas in the contemplation of the Creator's power, wisdom, and majesty. It is never to be forgotten, also, that the error was seldom all on one side; that science, too, has in numberless cases put forth its hasty and unwarrantable theories and has often had to retract even its truer speculations within limits which brought them into more perfect harmony with revealed truth. If theology has resisted novelties of science, it has often had good reason for so doing.

It is well in any case that this alleged conflict of Christianity with science should be carefully probed, and that it should be seen where exactly the truth lies in regard to it.

I. Science and Law — Miracle

It is perhaps more in its *general outlook* on the world than in its specific results that science is alleged to be in conflict with the Bible and Christianity. The Bible is a record of divine revelation. Christianity is a supernatural system, and miracle, in the sense of a direct entrance of God in word and deed into human history for gracious ends, is of the essence of it. On the other hand, the advance of science has done much to deepen the impression of the universal reign of *natural law*. The effect has been to lead multitudes whose faith is not grounded in direct spiritual experience to look askance on the whole idea of the supernatural. God, it is assumed, has his own mode of working, and that is by means of secondary agencies operating in absolutely uniform ways; miracles, therefore, cannot be admitted. And, since miracles are found in Scripture — since the entire Book rests on the idea of a supernatural economy of grace — the whole must be dismissed as in conflict with the modern mind. Professor G. B. Foster goes so far as to declare that a man can hardly be intellectually honest who in these days professes to believe in the miracles of the Bible.

It would be overstating the case to speak of this present *repugnance to miracle*, and rejection of it in the Bible, as if it were really new. It is as old as rationalism itself. You find it in Spinoza, in Reimarus, in Strauss, and in numberless others. DeWette and Vatke, among earlier Old Testament critics, manifested it as strongly as their followers do now, and made it a pivot of their criticism. It governed the attacks on Christianity made in the age of the deists. David Hume wrote an essay against miracles which he thought had settled the question forever. But, seriously considered, can this attack on the idea of miracle, derived from our experience of the uniformity of nature's laws, be defended? Does it not in itself involve a huge assumption, and run counter to experience and common sense? The question is one well worth asking.

First, what *is* a miracle? Various definitions have been given, but it will be enough to speak of it here as *any effect in nature, or deviation from its ordinary course, due to the interposition of a supernatural cause.* It is no necessary part, it should be observed, of the biblical idea of miracle, that natural agencies should not be employed as far as they will go. If the drying of the Red Sea to let the Israelites pass over was due in part to a great wind that blew, this was none the less of God's ordering, and did not detract from the supernatural character of the event as a whole. It was still at God's command that the waters were parted and that a way was made at that particular time and place for the people to go through. These are what theologians call "providential" miracles, in which, so far as one can see, natural agencies under divine direction suffice to produce the result. There is, however, another and more conspicuous class, such as the instantaneous cleansing of the leper, or the raising of the dead, in which natural agencies are obviously altogether transcended. It is this class about which the chief discussion goes on. They are miracles in the stricter sense of a complete transcendence of nature's laws.

What, in the next place, is meant by the *uniformity of nature?* There are, of course, laws of nature — no one disputes that. It is quite a mistake to suppose that the Bible, though not written in the twentieth century, knows nothing of a regular order and system of nature. The world is God's world; it is established by his decree; he has given to every creature its nature, its bounds, its limits; all things continue according to his ordinances (Psa. 119: 91). However, law in the Bible is never viewed as having an independent existence. It is always regarded as an expression of the power or wisdom of God. It is this which gives the right point of view for considering the relation of law to miracle. What then do we mean by a "law" of nature? It is, as science will concede, only our registered observation of the order in which we find causes and events linked together in our experience. That they are so linked no one questions. If they were not, we should have no world in which we could live at all. Next, what do we mean by "uniformity" in this connection? We mean no more than this — that, given like causes, operating under like conditions, like effects will follow. This is quite true, and it is doubtful if any will deny it.

But then, as J. S. Mill in his *Logic* pointed out long ago, a miracle in the strict sense is not a denial of either of these truths. A miracle is not the assertion that, the same causes operating, a different result is produced. It is, on the contrary, the assertion that a *new* cause has intervened, and this a cause which the theists cannot deny to be a *vera causa* — the will and power of God. Just as, when I lift my arm, or throw a stone high in the air, I do not abolish the law of gravitation but counteract or overrule its purely natural action by the introduction of a new transcending force; so, but in an infinitely higher way, is a miracle due to the interposition of the first cause of all, God himself. What the scientific man needs to prove to establish his objection to miracle is, not simply that natural causes operate uniformly, but that *no other than natural causes exist;* that natural causes exhaust all the causation in the universe. And that, we hold, he can never do.

It is obvious from what has now been said that the real question at issue in miracle is not natural law, but *theism.* It is to be recognized at once that miracle can profitably be discussed only on the basis of a theistic view of the universe. It is not disputed that there are views of the universe which exclude miracle. The atheist cannot admit miracle, for he has no God to work miracles. The pantheist cannot admit miracle, for to him God and nature are one. The deist cannot admit miracle, for he has separated God and the universe so far that he can never bring them together again. The question is not, "Is miracle possible on an atheistic, a materialistic, or a pantheistic, view of the world," but, "Is it possible on a theistic view — on the view of God as at once immanent in his world, and in infinite ways transcending it?" I say nothing of intellectual "honesty," but I do marvel at the *assurance* of any one who presumes to say that, for the highest and holiest ends in his personal relations with his creatures, God can work only within the limits which nature imposes; that he cannot act without and above nature's order if it pleases him to do so. Miracles stand or fall by their evidence, but the attempt to rule them out by any *a priori* dictum as to the uniformity of natural law must inevitably fail. The same applies to the denial of providence or of answers to prayer on the ground of the uniformity of natural law. Here no breach of nature's order is affirmed, but only a governance or direction of nature of which man's own use of natural laws, without breach of them, for special ends, affords daily examples.

II. SCRIPTURE AND THE SPECIAL SCIENCES

Approaching more nearly the alleged conflict of the Bible or Christianity with the special sciences, a first question of importance is, "What is the *general relation* of the Bible to science? How does it claim to relate itself to the advances of natural knowledge?" Here, it is to be feared, mistakes are often made on both sides — on the side of science in affirming contrariety of the Bible with scientific results where none really exists; on the side of believers in demanding that the Bible be taken as a textbook of the newest scientific discoveries, and trying by forced methods to read these into them. The truth on this point lies really on the surface. The Bible clearly does not profess to anticipate the scientific discoveries of the nineteenth and twentieth centuries. Its design is very different; namely, to reveal God and his will and his purposes of grace to men, and, as involved in this, his general relation to the creative world, its dependence in all its parts on him, and his orderly government of it in Providence for his wise and good ends. Natural things are taken as they are given, and spoken of in simple, popular language, as we ourselves every day speak of them. The world it describes is the world men know and live in, and it is described as it appears, not as, in its recondite researches, science reveals its inner constitution to us. Wise expositors of the Scriptures, older and younger, have always recognized this, and have not attempted to force its language further. To take only one example, John Calvin, who wrote before the Copernican system of astronomy had obtained common acceptance, in his commentary on the first chapter of Genesis penned these wise words: "He who would learn astronomy and other recondite arts," he said, "let him go elsewhere. Moses wrote in a popular style things which, without instruction, all ordinary persons indued with common sense are able to understand. . . . He does not call us up to heaven, he only proposes things that lie open before our eyes." To this hour, with all the light of modern science around us, we speak of sun, moon and stars "rising" and "setting," and nobody misunderstands or affirms contradiction with science. There is no doubt another side to this, for it is just as true that in depicting natural things, the Bible, through the Spirit of revelation that animates it, seizes things in such a light—still with reference to its own purposes—that the mind is prevented from being led astray from the great truths intended to be conveyed.

It will serve to illustrate these positions as to the relation of the Bible to science if we look at them briefly in their application to the two sciences of *astronomy* and *geology,* in regard to which conflict has often been alleged.

1. The change from the *Ptolemaic* to the *Copernican* system of astronomy — from the view which regarded the earth as the center of the universe to the modern and undoubtedly true view of the earth moving round the sun, itself, with its planets, but one of innumerable orbs in the starry heavens — of necessity created great searchings of heart among those who thought that the language of the Bible committed them to the older system. For a time there was strong opposition on the part of many theologians, as well as of students of science, to the new discoveries of the telescope. Galileo was imprisoned by the church. But truth prevailed, and it was soon perceived that the Bible, using the language of appearances, was no more committed to the literal moving of the sun around the earth than are our modern almanacs, which employ the same forms of speech. One would have to travel far in these days to find a Christian who feels his faith in the least affected by the discovery of the true doctrine of the solar system. He rejoices that he understands nature better, and reads his Bible without the slightest sense of contradiction. Yet Strauss was confident that the Copernican system had given its death-blow to Christianity; as Voltaire before him had affirmed that Christianity would be overthrown by the discovery of the law of gravitation and would not survive a century. Newton, the humble-minded Christian discoverer of the law of gravitation, had no such fear, and time has shown that it was he, not Voltaire, who was right. These are specimens of the "conflicts" of Christianity with science.

The so-called "astronomical objection" to Christianity more specially takes the form of enlarging on the *illimitableness* of the universe disclosed by science in contrast with the *peculiar* interest of God in man displayed in the Christian Gospel. "What is man that thou art mindful of him?" (Psa. 8:4). Is it credible that this small speck in an infinity of worlds should be singled out as the scene of so tremendous an exhibition of God's love and grace as is implied in the incarnation of the Son of God, the sacrifice of the cross, the redemption of man? The day is well-nigh past when even this objection is felt to carry much weight. Apart from the strange fact that up to this hour no evidence seems to exist of other worlds inhabited by rational intelligences like man — no planets, no known systems — thoughtful people have come to realize that quantitative bigness is no measure of God's love and care; that the value of a soul is not to be estimated in terms of stars and planets; that sin is not less awful a fact even if it were proved that this is the only spot in the universe in which it has emerged. It is of the essence of God's infinity that he cares for the little as well as for the great; not a blade of grass could wave, or the insect of a day live its brief life upon the wing, if God were not actually present, and minutely careful of it. Man's position in the universe remains, by consent, or rather by proof, of science, an altogether peculiar one. Link between the material and the spiritual, he is the one being that seems fitted, as Scripture affirms he is, to be the bond of unity in the creation (Heb. 2:6-9). This is the hope held out to us in Christ (Eph. 1:10).

One should reflect also that, while the expanse of the *physical* universe is a modern thought, there has never been a time in the Christian Church when God — himself infinite — was not conceived of as adored and served by *countless hosts* of ministering spirits. Man was never thought of as the only intelligence in creation. The mystery of the divine love to our world was in reality as great before as after the stellar expanses were discovered. The sense of "conflict," therefore, though not the sense of wonder, awakened by the "exceeding riches" of God's grace to man in Christ Jesus, vanishes with increasing realization of the depths and heights of God's love "which passeth knowledge" (Eph. 3:19). Astronomy's splendid demonstration of the majesty of God's wisdom and power is undiminished by any feeling of disharmony with the Gospel.

2. As it is with astronomy, so it has been with the revelations of geology of the age and gradual formation of the earth. Here also doubt and suspicion were — naturally enough in the circumstances — at first awakened. The gentle Cowper could write in his "Task" of those:

> . . . *who drill and bore*
> *The solid earth and from the strata there*
> *Extract a register, by which we learn*
> *That He who made it, and revealed its date*
> *To Moses, was mistaken in its age.*

If the intention of the first chapter of Genesis was really to give us the "date" of the creation of the earth and heavens, the objection would be unanswerable. But things, as in the case of astronomy, are now better understood, and few are disquieted in reading their Bibles because it is made certain that the world is immensely older than the 6,000 years which the older chronology gave it. Geology is felt only to have expanded our ideas of the vastness and marvel of the Creator's operations through the aeons of time during which the world, with its teeming populations of fishes, birds, reptiles, mammals, was preparing for man's abode — when the mountains were being upheaved, the valleys being scooped out, and veins of precious metals being inlaid into the crust of the earth.

Does science, then, really contradict Genesis 1? Not surely if what has been above said of the essentially popular character of the allusions to natural things in the Bible be remembered. Here certainly is no detailed description of the process of the formation of the earth in terms anticipative of modern science — terms which would have been unintelligible to the original readers — but a sublime picture, true to the order of nature, as it is to the broad facts even of geological succession. If it tells how God called heaven and earth into being, separated light from darkness, sea from land, clothed the world with vegetation, gave sun and moon their appointed rule of day and night, made fowl to fly, and sea-monsters to plow the deep, created the cattle and beasts of the field, and finally made man, male and female, in his own image, and established him as ruler over all God's creation, this orderly succession of created forms, man crowning the whole, these deep ideas of the narrative, setting the world at the very beginning in its right relation to God and laying the foundations of an enduring philosophy of religion, are truths which science does nothing to subvert, but in myriad ways confirms. The "six days" may remain as a difficulty to some, but, if this is more than a symbolic setting of the picture — a great divine "week" of work — one may well ask, as was done by Augustine long before geology was thought of, what kind of "days" these were which rolled their course before the sun, with its twenty-four hours of diurnal measurement, was appointed to that end? There is no violence done to the narrative in substituting in thought "aeonic" days — vast cosmic periods — for "days" on our narrower, sun-measured scale. Then the last trace of apparent "conflict" disappears.

The conclusion of the matter is, that, up to the present hour, science and the biblical views of God, man, and the world do not stand in any real relation of conflict. Each book of God's writing reflects light upon the pages of the other, but neither contradicts the other's essential testimony. Science itself seems now disposed to take a less materialistic view of the origin and nature of things than it did a decade or two ago, and to interpret the creation more in the light of the spiritual. The experience of the Christian believer, with the work of missions in heathen lands, furnishes a testimony that cannot be disregarded to the reality of this spiritual world, and of the regenerating, transforming forces proceeding from it. To God be all the glory!

JAMES MARTIN GRAY (1851-1935) was called by D.L. Moody, "the best Bible teacher I ever met." Although he was not converted until he was 21, Gray became a noted Bible expositor, lecturer, writer, and educator. After serving as rector of First Reformed Episcopal Church in Boston (1979-1894) and as professor of Bible at A.J. Gordon's Missionary and Training School (now Gordon College), he became dean of Moody Bible Institute in 1924. He was named president of Moody Bible Institute in 1925. Other pursuits included serving as an editor of the *Scofield Reference Bible*, traveling to Great Britain to speak, authoring several books, and writing numerous hymns. Important books include *How to Master the English Bible, Christian Worker's Commentary* (republished by Kregel Publications as *Home Bible Study Commentary*), and *Why a Christian Cannot Be an Evolutionist.*

14

The Inspiration of the Bible—
Definition, Extent and Proof

By Rev. James M. Gray, D.D.
DEAN OF MOODY BIBLE INSTITUTE, CHICAGO, IL

Revised and edited by Gerald B. Stanton, Th.D.

In this paper the authenticity and credibility of the Bible are assumed, by which is meant: (1) that its books were written by the authors to whom they are ascribed, and that their contents are in all material points as when they came from their hands; and (2) that those contents are worthy of entire acceptance as to their statements of fact. Were there need to prove these assumptions, the evidence is abundant, and abler pens have dealt with it.

Let it not be supposed, however, that because these things are assumed their relative importance is undervalued. On the contrary, they underlie inspiration, and, as President Patton says, come in on the ground floor. They have to do with the historicity of the Bible, which for us just now is the basis of its authority. Nothing can be settled until this is settled, but admitting its settlement which, all things concerned, we now may be permitted to do, what can be of deeper interest than the question as to how far that authority extends?

For a long while the enemy's attack has directed our energies to another part of the field, but victory there will drive us back here again. The other questions are outside of the Bible itself, this is inside. They lead men away from the contents of the book to consider how they came; this brings us back to consider what they are. Happy the day when the inquiry returns here, and happy the generation which has not forgotten how to meet it.

I. DEFINITION OF INSPIRATION

1. *Inspiration is not revelation.* As Dr. Charles Hodge expressed it, revelation is the act of communicating divine knowledge

to the mind, but inspiration is the act of the same Spirit controlling those who make that knowledge known to others. Sometimes both of these experiences met in the same person; indeed Moses himself is an illustration of it, having received a revelation at another time and also the inspiration to make it known, but it is of importance to distinguish between the two.

2. *Inspiration is not illumination.* Every regenerated Christian is illuminated in the simple fact that he is indwelt by the Holy Spirit, but every such an one is not also inspired, but only the writers of the Old and New Testaments. Spiritual illumination is subject to degrees, some Christians possessing more of it than others; but inspiration is not subject to degrees, being in every case the breath of God, expressing itself through a human personality.

3. *Inspiration is not human genius.* The latter is simply a natural qualification, however exalted it may be in some cases, but inspiration in the sense now spoken of is supernatural throughout. It is an enduement coming upon the writers of the Old and New Testaments directing and enabling them to write those books, and on no other men, and at no other time, and for no other purpose. No human genius of whom we ever heard introduced his writings with the formula, "Thus saith the Lord," or words to that effect, and yet such is the common utterance of the Bible authors. No human genius ever yet agreed with any other human genius as to the things it most concerns men to know, and, therefore, however exalted his equipment, it differs not merely in degree but in kind from the inspiration of the Scriptures.

4. When we speak of the Holy Spirit coming upon the men in order to the composition of the books, it should be further understood that *the object is not the inspiration of the men but the books* — not the writers but the *writings*. It terminates upon the record, in other words, and not upon the human instrument who made it.

To illustrate: Moses, David, Paul, John, were not always and everywhere inspired, for then always and everywhere they would have been infallible and inerrant, which was not the case. They sometimes made mistakes in thought and erred in conduct. But however fallible and errant they may have been as men compassed with infirmity like ourselves, such fallibility or errancy was never under any circumstances communicated to their sacred writings.

This disposes of a large class of objections sometimes brought against the doctrine of inspiration—those, for example, associated with the question as to whether the Bible is the Word of God or only contains that Word. If by the former be meant that God spake every word in the Bible, and hence that every word is true, the answer must be *no;* but if it be meant that God caused every word in the Bible, true or false, to be recorded, the answer should be *yes.* There are words of Satan in the Bible, words of false prophets, words of the enemies of Christ, and yet they are God's words, not in the sense that he uttered them, but that he caused them to be recorded, infallibly and inerrantly recorded, for our profit. In this sense, the Bible does not merely contain the Word of God, it *is* the Word of God.

5. Let it be stated further in this definitional connection, that *the record for whose inspiration we contend is the original record—* the autographs or parchments of Moses, David, Daniel, Matthew, Paul or Peter, as the case may be, and not any particular translation or translations of them whatever. There is no translation absolutely without error, nor could there be, considering the infirmities of human copyists, unless God were pleased to perform a perpetual miracle to secure it.

But does this make nugatory our contention? Some would say it does, and they would argue speciously that to insist on the inerrancy of a parchment no living being has ever seen is an academic question merely, and without value. But do they not fail to see that the character and perfection of the Godhead are involved in that inerrancy?

Some years ago a "liberal" theologian, deprecating this discussion as not worthwhile, remarked that it was a matter of small consequence whether a pair of trousers were originally perfect if they were now rent. To which the valiant and witty David James Burrell replied, that it might be a matter of small consequence to the wearer of the trousers, but the tailor who made them would perfer to have it understood that they did not leave his shop that way. And then he added, that if the Most High must train among knights of the shears he might at least be regarded as the best of the guild, and One who drops no stiches and sends out no imperfect work.

But if this question be so purely speculative and valueless, what becomes of the science of biblical criticism by which properly we set such store today? Do builders drive piles into soft earth if they never expect to touch bottom? Do scholars dispute about the Scripture text and minutely examine the history and meaning of single words, "the delicate coloring of mood, tense and accent," if at the end there is no approximation to an absolute? As Dr. George H. Bishop says, does not our concordance, every time we take it up, speak loudly to us of a once inerrant parchment? Why do we not possess concordances for the very words of other books?

Nor is that original parchment so remote a thing as some suppose. Do not the number and variety of manuscripts and versions extant render it comparatively easy to arrive at a knowledge of its text, and does not competent scholarship today affirm that as to the New Testament at least, we have in 999 cases out of every thousand the very word of that original text? Let candid consideration be given to these things, and it will be seen that we are not pursuing a phantom in contending for an inspired autograph of the Bible.

II. Extent of Inspiration

1. *The inspiration of Scripture includes the whole and every part of it.* There are some who deny this and limit it to only the prophetic portions, the words of Jesus Christ, and, say, the profounder spiritual teachings of the epistles. The historical books in their judgment, and as an example, do not require inspiration because their data were obtainable from natural sources.

The Bible itself, however, knows of no limitations, as we shall see: "*All* scripture is given by inspiration of God." The historical data, most of it at least, might have been obtained from natural sources, but what about the supernatural guidance required in their selection and narration? Compare, for example, the records of creation, the fall, the deluge, etc., found in Genesis with those already discovered by excavations in Bible lands. Do not the results of the pick-axe and the spade point to the same original as the Bible, and yet do not their childishness and grotesqueness often bear evidence of the human and sinful mould through which they ran? Do they not show the need of some power other than man himself to lead him out of the labyrinth or error into the open ground of truth?

Furthermore, are not the historical books in some respects the most important in the the Bible? Are they not the bases of its doctrine? Does not the doctrine of sin need for its starting point the record of the fall? Could we so satisfactorily understand justification did we not have the story of God's dealings with Abraham? And what of the priesthood of Christ? Dismiss Leviticus and what can be made of Hebrews? Is not the Acts of the Apostles historical, but can we afford to lose its inspiration?

Indeed, the historical books have the strongest testimony borne to their importance in other parts of the Bible. This will appear more particularly as we proceed, but take, in passing, Christ's use of Deuteronomy in his conflict with the tempter. Thrice does he overcome him by a citation from that historical book without note or comment. Is it not difficult to believe that neither he nor Satan considered it inspired?

Thus without going further, we may say that it is impossible to secure the *religious* infallibility of the Bible — which is all the objector regards as necessary — if we exclude Bible history from the sphere of its inspiration. But if we include Bible history at all, we must include the whole of it, for who is competent to separate its parts?

2. *The inspiration includes not only all the books of the Bible in general but in detail, the form as well as the substance, the word as well as the thought.* This is sometimes called the verbal theory of inspiration and is vehemently spoken against in some quarters. It is too mechanical, it degrades the writers to the level of machines, it has a tendency to make skeptics, and all that.

This last remark, however, is not so alarming as it sounds. The doctrine of the eternal retribution of the wicked is said to make skeptics, and also that of a vicarious atonement, not to mention other revelations of Holy Writ. The natural mind takes to none of these things. But if we are not prepared to yield the point in one case for such a reason, why should we be asked to do it in another?

But we are insisting upon no theory that altogether excludes the human element in the transmission of the Sacred Word. As Dr. Henry B. Smith says, "God speaks through the personality as well as the lips of his messengers," and we may pour into that word "personality" everything that goes to make it — the age in which the person lived, his environment, his degree of culture, his temperament and all the rest. It is limiting the Holy One of Israel to say that he is unable to do this without turning a human being into an automaton. Has he who created man as a free agent left himself no opportunity to mould his thoughts into forms of speech inerrantly expressive of his will, without destroying that which he has made?

Indeed, wherein resides man's free agency, in his mind or in his mouth? Shall we say he is free while God controls his thought, but that he becomes a mere machine when that control extends to the *expression* of his thought?

In the last analysis, it is the Bible itself which must settle the question of its inspiration and the extent of it, and to this we come in the consideration of the proof, but we may be allowed a final question. Can even God himself give a thought to man without the words that clothe it? Are not the two inseparable, as much so "as a sum and its figures, or a tune and its notes?" Has any case been known in human history where a healthy mind has been able to create ideas without expressing them to its own perception? In other words, as Dr. A. J. Gordon once observed: "To deny that the Holy Spirit speaks in scripture is an intelligible proposition, but to admit that he speaks, it is impossible to know what he says except as we have his words."

III. Proof of Inspiration

1. *The inspiration of the Bible is proven by the philosophy, or what may be called the nature of the case.*

The proposition may be stated thus: The Bible is the history of the redemption of the race, or from the side of the individual, a supernatural revelation of the will of God to men for their salvation. But it was given to certain men of one age to be conveyed in writing to other men in different ages. Now all men experience difficulty in giving faithful reflections of their thoughts to others because of sin, ignorance, defective memory and the inaccuracy always incident to the use of language.

Therefore, it may be easily deduced that if the revelation is to be communicated precisely as originally received, the same supernatural power is required in the one case as in the other. This has been sufficiently elaborated in the foregoing and need not be dwelt upon again.

2. *It may be proven by the history and character of the Bible, i.e.,* by all that has been assumed as to its authenticity and credibility. All that goes to prove these things goes to prove its inspiration.

To borrow in part, the language of the Westminster Confession, "the heavenliness of its matter, the efficacy of its doctrine, the unity of its various parts, the majesty of its style and the scope and completeness of its design," all indicate the divinity of its origin.

The more we think upon it the more we must be convinced that men unaided by the Spirit of God could neither have conceived, nor put together, nor preserved in its integrity that precious deposit known as the Sacred Oracles.

3. The strongest proof is the declarations of the Bible itself and the inferences to be drawn from them. Nor is this reasoning in a circle as some might think. In the case of a man as to whose veracity there is no doubt, no hesitancy is felt in accepting what he says about himself; and since the Bible is demonstrated to be true in its statements of fact by unassailable evidence, may we not accept its witness in its own behalf?

Take the argument from Jesus Christ as an illustration. He was content to be tested by the prophecies of himself that went before, and the result was the definite establishment of his claims to be the Messiah. That complex system of prophecies, rendering collusion or counterfeit impossible, is the incontestable proof that he was what he claimed to be.

It is so with the Bible. The character of its contents, the unity of its parts, the fulfillment of its prophecies, the miracles wrought in its attestation, the effects it has accomplished in the lives of nations and of men, all these go to show that it is divine, and if so, that it may be believed in what it says about itself.

A.   Argument for the Old Testament.

To begin with the Old Testament, (a) consider how the writers speak of the origin of their messages.   Dr. James H. Brookes is authority for saying that the phrase, "Thus saith the Lord" or its equivalent is used by them 2,000 times.   Suppose we eliminate this phrase and its necessary context from the Old Testament in every instance, one wonders how much of the Old Testament would remain.

(b)   Consider how the utterances of the Old Testament writers are introduced into the New.   Take Matthew 1:22 as an illustration, "Now all this was done that it might be fulfilled which was spoken by the Lord through the prophet."   It was not the prophet who spake, but the Lord who spake through the prophet.

(c)   Consider how Christ and his apostles regard the Old Testament.   He came "not to destroy but to fulfill the law and the prophets" (Matt. 5:17).   "The Scripture cannot be broken" (John 10:35).   He sometimes used single words as the bases of important doctrines, twice in Matthew 22, at verses 31, 32 and 42-45.   The apostles do the same (see Gal. 3:16; Heb. 2:8, 11 and 12:26, 27).

(d)   Consider what the apostles directly teach upon the subject.   Peter tells us that "No prophecy ever came by the will of man, but men spake from God, being moved by the Holy Spirit" (II Pet. 1:21, ASV).   "Prophecy" here applies to the word written as is indicated in the preceding verse, and means not merely the foretelling of events, but the utterances of any word of God without reference as to time past, present or to come. As a matter of fact, what Peter declares is that the will of man had nothing to do with any part of the Old Testament, but that the whole of it, from Genesis to Malachi, was inspired by God.

Of course, Paul says the same, in language even plainer, in II Timothy 3:16, "All scripture is given by inspiration of God, and is profitable."   The phrase "inspiration of God" means literally *God-breathed*.   The whole of the Old Testament is God-breathed, for it is to that part of the Bible the language particularly refers, since the New Testament as such was not then generally known.

As this verse is given somewhat differently in the Revised Version we dwell upon it a moment longer. It there reads, "Every scripture inspired of God is also profitable," and the caviller is disposed to say that therefore some scripture may be inspired and some may not be, and that the profitableness extends only to the former and not the latter.

But aside from the fact that Paul would hardly be guilty of such a weak truism as that, it may be stated in reply first, that the King James rendering of the passage is not only the more consistent Scripture, but the more consistent Greek. Several of the best Greek scholars of the period affirm this, including some of the revisers themselves who did not vote for the change. And secondly, even the revisers place it in the margin as of practically equal authority with their preferred translation, and to be chosen by the reader if desired. There are not a few devout Christians, however, who would be willing to retain the rendering of the Revised Version as being stronger than the King James, and who would interpolate a word in applying it to make it mean, "Every scripture (*because*) inspired of God is also profitable." We believe that both Gaussen and Wordsworth take this view, two as staunch defenders of plenary inspiration as could be named.

B. Argument for the New Testament

We are sometimes reminded that, however strong and convincing the argument for the inspiration of the Old Testament, that for the New Testament is only indirect. "Not one of the evangelists tells us that he is inspired," says a certain theological professor, "and not one writer of an epistle, except Paul."

While we are prepared to dispute this statement, let us first reflect that the inspiration of the Old Testament being assured as it is, why should similar evidence be required for the New? Whoever is competent to speak as a Bible authority knows that the *unity* of the Old and New Testaments is the strongest demonstration of their common source. They are seen to be not two books, but only two parts of one book.

It is somewhat as follows that Dr. Gaussen in his exhaustive *Theopneustia* (now published by Moody Press under the title, *The*

Inspiration of the Holy Scripture) gives the argument for the inspiration of the New Testament.

(a)   The New Testament is the later, and for that reason the more important revelation of the two, and hence if the former were inspired, it certainly must be true of the latter.   The opening verses of the first and second chapters of Hebrews plainly suggest this: "God, who at sundry times and in divers manners spake in time past unto the fathers by the prophets, hath in these last days spoken unto us by his Son . . . . *Therefore* we ought to give the more earnest heed to the things which we have heard."

This inference is rendered still more conclusive by the circumstance that the New Testament sometimes explains, sometimes proves, and sometimes even repeals ordinances of the Old Testament.   See Matthew 1:22, 23 for an illustration of the first, Acts 13:19 to 39 for the second, and Galatians 5:6 for the third.   Assuredly, these things would not be true if the New Testament were not of equal, and in a certain sense, even greater authority than the Old.

(b)   The writers of the New Testament were of an equal or higher rank than those of the Old.   That they were prophets is evident from such allusions as Romans 16:25-27, and Ephesians 3:4, 5.   But that they were more than prophets is indicated in the fact that wherever in the New Testament prophets and apostles are both mentioned, the last-named is always mentioned first (see I Cor. 12:28; Eph. 2:20; 4:11).   It is also true that the writers of the New Testament had a higher mission than those of the Old, since they were sent forth by Christ, as he had been sent forth by the Father (John 20:21).   They were to go, not to a single nation only (as Israel), but into all the world (Matt. 28:19).   They received the keys of the kingdom of heaven (Matt. 16:19), and they are to be pre-eminently rewarded in the regeneration (Matt. 19:28). Such considerations and comparisons as these are not to be overlooked in estimating the authority by which they wrote.

(c)   The writers of the New Testament were especially qualified for their work, as we see in Matthew 10:19, 20; Mark 13:11; Luke 12:2; John 14:26 and 16:13, 14.   It may be noticed that in some instances, inspiration of the most absolute character was promised as to what they should *speak* — the inference being warranted that none the less would they be guided in what they wrote. Their spoken words were limited and temporary in their sphere, but their written utterances covered the whole range of revelation and were to last forever. If in the one case they were inspired, how much more in the other?

(d) The writers of the New Testament directly claim divine inspiration. See Acts 15:23-29, where, especially at verse 28, James is recorded as saying, "for it seemed good to the Holy Ghost and to us, to lay upon you no greater burden than these necessary things." Here it is affirmed very clearly that the Holy Ghost is the real writer of the letter in question and simply uses the human instruments for his purpose. Add to this I Corinthians 2:13, where Paul says "Which things also we speak, not in the words which man's wisdom teacheth, but which the Holy Ghost teacheth, comparing spiritual things with spiritual," or as the margin of the Revised Version puts it, "imparting spiritual things to spiritual men." In I Thessalonians 2:13 the same writer says: "For this cause also thank we God without ceasing, because when ye received the word of God which ye heard of us, ye received it not as the word of man, but as it is in truth the word of God." In II Peter 3:2 the apostle places his own words on a level with those of the prophets of the Old Testament, and in verses 15 and 16 of the same chapter he does the same with the writings of Paul, classifying them "with the other scriptures." Finally, in Revelation 2:7, although it is the Apostle John who is writing, he is authorized to exclaim: "He that hath an ear let him hear what the Spirit saith unto the churches," and so on throughout the epistles to the seven churches.

C. Argument for the Words

The evidence that the inspiration includes the form as well as the substance of the Holy Scriptures, the word as well as the thought, may be gathered in this way.

1. *There were certainly some occasions when the words were given to the human agents.* Take the instance of Balaam (Num. 22:38; 23:12, 16). It is clear that this self-seeking prophet *thought*, *i.e.*, desired to speak differently from what he did, but was obliged to speak the word that God put in his mouth. There are two

incontrovertible witnesses to this, one being Balaam himself and the other God.

Take Saul (I Sam. 10:10), or at a later time, his messengers (19:20-24). No one will claim that there was not an inspiration of the words here. And Caiaphas also (John 11:49-52), of whom it is expressly said that when he prophesied that one man should die for the people, "this spake he not of himself." Who believes that Caiaphas meant or really knew the significance of what he said?

How entirely this harmonizes with Christ's promise to his disciples in Matthew 10:19, 20 and elsewhere. "When they deliver you up take no thought [be not anxious] how or what ye shall speak; for it shall be given you in that hour what ye shall speak. For it is not ye that speak but the Spirit of your Father which speaketh in you." Mark is even more emphatic: "Neither do ye *premeditate,* but whatsoever shall be given you in that hour, that speak ye, for it is not ye that speak, but the Holy Ghost."

Take the circumstance of the day of Pentecost (Acts 2:4-11), when the disciples "began to speak with other tongues as the Spirit gave them utterance." Parthians, Medes, Elamites, the dwellers in Mesopotamia, in Judea, Cappadocia, Pontus, Asia, Phrygia, Pamphylia, Egypt, in the parts of Libya about Cyrene, the strangers of Rome, Cretes and Arabians all testified, "we do hear them speak in our tongues the wonderful works of God!" Did not this inspiration include the words? Did it not indeed *exclude* the thought? What clearer example could be desired?

Now, consider the utterance of I Peter 1:10, 11, where he speaks of them who prophesied of the grace that should come, as "searching what, or what manner of time, the Spirit of Christ which was in them did signify when he testified beforehand the sufferings of Christ and the glory that should follow, to whom it was revealed," etc.

"Should we see a student who, having taken down the lecture of a profound philosopher, was now studying diligently to comprehend the sense of the discourse which he had written, we should understand simply that he was a pupil and not a master; that he had nothing to do with originating either the thoughts or the words of the lecture, but was rather a disciple whose province it was to understand what he had transcribed, and so be able to communicate it to others.

"And who can deny that this is the exact picture of what we have in this passage from Peter? Here were inspired writers studying the meaning of what they themselves had written. With all possible allowance for the human peculiarities of the writers, they must have been reporters of what they heard, rather than formulators of that which they had been made to understand" (A J. Gordon, *The Ministry of the Spirit*, pp. 173, 174).

2. *The Bible plainly teaches that inspiration extends to its words.* We spoke of Balaam as uttering that which God put in his mouth, but the same expression is used by God himself with reference to his prophets. When Moses would excuse himself from service because he was not eloquent, he who made man's mouth said, "Now therefore go, and I will be with thy mouth, and teach thee what thou shalt say" (Ex. 4:10-12). And Dr. James H. Brookes' comment is very pertinent: "God did not say I will be with thy mind, and teach thee what thou shalt think; but I will be with thy mouth and teach thee what thou shalt say. This explains why, forty years afterwards, Moses said to Israel, 'Ye shall not add unto the word I command you, neither shall ye diminish ought from it' (Deut. 4:2)." Seven times Moses tells us that the tables of stone containing the commandments were the work of God, and the writing was the writing of God, graven upon the tables (Ex. 31:16).

Passing from the Pentateuch to the poetical books we find David saying, "The Spirit of the Lord spake by me, and his word was in my tongue" (II Sam. 23:1, 2). He, too, does not say, God thought by me, but spake by me.

Coming to the prophets, Jeremiah confesses that, like Moses, he recoiled from the mission on which he was sent and for the same reason. He was a child and could not speak. "Then the Lord put forth his hand and touched my mouth. And the Lord said unto me, Behold, I have put my word in thy mouth" (Jer. 1:6-9).

All of which substantiates the declaration of Peter quoted earlier, that "no prophecy ever came by the will of man, but man spake from God, being moved by the Holy Spirit." Surely, if the will of man had *nothing* to do with the prophecy, he could not have been at liberty in the selection of the words.

So much for the Old Testament. When we reach the New, we have the same unerring and verbal accuracy guaranteed to the apostles by the Son of God, as we have seen. And we have the apostles making claim of it, as when Paul in I Corinthians 2:12, 13 distinguishes between the "things" or the thoughts which God gave him and the words in which he expressed them, and insisting on the divinity of both; "Which things also we speak," he says, "not in the words which man's wisdom teacheth, but which the Holy Ghost teacheth." In Galatians 3:16, following the example of his divine Master, he employs not merely a single word, but a single letter of a word as the basis of an argument for a great doctrine. The blessing of justification which Abraham received has become that of the believer in Jesus Christ. "Now to Abraham and his seed were the promises made. He saith not, And to seeds, as of many; but as of one, And to thy *seed,* which is Christ."

The writer of the epistle to the Hebrews bases a similar argument on the word "all" in chapter 1:8, on the word "one" in 1:11, and on the phrase "yet once more" in 12:26, 27.

3. *The most unique argument for the inspiration of the words of Scripture is the relation which Jesus Christ bears to them.* In the first place, he himself was inspired as to his words. In the earliest reference to his prophetic office (Deut. 18:18), Jehovah says, "I will put my words in his mouth, and he shall speak . . . all that I shall command him." This was a limitation on his utterance which Jesus everywhere recognizes. "As my Father hath taught me, I speak these things"; "the Father which sent me, he gave me a commandment what I should say, and what I should speak"; "whatsoever I speak therefore, even as the Father said unto me, so I speak"; "I have given unto them the words which thou gavest me"; "the words that I speak unto you, they are spirit and they are life" (John 6:63; 8:26, 28, 40; 12:49, 50).

The thought is still more impressive as we read of the relation of the Holy Spirit to the God-man. "The Spirit of the Lord is upon me because he hath anointed me to preach the gospel to the poor; "He through the Holy Ghost had given commandments unto the apostles"; "the revelation of Jesus Christ which God gave unto him";

"these things saith he that holdeth the seven stars in his right hand"; "He that hath an ear let him hear what the *Spirit* saith unto the churches" (Luke 4:18; Acts 1:2; Rev. 1:1; 2:1, 11). If the incarnate Word needed the unction of the Holy Ghost to give to men the revelation he received from the Father in whose bosom he dwells, and if the agency of the same Spirit extended to the words he spake in preaching the gospel to the meek, how much more must these things be so in the case of ordinary men when engaged in the same service? With what show of reason can one contend that any Old or New Testament writer stood, so far as his words were concerned, in need of no such agency" (*The New Apologetic*, pp. 67, 68).

In the second place, Christ used the Scriptures as though they were inspired as to their words. In Matthew 22:31-32 he substantiates the doctrine of the resurrection against the skepticism of the Sadducees by emphasizing the present tense of the verb "to be," *i.e.*, the word "am" in the language of Jehovah to Moses at the burning bush. In verses 42-45 of the same chapter he does the same for his own deity by alluding to the second use of the word "Lord" in Psalm 110. "The LORD said unto my Lord . . . If David then call him Lord, how is he his son?" In John 10:34-36, he vindicates himself from the charge of blasphemy by saying, "Is it not written in your law, I said, ye are gods? If he called them gods, unto whom the word of God came, and the scripture cannot be broken; say ye of him, whom the Father hath sanctified, and sent into the world, thou blasphemest; because I said, I am the Son of God?"

We see him in Matthew 4 overcoming the tempter in the wilderness by three quotations from Deuteronomy without note or comment except, "*It is written.*" Referring to this Adolphe Monod says, "I know of nothing in the whole history of humanity, nor even in the field of divine revelation, that proves more clearly than this the inspiration of the Scriptures. What! Jesus Christ, the Lord of heaven and earth, calling to his aid in that solemn moment Moses his servant? He who speaks from heaven fortifying himself against the temptations of hell by the word of him who spake from earth? How can we explain that spiritual mystery, that wonderful reversing of the order of things, if for Jesus the words of Moses were not the words of God rather than those of men? How shall we explain it if Jesus were not fully aware that holy men of God spake as they were moved by the Holy Ghost? . . . Let that which was sufficient for him suffice for you. Fear not that the rock which sustained the Lord in the hour of his temptation and distress will give way because you lean too heavily upon it."

In the third place, Christ teaches that the Scriptures are inspired as to their words. In the Sermon on the Mount he said, "Think not that I am come to destroy the law, or the prophets: I am not come to destroy, but to fulfil. For verily I say unto you, till heaven and earth pass, one jot or one tittle shall in no wise pass from the law, till all be fulfilled."

Here is testimony confirmed by an oath, for "verily" on the lips of the Son of Man carries such force. He affirms the indestructibility of the law, not its substance merely but its form, not the thought but the word.

"One jot or tittle shall in no wise pass from the law." The "jot" means the *yod,* the smallest letter in the Hebrew alphabet, while the "tittle" means the *horn,* a short projection in certain letters extending the base line beyond the upright one which rests upon it. A reader unaccustomed to the Hebrew needs a strong eye to see the tittle, but Christ guarantees that as a part of the sacred text, neither the tittle nor the *yod* shall perish.

IV. Difficulties and Objections

That there are difficulties in the way of accepting a view of inspiration like this goes without saying. But to the finite mind there must always be difficulties connected with a revelation from the Infinite, and it cannot be otherwise. Men of faith, and it is such we are addressing and not men of the world, do not wait to understand or resolve all the difficulties associated with other mysteries of the Bible before accepting them as divine, and why should they do so in this case?

Moreover, Archbishop Whately's dictum is generally accepted, that we are not obliged to clear away every difficulty about a doctrine in order to believe it, always provided that the facts on which it rests are true. Particularly is this the case where the rejection of such a doctrine involves greater difficulties than its belief, as it does here.

For if this view of inspiration be rejected, what have its opponents to give in its place? Do they realize that any objections to it are slight in comparison with those to any other view that can be named? And do they realize that this is true, because this view has the immeasurable advantage of agreeing with the plain declarations of Scripture on the subject? In other words, as Dr. Burrell says, those who assert the inerrancy of the scripture autographs do so on the authority of God himself, and to deny it is of a piece with the denial that they teach the forgiveness of sins or the resurrection from the dead. No amount of exegetical turning and twisting can explain away the assertions already quoted in these pages, to say nothing of the constant undertone of evidence we find in the Bible everywhere to their truth. But now let us consider some of the same difficulties.

1. *There are the so-called discrepancies or contradictions be-tween certain statements of the Bible and the facts of history or natural science.* The best way to meet these is to treat them separately as they are presented, but when you ask for them you are not infrequently met with silence. They are hard to produce, and when produced, who is able to say that they belong to the original parchments? As we are not contending for an inerrant translation, does not the burden of proof rest with the objector?

But some of these "discrepancies" are easily explained. They do not exist between statements of the Bible and facts of science, but between erroneous interpretations of the Bible and immature conclusions of science. The old story of Galileo is in point, who did not contradict the Bible in affirming that the earth moved round the sun, but only the false theological assumption about it. In this way advancing light has removed many of these discrepancies, and it is fair to presume that further light would remove all.

2. *There are the differences in the narratives themselves.* In the first place, the New Testament writers sometimes change important words in quoting from the Old Testament, which it is assumed could not be the case if in both instances the writers were inspired. But it is forgotten that in the Scriptures we are dealing not so much with different human authors as with one Divine

Author. It is a principle in ordinary literature that an author may quote himself as he pleases, and give a different turn to an expression here and there as a changed condition of affairs renders it necessary or desirable. Shall we deny this privilege to the Holy Spirit? May we not find, indeed, that some of these supposed misquotations show such progress of truth, such evident application of the teaching of an earlier dispensation to the circumstances of a later one, as to afford a confirmation of their divine origin rather than an argument against it? We offer as illustrations of this principle Isaiah 59:20 quoted in Romans 11:26, and Amos 9:11 quoted in Acts 15:16.

Another class of differences, however, is where the *same event* is sometimes given differently by different writers. Take that most frequently used by the objectors, the inscription on the cross, recorded by all the evangelists and yet differently by each. How can such records be inspired, it is asked.

It is to be remembered in reply, that the inscription was written in three languages calling for a different arrangement of the words in each case, and that one evangelist may have translated the Hebrew, and another the Latin, while a third recorded the Greek. It is not said that any one gave the *full* inscription, nor can we affirm that there was any obligation upon them to do so. Moreover, no one contradicts any other, and no one says what is untrue.

Recalling what was said about our having to deal not with different human authors but with one Divine Author, may not the Holy Spirit here have chosen to emphasize some one particular fact, or phase of a fact of the inscription for a specific and important end? Examine the records to determine what this fact may have been. Observe that whatever else is omitted, all the narratives record the momentous circumstances that the Sufferer on the cross was THE KING OF THE JEWS.

Could there have been a cause for this? What was the charge preferred against Jesus by his accusers? Was he not rejected and crucified, because he said he was the King of the Jews? Was not this the central idea Pilate was providentially guided to express in the inscription? And if so, was it not that to which the evangelists should bear witness? And should not that witness have been borne in a way to dispel the thought of collusion in the premises? And did not this involve a variety of narrative which should at the same time be in harmony with truth and fact? And do we not have this very thing in the four gospels?

These accounts supplement, but do not contradict each other. We place them before the eye in the order in which they are recorded.

This is Jesus	THE KING OF THE JEWS
	THE KING OF THE JEWS
This is	THE KING OF THE JEWS
Jesus of Nazareth	THE KING OF THE JEWS

The entire inscription evidently was "This is Jesus of Nazareth the King of the Jews," but we submit that the foregoing presents a reasonable argument for the differences in the records.

3. *There is the variety in style.* Some think that if all the writers were alike inspired and the inspiration extended to their words, they must all possess the same style — as if the Holy Spirit had but one style!

Literary style is a method of selecting words and putting sentences together which stamps an author's work with the influence of his habits, his condition in society, his education, his reasoning, his experience, his imagination and his genius. These give his mental and moral physiognomy and make up his style.

But is not God free to act with or without these fixed laws? There are no circumstances which tinge his views or reasonings, and he has no idiosyncrasies of speech, and no mother tongue through which he expresses his character, or leaves the finger mark of genius upon his literary fabrics.

It is a great fallacy then, as Dr. Thomas Armitage once said, to suppose that uniformity of verbal style must have marked God's authorship in the Bible, had he selected its words. As the author of all styles, rather does he use them all at his pleasure. He bestows all the powers of mental individuality upon his instruments for using the Scriptures, and then uses their powers as he will to express his mind by them.

Indeed, the variety of style is a necessary proof of the freedom of the human writers, and it is this which among other things convinces us that, however controlled by the Holy Spirit, they were not mere machines in what they wrote.

William Cullen Bryant was a newspaper man but a poet; Edmund Clarence Stedman was a Wall Street broker and also a poet. What a difference in style there was between their editorials and commercial letters on the one hand, and their poetry on the other! Is God more limited than a man?

4. *There are certain declarations of Scripture itself.* Does not Paul say in one or two places "I speak as a man," or "After the manner of man"? Assuredly, but is he not using the arguments common among men for the sake of elucidating a point? And may he not as truly be led of the Spirit to do that, and to record it, as to do or say anything else? Of course, what he quotes from men is not of the same essential value as what he receives directly from God, but the *record* of the quotation is as truly inspired.

There are two or three other utterances of his of this character in the 7th chapter of I Corinthians, where he is treating of marriage. At verse 6 he says, "I speak this by permission, not of commandment," and what he means has no reference to the source of his message but the subject of it. In contradiction to the false teaching of some, he says Christians are permitted to marry, but not commanded to do so. At verse 10 he says, "Unto the married I command, yet not I, but the Lord," while at verse 12 there follows, "but to the rest speak I, not the Lord." Does he declare himself inspired in the first instance, and not in the second? By no means, but in the first he is alluding to what the Lord spake on the subject while here in the flesh, and in the second to what he, Paul is adding thereto on the authority of the Holy Spirit speaking through him. In other words, putting his own utterances on equality with those of our Lord, he simply confirms their inspiration.

At verse 40 he uses a puzzling expression, "I think also that I have the Spirit of God." As we are contending only for an inspired record, it would seem easy to say that here he records a doubt as to whether he was inspired, and hence everywhere else in the absence of such record of doubt the inspiration is to be assumed. But this would be begging the question, and we prefer the solution of others that the answer is found in the condition of the Corinthian church at that time. His enemies had sought to counteract his teachings, claiming that they had the Spirit of God. Referring to the claim, he says with justifiable irony, "I think also that I have the Spirit of God" (A.S.V.). "I think" in the mouth of one having apostolic authority, says Professor Watts, may be taken as carrying the strongest assertion of the judgment in question. The passage is something akin to another in the same epistle at the 14th chapter, verse 37, where he says, "If any man think himself to be a prophet, or spiritual, let him acknowledge that the things I write unto you are the commandments of the Lord."

Time forbids further amplification on the difficulties and objections nor is it necessary, since there is not one that has not been met satisfactorily to the man of God and the child of faith again and again. Furthermore, it is safe to challenge the whole Christian world for the name of a man who stands out as a winner of souls who does not believe in the inspiration of the Bible as it has been sought to be explained in these pages.

But we conclude with a kind of concrete testimony — that of the General Assembly of the Presbyterian Church of America, and as long ago as 1893. The writer is not a Presbyterian, and therefore with the better grace can ask his readers to consider the character and the intellect represented in such an Assembly. Here are some of our greatest merchants, our greatest jurists, our greatest educators, our greatest statesmen, as well as our greatest missionaries, evangelists and theologians. There may be seen as able and august a gathering of representatives of Christianity in other places and on other occasions, but few that can surpass it. For sobriety of thought, for depth as well as breadth of learning, for wealth of spiritual experience, for honesty of utterance, and virility of conviction, the General Assembly of the Presbyterian Church in America must in this day command attention and respect throughout the world. And this is what it said on the subject we are now considering at its gathering in the city of Washington, the capital of the nation, at the date named:

"The Bible as we now have it, in its various translations and revisions, when freed from all errors and mistakes of translators, copyists and printers, (is) the very Word of God, and consequently wholly without error."

LEANDER WHITCOMB MUNHALL (1843-1934) was a largely self-educated Methodist evangelist who preached the gospel for more than fifty years. He served with distinction during the Civil War, participating in thirty-three battles. He edited *The Methodist*, a weekly publication out of Philadelphia, and served as a representative to denominational conferences. A crusader for biblical orthodoxy, he warned his denomination of liberalism in his book *Breakers! Methodism Adrift* (1913).

15

Inspiration

By L. W. Munhall, M.A., D.D.
AUTHOR OF "THE HIGHEST CRITICS VS. THE HIGHER CRITICS"

Revised and edited by Gerald B. Stanton, Th.D.

The Bible is inspired. It is therefore God's Word. This is fundamental to the Christian faith. "Faith cometh by hearing, and hearing by the Word of God" (Rom. 10:17).

But, it is asked, what do you mean by inspiration? Since there are many who insist that only the thoughts of Scripture, and not the words, are inspired this is a proper question.

The General Assembly of the Presbyterian Church, in 1893, by a unanimous vote made the following deliverance: "The Bible as we now have it in its various translations and revisions when freed from all errors and mistakes of translators, copyists and printers, is the very Word of God, and consequently, wholly without error."

We mean by verbal inspiration that the words composing the Bible are God-breathed. If they were not, then the Bible is not inspired at all, since it is composed only and solely of words.

"All Scripture is given by inspiration of God" (II Tim. 3:16). The word rendered Scripture in this passage is *graphe*. It means writing, anything written. The writing is composed of words. What else is this but verbal inspiration; and they wrest the "Scriptures unto their own destruction," who teach otherwise.

Prof. A. A. Hodge says: "The line can never rationally be drawn between the thoughts and words of Scripture . . . That we have an inspired Bible, and a verbally inspired one, we have the witness of God himself."

Prof. Gaussen says: "The theory of a Divine Revelation, in which you would have the inspiration of thoughts, without the inspiration of the language, is so inevitably irrational that it cannot be sincere, and proves false even to those who propose it."

Canon Westcott says: "The slightest consideration will show that words are as essential to intellectual processes as they are to mutual intercourse . . . Thoughts are wedded to words as necessarily as soul to body. Without it the mysteries unveiled before the eyes of the seer would be confused shadows; with it, they are made clear lessons for human life."

Dean Burgon, a man of vast learning, says: "You cannot dissect inspiration into substance and form. As for thoughts being inspired, apart from the words which give them expression, you might as well talk of a tune without notes, or a sum without figures. No such theory of inspiration is even intelligible. It is as illogical as it is worthless, and cannot be too sternly put down."

This doctrine of the inspiration of Scripture, in all its elements and parts, has always been the doctrine of the Church. Dr. Westcott has proved this by a copious catena of quotations from *Ante-Nicene Fathers* (in Appendix B to his *Introduction to the Study of the Gospels*). For example, he quotes Clemens Romanus as saying that the Scriptures are "the true utterances of the Holy Ghost."

Let us consider a few quotations from the Fathers: (1) Justin, speaking of the words of Scripture, says: "We must not suppose that the language proceeds from the men that are inspired, but from the Divine Word himself, who moves them. Their work is to announce that which the Holy Spirit proposes to teach, through them, to those who wish to learn the true religion." "The history Moses wrote was by the Divine Inspiration." And so, of all the Bible.

(2). Irenaeus. "The writers spoke as acted on by the Spirit. All who foretold the coming of Christ received their inspiration from the Son, for how else could Scripture 'testify' of him alone?" "Matthew might have written, 'The generation of Jesus was on this wise,' but the Holy Spirit, foreseeing the corruption of the truth, and fortifying us against deception says, through Matthew, 'The generation of Jesus the Messiah was on this wise.'" "The writers are beyond all falsehood," i.e., they are inerrant.

(3). Clement of Alexandria. "The foundations of our faith rest on no insecure basis. We have received them through God himself through the Scripture, not one jot or tittle of which shall pass away till all is accomplished, for the mouth of the Lord, the Holy Spirit, spoke it. He ceases to be a man who spurns the tradition of the Church, and turns aside to human opinions; for the Scriptures are truly holy, since they make us holy, God-like. Of these Holy Writings or Words, the Bible is composed. Paul calls them God-breathed (II Tim. 3:15, 16). The Sacred Writings consist of these holy letters or syllables, since they are "God-breathed." Again, "The Jews and Christians agree as to the inspiration of the Holy Scriptures but differ in interpretation. By our faith, we believe that every Scripture, since it is God-breathed, is profitable."

(4). Origen. "It is the doctrine acknowledged by all Christians, and evidently preached in the churches that the Holy Spirit, inspired the Saints, Prophets and Apostles, and was present in those he inspired at the Coming of Christ; for Christ, the Word of God, was in Moses when he wrote, and in the Prophets, and by his Spirit he did speak to them all things. The records of the Gospels are the Oracles of the Lord, pure Oracles purified as silver seven times tried. They are without error, since they were accurately written, by the cooperation of the Holy Spirit." "It is good to adhere to the words of Paul and the Apostles as to God and our Lord Jesus Christ. There are many writings, but only one Book; four Evangelists, but only one Gospel. All the Sacred Writings breathe the same fullness. There is nothing, in the Law, the Prophets, the Gospel, the Apostles, that did not come from the fullness of God."

(5). Augustine. The view of the Holy Scriptures held by Augustine was that held by Tertullian, Cyprian and all Fathers of the North African Church. No view of verbal inspiration could be more rigid. "The Scriptures are the letters of God, the voice of God, the writings of God." "The writers record the words of God. Christ spoke by Moses, for he was the Spirit of the Creator, and all the prophecies are the voice of the Lord. From the Spirit came the gift of tongues. All Scripture is profitable since it is inspired of God. The Scriptures, whether in History, Prophecy,

Psalms or Law are of God. They cannot stand in part and fall in part. They are from God, who spake them all." "As it was not the Apostles who spoke, but the Spirit of the Father in them, so it is the Spirit that speaks in all Scriptures." "It avails nothing what I say, what he says but what saith the Lord."

Prof. B. B. Warfield, of Princeton Theological Seminary, summarizes the case in an article on The Westminster Doctrine of Inspiration: "Doubtless enough has been said to show that the confession teaches precisely the doctrine which is taught in the private writings of the framers which was also the General Protestant Doctrine of the time, and not of that time only or of the Protestants only; for despite the contrary assertion that has recently become tolerably current, essentially this doctrine of inspiration (verbal) has been the doctrine of the Church of all ages and of all names."

Some Proofs of Verbal Inspiration

The Bible plainly teaches that its words are inspired, and that it *is* the Word of God. Let us examine into this matter a little, by considering briefly three kinds of evidence.

First. Let us note the direct testimony of the Bible to the fact of verbal inspiration.

"And Moses said unto the Lord, I am not eloquent [a man of words], neither heretofore nor since thou hast spoken unto thy servant: for I am slow of speech, and of a slow tongue. And the Lord said unto him, Who hath made man's mouth? . . . Now therefore go, and I will be with thy mouth, and teach thee what thou shalt speak" (Ex. 4:10-12). "And the Lord said unto Moses, Write thou these words: for after the tenor of these words I have made a covenant with thee, and with Israel" (Ex. 34:27). "And he said, Hear now my words: if there be a prophet among you, I the Lord will make myself known unto him in a vision, and will speak unto him in a dream . . . With him [Moses] will I speak mouth to mouth, even apparently, and not in dark speeches; and the similitude of the Lord shall he behold" (Num. 12:6, 8). "Ye shall not add unto the word which I command you, neither shall ye diminish from it" (Deut. 4:2). "But the prophet which shall speak a word presumptuously in my name, which I have not commanded him to speak, . . . that prophet shall die" (Deut. 18:20).

In Mark 12:36, Jesus said: "David himself said in the Holy Spirit." If we turn to II Samuel 23:2, we will find what it was David said: "The Spirit of the Lord spake by me, and his word was upon my tongue."

Jeremiah said: "Ah! Lord God! behold I cannot speak, for I am a child. But the Lord saith unto me, Say not I am a child, for thou shalt go to all that I shall send thee, and whatsoever I command thee thou shalt speak. Be not afraid of their faces, for I am with thee to deliver thee, saith the Lord. Then the Lord put forth his hand and touched my mouth. And the Lord said unto me, Behold, I have put my words in thy mouth" (Jer. 1:6-9).

Balaam was compelled to speak against his will. He said: "Lo, I am come unto thee; have I now any power at all to say anything? the word that God putteth in my mouth, that shall I speak." He did his very utmost to curse the Israelites, but as often as he tried it, he blessed them. Balak at last said, "Neither curse them at all, nor bless them at all." But Balaam answered, "Told not I thee, saying, All the Lord speaketh, that must I do" (Num. 22:38; 23:26).

In the five books of Moses, in the books called historical, the books included under the general title of the Psalms, such expressions as the following occur hundreds of times: "Thus saith the Lord"; "The Lord said"; "The Lord spake"; "The Lord hath spoken"; "The saying of the Lord"; and "The word of the Lord." There is no other thought expressed in these books concerning inspiration than that the writers spoke and wrote the very words that God gave them.

Turning to the books called prophetical, we find Isaiah saying, "Hear the word of the Lord" (Isa. 1:10); and no fewer than twenty times does he explicitly declare that his writings are the "words of the Lord." Almost one hundred times does Jeremiah say, "The word of the Lord came unto me," or declare he was uttering the "words of the Lord," and the "word of the living God." Ezekiel says that his writings are the "words of God" quite sixty times. Here is a sample: "Son of man, all my words that I shall speak unto thee receive in thine heart, and hear with thine ears. And go get thee to them of the captivity, unto the children of thy

people, and speak unto them, and tell them, Thus saith the Lord
God" (Ezek. 3:10-11). Daniel said, "And when I heard the voice
of his words" (Dan. 10:9). Hosea said, "The word of the Lord"
(Hosea 1:1). "The word of the Lord that came to Joel" (Joel
1:1). Amos said "Hear the word of the Lord" (Amos 3:1).
Obadiah said, "Thus saith the Lord God" (Oba. 1:1). "The word
of the Lord came unto Jonah" (Jonah 1:1). "The word of the
Lord that came to Micah" (Micah 1:1). Nahum said, "Thus
saith the Lord" (Nah. 1:12). Habakkuk wrote, "The Lord
answered me and said" (Hab. 2:2). "The word of the Lord
which came to Zephaniah" (Zeph. 1:1). "Came the word of the
Lord by Haggai the prophet" (Hag 1:1). "Came the word of
the Lord unto Zechariah" (Zech. 1:1). "The word of the Lord
to Israel by Malachi" (Mal 1:1). And in this last of the Old
Testament books, is it twenty-four times said, "Thus saith the
Lord."

The words Jesus himself uttered were inspired. The words he
spoke were not his own, but actually put into his mouth. In the
most express manner it was ,foretold that Christ should thus
speak, just as Moses spake. "A prophet shall the Lord your God
raise up, *like* unto me. To him ye shall hearken." Twice it is
said, *"like unto me."* And how like to Moses, except as the whole
context shows, *"like unto* him in *verbal inspiration?* To Moses
God said: "I will be with thy mouth, and teach thee what to say.
Thou shalt put words in Aaron's mouth, and I will be with thy
mouth, and teach you what you shall say. And he shall be thy
spokesman to the people. And he shall be to thee instead of a
mouth, and thou shalt be to him instead of God" (Ex. 4:11-16).
Therefore did Jesus, as Prophet, utter inspired words "like unto
Moses." The very *words* he spoke God put into his mouth and
on his tongue. Therefore did he say, assuring the Jews that
Moses wrote of him: "I have not spoken from myself, but the
Father who sent me gave me commandment what I should say and
what I should speak. I speak therefore even as the Father said to
me, even so I speak" (John 12:49, 50). "I have given unto them
the *words Thou gavest Me,* and they have received them" (John
17:8). "The Son can do nothing from himself" (5:19). Since
Jesus Christ was divinely helped, "like unto Moses," the very words

put into his mouth, how should not the Evangelists and Apostles need the same divine guidance and help to qualify them for their work, and guarantee its inerrant truthfulness and its divine authority? If Moses and Isaiah, if Jesus Christ himself, had to be divinely assisted, how should the narrators of New Testament history and oracles be exempted from the same divine activity of the Spirit, all-controlling and guiding into the full truth?

Jesus said to the disciples, "And when they lead you to the judgment, and ·deliver you up, be not anxious beforehand what ye shall speak : but whatsoever shall be given you in that hour, that speak ye : for it is not ye that speak, but the Holy Ghost" (Mark 13 :11).

This same gift included all the disciples on the day of Pentecost, for "They were all filled with the Holy Ghost, and began to speak with other tongues as the Spirit gave them utterance" (Acts 2 :1, 4). The multitude that heard "marveled, saying, Behold, are not all these which speak Galileans? And how hear we every man in our own language? . . . We do hear them speaking in our tongues the mighty works of God" (Acts 2 :7, 11).

Paul says : "Which things also we speak, not in words which man's wisdom teacheth, but which the Spirit teacheth" (I Cor. 2 :13). "And for this cause we also thank God without ceasing, that, when ye received from us the word of the message *even the word* of God, ye accepted it not as the word of men, but, as it is in truth, the word of God" (I Thess. 2 :13).

So the Bible uniformly teaches the doctrine of verbal inspiration. It *is* the Word of God. This is the invariable testimony of the Book itself. It never, in a single instance, says that the mere thoughts of the writers were inspired; or, that these writers had a "concept." The Scriptures are called "the oracles of God" (Rom. 3 :2) ; "the Word of God" (Luke 8 :11) ; "the Word of the Lord" (Acts 13 :48) ; "the Word of life" (Phil. 2 :16) ; "the Word of Christ" (Col. 3 :16) ; "the Word of truth" (Eph. 1 :13) ; "the Word of faith" (Rom. 10 :8) ; and, by these and similar statements, do they declare, *more than two thousand times,* that the Bible is the Word of God — that the words are God-breathed, are inspired.

Second.   What of the inferential testimony to the fact of verbal inspiration? I mean by inferential testimony that which is assumed by the Bible, and the natural implication belonging to many of its statements.

The Bible assumes to be from God in that it meets man face to face with drawn sword and says: "Thou shalt!" and "Thou shalt not!" and demands immediate, unconditional and irreversible surrender to the authority of heaven, and submission to all the laws and will of God, as made known in its pages. This of itself would not signify a great deal, though unique, were it not for the striking and significant results of such submission; but, the natural inference of such assumption is, that the words of demand and command are from God.

A great many statements of the Bible plainly indicate that the words are inspired. The following are a few instances: "Forever, O Lord, thy Word is settled in heaven" (Psa. 119:89). This is characteristic of the entire Psalm. "The words of the Lord are pure words" (Psa. 12:6). "Is not my word like as a fire? saith the Lord; and like a hammer that breaketh the rock in pieces?" (Jer. 23:29). "The Word of our God shall stand forever" (Isa. 40:8); and so on, almost *ad infinitum.* Everywhere in the sacred record you find this same suggestion of divine authorship. Jesus and the Apostles always recognized it, and gave it prominence and emphasis. Its importance and value should not be underestimated.

Third.   The resultant testimony. What of it? Paul tells us that "every sacred writing" is God-breathed." "No prophecy ever came by the will of man; but men spake from God, being moved (*pheromenoi,* borne along) by the Holy Spirit" (II Pet. 1:21). "This passage does not justify the so-called "mechanical theory of inspiration." Such theory is nowhere taught in the Scriptures. Indeed, the obvious fact that the individual characteristics of the writers were in no way changed or destroyed, disproved such theory. It is said: "The Lord God formed man of the dust of the ground, and breathed into his nostrils the breath of life; and man became a living soul" (Gen. 2:7). Elihu said, "The Spirit of God hath made me, and the breath of the Almighty hath given me life" (Job 33:4). Now, then, the very same almighty power that gave life to Adam and Elihu, and which made the

"Heavens . . . and all the host of them," is, in some mysterious sense, in the words of the Sacred Record. Therefore are we told: "For the Word of God is living and active, and sharper than any two-edged sword, and piercing even to the dividing of soul and spirit, of both joints and marrow, and quick to discern the thoughts and intents of the heart" (Heb. 4:12). What results will follow believing the Word and submission to its requirements?

1. It will impart spiritual life and save the soul. "Receive with meekness the implanted Word, which is able to save your souls" (James 1:21). "Having been begotten again, not of corruptible seed, but of incorruptible, through the Word of God, which liveth and abideth" (I Pet. 1:23). "Of his own will begat he us by the word of truth" (James 1:18). Jesus said: "The words I have spoken unto you are spirit, and are life" (John 6:63).

As a good seed contains the germ of life, so that when cast into the soil of earth at the proper season, under the influence of sunshine and showers, it germinates and springs up to reproduce itself in kind; even so the words of the Bible, if received into the mind and heart to be believed and obeyed, germinate, and spiritual life is the result, reproducing its kind; and that believing soul is made partaker of the Divine nature (II Pet. 1:4). "He is a new creature [creation]; the old things are passed away; behold, they are become new" (II Cor. 5:17). The power and life of the Almighty lie hidden in the words of the Sacred Record; they are God-breathed, and that power and life will be manifest in the case of every one who will receive them with meekness, believing them and submitting to their requirements. All the books men have written cannot do this.

2. It has cleansing power. "Wherewithal shall a young man cleanse his way? By taking heed thereto according to thy word" (Psa. 119:9). Jesus said: "Already ye are clean because of the word which I have spoken unto you" (John 15:3). "That he might sanctify it, having cleansed it, by the washing of water with the Word" (Eph. 5:26).

3. By the Word we are kept from evil and the power of the evil one. The Psalmist said: "By the words of thy lips I have kept me from the paths of the destroyer" (Psa. 17:4); and, "Thy

word have I hid in my heart, that I might not sin against thee" (Psa. 119:11). Therefore, Jesus said: "I have given them thy word . . . Sanctify them through [in] the truth. Thy word is truth" (John 17:14, 17).

The voice said: Cry. And he said, What shall I cry? All flesh is grass, and all the goodliness thereof is as the flower of the field . . . The grass withereth, the flower fadeth: but the word of our God shall stand forever" (Isa. 40:6, 8). "For we can do nothing against the truth, but for the truth" (II Cor. 13:8).

This, then, is the sum of our contention: The Bible is made up of writings, and these are composed of words. The words are inspired — God-breathed. Therefore is the Bible inspired — *is* God's Word.

This is plainly seen, *first,* in the uniform declaration of the Book. All the Old Testament prophets, Jesus our Lord, and all the New Testament writers, bear the same testimony concerning this transcendentally important matter. Not a single word or thought to the contrary can anywhere be found in all their declarations. The attitude of Jesus toward the Old Testament and his utterances confirm beyond question our contention. He had the very same Old Testament we have today. He believed it to be the Word of God, and proclaimed it as such. He said, "One jot or one tittle shall in no wise pass from the laws, till all be fulfilled." In thwarting the tempter he said: "It is written! it is written! it is written!" In confounding the Jews, he said: "If ye believed Moses ye would believe me, for he wrote of me." He never criticized the Scriptures, but always appealed to them as his Father's words, authoritative and final.

Jesus is the life and the light of man. The same is true of the Scriptures. Jesus said: "The words that I speak unto you, they are spirit, and they are life." The Psalmist said, "Thy word is a lamp unto my feet, and a light unto my path." In an inexplicable way Jesus is identified with the Word. "The word was God . . . and the word became flesh." And when the victories of the Gospel shall have been finally accomplished, and Jesus shall assert his regal rights, his name is called, "The Word of God" (see Rev. 19:11, 13).

Second. The Bible assumes to be God's Word by its imperious demands. Who but God has a right to require of men what the Bible does?

Third. The Bible has fulfilled all its claims and promises. The marvelous, far-reaching results of proclaiming and believing it, demonstrably prove its supernatural origin and character.

That there are difficulties, I well enough know. But many difficulties have disappeared as a result of patient, reverent, scholarly research; and without doubt others will soon go the same way. So, while I bid the scholars and reverent critics God-speed in their noble work, with the late learned Bishop Ryle I say: "Give me the plenary verbal theory with all its difficulties, rather than the doubt. I accept the difficulties, and humbly wait for their solution; but while I wait I am standing on a rock."

Let this, then, be our *attitude*, to tell it out to the wide world that the blessed Bible, the "Holy Scriptures" of both Testaments, are the product of the *"breath of God,"* who made heaven and earth, and "breathed" into man His soul; the product of that divine "breath" that regenerates, that illuminates and sanctifies the soul; a *"God-breathed Scriptures,"* whose "words" are the "words of God." Tell it to the Church in her seminaries, universities and colleges, from her pulpits, Sunday Schools and Bible classes, and sound it in every convention, conference and assembly that her conception and estimate of the Scriptures must be no lower and no less than were the high conception and estimate of the "Volume of the Book" by our Lord and his Apostles. That which they regarded as the *"Breath of God,"* she must so regard in opposition to every breath of man that dares to breathe otherwise. Say, with the immortal Athanasius, who knew how to read Greek better than the "drift of scholarly opinion"; "O my child, not only the ancient, but the new Scriptures are God-breathed, as Paul saith, 'Every Scripture is God-breathed.'" Say to the rising ministry, "Speak as the Oracles of God speak" — the words that "God hath spoken," the words that Christ has written. Tell it to every reader and hearer of the Word, that what "Moses saith" and "David saith" and "Isaiah, Peter, Paul, John and the Scripture saith," is what *"God saith."* Tell it to the dying saint, when his last pulse quivers at the wrist, and friends are weeping by his bed, and "Science" has exhausted in vain all her poor resources, that God, who breathed the Scriptures, "cannot lie," that Jesus is a Rock and that the "firm Foundation" laid in the Word for his faith can never disappoint his trust.   To every question of exegesis or of criticism, return the answer, "What saith the Scriptures?" "How readest thou?" "It is written!"   And cease to deride the most sacred, age-established, and time-honored tradition the Apostolic Church has left us.   With such an *attitude* as this, the days will revisit the Church as once they were "in the beginning," and God, honored in his Word, will no longer restrain the Spirit, but open the windows of heaven and pour upon her a blessing so great that there will not be room to receive it. God hasten the day!

WILLIAM GALLOGLY MOOREHEAD (1836-1914) was a conservative, evangelical writer, missionary, and pastor. Ohio-born, he graduated from Muskingum College, Allegheny Theological Seminary, and Xenia Theological Seminary. After his 1862 ordination, Moorehead traveled to Italy as a missionary with the American and Foreign Union. Upon his return to the States in 1869, he pastored churches in Ohio and Pennsylvania. In 1873, while pastoring First Church in Xenia, he began teaching at Xenia Theological Seminary where he taught New Testament until becoming president of the school in 1899. He wrote many books, including *Studies in Mosaic Institutions*, and a series of outline studies of books of the Bible. Moorehead was one of the editors of the *Scofield Reference Bible*.

16

The Moral Glory of Jesus Christ a Proof of Inspiration

By Rev. Wm. G. Moorehead, D.D.
PRESIDENT OF XENIA THEOLOGICAL SEMINARY, XENIA, OHIO

Abridged and emended by James H. Christian, Th.D.

The glories of the Lord Jesus Christ are threefold: essential, official and moral. His essential glory is that which pertains to him as the Son of God, the equal of the Father. His official glory is that which belongs to him as the Mediator. It is the reward conferred on him, the august promotion he received when he had brought his great work to a final and triumphant conclusion. His moral glory consists of the perfections which marked his earthly life and ministry; perfections which attached to every relation he sustained, and to every circumstance in which he was found. His essential and official glories were commonly veiled during his earthly sojourn. His moral glory could not be hid; he could not be less than perfect in everything; it belonged to him; it was himself. The moral glory now illumines every page of the four Gospels, as once it did every path he trod.

The thesis which we undertake to illustrate and establish is this: That the moral glory of Jesus Christ as set forth in the four Gospels cannot be the product of the unaided human intellect, that only the Spirit of God is competent to execute this matchless portrait of the Son of Man. The discussion of the theme falls into two parts: I. A brief survey of Christ's moral glory as exhibited in the Gospels. II. The application of the argument.

I. CHRIST'S MORAL GLORY

The Humanity of Jesus

1. The moral glory of Jesus appears in his development as Son of Man. The nature which he assumed was our nature, sin and sinful propensities only excepted. His was a real and a true

humanity, one which must pass through the various stages of growth like any other member of the race. From infancy to youth, from youth to manhood, there was steady increase both of his bodily powers and mental faculties; but the progress was orderly.

As Son of Man he was compassed about with the sinless infirmities that belong to our nature. He had needs common to all; need of food, of rest, of human sympathy, and of divine assistance. He was subject to Joseph and Mary, he was a worshiper in the synagogue and the Temple; he wept over the guilty and hardened city, and at the grave of a loved one; he expressed his dependence on God by prayer.

Nothing is more certain than that the Gospel narratives present the Lord Jesus as a true man, a veritable member of our race. But we no sooner recognize this truth, than we are confronted by another which sets these records alone and unapproachable in the field of literature. This second fact is this: At every stage of his development, in every relation of life, in every part of his service he is absolutely perfect. To no part of his life does a mistake attach, over no part of it does a cloud rest, nowhere is there defect. Nothing is more striking, more unexampled, than the profound contrast between Jesus and the conflict and discord around him, than between him and those who stood nearest him, the disciples, John Baptist, and the mother, Mary. All fall immeasurably below him.

The Pattern Man

2. The Gospels exalt our Lord infinitely above all other men as the representative, the ideal, the pattern man. Nothing in the judgment of historians stands out so sharply distinct as race, national character — nothing is more ineffaceable. The very greatest men are unable to free themselves from the influences amid which they have been born and educated. Peculiarities of race and the spirit of the age leave in their characters traces that are imperishable. To the last fiber of his being Luther was German, Calvin was French, Knox was Scotch; Augustine bears the unmistakable impress of the Roman, and Chrysostom is as certainly Greek. Paul, with all his large-heartedness and sympathies was a Jew, always a Jew. Jesus Christ is the only one who

is justly entitled to be called the Catholic Man. Nothing local, transient, individualizing, national, or sectarian dwarfs the proportions of his wondrous character. "He rises above the parentage, the blood, the narrow horizon which bounded, as it seemed, his life; for he is the archetypal man in whose presence distinctions of race, intervals of ages, types of civilization and degrees of mental culture are as nothing" (Liddon). He belongs to all ages, he is related to all men, whether they shiver amid the snows of the arctic circle, or pant beneath the burning heat of the equator; for he is the Son of mankind, the genuine offspring of the race.

Unselfishness and Dignity

3. The Lord's moral glory appears in his unselfishness and personal dignity. The entire absence of selfishness in any form from the character of the Lord Jesus is another remarkable feature of the Gospels. He had frequent and fair opportunities of gratifying ambition had his nature been tainted with that passion. But "even Christ pleased not himself"; he "sought not his own glory"; he came not "to do his own will." His body and soul with all the faculties and activities of each were devoted to the supreme aims of his mission. His self-sacrifice included the whole range of his human thought, affection, and action; it lasted throughout his life; its highest expression was his ignominious death on the cross of Calvary.

The strange beauty of his unselfishness as it is displayed in the Gospel narratives appears in this, that it never seeks to draw attention to itself, it deprecates publicity. In his humility he seems as one naturally contented with obscurity; as wanting the restless desire for eminence which is common to really great men; as eager and careful that even his miracles should not add to his reputation. But amid all his self-sacrificing humility he never loses his personal dignity nor the self-respect that becomes him. He receives ministry from the lowly and the lofty; he is sometimes hungry, yet feeds the multitudes in desert places; he has no money, yet he never begs, and he provides the coin for tribute to the government from a fish's mouth. He may ask for a cup of water at the well, but it is that he may save a soul. He never flies from enemies; he quietly withdraws or passes by unseen. Hostility neither excites nor exasperates him. He is always calm, serene. He seems to care little for himself, for his own ease or comfort or safety, but everything for the honor and the glory of the Father. If multitudes, eager and expectant, press upon him, shouting, "Hosanna to the son of David," he is not elated; if all fall away, stunned by his words of power, he is not cast down. He seeks not a place among men; he is calmly content to be the Lord's Servant, the obedient and the humble one. It is invariably true of him that he pleased not himself."

And yet through all his amazing self-renunciation, there glances ever and anon something of the infinite majesty and supreme dignity which belong to him because he is the Son of God. The words of Van Oosterzee are as true as they are beautiful and significant: "It is the same King's Son who today dwells in the palace of his Father, and tomorrow, out of love to his rebellious subjects in a remote corner of the Kingdom, renouncing his princely glory, comes to dwell amongst them in the form of a servant . . . and is known only by the dignity of his look, and the star of royalty on his breast, when the mean cloak is opened for a moment, apparently by accident."

Superiority to Human Judgment and Intercession

4. The Gospels exhibit the Lord Jesus as superior to the judgment and the intercession of men. When challenged by the disciples and by enemies, as he often was, Jesus never apologized, never excused himself, never confessed to a mistake. When the disciples, terrified by the storm on the lake, awoke him saying, "Master, carest thou not that we perish?", he did not vindicate his sleep, nor defend his apparent indifference to their fears. Martha and Mary, each in turn, with profound grief, say, "Lord, if thou hadst been here, my brother had not died." But Jesus did not excuse his not being there, nor his delay of two days in the place where he was when the urgent message of the sisters reached him. In the consciousness of the perfect rectitude of his ways, he only replied, "Thy brother shall rise again." Peter once tried to admonish him, saying, "This be far from thee, Lord; this shall not be unto thee." But Peter had to learn that it was Satan that prompted the admonition. Nor did he recall a word when the Jews rightly

inferred from his language that he "being man made himself God" (John 10:30-36). He pointed out the application of the name Elohim implied that his title to divinity is higher than, and distinct in kind from, that of the Jewish magistrates. He thus arrived a second time at the assertion which had given so great offense, by announcing his identity with the Father, which involves his own proper deity. The Jews understood him. He did not retract what they accounted blasphemy, and they again sought his life.

So likewise he is superior to human intercession. He never asked even his disciples nor his nearest friends, and certainly never his mother Mary, to pray for him. In Gethsemane he asked the three to watch with him, he did not ask them to pray for him. He bade them pray that they might not enter into temptation, but he did not ask them to pray that he should not, nor that he should be delivered out of it. Paul wrote again and again, "Brethren, pray for us" — "pray for me." But such was not the language of Jesus. In his intercession he never used plural personal pronouns in his petitions. He always said, "I" and "me," "these" and "them that thou hast given me."

The Sinlessness of Jesus

5. The sinlessness of the Saviour witnesses to his moral glory. The Gospels present us with one solitary and unique fact of human history — an absolutely sinless Man! Hear some witnesses. There is the testimony of his enemies. For three long years the Pharisees were watching their victim. As another writes, "There was the Pharisee mingling in every crowd, hiding behind every tree. They examined his disciples, they cross-questioned all around him. They looked into his ministerial life, into his domestic privacy, into his hours of retirement. They came forward with the sole accusation they could muster — that he had shown disrespect to Caesar. The Roman judge who ought to know, pronounced it void." There was another spy — Judas. Had there been one failure in the Redeemer's career, in his awful agony Judas would have remembered it for his comfort; but the bitterness of his despair, that which made his life intolerable, was, "I have betrayed the innocent blood."

There is the testimony of his friends. His disciples affirm that during their intercourse with him his life was unsullied. Had there been a single blemish they would have detected it, and they would have recorded it, just as they did their own shortcomings and blunders. The purest and most austere man that lived in that day, John the Baptist, shrank from baptizing the Holy One, and in conscious unworthiness he said, "I have need to be baptized of thee, and comest thou to me?" Nor is his own testimony to be overlooked. Jesus never once confesses sin. He never once asks for pardon. Yet is it not he who so sharply rebukes the self-righteousness of the Pharisees? But yet he never lets fall a hint, he never breathes a prayer which implies the slightest trace of blameworthiness. He paints the doom of incorrigible and unrepentant sinners in the most dreadful colors found in the entire Bible, but he himself feels no apprehension, he expresses no dread of the penal future; his peace of mind, his fellowship with Almighty God is never disturbed nor interrupted. He challenges his bitterest enemies to convict him of sin (John 8:46). In Jesus Christ this self-revelation was not involuntary, nor accidental, nor forced: it was in the highest degree deliberate. There is about him an air of superior holiness, of aloofness from the world and its ways, a separation from evil in every form and of every grade, such as no other that has ever lived has displayed. Although descended from an impure ancestry, he brought no taint of sin into the world with him; and though he mingled with sinful men and was assailed by fierce temptations, he contracted no guilt, he was touched by no stain. He was not merely undefiled, but was undefilable. He came down into all the circumstances of actual humanity in its sin and misery, and yet he kept the infinite purity of heaven with him. In the annals of our race there is none next to or like him.

Assemblage and Correlation of Virtues

6. The exquisite assemblage and correlation of virtues and excellencies in the Lord Jesus form another remarkable feature of the Gospel narratives. There have been those who have displayed distinguished traits of character; those who by reason of extraordinary gifts have risen to heights which are inaccessible to the great mass of men. But who among the mighest of men has shown himself to be evenly balanced and rightly poised in all his faculties and powers? In the very greatest and best, inequality and disproportion are encountered. In Jesus Christ there is no uneven-

ness. In him there is no preponderance of the imagination over the feeling, of the intellect over the imagination, of the will over the intellect. There is in him an uninterrupted harmony of all the powers of body and soul, in which that serves which should serve, and that rules which ought to rule, and all works together to one adorable end. In him every grace is in its perfectness, none in excess, none out of place, and none wanting. His justice and his mercy, his peerless love and his truth, his holiness and his freest pardon never clash; one never clouds the other. His firmness never degenerates into obstinacy, or his calmness into indifference. His gentleness never becomes weakness, nor his elevation of soul forgetfulness of others. In his best servants virtues and graces are uneven and often clash. Paul had hours of weakness and even of petulance. John the Apostle of love even wished to call down fire from heaven to consume the inhospitable Samaritans. And the virgin mother must learn that even she cannot dictate to him as to what he shall do or not do.

In his whole life one day's walk never contradicts another, one hour's service never clashes with another. While he shows he is master of nature's tremendous forces, and the Lord of the unseen world, he turns aside and lays his glory by to take little children in his arms and to bless them. "He never speaks where it would be better to keep silence, He never keeps silence where it would be better to speak; and he always leaves the arena of controversy a victor."

Omnipotence and Omniscience

7. The evangelists do not shrink from ascribing to the Lord Jesus divine attributes, particularly omnipotence and omniscience. They do so as a mere matter of fact, as what might and should be expected from so exalted a personage as the Lord Jesus was. How amazing the power is which he wields when it pleases him to do so! It extends to the forces of nature. At his word the storm is hushed into a calm, and the raging of the sea ceases. At his pleasure he walks on the water as on dry land. It extends to the world of evil spirits. At his presence demons cry out in fear and quit their hold on their victims. His power extends into the realm of disease. Every form of sickness departs at his command,

and he cures the sick both when he is beside them and at a distance from them. Death likewise, that inexorable tyrant that wealth has never bribed, nor tears softened, nor human power arrested, yielded instantly his prey when the voice of the Son of God bade him.

But Jesus equally as certainly and as fully possessed a superhuman range of knowledge as well as a superhuman power. Thus he saw into the depths of Nathaniel's heart when he was under the fig tree; he saw into the depths of the sea, and the exact coin in the mouth of a particular fish; he read the whole past life of the woman at the well, although he had never before met with her. John tells us, "He needed not that any should testify of man: for he knew what was in man" (John 2:25). He knew the world of evil spirits. He was perfectly acquainted with the movements of Satan and of demons. He said to Peter, "Simon, Simon, behold, Satan asked to have you that he might sift you as wheat: I made supplication for thee that thy faith fail not" (Luke 22: 31, 32). He often spoke directly to the evil spirits that had control of people, ordering them to hold their peace, to come out and to enter no more into their victims. He knew the Father as no mere creature could possibly know him. "All things are delivered unto me of my Father: and no man knoweth the Son, save the Father; neither doth any know the Father, save the Son, and he to whomsoever the Son, willeth to reveal him" (Matt. 11:27).

II. THE APPLICATION OF THE ARGUMENT

Nothing is more obvious than the very commonplace axiom, that every effect requires an adequate cause. Here are four brief records of our Lord's earthly life. They deal almost exclusively with his public ministry; they do not profess even to relate all that he did in his official work (cf. John 21:25). The authors of these memorials were men whose names are as household words the world over; but beyond their names we know little more. The first was tax collector under the Roman government; the second was, it is generally believed, that John Mark who for a time served as an attendant on Paul and Barnabas, and who afterward became the companion and fellow-laborer of Peter; the third was a physician and the devoted friend and co-worker of Paul; and the fourth was a fisherman. Two of them, Matthew and John, were disciples of Jesus; whether the others, Mark and Luke, ever saw him during his earthly sojourn cannot be determined.

These four men, unpracticed in the art of writing, unacquainted with the ideals of antiquity, write the memorials of Jesus' life. Three of them traverse substantially the same ground, record the same incidents, discourses and miracles. While they are penetrated with the profoundest admiration for their Master, they never once dilate on his great qualities. All that they do is to record his actions and his discourses with scarcely a remark. One of them, indeed, John, intermingles reflective commentary with the narrative; but in doing this he carefully abstains from eulogy and panegyric. He pauses in his narrative only to explain some reference, to open some deep saying of the Lord, or to press some vital truth. Yet, despite this absence of the smallest attempt to delineate a character, these four men have accomplished what no others have done or can do — they have presented the world with the portrait of a Divine Man, a glorious Saviour. Matthew describes him as the promised Messiah, the glory of Israel, the Son of David, the Son of Abraham; the One in whom the covenants and the promises find their ample fulfillment; the One who accomplishes all righteousness. Mark exhibits him as the mighty Servant of Jehovah who does man's neglected duty, and meets the need of all around. Luke depicts him as the Friend of man, whose love is so intense and comprehensive, whose pity is so divine, that his saving power goes forth to Jew and Gentile, to the lowliest and the loftiest, to the publican, the Samaritan, the ragged prodigal, the harlot, the thief, as well as to the cultivated, the moral, the great. John presents him as the Son of God, the Word made flesh; as Light for a dark world, as Bread for a starving world, as Life for a dead world. Matthew writes for the Jew, Mark for the Roman, Luke for the Greek, and John for the Christian; and all of them write for every kindred, and tribe, and tongue and people of the entire globe, and for all time! What the philosopher, the poet, the scholar, the artist could not do; what men of the greatest mind, the most stupendous genius have failed to do, these four unpracticed men have done — they have presented to the world the Son of Man and the Son of God in all his perfections and glories.

A Fact to be Explained

How comes it to pass that these unlearned and ignorant men (Acts 4:13) have so thoroughly accomplished so great a task? Let us hold fast our commonplace axiom, every effect must have an adequate cause. What explanation shall we give of this marvellous effect? Shall we ascribe their work to genius? But multitudes of men both before and since their day have possessed genius of the very highest order; and these gifted men have labored in fields akin to this of our four evangelists. The mightiest minds of the race — men of Chaldea, of Egypt, of India, of China, and of Greece — have tried to draw a perfect character, have expended all their might to paint a god-like man. And with what result? Either he is invested with the passions and the brutalities of fallen men, or he is a pitiless and impassive spectator of the world's sorrows and woes. In either case, the character is one which may command the fear but not the love and confidence of men.

Again, we ask, How did the evangelists solve this mighty problem of humanity with such perfect originality and precision? Only two answers are rationally possible: 1. They had before them the personal and historical Christ. Men could no more invent the God-man of the Gospels than they could create a world. The almost irreverent words of Theodore Parker are grounded in absolute truth: "It would have taken a Jesus to forge a Jesus." 2. They wrote by inspiration of the Spirit of God. It cannot be otherwise. It is not enough to say that the divine model was before them: they must have had something more, else they never could have succeeded.

Let it be assumed that these four men, Matthew, Mark, Luke, and John, were personally attendant on the ministry of Jesus — that they saw him, heard him, companied with him for three years. Yet on their own showing they did not understand him. They testify that the disciples, the apostles among the number, got but the slenderest conceptions of his person and his mission from his very explicit teachings. They tell us of a wonderful incapacity and weakness in all their apprehensions of him. The Sun of Righteousness was shining on them and around them, and they could see only the less! He told them repeatedly of his approaching death, and of his resurrection, but they did not understand him; they even questioned among themselves what the rising from the dead should mean (Mark 9:10) — poor men! And yet these men, once so blind and ignorant, write four little pieces about the person and the work of the Lord Jesus which the study and the research of Christendom for nineteen hundred years have not exhausted, and which the keenest and most hostile criticism has utterly failed to discredit.

But this is not all. Others have tried their hand at composing the Life and Deeds of Jesus. Compare some of these with our Four Gospels.

Spurious Gospels

The Gospel narrative observes an almost unbroken silence as to the long abode of Jesus at Nazareth. Of the void thus left the church became early impatient. During the first four centuries many attempts were made to fill it up. Some of these apocryphal gospels are still extant, notably that which deals with the infancy and youth of the Redeemer; and it is instructive to notice how those succeeded who tried to lift the veil which covers the earlier years of Christ. Let another state the contrast between the New Testament records and the spurious gospels: "The case stands thus: our Gospels present us with a glorious picture of a mighty Saviour, the mythic gospels with that of a contemptible one. In our Gospels he exhibits a superhuman wisdom; in the mythic ones a nearly equal superhuman absurdity. In our Gospels he is arrayed in all the beauty of holiness; in the mythic ones this aspect of character is entirely wanting. In our Gospels not one strain of sinfulness defiles his character; in the mythic ones the boy Jesus is both pettish and malicious. Our Gospels exhibit to us a sublime morality; not one ray of it shines in those of the mythologists. The miracles of the one and of the other stand contrasted on every point" (Row).

These spurious gospels were written by men who lived not long after the apostolic age; by Christians who wished to honor the Saviour in all they said about him; by men who had the portraiture of him before them which the Gospels supply. And yet these men,

many of them better taught than the apostles, with the advantage
of two or three centuries of Christian thought and study, could not
produce a sketch of the Child Jesus without violating our sense of
propriety, and shocking our moral sense.   The distance between
the Gospels of the New Testament and the Pseudo-gospels is
measured by the distance between the product of the Spirit of God,
and that of the fallen human mind.

Uninspired "Lives of Christ"

Let us take another illustration.   The nineteenth century has
been very fruitful in the production of what are commonly called
"Lives of Christ."   Contrast with the Gospels four such "Lives,"
perhaps the completest and the best, taken altogether, of those
written by English-speaking people — Andrews', Geikie's, Hanna's,
and Edersheim's.   Much information and helpfulness are to be
derived from the labors of these Christian scholars, and others who
have toiled in the same field; but how far they all fall below the
New Testament record it is needless to show.

Let the contrast be noted as to size or bulk.   The four combined
have no less than 5,490 pages, enough in these busy days to require
months of reading to go but once through their contents.   Bagster
prints the four Gospels in 82 pages; the American Revised in about
100 pages of the four Gospels against more than five thousand
four hundred of the four "Lives."

How happens it that such stores of wisdom and knowledge lie
garnered in these short pieces?   Who taught the evangelists this
superhuman power of expansion and contraction, of combination
and separation, of revelation in the words and more revelation
below the words?   There is but one answer to these questions,
there can be no other.   The Spirit of the living God filled their
minds with his unerring wisdom and controlled their human speech.
To that creative Spirit who has peopled the world with living
organisms so minute that only the microscope can reveal their
presence, it is not hard to give us in so brief a compass the
sublime portrait of the Son of Man.

GEORGE SALES BISHOP (1836-1914) was born in Rochester, NY, and graduated from Princeton Theological Seminary in 1864. Ordained that year into the Presbyterian ministry, he pastored churches in Trenton and Orange, NJ, and Newburgh, NY. He served the First Reformed Church of Orange, NJ, for thirty-one years, and served as president of the General Synod of the Reformed Church in America from 1899-1900. He was awarded an honorary D.D. by Rutgers University in 1877. Beside his contribution to *The Fundamentals*, he wrote for several evangelical publications and was the author of *The Person and Work of the Holy Spirit* (1897), *The Sweep of Time* (1909), *The Doctrines of Grace* (1910), and *A Commentary on Galatians* (1912).

17

The Testimony of the Scriptures to Themselves

By Rev. George S. Bishop, D.D.
EAST ORANGE, NEW JERSEY

Revised and edited by Charles L. Feinberg, Th.D., Ph.D.

The subject under consideration in this chapter is the testimony of the Scriptures to themselves, that is, their own self-evidence, the overpowering, unparticipated witness that they bring. This witness can be treated under four heads: (1) Immortality, (2) Authority, (3) Transcendent Doctrine, and (4) Direct Assertion.

1. Immortality. All other books die. Few books survive, and of these fewer have any influence. Most of the books from which we quote have been written in recent times. But here is a book whose antemundane voices had grown old, when voices spoke in Eden. It is a book which has survived not only with continued, but increasing lustre, vitality, and influence. Through all the shocks it has come without a wrench, and through all the furnaces of the ages with every document in its place without the smell of smoke. Of this book it may be said, as of Christ himself: "Thou hast the dew of thy youth from the womb of the morning." It dates from days as old as the Ancient of Days, and when the universe is dissolved, it will still speak in thunder-tones of majesty and music-tones of love. It wraps in itself the everlasting past, and opens from itself the everlasting future, the one unchanging, changeless revelation of God.

2. Immortality is here, and authority sets her seal. It is useless to talk of no standard. Nature points to one; conscience cries out for one. There must be a standard and an inspired one; for inspiration is the essence of authority, and authority is in proportion to inspiration. Verbal inspiration is, therefore, the "Thermopylae" of Biblical faith. No breath, no syllable; no syllable, no word; no word, no book; no book, no religion. There can

be no possible advance in revelation no new light. What was written at first, the same stands written today, and will stand forever. The product of the mind of God is complete, perfect, final (Rev. 22:18, 19).

The Bible is the Word of God, not merely contains it. The Bible calls itself the Word of God, and by that very title is distinguished from all other books. If the Bible is not called the Word of God, then it cannot be called anything else. The Bible is the Word of God, because it comes from God; because its every word was penned by God; because it is the only exponent of God; the only rule of his procedure; and the only book by which all must at last be judged.

(1) The Bible is authority because throughout God is the speaker. In the Bible God speaks, God is listened to, and men are born again by God's Word (Rom. 10:17). (2) The Bible comes announced by miracles and heralded with fire. In the Old Testament it is Mount Sinai, in the New, Pentecost. Would God himself write on tables in the giving, and send down tongues of fire for the proclamation of a revelation, every particle of which was not his own? In short, would he work miracles and send fire to signalize a work merely human, or even partly human and partly divine? How unworthy of God, how utterly impossible the supposition!

(3) The Bible comes clothed with authority in the exalted terms of its address. God in the Bible speaks out of a whirlwind, with the voice of an Elijah, with the imperative tone of prophets and apostles which enabled them to brave and boldly teach the world from Pharaoh to Nero and beyond. See Jeremiah 20:9 and Amos 3:8. (4) The Bible is the height of authority, because it is from first to last a glorious projection on the widest scale of the decrees of God. The sweep of the Bible is from the creation of the angels to a new heaven and new earth, across a lake of fire. What a field for events! When the Bible is considered as an exact projection of the decrees of God into the future, this argument is seen to move to a climax; in fact, it does reach to the very crux of controversy. The hardest thing to believe about God is that he exactly, absolutely knows, because he has ordained,

the future. The attribute of infallible omniscience is hard to grasp, and it calls for direct inspiration.

(5) The Bible is the acme of authority, because the hooks at the end of the chain prove the inspiration of its every link. Compare the fall in Genesis with the resurrection in the Apocalypse. Compare the old creation in the first chapters of the Old Testament with the new creation in the last chapters of the New. One is the prologue, while the other is the epilogue of a vast, infinite drama. (6) Another argument for the supreme authority of Scripture is the character of the investigation challenged for the Word of God. The Bible courts the closest scrutiny. Its open pages blaze the legend, "Search the Scriptures!" The Scriptures may be analyzed, sifted, pulverized as in a mortar to the last thought. Only a divine book would dare speak such a challenge. God has written it, and none can exhaust it. Apply your microscopes, apply your telescopes, to the Scriptures. They separate, but do not fray, its threads. They broaden out its nebulae, but find them clustered stars. With the Word of God it is the more scrutiny, the more divinity; the more dissection, the more perfection. It is impossible to bring to it a test too penetrating, nor a light too piercing, nor a touchstone too exacting.

3. In the third place, the Scriptures testify to their divine original by their transcendent doctrine, the glow of the divine, the witness of the Spirit. We should expect to find a book that came from God to be penciled with points of jasper and of sardine stone, enhaloed with a brightness from the everlasting hills. We should look for that about the book which, flashing conviction at once, should carry overwhelmingly and everywhere by its bare, naked witness, by what it simply is.

The Bible is the Word of God, because it is the book of infinites, the revelation of what nature never could have attained. The greatest need of the soul is salvation. It is such a knowledge of God as will assure us of comfort here and hereafter. Nature outside the Bible does not contain such a knowledge. Groping in his darkness, man is confronted by two changeless facts: his guilt and the justice of God. Nature helps to no bridge; it nowhere speaks of redemption.

The Scriptures are divine in their very message, because they deal with three infinites: infinite guilt, infinite holiness, and infinite redemption.

Infinite guilt! Has my guilt any bottom? Is hell any deeper? Infinitely guilty! That is what I am. As soon as the Bible declares it, I know it, and with it I know that witnessing Bible is divine. I know it by conscience, by illumination, by the power of the Spirit of God, by the Word, and by the flashed conviction in me which agree.

And counterpoised above me, a correlative infinite—God! What can be higher? What zenith loftier? Infinite God, above me, coming to judge me! I know it as soon as the Bible declares it.

Then the third and that which completes the triangle, and makes its sides eternally, divinely equal, infinite redemption, an infinite Saviour, God on the cross making answer to God on the throne, my Jesus, my Refuge, my Everlasting God. By these three infinites, especially the infinite redemption for which man's whole being cries out its last cry of exhaustion, the Bible proves itself the soul's geometry, the one eternal mathematics, the true revelation of God.

The Scriptures are their own self-evidence. The sun requires no critic, truth no diving-bell. When God speaks, his evidence is in the accent of his words. How did the prophets of old know, when God spoke to them, that it was God? Did they subject the voice, that shook their every bone, to a critical test? Did they put God, as it were, into a crucible, into a chemist's retort, in order to certify that he was God? Did they find it necessary to hold the handwriting of God in the light of anxious philosophical examination, in order to bring out and to make the invisible, visible? The very suggestion is madness.

4. In the fourth place, the Scriptures say of themselves that they are divine. They not only assume it; they say it. "Thus saith the Lord" is intrinsic, a witness inside of the witness. The argument from the self-assertion of Scripture is cumulative.

(1) The Bible claims that, as a book, it comes from God. In various ways it urges this claim. It says so (Heb. 1:1, 2). The question of inspiration is, in its first statement, the question of

revelation itself. The question is simply one of divine testimony, and our business is simply to receive that testimony. When God speaks, there is the whole of it. He is bound to be heard and obeyed.

In the Bible God speaks, and speaks not only by proxy. Again and again it is "the Lord spake." The self-announced speaker is God. God himself comes down and speaks, not in the Old Testament alone, and not alone by proxy. Christ everywhere received the Scripture, and speaks of the Old Testament in its entirety, the Law, the Prophets, and the Psalms, as the living oracle of God. He accepts and he endorses everything written, and even makes most prominent those miracles which infidelity regards as most incredible. And he does all this upon the ground of the authority of God. Too, this position of our Saviour, which exalted Scripture as the mouthpiece of the living God, was steadily maintained by the apostles and the apostolic church. Again and again in the Book of Acts and in all the epistles, the expression is "God saith," "he saith," and "the Holy Spirit saith."

(2) If the Scriptures are divine, then what they say of themselves is divine. Here two words constitute the apostolic keys to the church's position: *"graphe"* (writing) and *"theopneustos"* (God-breathed). The sacred assertion is not of the instruments, but of the author, not of the agents, but of the product. It is the sole and sovereign vindication of what has been left on the page when inspiration gets through. God inspires not men, but language. Holy men were moved, borne along, but their writing, what they put down on the page, was God-breathed. You breathe on a pane of glass. Your breath congeals there; stays there; fixes an ice-picture there. That is the idea. The writing on the page beneath the hand of Paul was just as much breathed on, breathed into that page, as was his soul breathed into Adam.

On the original parchment every sentence, word, line, mark, point, pen-stroke, jot, tittle was put there by God. There is no question of other, anterior parchments. Men may destroy the parchments. Time may destroy them, but the writing remains.

The Scriptures say that the laws the writers promulgated, the doctrines they taught, the accounts they recorded, their prophecies of Christ, were not their own, were not conceived by them from outside sources, but were immediately from God. Some of the speakers of the Bible, like Balaam and Caiaphas, are made to speak in spite of themselves. The prophets themselves did not know what they wrote (I Pet. 1:10, 11). That lifts the Bible from all human hands and places it back, as his original deposit, in the hands of God.

It is said that "the word of the Lord came" to such and such a writer. It is not said that the Spirit came, which is true; but that the Word itself came. It is denied, and most emphatically, that the words are the words of man, of the agent. "The word was in my tongue" (II Sam. 23:2). Paul asserts that "Christ spake in me" (II Cor. 13:3). Could language more plainly assert or defend a verbal, direct, and plenary inspiration?

The Scripture declares that holy men were moved, or rather carried along in a supernatural ecstatic current. They were not left one instant to their wit alone, their wisdom, fancies, memories, or judgments, either to order, arrange, dispose or write out. They were intelligent, conscious, exact, and accurate instruments. Ultimately, it was God who wrote the whole Bible.

The danger of our day, the decline in doctrine, conviction, moral sentiment—does it not find its first step in our lost hold upon the verbal, plenary inspiration of the Word of God? A fresh conviction here lies at the root of every remedy we desire, as its sad lack lies at the root of every ruin we deplore.

ARTHUR TAPPAN PIERSON (1837-1911) had the unenviable task of following C.H. Spurgeon in the pulpit of London's Metropolitan Tabernacle when Spurgeon became ill. Before succeeding Spurgeon, Pierson had served Congregational and Presbyterian churches in New York and Pennsylvania from 1860-1911. He was an editor of the *Scofield Reference Bible*. Notable among his books are *Crisis of Missions, The Coming of the Lord,* and *Miracle of Missions*. Besides his theological work, Pierson founded the First Penny Saving Bank of Philadelphia.

18

The Testimony of the Organic Unity of the Bible to Its Inspiration

by Arthur T. Pierson, D.D.

PASTOR, SPURGEON'S TABERNACLE, LONDON

Revised and edited by Charles L. Feinberg, Th.D., Ph.D.

The argument for the inspiration of the Bible to be presented is that drawn from its unity. This unity may be seen in several conspicuous particulars.

1. *The unity is structural.* In the book itself appears a certain archetypal, architechural plan. The two Testaments are built on the same general scheme. Each is in three parts: historic, didactic, prophetic; looking to the past, the present, and the future. Here is a collection of books; in their style and character there are great variety and diversity. Some are historical, others poetical; some contain laws, others lyrics; some are prophetic, some symbolic. In the Old Testament we have historical, poetical, and prophetical divisions; and in the New Testament we have historic narratives, then twenty-one epistles, then a symbolic apocalyptic poem in oriental imagery. Yet this is no artificial arrangement of fragments. We find "the Old Testament patent in the New; the New latent in the Old."

In such a book, then, it is not likely that there would be unity; for all the conditions were unfavorable to a harmonious moral testimony and teaching. Here are some sixty or more separate documents, written by some forty different persons, scattered over wide intervals of space and time, strangers to each other. These documents are written in three different languages, in different lands, among different and sometimes hostile peoples, with marked diversities of literary style, and by men of all grades of culture and mental capacity, from Moses to Malachi. When we look into these productions, there is even in them great unlikeness, both in matter and manner of statement; yet they all constitute one volume.

All are entirely at agreement. There is diversity in unity, and unity in diversity. The more we study it, the more do its unity and harmony appear. All the criticism of more than three thousand years has failed to point out one important or irreconcilable contradiction in the testimony and teachings of those who are farthest separated. There is no collision, yet there could be no collusion! How can this be accounted for? There is no answer which can be given unless you admit the supernatural element. If God actually superintended the production of this book, then its unity is the unity of a divine plan, and its harmony the harmony of a Supreme Intelligence.

The temple, first built upon Mount Moriah, was built of stone, made ready before it was brought thither. There was neither hammer nor ax nor any tool of iron heard in the house while it was in building. What insured symmetry in the temple when constructed, and harmony between the workmen in the quarries and shops, and the builders on the hill? One presiding mind planned the whole; one intelligence built that whole structure in ideal before it was in fact. Only so can we account for the structural unity of the Word of God. The structure was planned and wrought out in the mind of a divine architect, who superintended his own workmen and work. Everything is in agreement with everything else, because the whole Bible was built in the thought of God before one book was laid in order. The building rose steadily from cornerstone to capstone, foundations first, then story after story, pillars on pedestals, and capitals on pillars, and arches on capitals, till like a dome flashing back the splendors of the noonday, the Apocalypse spans and crowns and completes the whole, glorious with celestial visions.

2. *The unity is historic.* The whole Bible is the history of the kingdom of God. Israel represents that kingdom. All centers about the Hebrew nation. With their origin and progress the main historical portion begins; with their apostasy and captivity it stops. The times of the Gentiles filled the interval and have no proper history. Prophecy, which is history anticipated, takes up the broken thread, and gives us the outline of the future when Israel shall again take its place among the nations.

3. *The unity is dispensational.* There are certain uniform dispensational features which distinguish every new period. Each dispensation is marked by seven features in this order: (a) increased light; (b) decline of spiritual life; (c) union between believers and the world; (d) a gigantic civilization worldly in type; (e) parallel development of good and evil; (f) apostasy on the part of God's people; (g) concluding judgment. The same seven marks have been upon all alike, showing one controlling power, God in history.

4. *The unity is prophetic.* Of all prophecy there is but one center, the kingdom and the King. Adam, the first king, lost his scepter by sin. His probation ended in failure and disaster. The last Adam, in his probation, gained the victory, routed the tempter, and stood firm. The two comings of this King constituted the two focal centers of the prophetic ellipse. His first coming was to make possible an empire in man and over man. His second coming will be to set that empire up in glory. All prophecy moves about these advents. It touches Israel only as related to the kingdom; and the Gentiles only as related to Israel. There are some six hundred and sixty-six general prophecies in the Old Testament, three hundred and thirty-three of which refer particularly to the coming Messiah, and meet only in him.

5. *The unity is, therefore, also personal.* Hebrews 10:7. There is but one book, and within it but one person. Christ is the center of Old Testament prophecy, as he is of New Testament history. From Genesis 3 to Malachi 3, he fills out the historic and prophetic profile. Not only do the predictions unite in him, but even the rites and ceremonies find in him their only interpreter. Historic characters prefigure him, and historic events are pictorial illustrations of his vicarious ministry. The Old Testament is a lock of which Christ is the key. Beginning at any point you may preach Jesus.

6. *The unity is symbolic.* There is a corresponding use of symbols, whether in form, color, or numbers. In form, we have the square, the cube, and the circle, and they are used as types of the same truths. In color, there is the white for purity, the lustrous white for glory, the red for guilt of sin and the sacrifice for sin, the blue for truth and fidelity to promise, the purple for royalty,

the pale or livid hue for death, and the black for woe and disaster. In numbers there is plainly a numerical system. One seems to represent unity, two correspondence and confirmation or contradiction; three is the number of Godhead; four of the world and man. Seven, the sum of three and four, stands for the combination of the divine and human; twelve the product of three and four, for the divine interpenetrating the human; ten, the sum of one, two, three, and four, is the number of completeness. Three and a half, the broken number, represents tribulation; six, which stops short of seven, is unrest; eight, which is beyond the number of rest, is the number of victory. All this implies one presiding mind, and it could not be man's mind.

7. *The unity is didactic.* In the entire range and scope of the ethical teaching of the Bible there is no inconsistency or adulteration. In not one respect are the doctrinal and ethical teachings in conflict from beginning to end; rather, we find in them a positive oneness of doctrine which amazes us. Even where at first glance there appears to be conflict, as between Paul and James, on closer examination it is found that, instead of standing face to face beating each other, they stand back to back, beating off common foes. We observe, moreover, a progressive development of revelation, not only from the Old Testament to the New but in the confines of the New itself. Most wonderful of all, this moral and didactic unity could not be fully understood till the book was completed. The progress of preparation, like a scaffolding about a building, obscured its beauty; but when John placed the capstone in position and declared that nothing further should be added, the scaffolding fell and a grand cathedral was revealed.

8. *The unity is scientific.* The Bible is not a scientific book, but it follows one consistent law. Like an engine on its own track, it thunders across the track of science, but is never diverted from its own. (1) No direct teaching or anticipation of scientific truth is found here. (2) No scientific fact is ever misstated, though common, popular phraseology may be employed. (3) An elastic set of terms is used, which contain in germ all scientific truth, as the acorn enfolds the oak. The language is so elastic and flexible as to contract itself to the narrowness of human ignorance, and yet expand itself to the dimensions of knowledge. If the Bible

may, from imperfect language, select terms which may hold hidden truths till ages to come shall disclose the inner meaning, that would seem to be the best solution of this difficult problem. Now when we come to compare the language of the Bible with modern science, we find just this to be the fact.

The general correspondence between the Mosaic account of creation and the most advanced discoveries of science, proves that only he who built the world, built the book. As to the order of creation, Moses and geology agree. Both teach that at first there was an abyss, or watery waste, whose dense vapors shut out light. Both make life to precede light; and the life to develop beneath the abyss. Both make the atmosphere to form an expanse by lifting watery vapors into cloud, and so separating the fountains of waters above from the fountains below. Both tell us that continents next lifted themselves from beneath the great deep, and brought forth grass, herbs, and tree. Both teach that the heavens became cleared of cloud, and the sun and moon and stars, which then appeared, began to serve to divide day from night, and to become signs for seasons and years. Both then represent the waters bringing forth moving and creeping creatures, and fowl flying in the expanse, followed next by the race of quadruped mammals, and, last of all, by man himself.

There is the same agreement as to the order of animal creation. Geology and comparative anatomy combine to teach that the order was from lower to higher types; first, the fish, then reptiles, then man. This is exactly the order of Moses. Take an example of this scientific accuracy from astronomy. Jeremiah in 30:22 said, "The host of heaven cannot be numbered, neither the sand of the sea measured." Before the time of Christ the number was thought to be about 1,000; during the last century the number had increased to millions; and now we know they must be numbered in the billions. So the exclamation of the prophet, six centuries before Christ, more than 2,000 years before Galileo, proves to be not poetic exaggeration, but literal truth. Who was Jeremiah's teacher in astronomy?

9. *Last of all, the unity of the Bible is organic.* It is the unity of organized being. Organic unity implies three things: first,

that all parts are necessary to a complete whole; secondly, that all are necessary to complement each other; and thirdly, that all are pervaded by one life-principle. (1) Organic unity is dependent on the existence and cooperation of organs. An oratorio is not an organic unity, because any part of it may be separated from the rest, or displaced by a new composition. But if the human body loses an eye, a limb, or the smallest joint of the finger, it is permanently maimed; its completeness is gone. Not one of the books of the Bible could be lost without maiming the body of truth here contained. Every book fills a place; none can be omitted.

For example, the Book of Esther has long been criticized as not necessary to the completeness of the canon, particularly because it does not once mention the name of God. But that book is the completest exhibition of the providence of God. It teaches a divine hand behind human affairs, unbiased freedom of resolution and action as consistent with God's overruling sovereignty, and all things working together to produce grand results.

The Epistle to Philemon seems at first only a letter to a friend about a runaway slave. But this letter is full of illustrations of grace. The sinner has run away from God, and robbed him besides. The law allows him no right of asylum; but grace concedes him the privilege of appeal. Christ, God's Partner, intercedes. He sends him back to the Father, no more a slave but a son.

(2) The law of unity has been framed in scientific statement. Organized being in every case forms a whole, a complete system, all parts of which mutually correspond. None of these parts can change without the other also changing; and consequently, each taken separately indicates and gives all the others. The Four Gospels are necessary to each other and to the whole Bible. Each presents the subject from a different point of view, and the combination gives us a divine Person reflected, projected before us, like an object with proportions and dimensions. Matthew wrote for the Jew, and shows Jesus as the King of the Jews, the Royal Lawgiver. Mark wrote for the Roman, and shows Him as the Power of God, the Mighty Worker. Luke wrote for Greek, and shows Him as the Wisdom of God, the human Teacher and Friend. John, writing to supplement and complement the other Gospels,

shows Him as Son of God, as well as Son of man, having and giving eternal life.

The Epistles are likewise all necessary to complete the whole and complement each other. There are five writers, each having his own sphere of truth. Paul's great theme is faith, and its relations to justification, sanctification, service, joy, and glory. James treats of works, their relation to faith, as its justification before man. He is the counterpart and complement of Paul. Peter deals with hope, as the inspiration of God's pilgrim people. John's theme is love, and its relation to the light and life of God as manifested in the believer. Jude sounds the trumpet of warning against apostasy, which implies the wreck of faith, the delusion of false hope, love grown cold, and the utter decay of good works. What one of all these writers could be dropped from the New Testament?

The unity of the Bible is the unity of one organic whole. The decalogue demands the Sermon on the Mount. Isaiah's prophecy makes necessary the narrative of the Evangelists. Daniel fits into the Revelation as bone fits socket. Leviticus explains, and is explained by, the Epistle to the Hebrews. The Psalms express the highest morality and spirituality of the Old Testament; they link the Mosaic code with the divine ethics of the Gospels and the Epistles. When you come to the last chapters of Revelation, you find yourself mysteriously touching the first chapters of Genesis; and lo! as you survey the whole track of your thought, you find you have been following the perimeter of a golden ring; the extremities actually bend around, touch, and blend.

(3) The life of God is in his Word. The Word is quick, living. Is it a mirror? yes, but such a mirror as the living eye. Is it a seed? yes, but a seed hiding the vitality of God. Is it a sword? yes, but a sword that omnisciently discerns and omnipotently pierces the human heart. Hold it reverently, for you have a living book in your hand. Speak to it, and it will anwer you. Bend down and listen; you will hear in it the heart-throbs of God.

This book, thus one, we are to hold forth as the word of life and the light of God in the midst of a crooked and perverse generation. We shall meet opposition. Like the birds that beat themselves into insensibility against the light in the Statue of Liberty in New York Harbor, the creatures of darkness will assult this Word, and vainly seek to put out its eternal light. But they shall only fall stunned and defeated at its base, while it still rises from its rock pedestal, immovable and serene!

ARNO CLEMENS GAEBELEIN (1861-1945) was a tireless, dedicated Bible scholar who came to the United States from Germany when he was 18 years old. Mostly self-taught in biblical matters, Gaebelein had a comprehensive knowledge of Hebrew. His expertise in prophecy was beneficial in his ministry to Jews in New York. His work as founder and editor of *Our Hope* magazine is still revered today by those who benefited by its monthly Bible studies. Also still valued by biblical scholars today are Gaebelein's books, such as *The Annotated Bible, Studies in Zechariah,* and *The Prophet Daniel* (republished in 1955 by Kregel Publications). Gaebelein served as an editor of the *Scofield Reference Bible.*

19

Fulfilled Prophecy a Potent Argument for the Bible

by Arno C. Gaebelein, D.D.
LATE EDITOR, OUR HOPE, NEW YORK

Revised and edited by Charles L. Feinberg, Th.D., Ph.D.

The challenge of the Lord to the idol-gods of Babylon was to predict future events. See Isaiah 41:21-23 and 46:10. God alone can declare the end from the beginning. The dumb idols of the heathen know nothing concerning the future, and man himself is powerless to find out things to come. However, the Lord, who made this challenge, has demonstrated his power to predict. None of the "sacred books" of the nations contains predictions of the future. If the authors of these writings had attempted to foretell the future, they would have furnished the strongest evidence of their deception. But the Bible is pre-eminently a book of prophecy. These predictions are declared to be the utterances of the Lord; they show that the Bible is a supernatural book, the revelation of God.

Prophecy Neglected and Denied

It is deplorable, then, that the professing church almost completely ignores or neglects the study of prophecy, resulting in the loss of one of the most powerful weapons against infidelity. The denial of the Bible as the inspired Word of God has become widespread. If prophecy were intelligently studied, such a denial could not flourish as it does, for the fulfilled predictions of the Bible give the clearest and most conclusive evidence that the Bible is the revelation of God.

Past, Present, and Future

The prophecies of the Bible may, first of all, be divided into three classes: (1) Prophecies which have found their fulfillment already. (2) Prophecies which are now in process of fulfillment. Many predictions written several thousand years ago are being fulfilled.   Among them are those which relate to the national and spiritual condition of Israel, and the predictions concerning the moral condition of the present age.   (3) Prophecies which are still unfulfilled.   Reference is to those which predict the second, glorious coming of our Lord, the regathering and restoration of Israel to the land of promise, judgments which await the nations of the earth, the establishment of the kingdom, the conversion of the world, universal peace and righteousness, the deliverance of creation, and others.

These great prophecies of future things are often robbed of their literal and solemn meaning by a process of spiritualization. The visions of the prophets concerning Israel and Jerusalem, and the glories to come in a future age, are almost generally explained as having their fulfillment in the church during the present age. However, our object is not to follow the unfulfilled prophecies, but prophecies fulfilled and in the process of fulfillment.

Fulfilled Prophecy a Vast Theme

Fulfilled prophecy is a vast theme of much importance.   History bears witness to the fact that the events which have transpired among the nations were pre-written in the Bible.   Attention will be directed to the fulfilled prophecies relating to the Person of Christ, the people of Israel, and a number of nations, whose history has been divinely foretold in the Bible.   Furthermore, mention will be made of the prophetic unfoldings given in the Book of Daniel with their interesting fulfillment.

Messianic Prophecies and Their Fulfillment

The Old Testament contains a remarkable chain of prophecies concerning the Person, life, and work of our Lord.   Radical destructive criticism has taken the position that there are no predictions concerning Christ in the Old Testament.   Such a denial is linked with the denial of his deity and his work on the cross. To follow the large number of prophecies concerning the coming of Christ into the world, and the work he was to accomplish, is beyond the scope of these pages.   However, highlights of Messianic prophecy will be pointed out.   Christ is first announced in Genesis 3:15 as the seed of the woman, and therefore of the human race. In Genesis 9:26-27 the supremacy of Shem is predicted.   In due time Abraham, a son of Shem, received the promise that the predicted seed was to come from him (Gen. 12:8).

Then the fact was revealed that he was to come from Isaac and not from Ishmael, from Jacob and not from Esau. Divine prediction pointed to Judah and later to the house of David of the tribe of Judah whence Messiah should spring. The prophecies of Isaiah disclose that his mother was to be a virgin (Isa. 7:14); the virgin born son was to be Immanuel, God with us. Deity and humanity are united in the Messiah (Isa. 9:6). Messiah, the Son of David, was to appear (Isa. 11:1) after the house of David had been stripped of its royal dignity and glory.

There are prophecies which speak of his life, his poverty, the works he was to do, his rejection by his own people (Isa. 53). During the time of his rejection by Israel, the Gentiles would be visited by his salvation (Isa. 49:5, 6).

His sufferings and death are even more minutely predicted. In the Book of Psalms the sufferings of Christ, the deep agony of his soul, the expressions of his sorrow and his grief, are pre-written by the Spirit of God. His death by crucifixion is prophesied in Psalm 22, a death unknown in David's time. The cry of the forsaken One is predicted in the very words which came from the lips of our Savior out of the darkness which enshrouded the cross. So also are the words of mockery by those who looked on; the piercing of his hands and feet; the parting of the garments and the casting of the lots. Finally, Psalm 110:1 prophesies that the rejected One would occupy the place at the right hand of God. It is indeed a wonderful chain of prophecies concerning Christ.

The Jewish People

When Frederick the Great, King of Prussia, asked the court chaplain for an argument that the Bible is an inspired book, he answered, "Your Majesty, the Jews." It was well said. The Scriptures are filled with predictions relating to Israel's history. Their unbelief, the rejection of the Messiah, the results of that rejection, their world-wide dispersion, the persecutions and sorrows they were to suffer, their miraculous preservation as a nation, their future great tribulation, and final restoration — all these were repeatedly announced by their own prophets. All the epochs of their eventful history were predicted long before they were reached. Their sojourn and servitude in Egypt were announced to Abraham. The Babylonian captivity and the return of a remnant were foretold by the pre-exilic prophets, who also predicted a greater and longer exile of world-wide proportions. In the prophecies of the return from Babylon, even the name of the Persian king through whom it was to be accomplished, is foretold. Two hundred years before Cyrus was born, Isaiah prophesied of him (Isa. 44:28; 45:1).

One of the most remarkable chapters in the Pentateuch is Deuteronomy 28. Here is prewritten the sad history of Israel. The Spirit of God through Moses outlined thousands of years ago the history of the scattered nation, their suffering and tribulation, as it has been for well nigh two millenniums and as it is still. These are arguments for the divine, supernatural origin of this book, which no infidel has ever been able to answer; nor will there be found an answer. Of much interest is the last verse of this great prophetic chapter. When Jerusalem was destroyed by the Romans in 70 A.D., all who did not die in the terrible calamity were sent to the mines of Egypt, where the slaves were kept constantly at work until they succumbed. According to Josephus, about 100,000 were made slaves, so that the market was glutted with them. Thus was fulfilled the word, "No man shall buy you."

Though without a land, Israel through the centuries was still a nation. All this is written beforehand in the Bible. Compare Leviticus 26:33; Deuteronomy 4:27; 28:64-67; and Jeremiah 30: 11. Herder called the Jews "the enigma of history." What human mind could have foreseen that this peculiar people, dwelling in a special land, was to be scattered among the nations, suffer there as no other nation ever suffered, and yet be kept and thus marked out still as the covenant people of the God whose gifts and callings are without repentance? Here indeed is an argument for the Word of God which no infidel can answer.

According to Hosea 5:15 the Lord is to be in the midst of Israel and is to return to his place. Reference is to the manifestation of the Lord Jesus Christ among his people. They rejected him; he returned to his place in glory. They are yet to acknowledge their offence. Elsewhere in the Word predictions are found that foretell the future national repentance of Israel when the remnant confesses their guilt in rejecting Messiah.

Prophecies of Other Nations

The prophets have much to say about the nations that touched Israel. Babylonia, Assyria, Egypt, Ammon, Moab, Tyre, Sidon, Idumea and others are mentioned in the prophetic Scriptures. Their ultimate fate was predicted by God long before their downfall and overthrow occurred. Ezekiel's precise prophecies of the judgment of these nations in chapters 25 to 37 have been fulfilled to the letter, as comparison with secular history will verify. Whether it be Ezekiel's prediction of the doom of Tyre (chapters 26 to 28) or Isaiah's prophecies of the judgment of Egypt (chapter 19), all was literally fulfilled.

Moreover, the Book of Daniel supplies some of the most startling evidences of fulfilled prophecy. No book of the Bible has been more attacked than this, but it has survived all attacks. The dream of Nebuchadnezzar is recorded in the second chapter. The heathen king was informed by God of the course of world rule from his day till the kingdom of Messiah. As foretold, the kingdoms have been four: Babylon, Medo-Persia, Greece, and Rome. The final division into ten kingdoms will yet be fulfilled. In the seventh chapter the vision of Daniel covers the same ground from God's viewpoint and with added detail concerning the fourth empire. History bears witness that these four powers came onto the stage of history and fell, just as indicated in these prophetic portions. In the eighth chapter the coming and career of Alexander the Great were revealed. The identification of the wicked ruler of 8:19-24 with Antiochus Epiphanes is without refutation. The greatest prophecy in the Book of Daniel is in the ninth chapter. Here the very time of Messiah's coming, his violent death, the rebuilding of Jerusalem in the time of Ezra and Nehemiah, and its subsequent destruction by the Romans in 70 A.D., are clearly predicted.

The greater part of the eleventh chapter of Daniel has been historically fulfilled. So accurately have these predictions been fulfilled, that the enemies of the Word have resorted to the subterfuge that the chapter was written after the events occurred.

Several prophecies and their fulfillments will be adduced; others equally clear could be set forth. The mighty king of verse 3 was Alexander the Great, son of Philip of Macedon. Verse 4 accurately states the disruption of the Alexandrian empire. The king of the south and the king of the north of verse 6 are Ptolemy II (Philadelphus) and Antiochus II (Theos), respectively. The invasion of the land of Palestine by Antiochus the Great is foretold in verse 16. The daughter of women of verse 17 has been historically verified in Cleopatra. Verses 21-45 found their fulfillment in the wicked deeds of Antiochus IV (Epiphanes). The heroic and godly deeds of the Maccabees (recounted in the apocryphal Books of Maccabees) are referred to in verses 32 to 34.

Other Fulfilled Prophecies

The New Testament contains prophecies which are now in process of fulfillment. The present apostasy from the historic faith is predicted in such passages as I Timothy 4:1, 2; II Timothy 3:1-5; 4:1-3; II Peter 2; the Epistle of Jude; and other portions in the Epistles and the Revelation.

Unfulfilled Prophecy

There are many unfulfilled prophecies in the Bible. The literal fulfillment of prophecies in the past vouches for the literal fulfillment of every prophecy in the Word of God. The world still waits for their accomplishment. In God's time he will bring about his eternal purposes. May we, the people of God, not neglect prophecy, for the prophetic testimony is the lamp which shines in a dark place.

PHILIP MAURO (1859-1952) was a successful lawyer, practicing before the United States Supreme Court, when he was converted after attending meetings at the Gospel Tabernacle in New York City, pastored by A. B. Simpson. That was on May 24, 1903. The next year, he published *From Reason to Revelation*, the first of more than forty books that would come from his pen. One of his most widely circulated books, *Life in the Word*, was published in 1909 and was included in *The Fundamentals* in a condensed version. He continued his law practice while speaking at Christian meetings and writing books and articles. It was Mauro who prepared the legal brief that William Jennings Bryan used at the famous "Scopes Trial" in 1925. In later years, he changed his views of the kingdom and prophecy, but he never strayed from the basic doctrines of the Christian faith.

20

Life in the Word

By Philip Mauro
ATTORNEY-AT-LAW, NEW YORK

Revised and edited by Rev. Glenn O'Neal, Ph.D.

Of the many statements which the Bible makes concerning the Word of God, none is more significant, and surely none is of greater importance to dying men than the statement that the Word of God is a LIVING Word. If men are able to apprehend, however feebly, this tremendous fact, it will cause them to give it the proper respect and the utmost emphasis in their preaching and teaching.

In Philippians 2:16 we have the expression, "The Word of Life." The same expression occurs in I John 1:1. It is here used of Jesus Christ, the Incarnate Word, whereas in Philippians it is apparently the Written Word that is spoken of. The Written Word and the Incarnate Word are so identified in Scripture that it is not alway clear which is meant. The same things are said of each, and the same characters attributed to each. The fundamental resemblance lies in the fact that each is the revealer or tangible expression of the Invisible God. As the written or spoken word expresses, for the purpose of communicating to another, the invisible and inaccessible thought, so Jesus Christ as the Incarnate Word, and the Holy Scriptures as the written Word, express and communicate knowledge of the invisible and inaccessible God. "He that hath seen me hath seen the Father." "Believe me that I am in the Father, and the Father in me" (John 14:9, 11).

In Hebrews 4:12 we find the statement that "The Word of God is LIVING and powerful, and sharper than any two-edged sword" (ASV). Clearly this refers to the written Word. But the very next verse, without any change of subject, directs our attention to the Searcher of hearts (Rev. 2:23), saying, "Neither is there any creature that is not manifest in his sight: but all things are naked and opened unto the eyes of him with whom we have to do."

Again in I Peter 1:23 we read of "the Word of God which liveth," or more literally, "the Word of God living." Here again there might be uncertainty as to whether the Incarnate Word or the Written Word be meant; but it is generally understood that the latter is in view, and the quotation from Isaiah 40:6-8 would confirm this idea.

From these passages we learn that the Word of God is spoken of as a "living" Word. This is a very remarkable statement, and is worthy of our closest examination and most earnest consideration. Why is the Word of God thus spoken of? Why is the extraordinary property of LIFE, or vitality, attributed to it? In what respects can it be said to be a living Word?

But the expression "living," as applied to the Word of God, manifestly means something more than partaking of the kind of life with which we are acquainted from observation. God speaks of himself as the "Living God." The Lord Jesus is the "Prince of Life" (Acts 3:15). He announced himself to John in the vision of Patmos as "he that liveth." Eternal life is in him (I John 5: 11).

It is clear, then, that when we read, "The Word of God is living," we are to understand thereby that it lives with a spiritual, an inexhaustible, an inextinguishable, in a word, a divine, life. If the Word of God be indeed living in this sense, then we have here a fact of the most tremendous significance. In the world around us the beings and things which we call "living" may just as appropriately be spoken of as "dying." What we call "the land of the living" might better be described as the land of the dying. Wherever we look we see that death is in possession, and is working according to its invariable method of corruption and decay. Death is the real monarch of this world, and we meet at every turn the gruesome evidence and results of the universal sway of him who has "the power of death, that is, the devil" (Heb. 2:14). "Death reigned" (Rom. 5:17), and still reigns over everything. The mighty and awful power of death has made this earth of ours a great burying ground — a gigantic cemetery.

Can it be that there is an exception to this apparently universal rule? Is there, indeed, in this world of dying beings, where the forces of corruption fasten immediately upon everything into which life has entered, and upon all the works of so-called living creatures, one object which is really LIVING, an object upon which corruption cannot fasten itself, and which resists and defies all the power of death? Such is the assertion of the passages of Scripture which we have quoted. Surely, then, if these statements be true, we have here the most astonishing phenomenon in all the accessible universe; and it will be well worth while to investigate an object of which so startling an assertion is seriously, if very unobtrusively, made.

Before we proceed with our inquiry let us note one of many points of resemblance between the Incarnate Word and the Written Word. When "the Word was made flesh and dwelt (tabernacled) among us" (John 1:14), there was nothing in his appearance to manifest his deity, or to show that "in him was life" (John 1:4). That fact was demonstrated not by his blameless and unselfish behavior, nor by his incomparable teachings and discourses, but by his *resurrection from the dead*. The only power which is greater than that of death is the power of life. He had, and exercised, that power, and holds now the keys of death and of Hades (Rev. 1:18, ASV).

Similarly, there is nothing in the appearance and behavior (so to speak) of the Bible to show that it has a characteristic, even divine life, which other books have not. It bears the same resemblance to other writings that Jesus, the Son of Mary, bore to other men. It is given in human language just as he came in human flesh. Yet there is between it and all other books the same difference as between him and all other men, namely, the difference *between the living and the dying*. "The word of God is living."

It will require, therefore, something more than a hasty glance or a casual inspection to discern this wonderful difference; but the difference is there, and with diligence and attention we may discover some clear indications of it.

We look then at the Written Word of God to see if it manifests characteristics which are found only in living things, and to see if it exhibits, not merely the possession of life of the perishable and corruptible sort with which we are so familiar by observation, but life of a different order, imperishable and incorruptible.

I. Perennial Freshness

The Bible differs radically from all other books in its perpetual freshness. This characteristic will be recognized only by those who know the Book in that intimate way which comes from living with it, as with a member of one's family. I mention it first because it was one of the first *unique* properties of the Bible which impressed me after I began to read it as a believer in Christ. It is a very remarkable fact that the Bible never becomes exhausted, never acquires sameness, never diminishes in its power of responsiveness to the quickened soul who comes to it. The most familiar passages yield as much (if not more) refreshment at the thousandth perusal, as at the first. It is indeed as a fountain of living water. The fountain is the same, but the water is always fresh, and always refreshing. We can compare this to nothing but what we find in a living companion, whom we love and to whom we go for help and fellowship. The person is always the same, and yet without sameness. New conditions evoke new responses; and so it is with the Bible. As a living Book it adapts itself to the new phases of our experience and the new conditions in which we find ourselves. From the most familiar passage there comes again and again *a new message;* just as our most familiar friend or companion will have something new to say, as changed conditions and new situations require it from time to time.

But while the Bible resembles in this important respect a living person, who is our familiar, sympathetic, and responsive companion, it differs from such a human companion in that the counsel, comfort, and support it furnishes are far above and beyond what any human being can supply; and the only explanation of this is that the source of its life and powers is not human, but divine.

II. The Bible Does Not Become Obsolete

One of the most prominent characteristics of books written by men for the purpose of imparting information and instruction, is that they very quickly become obsolete, and must be cast aside and replaced by others. This is particularly true of books on science, textbooks and the like. Indeed, it is a matter of boasting (though it would be hard to explain why) that "progress" is so rapid in all departments of learning as to render the scientific books of one generation almost worthless to the next. Changes in human knowledge, thought and opinion occur so swiftly, that books, which were the standards yesterday, are set aside today for others, which in turn will be discarded for yet other "authorities" tomorrow. In fact, every book which is written for a serious purpose begins to become obsolete before the ink is dry on the page. This may be made the occasion of boasting of the great progress of humanity, and of the wonderful advances of "science"; but the true significance of the fact is that man's books are all, like himself, dying creatures.

The Bible, on the other hand, although it treats of the greatest and most serious of all subjects, such as God, Christ, eternity, life, death, sin, righteousness, judgment, redemption — is always the latest, best, and *only* authority on all these and other weighty matters whereof it treats. Centuries of "progress" and "advancement" have added *absolutely nothing* to the sum of knowledge on any of these subjects. The Bible is always fresh and thoroughly "up-to-date." Indeed, it is far, far ahead of human science. Progress cannot overtake it, or go beyond it. Generation succeeds generation, but each finds the Bible waiting for it with its ever fresh and never failing stores of information touching matters of the highest concern, touching *everything* that affects the welfare of human beings.

We may say then that, considered merely as a book of instruction, the Bible is, as to every subject whereof it treats, not merely abreast of, but far ahead of the learning of these and all other times, whether past or future. The impressions it makes upon believing minds are the impressions of *truth*, even though contemporary science may give, as its settled conclusions, impressions directly to the contrary.

Unlike other books of instruction, *the Bible does not become obsolete*. This is a fact of immense significance; and its only explanation is that the Bible is a LIVING book, the Word of the living God. All other books partake of the infirmity of their authors, and are either dying or dead.

III. THE BIBLE IS INDESTRUCTIBLE

The Bible manifests the possession of inherent and imperishable life in that it survives all the attempts that have been made to destroy it.

The Bible is the only book in the world that is truly hated. The hatred it arouses is bitter, persistent, murderous. From generation to generation this hatred has been kept alive. There is doubtless a supernatural explanation for this continuous display of hostility towards the Word of God, for that Word has a supernatural enemy who has personally experienced its power (Matt. 4:1-10).

But the natural explanation of this hatred is that the Bible differs notably from other books in that it gives no flattering picture of man and his world, but just the reverse. The Bible does not say that man is a noble being, ever aspiring towards the attainment of exalted ideals. It does not describe the career of humanity as "progress," as the brave and successful struggle of man against the evils of his environment; but quite the contrary, declares it to be a career of disobedience and departure from God, a preference for darkness rather than for light, "because their deeds are evil."

The Bible does not represent man as having come, without any fault of his own, into adverse circumstances, and as being engaged in gradually overcoming these by the development and exercise of his inherent powers. It does not applaud his achievements, and extol his wonderful civilization. On the contrary, it records how God saw that the *wickedness* of man was great in the earth, and that every imagination of the thoughts of his heart was only evil continually (Gen. 6:5). It speaks of man as "being filled with all unrighteousness, fornication, wickedness, covetousness, malicious- ness, full of envy, murder, strife, guile, evil dispositions; whis- perers, slanders, hateful to God, insolent, proud, vaunting in- ventors of evil things, disobedient to parents, without understand- ing, perfidious, without natural affection, implacable, unmerciful" (Rom. 1:29-31 *Gr.*). It says that "They are all under sin," that "there is none righteous, no, not one. There is none that under- standeth, there is none that seeketh after God. They are all gone out of the way, they are together become unprofitable; there is none that doeth good, no, not one" (Rom. 3:10-12). Man's condition by nature is described as *"dead* in trespasses and sins," "children of disobedience; among whom also we *all* had our conduct in times past in the lusts of our flesh, fulfilling the desires of the flesh and of the mind; and were *by nature* the children of wrath" (Eph. 2:1-3).

The Bible has nothing to say in praise of man or of his natural endowments. On the contrary, it derides his wisdom as "foolishness with God." It declares that God has made foolish the wisdom of this age (I Cor. 1:20); that the natural man is incapable of receiving the things of the Spirit of God (I Cor. 2:14); and that if any man thinks that he knows anything, he knows nothing yet as he ought to know (I Cor. 8:2).

Nor does the Bible predict the ultimate triumph of "civilization." It does not say that the progress of humanity shall bring it eventually to a vastly better state of things. It does not say that human nature shall improve under the influences of education and self-culture, even with that of Christianity added. On the contrary, it declares that evil men "shall wax worse and worse, deceiving, and being deceived" (II Tim. 3:13).

Even of "this present evil age" (Gal. 1:4), during which the professing church is the most conspicuous object on earth, and during which the world has the enormous benefit resulting from the light of revelation and an open Bible, it is not predicted that man and his world would undergo any improvement, or that the developments of the age would be in the direction of better conditions on earth. On the contrary, the Bible declares that "in the last days perilous (or difficult) times shall come. For men shall be lovers of their own selves, lovers of money, vaunting, proud, evil speakers, disobedient to parents, untruthful, unholy, without natural affection, implacable, slanderers, inconsistent, savage, not lovers of good, betrayers, headstrong, puffed up, lovers of pleasure rather than lovers of God; having a form of piety, but denying the power of it" (II Tim. 3:1-5 *Gr.*),

Such is the character of man, and such is to be the result as Scripture foretells it, of all his schemes of betterment, education, development, self-culture, civilization and character-building. And because of this the Bible is heartily detested. Men have sought nothing more earnestly than they have sought to destroy this appallingly accurate portrait of themselves and their doings. How astonishing it is that any intelligent person should suppose that man drew this picture of himself, and predicted this as the outcome of all his own efforts! No wonder the Bible is hated, and for the simple and sufficient reason that it declares the truth about man and his world. The Lord Jesus set forth clearly both the fact and its explanation when he said to his unbelieving brethren, "The world cannot hate you; but me it hateth, because I testify of it that *the works thereof are evil*" (John 7:7).

Again, the Bible is hated because it claims the right to exercise, and assumes to exercise, *authority over man*. It speaks as one *having authority*. It issues commands to all. It says, "Thou shalt" and "Thou shalt not." It does not simply advise or commend one course of action rather than another, as one would address an equal, but it directs men imperatively what they shall do, and what they shall not do. In this manner it addresses all ranks and conditions of men — kings and governors, parents and children, husbands and wives, masters and servants, rich and poor, high and low, free and bond. In this, too, we have a characteristic of the Bible which distinguishes it from all other books. It is no respecter of persons. But for this cause also it is hated; for men are becoming more and more impatient of all external authority. The principles of democracy, the essence of which is the supremacy (virtually the *divinity*) of man, leave thoroughly leavened all society in the progressive nations of the earth. There is a sentiment abroad, which finds frequent expression and meets always with a sympathetic reception, to the effect that man has been shackled through the ages by narrow theological ideas whereof the Bible is the source, and that the time has arrived for him to throw off this bondage, to arise in his true might and majesty, and to do great things for himself.

It is a most impressive fact that, in all the visible universe, there is nothing that assumes authority over man, or that imposes laws upon him, *except the Bible*. Once thoroughly rid of that troublesome book, and man will be finally rid of all authority, and will have arrived at that state of lawlessness predicted in the New Testament prophecies, wherein society will be ready to accept the leadership of that "lawless one," whose coming is to be after the working of Satan, with all power, and signs, and wonders of falsehood, and with all deceit of unrighteousness in them that perish because they received not a love of the truth that they might be saved (II Thess. 2:7-10).

This is perhaps the main purpose of the persistent attempts in our day, mostly in the name of scholarship and liberal theology, to break down the authority of Scripture; and we may see with our own eyes that the measure of success of this great apostasy is just what the Bible has foretold.

Other books arouse no hatred. There may be books which men dislike, and such they simply let alone. But the Bible is, and always has been, hated to the death. It is the *one book* that has been pursued from century to century, as men pursue a mortal foe. At first its destruction has been sought by violence. All human powers, political and ecclesiastical, have combined to put it out of existence. Death has been the penalty for possessing or reading a copy; and such copies as were found have been turned over to the public executioner to be treated as was the Incarnate Word. No expedient that human ingenuity could devise or human cruelty put into effect, has been omitted in the desperate attempt to put this detested book out of existence.

But, violence having failed to rid man of the Bible other means have been resorted to in the persistent effort to accomplish that object. To this end the intellect and learning of man have been enlisted. The Book has been assailed from very side by men of the highest intelligence, culture and scholarship. Since the art of printing has been developed, there has been in progress a continuous war of books. Many books against *the* Book — man's books against God's Book. Its authority has been denied, and its veracity and even its morality have been impugned, its claims upon the consciences of men have been ridiculed; but all to no purpose, except to bring out more conspicuously the fact that the "Word of God is LIVING," and with an indestructible life.

A little less than two centuries ago a book made its appearance which attracted wide attention, particularly in the upper circles of intellect and culture. It was vauntingly entitled the "Age of

Reason," and its author, Thomas Paine, was probably without superior in intelligence among his contemporaries. So confident was the author of this book that his reasonings proved the untrustworthiness of Scripture, and destroyed its claim upon the consciences of men as the revelation of the living God, that he predicted that in fifty years the Bible would be practically out of print. But nearly two hundred years have passed since this boast was uttered. The boaster and his book have passed away; and their very names are well-nigh forgotten. But the Word of God has maintained its place, and not by human power. They who believe and cherish it are a feeble folk. Not many wise, not many mighty, not many high-born are among them. They have no might of their own to stand against the enemies of the Bible. The situation resembles a scene recorded in I Kings 20:27, where the Israelites went out against the Syrians, and we read that "The children of Israel pitched before them like two little flocks of kids; but the Syrians filled the country." But notwithstanding such great odds, the victory is certain. The enemies of the Bible have indeed filled the country. Yet, they shall all pass away; but the Word of the Lord shall not pass away.

IV. The Bible Is a Discerner of Hearts

The power of discernment belongs only to an intelligent living being; and the power of discernment possessed by man does not go beneath the surface of things. Yet the passage in Hebrews, already quoted (4:12), asserts that Word of God is a "discerner of the thoughts and intents of the heart."

This is a very remarkable statement, yet it is true and millions of men have felt and recognized the searching and discerning power of the Word of God. We go to it not so much to learn the thoughts of other men, as to learn our own thoughts. We go to other books to find what was in the hearts and minds of their authors; but we go to this Book to find what is in our hearts and minds. To one who reads it with ever so little spiritual intelligence, there comes a perception of the fact that this Book understands and knows all about him. It lays bare the deepest secrets of his heart, and brings to the surface of his consciousness, out of the unfathomable depths and unexplorable recesses of his own being, "thoughts and intents" whose existence was unsuspected. It reveals man to himself in a way difficult to describe, and absolutely peculiar to itself. It is a faithful mirror which reflects us exactly as we are. It detects our motives, discerns our needs; uncovers our repressions and having truthfully revealed to us our true selves, it counsels, reproves, exhorts, guides, refreshes, strengthens, and illuminates.

The living Word shall continue to be the discerning companion of all who resort to it for the help which is not to be had elsewhere in this world of the dying. In going to the Bible we never think of ourselves as going *back* to a book of the distant past, to a thing of *antiquity;* but we go to it as to a book of the *present* —a living book.

V. The Word Exhibits the Characteristics of Growth

Growth is one of the characteristics of a living being. The Word of God lodges and grows in human hearts, for there is its real lodgment, rather than in the printed page. The Psalmist says, "Thy Word have I hid in my heart" (Ps. 119:11).

The Book of Deuteronomy has much to say about the Word of God. In chapter 30 it declares (verse 14) that "The Word is very nigh unto thee, in thy mouth and in thy heart." This is repeated in Romans 10:8, with the addition, "that is, the word of faith which we preach."

In I Thessalonians 2:13 Paul says to the Thessalonians, "When ye received the Word of God which ye heard of us, ye received it not as the word of men, but as it is in truth, the Word of God, which *effectually worketh also in you* that believe." The believing heart is its lodgment, and there it works to effect some definite results.

In Colossians 3:16 we have the admonition, "Let the word of Christ dwell *in* you richly in all wisdom." It is in the believing heart that the Word dwells richly.

The Lord Jesus, in explaining the parable of the sower, said "The seed is the Word of God" (Luke 8:11); and again, "The sower soweth *the Word*" (Mark 4:14). (A seed, of course, is worthless except it have life in it.) And he further explained that the seed which fell on good ground "are they which, *in an honest and good heart,* having heard the Word keep it, and bring forth fruit with patience" (Luke 8:15). To the unbelieving Jews the Lord said, "And ye have not his Word *abiding in you;* for whom he hath sent, him ye believe not" (John 5:38).

In Colossians 1:5, 6, Paul speaks of the "Word of the truth of the Gospel, which is come unto you, as it is in all the world, and bringeth forth fruit."

In these passages we have presented to us the thought of the Word as a living seed or germ, first finding lodgment in the heart of man, and then abiding and growing there.

The growth of the Word of God is specifically mentioned in several striking passages in the Acts of the Apostles. Acts 6:7: *"And the Word of God increased;* and the number of the disciples multiplied in Jerusalem greatly." Here we are told specifically that the Word of God increased. We learn from this that the mere multiplication of copies of the Scriptures is in itself of no importance. It is of no avail to have the Book in the house, and on the shelf or table, if it be not taken into the heart. But when so received into the heart, the Word of God grows and increases. It is assimilated into the life of him who receives it, and henceforth is a part of himself.

Happy is the man who has "received the Word of God" (Acts 8:14; 11:1, etc.), who has made room for it in his life, and in whose heart and mind it has grown and prevailed.

VI. A LIFE-GIVING WORD

We come now to something higher and deeper. The great mystery of a living thing is the power it possesses of propagating its kind.

The fact of spiritual conception, and the nature of the seed whereby it is effected, are plainly declared in I Peter 1:23: "Being born (or having been begotten) again, not of corruptible *seed,* but of incorruptible, by THE WORD OF GOD WHICH LIVETH and abideth for ever."

There is an immense amount of truth of the highest importance contained in this passage; but the statement which especially concerns us is that the seed of the new birth is from the living Word ("the Word which LIVETH"). This statement plainly teaches that the Word of God possesses the highest endowment of a living being, namely, that of imparting life. And with this agrees the teaching of the Lord Jesus in the parable of the sower, in the explanation of which he said, "The *seed* is the Word of God" (Luke 8:11).

In consequence of the transgression and fall of the first man, who was the original depository of the life of humanity (Gen. 2:7), the life in him, being "corruptible," became vitiated. Hence, by inexorable law, the seed of his generations also became corrupted. It follows that all men in their natural generation are begotten of corruptible (and corrupted) seed; and have received (and hence must impart to their succeeding generations) a corrupted life. What, therefore, was needed, in order to bring into existence a human family answering to God's purpose in the creation of man (Gen. 1:26), was a new and *incorruptible seed.* This has been supplied in the Word of God. All who believe that Word are begotten again (or from above); not this time of corruptible seed, "but of incorruptible, by the Word of God *which liveth.*" It is a living Word.

It is to be noted that this Scripture testifies that the seed of the living Word is not merely uncorrupted, but is "incorruptible." It partakes, therefore, of the nature of the "uncorruptible God" (Rom. 1:23).

This is the guaranty to us that the Word of God is not subject to the corrupting influences of the corrupted and decaying world into which it is come. It is the *only thing* which has not succumbed to the forces of decay and death which reign universally in the earth. Indeed, it has not been affected in the slightest degree by those forces. This has been pointed out at length in the foregoing pages; but the grand truth comes to us with peculiar force in connection with the passage in I Peter. We need not be at all concerned as to whether the truth of God, embodied by him in his Word, has been corrupted, for it is incorruptible. And by that Word they who believe are begotten again through the operation of the Holy Spirit. To them "the Spirit is life" (Rom. 8:10).

The same truth is declared in James 1:18, in the words, "Of his own will begat he us with the word of truth."

Such is the spiritual conception of the "sons of God." These are born, or begotten. In no other way is a "son" brought into existence save by being begotten of a father. The sons of God must be begotten of God. The Apostle John tells us that they are begotten, "not of the will of the flesh, nor of the will of man" (John 1:13). The Apostle James tells us that "of his own will" they are begotten. Therefore, though the process be inscrutably mysterious, there can be no doubt as to the fact. When the Word of God is truly "heard" and thereby received into a prepared heart, that word becomes truly a seed, spiritual and incorruptible in nature, which, when quickened by the Spirit of God, becomes the life-germ of a new creature—a son of God.

The same truth is very clearly taught in our Lord's explanation of his parable of the sower, to which reference has already been made. Inasmuch as we have his own interpretation of this parable, we need be in no uncertainty as to its meaning. He says, "Those by the wayside are they that hear; then cometh the Devil and taketh away *the Word out of their hearts,* lest they should *believe* and be saved" (Luke 8:12). And again: "But that on the good ground are they which, in *an honest and good heart,* having heard the Word keep it and bring forth fruit with patience" (Luke 8:15).

The method of spiritual conception set forth in these Scriptures, which is effected in a manner quite analogous to natural conception, furnishes the explanation of the connection between "believing" and "life" referred to in many passages of Scripture. One of the most familiar of these is John 5:24 where the Lord Jesus states in the simplest language that the man who hears his Word and believes on him who sent him has everlasting life, and is passed out of death into life. Such a man receives the seed in his heart, and the \seed is there quickened into life.

Indeed, the great purpose of the Written Word is to impart life—even eternal (that is to say divine) life — to those who are dead through trespasses and sins. The Gospel of John, which is devoted largely to the great subject of eternal life, and from which a large part of our information concerning it is derived, was "written that ye might believe that Jesus is the Christ, the Son of God and that *believing* ye might have *life* through his name" (John 20:31).

The same truth is declared in the familiar passage in Romans 10:9, which sets forth very definitely the special truth which constitutes the substance and marrow of God's revelation in his Word, and which he calls upon men to believe and obey through the preaching of the Gospel, namely that Jesus Christ, who died for sinners, has been *raised from the dead,* and that he is Lord of all, to the glory of God the Father.

The main point to be apprehended in this connection is that a certain state of preparedness of heart is necessary in order that the "good seed" of the Word may germinate and grow there. Such a prepared heart is described in Scripture as a *believing* heart. That prepared state is manifested when a man *believes God,* as Abraham did (Rom. 4:17); or, in other words, when a man is ready to receive the Word of God *as* the Word of God, as the Thessalonians did (I Thess. 2:13). When a man has been brought, by the operation of the Spirit of God, who is the "Spirit of LIFE in Christ Jesus" (Rom. 8:2, 10), into this state of preparation, then the Word of God, being received into the heart, acts as a seed falling into good soil.

Such is the power of the *living* truth to impart life; and herein lies the difference between the truth which God has revealed in his Word, and truth which may be found elsewhere. For there is much truth which is not *living* truth. The multiplication table is truth; but it is not living truth. It has no quickening power. The theorems of geometry are truth; but they are not living truth. Never yet has any man been heard to testify that he had been the wretched and hopeless slave of sin, and had continued in spiritual darkness, fast bound in misery and vice until his eyes were opened by the great truth that two and two make four, or that three angles of a triangle are equal to two right angles; and that thereby his life had been transformed, his soul delivered from bondage, and his heart filled with joy and peace in believing. On the other hand, in the case of a true conversion, it may have been but the shortest and simplest statement of "the Word of the truth of the Gospel"

(Col. 1:5) that was heard and believed, such as that "Christ died for the ungodly" (Rom. 5:6), yet it suffices, through the mighty power of him who raised up Christ from among the dead, to quicken together with Christ a soul that previously was dead in trespasses and sins (Eph. 1:20; 2:5). Thus the Word of truth becomes, in some inscrutible way, the vehicle for imparting that life of which the risen Christ, the Incarnate Word, is the only Source. Eternal life for the individual soul begins through believing "the testimony of God" (I Cor. 1:2), and the testimony of God which he has in grace given to perishing sinners that they may believe and be saved, is *"concerning his Son"* (Rom. 1:3; I John 5:10). "And this is the record (or testimony), that God hath given to us eternal life, and this life is in his Son" (I John 5:11). Therefore, it is written of those who experienced the new birth, "For ye are all the children of God by faith in Christ Jesus" (Gal. 3:26).

VII. The Life-Sustaining Word

The life possessed by human beings is not only a derived life, that is, a life obtained from an external source, but it is a dependent life, requiring continual sustenance. It must be sustained by constant and suitable nutrition, received into the body at short intervals. Man's strength whereof he boasts, and indeed his very existence in the body, are dependent on food, and this food itself must be organic matter, that is to say, matter which has once been living. The fact of this dependence upon food, and upon food which man is utterly unable to make for himself out of inorganic matter, though all the materials are within his reach, should teach him a lesson in humility; but it seems not to have that effect.

Men boast in these days of their "independence," and make much of "self-reliance." But this is the height of presumptuous folly; for man is a most helplessly dependent creature, not even able like the plant, to prepare his own food from the mineral elements, but dependent daily upon living creatures much lower than himself in the scale of being. And so far from having a basis for self-reliance, he does not know how to conduct the simplest of the vital processes of his own body. If his Creator, of whom principally man loves to fancy himself independent, should turn over to him the operation of the least of those essential processes for the briefest time, the poor creature would miserably perish.

As with the physical life, so is it with the spiritual life of those who have been begotten again of the incorruptible seed of the Word. These spiritual beings require appropriate food; and God has abundantly provided for this need. In studying the important subject of spiritual nutrition we shall learn again the relation between Christ, the Incarnate Word, and the Written Word. Both are spoken of repeatedly as food for the children of God.

The third, fourth and fifth chapters of the Gospel of John treat of the imparting of eternal life as the free gift of God through Jesus Christ, the Son of God, to all who believe on him; and the sixth chapter treats of spiritual nutrition. Therein, after feeding the multitude miraculously, thus showing himself as the one by whose power food is multiplied in the earth, he reveals himself as "the Bread of Life." Twice he says, "I am that bread of life" (verses 35 and 48) and in verse 33, "For the bread of God is he which cometh down from heaven, and giveth life unto the world." He who gives the life is the One who also sustains it. Again he says, "I am the living bread which came down from heaven" (verse 51). And of his words he says, "It is the spirit that quickeneth; the flesh profiteth nothing; *the words* that I speak unto you, they are spirit and they are life" (verse 63).

These sayings to the natural mind are, of course, meaningless; but they are addressed to faith. "How can this man give us his flesh to eat?" is the question which the unbelieving heart asks. How Christ can impart himself to sustain the "inner man" is a question to which no answer can now be had. The process of physical nutrition is equally beyond human comprehension and contrary to all *a priori* probabilities.

Looking more particularly at what is said in this connection concerning the written or spoken Word of God, we find that the Word of God is "living" in the sense that, like other living substance, it has the property of furnishing nutrition, and thereby sustaining life. It is a life-sustaining Word. But here a notable difference attracts our attention. Physical food comes up out of the earth (Ps. 104:14), while spiritual food comes down out of heaven. (John 6:50.)

Reference has already been made to the fact that, after setting forth the great truth of spiritual conception and generation through the incorruptible seed of the Word of God, the Apostle Peter enjoins attention to spiritual nutrition. "Wherefore," he says, "as newborn babes, desire the sincere milk of the word, that ye may grow thereby" (I Peter 2:1, 2). Evidently his Lord's three-fold injunction, "Feed my sheep," "Feed my lambs," had impressed upon him the importance of spiritual nutrition. But proper feeding requires appetite for wholesome food, and so he seeks to excite a desire in young Christians for that whereby they may grow. And he immediately connects the Word with Christ saying, "If so be ye have tasted that the Lord is gracious."

The importance of nourishing and sustaining the new life received upon coming to Christ, and the unhappy consequences which always result from neglect of the appropriate diet, have been so often and so forcibly stated by the servants of Christ, that it seems hardly necessary to dwell upon this matter. What our subject specially calls for is to note the correspondence between God's way of sustaining man's physical life by food derived from a living source, and his way of sustaining the believer's spiritual life by food from a living source, that is to say from the living Word.

The passages which present the Word of God as the food for his children are very familiar; and in bringing them to mind again we would impress it upon our readers that these statements are not to be taken as if they were poetical or figurative, but as very literal, practical and immensely important. In making man it was not God's plan that he should live by bread, or physical food alone, but "by every word that proceedeth out of the mouth of the Lord" (Deut. 8:3). The manna was given to his people in the wilderness to teach them this lesson, and that they might learn their dependence upon God. Hence, this passage was used by the Second Man in his combat with the devil in the wilderness, it being the purpose of the latter to inculcate in man the idea of independence of God. Thus did the Man Jesus Christ, with the Sword of the Spirit, strike sure and true at the central purpose of his great adversary.

It is by *every* word of God that man is to be fed. No part of the Bible can be neglected without loss and detriment; and it will be observed that there is, in the Bible, a variety of spiritual nutriment analogous to the variety of physical food which God has provided for the needs of the physical man. If there be milk for babes, there is also strong food for those who are mature. And there is the penalty of arrested growth paid by those who remain content with the relatively weak diet suitable for infants who know, perhaps, only that their sins are forgiven; as the Apostle John says: "I write unto you, little children, because your sins are forgiven you" (I John 2:12). But those who have to be fed on a milk diet, that is to say, the simplest elementary truths of the Gospel, are unskillful in the word of righteousness. Infants cannot do anything for themselves, much less can they prepare food, or render any service to others. Hence, the Apostle Paul, writing to the Hebrews, upbraids some of them because, at a time when they ought to have been teachers, they had need to be taught again the first principles, and were become "such as have need of milk and not of strong food. For every one that useth milk is unskillful in the word of righteousness: for he is a babe. But strong food belongeth to them that are of full age" (Heb. 5:12-14).

Jeremiah says, "Thy words were found and I did eat them" (Jer. 15:16). Thereby he found spiritual strength to sustain him in his most difficult and trying ministry, from which, because of his timid and sensitive disposition, he shrank back in agony of soul. To be a good and effective minister of Christ it is necessary that one be well nourished through partaking largely of the abundant spiritual food which the living Word supplies. Thus Paul admonished his child in the faith, Timothy, to whom he wrote, "If thou put the brethren in remembrance of these things, thou shalt be a good minister of Jesus Christ, *nourished up in the words of faith and of good doctrine*" (I Tim. 4:6).

VIII. THE LIFE-TRANSFORMING WORD

Feeding upon the Word of God, the bread of life, must necessarily be beneficial to the whole man, including his intellectual and physical being as well as his spiritual. The new man requires a new mind and provision is made to that end. Paul said, "Be renewed in the spirit of your mind" (Eph. 4:23), and, "Be not conformed to this world (or age), but be ye transformed by the renewing of your mind" (Rom. 12:2). The old mind, with all its habits of self-occupation (a sure breeder of unhappiness and discontent), its morbid tendencies, its craving for excitement and sensation, its imaginations, appetites, tastes, inclinations and desires, and every high thing that exalteth itself against the knowledge of God, is to be displaced and a new mind substituted; for godliness has the promise of the vigor of the life that now is, as well as of that which is to come.

How, then is this injunction to be carried out? It is of importance to millions of anxious souls to have a clear answer to this question. And it may be had. The everyday incidents and the atmosphere amid which the average man and woman spend their time, are such as to produce mental disturbances and disorders to an extent which, if understood, and if anything could impress this thoughtless and excited age, would create widespread alarm. The frequency with which one encounters cases of mental depression, insomnia, melancholia, and other nervous disorders, tells of widespread and insidious foes which attack the seat of reason, and which call for methods and means of defense and repair which are beyond the resources of medicine.

The writer knows by experience the indescribable horrors of depressed and morbid mental states, and knows, too, what a transformation is effected by the "renewing of the mind" according to the Biblical injunction. Full provision is made for this marvelous transformation, and the conditions wherin it is effected are plainly set forth and are accessible to every believer. In this case the study of the word used in the command ("be transformed") will make us acquainted with the conditions essential to the transformation. The word in question seems to have been set apart by the Holy Spirit for the purpose of teaching the important and wonderful secret of the transformation of the believer, during his existence in the body, into the likeness of Christ; so that all believers might be able to say with Paul, "We have the mind of Christ."

It will, therefore, surely repay the reader to note carefully the usages of this particular word. Its first occurrence is in the Gospel narratives ot the Transfiguration of Jesus Christ, and is in fact the very word there translated "transfigured" (Matt. 17:2; Mark 9:2). The word is literally "metamorphosed." "His face did shine as the sun, and his raiment was white as the light." This may well serve to teach the nature of the change contemplated. It is one that brings the radiance of heaven into the mind and tinges even the commonplace things with a glow of heavenly light.

The next occurrence of the word is, as we have already seen, in Romans 12:2, where believers are enjoined to be not cut out on the pattern of this age, but to be metamorphosed or transfigured by the renewing of their minds.

The third and last occurrence of the word tells us plainly *how* this great transformation is brought about. For the Bible is a very practical book. It comes moreover, from One who understands perfectly the limitations of man, who knows and declares that the latter is, in his natural state, "without strength," that is to say utterly impotent (Rom. 5:6). We may be sure, therefore, that when God calls upon the quickened soul to do a thing, he puts the means required for it within his reach. And so, in these plain words we read the conditions requisite for effecting the desired transformation: "We all, with unveiled face, beholding as in a mirror the glory of the·Lord, *are changed* into the same image from glory to glory, even as by the Spirit of the Lord" (II Cor. 3:18).

The word here translated "are changed" is the same word (metamorphosed or transfigured) used in the other passages cited; and these are the only occurrences of that word in the Bible.

The teaching is very clear. When the Jews read the Word of God a veil is over their hearts, their minds being blinded (verse 14). Or, as stated in Romans 11:25, "blindness in part is happened to Israel, until the fullness of the Gentiles be come in." Hence, they do not behold there him of whom the Scriptures testify. But, for us who believe the veil is done away in Christ, and consequently, all we beholding are transfigured into the same image by the divine and irresistible operation of the Holy Spirit.

If, when we look into the Word of God, *we do not see Christ there,* we look to no purpose, for he is everywhere in the Book.

Let it be carefully noted that this transformation is not the work of the man who beholds Christ in the Word; for the process is carried on while the former is not occupied with himself at all, or with his transformation, but is absorbed in the contemplation of the glory of the Lord. The transformation is effected by the power of the Spirit of God; and we may learn from this passage the important lesson that occupation with, and concern about, the work of the Spirit in us can only hinder that work. Let it suffice us that he who has begun a good work *in us* will perform it until the day of Christ. (Phil. 1:6.) Our part, and it should be also our delight, is to be continually beholding or contemplating the glory of the Lord; and while so doing we *"are* changed" into the same image, and all the faster if we are unconscious of ourselves.

Let it be also noted that the transformation is a gradual operation, calling for steadfastness in contemplating the One who is the object placed before us by the Holy Spirit. Little by little, as our gaze is fixed upon him, the old traits and dispositions which are unlike him are replaced by his own characteristics. Thus the work proceeds "from glory to glory." The conformation to his image, which is God's purpose for all the sons of God (Rom. 8:29), is not accomplished, as some would have it, by an instantaneous transfiguration, a convulsive upheaval and displacement of the old nature, brought about by working one's emotions into an ecstatic state; but is accomplished gradually while the believer is continually occupied with Christ ("beholding"). There is no hysterical short-cut to the desired result. For Christ must be known from the Written Word by the application of the Holy Spirit; and the process should continue during the whole term of the believer's existence in the body.

Thus the living Word becomes the regulator and transformer of the minds of those who diligently seek it. Under its potent influence confusion of thought, perplexities, depressed mental states, and other hurtful conditions are dissipated, and the serene tranquillity and repose of the mind of Christ are reproduced in those who are redeemed by his precious blood.

We are passing through the domain of death, the country of the last enemy that is to be destroyed, and who has put all things in this scene under his feet (I Cor. 15:26, 27). On every hand our eyes meet the unmistakable evidences of the supreme sovereignty of death. But in this domain of death there is a Living Word — a Living Word in a dying world. The forces of corruption and decay cannot fasten upon it, and it laughs at the attacks of its enemies.

But that Word is here, not merely to manifest life, but rather to impart life to those who are perishing, and to bring them into vital contact with the new Life-Source of humanity, the Son of God, the Second Man, the Lord from heaven, who liveth and was dead, and behold he is alive forevermore, and has the keys of death and of Hades (I Cor. 15:47; Rev. 1:18). He, as man, has crossed the gulf between the realm of death and that of life. To that end he became "a partaker of flesh and blood," not to improve flesh and blood, but in order that "through death he might destroy him that had the power of death, that is, the devil; and deliver them who through fear of death were all their lifetime subject to bondage" (Heb. 2:14, 15). Having himself crossed that gulf he is the way of life to all who believe on him, who, having heard his Word — the Word of life — have likewise passed out of death into life (John 5:24).

This is the wonderful provision of God for the deliverance of dying men. In order that they might not die, and because God wills not that any should perish (II Peter 3:9), he has sent into this dying world a Word of Life. For God is not the God of the dead, but of the living (Matt. 22:32).

In comparison with the provision of divine wisdom, power and grace, from the God who quickeneth the dead (Rom. 4:17), how pitifully foolish and vain are all human schemes for the betterment, reform and cultivation of that old man who has fallen under the sovereignty of death! Men are very ingenious, but none has yet brought forward a scheme for abolishing or escaping death, or for raising the dead. Without that, of what avail are plans of improvement? And what end do they serve but to blind men's minds to the truth that they are dead, and so are beyond all but the power of a God who raises the dead? Surely these schemes are the most successful devices of "the god of this age."

What men need is not morality, but life; not to make death respectable, but to receive the gift of eternal life; not decent interment, but a pathway out of the realm of death. Many men have brought forward their schemes for the "uplift of humanity" (though the results thereof are not yet discernible); but there is only One man who makes, or ever made, the offer of eternal life. None other has ever said, "I am the resurrection and the life; he that believeth on me though he were dead yet shall he live. And whosoever liveth and believeth on me shall never die" (John 11 :25, 26). He only claims to be the "Fountain of Living Waters" (Jer. 2 :13; John 4 :14; 7 :37), and says to all who are suffering the thirst of death, "Come unto me and drink" (John 7 :37).

Therefore, in concluding these reflections upon the Living Word, we obey the command, "Let him that heareth say, Come," and would lovingly repeat the last invitation of grace recorded in the Word of Life: "Let him that is athirst come. And whosoever will, let him take the water of life freely" (Rev. 22 :17).

THOMAS WHITELAW (1840-1917) was ordained in 1864 after receiving his formal education at the United Presbyterian Hall in Edinburgh, Scotland. Working with both Presbyterian churches and the United Free Church, Whitelaw served as pastor and adminstrator. His comentaries include studies in Genesis and Acts. He also wrote a book about the divinity of Christ.

21

Is There a God?

By Rev. *Thomas Whitelaw, M.A., D.D.*
Presbyterian minister, Kilmarnock, Scotland

Abridged and emended by James H. Christian, Th.D.

Whether or not there is a supreme personal intelligence, infinite and eternal, omnipotent, omniscient and omnipresent, the Creator, upholder and ruler of the universe, immanent in and yet transcending all things, gracious and merciful, the Father and Redeemer of mankind, is surely the profoundest problem that can agitate the human mind. Lying as it does at the foundation of all man's religious beliefs — as to responsibility and duty, sin and salvation, immortality and future blessedness, as to the possibility of a revelation, of an incarnation, of a resurrection, as to the value of prayer, the credibility of miracle, the reality of providence — with the reply given to it are bound up not alone the temporal and eternal happiness of the individual, but also the welfare and progress of the race. Nevertheless, to it have been returned the most varied responses.

The atheist, for example, asserts that there is no God. The agnostic professes that he cannot tell whether there is a God or not. The materialist boasts that he does not need a God, that he can run the universe without one. The Christian answers that he cannot do without a God.

I. The Answer of the Atheist

"There Is No God"

In these days it will hardly do to pass by this bold and confident negation by simply saying that the theoretical atheist is an altogether exceptional specimen of humanity, and that his audacious utterance is as much the outcome of ignorance as of impiety. It is apparent that theoretical atheism is not extinct, even in cultured circles, and that some observations with regard to it are needed. Let these observations be the following:

1. *Disbelief in the existence of a Divine Being is not equivalent to a demonstration that there is no God.*

2. *Such a demonstration is from the nature of the case impossible.* It was well observed by the late Prof. Calderwood of the Edinburgh University that "the divine existence is a truth so plain that it needs no proof, as it is a truth so high that it admits of none." As Dr. Chalmers long ago observed, before one can positively assert that there is no God, he must arrogate to himself the wisdom and ubiquity of God. He must explore the entire circuit of the universe to be sure that no God is there. He must have interrogated all the generations of mankind and all the hierarchies of heaven to be certain they had never heard of a God. In short, as Chalmers puts it, "for man not to know God, he has only to sink beneath the level of our common nature. But to deny God he must be God himself."

3. *Denial of the divine existence is not warranted by inability to discern traces of God's presence in the universe.* "I cannot see,'" Huxley wrote, "one shadow or tittle of evidence that the Great Unknown underlying the phenomena of the universe stands to us in the relation of a Father, loves and cares for us as Christianity asserts." Blatchford also with equal emphasis affirms: "I cannot believe that God is a personal God who interferes in human affairs. I cannot see in science, or in experience, or in history, any signs of such a God or of such intervention." The incapacity of Huxley and Blatchford either to see or hear God may, and no doubt does, serve as an explanation of their atheistical creed, but assuredly it is not justification of the same, since a profounder reasoner than either has said: "The invisible things of God since creation of the world are clearly seen, being perceived through the things that are made, even his everlasting power and divinity; so that they [who believe not] are without excuse."

The majority of mankind, not in Christian countries only, but also in heathen lands, from the beginning of the world onward, have believed in the existence of a Supreme Being. They may frequently, as Paul says, have "changed the glory of the incorruptible God into an image made like to corruptible man, and to birds and four-footed beasts and creeping things"; but deeply seated in their natures, debased though these were by sin, lay the conception of a Superhuman Power to whom they owed allegiance and whose favor was indispensable to their happiness. It was a saying of Plutarch that in his day a man might travel the world over without finding a city without temples and gods. It may be set down as incontrovertible that the vast majority of mankind have possessed some idea of a Supreme Being; so that if the truth or falsehood of the proposition, "There is no God," is to be determined by the counting of votes, the question is settled in the negative, that is, against the atheist's creed.

II. The Confession of the Agnostic

"I Cannot Tell Whether There Is A God Or Not"

Without dogmatically affirming that there is no God, the agnostic practically insinuates that whether there is a God or not, nobody can tell and it does not much matter. The agnostic does not deny that behind the phenomena of the universe there may be a Power; but whether there is or not, and if there is, whether that Power is a Force or a Person, are among the things unknown and unknowable, so that practically, it can never be more than a subject of curious speculation, like that which engages the leisure time of some astronomers, whether there be inhabitants in the planet Mars or not.

As thus expounded, the creed of the agnostic is open to serious objections.

1. *It entirely ignores the spiritual factor in man's nature* — either denying the soul's existence altogether, or viewing it as merely a function of the body; or, if regarding it as a separate entity distinct from the body, and using its faculties to apprehend and reason about external objects, yet denying its ability to discern spiritual realities. On either alternative, it is contradicted by both Scripture and experience. From Genesis to Revelation the Bible proceeds upon the assumption that "there is a spirit in man," which has power not only to apprehend things unseen but to see and know God and to be seen and known by him. Nor can it be denied that man is conscious of being more than

animated matter, and of having power to apprehend more than comes within the range of his senses; for he can and does entertain ideas and cherish feelings that have at least no direct connection with the senses, and can originate thoughts, emotions and volitions that have not been excited by external objects. It is as certain as language can make it that Abraham and Jacob, Moses and Joshua, Samuel and David, Isaiah and Jeremiah, had no doubt whatever that they knew God and were known of him; and multitudes of Christians exist today whom it would not be easy to convince that they could not and did not know God, although not through the medium of the senses or even of the pure reason.

2. *It takes for granted that things cannot be adequately known unless they are fully known.* This proposition, however, cannot be sustained in either science or philosophy, in ordinary life or in religious experience. Science knows there are such things as life and force, but confesses its ignorance of what life and force are as to their essence; all that is understood about them being their properties and effects. Philosophy can expound the laws of thought, but is baffled to explain the secret of thought itself; how it is excited in the soul by nerve-movements caused by impressions from without, and how it can express itself by originating counter-movements in the body. Nor is the case different in religious experience. The Christian, like Paul, may have no difficulty in saying, "Christ liveth in me," but he cannot explain to himself or others, how. Hence the inference must be rejected that because the finite mind cannot fully comprehend the infinite, therefore it cannot know the infinite at all, and must remain forever uncertain whether there is a God or not. Scripture, it should be noted, does not say that any finite mind can fully find out God; but it does say that men may know God from the things which he has made, and more especially from the image of himself which has been furnished in Jesus Christ, so that if they fail to know him, they are without excuse.

3. *It virtually undermines the foundations of morality.* For if one cannot tell whether there is a God or not, how can one be sure that there is any such thing as morality? The distinctions between right and wrong which one makes in the regulation of his conduct may be altogether baseless. It is true a struggle may

be made to keep them up out of a prudential regard for future safety, out of a desire to be on the winning side in case there should be a God. But it is doubtful if the imperative "ought" would long resound within one's soul, were the conclusions once reached that no one could tell whether behind the phenomena of nature or of consciousness there was a God or not. Morality no more than religion can rest on uncertainties.

III. The Boast of the Materialist

"I Do Not Need a God, I Can Run the Universe Without One"

Only grant him to begin with an ocean of atoms and a force to set them in motion and he will forthwith explain the mystery of creation. If we have what he calls a scientific imagination, he will let us see the whole process — the molecules or atoms combining and dividing, advancing and retiring, forming groups, building up space-filling masses, growing hotter and hotter as they wheel through space, whirling swifter and swifter, till through sheer velocity they swell and burst, after which they break up into fragments and cool down into a complete planetary system.

Inviting us to light upon this globe, the materialist will show us how through long centuries, mounting up to millions of years, the various rocks which form the earth's crust were deposited. Nay, if we will dive with him to the bottom of the ocean he will point out the first speck of dead matter that sprang into life, protoplasm, though he cannot tell when or how.

Concerning this theory of the universe, however, it is pertinent to make these remarks:

1. Taken at its full value, with unquestioning admission of the alleged scientific facts on which it is based, *it is at best only an inference or working hypothesis, which may or may not be true and which certainly cannot claim to be beyond dispute.*

2. *Conceding all that evolutionists demand,* that from matter and force the present cosmos has been developed, *the question remains, whether this excluded or renders unnecessary the intervention of God as the prime mover in the process.* If it does, one would like to know whence matter and force came. Moreover, one would like to know how these atoms or electrons came to attract

and repel one another and form combinations, if there was no original cause behind them and no aim before them.

Against this pantheistical assumption must ever lie the difficulty of explaining how or why the God that was latent in matter or force, was so long in arriving at consciousness in man, and how before man appeared, the latent God being unconscious could have directed the evolutionary process which fashioned the cosmos. Till these inquires are satisfactorily answered, it will not be possible to accept the materialistic solution of the universe.

IV. The Declaration of the Christian

"I Cannot Do Without a God. Without a God I Can Neither Account for the Universe Around Me, Nor Explain Jesus Christ Above Me, Nor Understand the Spiritual Experiences Within Me."

1. *Without a God the material universe around the Christian is and remains a perplexing enigma.*

When he surveys that portion of the universe which lies open to his gaze, he sees marks of wisdom, power and goodness that irresistibly suggest the idea of a God. When he looks upon the stellar firmament with its innumerable orbs, and considers their disposition and order, their balancing and circling, he instinctively argues that these shining suns and systems must have been created, arranged and upheld by a Divine Mind. When, restricting his attention to the earth on which he stands, he notes the indications of design which are everywhere visible, as witnessed, for example, in the constancy of nature's laws and forces, in the endless variety of nature's forms, inanimate and animate, as well as in their wonderful gradation not only in their kinds but also in the times of their appearing, and in the marvelous adjustment of organs to environment; he feels constrained to reason that these things are not the result of chance which is blind or the spontaneous output of matter, which in itself, so far as known to him, is powerless, lifeless and unintelligent, but can only be the handiwork of a Creative Mind. When further he reflects that in the whole round of human experience, effects have never been known to be produced without causes; that designs have never been known to be conceived or worked out without designers and artificers; that dead matter has never been known to spring into life either spontaneously or by the application of means; that one kind of life has never been known to transmute itself spontaneously or to be transmuted artificially into another, neither a vegetable into an animal, nor an animal into a man; he once more feels himself shut up to the conclusion that the whole cosmos must be the production of mind, even of a Supreme Intelligence infinitely powerful, wise and good. Like the Hebrew psalmist he feels impelled to say, "O Lord! how manifold are thy works: in wisdom hast thou made them all!"

Should the philosopher interject, that this argument does not necessarily require an Infinite Intelligence, but only an artificer capable of constructing such a universe as the present, the answer is that, if such an artificer existed, he himself would require to be accounted for, since beings that are finite must have begun to be, and therefore must have been caused. Accordingly, this artificer must have been preceded by another greater than himself, and that by another still greater, and so on travelling backwards forever.

2. *Without a God the Christian cannot explain to himself the Person of Jesus.*

Fixing attention solely on the Gospels, the Christian discerns a personality that cannot be accounted for on ordinary principles. It is not merely that Jesus performed works such as none other man did, and spoke words such as never fell from mortal lips; it is that in addition his life was one of incomparable goodness — of unwearied philanthropy, self-sacrificing love, lowly humility, patient meekness and spotless purity — such as never before had been witnessed on earth, and never since has been exhibited by any of his followers. It is that Jesus, being such a personality as described by those who beheld his glory to be that of the only-begotten from the Father, full of grace and truth, put forth such pretensions and claims as were wholly unfitting in the lips of a mere man, and much more of a sinful man, declaring himself to be the Light of the World and the Bread of Life: giving out that he had power to forgive sins and to raise the dead; that he had pre-existed before he came to earth and would return to that pre-existent state when his work was done, which work was to die for men's sins; that he would rise from the dead and ascend up into heaven, both of which he actually did; and asserting that he was the Son of God, the equal of the Father and the future Judge of mankind. The Christian studying this picture perceives that, while to it belong the lineaments of a man, it also wears the likeness of a God, and he reasons that if that picture was drawn from the life (and how otherwise could it have been drawn?), then a God must once have walked this earth in the person of Jesus. For the Christian no other conclusion is possible.

3. *Without a God the Christian cannot understand the facts of his own consciousness.*

Take first the idea of God of which he finds himself possessed on arriving at the age of intelligence and responsibility. How it comes to pass that this great idea should arise within him if no such being as God exists, is something he cannot understand. To say that he has simply inherited it from his parents or absorbed it from his contemporaries, is not to solve the problem, but only to put it back from generation to generation. The question remains, How did this idea first originate in the soul? To answer that it gradually grew up out of totemism and animism as practiced by the low-grade races who, impelled by superstitious fears, conceived material objects to be inhabited by ghosts or spirits, is equally an evasion of the problem. Because again the question arises, How did these low-grade races arrive at the conception of spirits as distinguished from bodies or material objects in general? Should it be responded that veneration for deceased ancestors begat the conception of a God, one must further demand by what process of reasoning they were conducted from the conception of as many gods as there were deceased ancestors to that of one Supreme Deity or Lord of all. The only satisfactory explanation of the latent consciousness of God which man in all ages and lands has shown himself to be possessed of is, that it is one of the soul's intuitions, a part of the intellectual and moral furniture with which it comes into the world; that at first this idea or intuition lies within the soul as a seed corn which gradually opens out as the ·soul rises into full possession of its powers and is appealed to by external nature; that had sin not entered into the world this idea or intuition would have everywhere expanded into full bloom, filling the soul with a clear and radiant conception of the Divine Being, in whose image it has been made; but that now in consequence of the blighting influence of sin this idea or intuition has been everywhere more or less dimmed or weakened and in heathen nations corrupted and debased.

Then rising to the distinctly religious experience of conversion, the Christian encounters a whole series or group of phenomena which to him are inexplicable, if there is no God. Conscious of a change partly intellectual but mainly moral and spiritual, a change so complete as to amount to an inward revolution, what Scripture calls a new birth or a new creation, he cannot trace it to education or to environment, to philosophical reflection or to prudential considerations. The only reasonable account he can furnish of it is that he has been laid hold of by an unseen but Superhuman Power, so that he feels constrained to say like Paul: "By the grace of God I am what I am." And not only so, but as the result of this inward change upon his nature, he realizes that he stands in a new relation to that Supreme Power which has quickened and renewed him, that he can and does enter into personal communion with him through Jesus Christ, addressing to him prayers and receiving from him benefits and blessings in answer to those prayers.

These experiences of which the Christian is conscious may be characterized by the non-Christian as illusions, but to the Christian they are realities; and being realities they make it simply impossible for him to believe there is no God. Rather they inspire him with confidence that God is, and is the Rewarder of them that diligently seek him, and that of him and through him and to him are all things; to whom be glory for ever. Amen.

ROBERT ELLIOTT SPEER (1867-1947) was one of America's most effective promoters of foreign missions. A graduate of Princeton University, in 1891 Speer interrupted his course at Princeton Seminary to become Secretary of Foreign Missions for the Presbyterian Board of Foreign Missions. He never returned to complete his seminary course but spent the next fifty-six years traveling and challenging Christians to invest their lives and wealth in the spreading of the gospel. In 1927 he was elected moderator of the Presbyterian Church of the United States, at that time the second layman to hold the position. Edinburgh University granted him an honorary doctorate in 1910. He wrote or edited sixty-seven books, among them *The Principles of Jesus, The Man Paul, Missions and Politics in Asia,* and *The Finality of Jesus Christ.*

22

God in Christ the Only Revelation of the Fatherhood of God

By Robert E. Speer
SECRETARY, PRESBYTERIAN BOARD OF FOREIGN MISSIONS

Abridged and emended by James H. Christian, Th.D.

They shall put you out of the synagogues: yea, the hour cometh, that whosoever killeth you shall think that he offereth service unto God. And these things will they do, because they have not known the Father nor me (John 16: 2, 3).

These words suggest to us that it is not enough for a man just to believe in God. Everything depends on what kind of a god it is in whom he believes. It is a rather striking and surprising comparison at first that our Lord institutes here between a mere belief in God and the possibly horrible moral consequences, on the one hand, and a knowledge of God in Christ and its sure moral effects, on the other. And the lesson would seem to be the inadequacy of any religious faith that does not recognize the revelation of the Father in Jesus Christ and that does not know Jesus Christ as God. It is a little hard for us to take such a great thought as this into our lives, and yet our Lord puts it in unmistakable clearness: on the one hand, the moral inadequacy of a mere belief in God; on the other hand, the moral and spiritual adequacy of a recognition of God as Father exposed in Christ as God.

Theism Not Sufficient

In the former of these two verses our Lord makes the first of these two points unmistakably clear. He saw no adequate guarantee of moral rectitude and justice in a mere theistic faith. He suffered in his own death the possibly bitter fruits of a mere theistic faith. The men who put him to death were ardent believers in God, and they thought they were doing a fine thing for God when they crucified the Son of God. And he told his disciples that the day would come when conscientious men would take out service of

God in executing them; and that those who would put them to death would not be bad men, but men who thought that by killing them they were doing God's will.

We see exactly the same great error in our own day. It is no sufficient protection to a man to believe in one God. Our Lord understood completely that a mere faith in God was not going to make a good man, that a man might believe in God and be a murderer, or an adulterer; he might believe in God and put the very apostles of Jesus Christ to death and think that thus he was doing God a great service.

Conscientiousness Not Sufficient

It seems to me that it is worthwhile to stop here for a moment incidentally to note how easy a thing it is for a man to be guilty of conscientious error and crime. It is no defense of a man's conduct to say that he is conscientiously satisfied with what he did. I suppose that most bad things have been done in all good conscience, and that most of the sins that we commit today we commit with a perfectly clean conscience. There is such a thing as a moral color-blindness that is just as real as a physical color-blindness. I was visiting a little while ago one of our well-known girl's schools, and had a discussion with one of the teachers, who said that she thought it did not make so much difference what a pupil believed or did, provided only she was conscientious in her belief and conduct. I told her that it must be quite easy to go to school to her if it did not matter whether you answered right or not, if only you were conscientiously honest in what you said. She might get two absolutely contrary answers to a question and mark each one of them perfect. The whole foundations of the moral universe fall out from beneath the man or the woman who will take that view of it, that there is not really any objective standard of right or wrong at all, that everything hinges on just how a person feels about it, and if they only feel comfortable over the thing it is all right. These men who were going to put the disciples of Jesus Christ to death had no qualms of conscience about it. They would think in doing it that they were doing God a service. The idea that our Lord means to bring out is this, that the standards of a man are dependent upon his conception of God, and he saw no guarantee of moral rectitude and justice in a man's life except as that man grasped the revelation of God as Father that had been made in Jesus Christ, and himself knew Jesus Christ as God.

Christ's Mention of "Father"

There is no room here to trace this great thought through all the teaching of our Lord. Lately, I read through the last discourses of Jesus in John with this in mind. Only four times does Jesus so much as mention the name of God, while he speaks of the Father at least forty times. Evidently our Lord conceived that his great message to men was a message of God as Father revealed in his own life, and he conceived this to be a great practical moral truth, that was to save men from those errors of judgment, of act, and of character about which a man has no sure guarantee under a mere monotheistic faith.

In Relation to Our Religious Faith

1. I think we might just as well now go right to the heart of the thing by considering, first of all, *the relationship of this revelation that Jesus Christ made of the Father-character of God in himself to our own religious faith.* We begin our Christian creed with the declaration, "I believe in God the Father Almighty." I believe that no man can say those words sincerely and honestly, with an intellectual understanding of what he is saying, who is not saying them with his feet solidly resting on the evangelical conviction; for we know practically nothing about God *as* Father except what we learn from the revelation of God as Father in Jesus Christ. Men say sometimes that the idea of God as Father was in the Old Testament, and there is a sense doubtless in which we can find it there: the Hebrews thought of God as the Father, the national Father of Israel.

Now and then there is some splendid burst in the prophets that contains that idea, as when Jeremiah, crying out for God, says, "I am a Father to Israel, and Ephraim is my firstborn." Or when Israel is itself crying out through Isaiah, "Jehovah is our Father. He is the potter and we are the clay." But in each sense it is a sort of nationalistic conception of God as the Father of the whole people, Israel. Turn some time to the 103rd Psalm, where there is the best expression of it, "Like as a father pitieth his children,.

so the Lord pitieth them that fear him," and even there it is the
national cry.   Or turn to the 89th Psalm, and there, too, it is
national and patriotic: "He shall cry unto me, thou art my Father,
my God, and the rock of my salvation."   And if in all the great
body of the religious poetry of Israel there are only two or three
distinct notes of the fatherhood of God, we cannot believe that
that idea filled any very large place in the heart of Israel.   And in
the very last of all the Old Testament prophecies, the complaint
of God is just this, that the Israelites would not conceive of him as
their Father, and that even the political conception of God as the
Father of the nation was no reality in the experience of the people.

A New Conception

The revelation of God as the Father of men was a practically
new conception exposed in the teaching and in the life of our
Lord Jesus Christ — not in his teaching alone.   We should never
have known God as Father by the message of Jesus Christ only;
we should never have been able to conceive what Christ's idea of
God was if we had not seen that idea worked out in the very person
of Jesus Christ himself.   It was not alone that he told us what
God was.   He said that when he walked before men, he was himself one with the Father on whom the eyes of men might gaze:
"I am the way, and the truth, and the life: no one cometh unto the
Father, but by me.   If ye had known me, ye would have known my
Father also; from henceforth ye have known him and have
seen him.   Philip saith unto him, Lord, show us the Father, and
it sufficeth us.   Jesus said unto him, Have I been so long time with
you, and dost thou not know me, Philip?   He that hath seen me
hath seen the Father; how sayest thou, Show us the Father?
Believest thou not that I am in the Father, and the Father in me?
The words that I say unto you I speak not from myself: but the
Father abiding in me doeth his works."

John and Matthew

We cannot separate the Christological elements of the Gospel
from the Gospel.   The effort is made by throwing the Gospel of
John out of court, and then we are told that with the Gospel of
John gone, the real work of Christ was just in his message,
making known the Father to men; and that the Christological

character that we impose upon the Gospel was something foisted upon it later, and not something lying in the mind and thought of Jesus Christ himself. But I do not see how men can take that view of it until they cut out also the 11th chapter of Matthew. Christ sets forth there the essentially Christological character of his Gospel just as unmistakably as it is set forth anywhere in the Gospel of John: "No man knoweth the Son save the Father; and no man knoweth the Father save the Son, and he to whomsoever the Son willeth to reveal him." You cannot tear Christ's revelation of the fatherhood of God away from the person of Christ. He did not expose the fatherhood of God by what he said; he exposed the fatherhood of God by what he was; and it is a species of intellectual misconception to take certain words of his and say those words entitle us to believe in God as our Father, while we reject Jesus Christ as his Divine Son, and think that it is possible to hold to the first article of our Christian creed without going on to the second article of it, "And I believe in Jesus Christ, his only Son, our Lord."

Christ Is All

If you and I subtract from our conception of God what we owe to the person of Jesus Christ, we have practically nothing left. The disciples knew that they would have little left. When it was proposed that they should separate themselves from Christ and the revelation that he was making, these men stood absolutely dumbfounded. "Why, Lord," they said, "what is to become of us? We have no place to go. Thou hast the words of eternal life. There is nothing for us in Judaism any more." Monotheism was in Judaism; the revelation of God was in Judaism; but that was nothing to the disciples now that they had seen that glorious vision of his Father made known to men in Jesus Christ his Son. It would seem to follow that our attitude towards Jesus Christ is determinative of our life in the Father, and that the imagination that we have a life in the Father that rests on a rejection of the claims of Jesus Christ is an imagination with no foundations under it at all. Take those great words of our Lord: "He that loveth me not keepeth not my words; and the word which ye hear is not mine, but the Father's who sent me. If a man love me, he will keep my word: and my Father will love him, and we will

come unto him and make our abode with him." What Jesus is
setting forth there as the condition of a right attitude toward God
is a man's acceptance of the inner secret of his own life, a man's
deliberate committing of himself to the great principles that underlie the character and the person of Jesus, a sympathetic union with
himself. And he summed it all up in those words to Philip, "He
that hath seen me hath seen the Father." It is in this sense, I say,
that you and I cannot honestly declare that we "believe in God the
Father" unless we go right on to say, "And in Jesus Christ, his
only Son, our Lord," for we know practically nothing about God
as Father except what was revealed of God as Father in him who
said, "I and the Father are one." Do we believe in the fatherhood
of God in that sense?

Practical Application

2. Perhaps we can answer that question better by going on to
ask, in the second place, whether we are *realizing in our lives all
the practical implications of this revelation of the Father-character
of God in Jesus Christ.* For one thing, think how it *interprets the
mystery and the testing of life.* Now life is simply an enigma on
the merely theistic hypothesis. We get absolutely no comfort, no
light, no illumination upon what we know to be the great problem
of life from a simple belief in God. It only becomes intelligible
to us as we understand God to be our Father in the sense in which
Jesus Christ revealed him. Dr. Babcock used to put it in the
simple phrase: "You have got to take one of two interpretations of
it. You have got to read it in the terms of fatherhood." Once I
accept the revelation of God made in Jesus Christ, my life is
still a hard problem to me. There are many things in it that are
terribly confused and difficult still; but I begin to get a little
light on its deep and impenetrable mysteries. It was just in this
point of view that the writer of the great Epistle to the Hebrews
thought he had some clue to the mystery of his own life, to the
chastening of it, to the hard and burning discipline through which
he sees we are all passing. It was only when he conceived of himself as being a son of the great Potter who was shaping the clay
himself that the mystery began to clear a little from his pathway.
And it was just so, you remember, that Christ got light on the
mystery of his life: "Father, not my will, but thine be done."

Only as he remembered and rested deeply upon the character of God as his Father did those great experiences through which he was passing have full intelligibility to him. After all, it was no fancy that connected the two great ideas of Isaiah, the living idea of the fatherhood of God and the metaphorical idea of God as the Potter shaping his clay. It is only so that we understand both aspects of our human life. When the wheel moves fast, and the hand of the Potter seems cruel upon the clay, and the friction is full of terrible heat, we begin to understand something of it all in realizing that the Potter's hand is the hand of a Father shaping in fatherly discipline the life of his son. "If ye endure chastening, God dealeth with you as sons."

Our Ideals

Or think, in the second place, how this conception of God *inspires and rectifies the ideals of our lives.* It was this that suggested the idea to Jesus here. He saw that there was absolutely no guarantee of right standards of life in a mere theistic faith, and there is none. We have no guarantee whatever of just and perfect moral ideals that we do not get from the exposure of the Father-character of God in the person of Jesus Christ and from personal union with God in him.

As a simple matter of fact the best ideals of our life we all owe to just that revelation. The ideal of purity — the Jews never had it. They had an ideal of ritual cleanliness, but they had no Christian ideal of moral purity. You cannot find the ideal of purity anywhere in the world where the conception of the Father-revelation of God in Christ has not gone. Explain it as you will, it is a simple fact of comparative religion. Can any man find the full ideal of moral purity anywhere in this world where it has not been created by the revelation of the Father-character of God in Christ? We owe it to that, and we cannot be sure of its perpetuation save where the conviction of that great revelation abides in the faith of man.

Or take our ideal of work. Where did Christ get his ideal of work? "My Father worketh hitherto, and I work." On what ground did he rest his claim upon men to work? "Son, go work today in my vineyard." Our whole ideal of a workingmen's life,

of a man's using his life to the fullness of its power in an unselfish service, is an ideal born of the revelation of the Father-
character of God in Christ.   And forgiveness is an ideal of the
same kind.   We owe all the highest and noblest ideals of our life
to that revelation.   And it seems to us something less than fair
for a man to take those ideals and then deny their origin, trampling
under foot the claims of him from whom those ideals came into
our lives.

Sweetens Obedience

And think *how rational and sweet this conception of God makes
obedience.*   There is something rational but hardly sweet in the
thought of obedience to him under the simple theistic conception.
All the joy of obedience comes when I think of myself as my
Father's son and sent to do my Father's will.   Our Lord thought
of his life just so.   "Simon," he said — that last night that Simon
tried to defend him by force — "put up thy sword into its sheath.
The cup which my Father hath given me, shall I not drink it?"
We get our ideals of obedience and the joy and the delight of
obedience from the thought that after all we are simply to obey
our Father.   In the 14th chapter of the Gospel of John, we get
a little vision of what Christ conceives to be the sweetness and the
tenderness and the beauty that can come into life from a real
acceptance of this revealing of his.   "In that day," he says, "ye
shall know that I am in my Father, and ye in me, and I in you.
He that hath my commandments and keepeth them, he it is that
loveth me; and he that loveth me shall be loved of my Father,
and I will love him and will manifest myself unto him.   If a man
love me, he will keep my word; and my Father will love him,
and we will come unto him and make our abode with him."

Relation to Prayer Life

3.   And, last of all, think on *the light that this conception
of God throws upon our life of prayer.*   I suspect that prayer
has been just a sham to many of us, or a thing that we have done,
because other people told us it was the thing to do.   We never
got anything out of it; it never meant anything to us.   We might
just as well have talked to stone walls as to pray the way we
have prayed.   We went out and said, "God," and we might
just as well have said, "hills," or "mountains," or "trees," or

anything else. Why have we not gone into the school of Christ and learned there, alike from his practice and his doctrine, what real prayer is and how a man can do it.

I hope I am not misunderstood. I am meaning only that Christ's conception of God and his practice of prayer did not rest merely on the theistic interpretation of the universe and the nature of its Creator in his majesty and almightiness. They rested on the Father-conception which he revealed in himself. Just run over in your thought his prayers: the prayer that he taught us to pray, "Our Father, who art in heaven"; the prayer he offered himself when the disciples of John the Baptist came to him: "I thank thee, Father, Lord of heaven and earth, that thou hast hidden these things from the wise and the understanding, and hast revealed them unto babes. Even so, Father, for it seemeth good in thy sight"; the prayer that he offered in the temple, when Philip and Andrew came to him with the message about the Greeks who were seeking to see him: "Now is my soul troubled, and what shall I say? Father, save me from this hour? But for this cause came I unto this hour"; the prayer that he offered before the grave of Lazarus, "Father, I thank thee that thou hearest me, and I know that thou hearest me always"; the prayer that he put up in Gethsemane, "My Father, if this cup cannot pass from me except I drink it, thy will be done"; and the last prayer of all, when, as a tired little child, he lay down in his Father's arms and fell asleep; "Father, into thy hands I commend my spirit." What a reality this conception of prayer gives to it. We are not praying to any cold theistic God alone; we are praying to our Father made real to us, warm with the warmth of a great tenderness for us, living with a great consciousness of all our human suffering and struggle and conflict and need.

It makes prayer, for one thing, a rational thing. I can go to my Father and ask him for the things that I need. There is an exquisite passage in Andrew Bonar's journals in which he speaks of sitting one day in his study, and looking out of his window and seeing two of his children pass through the fields. He said as he saw those little children making their way across the fields, the love in his heart overcame him, and he pushed his books away from him on the table, and went to the door and called out across the field to them, and they came running eagerly in response to their father's loving call. And when they had come and he had carressed them, he said he gave each one of them something simply because the ecstasy of his fatherly love made it impossible that he should not do something then for those two children who were so dear to his heart. Do you suppose that God is an inferior sort of a father? Prayer in the sense of supplication for real things becomes a rational reality to men who believe in God in Jesus Christ.

Fellowship

And how sweet it makes prayer in the sense of living fellowship. Do you suppose that we are nobler characters than that great Father after whom these human fatherhoods of ours are named? Do you suppose that if it is sweet to us to have our little children come creeping to us in the dark, it is not sweet to our heavenly Father here, everywhere, to have men, his sons, come stealing to his side and his love? This is no excessive way of putting it. Is it not guaranteed to us by those words which our Lord spoke that Easter morning as he stood there by his open grave, and the woman who adored him was about to clasp his feet, "Mary, go and tell my disciples that I ascend unto my Father, and your Father, my God and your God." Yes, that is the right way to put it today. No God for us, nowhere through the whole universe a real and satisfying God for us, except the God who is discovered to us in Jesus Christ, and who is calling to us today by the lips of Christ, "My son, O my son," and who would have us call back to him, if we be true men, "My Father, O my Father."

BENJAMIN BRECKINRIDGE WARFIELD (1851-1921) studied at Princeton College, Princeton Seminary and the University of Leipzig, Germany. Ordained in 1879, Warfield taught at Western Theological Seminary, Allegheny, PA, from 1878 until he went to Princeton Seminary in 1887, where he remained until his death in 1921. He followed Dr. A. A. Hodge and maintained the conservative Calvinistic position of that great theologian. From 1890 to 1902, he edited *The Presbyterian and Reformed Review*. Many of his books are still read today, including *Biblical and Theological Studies*, *Calvin and Augustine*, *Inspiration and Authority of the Bible*, *The Person and Work of Christ*, *Perfectionism*, and *Counterfeit Miracles*.

23

The Deity of Christ

By Professor Benjamin B. Warfield, D.D., LL.D.
PRINCETON THEOLOGICAL SEMINARY

Revised and edited by Gerald B. Stanton, Th.D.

A noted writer has remarked that our assured conviction of the deity of Christ rests, not upon "proof-texts or passages, nor upon old argument drawn from these, but upon the general face of the whole manifestation of Jesus Christ, and of the whole impression left by him upon the world." His antithesis is too absolute, and possibly betrays an unwarranted distrust of the evidence of Scripture. To make it acceptable, we should read the statement rather: "Our conviction of the deity of Christ rests not alone on the scriptural passages which assert it, but also upon his entire impression on the world." Or perhaps: "Our conviction rests not more on the scriptural assertions than upon his entire manifestation." Both lines of evidence are valid, and when twisted together form an unbreakable cord. The proof-texts and passages do prove that Jesus was esteemed divine by those who companied with him; that he esteemed himself divine; that he was recognized as divine by those who were taught by the Spirit; that, in fine, he was divine. But over and above this biblical evidence, the impression Jesus has left upon the world bears independent testimony to his deity, and it may well be that to many minds this will seem the most conclusive of all its evidences. It certainly is very cogent and impressive.

The Nature of Evidence

A man recognizes on sight the face of his friend, or his own handwriting. Ask him how he knows this face to be that of his friend, or this handwriting to be his own, and he may be dumb, or, seeking to reply, may babble nonsense. Yet his recognition rests on solid grounds, though he lacks analytical skill to isolate and state these solid grounds. We believe in God and freedom and immortality on good grounds, though we may not be able satisfactorily to analyze these grounds. No true conviction exists without adequate rational grounding in evidence. So, if we are solidly assured of the deity of Christ, it will be on adequate grounds, appealing to the reason. But it may well be on grounds not analyzed, perhaps not analyzable, by us, so as to exhibit themselves in the forms of formal logic.

We do not need to wait to analyze the grounds of our convictions before they operate to produce convictions, any more than we need to wait to analyze our food before it nourishes us. The Christian's conviction of the deity of his Lord does not depend for its soundness on the Christian's ability convincingly to state the grounds of his conviction. The evidence he offers for it may be wholly inadequate, while the evidence on which it rests may be absolutely compelling.

Testimony in Solution

The very abundance and persuasiveness of the evidence for the deity of Christ greatly increases the difficulty of stating it adequately. This is true even of the scriptural evidence, as precise and definite as much of it is. For it is a true remark of Dr. Dale's that the particular texts in which it is definitely asserted are far from whole, or even the most impressive, proofs which the Scriptures supply of our Lord's deity. He compares these texts to the salt-crystals which appear on the sand of the sea-beach after the tide has receded. "These are not," he remarks, "the strongest, though they may be the most apparent, proofs that the sea is salt; the salt is present in solution in every bucket of sea-water." The deity of Christ is in solution in every page of the New Testament. Every word that is spoken of him, every word which he is reported to have spoken of himself, is spoken on the assumption that he is God. That is the reason why the "criticism" which addresses itself to eliminating the testimony of the New Testament to the deity of our Lord has set itself a hopeless task. The New Testament itself would have to be eliminated. Nor can we get behind this testimony. Because the deity of Christ is the presupposition of every word of the New Testament, it is impossible to select words out of the New Testament from which to construct earlier documents in which the deity of Christ shall not be assumed. The assured conviction of the deity of Christ is contemporary with Christianity itself. There never was a Christianity, neither in the times of the Apostles nor since, of which this was not a prime tenet.

A Saturated Gospel

Let us observe in an example or two how thoroughly saturated the Gospel narrative is with the assumption of the deity of Christ, so that it crops out in the most unexpected ways and places.

In three passages of Matthew, reporting words of Jesus, he is represented as speaking familiarly and in the most natural manner in the world, of "*his* angels" (13:41; 16:27; 24:31). In all three he designates himself as the "Son of man"; and in all three there are additional suggestions of his majesty. "The Son of man shall send forth *his* angels, and they shall gather out of *his* kingdom all things that cause stumbling and those that do iniquity, and shall cast them into the furnace of fire."

Who is this Son of man who has angels, by whose instrumentality the final judgment is executed at his command? "The Son of man shall come in the glory of his Father with *his* angels; and then shall *he* reward every man according to his deeds." Who is this Son of man surrounded by *his* angels, in whose hand are the issues of life? The Son of man "shall send forth *his* angels with a great sound of a trumpet, and they shall gather together *his* elect from the four winds, from one end of heaven to the other." Who is this Son of man at whose behest his angels winnow men? A scrutiny of the passages will show that it is not a peculiar body of angels which is meant by the Son of man's angels, but just the angels as a body, who are his to serve him as he commands. In a word, Jesus Christ is above angels (Mark 13:32) — as is argued at explicit length at the beginning of the Epistle to the Hebrews. "To which of the angels said he at any time, Sit on my right hand . . ." (Heb. 1:13).

Heaven Come to Earth

There are three parables recorded in the fifteenth chapter of Luke as spoken by our Lord in his defense against the murmurs of the Pharisees at his receiving sinners and eating with them. The essence of the defense which our Lord offers for himself is, that there is joy *in heaven* over repentant sinners! Why "in heaven," "before the throne of God"? Is he merely setting the judgment of heaven over against that of earth, or pointing forward to his future vindication? By no means. He is representing his action in receiving sinners, in seeking the lost, as his proper action because it is the normal conduct of heaven manifested in him. He is heaven come to earth. His defense is thus simply the unveiling of the real nature of the transaction. The lost when they come to him are received because this is heaven's way; and *he* cannot act otherwise than in heaven's way. He tacitly assumes the good Shepherd's part as his own.

The Unique Position

All the great designations are not so much asserted as assumed by him for himself. He does not call himself a prophet, though he accepts this designation from others. He places himself above all the prophets, even above John, the greatest of the prophets, as him to whom all the prophets look forward. If he calls himself Messiah, he fills that term by doing so with a deeper significance, dwelling over on the unique relation of Messiah to God as his representative and his Son. Nor is he satisfied to represent himself merely as standing in unique relation to God. He proclaims himself to be the recipient of the divine fullness, the sharer in all that God has (Matt. 11:28). He speaks freely of himself indeed as God's Other, the manifestation of God on earth, whom to have seen was to have seen the Father also, and who does the work of God on earth. He openly claims divine prerogatives — the reading of the heart of man, the forgiveness of sins, the exercise of all authority in heaven and earth. Indeed, all that God has and is he asserts himself to have and be; omnipotence, omniscience, perfection belong as to the one so to the other. Not only does he perform all divine acts, his self-consciousness coalesces with the divine consciousness. If his followers lagged in recognizing his deity, this was not because he was not God or did not sufficiently manifest his deity. It was because they were foolish and slow of heart to believe what lay so patently before their eyes.

The Greatest Proof

The Scriptures give us evidence enough, then, that Christ is God. But the Scriptures are far from giving us all the evidence we have. There is, for example, the revolution which Christ has wrought in the world. If, indeed, it were asked what the most convincing proof of the deity of Christ is, perhaps the best answer would be, just Christianity. The new life he has brought into the world; the new creation which he has produced by his life and work in the world; here are at least his most palpable credentials.

Take it objectively. Read the historical account of the advance and conquest of Christianity in the days of the primitive Church, and then ask: Could these things have been wrought by power less than divine? And then remember that these things were not only wrought in that heathen world two thousand years ago, but have been wrought over again every generation since, for Christianity has re-conquered the world to itself each generation. Think of how the Christian proclamation spread, eating its way over the world like fire in the grass of a prairie. Think how, as it spread, it transformed lives. The thing, whether in its objective or in its subjective aspect, were incredible, had it not actually occurred. "Should a voyager," says Charles Darwin, "chance to be on the point of shipwreck on some unknown coast, he will most devoutly pray that the lesson of the missionary may have reached thus far. The lesson of the missionary is the enchanter's wand." Could this transforming influence, undiminished after two millenniums, have proceeded from a mere man? It is historically impossible that the great movement which we call Christianity, which remains unspent after all these years, could have originated in a merely human impulse, or could represent today the working of a merely human force.

The Proof Within

Or take it subjectively. Every Christian has within himself the proof of the transforming power of Christ, and can repeat the blind man's syllogism: Why herein is the marvel that ye know not whence he is, and yet he opened my eyes. "Shall we trust," demands an eloquent reasoner, "the touch of our fingers, the sight of our eyes, the hearing of our ears, and not trust our deepest consciousness of our higher nature — the answer of conscience, the flower of spiritual gladness, the glow of spiritual love? To deny that spiritual experience is as real as physical experience is to slander the noblest faculties of our nature. It is to say that one half of our nature tells the truth, and the other half utters lies. The proposition that facts in the spiritual region are less real than facts in the physical realm contradicts all philosophy." The transformed hearts of Christians, registering themselves "in gentle tempers, in noble motives, in lives visibly lived under the empire of great aspirations" — these are the ever-present proofs of the divinity of the Person from whom their inspiration is drawn.

The supreme proof to every Christian of the deity of his Lord is then his own inner experience of the transforming power of his Lord upon the heart and life. Not more surely does he who feels the present warmth of the sun know that the sun exists, than he who has experienced the recreative power of the Lord know him to be his Lord and his God. Here is, perhaps we may say the proper, certainly we must say the most convincing, proof to every Christian of the deity of Christ; a proof which he cannot escape, and to which, whether he is capable of analyzing it or drawing it out in logical statement or not, he cannot fail to yield his sincere and unassailable conviction. Whatever else he may or may not be assured of, he knows that his Redeemer lives. Because he lives, we shall live also — that was the Lord's own assurance. Because we live, he lives also — that is the ineradicable conviction of every Christian heart.

JAMES ORR (1844-1913) graduated from Glasgow University in his native Scotland. Between 1874 and 1891, he was a parish minister at East Bank United Presbyterian Church in Hawick. He left the pastorate to teach church history at the United Presbyterian Theological College in Glasgow until 1901, when he became professor of apologetics and dogmatics at Glasgow (later called Trinity) College. Orr enjoyed studying the progress of church doctrine, which he saw as following a divine logic. His major works included *The Christian View of God and the World* (1893, republished in 1989 by Kregel Publications) and *The Progress of Dogma* (1897).

24

The Virgin Birth of Christ

By Professor James Orr, D.D.
UNITED FREE CHURCH COLLEGE, GLASGOW, SCOTLAND

Revised and edited by Gerald B. Stanton, Th.D.

It is well known that the last half century has been marked by a determined assault upon the truth of the virgin birth of Christ. In the year 1892 a great controversy broke out in Germany, owing to the refusal of a pastor named Schrempf to use the Apostles' Creed in baptism because of disbelief in this and other articles. Schrempf was deposed, and an agitation commenced against the doctrine of the virgin birth which has grown in volume ever since. Other tendencies, especially the rise of an extremely radical school of historical criticism, added force to the negative movement. The attack is not confined, indeed, to the article of the virgin birth. It affects the whole supernatural estimate of Christ — his life, his claims, his sinlessness, his miracles, his resurrection from the dead. But the virgin birth is assailed with special vehemence, because it is supposed that the evidence for this miracle is more easily got rid of than the evidence for public facts, such as the resurrection. The result is that in very many quarters the virgin birth of Christ is openly treated as a fable, and belief in it is scouted as unworthy of the twentieth century intelligence.

The Unhappiest Feature

It is not only in the circles of unbelief that the virgin birth is discredited; in the church itself the habit is spreading of casting doubt upon the fact, or at least of regarding it as no essential part of Christian faith. This is the unhappiest feature in this unhappy controversy. The article, it is affirmed, did not belong to the earliest Christian tradition, and the evidence for it is not strong. Therefore, let it drop.

From the side of criticism, science, mythology, history and comparative religion, assault is thus made on this doctrine long so dear to the hearts of Christians and rightly deemed by them so vital to their faith. For loud as is the voice of denial, one fact must strike every careful observer of the conflict. Among those who reject the virgin birth of the Lord, few will be found — I do not know any — who take in other respects an adequate view of the person and work of the Saviour. Those who accept a full doctrine of the incarnation — that is, of a true entrance of the eternal Son of God into our nature for the purposes of man's salvation — with hardly an exception accept with it the doctrine of the virgin birth of Christ, while those who repudiate or deny this article of faith either hold a lowered view of Christ's person, or more commonly, reject his supernatural claims altogether. The great bulk of the opponents of the virgin birth — those who are conspicuous by writing against it — are in the latter class.

The Case Stated

It is the object of this paper to show that those who take the lines of denial on the virgin birth just sketched do great injustice to the evidence and importance of the doctrine they reject. The evidence, if not of the same public kind as that for the resurrection, is far stronger than the objector allows, and the fact denied enters far more vitally into the essence of the Christian faith than he supposes. Placed in its right setting among the other truths of the Christian religion, it is not only no stumbling-block to faith, but is felt to fit in with self-evidencing power into the connection of these other truths, and to furnish the very explanation that is needed of Christ's holy and supernatural person. The ordinary Christian is a witness here. In reading the Gospels, he feels no incongruity in passing from the narratives of the virgin birth to the wonderful story of Christ's life in the chapters that follow, then from these to the pictures of Christ's divine dignity given in John and Paul. The whole is of one piece: the virgin birth is as natural at the beginning of the life of such an one — the divine Son — as the resurrection is at the end. And the more closely the matter is considered, the stronger does this impression grow. It is only when the scriptural conception of Christ is parted with that various difficulties and doubts come in.

A Superficial View

It is, in truth, a *very superficial* way of speaking or thinking of the virgin birth to say that nothing depends on this belief
for our estimate of Christ. Who that reflects on the subject carefully can fail to see that if Christ was virgin born — if he was
truly "conceived," as the creed says, "by the Holy Ghost, born of
the Virgin Mary" — there must of necessity enter a supernatural
element into his person; while, if Christ was sinless, much more,
if he was the very Word of God incarnate, there must have been a
miracle — the most stupendous miracle in the universe — in his
origin? If Christ was, as John and Paul affirm and his Church
has ever believed, the Son of God made flesh, the second Adam,
the new redeeming Head of the race, a miracle was to be expected
in his earthly origin; without a miracle such a person could never
have been. Why then cavil at the narratives which declare the
fact of such a miracle? Who does not see that the Gospel history
would have been incomplete without them? Inspiration here only
gives to faith what faith on its own grounds imperatively demands
for its perfect satisfaction.

The First Promise

It is time now to come to the *Scripture itself,* and to look
at the fact of the virgin birth in its historical setting, and its
relation with other truths of the Gospel. As preceding the examination of the historical evidence, a little may be said, first, on the
Old Testament preparation. Was there any such preparation?
Some would say there was not, but this is not God's way, and we
may look with confidence for at least some indications which point
in the direction of the New Testament event.

One's mind turns first to that *oldest of all evangelical promises,*
that the seed of the woman would bruise the head of the serpent.
"I will put enmity," says Jehovah to the serpent-tempter, "between
thee and the woman, and between thy seed and her seed; he shall
bruise thy head, and thou shalt bruise his heel" (Genesis 3:15,
ASV). The "serpent" in this passage is Satan, and the "seed"
who should destroy him is described emphatically as the *woman's*
seed. It was the woman through whom sin had entered the race;
by the seed of the woman would salvation come. The early church
writers often pressed this analogy between Eve and the Virgin

Mary. We may reject any element of overexaltation of Mary they connected with it, but it remains significant that this peculiar phrase should be chosen to designate the future deliverer. I cannot believe the choice to be of accident. The promise to Abraham was that in *his* seed the families of the earth would be blessed; there the *male* is emphasized, but here it is the *woman* — the woman distinctively.

The Immanuel Prophecy

The idea of the Messiah, gradually gathering to itself the attributes of a divine King, reaches one of its clearest expressions in *the great Immanuel prophecy,* extending from Isaiah 7 to 9:7, and centering in the declaration: "The Lord himself will give you a sign; behold, a virgin shall conceive, and bear a son, and shall call his name Immanuel" (Isa. 7:14; Cf. 8:8, 10). This is none other than the child of wonder extolled in chapter 9:6, 7. This is the prophecy quoted as fulfilled in Christ's birth in Matthew 1:23, and it seems also alluded to in the glowing promises to Mary in Luke 1:32, 33. It is pointed out in objection that the term rendered "virgin" in Isaiah does not necessarily bear this meaning; it denotes properly only a young unmarried woman. The context, however, seems clearly to lay an emphasis on the unmarried state, and the translators of the Greek version of the Old Testament (the Septagint) plainly so understood it when they rendered it by *parthenos,* a word which *does* mean "virgin." It is singular that the Jews themselves do not seem to have applied this prophecy at any time to the Messiah — a fact which disproves the theory that it was this text which suggested the story of a virgin birth to the early disciples.

Testimony of the Gospel

This record found in the prophetic Scriptures had apparently borne no fruit in Jewish expectations of the Messiah, when *the event took place* which to Christian minds made them luminous with predictive import. In Bethlehem of Judea, as Micah had foretold, was born of a virgin mother he whose "goings forth" were "from of old, from everlasting" (Micah 5:2; Matt. 2:6). Matthew, who quotes the first part of the verse, can hardly have been ignorant of the hint of pre-existence it contained. This brings us to the testimony to the miraculous birth of Christ in our first and third Gospels — the only Gospels which record the circumstances of Christ's birth at all. By general consent the narratives in Matthew (chapters 1, 2) and in Luke (chapters 1, 2) are independent — that is, they are not derived one from the other — yet they both affirm, in detailed story, that Jesus, conceived by the power of the Holy Spirit, was born of a pure virgin, Mary of Nazareth, espoused to Joseph, whose wife she afterwards became. The birth took place at Bethlehem, whither Joseph and Mary had gone for enrollment in a census that was being taken. The announcement was made to Mary beforehand by an angel, and the birth was preceded, attended, and followed by remarkable events that are narrated (birth of the Baptist, with annunciations, angelic vision to the shepherds, visit of wise men from the east, etc.) The narratives should be carefully read at length to understand the comments that follow.

The Testimony Tested

There is no doubt, therefore, about the testimony to the virgin birth, and the question which now arises is — what is the *value* of these parts of the Gospels as evidence? Are they genuine parts of the Gospels? Or are they late and untrustworthy additions? From what sources may they be presumed to be derived? It is on the truth of the narratives that our belief in the virgin birth depends. Can they be trusted? Or are they mere fables, inventions, legends, to which no credit can be attached?

The answer to several of these questions can be given in very brief form. The narratives of the nativity in Matthew and Luke are undoubtedly *genuine parts* of their respective Gospels. They have been there since ever the Gospels themselves had an existence. The proof of this is convincing. The chapters in question are found in every manuscript and version of the Gospels known to exist. There are hundreds of manuscripts, some of them very old, belonging to different parts of the world, and many versions in different languages (Latin, Syriac, Egyptian, etc.), but these narratives of the virgin birth are found in all. We know, indeed, that a section of the early Jewish Christians — the Ebionites, as they are commonly called — possessed a Gospel based on Matthew from which the chapters on the nativity were absent. But this was not the real Gospel of Matthew: it was at best a mutilated and corrupted form of it. The genuine Gospel, as the manuscripts attest, always had these chapters.

Next, as to the Gospels themselves, they were not of late and non-apostolic origin; but were written by apostolic men, and were from the first accepted and circulated in the church as trustworthy embodiments of sound apostolic tradition. Luke's Gospel was from Luke's own pen and Matthew's Gospel, while some dubiety still rests on its original language (Aramaic or Greek), passed without challenge in the early church as the genuine Gospel of the Apostle Matthew. The narratives come to us, accordingly, with high apostolic sanction.

As to the sources of the narratives concerning the virgin birth in these two Gospels, the information they convey was derived from no lower source than Joseph and Mary themselves. This is a marked feature of contrast in the narratives — that Matthew's account is all told from Joseph's point of view, and Luke's is all told from Mary's. The signs of this are unmistakable. Matthew tells about Joseph's difficulties and action, and says little or nothing about Mary's thoughts and feelings. Luke tells much about Mary — even her inmost thoughts — but says next to nothing directly about Joseph. The narratives are not, as some would have it, contradictory, but are independent and complementary. The one supplements and completes the other. Both together are needed to give the whole story. They bear in themselves the stamp of truth, honesty, and purity, and are worthy of all acceptation, as they were evidently held to be in the early church.

Unfounded Objections

Against the acceptance of these early, well-attested narratives, what, now, have the critics to allege? The objection on which most stress is laid is the *silence* on the virgin birth in the remaining Gospels, and other parts of the New Testament. This, it is held, conclusively proves that the virgin birth was not known in the earliest Christian circles, and was a legend of later origin. As respects the Gospels — Mark and John — the objection would only apply if it was the design of these Gospels to narrate, as the others do, the circumstances of the nativity. But this was not their design. Both Mark and John knew that Jesus had a human birth — an infancy and early life — and that his mother was called Mary, but of deliberate purpose they tell us nothing about it. Mark begins his Gospel with Christ's entrance on his public ministry and says nothing of the period before, especially of how Jesus came to be called "the Son of God" (Mark 1:1). John traces the divine descent of Jesus, and tells us that the "Word became flesh" (John 1:14); but how this miracle of becoming flesh was wrought he does not say. It did not lie within his plan. He knew the church tradition on the subject: he had the Gospels narrating the birth of Jesus from the virgin in his hands, and he takes the knowledge of their teaching for granted. To speak of contradiction in a case like this is out of the question.

How far Paul was acquainted with the facts of Christ's earthly origin it is not easy to say. To a certain extent these facts would always be regarded as among the privacies of the innermost Christian circles — so long at least as Mary lived — and the details may not have been fully known till the Gospels were published. Paul admittedly did not base his preaching of his Gospel on these private, interior matters, but on the broad, public facts of Christ's ministry, death, and resurrection. It would be going too far, however, to infer from this that Paul had no knowledge of the miracle of Christ's birth. Luke was Paul's companion, and doubtless shared with Paul all the knowledge which he himself had gathered on this and other subjects. One thing certain is, that Paul could not have believed in the divine dignity, the pre-existence, the sinless perfection, and the redeeming headship of Jesus as he did, and not have been convinced that his entrance into humanity was no ordinary event of nature, but implied an unparalleled miracle of some kind. This Son of God, who "emptied" himself, who was "born of a woman, born under the law," "who knew no sin" (Phil. 2:7, 8; Gal. 4:4; II Cor. 5:21), was not and could not be a simple product of nature. God must have wrought creatively in his human origin. The virgin birth would be to Paul the most reasonable and credible of events. So also to John, who held the same high view of Christ's dignity and holiness.

Christ's Sinlessness a Proof

It is sometimes argued that a virgin birth is no aid to the explanation of Christ's *sinlessness*. Mary being herself sinful in nature, it is held the taint of corruption would be conveyed by one parent as really as by two. It is overlooked that the whole fact is not expressed by saying that Jesus was born of a virgin mother. There is the other factor — "conceived by the Holy Ghost." What happened was a divine, creative miracle wrought in the production of this new humanity which secured, from its earliest germinal beginnings, freedom from the slightest taint of sin. Paternal generation in such an origin is superfluous. The birth of Jesus was not, as in ordinary births, the creation of a new personality. It was a divine Person — already existing — entering on this new mode of existence. Miracle could alone effect such a wonder.

The Early Church a Witness

The history of the early Church is occasionally appealed to in witness that the doctrine of the virgin birth was not primitive. No assertion could be more futile. The early Church as far as we can trace it back, in all its branches, held this doctrine. No Christian sect is known that denied it, save the Jewish Ebionites formerly alluded to. The general body of the Jewish Christians — the Nazarenes as they are called — accepted it. Even the greater Gnostic sects in their own way admitted it. Those Gnostics who denied it were repelled with all the force of the church's greatest teachers. The Apostle John is related to have vehemently opposed Cerinthus, the earliest teacher with whom this denial is connected.

Doctrinally, the belief in the virgin birth of Christ is of the highest value for the right apprehension of Christ's unique and sinless personality. Here is one, as Paul brings out in Romans 5:12 ff., who, free from sin himself, and not involved in the Adamic liabilities of the race, reverses the curse of sin and death brought in by the first Adam, and establishes the reign of righteousness and life. Had Christ been naturally born, not one of these things could be affirmed of him. As one of Adam's race, not an entrant from a higher sphere, he would have shared in Adam's corruption and doom — would himself have required to be redeemed. Through God's infinite mercy he came from above, inherited no guilt, needed no regeneration or sanctification, but became himself the Redeemer, Regenerator, Sanctifier, for all who receive him. "Thanks be unto God for his unspeakable gift" (II Cor. 9:15).

JOHN STOCK (1817-1884) wrote books with such varied titles as *Confessions of an Old Smoker*, *Advice to a Young Christian*, and *A Handbook of Revealed Theology*. Born in London and educated at the University College of London, Stock occupied the pulpit at Chatham, Salendine Nook, and Morice Square Davenport in his 42 years of preaching. In 1868, Stock received the LL.D. degree from Madison University in the United States.

25

The God-Man

By John Stock

Revised and Edited by Rev. Glenn O'Neal, Ph.D.

Jesus of Nazareth was not mere man, excelling others in purity of life, sincerity of purpose, and fulness of his knowledge. He is the God-man. Such a view of the person of Messiah is the assured foundation of the entire Scriptural testimony to him, and it is to be irresistibly inferred from the style and strain in which he habitually spake of himself. Of this inferential argument of the Saviour we can give here the salient points only in briefest presentation.

1. *Jesus claimed to be the Son of God.* In his interview with Nicodemus he designated himself "The Only Begotten Son of God" (John 3:18). This majestic title is repeatedly appropriated to himself by our Master. When confronted with the Sanhedrin, Jesus was closely questioned about his use of this title; and he pleaded guilty to the indictment (see Matt. 26:63, 64, and 27:43; cf. Luke 22:70, 71, and John 19:7). It is clear from the narrative that the Jews understood this glorious name in the lips of Jesus to be a blasphemous assertion of divine attributes for himself.

They understood Jesus to thus claim *equality with God* (see John 5:18); and to *make himself God* (see John 10:33). Did they understand him? Did they overestimate the significance of this title as claimed by our Lord? How easy it would have been for him to set them right. How imperative were his obligations to do so, not merely to himself, but to these unhappy men who were thirsting for his blood under a misapprehension. Did not every principle of philanthropy require him to save them from the perpetration of the terrible murder which he knew they were contemplating? Yes, if they were mistaken, it was a heinous crime in our Lord not to correct the deception. But not a word did he say to soften down the offensiveness of his claim. He allowed it to stand in all its repulsiveness to the Jewish mind, and died without making any sign that he had been misapprehended. He thus accepted the Jewish interpretation of his meaning, and sealed that sense of the title, *Son of God,* with his heart's blood. Nothing can be clearer, then, than the fact that Jesus died without a protest for claiming equality with God, and thus making himself God. We dare not trust ourselves to write what we must think of him under such circumstances, if he were a mere man.

2. *Jesus, on several occasions, claimed a divine supremacy in both worlds.* He claimed authority over the angels. Take for example his description of the final judgment: "The Son of man shall send forth his angels, and they shall gather out of his kingdom all things that offend, and them which do iniquity: and shall cast them into the furnace of fire: there shall be wailing and gnashing of teeth" (Matt. 13:41). The kingdom is his, and all the angels of God are his obedient servants.

He declared in the plainest terms that he will preside as the Universal Judge of men at the last great day, and that his wisdom and authority will award to every man his appropriate doom. "When the Son of man shall come in his glory, and all the holy angels with him, then shall he sit upon the throne of his glory; and before him shall be gathered all nations; and he shall separate them one from another, as a shepherd divideth his sheep from the goats; and he shall set the sheep on his right hand, but the goats on the left" (Matt. 25:31-33). His voice will utter the cheering words, "Come, ye blessed," and the awful sentence, "Depart, ye cursed" (Matt. 25:31-46). Without hesitation, equivocation, or compromise Jesus of Nazareth repeatedly assumed the right and the ability to discriminate the moral character and desserts of all mankind from Adam to the day of doom. His sublime consciousness of universal supremacy relieved the claim of everything like audacity, and only made it the natural sequence of his incarnate Godhead. "All power," he said, "is given unto me in heaven and in earth" (Matt. 28:18).

This idea germinated in the minds of his followers and apostles. The vivid picture recorded in the twenty-fifth chapter of Matthew gave a coloring to all their subsequent thoughts about their divine

Master. They ever after spake of him as "ordained to be the Judge of the quick and the dead" (Acts 10:42; 17:31). They testified that "We must all appear before the judgment seat of Christ; that every one may receive the things done in his body, according to that he hath done, whether it be good or bad" (II Cor. 5:10; Rom. 14:10).

Thus the mind of John the Apostle was prepared for the subsequent revelations of Patmos, when he heard his glorified Lord claim to "have the keys of hell and of death" (Rev. 1:18), and saw the vision of the "great white throne, and him that sat on it, from whose face the earth and the heaven fled away" (Rev. 20:11).

But who is this that claims to grasp and wield the thunderbolts of eternal retribution; who professes to be able to scrutinize the secret purposes and motives, as well as the words and deeds, of every man that has been born, from the first dawn of personal responsibility to the day of death? Can anything short of indwelling omniscience qualify him for such an intricate and complicated and vast investigation? If he could not search *"the reins and the hearts"* (to use his own words to John), how could he give to every one of us according to his works (Rev. 2:23)? The brain reels when we think of the tremendous transactions of the last day, and the momentous interests then to be decided forever and ever; and reason tells us, that if the Judge who is to preside over these solemnities be a man, he must be a God-man. If Jesus is to be the universal and absolute Judge of our race — a Judge from whose decisions there will be no appeal, he must be "God manifest in the flesh." But what can we think of him, if in setting up this claim he mislead us?

3. *Jesus always claimed absolute and indisputable power in dealing with every question of moral duty and destiny.* Jesus claimed to be absolute Lord in the whole region of morals. He settled the meaning and force of old laws, and instituted new ones by his own authority. Take the Sermon on the Mount as an illustration. With what a self-possessed peremptoriness does he define the existing legislation of God, and enlarge its limits! With what conscious dignity does he decide every question in the whole range of human duty with the simple — "But I say unto you!" Seven times in one chapter does he use this formula (see Matt. 5:20, 22, 28, 32,

34, 39, 44). And in the application of the sermon he declared him only to be the wise man and built upon solid rock, who hears his sayings and does them (Matt. 7:24). Well might the people be astonished at his doctrine; for verily "He taught them as one having authority, and not as the scribes" (Matt. 7:28, 29). But the tone which pervades the Sermon on the Mount runs through the whole of the teaching of Jesus of Nazareth. He ever speaks as if he were the Author and Giver of the law; as if he had the power to modify any of its provisions according to his own ideas of fitness; and as if he were the Supreme Lord of human consciences. His style is utterly unlike that of any inspired teacher before or after him. They appealed to the law and to the testimony (see Isa. 8:20). But Jesus claimed an inherent power to modify and to alter both.

The Sabbath was the symbol of the entire covenant made by God with Israel through the ministry of Moses (see Exod. 31:12-17). But Jesus asserted his complete supremacy over this divine institution. These were his emphatic words: *"For the Son of man is Lord also of the Sabbath day"* (Matt. 12:8; Mark 2:28; Luke 6:5). He could, of his own will, relax the terrors of the Jewish Sabbath, and even supersede it altogether by the Christian "Lord's Day." He was Lord of all divine institutions.

And in the Church he claims the right to regulate her doctrines and her ordinances according to his will. The apostles he commissioned to baptize in his name, and charged them to teach their converts to observe all things whatsoever he had commanded them (Matt. 28:19-20). Thus John was prepared for the sublime vision of the Son of man as "He that holdeth the seven stars in his right hand, who walketh in the midst of the seven golden candlesticks" (Rev. 2:1); and as "He that hath the key of David, he that openeth, and no man shutteth; and shutteth, and no man openeth" (Rev. 3:7).

And the authority which Jesus claimed extends into heaven, and to the final state of things. He affirmed that he would ascend to share his Father's dominion, and to sit in the throne of his glory (see Matt. 19:28). The counterpart to which announcement is found in his declaration to John in Patmos: "to him that overcometh will I grant to sit with me in my throne, even as I also overcame, and am set down with my Father in his throne" (Rev. 3:21). The manner in which the Lord spake of himself in connection with the heavenly state bore much fruit in the hearts and sentiments of his disciples. To them this life was being "absent from the Lord" as to his visible presence; and their one beautiful idea of heaven was that it was being "present with the Lord" (II Cor. 5:6, 8). He had taught them to regard him as their "all in all," even in their eternal state; and with unquestioning faith they cherished the one blessed hope of being forever with the Lord. All other ideas of the celestial world were lost sight of in comparison with this absorbing anticipation.

The very mansions which they were to occupy in the Eternal Father's house, Jesus said, he would assign to them (John 14:2). He asserted his right to give away the crowns and glories of immortal blessedness as if they were his by indisputable right. He wills it, and it is done. He constantly reminded his disciples of rewards which he would give to every servant whom, at his coming, he found to be faithful (cf. Matt. 24:44 with 45, 46, 47; 25: 14-46, etc.).

It is true Jesus will give these honors only to those for whom they are prepared by his Father; for in their designs of mercy, the Father, the Son, and the Holy Spirit are *one*. Still he will, of right, dispense the blessing to all who receive it. For these were our Lord's true words: "To sit on my right hand, and on my left, is not mine to give, but (or, except) it shall be given to them for whom it is prepared of my Father" (Matt. 20:23). The language logically implies our Lord's absolute right to give the crowns; but only to such as are appointed to these honors by the Father.

These ideas are repeated in vision to John. Jesus gives the "right to the tree of life" (Rev. 2:7). In the praises of the redeemed host, as described in that marvelous Apocalypse, they ever ascribe their salvation and glory to Jesus, and the sinless angels swell the chorus of Immanuel's praises, while the universe, from its myriad worlds, echoes the strain (Rev. 5:8-14).

In the description of the final state of things — a state which shall be subsequent to the millennium (Rev. 20:1-10), and also to the final judgment of both righteous and wicked (Rev. 20:11-15), and to the act of homage and fealty described in I Cor. 15:24-28, we find the Lamb still and forever on the throne. The Church is still "the bride, the Lamb's wife" (Rev. 21:9). In that consummated state of all things, "The Lord God Almighty and the Lamb are the temple of it" (Rev. 21:22); the glory of God lightens it; "and the Lamb is the light thereof" (Rev. 21:23); the pure river of water of life still flows from beneath the throne of God and of the Lamb (Rev. 22:10), "the throne of God and of the Lamb shall be in it; and his servants shall serve him: and they shall see his face; and his name shall be in their foreheads" (Rev. 22:3, 4). Throughout the Apocalypse we never find Jesus among the worshipers. He is there the worshiped One on the throne, and with that picture the majestic vision closes.

The inspired Apostles had imbibed these ideas from the personal teaching of their Lord, and subsequent revelations did but expand in their minds the seed-thoughts which he had dropped there from his own sacred lips. Paul nobly expressed the sentiments of all his brethren when he wrote, "Henceforth there is laid up for me a crown of righteousness, which the Lord, the righteous judge, shall give me at that day; and not to me only, but unto all them also that love his appearing" (II Tim. 4:8). But surely he who claims supremacy, absolute and indisputable, in morals, in divine institutions, in the Church on earth, in heaven, and in a consummated universe forever, must be Lord of all, manifest in human form. If he were not, *what* must he have been to advance such assumptions, and what must the book be which enforces them?

4. *Jesus asserted his full possession of the power to forgive sins.* The moral instincts of the Jews were right when they put the question, "Who can forgive sins but God only?" (Mark 2:7). We do not wonder that, with their ideas of Christ, they asked in amazement, "Who is this that forgiveth sins also?" (Luke 7:49), or that they exclaimed, in reference to such a claim, from such a quarter, "This man blasphemeth" (Matt. 9:3).

And yet Christ declared most emphatically, on more than one occasion, his possession of this divine prerogative, and healed the palsied man in professed attestation of the fact (Luke 5:24). Those who would eliminate the miraculous element from the second narrative altogether, must admit that Mathew, Mark, and Luke all relate most circumstantially that Jesus did at least profess to work a miracle in support of his claim to possess power to forgive sins. If he wrought the miracle, his claim is established; and if he did not work it, but cheated the people, then away with him forever as an arrant impostor! But if he wrought it, and proved his claim, he must be equal with his Father; for the Jews were right, and no one "can forgive sins but God only." Could a mere man cancel with a word the sin of a creature against his Maker? The very thought is a blasphemy.

5. *Jesus claimed the power to raise his own body from the grave, to quicken the souls of men into spiritual life, and to raise all the dead at the last great day.* Jesus likened his body to a temple which the Jews should destroy, and which he would raise up again in three days (John 2:19-21). He affirmed that he had power to lay down his life, and power to take it up again (John 10:18). He declared that the *spiritually* dead — for the physical resurrection is spoken of afterward as a distinct topic — should hear his voice and live (John 5:25). And then he tells us not to wonder at this, for the day is coming when, by his omnific fiat, all the generations of the dead "Shall come forth; they that have done good, unto the resurrection of life; and they that have done evil unto the resurrection of damnation" (John 5:28, 29).

But if Jesus were not, in some mysterious sense, the Lord of his own life, what power had he to dispose of it as he pleased? And how could he recall it when gone? And how could he communicate spiritual life, if he were not its Divine Fountain? And how could he raise the dead from their graves, if he were not the Almighty Creator? All these claims, if genuine, necessitate faith in the Godhead of Jesus.

6. *Jesus declared that he had the ability to do all his Father's works.* The Saviour had healed the impotent man at the pool of Bethesda on the Sabbath day. When accused by the Jews of sin for this act, our Lord justified himself by the ever-memorable words, "My Father worketh hitherto (that is, on the Sabbath day in sustaining and blessing the worlds), and I work" — on the same day, *therefore*, in healing the sick, — thus indirectly asserting his right to do all that his Father did, and, as the Jews put it,

claiming *such* a Sonship as made him "equal with God." But our Lord did not abate one iota of his claim. True, he admitted that, as the *Incarnate Mediator,* he had received his authority from the Father, but he declared that "What things soever the Father doeth, these also doeth the Son likewise" (John 5:17-19). Now, no language can overestimate the sublimity of this claim. Christ affirmed that he possessed full right and ability to do all that the Eternal Father had the right and ability to do. Was such language ever used by the most inspired or the most daring of mere mortals? We do not forget that our Lord was careful to declare that the Father had committed all judgment to him (John 5:22); but had he not himself been a partaker of the Godhead how could he, as the Incarnate One, have been qualified to be armed with the prerogative so vast? He who can do all the works of God must be God!

7. *Jesus spake of himself as the greatest gift of infinite mercy.* In his conversation with Nicodemus, Christ spake of himself in these terms: "God so loved the world, that he gave his only begotten Son, that whosoever believeth in him, should not perish, but have everlasting life" (John 3:16), by which our Lord evidently meant to convey the idea that the gift of the Son was the richest gift of divine love. Imagine a mere man to stand forward and proclaim himself the choicest gift of God's love to our race. What a monstrous exaggeration and egotism! If Christ be greater than all other divine gifts combined, must he not be the God-man? On the evangelical hypothesis such representations are seen to be neither bombast nor rhetorical exaggeration, but sober, solid truth; and we can say with Paul, without reserve: "Thanks be unto God for his *unspeakable gift*" (II Cor. 9:15).

8. *Jesus announced himself as the center of rest for the human soul.* Who has not thrilled under the mighty spell of those mighty words: "Come unto me, all ye that labor and are heavy laden, and I will give you rest. Take my yoke upon you, and learn of me; for I am meek and lowly in heart; and ye shall find rest unto your souls. For my yoke is easy and my burden is light" (Matt. 11:28-30). In this invitation our Lord proclaims himself to be everything to the soul. We are to come to him, to take his

yoke upon us, and to learn of him. In receiving *him* we shall find rest unto our souls, for he will give us rest.

Now, God alone is the resting-place of the human spirit. In him, and in him only, can we find assured peace. But Jesus claims to be our rest. Must he not, then, be God Incarnate? And very noticeable is the fact that, in the same breath in which he speaks of himself in these august terms, he says: "I am meek and lowly in heart." But where were his meekness and lowiness in making such a claim, if he were simply a man like ourselves?

In the same spirit are those memorable passages in which this wonderful personage speaks of himself as our peace. "Peace I leave with you, my peace I give unto you; not as the world giveth, give I unto you" (John 14:27). "These words have I spoken unto you, that in *me* ye might have peace" (John 16:33). Thus ever does the Lord concentrate our thoughts upon *himself*. But what must he be to be worthy of such supreme attention?

9. *Jesus permitted Thomas to adore him as his Lord and his God, and pronounced a blessing upon the faith thus displayed* (John 20:28). On this fact we quote the admirable comment of Dean Alford: "The Socinian view, that these words, '*my Lord and my God,*' are merely an exclamation, is refuted, (1) By the fact that no such exclamations were in use among the Jews. (2) By the *eipen auto* (he said to *him*, that is Christ). (3) By the impossibility of referring *ho Kurios mou*, my Lord, to another than Jesus (see verse 13). (4) By the New Testament usage of expressing the vocative by the nominative with an article. (5) By the utter psychological absurdity of such a supposition; that one just convinced of the presence of him whom he deeply loved, should, instead of addressing him, break out into an irrelevant cry. (6) By the further absurdity of supposing that if such were the case, the Apostle John, who, of all the sacred writers, most constantly keeps in mind the object for which he is writing, should have recorded anything so beside that object. (7) By the intimate connection of *pepisteukas, thou hast believed* (see next verse).

"Dismissing it, therefore, we observe that this is the *highest confession* of faith which has yet been made; and that it shows that (though not yet fully) the meaning of the previous confessions of

his being *'the Son of God'* was understood. Thus John, in the
very close of his Gospel iterates the testimony with which he began
it — to the Godhead of the Word who became flesh, and, by this
closing confession, shows how *the testimony of Jesus to himself*
had gradually deepened and exalted the apostles' conviction, from
the time when they knew him only as *ho huios tou Ioseph* (1:46),
'the son of Joseph,' till now, when he is acknowledged as their
Lord and their God" (cf. Alford's *Greek New Testament* on the
passage).

These judicious remarks leave nothing to be added as to the
real application of the words, "my Lord and my God." But how
did the Saviour *receive* this act of adoration? He commended it,
and held it up for the imitation of the coming ages. "Jesus saith
unto him, Thomas, because thou hast seen me, thou hast believed:
blessed are they that have not seen, and yet have believed" (29).
He thus most emphatically declared his Lordship and Godhead.
But how fearful was his crime in so doing, if he was only a
Socinian Christ!

10. *Jesus demands of us an unhesitating and unlimited faith
in himself; such faith, in short, as we should only exercise in God.*
We are to believe in him for the salvation of our entire being;
not merely as pointing out to us the way to heaven, but as being
himself the way. He puts faith in him in the same category as
faith in the Father (John 14:1). The spirit of his teaching about
the faith to be reposed in him is given in his words to the woman
of Samaria: "If thou knewest the gift of God, and who it is
that saith unto thee, Give me to drink, thou wouldest have asked
of him, and he would have given thee living water." "Whosoever
drinketh of the water that I shall give him shall never thirst; but
the water that I shall give him shall be in him a well of water
springing up into everlasting life" (John 4:10-14). Unless we
exercise faith in his person and work, figuratively called eating
his flesh and drinking his blood, we have no life in us (John 6:53);
but if any man eat of this bread, he shall live forever (51). Those
who have given themselves up into the arms of Christ by faith
receive eternal life from him, and shall never perish (John 10:28).
They are as much in the arms of Jesus as in the arms of the Father;
and their safety is as much secured by one as by the other (cf. 28,

29, 30). In fact, in this gracious transaction the Son and the Father are one (30). Well might the Jews, with their views of his origin, take up stones to stone him for these claims, saying as they did it, "We stone thee for blasphemy, because that thou, being a man, makest thyself God" (33). Our Lord's vindication of himself, by a reference to the language of Psalm 82:6, is an illustration of the *argument from the less to the greater*. If in *any* sense the Jewish rulers might be called gods, how much more properly might *he*, the only begotten Son of the Father, be so designated? "Without me ye can do nothing," is in short the essence of the Saviour's teaching about himself (see John 15:1-5).

This is the sum of the Gospel message: Believe in the Lord Jesus Christ and ye shall be saved. It was a demand repeatedly and earnestly pressed by the Saviour, and inculcated by his apostles; and we say deliberately, that to exercise such a faith in Jesus as he required and the Gospel enforces, would, *with Socinian views*, be to expose ourselves to the terrible anathema: "Cursed is the man that trusteth in man, and that maketh flesh his arm" (Jer. 17:5). How could my soul be safe in the arms of a mere man? How dare I trust my eternal redemption to the care of such a Christ? And on what principle did Paul say: "I can do all things through Christ who strengtheneth me" (Phil. 4:13). And how can Jesus be "All in all" to true believers of every nation? (Col. 3:11).

11. *The affection and devotion which Jesus demands, are such as can be properly yielded only to God.* As we are to trust Christ for everything, so we are to give up everything for him, should he demand the sacrifice. This was a doctrine which the Lord repeatedly taught. Let our readers study Matt. 10:37-39, and the parallel passage, Luke 14:26, 27, and they will see at once how uncompromising is the Saviour's demand. Father, mother, son, daughter, wife, and even life itself are all to be sacrificed, if devotion to Christ necessitates the surrender. All creatures, and all things, and our very lives are to be to us as nothing when compared with Christ. God himself demands no less of us, and no more. What more *could* the Eternal Creator require? The moral law says: "Thou shalt love the Lord thy God with all thy soul, and with all thy strength, and him only shalt thou serve." But Christ bids us lov*e him* thus, and demands of us the homage

and sacrifice of our whole being; now, if he be not the *Author* of our being, what right has he to urge such a demand upon us? I could not love Christ as he requires to be loved, if I did not believe in him as the Incarnate God. To do so with Socinian views would be idolatry. Yet the motives which reigned in the hearts of inspired apostles are summed up in this one: "The love of Christ constraineth us," and they laid down the law, that all men are henceforth to live "not to themselves, but to him who died for them and rose again" (II Cor. 5:14, 15). And Jesus declared that our eternal destiny will take its character from our compliance or non-compliance with his demands: "Whosoever therefore shall confess me before men, him will I confess also before my Father who is in heaven. But whosoever shall deny me before men, him will I also deny before my Father who is in heaven" (Matt. 10:32, 33, 38-42, cf. Matt. 25:45, 46), and the sentiment is echoed in apostolical teaching, the langugage of which is, "If any man love not the Lord Jesus Christ, let him be Anathema Maranatha" (I Cor. 16:22). But clearly the suspension of such tremendous issues on the decree of our love for the person of a mere creature, is an idea utterly revolting to our moral sense. He must be the God-man.

12. *Very suggestive, too, are those passages in which Jesus promised his continued presence to his disciples after his ascension.* Beautiful are the words: "Where two or three are gathered together in my name, there am I in the midst of them" (Matt. 18:20). One of the last promises of our Lord was, "Lo, I am with you alway, even unto the end of the world" (Matt. 28:20). No perverse criticism can explain away these assurances; they guarantee the perpetual, personal presence of Jesus with all his disciples to the end of time.

And this idea had a wonderful influence over the thoughts and actions of the men whom Jesus inspired. They lived as those who were perpetually under their Lord's eye. Thus one speaks in the name of all: "Wherefore we labor, that, whether present or absent (from Christ as to his bodily presence, see 6 and 8), we may be accepted of him (Christ)" (II Cor. 5:9). Though denied his bodily presence, his divine they knew to be ever with them, hence they labored to please him, and the best wish they could breathe for each other was, "The Lord Jesus Christ be with thy spirit" (II Tim. 4:22). And John saw him in vision ever holding the ministerial stars in his right hand, and walking in the midst of the golden lamps — the churches (Rev. 2:1).

But how can we explain such representations as these, if Messiah be possessed of but one nature — the human, which must of necessity be local and limited as to its presence? Who is this that is always with his disciples in all countries at the same moment, but the Infinite One in a human form? We feel his presence; we know he is with us; and in this fact we have evidence that he is more than a man.

Some who reject the idea of the deity of Christ find solace in such passages as "My Father is greater than I" (John 14:28). No one denies that, as man and mediator, our Lord was inferior to the Father. Philippians 2:5-8 describes the process by which God the Son emptied himself of the voluntary exercise of his attributes in order to become man and die for us.

There are two classes of Scriptures relating to our Lord: the first, affirming his possession of a human nature, with all its innocent frailities and limitations; and second, ascribing to him a divine nature, possessed of the attributes of Godhood, performing divine work, and worthy of supreme honor and worship. Unitarians can only fairly explain one of these classes of Scriptures, the former; but Trinitarians can accept both classes, and expound them in their integrity and fullness. We do not stumble at evidences that Jesus was "bone of our bone, and flesh of our flesh." We rejoice in him as in one "touched with a feeling of our infirmities"; but we have no need to refine away, by a subtle and unfair criticism, the ascription to his person of divine perfections and works.

The times demand of us a vigorous re-assertion of the old truths, which are the very foundations of the Gospel system. *Humanity needs a Christ whom all can worship and adore.* The mythical account of Strauss' "Leben Jesu"; the unreal and romantic Christ of Renan's "Vie de Jesus"; and even the merely human Christ of "Ecce Homo," can never work any deliverance in the earth. Such a Messiah does not meet the yearnings of fallen human nature. It does not answer the pressing query, "How shall man be just with God?" It supplies no effective or sufficient agency for the regeneration of man's moral powers. It does not bring God down to us in our nature. Such a Christ we may criticise and admire, as we would Socrates, or Plato, or Milton, or Shakespeare; but we cannot trust him with our salvation; we cannot love him with all our hearts; we cannot pour forth at his feet the homage of our whole being; for to do so would be idolatry.

A so-called Saviour, whose only power to save lies in the excellent moral precepts that he gave, and the pure life that he lived; who is no longer the God-man, but the mere man; whose blood had no sacrificial atoning or propitiatory power in the moral government of Jehovah, but was simply a martyr's witness to a superior system of ethics — is not the Saviour of the four Gospels, or of Paul, or Peter, or John. It is not under the banners of such a Messiah that the Church of God has achieved its triumphs. The Christ of the New Testament, of the early Church, of universal Christendom; the Christ, the power of whose name has revolutionized the world and raised it to its present level, and under whose guidance the sacramental host of God's redeemed are advancing and shall advance to yet greater victories over superstition and sin, is Immanuel, God with us, in our nature, whose blood "cleanseth us from all sin," and who is "able to save, even to the uttermost, all that come unto God through him."

REUBEN ARCHER TORREY (1856-1928) was at one time early in his Christian life a higher critic. Yet, during a year of study in Germany, he rejected that philosophy, and he later became one of the leading thinkers among the early Fundamentalists. A powerful preacher, Torrey made his mark on world evangelism. Among his other achievements were being the first superintendent of Moody Bible Institute, pastor of the Moody Memorial Church, the Church of the Open Door in Los Angeles, and dean of the Bible Institute of Los Angeles (now Biola University). Torrey wrote many books, including *The Real Christ* (1920), *Is the Bible the Inerrant Word of God?* (1922), and *The Power of Prayer*.

26

The Certainty and Importance
of the Bodily Resurrection
# of Jesus Christ From the Dead

By Rev. R. A. Torrey, D.D.
FORMERLY DEAN, THE BIBLE INSTITUTE OF LOS ANGELES

Revised and edited by Gerald B. Stanton, Th.D.

The resurrection of Jesus Christ from the dead is the cornerstone of Christian doctrine. It is mentioned directly one hundred
and four or more times in the New Testament. It was the most
prominent and cardinal point in the apostolic testimony. When the
apostolic company, after the apostasy of Judas Iscariot, felt it
necessary to complete their number again by the addition of one to
take the place of Judas Iscariot, it was in order that he might "be a
witness with us of his resurrection" (Acts 1:21, 22). The resurrection of Jesus Christ was the one point that Peter emphasized
in his great sermon on the Day of Pentecost. His whole sermon
centered in that fact. Its keynote was, "This Jesus hath God
raised up, whereof we all are witnesses" (Acts 2:32; cf. vs. 24-31).
When the Apostles were filled again with the Holy Spirit some
days later, the one central result was that "with great power gave
the apostles *witness of the resurrection of the Lord Jesus.*" The
central doctrine that the Apostle Paul preached to the Epicurean
and Stoic philosophers on Mars Hill was Jesus *and the resurrection*
(Acts 17:18; cf. Acts 23:6; I Cor. 15:15).

The resurrection of Jesus Christ is one of the two fundamental
truths of the Gospel, the other being his atoning death (I Cor.
15:1, 3, 4). This was the glad tidings, first, that Christ died for
our sins, and second, that he arose again. The crucifixion loses
its meaning without the resurrection. Without the resurrection,
the death of Christ was only the heroic death of a noble martyr.
With the resurrection, it is the atoning death of the Son of God.
It shows that death to be of sufficient value to redeem us from all
our sins, for it was the sacrifice of the Son of God. Disprove

the resurrection of Jesus Christ and Christian faith is vain. "If Christ be not risen," cries Paul, "then is our preaching vain and your faith is also vain" (I Cor. 15:14). Later he adds, "If Christ be not risen, your faith is vain. You are yet in your sins." Paul, as the context clearly shows, is talking about the bodily resurrection of Jesus Christ. The doctrine of the resurrection of Jesus Christ is the one doctrine that has power to save any one who believes it with the heart (Rom. 10:9). To know the power of Christ's resurrection is one of the highest ambitions of the intelligent believer, to attain which he sacrifices all things and counts them but refuse (Phil. 3:8-10 ASV).

While the literal bodily resurrection of Jesus Christ is the cornerstone of Christian doctrine, it is also the Gibraltar of Christian evidence, and the Waterloo of infidelity and rationalism. If the scriptural assertions of Christ's resurrection can be established as historic certainties, the claims and doctrines of Chritianity rest upon an impregnable foundation. On the other hand, if the resurrection of Jesus Christ from the dead cannot be established, Christianity must go. It is a true instinct that led a leading and brilliant agnostic in England to say, that there is no use wasting time discussing the other miracles. The essential question is, Did Jesus Christ rise from the dead? If he did, it was easy enough to believe the other miracles; but, if not, the other miracles must go.

Are the statements contained in the four Gospels regarding the resurrection of Jesus Christ statements of fact or are they fiction, fables, myths? There are three separate lines of proof that the statements contained in the four Gospels regarding the resurrection of Jesus Christ are exact statements of historic fact.

I. *The External Evidence of the Authenticity and Truthfulness of the Gospel Narratives*

This is an altogether satisfactory argument. The external proofs of the authenticity and truthfulness of the Gospel narratives are overwhelming, but the argument is long and intricate and it would take a volume to discuss it satisfactorily. The other arguments are so completely sufficient and overwhelming and convincing to a candid mind that we can pass this present argument by, good as it is in its place.

II. *The Internal Proofs of the Truthfulness of the Gospel Records*

This argument is thoroughly conclusive, and we shall state it briefly in the pages which follow. We will assume absolutely nothing. We will start out with a fact which we all know to be a fact, namely, that we have the four Gospels today, whoever wrote them and whenever they were written. We shall place these four Gospels side by side, and see if we can discern in them the marks of truth or of fiction.

1. The first thing that strikes us as we compare these Gospels one with another is that they are *four separate and independent accounts*. This appears plainly from the apparent discrepancies in the four different accounts, which are marked and many. It would have been impossible for these four to have been made up in collusion with one another, or to have been derived from one another, when so many and so marked differences are found in them. There is harmony between the four accounts, but the harmony does not lie upon the surface; it comes out only by protracted and thorough study. It is precisely such a harmony as would exist between accounts written by several different persons, each looking at the events from his own standpoint. It is precisely such a harmony as would not exist in four accounts manufactured in collusion, or derived one from the other. In four accounts manufactured in collusion, whatever of harmony there might be would appear on the surface. Whatever discrepancy there might be would only come out by minute and careful study. But with the four Gospels the case is just the opposite. Harmony comes out by minute and careful study, and the apparent discrepancy lies upon the surface. Whether true or false, these four accounts are separate and independent from one another. (The four accounts also supplement one another, the third account sometimes reconciling apparent discrepancies between two.)

These accounts must be either a record of facts that actually occurred or else fictions. If fictions, they must have been fabricated independently of one another; the agreements are too marked and too many. It is absolutely incredible that four persons sitting down to write an account of what never occurred independently of one another, should have made their stories agree to the extent that these do. On the other hand, they cannot have been made up, as we have already seen, in collusion with one another; the apparent discrepancies are too numerous and too noticeable. It is proven they were not made up independently of one another; it is proven they were not made up in collusion with one another, so we are driven to the conclusion that they were not made up at all, that they are a true relation of facts as they actually occurred. We might rest the argument here and reasonably call the case settled, but we will go on still further.

2. The next thing we notice is that *each of these accounts bears striking indications of having been derived from eye witnesses.*

The account of an eyewitness is readily distinguishable from the account of one who is merely retailing what others have told him. Any one who is accustomed to weigh evidence in court or in historical study soon learns how to distinguish the report of an eye witness from mere hearsay evidence. Any careful student of the Gospel records of the resurrection will readily detect many marks of the eye witness. Some years ago when lecturing at an American university, a gentleman was introduced to me as being a skeptic. I asked him, "What line of study are you pursuing?" He replied that he was pursuring a postgraduate course in history with a view to a professorship in history. I said, "Then you know that the account of an eye witness differs in marked respects from the account of one who is simply telling what he has heard from others?" "Yes," he replied. I next asked, "Have you carefully read the four Gospel accounts of the resurrection of Christ?" He replied, "I have." "Tell me, have you noticed clear indications that they were derived from eye witnesses?" "Yes," he replied, "I have been greatly struck by this in reading the accounts." Any one who carefully and intelligently reads them will be struck with the same fact.

3. The third thing that we notice about these Gospel narratives is their *naturalness, straightforwardness, artlessness* and *simplicity.*

The accounts it is true, have to do with the supernatural, but the accounts themselves are most natural. There is a remarkable absence of all attempt at coloring and effect. There is nothing but the simple, straightforward telling of facts as they actually occurred. Dr. William Furness, the great Unitarian scholar and critic, who certainly was not over-much disposed in favor of the supernatural, says, "Nothing can exceed in artlessness and simplicity the four accounts of the first appearance of Jesus after his crucifixion. If these qualities are not discernible here, we must despair of ever being able to discern them anywhere."

Suppose we should find four accounts of the Battle of Monmouth. We found them all marked by that artlessness, straightforwardness and simplicity that always carries conviction; we found that, while apparently disagreeing in minor details, they agreed substantially in their account of the battle — even though we had no knowledge of the authorship or date of these accounts, would we not, in the absence of any other accounts, say, "Here is a true account of the Battle of Monmouth?" Now this is exactly the case with the four Gospel narratives. Manifestly separate and independent from one another, bearing the clear marks of having been derived from eye witnesses, characterized by an unparalleled artlessness, simplicity and straightforwardness, apparently disagreeing in minor details, but in perfect agreement as to the great central facts related. If we are fair and honest, if we follow the canons of evidence followed in court, if we follow any sound and sane law of literary and historical criticism, are we not logically driven to say, "Here is a true account of the resurrection of Jesus"?

4. The next thing we notice is the *unintentional evidence of words, phrases, and accidental details.*

It oftentimes happens that when a witness is on the stand, the unintentional evidence that he bears by words and phrases which he uses, and by accidental details which he introduces, is more convincing than his direct testimony of the truth to itself. The Gospel accounts abound in evidence of this sort.

Take, as the first instance, the fact that in all the Gospel records of the resurrection, we are given to understand that Jesus was not at first recognized by his disciples when he appeared to them after his resurrection (e.g., Luke 24:16; John 21:4). The Gospel narratives simply record the fact without attempting to explain it. If the stories were fictitious, they certainly would never have been made up in this way, for the writer would have seen at once the objection that would arise in the minds of those who did not wish to believe in his resurrection, that is, that it was not really Jesus whom the disciples saw. Why, then, is the story told in this way? For the self-evident reason that the evangelists were not making up a story for effect, but simply recording events precisely as they occurred. This is the way in which it occurred, therefore, this is the way in which they told it. It is not a fabrication of imaginary incidents, but an exact record of facts carefully observed and accurately recorded.

Take a second instance: In all the Gospel records of the appearances of Jesus after his resurrection, there is not a single recorded appearance to an enemy or opponent of Christ. All his appearances were to those who were already believers. Why this was so we can easily see by little thought, but nowhere in the Gospels are we told why it was so. If the stories had been fabricated, they certainly would never have been made up in this way. If the Gospels were, as some would have us believe, fabrications constructed one hundred, two hundred, or three hundred years after the alleged events recorded, when all the actors were dead and gone and no one could gainsay any lies told, Jesus would have been represented as appearing to Caiaphas, and Annas, and Pilate, and Herod, and confounding them by his reappearance from the dead. But there is no suggestion of anything of this kind in the Gospel stories. Every appearance is to one who is already a believer. Why is this so? For the self-evident reason that this was the way that things occurred, and the Gospel narratives are not concerned with producing a story for effect, but simply with recording events precisely as they occurred and as they were observed.

We find another very striking instance in what is recorded concerning the words of Jesus to Mary at their first meeting (John 20:17). Jesus is recorded as saying to Mary, "Touch me not, for I am not yet ascended to my Father." We are not told why Jesus said this to Mary. We are left to discover the reason for it, and the explanations vary widely one from another. Why then is this little utterance of Jesus put in the Gospel record without a word of explanation? Certainly a writer making up a story would not put in a detail like that without apparent meaning and without an attempt at an explanation of it. Why then do we find it here? Because this is exactly what happened. This is what Jesus said; this is what Mary heard Jesus say; this is what Mary told, and therefore this is what John recorded. We cannot have a fiction here, but an accurate record of words spoken by Jesus after his resurrection.

We find still another instance in John 20:4-6. This is all in striking keeping with what we know of John and Peter from other sources. Mary, returning hurriedly from the tomb, bursts in upon the two disciples and cries, "They have taken away the Lord out of the sepulchre, and we know not where they have laid him." The men sprang to their feet and ran at the top of their speed to the tomb. John, the younger of the two disciples (it is all the more striking that the narrative does not tell us here that he was the younger of the two disciples) was fleeter of foot and out-ran Peter and reached the tomb first, but man of retiring and reverent disposition that he was (we are not told this here but we know it from a study of his personality as revealed elsewhere) he did not enter the tomb, but simply stooped down and looked in. Impetuous but older Peter comes lumbering on behind as fast as he can, but when once he reaches the tomb, he never waits a moment outside but plunges headlong in. Is this made up, or is it life? He was indeed a literary artist of consummate ability who had the skill to make this up if it did not occur just so. There is incidentally a touch of local coloring in the report. When one visits today the tomb which scholars now accept as the real burial place of Jesus, he will find himself unconsciously obliged to stoop down in order to look in.

We find another instance in Mark 16:7: "But go your way, tell his disciples *and Peter* that he goeth before you into Galilee: there shall ye see him, as he said unto you." What I would have you notice here are the two words, *"and Peter."* Was not Peter one of the disciples? Why then, "and Peter"? No explanation is given in the text, but reflection shows it was the utterance of love toward the despondent, despairing disciple who had thrice denied his Lord. If the message had been simply to the disciples Peter would have said, "Yes, I was once a disciple, but I can no longer be counted such. I thrice denied my Lord on that awful night with oaths and curses. It does not mean me." But our tender compassionate Lord through his angelic messenger sends the message, "Go tell his disciples, and whoever you tell, be sure you tell poor, weak, faltering, backslidden, broken-hearted Peter." Is this made up, or is this a real picture of our Lord? I pity the man who is so dull that he can imagine this is fiction. Incidentally let it be noted that this is recorded only in the Gospel of Mark, which, as is well known, is Peter's Gospel. As Peter narrated to Mark one day what he should record, with tearful eyes and grateful heart he would turn to him and say, "Mark, be sure you put that in, 'Tell his disciples *and Peter.*'"

Take still another instance: In John 20:16 we read, "Jesus saith unto her, Mary. She turned and saith unto him, Rabboni; which is to say, Master." What a delicate touch of nature we have here! Mary is standing outside the tomb overcome with grief. She has not recognized her Lord, though he has spoken to her. She has mistaken him for the gardner. She has said, "Sir, if thou hast borne him hence, tell me where thou hast laid him, and I will take him away." Then Jesus utters just one word. He said, "Mary." As that name came trembling on the morning air, uttered with the old familiar tone, spoken as no one else had ever spoken it but he, in an instant her eyes were opened. She falls at his feet and tries to clasp them, and looks up into his face, and cries, "Rabboni, my Master." Is this made up? Impossible! This is life. This is Jesus, and this is the woman who loved him. No unknown author of the second, third, or fourth century could have produced such a masterpiece as this. We stand here unquestionably face to face with reality, with life, with Jesus and Mary as they actually were.

One more important illustration: In John 20:7 we read, "And the napkin, that was about his head, not lying with the linen clothes, but wrapped together in a place by itself." How strange that such a little detail as this should be added to the story with absolutely no attempt at explaining. But how deeply significant this little unexplained detail is. Recall the circumstances. Jesus is dead. For three days and three nights his body is lying cold and silent in the sepulchre, as truly dead as any body was ever dead, but at last the appointed hour has come, the breath of God sweeps through the sleeping and silent clay, and in that supreme moment of his own earthly life, that supreme moment of human history, when Jesus rises triumphant over death and the grave and Satan, there is no excitement upon his part, but with that same majestic self-composure and serenity that marked his whole career, that same divine calm that he displayed upon storm-tossed Galilee, so now again in this sublime, this awful moment, he does not excitedly tear the napkin from his face and fling it aside, but absolutely without human haste or flurry or disorder, he unties it calmly from his head, rolls it up and lays it away in an orderly manner in a place by itself. Was that made up? Never! We do not behold here an exquisite masterpiece of the romancer's art; we read here the simple narrative of a matchless detail in a unique life that was actually lived here upon earth, a life so beautiful that one cannot read it with an honest and open mind without feeling the tears coming into his eyes.

But some one will say, all these things are little things. True, and it is from that very fact that they gain much of their significance. It is just in such little things that fiction would disclose itself. Fiction displays itself to be different from fact in the minute; in the great outstanding outlines you can make fiction look like truth, but when you come to examine it minutely and microscopically, you will soon detect that it is not reality but fabrication. But the more microscopically we examine the Gospel narratives, the more we become impressed with their truthfulness. There is an artlessness and naturalness and self-evident truthfulness in the narratives, down to the minutest detail, that surpasses all the possibilities of art.

The third line of proof that the statements contained in the four Gospels regarding the resurrection of Jesus Christ are exact statements of historic fact, is

III. *The Circumstantial Evidence for the Resurrection of Christ*

There are certain proven and admitted facts that demand the resurrection of Christ to account for them.

1. Beyond a question, the foundation truth preached in the early years of the Church's history was the resurrection.

Whether Jesus did actually rise from the dead or not, it is certain that the one thing the apostles constantly proclaimed was that he had risen. Why should the apostles use this as the very cornerstone of their creed, if not well attested and firmly believed?

But this is not all: They laid down their lives for this doctrine. Men never lay down their lives for a doctrine which they do not firmly believe. They stated that they had seen Jesus after his resurrection, and rather than give up their statement, they laid down their lives for it. Of course, men may die for error and often have, but it was for error that they firmly believed. In this case they would have known whether they had seen Jesus or not, and they would not merely have been dying for error but dying for a statement which they knew to be false. This is not only incredible but impossible. Furthermore, if the apostles really firmly believed, as is admitted, that Jesus rose from the dead, they had some facts upon which they founded their belief. These would have been the facts that they would have related in recounting the story. They certainly would not have made up a story out of imaginary incidents when they had real facts upon which they founded their belief. But if the facts were as recounted in the Gospels, there is no possible escaping the conclusion that Jesus actually arose. Still further, if Jesus had not arisen, there would have been evidence that he had not. His enemies would have sought and found this evidence, but the apostles went up and down the very city where he had been crucified and proclaimed right to the faces of his slayers that he had been raised, and no one could produce evidence to the contrary. The very best they could do was to say the guards went to sleep and the disciples stole the body while the guards slept. Men who bear evidence of what happens while they are asleep are not usually regarded as credible witnesses. Further still, if the Apostles had stolen the body, they would have known it themselves and would not have been ready to die for what they knew to be a fraud.

2. Another known fact is the change in the day of rest. The early Church came from among the Jews. From time immemorial the Jews had celebrated the seventh day of the week as their day of rest and worship, but we find the early Christians in the

Acts of the Apostles, and also in early Christian writings, assembling on the first day of the week. Nothing is more difficult of accomplishment than the change in a holy day that has been celebrated for centuries and is one of the most cherished customs of the people. What is especially significant about the change is that it was changed by no express decree but by general consent. Something tremendous must have occurred that led to this change. The apostles asserted that what had occurred on that day was the resurrection of Christ from the dead, and that is the most rational explanation. In fact, it is the only reasonable explanation of the change.

3. But the most significant fact of all is the change in the disciples themselves, the moral transformation. At the time of the crucifixion of Christ, we find the whole apostolic company filled with blank and utter despair. We see Peter, the leader of the apostolic company, denying his Lord three times with oaths and cursings, but a few days later we see this same man, filled with a courage that nothing could shake. We see him standing before the council that had condemned Jesus to death and saying to them, "Be it known unto you all, and to all the people of Israel, that by the name of Jesus Christ of Nazareth, whom ye crucified, whom God raised from the dead, even by him doth this man stand before you whole" (Acts 4:10). A little further on when commanded by the council not to speak at all nor teach in the name of Jesus, we hear Peter and John answering, "Whether it be right in the sight of God to hearken unto you more than unto God, judge ye. For we cannot but speak the things which we have seen and heard" (Acts 4:19, 20). A little later still after arrest and imprisonment, in peril of death, when sternly arraigned by the council, we hear Peter and the apostles answering their demand that they should be silent regarding Jesus, with the words, "We ought to obey God rather than man. The God of our fathers raised up Jesus whom ye slew and hanged on a tree. Him hath God exalted with his right hand to be a Prince and a Saviour, for to give repentance to Israel, and forgiveness of sins. And we are his witnesses of these things" (Acts 5:29-32). Something tremendous must have occurred to account for such a radical and astounding moral transformation as this. Nothing short of the

fact of the resurrection and of their having seen the risen Lord will explain it.

These unquestionable facts are so impressive and so conclusive that even infidel and Jewish scholars now admit that the apostles believed that Jesus rose from the dead. Even Ferdinand Baur, father of the Tübingen School, admitted this. David Strauss, who wrote the most masterly "Life of Jesus" from the rationalistic standpoint that was ever written, said, "Only this much need be acknowledged that the apostles firmly believed that Jesus had arisen." Strauss evidently did not wish to admit any more than he had to, but he felt compelled to admit this much. Schenkel went even further and said, "It is an indisputable fact that in the early morning of the first day of the week following the crucifixion, the grave of Jesus was found empty. It is a second fact that the disciples and other members of the apostolic communion were convinced that Jesus was seen after the crucifixion." These admissions are fatal to the rationalists who make them. The question at once arises, "Whence these convictions and belief, if not from a literal resurrection?"

Renan attempted an answer by saying that "the passion of a hallucinated woman (Mary) gives to the world a resurrected God." (Renan, *Life of Jesus,* p. 357). By this, Renan means that Mary was in love with Jesus; that after his crucifixion, brooding over it, in the passion of her love, she dreamed herself into a condition where she had a hallucination that she had seen Jesus risen from the dead. She reported her dream as a fact, and thus the passion of a hallucinated woman gave to the world a resurrected God. But the reply to all this is self-evident, namely, the passion of a hallucinated woman was not competent to this task. Remember the makeup of the apostolic company; in the apostolic company were a Matthew and a Thomas to be convinced, outside was a Saul of Tarsus to be converted. The passion of a hallucinated woman will not convince a stubborn unbeliever like Thomas, nor a Jewish tax-gatherer like Matthew. Whoever heard of a tax-gatherer, and most of all of a Jewish tax-gatherer, who could be imposed upon by the passion of a hallucinated woman? Neither will the passion of a hallucinated woman convince a fierce and conscientious enemy like Saul of Tarsus. We must look for some saner explanation than this. Strauss tried to account for it by inquiring whether the appearance might not have been visionary. Strauss has had, and still has, many followers in this theory. But to this we reply, first of all, there was no subjective starting point for such visions. The apostles, so far from expecting to see the Lord, would scarcely believe their own eyes when they did see him. Furthermore, whoever heard of eleven men having the same vision at the same time, to say nothing of five hundred men (I Cor. 15:6) having the same vision at the same time. Strauss demands of us that we give up one reasonable miracle and substitute five hundred impossible miracles in its place. Nothing can surpass the credulity of unbelief.

The third attempt at an explanation is that Jesus was not really dead when they took him from the cross, that his friends worked over him and brought him back to life, and what was supposed to be the appearance of the raised Lord was the appearance of one who never had been really dead and was now merely resuscitated. This theory of Paulus has been brought forward and revamped by various rationalistic writers in our own time and seems to be a favorite theory of those who today would deny the reality of our Lord's resurrection. To sustain this view, appeal has been made to the short time Jesus hung upon the cross, and to the fact that history tells us of one in the time of Josephus taken down from the cross and nursed back to life. But to this we answer: Remember the events preceding the crucifixion, the agony in the garden of Gethsemane, the awful ordeal of the four trials, the scourging and the consequent physical condition in which all this left Jesus. Remember, too, the water and the blood that poured from his pierced side. In the second place, his enemies would have taken, and did take, all necessary precautions against such a thing as this happening (John 19:34). In the third place, if Jesus had been merely resuscitated, he would have been so weak, such an utter physical wreck, that his reappearance would have been measured at its real value, and the moral transformation in the disciples would still remain unaccounted for. In the fourth place, if brought back to life, the apostles and friends of Jesus, who are the ones who are supposed to have brought him back to life, would have known that it was not a case of resurrection but of resuscitation, and the main fact to be accounted for, namely, the change in themselves would remain unaccounted for. The attempted explanation is an explanation that does not explain. In the fifth place, we reply, that the moral difficulty is the greatest of all, for if it was really a case of resuscitation, then Jesus tried to palm himself off as one risen from the dead, when in reality he was nothing of the sort. In that case, he would be an arch-impostor, and the whole Christian system rests on a fraud as its ultimate foundation. Is it possible to believe that such a system of religion as that of Jesus Christ, embodying such exalted principles and precepts of truth, purity, and love, "originated in a deliberately planned fraud"? No one whose own heart is not cankered by fraud and trickery can believe Jesus to have been an impostor, and his religion to have been founded upon fraud.

A leader of the rationalistic forces in England has recently tried to prove the theory that Jesus was only apparently dead by appealing to the fact that when the side of Jesus was pierced blood came forth and asks, "Can a dead man bleed?" To this the sufficient reply is that when a man dies of what is called in popular language, a broken heart, the blood escapes into the pericardium, and after standing there for a short time it separates into serum (the water) and clot (the red corpuscles, blood), and thus if a man were dead, if his side were pierced by a spear, and the point of the spear entered the pericardium, "blood and water" would flow out just as the record states it did. What is brought forth as a proof that Jesus was not really dead, is in reality a proof that he was, and an illustration of the minute accuracy of the story. It could not have been made up in this way, if it were not actual fact.

We have eliminated all other possible suppositions. We have but one left, namely, Jesus really was raised from the dead the third day as recorded in the four Gospels. The desperate straits to which those who attempt to deny it are driven are themselves proof of the fact.

We have then several independent lines of argument pointing decisively and conclusively to the resurrection of Christ from the dead. Some of them taken separately prove the fact, but taken together they constitute an argument that makes doubt of the resurrection of Christ impossible to the candid mind. Of course, if one is determined not to believe, no amount of proof will convince him. Such a man must be left to his own deliberate choice of error and falsehood; but any man who really desires to know the truth and is willing to obey it at any cost must accept the resurrection of Christ as an historically proven fact.

REUBEN ARCHER TORREY (1856-1928) was at one time early in his Christian life a higher critic. Yet, during a year of study in Germany, he rejected that philosophy, and he later became one of the leading thinkers among the early Fundamentalists. A powerful preacher, Torrey made his mark on world evangelism. Among his other achievements were being the first superintendent of Moody Bible Institute, pastor of the Moody Memorial Church, the Church of the Open Door in Los Angeles, and dean of the Bible Institute of Los Angeles (now Biola University). Torrey wrote many books, including *The Real Christ* (1920), *Is the Bible the Inerrant Word of God?* (1922), and *The Power of Prayer*.

27

The Personality and Deity of the Holy Spirit

By R. A. Torrey, D.D.
FORMERLY DEAN, THE BIBLE INSTITUTE OF LOS ANGELES

Revised and edited by Charles L. Feinberg, Th.D., Ph.D.

One of the most distinctive doctrines of the Christian faith is that of the personality and deity of the Holy Spirit. It is of the highest importance from the standpoint of worship. If the Holy Spirit is a divine Person, worthy to receive our adoration, our faith, and our love, and we do not know and recognize him as such, then we are robbing a divine Being of the adoration and love and confidence which are his due.

The doctrine of the personality of the Holy Spirit is also of the highest importance from the practical standpoint. If we think of the Holy Spirit only as an impersonal power or influence, then our thought will constantly be, "How can I get hold of and use the Holy Spirit"; but if we think of him in the biblical way as a divine Person, infinitely wise infinitely holy, infinitely tender, then our thought will constantly be, "How can the Holy Spirit get hold of and use me?" The former conception leads to self-exaltation; the latter to self-humiliation, self-emptying, and self-renunciation. If we think of the Holy Spirit merely as a divine power or influence, and then imagine that we have received the Holy Spirit, there will be the temptation to feel as if we belonged to a superior order of Christians. But if we think of the Holy Spirit in the biblical way as a divine Being of infinite majesty, condescending to dwell in our hearts and take possession of our lives, it will put us in the dust, and make us walk very softly before God.

It is of the highest importance from an experimental standpoint that we know the Holy Spirit as a person. Many can testify of the blessing that has come into their own lives from coming to know the Holy Spirit, as an ever-present, living, divine friend and helper. There are four lines of proof in the Bible that the Holy Spirit is a person.

Characteristics of the Holy Spirit

1. All the distinctive characteristics of personality are ascribed to the Holy Spirit. What are the distinctive marks of personality? Knowledge, feeling, and will. Any being who knows and feels and wills is a person. When you say that the Holy Spirit is a person, some understand you to mean that the Holy Spirit has hands, feet, eyes, and so on, but these are marks, not of personality, but of corporeity. When we say that the Holy Spirit is a person, we mean that he is not a mere influence or power that God sends into our lives, but that he is a Being who knows, feels, and wills. These three characteristics of personality, knowledge, feeling, and will, are ascribed to the Holy Spirit over and over again.

In I Corinthians 2:10, 11 knowledge is ascribed to the Holy Spirit. He is not merely an illumination that comes into our minds, but he is a being who himself knows the deep things of God, teaching us what he himself knows. Will is ascribed to the Holy Spirit in I Corinthians 12:11 (ASV). The Holy Spirit is not a mere influence or power which we are to use according to our wills, but a divine Person who uses us according to his will. This is a truth of fundamental importance in getting into right relation with the Holy Spirit. We read in Romans 8:27 that the quality of mind is attributed to the Holy Spirit. "Mind" includes the ideas of thought, feeling, and purpose. Thus, personality in the fullest sense is ascribed to the Holy Spirit.

In Romans 15:30 love is stated as an attribute of the Holy Spirit. The Holy Spirit is not a mere blind, unfeeling influence or power that comes into our lives. The Holy Spirit is a person who loves as tenderly as God the Father or Jesus Christ the Son. We think daily of the love of God the Father and of Christ the Son, but very few meditate as we ought upon the love of the Holy Spirit. Yet we owe our salvation just as truly to the love of the Spirit, as we do to the love of the Father and the love of the Son. Again, we read in Nehemiah 9 :20 (ASV) that intelligence and goodness are characteristics of the Holy Spirit. There are those who tell us that the personality of the Holy Spirit is not found in the Old Testament. While this truth is not so fully developed as in the New Testament, nonetheless the basic concept is there also. Finally, Ephesians 4 :30 attributes grief to the Holy Spirit. He is a person who comes to dwell in our hearts, observing all that we do, say, and think. If there is anything in act, word, or thought that is impure, unkind, selfish, or evil in any way, he is deeply grieved by it. This thought once fully comprehended becomes one of the strongest motives to a holy life and careful walk.

The Acts of the Spirit

2. The second line of proof in the Bible of the personality of the Holy Spirit is that many acts that only a person can perform are ascribed to the Holy Spirit. I Corinthians 2 :10 states that the Spirit searches the deep things of God. He is not merely an illumination, but a person who searches into the deep things of God. In Revelation 2 :7 he is represented as speaking; Galatians 4 :6 declares he cries out. Romans 8 :26 is proof of the praying ministry of the Spirit. It is not only that he teaches us to pray, but he personally prays in and through us. The believer has Christ praying for him at the right hand of the Father (Heb. 7 :25), and the Holy Spirit praying through him here (Rom. 8 :26).

In John 15 :26, 27; 14 :26; and 16 :12-14 the Holy Spirit is set forth as a teacher of the truth, not merely an illumination that enables our mind to see the truth, but one who personally comes to us and teaches us the truth. It is the privilege of the humblest believer to have this divine Person as his daily teacher of the truth of God (I John 2 :20, 27). The Holy Spirit is represented in Romans 8 :14 as our personal guide. directing us what to do, taking us by the hand, as it were, and leading us into that line of action that is well-pleasing to God. From Acts 16 :6, 7; 13 :2; and 20 :28 we learn that the Holy Spirit takes command of the life and conduct of a servant of Jesus Christ; he is also seen calling men to work and appointing them to office. Repeatedly in the Scriptures actions are ascribed to the Holy Spirit which only a person could perform.

The Office of the Spirit

3. The third line of proof of the personality of the Holy Spirit is that an office is predicated to the Holy Spirit that could only be predicated of a person. In John 14:16, 17 we are told it is the office of the Spirit to be another Comforter to take the place of our absent Savior. Christ promised that during his absence he would not leave the disciples orphaned (John 14:18). Is it possible that Jesus should have promised another Comforter to take his place, if that One was not a person, but only an influence or power, no matter how beneficent and divine? Still further is it conceivable that he would have said it was expedient for him to go away (John 16:7), if the other Comforter that was coming to take his place was only an influence or power? Moreover, the Greek word "Paraclete" connotes one who is constantly at the side as helper, counselor, comforter, friend. This demands personality. While we await Christ's return from the throne of the Father, we have another Person just as divine as he, just as wise, just as strong, just as able to help, just as loving, always by our side ready at any moment that we look to him, to counsel us, to teach us, to give us victory to take the entire control of our lives.

This is one of the most comforting thoughts in the New Testament for this dispensation. It is a cure for loneliness. It is a cure for breaking hearts, separated from loved ones. It is a cure from the fear of darkness and danger. But it is in our service for Christ that this thought of the Holy Spirit comes to us with greatest helpfulness. We need not be robbed of joy and liberty in our service because fear hampers our efforts. We need only remember that the responsibility is not really upon us but upon another, the Holy Spirit, and he knows just what ought to be done and what ought to be said. If he is permitted to do the work which he is so perfectly competent to do, our fears and cares will vanish.

Treatment of the Holy Spirit

4. The fourth line of proof of the personality of the Holy Spirit is: a treatment is predicated of the Holy Spirit that could only be predicated of a person. The Holy Spirit can be opposed, resisted and grieved, according to Isaiah 63:10 (ASV). You

cannot rebel against an influence or power. You can only rebel against and grieve a person. You can only treat a person with contumely, and this is stated with reference to the Holy Spirit (Heb. 10:29). Ananias and Sapphira lied to the Holy Spirit (Acts 5:3). You cannot tell lies to a blind, impersonal influence or power, but only to a person. Matthew 12:31, 32 states that the Holy Spirit may be blasphemed. It is impossible to blaspheme an influence or power; only a person can be blasphemed, and a divine Person at that. We are still further told that the blasphemy of the Holy Spirit is a more serious sin than even the blasphemy of the Son of man himself. Could anything make more clear that the Holy Spirit is a person and a divine Person?

Summary

To summarize, the Holy Spirit is a person. The Scriptures make this plain beyond a question to anyone who candidly goes to the Scriptures to find out what they really teach. Do we walk in conscious fellowship with him? Do we realize that he is our constant Indweller? Do we know the communion of the Holy Spirit (II Cor. 13:14)? Herein lies the secret of a Christian life of liberty, joy, power and fullness. To have as one's ever-present friend, and to be conscious that one has as his ever-present friend, the Holy Spirit, and to surrender one's life in all its departments entirely to his control, this is true Christian living.

W. J. ERDMAN (1833-1923) was the second pastor of Moody Church in Chicago. His son, Charles R. Erdman (1876-1878), a fine pastor and author in his own right, called his father "one of the most devout and diligent and influential of modern Bible students." Erdman's influence was also felt in his interest in the Niagara Bible Conference, the forerunner of later Bible conferences throughout America.

28

The Holy Spirit and the Sons of God

By Rev. W. J. Erdman, D.D.
GERMANTOWN, PENNSYLVANIA

Revised and edited by Charles L. Feinberg, Th.D., Ph.D.

It is evident from many writings on the baptism of the Holy Spirit that due importance has not been given to the peculiar characteristic of the gift of Pentecost in its relation to the sonship of believers. Before considering this subject a few brief remarks may be made concerning the Holy Spirit and his relation to the people of God in the dispensations and times preceding the Day of Pentecost.

1. The Holy Spirit is another Person of the Godhead, but not a different Being. To him as a personal Being are ascribed names, affections, words, and acts, interchanged with those of God. His acts and dealings are not those of an impersonal medium or influence, but of a person, and One who in the nature of the case cannot be less than God in wisdom, love, and power, who is one with the Father and the Son. He is another Person, indeed, but not a different Being.

2. The spiritual, divine life in the people of God is the same in kind in every age and dispensation, but the relation to God in which the life was developed of old was different from that which now exists between believers as sons and God as Father. In accordance with that relationship the Holy Spirit acted. He was of old the author and nourisher of all spiritual life and power in righteous men and women of past ages, in patriarch and friend of God, in Israelites as minors and servants, in pious kings and adoring psalmists, in consecrated priests and faithful prophets. Whatever truth had been revealed, he employed to develop the divine life he had imparted. From the beginning he used promise and precept, law and type, psalm and ritual to instruct,

quicken, convince, teach, lead, warn, comfort, and promote the growth and establishment of the people of God.

When at last all righteousness and holy virtues appeared in Christ, then the mold and image of the spiritual life of the saints of the old covenant was seen perfect and complete. In ways Godward and manward, in self-denial and in full surrender to his Father's will, in hatred of sin and in grace to sinners, in purity of heart and forgiveness of injuries, in gentleness and all condescension, in restful yet ceaseless service, in unity of purpose and faultless obedience — in a word, in all excellencies and graces, in all virtues and beauties of the Spirit, in light and in love, the Lord Jesus set forth the mold and substance of the life spiritual, divine, eternal.

3. Redemption precedes sonship and the gift of the Spirit. This proposition is clearly seen in Paul's argument in Galatians 4:4-6. The word "adoption" signifies the placing in the state and relation of a son (Rom. 9:4 and Eph. 1:5). In the writings of John believers are never called sons, but "chidren" ("born ones"), a word indicating nature, kinship. Sonship relates not to nature, but to legal standing; it is associated not with regeneration, but with redemption. It was on the redeemed disciples that the Spirit of God was poured at Pentecost, not to make believers sons, but because they had become sons through redemption. In brief, sonship, though ever since redemption inseparable from justification, does in the order of salvation succeed justification.

Through redemption the new dignity of sonship was conferred, the new name "sons" was given to them as a new name "Father" had been declared of him. A new name was given to the life in this new relation, "the life eternal," and a new name, "Spirit of his Son," was given to the Holy Spirit, who henceforth would nourish and develop this life, and illumine and lead believers into all the privileges and duties of the sons of God.

These facts are then all related to and dependent upon each other. Jesus Christ must first lay the ground of the forgiveness of sins of past and future times in his work of redemption and reconciliation; as risen and glorified not before, he is "the first-born of many brethren," to whose image they are predestined to be conformed. As the Son, he declared to them the name of God as Father, the crowning name of God corresponding to their highest name, sons of God. As his brethren in this high and peculiar sense, he did not call them until he had first suffered, died, and risen again from the dead, but that name is the first word he spoke of them on the morning of the resurrection, as if it were the chiefest joy of his soul to name and greet them as his brethren, and sons of God, being in and with him "sons of the resurrection." Because they were sons, the Father through the Son sent forth the Spirit of his Son into their hearts, crying, "Abba, Father!" It is the marvelous dignity of a sonship in glory, like that of our Lord Jesus, with all its attendant blessings and privileges, services and rewards, suffering and glories, to which the gift of the Holy Spirit is related in this present dispensation.

Accordingly, when the disciples were baptized with the Spirit on the Day of Pentecost, they were not only endued with ministering power, but they also then entered into the experience of sonship. Then they knew, as they could not have known before, though the Book of Acts records but little of their inner life, that through the heaven-descended Spirit, the sons of God are forever united with the heaven-ascended, glorified Son of God. Whether they at first fully realized the fact or not, they were in him and he in them. Was Jesus begotten of the Spirit, so were they; was he not of the world as to origin and nature, neither were they. Was he loved of the Father, so were they, and with the same love; was he sanctified and sent into the world to bear witness to the truth, so likewise he sent them. Did he receive the Spirit as the seal of God to his Sonship, so were they sealed; was he anointed with power and light to serve, so they received the unction from him. Did he begin to serve when there came the attesting Spirit and confirming word of the Father, so they began to serve when the Spirit of the Son, the Witness, was sent forth into their hearts, crying, "Abba, Father." Was he, after service and suffering, received up in glory, so shall they obtain his glory when he comes again to receive them unto himself. Verily, "we are as he is in this world" (I John 4:17).

4. In the gift of the Holy Spirit on the Day of Pentecost all gifts for believers in Christ were contained, and were related to

them as sons of God, both individually and corporately as the church, the body of Christ. In kind, as can be seen on comparison, there was no difference in his gifts and acts before and after that day, but the new gift was now to dwell in the hearts of men as sons of God, and with more abundant life and varied manifestations of power and wisdom. But by the Spirit the one body was formed, and all gifts are due to his perpetual presence (I Cor. 12:14). John 7:37-39 is an example of the anticipative sayings of our Lord, not to be made good until he had died and risen again.

It is significant that after Pentecost only the words, "filled with the Spirit," are used. Nothing is said of an individual's receiving a new or fresh "baptism of the Spirit." It would imply that the baptism is one for the whole body until all the members are incorporated; one the outpouring, many the fillings; one fountain, many the hearts to drink, to have in turn a well of water springing up within them.

The disciples were indeed endued with power for service according to promise; on that factor especially their eyes and hearts had been fixed. That was the chief thing for them; but in the light of later Scriptures it is seen that the principal thing with God was not only to attest the glory of Jesus by the gift of the Spirit, but also in one Spirit to baptize into one body the children of God, who until then were looked upon as scattered abroad, as unincorporated members (I Cor. 12:13; John 11:52; Gal. 3:27, 28). And the gift, whether to the body or to the individual member, is once for all. As the Christian is once for all in Christ, so the Holy Spirit is once for all in the Christian; but the purpose of the presence of the Spirit is often but feebly understood by the believer, just as his knowledge of what it is to be in Christ is often most defective.

5. The Holy Spirit is given at once on the remission of sins to them that believe in Christ Jesus as their Saviour and Lord. It is, however, to be observed that as the Spirit acts according to the truth known or believed or obeyed, an interval unspiritual or unfruitful may come between the remission of sins and the marked manifestation of the Spirit, either in relation to holiness of life, or to power for service or to patience in trials. It certainly is the divine ideal of a holy life, that the presence of the Spirit should at

once be made manifest on the forgiveness of sins, and continue in increasing light and power to the end (Rom. 5:1-5). This steady progress unto the perfect day has been and is true of many, who from early childhood or from the day of conversion in the case of adults, were led continually by the Spirit and never came to one great crisis. With others it is not so, for it is the confession of a large number of men and women, afterward eminent for holiness, that their life previous to such crisis had been hardly worth the name of Christian. It was a definite act of dedication to the full will of God that explains the change.

Their experience may be set forth in this way. The full truth of the sonship and salvation of believers may not have been taught them when they first believed; the life may have begun under a yoke of legal bondage. The freedom of filial access may have been doubted, even though their hearts often burned because of the presence of the unknown Spirit. Thus, weary, ineffective years passed, attended with little growth in grace or fruitful service or patient resignation, until a point was reached in various ways, when at last through dedication of heart the Holy Spirit made himself manifest in the fulness of his love and power. That there is with God an interval between justification and the giving of the Spirit (an interval such as certain theories contend for), cannot be proved. The unsatisfactory experience of the ignorant or disobedient Christian may lead him to think he never had the Spirit.

There are, however, certain intervals recorded in the New Testament which should be considered. The one between the ascension and Pentecost was for a peculiar preparation through prayer and waiting on the Lord. That in the case of the converts on the Day of Pentecost was doubtless for the confirmation of the apostolic authority; that of the Samaritans when Philip preached may be accounted for by remembering the religious feud between Jew and Samaritan which now must be settled for all time, and the unity of the church established. In regard to Paul, it is evident from the narrative that he knew not the full import of the appearing of Jesus until Ananias came (Acts 9:10-19). But the case of Cornelius proves that no interval at all need exist, for the moment Peter spoke this word, received by faith by Cornelius and those present, the Holy Spirit who knew their hearts fell on them. Neither does the remaining instance of the twelve disciples of John the Baptist at Ephesus, prove that such an interval is necessary today; for they had not even heard that Jesus had come, and that redemption had been accomplished, and the Spirit given. But as soon as remission of sins in the name of Jesus was preached to them, they believed, were baptized, and through prayer and the laying on of hands, received the Holy Spirit (Acts 19:1-6). The question Paul addressed to them has been most strangely applied in these days to Christians, whereas it was pertinent to these disciples of John only. To address it to Christians now is to deny a finished redemption, the sonship of believers, and the once-for-all out-pouring of the Holy Spirit.

6. The conditions of the manifestation of the presence and power of the Spirit are the same, at conversion or at any later, deeper experience of the believer, whether in relation to fuller knowledge of Christ, or to more effective service, or to more patient endurance of trials, or to growth in likeness to Christ. The experience in each case is run in the same mold: each word or fact of Christ must be received in the same attitude and condition of mind as the first, when he was seen as the bearer of our sins, that is, by faith alone. Negatively, it may be said that the conditions are confessed weakness and inability to help oneself, then a willingness to look to God alone for help.

The Scriptures do not teach, as implied or expressed in certain theories, that there is an interval between the remission of sins and the sealing of the Spirit, and that justified believers may die during such interval having never been sealed, and so never having been in Christ, and never having been attested sons of God. Such belief contradicts the very grace of God and implies that sonship depends upon the gift of the Spirit, and not upon redemption and the remission of sins (Gal. 4:5). It also follows that such justified ones devoid of the Spirit are not Christ's (Rom. 8:9; I Cor. 12:3). As to the proof of the presence of the Spirit, whatever emotions may attend the discoveries of the love and power of God in the case of some, they are not to be the tests and measures for all. Conversions are not alike in all, neither are the manifestations of the Spirit. More than all, the proof is seen in growth in holiness, in self-denial for Christ's sake, in the manifold graces, and abiding fruit of the Spirit.

Positively, the requirements or inseparable accompaniments of the manifestation of the indwelling Spirit, whether for holy living or faithful service, must be drawn from the example of our Lord Jesus Christ. And they are prayer, obedience, faith, and above all a desire and purpose to glorify Christ. All, indeed, may be summed up in one condition and that is, to let God have his own will and way with us. If Christ is truly the wisdom of God unto salvation, the Holy Spirit alone can demonstrate it unto the minds and hearts of men; and he has no mission in the world separable from Christ and his work of redemption. The outer work of Christ and the inner work of the Spirit go together. The work for us by Christ is through the blood, the work in us by the Spirit is through the truth. The latter rests upon the former; and without the Spirit, substitutes for the Spirit and his work will be accompanied by substitutes for Christ and his work. The importance, therefore, of the presence and work of the Holy Spirit should be estimated according to that far-reaching word of Christ, "he shall glorify me" (John 16:13-15).

7. In conclusion, the sum of all his mission is to perfect in saints the good work he began, and he molds it all according to this reality of a high and holy sonship. He establishes the saints in and for Christ (II Cor. 1:21). According to this reality their life partakes of thoughts and desires, hopes and objects, spiritual and heavenly. Born of God, knowing whence they came and whither they are going, they live in a world not realized by flesh and blood. Their life is hid with Christ in God; their work of faith is wrought out in the unseen abode of the Spirit; their labor of love is prompted by a loyal obedience to their Lord, who is absent in a far country to which both he and they belong. Their sufferings are not their own but his, who from heaven could ask, "Why persecutest thou me?" Their worship is of the Father in spirit and in truth before the mercy-seat; their peace is the peace of God, which cannot be disturbed by any fear which eternal ages may disclose. Their joy is joy in the Lord, whose spring is in God and ever deepens in its perpetual flow; their hope is the coming of the Son of God from heaven and the vision of the King

in his beauty amidst the unspeakable splendors of his Father's house. And all through the way, thorn and flower, by which they are journeying to the heavenly country, it is the good Spirit who is leading them.

29

Christianity No Fable

By Rev. *Thomas Whitelaw, M.A., D.D.*
PRESBYTERIAN MINISTER, KILMARNOCK, SCOTLAND

Edited by Arnold D. Ehlert, Th.D.

I. ITS SUPREME EXCELLENCE

The first mark of the truthfulness of Christianity is to be found in its supreme excellence as a religious system. The unapproachable beauty and resistless charm of its conception, and the unique character of the means by which it seeks to carry out its aims, are not reconcilable with the notion of fable.

If, however, nothwithstanding, Christianity is a fable, then it is the divinest fable ever clothed in human speech. Nothing like it can be found in the literature of the world. Paul only spoke the unvarnished truth when he declared that eye had not seen nor ear heard, neither had the mind of man conceived the things which God had revealed to men in the Gospel.

Not of Human Origin

1. The very conception of the Gospel as a scheme for rescuing a lost world from the guilt and power of sin, for transforming men into servants of righteousness, followers of Christ, and children of God, each one resembling himself and partaking of his nature, and for eventually lifting them up into a state of holy and blessed immortality like that in which he himself dwells — that conception never took its rise in the brains of a human fable-monger and least of all in that of a crafty priest or political deceiver — no, not even in that of the best and most brilliantly endowed thinker, poet, prophet or philosopher that ever lived. Men do not write novels and compose fiction in order to redeem their fellows from guilt and sin, to comfort and support them in death, and to prepare them for immortality. Even those who regard Christianity as being based on delusions and deceptions do not assert that the object of

its instructors was anything so lofty and spiritual, but rather that
its fabricators sought thereby to enrich themselves by imposing on
their credulous fellows, blinding them to the truth by setting before
them fictions as if they were facts, frightening them with ghostly
terrors and so securing a hold upon their services or their means.
One of the claims of German speculation was that Christianity was
manufactured in Rome in the time of Trajan, i.e., about the beginning of the second century, in order to help on a great liberation
movement amongst the Jewish slave proletariat against their tyran-
nical masters, and that in fact it was an imaginary compound of
Roman Socialism, Greek Philosophy and Jewish Messiahism.
Neither of these, however, is the account furnished by Christianity
itself in its accredited documents, of its aim, which, as already
stated, is to deliver men from sin and death. The very grandeur
of this aim proves that Christianity has not emanated from the
mind of man, but must have proceeded from the heart of God.
And it may be safely contended that Infinite Wisdom and Love
makes no use of fables and deceptions, legends and fictions to
further its purposes and realize its aims.

2. If, in addition, the details of the Christian scheme be considered, that is to say, the particular means by which it proposes
to effect its aim, it will further appear that the idea of fiction and
fable must be laid aside and that of reality and truth set in its
place. It will not be seriously questioned that the details of the
Christian scheme are substantially and briefly these: (1) that God
in infinite love and out of pure grace, from eternity purposed to
provide salvation for the fallen race of man; (2) that in order to
carry out that purpose he sent his own Son, only begotten and well-
beloved, the brightness of his glory and the express image of his
Person, into this world in the likeness of sinful flesh, to die for
men's sins, thereby rendering satisfaction for the same, and to rise
again from the dead, thereby showing that God had accepted the
sacrifice and could on the ground of it be just and the justifier
of the ungodly as well as bringing life and immortality to light;
and (3) that on the ground of this atoning work salvation is
offered to all on the sole condition of faith. This being so, can
any one for a moment believe that forgers and fable-mongers would

or could have invented so divine a tale? All experience certifies the contrary.

Whensoever men have attempted to construct schemes of salvation, they have not sought the origin of these schemes in God but in themselves. Human schemes have always been plans by which men might be able to save themselves, with such salvation as they have supposed themselves to need — not always a salvation from sin and death; more frequently a salvation from material poverty, bodily discomfort, mental ignorance and generally temporal needs. Nor have they ever dreamt of a salvation that should come to them through the mediation of another, and certainly not of God himself in the Person of his Son; but always of a salvation through their own efforts. Never of a salvation by grace through faith and therefore free; but always of a salvation by works and through merit and therefore as a debt — a salvation by outward forms and magical rites, or by education and culture.

Who Invented It?

3. Then, it may be added: If the Christian scheme is a fable, who invented the idea of an Incarnation? For to Jewish minds at any rate such an idea was foreign, being forbidden by their strong monotheism. Who put together the picture of Jesus as it appears in the Gospels? Who conceived the notion of making it that of a sinless man, and doing it so successfully that all subsequent generations of beholders, with a few exceptions at most, have regarded him as sinless? Yet a sinless man had never been seen before nor has ever been beheld since his appearance. Who supplied this Jesus with the superhuman power that performed works only possible to God and with the superhuman wisdom that fell from his lips, if such wisdom was never spoken but only imagined? It is universally allowed that the power and wisdom of Jesus have never been surpassed or even equalled. Whose was the daring genius that struck out the notion not merely of making atonement for sin, but of doing this by Christ's giving his life a ransom for many and demonstrating its reality through his rising from the dead? These conceptions were so incredible to his followers at the first and have been so unacceptable to natural man since, that it is hard to believe any fable-monger would have selected them for his work, even though they had occurred to him.

And who suggested the doctrine of a twofold resurrection at the end of time? — a doctrine to which unaided human science or philosophy has never been able to attain.

The impartial reasoner must perceive that in all these themes we are dealing not with purely human thoughts but with thoughts that are divine, and that it is idle to talk of them as fabulous or untrue. "God is not a man that he should lie." He is neither a tyrant that he should seek to oppress men, nor a false priest that he should want to cheat men, nor a novel writer that he should study to amuse men, but a Father whose dearest interest is to save men, who is Light and in him is no darkness at all, and whose words are like himself, the same yesterday, today and forever.

II. Its Perfect Adaptation

The second mark of truthfulness in the Christian scheme is its perfect adaptation to the end for which it was designed.

1. Assuming for the moment that the Christian system is entirely a product of the human mind, or a pure fabrication, the question to be considered is, whether it is at all likely that it would perfectly answer the end for which it was intended. If that end was to deceive men in order to enslave and degrade them, then its concocters have signally outwitted themselves; for no sooner does a man accept Christianity, than he finds that if he is deceived thereby, it is a blessed deception which makes it impossible to keep him in subjection or degradation, since it illuminates his understanding, purifies his heart, cleanses his imagination, quickens his conscience, strengthens his will and ennobles his whole nature. "Ye shall know the truth and the truth shall make you free," said Christ. On the other hand, if its end was to do this very thing, then undoubtedly its end has been reached; but the mere fact that it has been reached, shows that the scheme has not proceeded from the human mind as a work of fiction, but from the heart of God as a Scripture of truth.

2. If there be one thing more characteristic of man's works than another, it is imperfection. Magnificent as some of man's inventions have been, few of them are absolutely free from defects, and those that are the freest have been brought to their present state of excellence only by slow and short stages and after repeated

modifications and improvements — witness the printing press, the steam engine, telegraphy, electrical power and lighting, musical instruments, airplanes, etc. And what is more, however perfect any human invention may appear to be at the present moment, there is no guarantee that it will not be in time superseded by something more adapted to the end it has in view.

The case, however, is different with God's works which like himself, are all perfect; and if it shall turn out on examination that the Christian system is perfectly adapted to the end it has in view, viz., salvation, and has never needed to be changed, modified or improved, then the inference will be unavoidable that it is God's work and not man's and as a consequence not a fiction but a fact, not fable but truth.

I am aware that at the present moment there are those who declare that Christianity is played out, that it has served its day, that it has lost its hold on men's minds, and will require to give place to some other panacea for the ills of life. But for the most part that is the cry of those who have not themselves tried Christianity and hardly understand what it means. And in any case no effective substitute for Christianity has ever been put forward by its opponents or critics. Nor has any attempt to modify or improve Christianity as a system of religious doctrine ever been successful. Perhaps one of the most strenuous efforts in this direction has been that of so-called liberal (alias rationalistic) theology which seeks to divest Christianity of all its supernatural elements, and in particular of its divine-human Jesus by reducing him to the dimensions of an ordinary man — in which case it is obvious, the whole superstructure of Christianity would fall to the ground. Yet a contributor to the *Hibbert Journal* (Jan. 1910), who himself does not accept orthodox Christianity, writes of "The Collapse of Liberal Christianity," and frankly confesses that "the simple Jesus of liberal Christianity cannot be found," which amounts to an admission that the picture of Jesus in the Gospels as a Divine Man, a supernatural Christ, is no fiction but a sublime truth.

3. A detailed examination of the Christian scheme shows that means better fitted to secure its ends could not have been devised.

a. It will not be denied that part of the aim of Christianity is to restore mankind in general and individuals in particular to the favor and fellowship of God, out of which they have been cast by sin. Whether the Bible is right in its explanation of the origin of sin, need not now be argued. Common observation as well as individual conscience testifies to the fact of sin; and the disastrous condition of the race induced by sin Christianity proposes to remedy — not by telling men that sin is only a figment of the imagination (which men know better than believe); or, if a reality, so trifling a matter that God will overlook it (which men in their best moments doubt); and certainly not by asking men to save themselvs (which they soon discover they cannot do); but by first setting forth sin in all its moral loathsomeness and legal guiltiness, and then announcing that God himself had provided a lamb for a burnt-offering, even his own Son, upon whom he has laid the iniquity of us all, and that now he is in Christ reconciling the world unto himself, not imputing unto men their trespasses.

b. A second thing proposed by Christianity is to make men holy, to free them from the love and practice of sin to conform them in the love and practice of truth and righteousness; and this it seeks to do by giving man a new heart and a right spirit, by changing his nature, implanting in it holy principles and putting it under the government of the divine and eternal spirit.

That the means are adequate has been proved by the experience of the past nineteen centuries, in which millions of human souls have been translated out of darkness into light and turned from the service of Satan to the service of the Living God. And what is more, other methods have been tried without effecting any permanent transformation of either hearts or lives. Magical incantations, meaningless mummeries, laborious ceremonies, painful penances, legislations, education, philanthropy, have in turn been resorted to, but in vain. Never once has the Gospel method been fairly tried and proved inefficient.

c. A third thing Christianity engages to do, is to confer on those who accept it a blessed immortality — to support them when they come to die, to cheer them with the prospect of a happy existence while their bodies are in the grave, to bring those bodies forth again, and in the end to bestow on their whole personality a glorious unending life beneath a new heaven and a new earth wherein dwelleth righteousness. And Christianity does this by first securing its adherents a title to eternal life through the obedience unto death of Christ, next by making them meet for the inheritance through the indwelling and operation of Christ's Spirit, then by opening for them the gates of immortality through Christ's resurrection, and finally by Christ's coming for them at the end of the age.

Now can anything more complete be thought of as a scheme of salvation? Is there any part of it that is not exactly fitted to its place and suited to its end? So far is this from being the case that not a single pin can be removed from the building without bringing down the whole superstructure. Abstract from Christianity the Incarnation, or the Atonement, or the Resurrection, or the Exaltation, or the Future Coming, and its framework is shattered. Take away pardon or purity or peace or sonship or heaven, and its value as a system of religion is gone. But these are not assertions that will hold good of fables and fictions, myths and legends, which might all be tampered with, taken from or added to, without endangering their worth. Hence, it is fair to argue, that a scheme so admirably adjusted in all its parts, so complete in its provisions and so exquisitely adapted to its design, could only have emanated from the mind of him who is wonderful in counsel and excellent in working, who is the true God and the Eternal Life.

III. Its Conspicuous Success

A third mark of truthfulness in the Christian system is its conspicuous success in effecting the end for which it was designed.

Had Christianity been a baseless imagination, or a superstitious legend, is there reason to suppose either that it would have lived so long or that it would have achieved the wonders it has done during the past nineteen centuries — either upon individuals or upon the world at large? It is true that mere length of time in which a religion has prevailed when considered by itself, is no sufficient guarantee of the truth of that religion, else Buddhism would possess a higher certificate of truthfulness than Christianity; but when viewed in connection with the beneficial results in elevating mankind, both individually and collectively, which have followed from a religion, the length of time during which it has continued is no small testimony to its truth. Still the practical effects of a religion upon individuals and upon the world at large, as has been said, form an argument in its favor which cannot easily be set aside.

1. As to the individual. Had the facts upon which Christianity is based been purely fictitious, had the story of the Incarnation, Death and Resurrection of Jesus been only a legend, and had the promise of pardon, purity and peace, of everlasting life and glory which Christianity holds out to men been a deception instead of a verity, does any one imagine it would have effected the transformations it has wrought on individual hearts and lives? I remember that the first lie told by the devil in Eden plunged the whole race of mankind into spiritual death. I have yet to learn that a lie hatched by even good people can save men from perdition and lift them to heaven, can bless them with inward happiness and assure them of divine favor, can comfort them in sorrow, strengthen them in weakness, sustain them in death and fit them for eternity. And yet that is what Christianity can do — has done in past ages to millions who have tried it, and is doing to-day to thousands who are trying it. It will take more than has been said by critics and scoffers to persuade me that these things have been done by a fable. I have heard of fables and fictions, legends and superstitions amusing men and women, diverting them when wearied, occupying them when idle, taking their thoughts off serious matters and even helping them to shut their eyes against death's approach; I never heard of their bringing souls to God, assuring them of his favor, cleansing them from sin, blessing them with peace, preparing them for eternity. But these again are what Christianity can do and does; and so I reason it is not a fable, but a fact, not a legend but a history, not an imaginary tale, but a solid truth.

2. And when to this I add what it has done on the broad theatre of the world, my faith in its truth is confirmed. Nineteen centuries ago Christianity started out on its conquering career. It had neither wealth nor power, nor learning, nor social influence, nor imperial patronage upon its side. It was despised by the great ones of the earth as a superstition. It was looked upon by Jew and Gentile as subversive of religion and morals. Its adherents were collected from the dregs of the population, from the poor and the

ignorant (at least in the world's estimation) ; and its apostles were a humble band, mostly of fishermen — though they soon had their ranks enlarged by the accession of one (Paul) whose mental force and religious earnestness were worth to Christianity whole battalions of common disciples or of average preachers. But what was one, even though he was an intellectual and spiritual giant, to the mighty task set before it of conquering the world and making all nations obedient to the Faith? Yet that task was immediately taken in hand and with what success the annals of the past centuries declare.

In the first century, which may be called the Apostolic Age, it practically defeated Judaism, by establishing itself as an organized religion, not in Palestine alone, but in Asia Minor, and in some of the chief cities of Europe. To this it was no doubt helped by the destruction of Jerusalem in the year 70 by the armies of Titus; but the undermining of Judaism was being gradually brought about by the spread of the Christian Faith.

In the next two centuries, which may be called the Age of the Fathers, it overcame paganism, substituting in wide circles the worship of Jesus for the worship of heathen divinities and of the Roman Emperor. Not without passing through fierce tribulation in the long succession of persecutions with which it was assailed, did it achieve the victory, but in its experience was repeated the experience of Israel in Egypt — "the more it was afflicted the more it multiplied and grew" so that by the end of the third and the beginning of the fourth century it had within its pale about a fifth of the Roman Empire.

From that time on Christianity applied itself to the task of making nominal Christians into real ones; and but for the mercy of God at the Reformation it might have been defeated. But God's Spirit brooded upon the moral and spiritual waste as erst he did upon the material in the beginning, and God's Word said — "Let there be light!" and there was light. Luther in Germany, Calvin in Geneva, and Knox in Scotland, with others in different parts arose as champions of the truth and recalled men's thoughts to the simplicities and certainties of the Gospel; and a great awakening overspread the nominally Christian world.

Thereafter Christianity took a forward step among the nations; and is now doing for the world what no other religion has done or can do — neither Buddhism nor Confucianism, nor Mohammedanism — what no modern substitute for Christianity can do — whether materialism, or agnosticism, or spiritism or socialism; and just because of this we may rest assured that Christianity is no cunningly devised fable but a divinely revealed truth — that it alone contains hope for the world, as a whole, and for generation after generation as it passes and that the day will yet come when it will fill the globe.

In short, when one remembers that Christianity has built up the Christian church and that the Christian church has been the most powerful factor in creating modern civilization, it becomes an impossibility to credit the allegation or even to harbor the suspicion, that it is founded on a lie. By its fruits it may be tested. Notwithstanding the imperfections that adhere to the Christian church so far as it is a human institution, few will deny that its existence in the world has been productive of preponderantly good results, and on that certificate alone it may be claimed that Christianity is no "cunningly devised fable" but a sure revelation of God's glorious redemptive purpose for sinful men.

30

The Biblical Conception of Sin

By Rev. Thomas Whitelaw, M.A., D.D.
PRESBYTERIAN MINISTER, KILMARNOCK, SCOTLAND

Revised by Charles L. Feinberg, Th.D., Ph.D.

Holy Scripture undertakes no demonstration of the reality of sin. In all its statements concerning sin, sin is presupposed as a fact which can neither be controverted nor denied. It is true that some, through false philosophy and materialistic science, refuse to admit the existence of sin, but their endeavors to explain it away by their theories is sufficient proof that sin is no figment of the imagination but a solid reality. Others may sink so far beneath the power of sin as to lose all sense of its actuality, because their moral natures have become so hardened as to be past feeling. In their case conviction of sin is not possible except by the inward operation of the Spirit of God, who can break up the hard crust of moral numbness in which their spirits are encased. A third class of persons, by simply declining to think about sin, may come in course of time to conclude that whether sin be a reality or not, it does not concern them; in which case once more they are merely deceiving themselves. The truth is that it is extremely doubtful whether any intelligent person whose moral intuitions have not been completely destroyed or whose mental perceptions have not been blunted by indulgence in wickedness, can successfully persuade himself permanently that sin is a myth or a creation of the imagination, and not a grim reality. Most men know that sin is in themselves a fact of consciousness they cannot deny, and in others a fact of observation they cannot overlook. The Bible assumes that any man will discover it who looks into his own heart.

Accordingly, the Bible devotes its efforts to imparting to mankind reliable knowledge about the nature and universality, the origin and culpability, and especially the removal of sin. To set forth these in succession will be the object of this chapter.

I. The Nature of Sin

It scarcely requires stating that modern ideas of sin receive no countenance from Scripture, which never speaks about sin as "good in the making," as "a necessity determined by heredity and environment," as "a stage in the upward development of finite being," as a "taint adhering to man's corporeal frame," and least of all "as a figment of the imperfectly enlightened, or theologically perverted, imagination," but always as the free act of an intelligent, moral and responsible being asserting himself against the will of his Maker, that will being discerned from the law written on his heart (Romans 2:15), or from the revelation of God to man in the Old Testament and in the New. Hence, sin is usually described in the Scriptures by terms that indicate with perfect clarity its relation to the divine will or law, and no uncertainty exists as to its essential character.

In the Old Testament (Ex. 34:5, 6; Psa. 32:1, 2) three words are used to give full definition of sin: (1) "Transgression" (*pesha'*) or a falling away from God, and therefore a violation of his commandments (Ex. 22:8) ; (2) "Sin" (*hatta'th*) or a missing of the mark, a coming short of one's duty, a failure to do what one ought (Gen. 4:7) ; (3) "Iniquity" (*'awon*) or a turning aside from the straight path, hence perversity, depravity, and inequality (Isa. 53:6).

The words employed in the New Testament to designate sin are not much, if at all, different in meaning — *hamartia,* a failure, a false step ; and *anomia,* lawlessness. Hence the biblical conception of sin may be fairly summed up in the words of the Westminster Confession: "Sin is any want of conformity unto or transgression of the law of God" ; or in those of Melancthon: "Sin is rightly defined as *anomia,* or dissimilarity to the law of God, that is, a failure of nature and deeds opposed to the law of God."

II. The Universality of Sin

According to the Bible, sin is not a quality or condition of soul that has revealed itself only in exceptional individuals like notorious offenders, or in exceptional circumstances, as in the early ages of man's existence on the earth, or among half developed races, or in lands where the arts and sciences are unknown, or in civilized communities where the local environment is prejudicial to morality. Sin is a quality or condition of soul which exists in every child born of woman, and not merely at isolated times but at all times, and at every stage of his career, though not always manifesting itself in the same forms of thought, feeling, word and action in every individual or even in the same individual. It has affected *extensively* the whole race of man in every age from the beginning of the world on, in every land beneath the sun, in every race into which mankind has been divided, in every situation in which the individual has found himself placed; and *intensively* in every individual in every department and faculty of his nature from the center to the circumference of his being.

Scripture utters no uncertain sound on the world-embracing character of moral corruption, in the prediluvian age (Gen. 6:12), in David's generation (Psa. 14:3), in Isaiah's time (Isa. 53:6), and in the Christian era (Rom. 3:23). Solomon's verdict holds good for every day, "There is no man that sinneth not" (I Kings 8:46). Not even the best of men who have been born again by the Spirit and the Word of God, renewed in their minds and created anew in Christ Jesus, are without sin (I John 1:8). How true this is may be learned from the fact that Scripture mentions only one person in whom there was no sin, Jesus of Nazareth, who could challenge his enemies to convict him of sin. Of those who knew him most intimately one testified that he "did no sin, neither was guile found in his mouth" (I Pet. 2:22; I John 3:5). Of this exception, of course, the explanation was and is that he was "God manifest in the flesh" (I Tim. 3:16). But besides him not a single person figures cn the page of the Holy Writ of whom it is said, or could have been said, that he was sinless. Neither Enoch nor Noah in the ante-diluvian age; neither Abraham nor Isaac in patriarchal times; neither Moses nor Aaron in the years of Israel's wanderings; neither David nor Jonathan in the days of the monarchy; neither Peter nor John, neither Barnabas nor Paul in the apostolic age, could have claimed such a distinction; and these were some of the best men that have ever appeared on this planet.

Nor is it merely extensively that the reign of sin over the human family is universal, but intensively as well. It is not a malady which has affected only one part of man's complex constitution; every part of it has felt its baneful influence. It has darkened his understanding and made him unable, without supernatural illumination, to apprehend spiritual things (I Cor. 2:14; Eph. 4:17, 18). It defiles the heart, so that if left to itself, it becomes deceitful above all things (Jer. 17:9, Eccl. 9:3; Gen. 6:5; Matt. 15:19). It paralyzes the will, at least partially in every case, so that even regenerated souls often complain like Paul, that when they would do good, evil is present with them (Rom. 7:14-25). It dulls the conscience, that vicegerent of God in the soul, renders it less quick to detect the approach of evil, less prompt to sound a warning against it, and sometimes so dead as to be past feeling about it (Eph. 4:19). In short, there is not a faculty of the soul that is not injured by it (Jas. 1:5).

III. The Origin of Sin

How a pure being, possessed of those intellectual capacities and moral intuitions which were needful to make him justly responsible to divine law, could and did lapse from his original innocence and fall into sin, is one of those dark problems which philosophers and theologians have vainly tried to solve. No more reliable explanation of sin's entrance into the universe in general and into this world in particular has ever been given than that furnished by Scripture.

According to the Bible, sin first made its appearance in the angelic hosts, though nothing more is recorded than the simple fact that the angels sinned, kept not their first estate, but left their proper habitation (II Pet. 2:4; Jude 6), their reason for doing so being passed over in silence. The obvious deduction is that the sin of these fallen spirits was a free act on their part, dictated by dissatisfaction with the place which had been assigned to them and by ambition to secure for themselves a higher station than that in which they had been placed. Yet this does not answer the question how such dissatisfaction and ambition could arise in beings created sinless. Inasmuch as external influence in the way of temptation from without, by intelligences other than themselves, is excluded, it does not appear that any other answer is possible than that in the creation of a finite personality endowed with freedom of will, there is necessarily involved the possibility of making a sinful choice.

In the case of man, however, sin's entrance into the world receives a somewhat different explanation from the sacred writers. With one accord they ascribe the sinful actions, words, feelings and thoughts of each individual to his own deliberate, free choice, so that he is thereby with perfect justice held responsible for his deviation from the path of moral rectitude. Some of the inspired writers make it clear that the entrance of sin into this world was effected through the disobedience of the first man who acted as the representative of his whole natural posterity (Rom. 5:12), and that the first man's fall was brought about by temptation from without, by the seductive influence of Satan (Gen. 2:1-6; John 8:44; II Cor. 11:3; Eph. 2:2). The Genesis story of the fall teaches unmistakably to this effect: That the first man's lapse from a state of innocence entailed disastrous consequences upon himself and his descendants. Upon himself it wrought immediate disturbance of his whole nature, implanting in it the seeds of degeneration, bodily, mental, moral and spiritual, filling him with fear of his Maker, laying upon his conscience a burden of guilt, darkening his perceptions of right and wrong, and interrupting the hitherto peaceful relations which had existed between himself and his Creator. Upon his descendants it opened the floodgates of corruption by which their natures even from birth fell beneath the power of evil, as was soon witnessed in the dark tragedy of fratricide with which the tale of human history began, and in the rapid spread of violence through the pre-diluvian world.

This is what theologians call the doctrine of original sin, by which they mean that the results of Adam's sin, both legal and moral, have been transmitted to Adam's posterity, so that now each individual comes into the world, not like his first father, in a state of moral equilibrium, but as the inheritor of a nature that has been weakened by sin.

That this doctrine, though frequently opposed, has a basis in science and philosophy as well as in Scripture, is becoming more apparent every day. But whether confirmed or contradicted by modern thought, the doctrine of Scripture shines like a sunbeam, that man is "conceived in sin and shapen in iniquity" (Psa. 51:5; see also Psa. 58:3; Eph. 2:3; Gen. 8:21; and Job 15:14). If these passages do not show that the Bible teaches the doctrine of original, or transmitted sin, it is difficult to see in what clearer or more emphatic language the doctrine could have been taught. The truth of the doctrine may be challenged by those who repudiate the authority of Scripture; that it is a doctrine of Scripture cannot be denied.

IV. The Culpability of Sin

By this is meant not merely the blameworthiness of sin as an act, inexcusable on the part of its perpetrator, who being such a personality as he is, endowed with such faculties as are his, ought never to have committed it; nor only the heinousness of it, as an act done against light and love, and in flagrant opposition to the holiness and majesty of the Lawgiver, who must regard it with abhorrence and repel from his presence and exclude from his favor the one guilty of it. But over and above these representations of sin which are all Scriptural, by the culpability of sin is intended its exposure to the penalty affixed by divine justice to transgression.

That a penalty was affixed by God in the first instance when man was created, the Genesis narrative declares (Gen. 2:16). That this penalty still hangs over the impenitent is not only distinctly implied in our Saviour's language, that apart from his redeeming work the world was in danger of perishing and already condemned (John 3:16-18); but it is expressly declared by John who says that "the wrath of God abideth" on the unbeliever (John 3:18), and by Paul who asserts that "the wages of sin is death" (Rom. 6:23).

It is manifest that Scripture includes in the just punishment of sin more than the death of the body. That this does form part of sin's penalty can hardly be disputed by a careful reader of the Bible; but Scripture unmistakably implies that the penalty equally includes spiritual and eternal death. When the Bible affirms that men are naturally dead in trespasses and sins (Eph. 2:1), it obviously purposes to convey the idea that until the soul is quickened by divine grace, it is incapable of doing anything spiritually good or religiously saving, of securing legal justification before a holy God, or of bringing about spiritual regeneration. When Scripture further asserts the unbeliever shall not see life (John 3:36), and that the wicked shall go away into everlasting punishment (Matt. 25:46), it assuredly does not suggest that on entering the other world, the unsaved on earth will have another opportunity to accept salvation (second probation), or that extinction of being will be their lot (annihilation), or that all mankind will eventually attain salvation (universalism). Meanwhile, it suffices to observe that the words just quoted teach that the penalty of sin continues beyond the grave. Granting that the words of Christ about the worm that never dies and the fire that shall not be quenched are figurative, they unquestionably signify that the figures stand for some terrible calamity — on the one hand, loss of happiness, separation from the source of life, exclusion from blessedness, and on the other, access of misery, suffering, wretchedness, woe, which will be realized by the wicked as the due reward of their impenitent and disobedient lives, and which no future years will relieve (see Revelation 22:11).

V. The Removal of Sin

Heinous and culpable as sin is, it is not left in Scripture to be contemplated in all the nakedness of its loathsome character in God's sight, and in all the heaviness of its guilt before the law, without hope of remedy for either; but in a comforting light it is set forth as an offense that may be forgiven and a defilement that will or may be ultimately cleansed.

As for the *pardonableness* of sin, that constitutes the heart of the good news for the propagation of which the Bible was written. From the first page of Genesis to the last in Revelation there is an undertone, swelling out as the end approaches into clear and joyous accents of love and mercy, proclaiming that the God of heaven, while himself holy and just, is nevertheless merciful and gracious (Ex. 34:6). It is announced that he has made full provision for harmonizing the claims of mercy and justice in his own character by laying help upon his only begotten Son, upon whom he laid the iniquity of us all (Isa. 53:6), that he might once for all as the Lamb of God, take away the sin of the world (John 1:29). The Bible declares that the whole work necessary for enabling sinful men to be forgiven, has been accomplished by

Christ's death and resurrection, and the world has been reconciled to God (2 Cor. 5:19). Men everywhere are invited to repent and be converted, that their sins may be blotted out (Acts 3:19). Nothing more is required of men in order to be freely and fully justified from all their transgressions than faith in the propitiation of the cross (Rom. 3:25); and nothing will shut a sinner out from forgiveness except refusal to believe (John 3:36).

The ultimate *removal* of sin from the souls of believers is left by Scripture in no uncertainty. It was foretold in the name given to the Saviour in no uncertainty. It was foretold in the name given to the Saviour at his birth (Matt. 1:21). It was implied in the purpose of his incarnation (I John 3:5). It is declared to have been the purpose of his death upon the cross (Tit. 2:14). It is held up before the Christian as his final destiny to be conformed to the image of Christ (Rom. 8:29) and to dwell in the heavenly city (Rev. 22:14).

That those who depart this life in impenitence and unbelief will be annihilated either at death or after the resurrection, is deemed by some to be a legitimate deduction from the use of the word death as the punishment of sin. But death, when applied to man, does not mean extinction of being. Long ago attention was drawn to the fact that the various organs of the body may be removed without extinguishing the indwelling spirit, and it is certain that the immaterial part of man will not be destroyed, though the entire material frame were reduced to dust. Solely on the assumption that mind is merely a function of matter, can the dissolution of the body be regarded as the extinction of being. Such an assumption is foreign to Scripture. In the Old Testament, David expected to "dwell in the house of the Lord forever" (Psa. 23:6). In the New Testament, Christ took for granted that Abraham, Isaac and Jacob, though long dead, were still living, and that Dives and Lazarus still existed in the unseen world, although their bodies were in the grave. Nowhere is it suggested that the soul is simply a function of the body, or that it ceases to be when the body dies.

As to the theory of a second probation, such texts as Matthew 12:32 and 25:48 give no hope of the ultimate destruction of sin through a second chance. Every attempt to find room for the idea shatters itself on the unchallengeable fact that the words "everlasting" and "eternal" are the same in Greek (*aionion*), and indicate that the punishment of the wicked and the blessedness of the righteous are of equal duration. Nor is it merely that the doctrine of a second probation is devoid of Scripture support, but contrary to all experiences, it takes for granted that every unsaved soul would accept the second offer of salvation, which is more than anyone can certainly affirm; and if all did not, sin would still remain. It may be argued that all would accept because of the greater light they would then have as to the paramount importance of salvation, or because of the stronger influences that will then be brought to bear upon them. But on this hypothesis a reflection would seem to be cast on God for not having done all he might have done to save men while they lived, a reflection good men will not make.

The third theory for banishing sin from the human family, if not from the universe, is that of universalism, the view that through discipline hereafter the souls of all will be brought into subjection to Christ. That the universal headship of Christ is taught in Scripture is true (I Cor. 15:28). But it is not implied that all will surrender in willing subjection to Christ. Subject to him must every power and authority be, human and angelic, hostile and friendly, believing and unbelieving. "He must reign till all his enemies have been placed beneath his feet" — not taken to his heart, received into his love and employed in his service. This does not look like universal salvation and the complete extinction of moral evil or sin in the universe.

A dark and insoluble mystery was the coming of sin into God's universe at the first. As dark a mystery is its continuance in a race that from eternity was the object of God's love, and in time was redeemed by the blood of God's Son, and graciously acted on by God's Spirit. Happily, we are not required to understand all mysteries; we can leave this one confidently in the Father's hand.

CHARLES BRAY WILLIAMS (1869-1952) was distantly related to Roger Williams, father of religious liberty in America; William Williams, signer of the Declaration of Independence; and Sir George Williams, founder of the Young Men's Christian Association (YMCA). He graduated from Wake Forest College (B.A.), Crozer Theological Seminary (B.D.), University of Chicago (M.A., Ph.D.) and was honored by Baylor University with a D.D. degree. He taught Greek at Southwestern Baptist Theological Seminary (1905-1919) and was Dean of the school (1913-1919). He became president of Howard College (Alabama) from 1919-1921; professor of New Testament Interpretation at Mercer University (1921-1925); and professor of Greek and Ethics at Union University (Tennessee) from 1925-1938. He also pastored Baptist churches in Pennsylvania, Texas, Florida Tennessee and North Carolina. Author of ten books, his most notable contributions was *A Translation of the New Testament in the Language of the People* (1937).

31

Paul's Testimony to the Doctrine of Sin

By Professor Charles B. Williams, B.D., Ph.D.
SOUTHWESTERN BAPTIST THEOLOGICAL SEMINARY,
FORT WORTH, TEXAS

Abridged and emended by James H. Christian, Th.D.

Theodore Parker once said: "I seldom use the word sin. The Christian doctrine of sin is the devil's own. I hate it utterly." His view of sin shaped his views as to the person of Christ, atonement, and salvation. In fact, the sin question is back of one's theology, soteriology, sociology, evangelism, and ethics. One cannot hold a scriptural view of God and the plan of salvation without having a scriptural idea of sin. One cannot proclaim a true theory of society unless he sees the heinousness of sin and its relation to all social ills and disorders. No man can be a successful New Testament evangelist, publishing the Gospel as "the power of God unto salvation to every one that believeth," unless he has an adequate conception of the enormity of sin. Nor can a man hold a consistent theory of ethics or live up to the highest standard of morality, unless he is gripped with a keen sense of sin's seductive nature.

SIN A FACT IN HUMAN HISTORY

Paul has an extensive vocabulary of terms denoting sin or sins. In the Epistle to the Romans, where he elaborates his doctrine of sin, he uses ten general terms for sin:

1. *Hamartia,* 58 times in all, 43 in Romans, missing of the mark, sin as a principle. 2. *Hamarteema,* twice, sin as an act. 3. *Parabasis,* five times, transgression, literally walking along by the line but not exactly according to it. 4. *Paraptoma,* 15 times, literally a falling, lapse, deviation from truth and uprightness

(Thayer), translated "trespass" in R.V. 5. *Adikia,* 12 times, unrighteousness. 6. *Asebeia,* four times, ungodliness, lack of reverence for God. 7. *Anomia,* lawlessness, six times. 8. *Akatharsia,* nine times, uncleanness, lack of purity. 9. *Parokoee,* twice, disobedience. 10. *Planee,* four times, wandering, error.

Besides these general terms for sin, Paul uses many specific terms for various sins, 21 of these being found in the category of Rom. 1:29-31. Twenty-one equals three times seven and seems to express the idea of completeness in sin reached by the Gentiles. It is literally true that Paul uses scores of terms denoting and describing various personal sins, sensual, social, ethical, and religious. Is this not an unmistakable lexical evidence that the Apostle to the Gentiles believed in sin as a fact in human history?

Again, in all Paul's leading epistles he deals with sin in the abstract or with sins in the concrete. In Romans 1:18-3:20, he discusses the failure of both Jews and Gentiles to attain righteousness. These chapters constitute the most graphic and comprehensive description of sin found in biblical, Greek, Roman, or any literature. It is so true to the facts in heathen life today that modern heathen often accuse Christian missionaries of writing it after they have had personal knowledge of their life and conduct.

In I Corinthians, gross sins are dealt with — envy, strife, divisions, incest, litigation, adultery, fornication, drunkenness, covetousness, idolatry, etc. In II Corinthians, some of the same sins are condemned. In Galatians, he implies the failure of man to attain righteousness in maintaining the thesis that no man is justified by the deeds of the law, but any man may be justified by simple faith in Christ Jesus (2:14ff), and mentions the works of the flesh, "fornication, uncleanness, lasciviousness, idolatry," etc. (5:19). In Ephesians, he recognizes that his readers were "once dead in trespasses and sins" (2:1), and exhorts them to lay aside certain sins (4:25ff). In Colossians, he does the same. In Philippians, he says less about sin or sins, but in 3:3-9 he tells his experience of failure to attain righteousness with all his advantages of birth, training, culture, and circumstances. In the pastoral epistles, he rebukes certain sins with no uncertain voice.

Paul's Experience the Psychological Proof to Him of His Doctrine of Sin

Paul was a Pharisee. Righteousness or right relation with God, was his religious goal. As a Pharisee he felt that he could and must, in himself, achieve righteousness by keeping the whole written and oral law. This kind of (supposable) righteousness he afterwards describes and repudiates. "For we are the circumcision, who worship by the Spirit of God, and glory in Christ Jesus, and have no confidence in the flesh: though I myself might have confidence even in the flesh: circumcised the eighth day, of the stock of Israel, of the tribe of Benjamin, a Hebrew of Hebrews: as touching zeal, persecuting the church; as touching the righteousness which is in the law, blameless. Howbeit, what things were gain to me, these have I counted loss for Christ. Yea, verily, and I count all things to be loss for the excellency of the knowledge of Christ Jesus my Lord; for whom I suffered the loss of all things and do count them but refuse, that I may gain Christ and be found in him, not having a righteousness of mine own, even that which is of the law, but that which is through faith in Christ, the righteousness which is from God by faith" (Phil. 3:3-9, ASV). All the righteousness he could achieve was insufficient. Only God's own righteousness, given through faith in Christ Jesus, could satisfy the conscience of the awakened sinner or be acceptable to God.

The Origin of Sin

The apostle does not discuss the larger problem, the origin of sin in God's moral universe. Only the relative and temporal origin of sin, its entrance into the human race on earth, not its absolute and ultimate source, engages the thought of Paul.

The classic passage on the source of human sin is Rom. 5:12-21. Paul testifies that sin entered our race in and through the disobedience of Adam. "As through one man sin [*hamartia*, the sin principle] entered into the world, and death by sin; and so death passed unto all men, for that all sinned . . . as through one trespass the judgment came unto all men to condemnation . . . for as through the one man's disobedience many were made sinners" (Rom. 5:12, 18-19). In this parallelism between Adam and Christ, Paul is seeking to show, by contrast, the excellence of grace and the transcendent blessedness of the justified man in Christ. He is not primarily discussing the origin of human sin. The fact that it is an incidental and not a studied testimony makes it all the more trustworthy and convincing.

Nor is Paul here simply voicing the thought of his uninspired fellow-countrymen as to the entrance of sin into our race. Dr. Edersheim says: "So far as their opinions can be gathered from their writings, the great doctrines of original sin and the sinfulness of our whole nature were not held by the ancient Rabbis." (*Life and Times of Jesus the Messiah,* I, 165.) Weber thus summarizes the Jewish view as expressed in the Talmud: "By the Fall man came under a curse, is guilty of death, and his right relation to God is rendered difficult. More than this cannot be said. Sin, to which the bent and leaning had already been planted by creation, had become a fact, 'the evil impulse' (*cor malignum,* 4 Es. 3:21) gained the mastery over mankind, who can only resist it by the greatest efforts; before the Fall it had power over him, but no such ascendancy" (*Altsyn. Theol.,* p. 216). The reader is referred to Wisd. 2:23ff; Ecclus. 25:24 (33); 4 Es. 3:7, 21ff; Apoc. Baruch 17:3; 54:15, 19, as expressions of the Jewish view of the entrance of sin into the world and the relation of Adam to the race in the transmission of guilt. One of these passages, Ecclus. 25:24 (33) even traces the sin of the race back to Eve.

Observe that Paul goes beyond the statement of any uninspired Jewish writers —

1. *In asserting that Adam and not Eve is the one through whom sin entered into the race.*

2. *That,* in some sense, *when Adam sinned, "all sinned", and in his sinning, "all were made"* (stood down or constituted) *"sinners"* (Rom. 5:19). The apostle here means, doubtless, that all the race was seminally in Adam as its progenitor, and that Adam by the process of heredity handed down to his descendants a depraved nature. He can scarcely mean that each individual was actually in person in Adam. If Adam had not sinned and thus depraved and corrupted the fountain head of the race, the race itself would not have been the heir of sin and the reaper of its fruits, sorrow, pain, and death.

3. *That in the introduction of sin into the race by its progen-itor the race itself was rendered helpless to extricate itself from sin and death.* This the apostle asserts over and over again and has already demonstrated before he reaches the parallelism be-tween Adam and Christ when he says: "That every mouth may be stopped and all the world brought under the judgment of God"; "because by the works of the law shall no flesh be justified in his sight" (3:19, 20).

The Essence and Nature of Sin

This brings us to ask, What constituted the essence or core of sin, as Paul saw it? Modern evolutionists emphasize the upward tendency of all things, and so sin is regarded by them as merely a step in the upward progress of the race; that is, sin is "good in the making." Christian Scientists go still farther and regard all pain and evil as merely imaginary creations of abnormal minds (see *Science and Health*). There is no actual evil, no real pain, say they. Does either of these views find endorsement in Paul? It must be noted that Paul nowhere gives a formal definition of sin. But by studying the terms he most frequently uses, we can determine his idea of sin. He uses mostly the noun *hamartia*, 58 times, from the verb *hamartano*, to miss the mark, to sin. In classical Greek it means "to miss an aim," "to err in judgment or opinion." *With Paul, to sin is to miss the mark* ETHICALLY and RELIGIOUSLY. Two other words used by Paul show us what the mark missed is: *adikia*, unrighteousness, lack of con-formity to the will of God; *anomia*, lawlessness, failure to act or live according to the standard of God's law. So the mark missed is the divine law. *Parabasis*, transgression, emphasizes the same idea, failure to measure up to the line of righteousness laid down in the law.

On the other hand, sin is not merely a negation. It is a positive quality. It is a "fall" (paraptoma 15 times). This is graphically illustrated by Paul in his description of the Gentile world's idola-try, sensuality, and immorality (Rom. 1:18-32). First, they knew God, for he taught them about himself in nature and in con-science (1:19, 20). Secondly, they refused to worship him as God, or to give thanks to him as the Giver of all good things (1:21). Thirdly, they began to worship the creature rather than the Creator, then gave themselves up to idolatry in a descending scale, worshipping first human images, then those of birds, then those of beasts, and finally of reptiles (1:22-25). Fourthly, this wrong idea of God and false relation to him degraded them into the grossest sensuality and blackest immorality (1:26-32). Is this progress of the race? If so, it is progress in the unfolding of sin's cumulative power, in the Roman Empire where human philosophy and culture were doing their utmost to stem the tide of vice and contribute to the advancement of human government, thought, art, and ethics. That is, if sin is a link in the chain of man's evolution, Paul would say it was a downward and not an upward step in the long road of man's development.

Let us look at another term used by Paul to express God's attitude toward sin. This is the term "wrath," occurring 20 times in Paul's epistles. (This count follows Moulton and Geden, *Concordance to the Greek Testament,* and excludes Hebrews from Paul's epistles.) Thayer defines this term thus: "That in God which stands opposed to man's disobedience, obduracy, and sin, and manifests itself in punishing the same" (*Greek English Lexicon to New Testament*). That is, *sin is diametrically opposite to the element of holiness and righteousness in God's character,* and so God's righteous character revolts at sin in man and manifests this revulsion by punishing sin. This manifestation of the divine displeasure at sin is not spasmodic or arbitrary. It is the natural expression of a character that loves right and goodness. Because he does approve and love right and goodness, he must disapprove and hate unrighteousness and evil. The spontaneous expression of this attitude of God's character toward sin is "wrath." How heinous and enormous sin must be, if the loving and gracious God, in whom Paul believes, thus hates and punishes it! Its nature must be the opposite of those highest attributes of God, holiness, righteousness, love.

Take another term used by Paul, *hupodikos*, guilty (Rom. 3:19). Thayer thus defines this term: "Under judgment, one who has lost his suit; with a dative of person, debtor to one, owing satisfaction (*ibid*). In this passage it is used with the dative of God, and so "all the world" is declared by Paul to be "under judgment of God, having lost its suit with God, owing satisfaction to God" (and by implication not able to render satisfaction to

him). This passage implies that *the essence of sin is "guilt."
Man by sin is "under judgment," "under sentence."* He has come
*into court with God, is found to have broken God's law, and so
is guilty* and liable to punishment. A secondary element in sin is
implied in this term, the helplessness of man in sin, "owing satisfaction to God," but not able to render it.

Paul uses the term sin to express three phases of sin: FIRST,
the sin principle, or sin in the abstract. He uses the term more
often in this sense than in any other. He often personifies the
sin principle, doubtless because he believes in the personal Satan.
SECONDLY, *by implication he teaches that man is in a state of sin*
(Rom. 5:18, 19). "All men unto condemnation" means that men
are in a state of condemnation — guilty of breaking God's law,
and therefore worthy of punishment. "Made sinners" signifies
that man's nature is essentially sinful, and so man may be said
to be under the sin principle, or in the state of sin (though this
phrase, "in the state of sin," does not occur in Paul, but first in
theologians of a later age). THIRDLY, *Paul uses several terms for
sin which signify acts of sin.* Here he views it in the concrete.
Men forget God, hate God, lie, steal, kill, commit adultery, hate
parents, love self, etc.

Relation of the Law to Sin

Does the law produce sin? Not at all, asserts Paul. "What
shall we say then? Is the law sin? God forbid. Howbeit, I had
not known sin, except through the law: for I had not known
coveting, except the law had said, Thou shalt not covet; but sin,
finding occasion, wrought in me through the commandment all
manner of coveting; for apart from the law sin is dead," etc., etc.
(Rom. 7:7-14, ASV). The following points seem clearly expressed in this passage:

1. *The law is not the real cause of man's sin.* Not even its
severest demands can be charged with causing man's sin.

2. *This is true, because the law is essentially "holy, righteous,
good"*; holy in the double sense of being a separate order of being and conduct ordained by God and also requiring holiness, or
the following of this separate order of being and conduct; righteous in the sense of being the expression of God's will and the
standard of man's thoughts and actions; good in the sense that it

is ordained for benevolent ends. It is also called "spiritual" in the sense that it was given through God's Spirit and conduces to spirituality if obeyed from the right motive.

3. *But this holy, righteous, good, and spiritual, law became* "THE OCCASION" *of sinning.* This Paul illustrates with the tenth commandment. He would not have coveted if the law had not said, Thou shalt not covet. The Greek word for "occasion" *aphormee* means literally "a base of operations" (Thayer). The sin principle makes the command of God its headquarters for a life-long campaign of struggle in man, urging him to evil actions and deterring him from good ones. There is something in man which revolts from doing the thing demanded and inclines him to do the thing forbidden. Hence, the sin principle, using this tendency in man, and so making the law the base of its operations, becomes the "occasion" to sinning.

4. *The law shows the sinfulness of sin* — shows it to be heinous in its nature and deadly in its consequences. This is what Paul intimated in Rom. 5:20, when he said, "the law came in besides that the trespass might abound." The law shows men that they are failures in the matter of achieving righteousness.

5. *The law thus* NEGATIVELY *prepares the way for leading men to Christ as their only Rescuer.* "Wretched man that I am! Who shall deliver me out of the body of this death? I thank God through Jesus Christ our Lord" (Rom. 7:24, 25). The apostle was driven to despair as he plunged headlong into persecution and its enormous sins, but when he reached the end of his own strength he looked up and accepted deliverance from the risen Christ.

Relation of the Flesh to Sin

Paul often uses the term "flesh" *sarx* in contrast with the term spirit. In this sense "flesh," according to Thayer, means "mere human nature, the earthly nature of man apart from divine influence, and therefore prone to sin and opposed to God." He regards the flesh (occurring 84 times) as the seat of the sin principle. "In me, that is, in my flesh, dwelleth no good thing" (Rom. 7:18). He does not mean to deny that sin as a guilty act rests on the human will. Yet he regards the lower nature of man (his *sarx*) as the element of weakness and corruption in man, which furnishes a field for the operation of the sin principle. *The law is the "*BASE *of operations"* (occasion), *but the flesh is the open* FIELD *where the sin principle operates.* This sin principle drags the higher man (called "the inner man," Rom. 7:22, "the mind, or reason," *nous* 7:25, or more usually, the spirit) down into the realm of the flesh and through the passions, appetites, etc. (Gal. 5:16; Eph. 2:3), leads the whole man into thoughts, acts, and courses of sin.

But we must hasten to say that Paul does not adopt the Platonic view that matter is evil per se. Paul does not think of man's physical structure as being in itself sinful and his spirit, or soul, in itself as holy. He merely emphasizes the serfdom of man under the sway of the sin principle on account of the weakness of human flesh. *Nor does Paul claim that human reason is free from sin because it approves the law of God.* His expression (Rom. 7:25) "I of myself with the mind [reason] indeed serve [am slave to] the law of God; but with the flesh the law of sin," only emphasizes the fact of struggle in man; that the higher nature does approve the requirements of God's law, though it cannot meet those demands because of the slavery of his lower nature (flesh) to the sin principle.

The Consequences of Sin

This point needs no prolonged discussion. Paul thinks of death, with its train of antecedents, sorrow, pain and all kinds of suffering, as the consequence of sin. This means physical as well as spiritual death, and the latter (separation of man from fellowship with God) is of prime import to Paul. He also asserted the great fact that all cosmic life, plant, animal, and human, has been made to suffer because of the presence of sin in man. (See Rom. 5:12-14, 21; 6:21; 7:10; 8:19-25; Eph. 2:1, etc.)

The Universality of Sin

Paul regards every man as a guilty sinner, however great may be his natural or cultural advantages. He feels that *he* had the greatest advantages "in the flesh" to attain righteousness (Phil. 3:3-9), but he had miserably failed (Rom. 7:24) as all men have failed (Rom. 1:18-2:29). But he is not satisfied with a mere experimental demonstration of the universality of sin. He likewise bases it on the dictum of Scripture (Rom. 3:9-20). More than that he studied the facts of human life, both Jewish and Gentile, and so by the inductive method is led by the Spirit to declare "by the works of the law shall no flesh be justified in his sight" (Rom. 3:20); "All have sinned and are coming short of the glory of God" (Rom. 3:23).

The Persistence of the Sin Principle

In Gal. 5:17-18, Paul tells the Galatian Christians that "the flesh lusteth against the Spirit, and the Spirit against the flesh; for these are contrary the one to the other, that ye may not do the things that ye would." Lightfoot says: "It is an appeal to their own consciousness: Have you not evidence of these two opposing principles in your own hearts?" (*"Commentary on Galatians in loco"*). The Galatian Christians are exhorted to "walk in the Spirit" and let not the sin principle, which is not utterly vanquished in the flesh at regeneration, prevail and cover them in defeat and shame. This same persistence of the sin principle is described in Rom. 8:5-9, where he surely is describing the experience of believers. Then in Phil. 3:12-14, he alludes to his own Christian experience thus: "I count not that I have already obtained; or am already made perfect; but I press on if so be that I may lay hold on that for which also I was laid hold on by Christ Jesus. Brethren, I count not myself yet to have laid hold. . . I press on toward the goal unto the prize of the high calling of God in Christ Jesus." Paul knew by experience that the old sin principle still pursued him and that on account of the weakness of the flesh he had not reached the "goal" of practical righteousness.

Sin Finally Vanquished in Christ Jesus

Paul has this thought of conquest in mind in that unique passage, Rom. 5:12-21. The conquest of sin by grace in Christ Jesus far transcends the demolishing power of sin handed down by Adam to his posterity. "But where sin abounded, grace abounded more exceedingly, that as sin reigned in death, even so might grace reign through righteousness unto eternal life through Jesus Christ our Lord." This is the apostle's paean of triumph as he draws the last pen stroke in describing the blessedness of the justified man.

The first historic conquest of sin in Christ was his conception without sin; though born of a sinful woman, her sinful nature was not handed down to him. Then followed victory after victory — in those thirty silent years in which he never yielded to a single sinful impulse; in the wilderness struggle when in that supreme moment he said, "Get thee hence, Satan"; on Calvary when he meekly submitted to the sufferings of human sin, in which submission he showed himself above sin; in the Resurrection when death was defeated and driven from his own battle field, the grave, while he as the Son of God arose in triumph and in forty days afterward sat down on the right hand of the Father, to send to men the Spirit to apply and enforce his mediatorial work.

This conquest of sin is *personalized* in each believer. At regeneration the sin principle is subdued by the Spirit in Christ and the divine nature so implanted as to guarantee the complete conquest of sin. In the life of consecration and service the sin principle goes down in defeat step by step, until in death whose sting is sin, the believer triumphs in Christ on the last field; he feels no sting and knows the strife with the sin monster is forever passed, and in exultation he receives "an abundant entrance" to the kingdom of glory, as Paul triumphantly received it (Phil. 1:21, 23; 2 Tim. 4:6-8).

SIR ROBERT ANDERSON (1841-1918) was converted to Christ at the age of nineteen and almost immediately began to preach in his native Dublin where he trained for a legal profession at Trinity College. He became a respected member of the Irish Home Office and an expert on criminal investigation. In 1888 he was summoned to Scotland Yard, London, to serve as Chief of the Criminal Investigation Department, an office he filled with distinction until his retirement in 1896. At his retirement, he was knighted by Queen Victoria; and in 1901, King Edward VII made him Knight Commander. In the midst of all his many duties, he managed to gain a profound knowledge of the Bible, preach in various conferences, and write seventeen books, including *The Coming Prince, Daniel in the Critics' Den, The Gospel and Its Ministry,* and *The Silence of God*, published by Kregel Publications. He also wrote numerous articles and pamphlets and was a declared foe of the higher critics.

32

Sin and Judgment to Come

By Sir Robert Anderson, K.C.B., LL.D.
AUTHOR, THE COMING PRINCE AND THE SILENCE OF GOD,
LONDON, ENGLAND

Revised by Charles L. Feinberg, Th.D., Ph.D.

Nearly two hundred times the Hebrew word *hata'*, translated "miss," is rendered "sin" in our English Bible; and this striking fact may teach us that, while "all unrighteousness is sin," the root-thought is far deeper. Man is a sinner because he fails to fulfill the purpose of his being. That purpose is, as the Westminster Confession aptly states it, "to glorify God and enjoy him forever." Our Maker intended that "we should be to the praise of his glory." But we utterly fail of this, for we "come short of the glory of God." Man is a sinner not merely because of what he does, but by reason of what he is.

Man a Failure

That man is a failure is denied by none except those who say in their heart, "There is no God." Are we not conscious of baffled aspirations and unsatisfied longings after the infinite? Some there are, we are told, who have no such aspirations. There are seeming exceptions, no doubt, but they can be explained. And these aspirations and longings are quite distinct from the groan of the lower creation. How, then, can we account for them? There is a mass of proof that man is by nature a religious being; and that indisputable fact points to the further fact that he is God's creature. Some attribute the intellectual and aesthetical phenomena of man's being to the great "primordial germ," a germ which was not created at all, but, in the words of Mark Twain, "only just happened." But most of us cannot rise to belief in an effect without an adequate cause; and if we accepted the almighty germ hypothesis we should regard it as a more amazing display of creative power than the Mosaic cosmogony.

Why a Failure?

But all this, which is so clear to every free and fearless thinker, gives rise to a difficulty of the first magnitude. If man be a failure, how can he be a creature of a God who is infinite in wisdom, goodness and power? God does not create imperfect creatures. We conclude that some evil has happened to our race. Here the fall affords an adequate explanation of the strange anomalies of our being, and no other explanation of them is forthcoming. It is certain that man is God's creature, and no less certain that he is a fallen creature. Even if Scripture were silent here, the patent facts would lead us to infer that some disaster such as that which Genesis records must have befallen the human race.

Man without Excuse

But while this avails to solve one difficulty, it suggests another. The dogma of the moral, irremediable depravity of man seemingly cannot be reconciled with divine justice in punishing sin. But that man is without excuse is the clear testimony of Holy Writ. In the antediluvian age the entire race was sunk in vice; and such was also the condition of the Canaanites in later times. But the divine judgments that fell on them are proof that their condition was not solely an inevitable consequence of the fall.

Depravity in Religious Nature

All unregenerate men are not equally degraded; in fact, the unconverted religionist can maintain as high a standard of morality as the spiritual Christian. In this respect the life of Saul the Pharisee was as perfect as that of Paul the apostle. His own testimony to this is unequivocal (Acts 26:4, 5; Phil. 3:4-6). No less so is his confession that, notwithstanding his life of blameless morality, he was a persecuting blasphemer and the chief of sinners (I Tim. 1:13).

The solution of this seeming enigma is to be found in the fact so plainly declared in the Scripture, that it is not in the moral, but in the religious or the spiritual sphere, that man is hopelessly depraved and lost. Hence the terrible word is true of all — "they that are in the flesh cannot please God." The natural man does not know his God.

Man a Sinner in Character

While sin has many aspects, man is a sinner primarily and essentially, not because of what he does, but because of what he is. Sin is to be judged from the divine, and not the human, standpoint. It relates to God's requirements and not to man's estimate of himself. And this applies to all the aspects in which sin may be regarded, whether as a missing of the mark, a transgressing, a disobedience, a falling, a non-observance of a law, a discord, and in many other ways. Original sin may sometimes find expression in "I cannot"; but "I will not" is behind all actual sin, for its root principle is the assertion of a will that is not subject to the will of God.

The Carnal Mind

Spiritual truths are spiritually discerned. When Paul declares that the mind of the unregenerate is enmity against God (Rom. 8:7), he is stating what is a fact in the experience of all thoughtful men. Speak to man of what is due to God, and the latent enmity of the carnal mind is at once aroused. In the case of one who has had religious training, the manifestations of that hatred may be modified or restrained, but he is conscious of it none the less. Thoughtful men of the world do not share the doubts which some entertain as to the truth of the Scripture on this subject. In every waking hour there is proof that, when man knows the will of God, there is something in him which prompts him to rebel against it. Such a state of things, moreover, is obviously abnormal, and if the divine account of it be rejected, it must remain a mystery unsolved and insoluble. The fall explains it, and no other explanation can be offered.

The Root of Sin

The Epistle of James declares that every sin is the outcome of an evil desire. Eating the forbidden fruit was the result of a desire excited by yielding to the tempter's wiles. Once our parents lent a willing ear to Satan's lies, their fall was an accomplished fact. The overt act of disobedience, which followed as of course, was but the outward manifestation of it. Since their ruin was brought about, not by the corruption of their morals, but by the undermining of their faith in God, it is not in the moral but in the spiritual sphere that the ruin is complete and hopeless.

Reconciliation the Great Need

Romans 2:6-11 applies to all whether with or without a divine revelation. Of course, the test and standard would be different with the Jew and the heathen, and the denial of this not only supplies an adequate apology for a life of sin, but impugns the justice of the divine judgment which awaits it. No amount of success, no measure of attainment in this sphere can avail to put us right with God. If a house be in darkness owing to the electric current having been cut off, no amount of care bestowed upon the plant and fittings will restore the light. The first need is to have the current renewed. So here; man by nature is alienated from the life of God, and his first need is to be reconciled to God. And apart from redemption reconciliation is impossible. A discussion of the sin question apart from God's remedy for sin would present the truth in a perspective so wholly false as to suggest positive error.

The Perfect Standard

The thoughtful will recognize that in divine judgment the standard must be perfection. If God accepted a lower standard than perfect righteousness, he would declare himself unrighteous. The great problem of redemption is not how he can be just in condemning, but how he can be just in forgiving. In a criminal court guilty or not guilty is the first question in every case, and this levels all distinctions. So it is here; all men come short, and therefore all the world is brought in guilty before God. After the verdict comes the sentence, and at this stage the question of degrees of guilt demands consideration. At the judgment of the wicked dead there will be many stripes for some, for others there will be few (Rev. 20:12).

Judgment to Come

The transcendent question of the ultimate fate of men must be settled before the advent of that day; for the resurrection will declare it, and the resurrection precedes the judgment. For there is a "resurrection unto life," and a "resurrection unto judgment" (John 5:29). But though the supreme issue of the destiny of men does not await that awful inquest, judgment to come is a reality for all. For it is of the people of God that the Word declares they are all to stand before the judgment seat of Christ

(Rom. 14:10, 12). That judgment will bring reward to some and loss to others. But this judgment of the Bema of Christ has only an incidental bearing on the theme of this chapter, and it must not be confounded with the judgment of the great white throne. From judgment in that sense the believer has absolute immunity (John 5:24). Believers are children of God (John 1:12), and it is not by recourse to a criminal court that the lapses and misdeeds of children are dealt with.

Degrees of Rewards and Punishments

It has been said that no two of the redeemed will have the same heaven; and in that sense no two of the lost will have the same hell. This is not a concession to popular heresies on this subject. For the figment of a hell of limited duration either traduces the character of God, or practically denies the work of Christ. If the extinction of being were the fate of the impenitent, to keep them in suffering for an eon or a century would be the cruelty of a tyrant who, having decreed the criminal's death, deferred the execution of the sentence in order to torture him. Far worse than this, for on this view the resurrection of the unjust could have no other purpose than to increase their capacity for suffering. If we adopt the alternative—that hell is a punitive discipline through which the sinner will pass to heaven — we disparage the atonement and undermine the truth of grace. If the prisoner gains his discharge by serving out his sentence, where is grace? And if the sinner's sufferings can expiate his sin, the most that can be said for the death of Christ is that it opened a short and easy way to the same goal that could be reached by a tedious and painful journey. Furthermore, unless the sinner is to be made righteous and holy before he enters hell (in this case, why not let him enter heaven at once?), he will continue to sin; since every fresh sin will involve a fresh penalty, his punishment can never end.

False Argument

Every treatise in support of these errors relies on the argument that the words in the English Bible, which connote endless duration, represent words in the original text which have no significance. But this argument is exploded by the fact that the critic would be compelled to use these very words, if he were set the task of retranslating the version into Greek. For that language has no other terminology to express the thought. But Christianity sweeps away all these errors. The God of Sinai has not repented of his thunders, but he has fully revealed himself in Christ. The wonder of the revelation is not punishment but pardon. The great mystery of the Gospel is how God can be just and yet the justifier of sinful men. The Scriptures which reveal that mystery make it clear as light that this is possible only through redemption (I John 2:2). Redemption is only and altogether by the death of Christ (John 3:16). To bring in limitations here is to limit God.

The Cross of Christ

In the wisdom of God the full revelation of eternal judgment and the doom of the lost, awaited the supreme manifestation of divine grace and love in the Gospel of Christ. When these awful themes are separated from the Gospel, truth is presented in such a false perspective that it seems to savor of error. Not even the divine law and the penalties for disobedience will enable us to realize aright the gravity of sin; this we can learn only at the Cross of Christ. Our estimate of sin will be proportionate to our appreciation of the cost of our redemption, the precious blood of Christ. Here, and only here, can we know the true character and depths of human sin, and here alone can we know, so far as the finite mind can ever know it, the wonders of a divine love that passes knowledge.

And the benefit is to every believer. It was by unbelief that man first turned away from God; how fitting, then, it is that our return to him should be by faith. If this Gospel is true, who can dare impugn the justice of everlasting punishment? Christ has opened the kingdom of God to all believers; the way to God is free, and whosoever will may come. There is no deceit in this and grace does not cover favoritism (I Tim. 2:3-6).

This much is as clear as words can make it, that the consequences of accepting or rejecting Christ are final and eternal. All related questions rest with a God of perfect justice and infinite love. And let this be our answer to those who demand a solution of them. Unhesitating faith is our right attitude in the presence of divine revelation, but where Scripture is silent let us keep silence.

WILLIAM C. PROCTER Croydon, England. (Additional biographical information unavailable).

33

What Christ Teaches Concerning Future Retribution

By Rev. Wm. C. Procter, F.Ph.
CROYDON, ENGLAND

Abridged and emended by James H. Christian, Th.D.

There are four reasons for confining our consideration of the subject of future retribution to the teaching of our Lord Jesus Christ:

(1) *It limits the range of our inquiry to what is possible in a brief essay.* We will concentrate our attention on the ten passages in which our Lord uses the word "Gehenna" (which was the usual appellation in his day for the abode of the lost) together with those other verses which evidently refer to the future state of the wicked.

(2) *It affords a sufficient answer to the speculation of those who do not know, to refer to the revelation of the One who does know.* In taking the words of Christ himself, we shall find the greatest ground of common agreement in these days of loose views of inspiration. Surely, he who is "the Truth" would never misrepresent or exaggerate it on a matter of such vital importance, and would neither encourage popular errors nor excite needless fears.

(3) *It also affords a sufficient answer to those who represent the doctrine as unreasonable and dishonoring to God, and who regard those who hold it as narrow-minded and hard hearted. It reminds them that all the very expressions which are most fiercely denounced in the present day fell from the lips of the Saviour who died for us, and came from the heart of the "Lover of souls."* Surely we have no right to seek to be broader minded than he was, or to nurture false hopes which have no solid foundation in his teaching; while to assume a greater zeal for God's honor, and a deeper compassion for the souls of men, is little short of blasphemy.

(4) *In cons:dering the subject as professing Christians, the words of the Master himself ought surely to put an end to all controversy; and these are clear and unmistakable when taken in their plain and obvious meaning, without subjecting them to any forced interpretation.*

Coming now to consider briefly Christ's teaching on the subject, let us ask, first of all:

1. WHAT DID OUR LORD TEACH AS TO THE CERTAINTY OF FUTURE RETRIBUTION? The word "retribution" is to be preferred to "punishment," because the Bible teaches us that the fate of the wicked is not an arbitrary (much less a vindictive) infliction, but the necessary consequence of their own sins. Taking the passages in their order, in Matt. 5:22 Christ speaks of causeless anger against, and contemptuous condemnation of, others as placing us "in danger of the hell of fire," while in verses 29 and 30 he utters a similar warning concerning the sin of lust; and these are in the Sermon on the Mount, which is the most generally accepted part of his teaching! In chapter 8:12 he speaks of unbelieving "children of the Kingdom" being "cast forth into the outer darkness," and adds, "There shall be the weeping and gnashing of teeth" — expressions which are repeated in chapters 22:13 and 25:30. In chapter 10:28 Jesus said: "Fear him which is able to destroy both soul and body in hell" — a wholesome fear which is decidedly lacking in the present day, and which many people regard as a remnant of superstition quite unsuited to this enlightened age! In our Lord's own explanation of the parable of the tares and wheat, he declared: "The Son of Man shall send forth his angels, and they shall gather out of his kingdom all things that cause stumbling, and them that do iniquity, and shall cast them into the furnace of fire; there shall be the weeping and gnashing of teeth. The angels shall come forth, and sever the wicked from among the righteous, and shall cast them into the furnace of fire; there shall be the weeping and gnashing of teeth" (Matt. 13:41, 42, 49, 50). In chapter 23:15 he speaks of the hypocritical Pharisees as "children of hell," showing that their conduct had fitted them for it, and that they would "go to their own place," like Judas (whom he describes as "the son of perdition" in John 17:12), while in verse 33 he asks: "How shall ye escape the judgment of hell?" The law of retribution can no more be repealed than that of grav-

itation; it is fixed and unalterable. That hell has not been prepared for human beings, but that they prepare themselves for it, is clear from the sentence which our Lord says that he will pronounce upon those on his left hand in the last great day: "Depart from me, ye cursed, into the eternal fire which is prepared for the devil and his angels" (Matt. 25:41).

Turning to the Gospel according to Mark, we find our Lord saying, in chapter 3:29: "Whosoever shall blaspheme against the Holy Spirit hath never forgiveness, but is guilty of an eternal sin." Whatever view may be taken of the character of blasphemy against the Holy Ghost, the cause and consequence are here closely linked together, eternal sin bringing eternal retribution. The words in the original undoubtedly indicate an inveterate habit rather than an isolated act, and would probably be better translated, "is held under the power of an eternal sin." This in itself precludes the possibility of forgiveness, because it assumes the impossibility of repentance; besides, each repetition involving a fresh penalty, the punishment is naturally unending. Similarly, in John 8:21, 24, our Lord's twice-repeated declaration to those Jews which believed not on him, "Ye shall die in your sins," indicates that unforgiven sin must rest upon the soul in condemnation and pollution; for death, so far from changing men's characters, only fixes them; and hence Christ speaks in chapter 5:29 of "the resurrection of damnation."

A careful study of the scriptural uses of the words "life" and "death" will clearly show that the root ideas are respectively "union" and "separation." Physical life is union of the spirit with the body; spiritual life is the union of the spirit with God; and everlasting life is this union perfected and consummated to all eternity. Similarly, physical death is the separation of the spirit from the body; spiritual death is the separation of the spirit from God; and eternal death is the perpetuation of this separation. Hence, for all who have not experienced a second birth, "the second death" becomes inevitable; for he who is only born once dies twice, while he who is "born again" dies only once.

2. WHAT DID CHRIST TEACH AS TO THE CHARACTER OF FUTURE RETRIBUTION? We have already seen that he spoke of it as full of sorrow and misery in his seven-fold repetition of the striking expression: "There shall be the weeping and gnashing of teeth"

(Matt. 8:12; 13:42, 50; 22:13; 24:51; 25:30; Luke 13:28). In Mark 9:43-48, our Lord twice speaks of "the fire that never shall be quenched," and thrice adds, "where their worm dieth not, and the fire is not quenched." Of course, he was using the common Jewish metaphors for Gehenna, taken from the perpetual fires that burned in the valley of Hinnom to destroy the refuse, and the worms that fed upon the unburied corpses that were cast there; but, as we have already seen, he would never have encouraged a popular delusion. Our Lord twice spoke of fruitless professors being "cast into the fire" (Matt. 7:19; John 15:6); twice of "the furnace of fire" (Matt. 13:42, 50); twice of the "hell of fire" (Matt. 5:22; 18:9); and twice of "eternal fire" (Matt. 18:8; 25:41).

In our Lord's parable of the rich man and Lazarus, the former is represented as being "in torments" and "in anguish" even in "Hades," and that memory survives the present life and accompanies us beyond the grave, is clear from Abraham's words to him: "Son, remember" (Luke 16:23-25). Could any material torments be worse than the moral torture of an acutely sharpened conscience, in which memory becomes remorse as it dwells upon misspent time and misused talents, upon omitted duties and committed sins, upon opportunities lost both of doing and of getting good, upon privileges neglected and warning rejected? It is bad enough here, where memory is so defective, and conscience may be so easily drugged; but what must it be hereafter, when no expedients will avail to banish recollection and drown remorse? Cecil puts the matter in a nutshell when he writes: "Hell is the truth seen too late."

Surely, such expressions as the undying worm and the unquenchable fire represent, not pious fictions, but plain facts; and we may be sure that the reality will exceed, not fall short of, the figures employed, as in the case of the blessedness of the redeemed. The woes thus pronounced are more terrible than the thunders of Sinai, and the doom denounced more awful than that of Sodom; but we should never forget that these terrible expressions fell from the lips of Eternal Love, and came from a heart overflowing with tender compassion for the souls of men.

3. WHAT DID CHRIST TEACH AS TO THE CONTINUITY OF FUTURE RETRIBUTION? Is there any solid basis in his recorded

words for the doctrine of eternal hope, or the shadow of a foundation for the idea that all men will be eventually saved? Much has been made of the fact that the Greek word "aionios" (used by our Lord in Matt. 18:8 and 25:41, 46, and translated "everlasting" in the Authorized Version and "eternal" in the Revised Version) literally means "age-long"; but an examination of the 25 places in which it is used in the New Testament reveals the fact that it is twice used of the Gospel, once of the Gospel covenant, once of the consolation brought to us by the Gospel, twice of God's own being, four times of the future of the wicked, and fifteen times of the present and future life of the believer. No one thinks of limiting its duration in the first four cases and in the last, why then do so in the other one? The dilemma becomes acute in considering the words of our Lord recorded in Matt. 25:46, where precisely the same word is used concerning the duration of the reward of the righteous and the retribution of the wicked, for only by violent perversion and distortion can the same word in the same sentence possess a different signification. It is certainly somewhat illogical for those who make so much of the love of God to argue that punishment will prove remedial hereafter in the case of those whom Divine Love has failed to influence here. Not only is there not the slightest hint in the teaching of our Lord that future punishment will prove remedial or corrective, but his words concerning Judas in Matt. 26:24 are inexplicable on that supposition. Surely his existence would still have been a blessing if his punishment was to be followed by ultimate restoration, and Christ would, therefore, never have uttered the sadly solemn words: "It had been good for that man if he had not been born." Similarly there is a striking and significant contrast between our Lord's words to the unbelieving Jews recorded in John 8:21: "Whither I go ye cannot come," and those to Peter in chapter 13:36: "Whither I go, thou canst not follow me now, but thou shalt follow me afterwards."

4. WHAT DID CHRIST TEACH AS TO THE CAUSES OF FUTURE RETRIBUTION? A careful study of our Lord's words shows that there are two primary causes, namely, deliberate unbelief and wilful rejection of him; and surely these are but different aspects of the same sin. In Matt. 8:12 it was the contrast between the faith of the Gentile centurion and the unbelief of the Jewish

nation which drew from his lips the solemn words: "The children of the kingdom shall be cast out into outer darkness"; while, in chapter 23 the awful denunciation in verse 33 is followed by the sad lamentation: "How often would I have gathered thy children together, even as a hen gathereth her chickens under her wings, and ye would not" (verse 37). Similarly, in Mark 3:29, ASV, the "eternal sin" spoken of can only be that of continued rejection of the offers of mercy; and in John 8:24, our Lord plainly declares: "If ye believe not that I am he, ye shall die in your sins." Finally, in Mark 16:16, we find the words: "He that believeth and is baptized shall be saved; but he that disbelieveth shall be condemned."

Another difficulty is removed when we realize that our Lord taught that there would be different degrees in hell as in heaven. Thus, in Matt. 11:20-24 he taught that it would be "more tolerable in the day of judgment" for Tyre and Sidon than for Chorazin and Bethsaida, and for Sodom than for Capernaum; and in Mark 12:40 he speaks of "greater damnation." It is clear that future retribution will be proportioned to the amount of guilt committed and of grace rejected. (See also Luke 12:47, 48; John 19:11.)

We have so far examined, as thoroughly as possible within this limited space, all the recorded words of our Lord which bear on this important subject. It only remains, in conclusion, very briefly to point out that *the whole drift of Christ's teaching confirms what we learn from these isolated passages,* and that *future retribution is not merely an incidental, but a fundamental part of the Gospel message.* It is the dark background on which its loving invitations and tender expostulations are presented, and the Gospel message loses much of its force when the doctrine is left out. But, worst of all, the earnest exhortations to immediate repentance and faith lose their urgency if the ultimate result will be the same if those duties are postponed beyond the present life. Is it seriously contended that Judas will eventually be as John, and Nero as Paul?

Finally, *the doctrines of heaven and hell seem to stand or fall together,* for both rest upon the same divine revelation, and both have the same word "everlasting" applied to their duration. If the threatening of God's Word are unreliable, so may the promises be; if the denunciations have no real meaning, what becomes of the invitations? Ruskin well terms the denial of hell "the most dangerous, because the most attractive, form of modern infidelity." But is it so modern? Is it not an echo of the devil's insinuating doubt: "Yea, hath God said?" followed by his insistent denial, "Ye shall not surely die," which led to the fall of man. Let us, therefore, believe God's truth, rather than the devil's lie; let us accept divine revelation, rather than human speculation; and let us heed what Christ so plainly taught, without mitigating, modifying, or minimizing his solemn warnings.

FRANKLIN JOHNSON (1836-1916) was a man of many talents and interests. In 1860 he was a member of the Republican National Convention that nominated Abraham Lincoln for President. He wrote books on such varied topics as evolution, womanhood, pysychic studies, missionaries, and romance. After receiving his degree from Colgate Theological Seminary in 1861, Johnson was ordained as a Baptist minister and took up his first pastorate in Bay City, Michigan. Between 1862 and 1889, Johnson led churches in New Jersey, Massachusetts, and Athens, Greece. Later, he taught at Ottawa University and the University of Chicago. Johnson also contributed to encyclopedias, and he translated Latin hymnals.

34

The Atonement

By Professor Franklin Johnson, D.D., LL.D.
AUTHOR OF OLD TESTAMENT QUOTATIONS IN THE NEW TESTAMENT
CHICAGO

Revised by Gerald B. Stanton, Th.D.

The Christian world as a whole believes in a substitutionary atonement. This has been its belief ever since it began to think. The doctrine was stated by Athanasius as clearly and fully as by any later writer. All the great historic creeds which set forth the atonement at any length set forth a substitutionary atonement. All the great historic systems of theology enshrine it as the very Ark of the Covenant, the central object of the Holy of Holies.

GROUNDS OF BELIEF IN SUBSTITUTION

If we should ask those who hold this doctrine on what grounds they believe that Christ is the substitute for sinners, there would be many answers, but perhaps in only two of them would all voices agree. The first of these grounds would be the repeated declarations of Holy Scripture, which are so clear, so precise, so numerous, and so varied that they leave no room to doubt their meaning. The other ground is the testimony of the human heart wherever it mourns its sin or rejoices in an accomplished deliverance. The declaration of the Scriptures that Christ bore our sins on the cross is necessary to satisfy the longings of the soul.

THE MORAL-INFLUENCE THEORY

While the Christian world as a whole believes in a substitutionary atonement, the doctrine is rejected by a minority of able men who present instead what has often been called the "moral-influence theory." According to this view, the sole mission of Christ was to reveal the love of God in a way so moving as to melt the heart and induce men to forsake sin. Now, no one calls in question the profound spiritual influence of Christ where he is preached as the propitiation of God, and where the Cross is lifted up as the sole appointed means of reaching and saving the lost. They object only when the "moral-influence theory" is presented as a sufficient account of the atonement, to the denial that the work of Christ has rendered God propitious toward man. One may appreciate the moon without wishing that it put out the sun and stars.

ARGUMENTS AGAINST SUBSTITUTION

The advocates of the "moral-influence theory" must clear the doctrine of substitution out of the way. They attempt to do this by advancing many arguments, only two of which need detain us here, since the others, of lighter moment, will fall of themselves.

a. *Substitution Impossible.*

It is said by them that the doctrine of substitution supposes that which is impossible. Guilt cannot be transferred from one person to another. Punishment and penalty cannot be transferred from a guilty person to an innocent one. An innocent person may be charged with sin, but if so he will be innocent still, and not guilty. An innocent person may suffer, but if so his suffering will not be punishment or penalty. Such is the objection: the Christian world, in believing that a substitutionary atonement has been made by Christ, believes a thing which is contrary to the necessary laws of thought.

The reader will observe that this objection has to do wholly with the definitions of the words *guilt* and *punishment* and *penalty,* and has no force beyond the sphere of verbal criticism. It is true that guilt and punishment, in the sense of personal blameworthiness, cannot be transferred from the wrongdoer to the welldoer. This is no discovery, for it is maintained as earnestly by those who believe in a substitutionary atonement as by those who deny it. But to recognize the fact that guilt belongs historically to the one who has committed it, and is in this sense non-transferable, in no way militates against the fact that guilt as an obligation to justice may, under certain conditions, be transferred.

b. *Substitution Immoral.*

The second argument by means of which the advocates of the "moral-influence theory" seek to refute the doctrine of a substitutionary atonement is equally unfortunate with the first, in that, it also criticizes words rather than the thoughts which they are employed to express. The doctrine of a substitutionary atonement, it is said, is immoral. Let us inquire what this immoral doctrine is. It is answered that it is immoral to say that our guilt was transferred to Christ and that he was punished for our sins. But they fail to see that this would be true only if the action were contrary to the will of Christ, which manifestly it was not.

The objector does not maintain that the doctrine of a substitutionary atonement has equally produced immorality whereever it has been proclaimed. He does not venture to test this charge by an appeal to history. The appeal would be fatal. For nineteen hundred years the only great moral advances of the human race have been brought about by the preaching of a substitutionary atonement. "A tree is known by its fruits." It is impossible that a doctrine essentially immoral should be the cause of morality among men.

MORAL-INFLUENCE THEORY NOT ADEQUATE

Let us turn now to the "moral-influence theory" and consider why it ought not to be accepted. First of all, it is *too circumscribed*.

As a complete theory of the atonement it is far too narrowly circumscribed. Were it universally adopted it would be the end of thought on this high theme. The substitutionary atonement promises an eternity of delightful progress in study. It cannot be exhausted.

As the adoption of this circumscribed view would be the end of thought, so it would be the end of emotion. The heart has always been kindled by the preaching of a Christ who bore our sins before God on the cross. By this truth the hardened sinner has been subdued and in it the penitent sinner has found a source of delight. An atonement of infinite cost, flowing from infinite love, and procuring deliverance from infinite loss, melts the coldest heart and inflames the warmest. To preach a lesser sacrifice would be to spread frost instead of fire.

But the will is reached through the reason and the emotions. That which would cease to challenge profound thought and would cut out the flames of emotion would fail to reach the will and transform the life. The theory makes the death of Christ predominantly scenic, spectacular, an effort to display the love of God rather than an offering to God which, by its nature, is necessary for the salvation of man. It struggles in vain to find a worthy reason for the awful sacrifice. Hence it may properly be charged with essential immorality. In any case, the work of Christ, if interpreted in this manner, will not prove "the power of God unto salvation." The speculation is called the "moral-influence theory," but when preached as an exclusive theory of the atonement it is incapable of wielding any profound moral influence. The man who dies to rescue one whom he loves from death is remembered with tears of reverence and gratitude; the man who puts himself to death merely to show that he loves is remembered with horror.

Still further, the view is *not scriptural.* The chief failure of those who advance this view is in the sphere of exegesis. The Bible is so full of a substitutionary atonement that the reader comes upon it everywhere. The texts which teach it are not rare and isolated expressions; they assemble in multitudes; they rush in troops; they occupy every hill and every valley. They occasion the greatest embarrassment to those who deny that the relation of God to the world is determined by the cross, and various methods are employed by various writers in an attempt to reduce their number and their force. Since they are most abundant in the epistles of the Apostle Paul, some depreciate his authority as a teacher of Christianity. The doctrine is implied in the words which our Lord uttered at the last supper, so some attack these as not genuine. Christ is repeatedly declared to be a propitiation. "Whom God hath set forth to be a propitiation, through faith, by his blood" (Rom. 3:25; see also I John 2:2; 4:10; Heb. 3:17). Many special pleas are entered against the plain meaning of these declarations. It does not seem difficult to understand them. A propitiation must be an influence which renders someone propitious, and the person rendered propitious by it must be the person who was offended. Yet some do not hesitate to affirm that these texts regard man as the only being propitiated by the cross.

Special tortures are applied to many other Scriptures to keep them from proclaiming a substitutionary atonement. Christ is "the Lamb of God, which taketh away the sin of the world" (John 1:29). "The Son of man came not to be ministered unto, but to minister, and to give his life a ransom for many" (Matt. 20:28; Mark 10:45). "Him that knew no sin he made to be sin on our behalf, that we might become the righteousness of God in him" (II Cor. 5:21). Such are a few examples of the countless declarations of a substitutionary atonement which the Scriptures make, and with which those who reject the doctrine strive in vain. Any speculation which sets itself against this mighty current flowing through all the Bible is destined to be swept away.

Yet further. A theological theory, like a person, should be judged somewhat by the company it keeps. If it shows an inveterate inclination to associate with other theories which lie wholly upon the surface, which sound no depths and solve no problems, and which the profoundest Christian experience rejects, it is evidently the same in kind.

The theory which I am here opposing tends to consort with an inadequate view of inspiration. Some of its representatives question the inerrancy of the Scripture, even in the matters pertaining to faith and conduct. It tends to consort with an inadequate view of God, for some of its representatives in praising his love forget his holiness and his awful wrath against incorrigible wrongdoers. It tends to consort with an inadequate view of sin, for some of its representatives make the alienation of man from God consist merely in acts, rather than in an underlying state from which they proceed. It tends, finally, to consort with an inadequate view of responsibility and guilt, some of its representatives teaching that these cease when the sinner turns, so that there is no need of propitiation, but only for repentance. A distinguished representative of this theory has written the following: "All righteous claims are satisfied if sin is done away." "Divine law is directed against sin, and is satisfied when sin is made to cease." "If grace brings an end of sinning, the end sought by law has been attained. It cannot be, therefore, that in the sight of God there is any need of satisfying law before grace can save sinners." These words are like the voice of "a very lovely song"; but many a pardoned soul uttered a more troubled strain. A man may cease to sin without reversing the injury he has wrought. In the course of his business, let us suppose, he has defrauded widows and orphans, and they are now dead. Or, in his social life, he has led the young into unbelief and vice, and they now laugh at his efforts to undo the mischief, or have gone into eternity unsaved. In a sense his sinning has come to an end, yet its baneful effects are in full career. His conscience tells him he is responsible not only for the commission of his sins, but for the ruin wrought by his sins. In other words, he is responsible for the entire train of evils which he has put into operation. The depths of his responsibility are far too profound for such light plummets to sound.

These are some of the reasons which lead the Christian world as a whole to reject the "moral-influence theory" of the atonement as inadequate.

The Adequacy of Substitutional Atonement

While the biblical doctrine of salvation will stand without attempting to construct a theory, nevertheless many Christian thinkers will never cease to seek for an adequate theory of the atonement. It may be well for us therefore to consider some of the conditions with which it is necessary for him to comply in order to succeed in casting any new light upon this vital theme.

1. Any theory of the atonement, to be adequate, must proceed from a fair and natural interpretation of all the biblical statements on the subject. It must not pick and choose among them. It must not throttle any into silence.

2. It must make use of the thought which other generations have contributed. It must not discard these old materials. Though they are not a completed building, they constitute a foundation which we cannot afford to destroy, and whoever would advance our knowledge of the peace made for us by Christ must not disdain to build upon them.

3. It must take account of all the moral attributes of God, for all are concerned in our salvation. It will find the chief motive for the atonement in the love of God (John 3:16). It will find one necessity of the atonement in the righteousness of God (Rom. 3:25, 26). It will find one effect of the atonement in the aversion from man of the wrath of God, the product of love and right-

eousness outraged by sin: "While we were yet sinners, Christ died for us. Much more then, being now justified by his blood, shall we be saved from wrath through him."

4. It must accord with a profound Christian experience. It must take into account the judgment of those wise souls who have learned "the deep things of God" in much spiritual conflict, and will reach conclusions acceptable to them.

5. It must view the sacrifice of Christ as an event planned from eternity. He is "the Lamb that hath been slain from the foundation of the world" (Rev. 13:8). He "was foreknown before the foundation of the world, but manifested at the end of the times" (1 Pet. 1:20). Sin did not take God by surprise. He had foreseen it and had provided a Redeemer before it had led us captive.

6. It must take an adequate view of the self-sacrifice of Christ. No mere man ever laid down his life for others in the sense in which Christ laid down his life for the world. Every man must die at some time; "there is no discharge in that warfare." When a man sacrifices his life he does but sacrifice a few days or years; he does but lay it down earlier instead of later. But Christ did not choose between dying at one time rather than at another; he chose between dying and not dying. Thus, viewed in any light whatever, the voluntary sufferings of Christ surpass our powers of thought and imagination, reaching infinitely beyond all human experience.

7. It must make much of the effect produced upon God by the infinite, voluntary, and unselfish sacrifice of Christ for the world. Here all human language breaks down, and it sounds feeble to say that God the Father admires with the utmost enthusiasm this holy and heroic career of suffering for the salvation of man. Yet we must use such words, though they are inadequate. The Scriptures speak of his attitude toward his incarnate Son as one of unbounded appreciation and approval, and tell us that his voice was heard repeatedly from heaven, saying: "This is my beloved Son, in whom I am well pleased." When we say that the sacrifice of Christ is meritorious with God, we mean that it calls forth his supreme admiration. Such was his feeling toward it as he foresaw it from eternity; such was his feeling toward it as he looked

upon it while being made; and such is his feeling toward it now, as he looks back upon it and glorifies Christ in honor of it.

8. It must find that the work of Christ has made a vast difference in the relations of God to the fallen world. It was infinite in the love which prompted it and in the self-sacrifice which attended it, and hence infinite in its moral value. We cannot but deem it fitting that it should procure for the world an administration of grace. Provided for eternity and efficacious with God from eternity, it has procured an administration of grace from the moment when the first sin was committed.

No doubt it is for this reason that God has suffered the world to stand through all the ages of its rebellious history. He has looked upon it from the beginning in Christ, and hence has treated it with forebearance, with love, with mercy. It did not first come under grace when Christ was crucified; it has always been under grace, because the sacrifice of Christ was always in the plan and purpose of God, and thus has always exercised a propitiatory influence. The grace of God toward man was not fully revealed and explained until it was made manifest in the person and work of Christ, but it has always been the reigning principle of the divine government. Men are saved by grace since the death of Christ, and they have always been saved by grace when they have been saved at all. The entire argument of the Apostle Paul in his epistles to the Romans and the Galatians has for its purpose the defense of the proposition, that God has always justified men by grace through faith, and that there has never been any other way of salvation. The entire administration of God in human history is set forth in the light of "the Lamb that hath been slain from the foundation of the world," as one of infinite kindness and leniency, notwithstanding those severities which have expressed his abhorrence of sin.

But if the self-sacrifice of Christ has made a difference in the practical attitude of God toward the world, it has also made a difference in his feeling toward the world. God is one. He is not at war with himself. He has not one course of action and a different course of feeling. If he has dealt patiently and graciously with our sinning race, it is because he has felt patient and gracious, and the work of his Son, by means of which his administration has been rendered patient and gracious, has rendered his feeling after the same order.

It is to this different administration and to its basis in a different feeling that the Scriptures refer when they present Christ to us as "the propitiation for our sins, and not for ours only, but for the whole world."

CANON DYSON HAGUE (1857-1935) was ordained in 1883 after studying the arts and divinity at the University of Toronto. He served as curate at St. James' Cathedral in Toronto and as rector of St. Paul's in Brockville, Ontario, and St. Paul's in Halifax, Nova Scotia. From 1897 to 1901, Hague taught apologetics, liturgics, and homiletics at Wycliffe College in Toronto. His writings include several books on Anglican liturgy.

35

At-one-ment by Propitiation

By Dyson Hague, M.A.
VICAR OF THE CHURCH OF THE EPIPHANY, TORONTO, CANADA;
PROFESSOR OF LITURGICS, WYCLIFFE COLLEGE, TORONTO;
CANON OF ST. PAUL'S CATHEDRAL, LONDON, CANADA, 1908-1912

Revised by Arnold D. Ehlert, Th.D.

The importance of the subject is obvious. The atonement is Christianity in epitome. It is the heart of Christianity as a system; it is the distinguishing mark of the Christian religion. For Christianity is more than a revelation; it is more than an ethic. Christianity is uniquely a religion of redemption. At the outset we take the ground that no one can clearly apprehend this great theme who is not prepared to take Scripture as it stands, and to treat it as the final and authoritative source of Christian knowledge, and the test of every theological theory. Any statement of the atonement, to satisfy completely the truly intelligent Christian, must not antagonize any of the biblical viewpoints. And further, to approach fairly the subject, one must receive with a certain degree of reservation the somewhat exaggerated representations of what some modern writers conceive to be the views of orthodoxy. We cannot deduce Scriptural views of the atonement from non-biblical conceptions of the person of Christ; and the ideas that Christ died because God was insulted and must punish somebody, or that the atonement was the propitiation of an angry monarch — God who let off the rogue while he tortured the innocent, and such like travesties of the truth, are simply the misrepresentations of that revamped Socinianism, which leavened the theology of many of the outstanding religious leaders of the latter part of the nineteenth century.

I. THE ATONEMENT FROM THE SCRIPTURAL VIEWPOINT
The Old Testament Witness

As we study *the Old Testament* we are struck with the fact that in the Old Testament system, without an atoning sacrifice there

could be no access for sinful men into the presence of the Holy
God. The heart and center of the divinely-revealed religious system of God's ancient people was that without a propitiatory sacrifice there could be no acceptable approach to God. There must be
acceptance before there is worship; there must be atonement before there is acceptance. This atonement consisted in the shedding
of blood. The blood-shedding was the effusion of life; for the life
of the flesh is in the blood — a dictum which the modern science
of physiology abundantly confirms (Lev. 17:11-14). The blood
shed was the blood of a victim which was to be ceremonially
blemishless (Ex. 12:5; 1 Pet. 1:19); and the victim that was slain
was a vicarious or substitutionary representative of the worshiper
(Lev. 1:4; 3:2, 8, 13; 4:4, 15, 24, 29; 16:21, etc.). The death of
the victim was an acknowledgement of the guilt of sin, and its
exponent.

In one word: the whole system was designed to teach the holiness and righteousness of God, the sinfulness of men, and the
guilt of sin; and, above all, to show that it was God's will that
forgiveness should be secured, not on account of any works of the
sinner or anything that he could do, any act of repentance or exhibition of penitence, or performance of expiatory or restitution-
ary works, but solely on account of the undeserved grace of God
through the death of a victim guilty of no offence against the
divine law, whose shed blood represented the substitution of an
innocent for a guilty life. (See *Lux Mundi*, p. 237. The idea,
on p. 232, that sacrifice is essentially the expression of unfallen
love, is suggestive, but it would perhaps be better to use the word
"also" instead of "essentially." See also, the extremely suggestive
treatment in Gibson's "Mosaic Era," of the *Ritual of the Altar*, p.
146.) It is obvious that the whole system was transitory and imperfect, as the eighth chapter of Hebrews shows. Not because it
was revolting as the modern mind objects, for God intended them
thereby to learn how revolting sin was and how deserving of
death; but because in its essence it was typical, and prophetical,
and intended to familiarize God's people with the great idea of
atonement, and at the same time to prepare for sublime revelation
of him who was to come, the despised and rejected of men who
was to be smitten of God and afflicted, who was to be wounded

for our transgressions and bruised for our iniquities, whose soul was to be made an offering for sin (Isa. 53:5, 8, 10, 12).

The New Testament Witness

When we come to *the New Testament* we are struck with three things:

First, the unique prominence given to the death of Christ in the four Gospels. This is unparalleled. It is without analogy, not only in Scripture, but in history, the most curious thing about it being that there was no precedent for it in the Old Testament (Dale, *Atonement,* p. 51). No particular value or benefit is attached to the death of anybody in the Old Testament; nor is there the remotest trace of anybody's death having an expiatory or humanizing or regenerative effect. There were plenty of martyrs and national heroes in Hebrew history, and many of them were stoned and sawn asunder, were tortured and slain with the sword, but no Jewish writer attributes any ethical or regenerative importance to their death, or to the shedding of their blood.

Second, it is evident to the impartial reader of the New Testament that the death of Christ was the object of his incarnation. His crucifixion was the main purport of his coming. While his glorious life was and is the inspiration of humanity after all, his death was the reason of his life. His mission was mainly to die. Beyond thinking of death as the terminus or the inevitable climax of life, the average man rarely alludes to or thinks of death. In all biography it is accepted as the inevitable. But with Christ, his death was the purpose for which he came down from heaven: "For this cause came I to this hour" (John 12:27). From the outset of his career it was the overshadowing event. It was distinctly foreseen. It was voluntarily undergone, and, in Mark 10:45, he says: "The Son of man came to give his life a ransom for many." We are not in the habit of paying ransoms, and the metaphor nowadays is unfamiliar. But, to the Jew, ransom was an everyday custom. It was what was given in exchange for the life of the first-born. It was the price every man paid for his life. It was the underlying thought of the Mosaic and prophetical writings (Lev. 25:25, 48; Num. 18:15; Psa. 49:7; Isa. 35:10; 51:11; 43:14; Ex. 13:13; 30:12, 16; 34:20; Hos. 13:14 etc.); and so, when Christ made the statement, it was a concept which would be immediately grasped. He came to give his life a ransom, that through the shedding of his blood we might receive redemption, or emancipation, both from the guilt and from the power of sin. (The modernists endeavor to evacuate this saying of Christ of all meaning. The text, unfortunately for them, is stubborn, but the German mind is never at a loss for a theory; so it is asserted that they are indications that Peter has been Paulinized, so reluctant is the rationalizer to take Scripture as it stands, and to accept Christ's words in their obvious meaning, when they oppose his theological aversions.)

Third, the object of the death of Christ was the forgiveness of sins. The final cause of his manifestation was remission. It would be impossible to summarize all the teaching of the New Testament on this subject. (The student is referred to Crawford, who gives 160 pages to the texts in the New Testament, and Dale's *Summary,* pp. 443-458.)

It is clear, though, that, to our Saviour's thought, his cross and passion was not the incidental consequence of his opposition to the degraded religious standards of his day, and that he did not die as a martyr because death was preferable to apostasy. His death was the means whereby men should obtain forgiveness of sins and eternal life (John 3:14, 16; Matt. 26:28). The consentient testimony of the New Testament writers, both in the Acts and in the Epistles, is that Christ died no accidental death, but suffered according to the will of God, his own volition, and the predictions of the prophets, and that his death was substitutionary, sacrificial, atoning, reconciling and redeeming (John 10:18; Acts 2:23; Rom. 3:25; 5:6, 9; I Cor. 15:3; II Cor. 5:15, 19, 21; Heb. 9:14, 26, etc.). In proof, it will be sufficient to take the inspired testimony of the three outstanding writers, St. Peter, St. John, and St. Paul.

St. Peter's Witness

To St. Peter's mind, the death of Jesus was the central fact of revelation and the mystery, as well as the climax, of the incarnation. The shedding of his blood was sacrificial; it was covenanting; it was sin-covering; it was redeeming; it was ransoming; it was the blood of the immaculate Lamb, which emancipates from sin

(I Pet. 1:2, 11, 18, 19). In all his post-Pentecostal deliverances he magnifies the crucifixion as a revelation of the enormity of human sin, never as a revelation of the infinitude of the divine love (Dale, p. 115). His death was not merely an example; it was substitutionary. It was the death of the sin-bearer. "Christ also suffered for us," "he bare our sins," meaning that he took their penalty and their consequence (Lev. 5:17; 24:15; Num. 9:13; 14:32, 34; Ezek. 18:19, 20). His death was the substitutionary, the vicarious work of the innocent on behalf of, in the place of, and instead of, the guilty (I Pet. 3:18). (It is surely an evidence of the bias of modernism to interpret this as bearing them in sympathy merely.)

St. John's Witness

According to St. John, the death of the Lord Jesus Christ was propitiatory, substitutionary, purificatory. It was the *hilasmos,* the objective ground for the remission of our sins.

The narrow and superficial treatment of modernism, which if it does not deny the Johannine authorship of the fourth Gospel and the Revelation, at least insinuates that the death of Christ has no parallel place in the writings of St. John to that which it has in the writings of St. Peter and St. Paul, and the other New Testament authors, is entirely contradicted by the plain statements of the Word itself.

The glory of the world to come is the sacrificed Lamb. The glory of heaven is not the risen or ascended Lord, but the Lamb that was slaughtered (Rev. 5:6-12; 7:10; 21:23, etc.). The foremost figure in the Johannine Gospel is the Lamb of God which taketh away the sin of the world, who lifts the sin-burden by expiating it as the Sin-Bearer. The center of the Johannine evangel is not the teaching Christ, but the uplifted Christ, whose death is to draw as a magnet the hearts of mankind, and whose life as the Good Shepherd is laid down for the sheep (John 12:32; 10:11-15).

No one who fairly faces the text could deny that the objective ground for the forgiveness of sin, in the mind of St. John, is the death of Christ, and that the most fundamental conception of sacrifice and expiation is found in the writings of him who wrote by the Spirit of God, "He is the propitiation of our sins, and not for ours only" (I John 2:2). "Hereby perceive we the love of

God because he laid down his life for us" (I John 3:16). "Herein is love," etc. (I John 4:10).

The propitiatory character of the blood, the substitutionary character of the atonement, and, above all, the expiating character of the work of Christ on Calvary, clearly are most indubitably set forth in the threefoldness of the historic, didactic, and prophetic writings of St. John.

St. Paul's Witness

St. Paul became, in the province of God, the constructive genius of Christianity. His place in history, through the Spirit, was that of the elucidator of the salient facts of Christianity, and especially of that one great subject which Christ left in a measure unexplained — his own death (Stalker's *St. Paul*, p. 13). That great subject, its cause, its meaning, its result, became the very fundamentum of his Gospel. It was the commencement, center, and consummation of his theology. It was the elemental truth of his creed; he began with it. It pervaded his life. He glorified in it to the last. The sinner is dead, enslaved, guilty, and hopeless without the atoning death of Jesus Christ. But Christ died for him, in his stead, became a curse for him, became sin for him, gave himself for him, was an offering and a sacrifice to God for him, redeemed him, justified him, saved him from wrath, purchased him by his blood, reconciled him by his death, etc. To talk of Paul using the language he did as an accommodation to Jewish prejudices, or to humor the adherents of a current theology, is not only, as Dale says, an insult to the understanding of the founders of the Jewish faith, it is an insult to the understanding of any man with sense today. Christ's death was a death for sin; Christ died for our sins; that is, on behalf of, instead of, our sins. There was something in sin that made his death a divine necessity. His death was a propitiatory, substitutionary, sacrificial, vicarious death. Its object was to annul sin; to propitiate divine justice, to procure for us God's righteousness; to ransom us, and to reconcile us. Christ's death was conciliating, in that by it men are reconciled to God, and sin's curse and the sinner's slavery and liability to death, and incapability of returning to God, are overcome by the death of the Lamb who was slaughtered as a victim and immolated as a sacrifice (I Cor. 5:7).

To Paul, the life of the Christian emerged from the death of Christ. All love, all regeneration, all sanctification, all liberty, all joy, all power, circles around the atoning work of the Lord Jesus Christ who died for us, and did for us objectively something that man could never do, and who wrought that incredible, that impossible thing, salvation by the substitution of his life in the place of the guilty.

The Bible Summary

To epitomize the presentation of the Bible: The root of the idea of atonement is estrangement. Sin, as iniquity and transgression, had the added element of egoistic rebellion and positive defiance of God (I John 3:4; Rom. 5:15, 19). The horror of sin is that it wrenched the race from God. It dashed God from his throne and placed self thereupon. It reversed the relationship of man and God. Its blight and its passion have alienated mankind, enslaved it, condemned it, doomed it to death, exposed it to wrath. The sacrifice of the cross is the explanation of the enormity of sin, and the measure of the love of the redeeming Trinity. Surely it is ignorance that says God loves because Christ died. Christ died because God loves. Propitiation does not awaken love; it is love that provides expiation. To cancel the curse, to lift the ban, to inoculate the antitoxin of grace, to restore life, to purchase pardon, to ransom the enslaved, to defeat Satan's work; in one word, to reconcile and restore a lost race; for this, Jesus Christ, the Son of God, and Son of man, came into this world and offered up his divine-human Person, body and soul.

Christ's death upon the cross, both as a substitute and as the federal representative of humanity, voluntary, altruistic, vicarious, sinless, sacrificial, purposed not accidental, from the standpoint of humanity, unconscionably brutal, but from the standpoint of love indescribably glorious, not only satisfied all the demands of the divine righteousness, but offered the most powerful incentive to repentance, morality, and self-sacrifice. The Scripture in its completeness thus sets forth the substance of the two great theories, the moral and the vicarious, and we find in the rotundity or allness of the scriptural presentment no mere partial or antagonistic segments of truth, but the completeness of the spiritual, moral, altruistic and atoning aspects of the death of Christ.

II. The Consensus of all the Churches

When we turn to this subject as set forth in the standards of
the representatives of the leading Protestant churches, it is refreshing to find what substantial unity there is among them. In all
the creeds and church confessions the death of Christ is set forth
as the central fact of Christianity; for it ought to be remembered
that the Reformed churches accepted equally with the Roman
church the historic platform of the three great creeds, and that in
all these creeds that subject stands pre-eminent. In the Apostles'
Creed, for instance, there is not the slightest mention of Christ's
glorious example as a man, or of the works and words of his
marvelous life. All is passed over, in order that the faith of the
church in all ages may at once be focused upon his sufferings
and his death. And as to the various doctrinal standards, a reference to the Articles of the Church of England, or the Westminster
Confession of Faith, or the Methodist, or Baptist formularies of
belief, at once shows that the atonement is treated as one of the
fundamentals of the faith. It may be stated in language that a modern theologian finds difficult to accept and would gladly explain
away; but is unquestionably asserted to be no mere at-one-ment in
the Ritschlian sense, but a real vicarious offering; a redemptive
death; a reconciling death; a sin-bearing death; a sacrificial death
for the guilt and sins of men. His death was the death of the
divine victim. It was a satisfaction for man's guilt. It propitiated
God. It satisfied the justice of the Father. The modern mind sees
only one side to reconciliation.

It looks at truth from only one standpoint. It fails to take into
account the fact of the wrath of God, and that I John 2:1 and
Romans 3:25 teach that Christ's death does something that can
only be expressed as "propitiating." The modern theory ignores
one side of the truth, and antagonizes the two complementary
sides, and is, therefore, not to be trusted. The Church standards
simply set forth, of course, in necessarily imperfect language, the
truth as it is in the Scriptures of God. Perhaps no finer summary
of their teaching could be found than the language of the Anglican communion service: "Jesus Christ, God's only Son, suffered
death upon the cross for our redemption, and made there, by his
one oblation of himself once offered, a full, perfect, and sufficient
sacrifice, oblation and satisfaction for the sins of the whole world."

III. THE PRACTICAL ASPECT

The Power of His Death

We finally consider the atonement in its actual power. As we glance through the vistas of history we see it exemplified in innumerable lives. Paul, Augustine, Francis of Assisi, Luther, Latimer, with a myriad of the sinful, struggling, weary, despondent, and sin-sick sons of men, laden with the sin-weight, haunted with the guilt-fear, struggling with the sin-force, tormented with the sin-pain, have found in him who died their peace. "The atonement," said the great scientist, Sir David Brewster, "Oh, it is everything to me! It meets my reason, it satisfies my conscience, it fills my heart." (See also that fine passage in Drummond, *The Ideal Life,* p. 187.)

Or, take our hymns. We want no better theology and no better religion than are set forth in these hymns, says a great theologian (Hodge, *Syst. Theol.,* ii: 591), which voice the triumph, and the confidence, and the gratitude, and the loyalty of the soul, such as:

> *Rock of Ages, cleft for me,*
> *Let me hide myself in Thee.*

> *My faith looks up to Thee,*
> *Thou Lamb of Calvary.*

> *When I survey the wondrous cross,*
> *On which the Prince of glory died.*

Or take the preacher's power. It must be built upon reality as real as life itself; on what the Son of God has done for him. One of the greatest of the nineteenth century preachers said, "Looking back upon all the chequered way, I have to say that the only preaching that has done me good is the preaching of a Saviour who bore my sins in his own body on the tree, and the only preaching by which God has enabled me to do good to others is the preaching in which I have held up my Saviour, not as a sublime example, but as the Lamb of God that taketh away the sins of the world!" And the work of Christ did not end with his death upon the cross. As the risen and ascended One, he continues it. The Crucified is still drawing souls to himself. He is still applying his healing blood to the wounded conscience. We do not preach a Christ who was alive and is dead; we preach the Christ who was dead and is alive. It is not the extension of the incarnation merely; it is the perpetuation of the crucifixion that is the vital nerve of Christianity.

But orthodoxy must not be dissevered from orthopraxy. Maclaren of Manchester tells us, in one of his charming volumes, that he once heard of a man who was of a very shady character, but was sound on the atonement. But what on earth is the good of being sound on the atonement if the atonement does not make you sound? Anyone who reads his New Testament or understands the essence of apostolic Christianity must understand that a mere theoretic acceptance of the atonement, unaccompanied by a penetration of the life and character of the principles of Jesus Christ, is of no value whatever. The atonement is not a mere formula for assent; it is a life principle for realization. But is it not a fact that, wherever the atonement is truly received, it generates love to God, and love to man; evokes a hatred and horror of sin; and offers not only the highest incentive to self-sacrifice, but the most powerful dynamic for the life of righteousness?

To the soul that beholds the Lamb of God, and finds peace through the blood of the cross, there comes a sense of joyous relief, a consciousness of deep satisfaction, that is newness of life.

Yes, a Christianity that is merely a system of morals, and the best only of natural religions, is not worth preserving. A Christianity without a Christ divine, an atonement vicarious, and a Bible inspired, will never carry power. A devitalized gospel, a diluted gospel, an attenuated gospel, will conceive no splendid program, inspire no splendid effort. It never did produce a martyr; it never will. It never inspired a reformer, and it never will. The two religious poverties of the day, a lost sense of sin, and a lost sense of God, are simply the result of this attenuated Socinianism that is becoming prevalent. No minister of Christ has any right to smooth off the corners of the cross. At the same time, a Christianity, that is merely orthodoxy, or an orthodoxy clasped in the dead hand of a moribund Christianity, is one of the greatest of curses. A church that is only the custodian of the great tradition of the past, and not the expression of a forceful spiritual life; a Christian who is simply conserving a traditional creed, and not exemplifying the life of the living God, is a cumberer of the ground. A dead church can never be the exponent of the living God, and a dead churchman can never be the exponent of a living church, for the test of every religious, political or educational system, after all, as Amiel says, is the man it forms (Amiel, p.27).

CYRUS INGERSON SCOFIELD (1843-1921) is best known for his *Scofield Reference Bible*. He served in the Confederate army, studied law in St. Louis, and in 1869 was admitted to the Kansas bar. He served in the Kansas State Legislature in 1871, was named District Attorney in 1873, but shortly after returned to St. Louis. Sometime during 1879, Scofield was converted to Christ. Feeling a call to preach, he was licensed in 1880, and the next year organized a small Congregational Church in Dallas, TX, now the Scofield Memorial Church. In 1895, Scofield became pastor of D. L. Moody's home church in Northfield, MA, as well as president of Moody's schools. In 1901 he conceived the plan for his reference Bible, and the Bible was published on January 15, 1909. Scofield spent the closing years of his life in Bible conference ministry. He helped to found the Philadelphia Bible College in 1914; and in 1917, a new edition of the *Scofield Reference Bible* was published. (A complete revision came out in 1967.) Scofield was one of the most influential leaders of the dispensational school of Bible interpretation in America, if not in the world.

36

The Grace of God

By C. I. Scofield, D.D.
EDITOR, SCOFIELD REFERENCE BIBLE

Edited by Charles L. Feinberg, Th.D., Ph.D.

Grace is an English word used in the New Testament to translate the Greek word, *charis,* which means "favor," without recompense. If there is any compensatory act or payment, however slight or inadequate, it is no more grace. When used to denote a certain attitude or act of God toward man, it is of the very essence of the matter that human merit or desert is utterly excluded. In grace God acts out from himself toward those who have deserved, not his favor, but his wrath. In the plan of the Epistle to the Romans grace does not enter, could not enter, till a whole race without one single exception stands guilty and speechless before God.

Condemned by creation, the silent testimony of the universe (Rom. 1:18, 20); by wilful ignorance, the loss of a knowledge of God once universal (Rom. 1:21); by senseless idolatry (Rom. 1:22, 23); by a manner of life worse than bestial (Rom. 1:24, 27); by godless pride and cruelty (Rom. 1:28, 32); by philosophical moralizings which had no fruit in life (Rom. 2:1, 4); by consciences which can only "accuse" or seek to "excuse" but never justify (Rom. 2:5, 16); and finally, by the very law in which those who have the law boast (Rom. 2:17; 3:20), "every mouth" is "stopped, and all the world becomes guilty before God."

In an absolute sense, the end of all flesh is come. Everything has been tried. Innocence, as of two unfallen creatures in an Eden of beauty; conscience, that is, the knowledge of good and evil with responsibility to do good and avoid evil; promises, with the help of God available through prayer; law, tried on a grand scale, and through centuries of forbearance, supplemented by the mighty ethical ministry of the prophets, without ever once presenting a human being righteous before God (Rom. 3:19, Gal. 3:10; Heb. 7:19; Rom. 3:10, 18; 8:3, 4); this is the biblical picture. And it is against this dark background that grace shines out.

Definition

The New Testament definitions of grace are both inclusive and exclusive. They tell us what grace is, but they are careful also to tell us what grace is not. The two great central definitions are found in Ephesians 2 and Titus 3. The inclusive or affirmative side is in Ephesians 2:7; the negative aspect, what grace is not, is found in Ephesians 2:8, 9. The Jew, who is under the law when grace comes, is under its curse (Gal. 3:10); and the Gentiles are "without Christ, being aliens from the commonwealth of Israel, and strangers from the covenants of promise, having no hope, and without God in the world" (Eph. 2:12). And to this race God comes to show "the exceeding riches of his grace in his kindness toward us," "through Christ Jesus."

The other great definition of grace is found in Titus 3:4, 5 with the positive and negative aspects also. Grace, then, characterizes the present age, as law characterized the age from Sinai to Calvary (John 1:17). And this contrast between law as a method and grace as a method runs through the whole biblical revelation concerning grace.

It is not, of course, meant that there was no law before Moses, any more than that there were no grace and truth before Jesus Christ. The forbidding to Adam of the fruit of the tree of the knowledge of good and evil (Gen. 2:17) was law, and surely grace was most sweetly manifested in the seeking by the Lord God of his sinning creatures, and in his clothing them with coats of skins (Gen. 3:21), a beautiful picture of Christ made our righteousness (I Cor. 1:30). Law, in the sense of some revelation of God's will, and grace, in the sense of some revelation of God's goodness, have always existed, and to this Scripture abundantly testifies. But the law as an inflexible rule of life was given by Moses, and from Sinai to Calvary dominates and characterizes the time; just as grace dominates, or gives its peculiar character to, the dispensation which begins at Calvary, and has its predicted termination in the rapture of the church.

Law and Grace Diverse

It is, however, of the most vital moment to observe that Scripture never in any dispensation mingles these two principles. Law always has a place and work distinct and wholly diverse from that of grace. Law is God prohibiting and requiring (Ex. 20:1, 17); grace is God beseeching and bestowing (II Cor. 5:18, 21). Law is a ministry of condemnation (Rom. 3:19); grace, of forgiveness (Eph. 1:7). Law curses (Gal. 3:10); grace redeems from that curse (Gal. 3:1). Law kills (Rom. 7:9, 11); grace makes alive (John 10:10). Law shuts every mouth before God; grace opens every mouth to praise him. Law puts a great and guilty distance between man and God (Ex. 20:18, 19); grace makes guilty man nigh to God (Eph. 2:13). Law says, "An eye for an eye, and a tooth for a tooth" (Ex. 21:24); grace says, "Resist not evil; but whosoever shall smite thee on thy right cheek, turn to him the other also" (Matt. 5:39). Law says, "Hate thine enemy"; grace, "Love your enemies, bless them that despitefully use you." Law says, do and live (Luke 10:26, 28); grace, believe and live (John 5:24). Law never had a missionary; grace is to be preached to every creature. Law utterly condemns the best man (Phil. 3:4, 9); grace freely justifies the worst (Luke 23:24; Rom. 5:5; I Tim. 1:15; I Cor. 6:9, 11). Law is a system of probation; grace, of favor. Law stones an adulteress (Deut. 22:21); grace says, "Neither do I condemn thee" (John 8:1, 11). Under the law the sheep dies for the shepherd; under grace the shepherd dies for the sheep (John 10:11).

The relation to each other of these diverse principles, law and grace, troubled the apostolic church. The first controversy concerned the ceremonial law. It was the contention of the legalists that converts from among the Gentiles could not be saved unless circumcised "after the manner of Moses" (Acts 15:1). This demand was enlarged when the apostles and elders had come together at Jerusalem to settle that controversy (Acts 15:5, 6). The demand then made, put in issue not circumcision merely or the ceremonial law, but the whole Mosaic system. The decision of the council negatived both demands, and the new law of love was invoked that Gentile converts should abstain from things especially offensive to Jewish believers (Acts 15:28, 29).

But the confusion of these two diverse principles did not end with the decision of the council. The controversy continued, and six years later the Holy Spirit through Paul launched against the legalists from Jerusalem the crushing thunderbolt of the Epistle to the Galatians. In this great letter every phase of the question of the respective spheres of law and grace comes up for discussion and final, authoritative decision.

The apostle had called the Galatians into the grace of Christ (Gal. 1:6). Now grace means unmerited, unrecompensed favor. It is essential to get this clear. Add never so slight an admixture of law-works or law effort, and "grace is no more grace" (Rom. 11:6). So absolutely is this true, that grace cannot even begin with us until the law has reduced us to speechless guilt (Rom. 3:19). So long as there is the slightest question of utter guilt, utter helplessness, there is no place for grace. If a man is not quite so good as he ought to be, but yet quite too good for hell, he is not an object for the grace of God, but for the illuminating and convicting and death-dealing work of His law.

The law is just (Rom. 7:12), and therefore heartily approves goodness, and unsparingly condemns badness; but, except Jesus of Nazareth, the law never saw a man righteous through obedience. Grace, on the contrary, is not looking for good men whom it may approve, for it is not grace, but mere justice to approve goodness. But it is looking for condemned, guilty, speechless and helpless men whom it may save through faith, then sanctify and glorify.

Into grace, then, Paul has called the Galatians. What was his controversy with them? (1:6). Just this: they were removed from the grace of Christ to another gospel which is not another (Gal. 1:7). There could not be another gospel. Change, modify the grace of Christ by the smallest degree, and you no longer have a gospel. A gospel is glad tidings; and the law is not glad tidings (Rom. 3:19). The law, then, has but one language; it pronounces all the world — good, bad, and "goody-good" — guilty.

But what is a simple child of God, who knows no theology, to do? Just this: to remember that any so-called gospel which is not pure, unadulterated grace is another gospel. If it proposes under whatever specious guise to win favor of God by works or goodness or character or anything else man can do, it is spurious. That is the unfailing test.

But it is more than spurious, it is accursed, or rather the preachers of it are (Gal. 1:8, 9). It is not man who says that, but the Spirit of God who says it by his apostle. This is unspeakably solemn. Not even the denial of the Gospel is so awfully serious as to pervert the Gospel. May God give his people in this day power to discriminate, to distinguish things that differ. Alas, it is discernment which seems so painfully wanting.

If a preacher is cultured, gentle, earnest, intellectual, and broadly tolerant, the sheep of God run after him. He, of course, speaks beautifully about Christ, and uses the old terms—redemption, the cross, sacrifice, and atonement — but what is his gospel? That is the crucial question. Is salvation perfect, entire, eternal — justification, sanctification, glory — the work of Christ alone, and the free gift of God to faith alone? Or does he claim that character is salvation, even though he may add that Christ helps to form that character?

The Two Errors

In the Epistle to the Galatians Paul answers the two great errors into which in different degrees, theological systems have fallen. The course of this demonstration is like the resistless march of an armed host. The reasonings of ancient and modern legalists are scattered like the chaff of the summer threshing floor. Most of us have been reared and now live under the influence of Galatianism. Protestant theology is for the most part thoroughly Galatianized, in that neither law nor grace is given its distinct and separate place as in the counsels of God, but they are mingled together in one incoherent system. The law is no longer, as in the divine intent, a ministration of death (II Cor. 3:7), of cursing (Gal. 3:10), of conviction (Rom. 3:19), because we are taught that we must try to keep it, and that by divine help we may. Nor does grace, on the other hand, bring us blessed deliverance from the dominion of sin, for we are kept under the law as a rule of life despite the plain declaration of Romans 6:14.

The First Error

The Spirit first meets the contention that justification is partly by law-works and partly by faith through grace (Gal. 2:5-3:24).

The steps are: 1. Even the Jews, who are not like the Gentiles, hopeless and without God in the world (Eph. 2:12), but already in covenant relations with God, even they, "knowing that a man is not justified by the works of the law, but by the faith of Jesus Christ" (Gal. 2:15, 16), have believed; "for by the works of the law shall no flesh be justified." 2. The law has executed its sentence upon the believer (Gal. 2:19); death has freed him. Identified with Christ's death by faith, in the reckoning of God he died with Christ (Rom. 6:3-10; 7:4). 3. But righteousness is by faith, not by law (Gal. 2:21). 4. The Holy Spirit is given to faith, not law-works (Gal. 3:1-9). 5. Those under the law are under the curse (Gal. 3:10). The law, then, cannot help, but can only do its great and necessary work of condemnation (Rom. 3:19, 20; II Cor. 3:7, 9; Gal. 3:19; James 2:10).

In Romans 5:1-5 the apostle sums up the results of justification by faith with every semblance of human merit carefully excluded. Grace through faith in Jesus Christ has brought the believer into peace with God, a standing in grace, and assured hope of glory. Tribulation can but serve to develop in him new graces. The very love that saved him through grace now fills his heart; the Holy Spirit is given him, and he joys in God. And all by grace, through faith!

The Second Error

The Spirit next refutes the second great error concerning the relations of law and grace — the notion that the believer, though assuredy justified by faith through grace wholly without law-works, is after justification put under law as a rule of life. This is the current form of the Galatian error. From Luther down, Protestantism has consistently held to justification by faith through grace. Most inconsistently Protestant theology has held to the second form of Galatianism.

An entire section of the Epistle to the Romans and two chapters of Galatians are devoted to the refutation of this error, and to the setting forth of the true rule of the believer's life. Romans 6, 7, 8 and Galatians 4 and 5 set forth the new Gospel of the believer's standing in grace. Romans 6:14 states the new principle. The apostle is not here speaking of the justification of a sinner, but of the deliverance of a saint from the dominion of indwelling sin. In Galatians, after showing that the law had been to the Jew like a pedagogue in a Greek or Roman household, a ruler of children in their nonage (Gal. 3:23, 24), the apostle says explicitly (3:25), "But after that faith has come, we are no longer under a schoolmaster" (pedagogue). No evasion is possible here. The pedagogue is the law (3:24); faith justifies, but the faith which justifies also ends the rule of the pedagogue. Modern theology claims that after justification we are under the pedagogue. Here is a clear issue, an absolute contradiction between the Word of God and theology. Which do you believe?

Equally futile is the timorous claim that this whole profound discussion in Romans and Galatians relates to the ceremonial law. No Gentile could observe the ceremonial law. Even the Jews since the destruction of the temple in 70 A.D., have not been able to keep the ceremonial law except in a few particulars of diet. It is not the ceremonial law which speaks of coveting (Rom. 7:7-9).

The believer is separated by death and resurrection from the Mosaic law (Rom. 6:3-15; 7:1-6; Gal. 4:19-31). The fact remains immutable that to God he is, as to the law, an executed criminal. Justice has been completely vindicated, and it is no longer possible even to bring an accusation against him (Rom. 8:33, 34).

It is not possible to know gospel liberty or gospel holiness until this great fundamental truth is clearly, bravely grasped. One may be a Christian and a worthy, useful man, and still be under bondage to the law. But one can never have deliverance from the dominion of sin, nor know the true blessedness and rest of the Gospel, and remain under the law. Therefore, note once more that it is death which has broken the connection between the believer and the law (Rom. 7:1-6). Nothing can be clearer.

But it must be added there is a mere carnal way of looking at our deliverance from the law, which is most unscriptural and most dishonoring to God. It consists in rejoicing in a supposed deliverance from the principle of divine authority over the life, a deliverance into mere self-will and lawlessness.

The true ground of rejoicing is quite another matter. The truth is that a Christian may get on after a sort under law as a rule of life. Not apprehending that the law is anything more than an ideal, he feels a kind of pious complacency in "consenting unto the law that it is good," and more or less languidly hoping that in the future he may succeed better in keeping it than in the past. So treated, the law is wholly robbed of its terror. Like a sword carefully fastened in its scabbard, the law no longer cuts into the conscience. It is forgotten that the law offers absolutely only two alternatives, exact obedience always in all things, or a curse. There is no third voice (Gal. 3:10; James 2:10). The law has but one voice (Rom. 3:19). The law, in other words, never says: "Try to do better next time." Of this the antinomian legalist seems entirely unaware.

The True Christian Life

And now turning from the negative to the positive side of a holy, victorious walk under grace, we find the principle and power of the walk defined in Galatians 5:16-24. The principle of the walk is briefly stated: "Walk in the Spirit, and ye shall not fulfill the lusts of the flesh" (Gal. 5:16).

The Spirit is revealed in Galatians in a threefold way. First, he is received by the hearing of faith (3:2). When the Galatians believed they received the Spirit. To what end? For his blessed enabling in the inner life. In Romans the Spirit is not even mentioned until we have a justified sinner trying to keep the law, utterly defeated in that attempt by the flesh, and crying out, not for help, but for deliverance (Rom. 7:15-24). Then the Spirit is brought in with what marvelous results! (Romans 8:2). Not the apostle's effort under the law, nor even the Spirit's help in that effort, but the might of the indwelling Spirit alone, breaks the power of indwelling sin (Gal. 5:16-18).

What is it to walk in the Spirit? The answer is in Galatians 5:18. But how else can one be led of him save by yieldedness to his sway? There is a wonderful sensitiveness in the Spirit's love. He will not act in and over our lives by way of almightiness, forcing us into conformity. That is why "yield" is the great word of Romans 6, where it is expressly said that we are not under the law, but under grace.

The results of walking in the Spirit are twofold, negative and positive. Walking in the Spirit we shall not fulfill the lusts of the flesh (Gal. 5:16). The "flesh" here is the exact equivalent of "sin" in Romans 6:14. And the reason is immediately given (5:17). The Spirit and the flesh are contrary, and the Spirit is greater and mightier than the flesh. Deliverance comes, not by self-effort under the law (Rom. 7), but by the omnipotent Spirit, who himself is contrary to the flesh (Gal. 6:7), and who brings the yielded believer into the experience of Romans 8.

THOMAS SPURGEON (1856-1917) was the son of the famous London preacher Charles Haddon Spurgeon. He and his twin brother Charles were baptized by their father on September 21, 1874, and it was always hoped that they would follow in his footsteps and perhaps one day succeed him. Charles entered a mercantile career, but Thomas felt a call to ministry and served successfully in New Zealand. After his father's death in 1892, Thomas Spurgeon was asked to preach for three months at the Metropolitan Tabernacle in London, and then for a year. He was called as pastor in 1894, and he remained until 1908. During his ministry, the great building burned to the ground; but he led the congregation in a reconstruction program and the work continued. Though overshadowed by his father's ministry, Thomas Spurgeon was an effective preacher in his own right.

37

Salvation by Grace

By Rev. *Thomas Spurgeon*
BAPTIST PASTOR, LONDON, ENGLAND

Edited by Arnold D. Ehlert, Th.D.

What Is "Grace"?

Once upon a time, I met, on board an Australian liner, an aged man of genial temperament, and of sound and extensive learning. He managed to dwell in well-nigh perpetual sunshine, for he followed the sun 'round the globe year after year, and he was himself so sunny that the passengers made friends with him, and sought information from him. It fell out that a discussion having arisen as to what "grace" was, someone said, "Let us ask 'the walking encyclopaedia,' he will be sure to know." So to him they went with their inquiry as to the meaning of the theological term, "grace." They returned woefully disappointed, for all he could say was, "I confess that I don't understand it." At the same time he volunteered the following extraordinary statement: "I don't think that they understand it either who so often speak of it." Like the medical man, of whom the Rev. T. Phillips told in his Baptist World Congress sermon, who said of grace, "It is utterly meaningless to me," this well-read traveler comprehended it not. Some among us were hardly astonished at this, but it did occur to us that he might have allowed that it was just possible that on this particular theme, at all events, some less learned folk might be more enlightened than himself. Now, it chanced that on that same vessel there was a Christian seaman, who, if he could not have given a concise and adequate definition of "grace," nevertheless knew perfectly well its significance, and would have said, "Ay, ay, sir; that's it," with bounding heart and beaming face, if one had suggested that "Grace is God's free, unmerited favor, graciously bestowed upon the unworthy and sinful." And if Mr. Phillips himself had been on board, and had preached his sermon there, and had declared, "Grace is something in God which is at the heart of all his redeeming activities, the downward stoop and reach of God, God bending from the heights of his majesty, to touch and grasp our insignificance and poverty," the weather-beaten face would have beamed again, and the converted sailor-man would have said within himself, "Oh, to grace how great a debtor, daily I'm constrained to be."

Verily, the world through its wisdom knows not God. The true meaning of "grace" is hidden from the wise and prudent, and is revealed to babes. "Cottage dames" are often wiser as to the deep things of God than savants and scientists. Our learned traveler dwelt in perpetual sunshine, but he was not able from experience to say, "God hath shined in our hearts to give the light of the knowledge of the glory of God, in the face of Jesus Christ."

Dr. Dale, long years ago, lamented that the word "grace" was becoming disused. It has, alas! been used a great deal less since then. His own definition of "grace" is worth remembering: "Grace is love which passes beyond all claims to love. It is love which after fulfilling the obligations imposed by law, has an unexhausted wealth of kindness." And here is Dr. Maclaren's: "Grace — what is that? The word means, first, love in exercise to those who are below the lover, or who deserve something else; stooping love that condescends, and patient love that forgives. Then it means the gifts which such love bestows; and then it means the effect of these gifts in the beauties of character and conduct developed in the receivers."

Dr. Jowett puts the matter strikingly: "Grace is energy. Grace is love-energy. Grace is a redeeming love-energy ministering to the unlovely, and endowing the unlovely with its own loveliness." Shall we hear Dr. Alexander Whyte here-upon? "Grace means favor, mercy, pardon. Grace and love are essentially the same, only grace is love manifesting itself and operating under certain conditions, and adapting itself to certain circumstances. As, for instance, love has no limit or law such as grace has. Love may exist between equals, or it may rise to those above us, or flow down to those in any way beneath us. But grace, from its nature, has only one direction it can take. *Grace always flows down.* Grace is love indeed, but it is love to creatures humbling itself. A king's love to his equals, or to his own royal house, is love; but his love to his subjects is called grace. And thus it is that God's love to sinners is always called *Grace* in the Scriptures. It is love indeed, but it is love to creatures, and to creatures who do not deserve his love. And therefore all he does for us in Christ, and all that is disclosed to us of his goodwill in the Gospel, is called Grace."

Is "Grace" Definable?

Delightful as these definitions are, we are conscious that the half has not been told. Oh! the exceeding riches of his grace. Whereunto shall we liken the mercy of God, or with what comparison shall we compare it? It defies definition, and beggars description. This is hardly to be wondered at, for it is so divine. There are some things of earth to which no human pen or brush has done justice — storms, rainbows, cataracts, sunsets, icebergs, snowflakes, dewdrops, the wings that wanton among summer flowers. Because God made them, man fails to describe them. Who, then, shall tell forth fully that which God has and is? The definition we have quoted from Dr. Jowett is worthy of his great reputation, yet he himself confesses that "grace" is indefinable. Thus choicely he puts it: "Some minister of the Cross, toiling in great loneliness, among a scattered and primitive people, and on the very fringe of dark primeval forests, sent me a little sample of his vast and wealthy environment. It was a bright and gaily colored wing of a native bird. The color and life of trackless leagues sampled within the confines of an envelope! And when we have made a compact little phrase to enshrine the secret of Grace, I feel that however fair and radiant it may be, we have only got a wing of a native bird, and bewildering stretches of wealth are untouched and unrevealed. No, we cannot define it."

Desire for Salvation

It cannot be pretended that all men desire to be saved. Would to God that it were so! A lack of the sense of sin is still the most perilous omen of today, as Mr. Gladstone declared it was in his time. Were he now alive, he would, we believe, repeat those portentous words with added emphasis, for this lack — this fatal lack — is approved and fostered by certain of those whose solemn endeavor it should be to prevent and condemn it. A fatal lack it assuredly is, for if a sense of sin be absent, what hope is there of a longing for salvation, of a cry for mercy, or of appreciation of a Saviour? So long as men imagine themselves to be potential Christs, there is little likelihood that they will be sufficiently discontent with self to look away to Jesus, or, indeed, to suppose that they are other than rich and increased in goods and in need of nothing. No, no; all men do not desiderate salvation, though we sometimes think that there has come to all men at some time or other, before the process of hardening was complete, some conscience of sin, some apprehension as to the future, some longings, faint and fitful it may be, to be right with God, and assured of heaven. There is, moreover, a much larger number than we suppose of really anxious souls. Deep desire is often hidden under a cloak of unconcern, and there is sometimes a breaking heart under a brazen breast. In addition to, and partly in consequence of, this lack of a sense of sin, there is much misconception as to the nature of salvation, and the way to secure it. It is even possible to entertain some true conception of sin, and of salvation, without comprehending, or, at all events, without submitting to God's method of salvation. One may realize that to be saved from sin is to overcome its power as well as to escape its penalty, and yet suppose that this is not impossible to fallen men by way of profound penitence, radical reformation, and precise piety.

Righteousness Is Essential

One thing is evident — righteousness is essential. But what must be the nature and quality of that righteousness, and how and whence is it to be obtained? Shall it be homemade, or shall it be of God and from above? Shall I go about to establish my own, or shall I subject myself to God's? Shall salvation be of works, or by faith? Is Christ to be a Substitute for the sinner, or will the sinner be a substitute for the Saviour? Shall the altar smell of sacrifice, God-appointed and God-provided, or will we prefer to deck it with flowers that wither and with fruits that shrivel, howsoever fair they seem at first? Is personal goodness, or is God's grace, as revealed in Jesus Christ, to bring us to the world where all is well? The one is a ladder that we ourselves set up, and painfully ascend; the other is an elevator which God provides, into which, indeed, we pass by penitential faith, but with which the lifting power is God's alone. Salvation by works is the choice of the Pharisee, salvation by grace is the hope of the Publican.

One or Other

Nor can these two principles be combined. They are totally distinct; nay, more, they are at variance the one with the other. A blend of the two is impossible. "If it is by grace, it is no more of works; otherwise grace is no more grace." One cannot merit mercy. This field must not be sown with mingled seed. The ox of mercy and the ass of merit must not be yoked together; indeed, they cannot be; they are too unequal. No linsey-woolsey garment can we weave of works and grace. As Hart quaintly puts it:

> *Everything we do we sin in,*
> *Chosen Jews*
> *Must not use*
> *Woollen mixt with linen.*

So the choice must be made between these two ways to heaven. The great question still is, "How can man be just with God?" and it appears that he must either himself be essentially and perfectly holy, or he must, by some means, acquire a justness which will bear the scrutiny of omniscience, and pass muster in the high court of heaven.

What Says the Book?

What has the Word of God to say about this all-important matter? It declares most plainly that all have sinned, that sin is exceeding sinful, that retribution follows iniquity as the cartwheel follows the footprints of the ox that draws it, that none can make his hands clean or renew his own heart. It tells us also that God, in his infinite mercy, has devised a way of salvation, and that none but Jesus can do helpless sinners good. Behold the bleeding victims and the smoking altars of the old dispensation! They speak of sin that needed to be put away, and they foreshadowed a sacrifice of nobler name and richer blood than they, the only Sacrifice which can make the comers thereunto perfect. Hearken to David as he cries: "Enter not into judgment with thy servant, for in thy sight shall no flesh living be justified."

The prophets tell the selfsame tale. "By the knowledge of him shall my righteous Servant justify many, for he shall bear their iniquities (Isa. 53:11). Then there is the wonderful word which broke the fetters that were on Luther's soul as he climbed the holy staircase on his knees: "The just shall live by faith."

The apostles bear similar witness. Peter tells of Jesus of Nazareth, and declares, "In none other is there salvation; for neither is there any other name under heaven, that is given among men, wherein we must be saved" (Acts 4:12, ASV).

Paul is insistent on justification by faith alone. "By the deeds of the law there shall no flesh be justified in his sight" (Rom. 3:20). "By grace ye are saved through faith; and that not of yourselves; it is the gift of God; not of works, lest any man should boast" (Eph. 2:8 and 9). "Not by works of righteousness which we have done, but according to his mercy he saved us, by the washing of regeneration, and renewing of the Holy Ghost, which he shed on us abundantly through Jesus Christ our Saviour; that being justified by his grace, we should be made heirs according to the hope of eternal life" (Titus 3:5, 6, 7). (See also Gal. 3:11; Phil. 3:8 and 9; Acts 13:39; and II Tim. 1:9).

No Thoroughfare

What need have we of further witness? It is evident that the way of works is closed. Athwart the narrow track have fallen the Tree of Life and the broken tables of the Law, and God has affixed a notice there, large and legible, so that he who reads may run into a better path — NO THOROUGHFARE! It is given "By Order," and the King's red seal is on it; therefore doth it stand fast for ever. Levitical instructions, Davidic confessions, prophetic and apostolic declarations are all the voice of the Lord — the voice that breaketh the cedars of Lebanon and strippeth the forests bare — declaring that salvation is by grace alone.

The Verdict of History

The history of man is the history of sin. It is one long, lurid record of fall and failure. Adam had the best opportunity of all. The law was fragmentary and rudimental then. There was but one command — a solitary test. But it was one too many for our first parents. Later, the flood-swept world was soon defiled again. Later still, there came a law to Israel, holy and just and good. Did they obey? Let the carcasses that strew the wilderness bear witness. Is there a perfect life in all time's annals? The Pharisees were pre-eminent as professional religionists, yet Jesus said, "Except your righteousness shall exceed the righteousness of the scribes and Pharisees, ye shall in no wise enter into the kingdom of heaven." They, as it were, traveled in an express train, and, of course, first-class, but it was the wrong train! Saul of Tarsus was a Pharisee of the Pharisees, and he was no hypocrite, mind you, but he, too, was on the wrong track, till he changed trains at Damascus junction. There, he relinquished all confidence in the flesh, and thenceforth exclaimed: "What things were gain to me, these have I counted loss for Christ. Yea, verily, and I count all things to be loss for the excellency of the knowledge of Christ Jesus my Lord, for whom I suffered the loss of all things, and do count them but dung that I may win Christ, and be found in him, not having mine own righteousness which is of the law, but that which is through faith in Christ, the righteousness which is of God by faith."

Grace, Not Graces

Personal experience bears similar testimony. Our own graces can never satisfy as does God's grace. He who is not far from the kingdom, nevertheless inquires, "What lack I yet?" One might as well think to lift himself by hauling at his boots, as expect to win heaven by the deeds of the law. The fact is, that fallen human nature is incapable of perfectly keeping the perfect law of God. It is well when this is understood and humbly acknowledged; it may be the dawn of better things, even as it was with one of whom I have heard, who was brought to Christ by the Spirit's application of the words, "The heart is deceitful above all things, and desperately wicked." Who can bring a clean thing out of an unclean? Gulliver tells of a man who had been eight years upon a process of extracting sunbeams out of cucumbers. The sunbeams were to be put in phials hermetically sealed, and let out to warm the air in inclement weather. This was folly indeed, but it is even more ridiculous to think of extracting righteousness from a depraved heart. "They that are in the flesh cannot please God." That was good advice given to a seeker: "You'll never know peace till you give up looking at self, and let all your graces go for nothing." The black devil of unrighteousness has slain its thousands, but the white devil of self-righteousness hath slain its tens of thousands. Salvation is by grace, not by graces. Sound aloud this truth, for it is glad tidings, for all save Pharisees. They, indeed, prefer another gospel, which is not another, and a modern one which is as old as Cain's offering. Their watchword is, "Believe in yourself," but for those who have seen themselves as God sees them, for such as can by no means lift up themselves, who are shut up under sin, and condemned already, oh! for these, this is summer news, in truth. If salvation is by grace, the graceless may be saved, prodigals may venture home, the vilest may be cleansed. Ah! yes, and there is a sense in which the guiltier, the better. Then is there less fear of the intrusion of other trust, and the glory gotten to God's grace is greater. I do perceive that if salvation be by works, then can none be saved. Equally sure am I that if salvation be by grace, none need be lost, for it is omnipotent, and greatly rejoiceth to be tested to the full. I read this sentence in a riveter's shop-window the other day: "No article can be broken beyond repair — the more it is smashed the better we like it," and I said within myself: "Thus it is with the grace of God, and long as I live I will tell poor sinners so."

As for the proud Pharisee, "God grant him grace to groan."

What Saith the Cross?

Grace and atonement go hand in hand. Dr. Adolph Saphir has well said: "The world does not know what grace is. Grace is not pity; grace is not indulgence nor leniency; grace is not long-suffering. Grace is as infinite an attribute of God as is his power, and as is his wisdom. Grace manifests itself in righteousness, grace has a righteousness which is based upon atonement or substitution, and through the whole Scripture there run the golden thread of grace and the scarlet thread of atonement, which together reveal to us, for man, a righteousness that comes down from heaven." The fact that Christ has died, a sacrifice for sin, surely settles the question as to whether salvation is or is not by grace. "If righteousness is through the law, then Christ died for nought." Yon great Sacrifice were worse than waste, if man can save himself. They who think to be saved through works of the flesh make void the grace of God. The unspeakable gift had never been donated; the substitutionary sacrifice had never been offered, had any other way been possible. Calvary says, more plainly than anything else, "Salvation is of the Lord." Away, ye merit-mongers from the cross, where "the sword of Justice is scabbarded in the jeweled sheath of grace." Penances, and pieties, and performances are less than vanity in view of the "unknown sufferings" of the spotless Lamb of God. It is impossible for self-righteousness to thrive on the slope of the hill called Calvary.

> *Oh bring no price; God's grace is free*
> *To Paul, to Magdalene, to me!*
> *All of Grace*

Salvation, then, is necessarily all of grace. Man's fall is so complete, God's justice is so inexorable, heaven is so holy, that nothing short of omnipotent love can lift the sinner, magnify the law which he has mutilated, and make him pure enough to dwell in light. The thought of saving sinners is God's, born in the secret places of his great loving heart. "Grace first contrived the way to save rebellious man." The accomplishment of the wondrous plan reveals God's grace throughout. He sent his Son to be the Saviour of the world. He freely delivered him up for us all. He acknowledged him in his humiliation as his beloved Son, but forsook him on the tree, because he was made sin for us. Moreover, he brought again from the dead our Lord Jesus, that great shepherd of the sheep, and enthroned him at the right hand of the majesty on high. There followed the shedding forth of the Spirit to convict the world of sin, and of righteousness, and of judgment. Here is grace at every turn.

"Through Faith"

A work of grace, too, has been effected in each believing heart. We are not saved merely because Christ died. The good news would be to us as rain upon Sahara, did not grace incline to penitence and prayer and faith.

> *Grace taught my soul to pray,*
> *And made my eyes o'erflow.*

Salvation by grace is appropriated by faith. Grace is the fountain, but faith is the channel. Grace is the lifeline, but faith is the hand that clutches it. And, thoroughly and finally to exclude all boasting, it is declared that the salvation and the faith are both the gift of God. "And that not of yourselves, it is the gift of God." That salvation is God's gift is evident. "The gift of

God is eternal life through Christ." "The free gift," "the gift of grace," "the gift of righteousness" — these phrases determine the fact that salvation is itself a divine present to man. "Salvation," cried C. H. Spurgeon in the great congregation, "is everything for nothing!—Christ free!—Pardon free!—Heaven free!" Thanks be to God for a gratuitous salvation!

But is faith, also, the gift of God? Assuredly it is, if only because it is one of the most precious faculties of the human heart. What have we that we have not received? But faith in Christ is, in a very special sense, a divine gift. "Not that something is given us which is different from absolute trust as exercised in other cases, but that such trust is divinely guided and fixed upon the right object. Gracious manifestations of the soul's need, and of the Lord's glory, prevail upon the will to repose trust upon that object." To trust is natural, but to trust Christ, rather than self, or ceremonies, is supernatural — it is the gift of God. Moreover, faith, to be worthy of the name, must not be dry-eyed, and who can melt the heart and turn the flint into a fountain of waters but the God of all grace?

> *The grace that made me feel my sin,*
> *It taught me to believe;*
> *Then, in believing, peace I found,*
> *And now I live, I live.*

Nor is it to be supposed that grace has done with us as soon as we have believed. The mighty call of grace that results in our awakening is but the beginning of good things. Grace keeps us to the end. It will not let us go. It is the morning and the evening star of Christian experience. It puts us in the way, helps us by the way, and takes us all the way!

"Lest Any Man Should Boast"

It is difficult to imagine by what other process salvation could have been secured, consistently with God's honor. Suppose, for a moment, that salvation by works were a possible alternative. Boasting, so far from being excluded, would be invited. Man would boast in prospect. How proud he would be of his purposes and hopes. On such a task as this, he would embark with bands playing and colors flying. There would be credit and eclat from the first. Alas! vain man; this can only end disastrously. Thou art building on the sand. This is not of God, and must therefore come to naught. The divine Spirit humbles men to conviction and deep repentance; he never prompts to self-righteousness and pride; as Hart's simple stanza has it:

> *He never moves a man to say,*
> *"Thank God, I am so good,"*
> *But turns his eye another way —*
> *To Jesus and His blood.*

He would boast in progress. How his meanest achievement would elate him? What crowing there would be over the slightest advance! There would be no need for indebtedness to God. The new birth, the cleansing blood, the converting Spirit — what call for these? The self-made man, they say, worships his creator, and the self-righteous man adores his saviour, that is to say, himself. While the Pharisee is bragging of what he does, the publican mourns over what he is. Because his heart smites him, he smites his heart; he cannot look up, for he has looked within, but because he cries for mercy he is justified. This is as God would have it, for he hath said: "My glory will I not give unto another."

He would boast when perfect. If real peace and lasting joy could come to him, he would boast anew. "I have made my heart clean, and washed my hands in innocency," he would cry. There would be no room for God, and for his sovereign claim to the whole praise of our salvation. Instead of the sweet chiming of the bells of St. Saviour's, "I forgave thee — I forgave thee — I forgave thee all that debt," we should be deafened with the hoarse brass of every man's own trumpet blaring about the good — some will even dare to say, the God — that is in all.

I know which music I prefer. Since first I hearkened to that pardoning word, like bells at evening pealing, my soul has scorned all other strains. Ring on, ring on, sweet bells!

Again, he would boast in Paradise. Think of it! Heaven as it is, is full of perfect praise to God. Its every song is in honor of Father, Son, or Spirit. "Unto him that loved us and washed us from our sins in his own blood, and hath made us kings and priests unto God and his Father, to him be glory and dominion for ever and ever." That is the chorus of the skies, the sweet refrain of the everlasting song. "Worthy is the Lamb," they cry, and again they say, "Hallelujah!"

But were salvation by works instead of by grace, the songs would be in praise of man. Each would laud his fellow or himself, and eternity would be spent in recounting personal virtues and victories. Oh, what a tiresome eternity that would be.

Ah! it is better as it is, with the Lamb in the midst of the throne, and the harps all tuned to Jesus' praise. There will be no self-admiration there, and, consequently, no comparisons and no rivalry, unless, indeed, we vie one with the other as to who shall honor grace the most. The motto of each will be, "He that glorieth, let him glory in the Lord." As McCheyne puts it, we shall be "dressed in beauty not our own." That is the beauty of it!

So, salvation is of grace, and of grace alone. God will have no man boasting, and boast he assuredly would, were he saved, even in part, by the works of his own hands. It is admittedly a humbling doctrine. We wonder not that it is not popular. Truth seldom is. "Truth is unwelcome, however divine." But is it not well to be humbled? We are not disposed to favor any teaching which belittles God, or magnifies man. It has been well and truly said that "the man who has been snatched from helplessness and despair by unmerited grace, will never forget to carry himself as a forgiven man" (Rev. T. Phillips). He will not fail to look back to the rock whence he was hewn, and to the hole of the pit whence he was digged. Gipsy Smith kept the hedgerow at the foot of his Cambridge garden that he might enjoy uninterrupted view of the common on which his father's tent was pitched, and whence he used to sally forth as a young timber-merchant. (He sold clothes-pegs, you remember.) We love him for this. Lifted to honor and usefulness by grace, he gave God the praise. Grace divine makes gracious men. Good works and graces are by no means excluded from believers' lives. They are the product of gratuitous salvation, the evidence of saving faith, the acknowledgment of grateful hearts. The grace-saved sinner works out the salvation that has been wrought in him. He is his Saviour's willing bond-slave. He cannot be content with triumphing in Christ's grace; he must grace his triumph, too. It is with him as it is with the inhabitants of the city of Bath, who record their appreciation of its healing waters on a tablet inscribed as follows:

These healing waters have flowed on from time immemorial,
Their virtue unimpaired, their heat undiminished,
Their volume unabated; they explain the origin,
Account for the progress, and demand the gratitude
Of the City of Bath.

The analogy is nearly perfect. God's grace may well be likened to flowing waters, to streams hot and health-giving, to streams that never cool nor fail. Moreover, "they account for our origin and progress," that is, we owe our spiritual being and well-being to them. And as for demanding gratitude — well, "Streams of mercy never ceasing call for songs of loudest praise."

Oh, let us preach up grace, even if it be not graciously received. "If the people don't like the doctrine of grace," said C. H. Spurgeon, "give them the more of it." Not what they want, but what they need we must supply. If the age is pleasure-loving, unbelieving, self-satisfied, the more call for faithful testimony as to the nature of sin, God's attitude towards it, and the terms on which he offers salvation. We must aim the more at heart and conscience. We must seek to arouse and even alarm the sinner, while we invite as wooingly as ever to the one Mediator. A full-orbed Gospel treats alike of abounding sin, and of much more abounding grace.

Surely, Dr. Watts sang truly when he pictured the ransomed recounting their experiences of grace:

Then all the chosen seed
Shall meet around the throne,
Shall bless the conduct of his grace,
And make his glories known.

To me it has been what the same poet calls "a drop of heaven," to review God's plan for my salvation, and to try to set it forth. Toward the stout ships that have carried me across the seas I have ever cherished a grateful feeling. How much more do I love the good ship of grace that has borne me thus far on my way to the Fair Havens. An unusual opportunity was once offered me of viewing the vessel on which I was a passenger, before the voyage was quite complete. After nearly three months in a sailing ship, we were greeted by a harbor tug, whose master doubtless hoped for the task of towing us into port. There was, however, a favorable breeze which, though light, promised to hold steady. So the tug's services were declined. Anxious to earn an honest penny, her master ranged alongside the clipper, and transshipped such passengers as cared to get a view from another deck of the good ship that had brought them some fifteen thousand miles. You may be sure that I was one of these. A delightful experience it was to draw away from our floating home, to mark her graceful lines, her towering masts, her tapering yards, her swelling sails — the white wave curling at her fore-foot, and the green wake winding astern. From our viewpoint items that had grown familiar were invested with fresh interest. There was the wheel to which we had seen six seamen lashed in time of storm, and there the binnacle, whose sheltered compass had been so constantly studied since the start, and there the chart-house with its treasures of wisdom, and yonder the huge-fluked anchors, and over all the network of ropes — a tangle to the uninitiated. Even the smoke from the galley fire inspired respect, as we remembered the many meals that appetites, sharpened by the keen air of the Southern Seas, had demolished. And yonder is the port of one's own cabin! What marvelous things had been viewed through that narrow peephole, and what sweet sleep had been enjoyed beneath it, "rocked in the cradle of the deep." Oh! it was a brave sight, that full-rigged ship, so long our ocean home, which, despite contrary winds and cross-currents, and terrifying gales and tantalizing calms, had half compassed the globe, and had brought her numerous passengers and valuable freight across the trackless leagues in safety. Do you wonder that we cheered the staunch vessel, and her skillful commander, and the ship's company again and again? I can hear the echoes of those hurrahs today. Do you wonder that we gave thanks for a prosperous voyage by the will of God, and presently stepped back from the tugboat to the ship without question that what remained of the journey would be soon and successfully accomplished?

Let me apply this incident. The good ship is *free grace*, and I have taken my readers aboard my tugboat to give them opportunity to view the means by which they have already come so near —

(how near we know not) — to the haven under the hill. We have sailed around about her, and told the towering masts thereof, and marked well her bulwarks. We have seen the breath of God filling her sails brightened by the smile of his love. We have noted the scarlet thread in all her rigging, and the crimson flag flying at the fore. We have seen at the stern the wheel of God's sovereignty by which the great ship is turned whithersoever the Governor listeth, and on the prow the sinner's sheet-anchor: "Him that cometh unto me, I will in no wise cast out." The chart-house is the Word, and the compass is the Spirit, and there are well-plenished store-rooms, and spacious salons, and never-to-be-forgotten chambers wherein he has given his beloved precious things in sleep, and outlooks whence they have seen his wonders in the deep. Through stress of storm and through dreary doldrums; through leagues of entangling weed, and past many a chilling and perilous iceberg, with varying speed and zigzag course, and changing clime, *free grace* has brought us hitherto. We have, perchance, a few more leagues to cover. We may even stand off and on a while, near the harbor mouth, but, please God, we shall have abundant entrance at the last. We have circled the ship, and I call on every passenger to bless her in the name of the Lord, and to shout the praise of him who owns and navigates her. All honor and blessing be unto the God of grace and unto the grace of God! Ten thousand, thousand thanks to Jesus! And to the blessed Spirit equal praise!

THOMAS BOSTON (1676-1732) was born into an evangelical Presbyterian home in Scotland. As a lad, he spent time in prison with his father who would not compromise his biblical convictions. Educated in Edinburgh, he was ordained in 1699 and became pastor of a small church in Simprin, Berwickshire. In 1707 he moved to Ettrick, in Selkirkshire, and remained there for the rest of his life. A powerful preacher of the Gospel, he magnified the grace of God and gave his people solid biblical theology. His collected writings are in twelve volumes. His most popular books are *The Crook in the Lot* and *Human Nature in Its Four-fold State*.

38

The Nature of Regeneration

By Thomas Boston (1676-1732)

Abridged and emended by James H. Christian, Th.D.

By false conceptions of the nature of regeneration, many are deluded, mistaking some partial changes made upon them for this great and thorough change. To remove such mistakes, let these few things be considered:

1. Many call the church their mother, whom God will not own to be his children. All that are baptized are not born again. Simon was baptized, yet still "in the gall of bitterness, and in the bond of iniquity" (Acts 8:13-23). Where Christianity is the religion of the nation, many are called by the name of Christ, who have no more of him than the name: and no wonder, for the devil had his goats among Christ's sheep in those places where but few professed the Christian religion. "They went out from us, but they were not of us" (I John 2:19).

2. Good education is not regeneration. Education may chain up men's lusts, but cannot change their hearts. A wolf is still a ravenous beast, though it be in chains. Joash was very devout during the life of his good tutor Jehoiada; but afterwards he quickly showed what spirit he was of, by his sudden apostasy (II Chron. 24:2-18). Good example is of mighty influence to change the outward man; but that change often goes when a man changes his company.

3. A turning from open profanity to civility and sobriety falls short of this saving change. Some are, for a while, very loose, especially in their younger years; but at length they reform, and leave their profane courses. This change may be found in men utterly void of the grace of God.

4. One may engage in all the outward duties of religion, and yet not be born again. Men may escape the pollutions of the

world and yet be unsaved (II Pet. 2:20-22). All the external acts of religion are within the compass of natural abilities. Yea, hypocrites may have the counterfeit of all the graces of the Spirit: for we read of "true holiness" (Eph. 4:23); and "faith unfeigned" (I Tim. 1:15); which shows us that there is a counterfeit holiness, and a feigned faith.

5. Men may advance to a great deal of strictness in their own way of religion, and yet be strangers to the new birth. "After the most straitest sect of our religion I lived a Pharisee" (Acts 26:5). Nature has its own unsanctified strictness in religion. The Pharisees had so much of it that they looked on Christ as little better than a mere libertine.

6. A person may have sharp soul-exercises and pangs, and yet die in the birth. Many "have been in pain," that have but, as it were, "brought forth wind." There may be sore pangs and throes of conscience, which turn to nothing at last. Pharaoh and Simon Magus had such convictions as made them desire the prayers of others for them. Judas repented himself; and under terrors of conscience, gave back his ill-gotten pieces of silver. Trees may blossom fairly in the spring, on which no fruit is to be found in the harvest: and some have sharp soul exercises, which are nothing but foretastes of hell.

The new birth, however in appearance hopefully begun, may be marred two ways: *First,* some, like Zerah (Gen. 38:28, 29), are brought to the birth, but go back again. They have sharp convictions for a while; but these go off, and they become as careless about their salvation, and as profane as ever and usually worse than ever; "their last state is worse than their first" (Matt. 12:45). They get awakening grace, but not converting grace, and that goes out by degrees as the light of the declining day till it issue in midnight darkness.

Secondly, some, like Ishmael, come forth too soon; they are born before the time of the promise (Gen. 16:2; compare Gal. 4:22, etc.). They take up with a mere law-work, and stay not till the time of the promise of the Gospel. They snatch at consolation, not waiting till it be given them; and foolishly draw their comfort from the law that wounded them. They apply the healing plaster to themselves, before their wound is sufficiently searched. The law severely beats them, and throws in curses and vengeance upon their souls. Then they fall to reforming, praying, mourning, promising, and vowing, till this fear is abolished. Finally, they fall asleep again in the arms of the law, and are never shaken out of themselves and their own righteousness, nor brought forward to Jesus Christ.

Lastly, there may be a wonderful moving of the affections, in souls that are not at all touched with regenerating grace. Where there is no grace, there may, notwithstanding, be a flood of tears, as in Esau, "who found no place of repentance, though he sought it carefully with tears" (Heb. 12:17). There may be great flashes of joy; as in the hearers of the Word, represented in the parable by the stony ground, who "anon with joy receive it" (Matt. 13:20). There may also be great desires after good things, and great delight in them too; as in those hypocrites described in Isa. 58:2: "Yet they seek me daily, and delight to know my ways: they take delight in approaching to God." See how high they may sometimes stand, who yet fall away (Heb. 6:4-6). They may be "enlightened, taste of the heavenly gift," be "partakers of the Holy Ghost, taste the good Word of God, and the powers of the world to come." Common operations of the divine Spirit, like a land flood, make a strange turning of things upside down; but when they are over, all runs again in the ordinary channel. All these things may be, where the sanctifying Spirit of Christ never rests upon the soul, but the stony heart still remains; and in that case these affections cannot but wither, because they have no root.

But regeneration is a real thorough change, whereby the man is made a new creature (II Cor. 5:17). The Lord God makes the creature a new creature, as the goldsmith melts down the vessel of dishonor, and makes it a vessel of honor. Man is, in respect of his spiritual state, altogether disjointed by the fall; every faculty of the soul is, as it were, dislocated: in regeneration the Lord loosens every joint, and sets it right again. Now this change made in regeneration, is:

1. *A change of qualities or dispositions:* it is not a change of the substance, but of the qualities of the soul. Vicious qualities are removed, and the contrary dispositions are brought in, in their room. "The old man is put off" (Eph. 4:22); "the new

man put on" (4:24). Man lost none of the rational faculties of his soul by sin: he had an understanding still, but it was darkened; he had still a will, but it was contrary to the will of God. So in regeneration, there is not a new substance created, but new qualities are infused; light instead of darkness, righteousness instead of unrighteousness.

2. *It is a supernatural change:* he that is born again, is born of the Spirit (John 3:5). Great changes may be made by the power of nature, especially when assisted by external revelation. Nature may be so elevated by the common influences of the Spirit, that a person may thereby be turned into another man, as Saul was (I Sam. 10:6), who yet never becomes a new man. But in regeneration, nature itself is changed, and we become partakers of the divine nature; and this must needs be a supernatural change. How can we, that are dead in trespasses and sins, renew ourselves, more than a dead man can raise himself out of his grave? Who but the sanctifying Spirit of Christ can form Christ in a soul, changing it into the same image? Who but the Spirit of sanctification can give the new heart? Well may we say, when we see a man thus changed: "This is the finger of God."

3. *It is a change into the likeness of God.* "We, beholding as in a glass, the glory of the Lord, are changed into the same image" (II Cor. 3:18). Everything that generates, generates its like; the child bears the image of the parent; and they that are born of God bear God's image. Man aspiring to be as God, made himself like the devil. In his natural state he resembles the devil, as a child doth his father. "Ye are of your father the devil" (John 8:44). But when this happy change comes, that image of Satan is defaced, and the image of God restored. Christ himself, who is the brightness of his Father's glory, is the pattern after which the new creature is made. "For whom he did foreknow, he also did predestinate, to be conformed to the image of his Son" (Rom. 8:29). Hence, he is said to be formed in the regenerate (Gal. 4:19).

4. *It is a universal change:* "all things become new" (II Cor. 5:17). Original sin infects the whole man; and regenerating grace, which is the salve, goes as far as the sore. This fruit of the Spirit is in all goodness; goodness of the mind, goodness of

the will, goodness of the affections, goodness of the whole man. He gets not only a new head, to know religion, or a new tongue to talk of it; but a new heart, to love and embrace it in the whole of his conversation.

GEORGE WILLIAM LASHER (1831-1920) was ordained into the Baptist ministry in 1859. He served churches in New York, New Jersey, Massachusetts and Connecticut, and then (1872) became director of the Baptist Education Society in New York. He was granted honorary degrees by Hamilton Theological Seminary and by Colgate University. He was the author of popular pamphlets such as *Theology for Plain People*, *What Did Peter Mean?*, and *Individualism in Religion*.

39

Regeneration—Conversion—Reformation

By Rev. George W. Lasher, D.D., LL.D.
AUTHOR OF *THEOLOGY FOR PLAIN PEOPLE*
CINCINNATI, OHIO

Abridged and emended by James H. Christian, Th.D.

In his *Twice-Born Men,* Harold Begbie gives us a series of instances wherein men of the lowest grade, or the most perverse nature, became suddenly changed in thought, purpose, will and life. Without intentionally ignoring the word "regeneration," or the fact of regeneration, he emphasizes the act of conversion in which he includes regeneration which, in our conception, is the origin of conversion and a true reformation as a permanent fact. A weakness in much of the teaching of modern times is that conversion and reformation are thrust to the front, while regeneration is either ignored, or minimized to nothingness.

I. REGENERATION

Jesus Christ did not say much about regeneration, using the equivalent word in the Greek *(palingenesis)* only once, and then (Matt. 19:28) having reference to created things, a new order in the physical universe, rather than to a new condition of the individual soul. But he taught the great truth in other words by which he made it evident that a regeneration is what the human soul needs and must have to fit it for the kingdom of God.

In the other Gospels, Jesus is represented as teaching things which involve a new birth, without which it is impossible to meet divine requirements; but in John's Gospel it is distinctly set forth in the very first chapter, and the idea is carried through to the end. When (in John 1:12, 13) it is said that those who received the Word of God received also "power," or right, to become God's children, it is expressly declared that this power, or right, is not inherent in human nature, is not found in the natural birth, but involves a new birth — "who are born not of blood, nor of the will of man, but of God." It is this new or second birth which produces children of God. The declaration of John (3:3) puts to confusion the very common claim that God is the Father of universal humanity, and makes it absurd to talk of "the Fatherhood of God," "the heavenly Father," "the divine Fatherhood," and other such phrases with which we are surfeited in these modern days. Nothing is farther from truth, and nothing is more dangerous and seductive than the claim that the children of Adam are, by nature, God's children. It is the basis of much false reasoning with regard to the future state and the continuity of future punishment. It is said that though a father may chastise his son, "for his profit," yet the relation of fatherhood and sonship forbids the thought that the father can thrust his son into the burning and keep him there forever. No matter what the offense, it can be expiated by suffering; the father heart will certainly relent and the prodigal will turn again and will be received with joy and gladness by the yearning father.

Of course, the fallacy of the argument is in the assumption that all men are, by nature, the children of God, a thing expressly denied by the Lord Jesus (John 8:42) who declared to certain ones that they were of their father the devil. The conversation with Nicodemus gives us the condition upon which once-born men may see the kingdom of God, namely, by being twice-born, once of the flesh, and a second time of the Spirit. "Except a man be born again [*anothen,* from above] he cannot see the kingdom of God." There must be a birth from heaven before there can be a heavenly inheritance. Nicodemus, though a teacher of Israel, did not understand it. He had read in vain the word through Jeremiah (31:31) relative to the "new covenant" which involves a new heart. He had failed to discern between the natural man and the spiritual man. He had no conception of a changed condition as the basis of genuine reformation. But Nicodemus was not alone in his misconception. After all these centuries, many students of the New Testament, accepting the Gospel of John as canonical and genuine, stumble over the same great truth and "pervert the right ways of the Lord." Taking the fifth verse of John 3, they accept the doctrine of regeneration, but couple it with an external act without which, in their view, the regeneration is not and cannot be completed. In their rituals they distinctly declare that water baptism is essential to and is productive of the regeneration which Jesus declares must be from heaven. They stumble over, or pervert the words used, and make "born of water" to be baptism, of which nothing is said in the verse in the chapter, and which the whole tenor of Scripture denied.

The lexicographers, the grammarians and evangelical theologians are all pronounced against the interpretation put upon the words of Jesus when he said: "Except a man [any one] be born of water *kai* spirit, he cannot enter into the kingdom of God." The lexicographers tell us that the conjunction *kai* (Greek) may have an epexegetical meaning and may be (as it frequently is) used to amplify what has gone before; that it may have the sense of "even," or "namely." And thus they justify the reading: "Except a man be born of water, even [or namely] spirit, he cannot enter into the kingdom of God." The grammarians tell us the same thing, and innumerable instances of such usage can be cited from both classic and New Testament Greek. The theologians are explicit in their denial that regeneration can be effected by baptism. They hold to a purely spiritual experience, either before baptism, or after it, and deny that the spiritual birth is effected by the water, no matter how applied. And yet some who take this position in discussions of the "new birth" fall away to the ritualistic idea when they come to treat of baptism, its significance and place in the Christian system.

Paul As an Interpreter of Jesus

The best interpreter of Jesus who ever undertook to represent him was the man who was made a "chosen vessel," to bear the Gospel of the kingdom to the pagan nations of his own time and to transmit his interpretations to us of the twentieth century. He could say: "The Gospel which was preached of me is not after man, neither was I taught it, but by revelation of Jesus Christ." And Paul speaks of this work wrought in the human soul as a "new creation" — something that was not there before. "If any man be in Christ, he is a new creature" (creation). "Neither circumcision availeth anything, nor uncircumcision, but a new creature" (creation). Never once, in all his discussions of the way of salvation, does Paul intimate that the new creation is effected by a ritual observance. He always and everywhere regarded and treated it as a spiritual experience wrought by the Spirit of God.

The Testimony of Experience

The prayers of the Bible, especially those of the New Testament, do not indicate that the suppliant asks for a regeneration — a new heart. He may have been taught the need of it, and may be brought face to face with the great and decisive fact; but his thought is not so much of a new heart as it is of his sins and his condemnation. What he wants is deliverance from the fact and the consequences of sin. He finds himself a condemned sinner, under the frown of a God of justice, and he despairs. But he is told of Jesus and the forgiving grace of God, and he asks that the gracious provision be applied to his own soul. But when the supplicating and believing sinner awakes to a consciousness that his prayer has been heard, he finds that he is a new creature. The work has been wrought without his consciousness of it at the moment. All he knows is that a great change has taken place within him. He is a new creature. He dares to hope and to believe that he is a son of God; and he cries in the ecstasy of a new life: "Abba, Father." "The Spirit himself beareth witness with our spirit that we are the children of God," and subsequently we learn that we are heirs of a rich Father — "heirs of God and joint-heirs with Jesus Christ," with whom we are both to suffer and reign.

II. Conversion

Conversion (which really means only "change"), we have said, is included in the idea of regeneration; but the words do not mean the same thing. Regeneration implies conversion; but there may be conversion without regeneration. The danger is that the distinction may not be observed and that, because there is a visible conversion, it may be supposed that there must be a prevenient regeneration. Conversion may be a mere mental process; the understanding convinced, but the heart unchanged. It may be effected as education and refinement are effected. The schools are constantly doing it. Regeneration involves a change of mind; but conversion may be effected while the moral condition remains unchanged. Regeneration can occur but once in the experience of the same soul; but conversion can occur many times. Regeneration implies a new life, eternal life, the life of God in the soul of man, a divine sonship, and the continuous indwelling of the Holy Spirit. Conversion may be like that of King Saul, when he took a place among the prophets of Jehovah, or like that of Simon the sorcerer, who said: "Pray ye the Lord for me, that none of these things which ye have spoken come upon me."

Conversion may be the result of a conviction that, after all, a change of life may be profitable for the life that is to come, as well as for the life that now is; that in the future world a man gets what he earns in this life. It does not imply a heart in love with God and the things of God. Men of the world are converted many times. They change their minds, and often change their mode of living for the better without being regenerated.

One of the most imminent dangers of the religious life of today is the putting of conversion in the place of regeneration, and counting converted men as Christian men, counting "converts" in revival meetings as regenerated and saved, because they have mentally, and, for the moment, changed. Men are converted, politically, from one party to another; from one set of principles to another. Christians, after regeneration, may change their religious views and pass from one denomination to another. Few Christians pass through many years without a need of conversion. They grow cold of heart, blind to the things of God, and wander from the straight path to which they once committed themselves; and they need conversion. Most revivals of religion begin with the conversion of saints. Rarely are souls, in considerable numbers, regenerated while regenerated men and women are in need of conversion and unconscious of their high calling. First, a converted church, then regenerated and converted souls.

III. REFORMATION

Reformation implies conversion, but it does not imply regeneration. Regeneration insures reformation, but reformation does not imply regeneration. Reformers have been abroad in all ages, and are known to paganism as well as to Christianity. The Buddha was a reformer. Mahomet was a reformer. Kings and priests have been reformers, while knowing nothing of the life of God in the human soul. The most glaring and fatal mistake in the religious world today is the effort to reform men and society by making the reformation a substitute for regeneration.

The social life of today is full of devices and expedients for bettering the physical condition of individuals, families and communities, while yet the soul-life is untouched. We have civic organizations without number, each of which has for its highest object the betterment not simply of worldly conditions, but of the character of the brotherhood. An argument for the existence of many of these organizations is that they may make better men by reason of the confidence and fraternity secured by the contact effected, by the oaths and vows taken, and by the cultivation of the social life.

That reformatory agencies are good and accomplish good is not denied. But a fatal mistake is in the notion that the elevation of society, the eliminating of its miseries, is conducive to a religious life and promotive of Christianity. Perhaps the greatest hindrances to the conquest sought by Christianity today, in civilized and nominally Christian countries, are the various agencies intended to reform society. They are improving the exterior, veneering and polishing the outside, while the inside is no better than before because the heart remains wicked and sinful. "Now do ye Pharisees make clean the outside of the cup and the platter, but your inward part is full of ravening and wickedness."

The Pharisees were the best people of their day; and yet they were the greatest failures. Against no others did Jesus hurl so fierce denunciations. Why? Because they put reformation in the place of repentance and faith; because they were employing human means for accomplishing what only the Holy Spirit could accomplish. And so, today, every device for the betterment of society which does not strike at the root of the disease and apply the remedy to the seat of life, the human soul, is Pharisaical and is doing a Pharisee's work. It is polishing the outside, while indifferent to the inside. "The good is always the enemy of the best"; and so reformation is always an enemy of the cross of Christ.

Fundamental to the Christian system is a conviction of sin which compels a cry for mercy, responded to by the Holy Spirit, who regenerates the soul, converts it, reforms it, and fits it for the blessedness of heaven.

HANDLEY C. G. MOULE (1841-1920) served the English crown as the chaplain to Queen Victoria. Moule received three degrees from Cambridge University: M.A., 1869; B.D., 1894; D.D., 1895. As a member of the faculty of theology at Cambridge University, he paved the way for D. L. Moody and Ira D. Sankey to speak to the students. A New Testament scholar, Moule's special area of expertise was the apostle Paul. One writer commented that Moule "could think and feel as Paul felt and thought." Although his prolific pen gave us numerous commentaries, essays, expository studies, and poems, his greatest contribution may well have been his *Colossian and Philemon Studies: Lessons in Faith and Holiness* (published by Kregel Publications).

40

Justification by Faith

By H. C. G. Moule, D.D.
Bishop of Durham, England

Revised by Gerald B. Stanton, Th.D.

"Justification by faith"; the phrase is weighty alike with Scripture and with history. In Holy Scripture it is the main theme of two great dogmatic epistles, Romans and Galatians. In Christian history it was the potent watchword of the Reformation movement in a vast spiritual upheaval of the church. It is not by any means the only great truth considered in the two epistles; we should woefully misread them if we allowed their message about justification by faith to obscure their message about the Holy Spirit, and the strong relation between the two messages. It was not the only great truth which moved and animated the spiritual leaders of the Reformation. Nevertheless, such is the depth and dignity of this truth, and so central is its reference to other truths of our salvation, that we may fairly say that it was *the* message of St. Paul, *the* truth that lay at the heart of the distinctive messages of the non-Pauline epistles, and *the* truth of the great Reformation of the Western church. With reason did Luther say that justification by faith was "the articles of a standing or a falling church."

Importance of Terms

There are two great terms before us, justification and faith. We shall, of course, consider in its place the word which, in our title, links them, and ask how justification is "by" faith. But first, what is justification, and then, what is faith?

By derivation, JUSTIFICATION means to make just, that is to say, to make conformable to a true standard. It would seem thus to mean a process by which wrong is corrected, and bad is made good, and good better, in the way of actual improvement of the thing or person justified. In one curious case, and, so far as I know, in that case only, the word has this meaning in actual use. "Justification" is a term of the printer's art. The compositor "justifies" a piece of typework when he corrects, brings into perfect order, as to spaces between words and letters, and so on, the type which he has set up.

But this is a solitary case. In the use of words otherwise, universally, justification and justify mean something quite different from improvement of condition. They mean establishment of position as before a judge or jury, literal or figurative. They mean the winning of a favorable verdict in such a presence, or the utterance of that verdict, the sentence of acquittal, or the sentence of vindicated right, as the case may be.

I am thinking of the word not at all exclusively as a religious word. Take it in its common, everyday employment; it is always thus. To justify an opinion, to justify a course of conduct, to justify a statement, to justify a friend, what does it mean? Not to readjust and improve your thoughts, or your actions, or your words; not to educate your friend to be wiser or more able. No, but to win a verdict for thought, or action, or word, or friend, at some bar of judgment, as for example the bar of public opinion, or of common conscience. It is not to improve, but to vindicate.

Take a ready illustration to the same effect from Scripture, and from a passage not of doctrine, but of public Israelite law: "If there be a controversy between men, and they come unto judgment, that the judges may judge them, then they shall justify the righteous and condemn the wicked" (Deut. 25:1). Here it is obvious that the question is not one of moral improvement. The judges are not to make the righteous man better. They are to vindicate his position as satisfactory to the law.

Non-theological passages, it may be observed, and generally non-theological connections, are of the greatest use in determining the true, native meaning of theological terms. For with rare exceptions, theological terms are terms of common thought, adapted to a special use, but in themselves unchanged. That is, they were thus used at first, in the simplicity of original truth. Later ages may have deflected that simplicity. It was so as a fact with our word justification, as we shall see immediately. But at first the word meant in religion precisely what it meant out of it. It meant the winning, or the consequent announcement, of a favorable verdict. Not the word, but the application was altered when salvation was in question. It was indeed a new and glorious application. The verdict in question was the verdict not of a Hebrew court, nor of public opinion, but of the eternal Judge of all the earth. But that left the meaning of the word the same.

Justification a "Forensic" Term

It is evident that the word justification, alike in religious and in common parlance, is a word connected with law. It has to do with acquittal, vindication, acceptance before a judgment seat. To use a technical term, it is a *forensic* word, a word of the law-courts (which in old Rome stood in the *forum*). In regard to our salvation, it stands related not so directly to our need of spiritual revolution, amendment, purification, holiness, as to our need of getting, somehow — in spite of our guilt, our liability, our debt, our deserved condemnation — a sentence of acquittal, a sentence of acceptance, at the judgment seat of a holy God.

Not that it has nothing to do with our inward spiritual purification. It has intense and vital relations that way. But they are not direct relations. The direct concern of justification is with man's need of a divine deliverance, not from the power of his sin, but from its guilt.

Justification Not the Same as Pardon

The problem raised by the word justification is, How shall man be just before God? To use the words of our Eleventh Article, it is, How shall we be "accounted righteous before God?" In other words, How shall we, having sinned, having broken the holy law, having violated the will of God, be treated, as to our acceptance before him? Its question is not, directly, How shall I a sinner become holy, but, How shall I a sinner be received by my God, whom I have grieved, as if I had not grieved him?

Here let us note what will be clear on reflection, that justification means properly no less than this, the being received by him as if we had not grieved him. It is not only the being forgiven by him. We do indeed as sinners most urgently need forgiveness,

the remission of our sins, the putting away of the holy vengeance
of God upon our rebellion. But we need more. We need the voice
which says, not merely, you may go; you are let off your penalty;
but, you may come; you are welcomed into my presence and fellowship. Justification means not merely a grant of pardon, but
a verdict in favor of our standing as satisfactory before the
Judge.

The Special Problem of Our Justification

Here in passing let us notice that the word justification does
not *of itself* imply that the justified person is a sinner. To see this
as plainly as possible, recollect that God himself is said to be
justified in Psalms 51:4, and Christ himself in I Timothy 3:16.
In a human court of law, as we have seen above, it is the supreme
duty of the judge to "justify *the righteous*" (Deut. 25:1), and
the righteous only. In all such cases justification bears its perfectly proper meaning, unperplexed, crossed by no mystery or
problem. But then the moment we come to the concrete, practical
question, how shall *we* be justified, and *before God*, or, to bring
it closer home, how shall *I, I the sinner*, be welcomed by my offended Lord as if I were satisfactory, then the thought of justification presents itself to us in a new and most solemn aspect. The
word keeps its meaning unshaken. But how about its application?
Here am I, guilty. To be justified is to be pronounced not guilty,
to be vindicated and accepted by Lawgiver and Law. Is it possible? Is it not impossible?

Justification by faith means the acceptance of guilty sinners
before God by faith. Great is the problem so indicated. And
great is the wonder and the glory of the solution given us by the
grace of God. But to this solution we must advance by some
further steps.

What Is Faith?

We may now fitly approach our second great term, FAITH, and
ask ourselves, What does it mean? As with justification, so with
faith, we may best approach the answer by first asking, What
does faith mean in common life and speech? Take such phrases
as, to have faith in a policy, faith in a remedy, faith in a political
leader, or a military leader, faith in a lawyer, faith in a physician.
Here the word faith is used in a way obviously parallel to that

in which our Lord uses it when he appeals to the apostles to have faith in him. The use is parallel also to its habitual use in the epistles, for example in Romans 4 where St. Paul makes so much of Abraham's faith, in close connection with the faith which he seeks to develop in us.

Now is it not plain that the word means, to all practical intents and purposes, trust, reliance? Is not this obvious without comment when a sick man sends for the physician in whom he has faith, and when the soldier follows, perhaps literally in utter darkness, the general in whom he has faith? Reliance upon thing or person supposed to be trustworthy, this is faith.

Practical Confidence

To note a further aspect of the word, faith, in actual common use, tends to mean a *practical* confidence. Rarely, if ever, do we use it of a mere opinion lying passive in the mind. To have faith in a commander does not mean merely to entertain a conviction that he is skillful and competent. We may entertain such a belief about the commander of the enemy — with very unpleasant impressions on our minds in consequence. We may be *confident* that he is a great general in a sense the very opposite to a personal *confidence in him.* No, to have faith in a commander implies a view of him in which we either actually do, or are quite ready to, trust ourselves and our cause to his command. Just the same is true of faith in a divine promise, faith in a divine Redeemer. It means a reliance, genuine and practical. It means a putting of ourselves and our needs, in personal reliance, into his hands.

Here we observe that faith accordingly always implies an element of the dark, of the unknown. Where everything is *visible* to the heart and mind there scarcely can be faith. I am on a dangerous piece of water, in a boat with a skilled and experienced boatman. I cross it, not without tremor perhaps, but with faith. Here faith is exercised on a trustworthy and known object, the boatman. But it is exercised regarding what are to me, uncertain circumstances — the amount of peril, and the way to handle the boat in it. Were there no uncertain circumstances my opinion of the boatman would not be faith but mere opinion; estimate, not reliance.

Our illustration suggests the remark that faith, as concerned with our salvation, needs a certain and trustworthy object, even Jesus Christ. Having him, we have the right condition for exercising faith — trust in his skill and power on our behalf in unknown or mysterious circumstances.

Hebrews XI:I Not a Definition

It seems well to remark here on that great sentence, Hebrews 11:1, sometimes quoted as a definition of faith: "Now faith is certainty of things hoped for, proof of things not seen." If this is a definition, it must negative the simple definition of faith which we have arrived at above, namely, reliance. For it leads us towards a totally different region of thought, and suggests that faith is a mysterious spiritual sense, a subtle power of touching and feeling th unseen and eternal, almost a "second-sight" in the soul. We on the contrary maintain that it is always the same thing in itself, whether concerned with common or with spiritual things, namely, reliance, reposed on a trustworthy object, and exercised more or less in the dark.

Therefore, we take the words of Hebrews 11:1 to be a description of faith. They do not define faith in itself; they describe it in its power. They form the sort of statement we make when we say, Knowledge is power. That is not a definition of knowledge by any means. It is a description of it in one of its great effects.

The whole chapter, Hebrews 11, illustrates this, and confirms our simple definition of faith. Noah, Abraham, Joseph, Moses — they all treated the hoped-for and the unseen as solid and certain because they all relied upon the faithful Promiser. Their victories were mysteriously great, their lives were related vitally to the Unseen. But the action to this end was on their part sublimely simple. It was reliance on the Promiser. It was taking God at his Word.

Faith Without Merit

"The virtue of faith lies in the virtue of its Object." That Object, in this matter of justification, so the Scriptures assure us abundantly and with the utmost clearness, is our Lord Jesus Christ himself, who died for us and rose again.

A momentous issue from this reflection is as follows: We are warned against the temptation to erect faith into a Saviour, that is, to rest our reliance upon our faith. To do so is a real temptation to many. Hearing that to be justified they must have faith, they are soon occupied with an anxious analysis of their faith. Do I trust enough? Is my reliance satisfactory in kind and quantity? But if saving faith is simply a reliant attitude, then the question of its effect and virtue is at once shifted to the question of the adequacy of its Object. They should not ask, Do I rely enough? but, Is Jesus Christ great enough and gracious enough for me to rely upon? The soul's open eyes turn upward to the face of our Lord Jesus Christ, and faith forgets itself in its own proper action. In other words, the man relies instinctively upon an Object seen to be so magnificently, so supremely, able to sustain him. His feet are on the Rock and he knows it, not by feeling for his feet, but by feeling the Rock.

Here let us note that faith, seen to be reliance, is obviously a thing as different as possible from merit. No one in common life thinks of a well-placed reliance as meritorious. It is right, but not righteous. It does not make a man deserving of rescue when, being in imminent danger, he implicitly accepts the guidance of his rescuer. The man who discovers himself to be a guilty sinner, and relies upon Christ as his all for pardon and peace, certainly does not earn merit to apply to his own salvation. He deserves nothing by virtue of the act of accepting all.

"By" Defined

Now we take up the question of that middle and connective word in our title, "by." Justification *by* faith, what does it mean? This divine welcome of the guilty as if they were not guilty, *by* reliance upon Jesus Christ — what have we to think about this?

We have seen that one meaning most certainly cannot be borne by the word "by." It cannot mean "on account of," as if faith were a valuable consideration which entitled us to justification. The surrendering rebel is not amnestied because of the valuable consideration of his surrender, but because of the grace of the sovereign or state which amnesties. On the other hand, his surrender is the necessary means to the amnesty becoming actually his. It is his only proper attitude (in a supposed case of unlawful rebellion) towards the offended power. That power cannot make peace with a subject who is in a wrong attitude towards it. It wishes him well, or it would not provide amnesty. But it cannot make peace with him while he declines the provision. Surrender is accordingly not the price paid for peace, but it is nevertheless the open hand necessary to appropriate the gift of it.

In a fair measure this illustrates our word "by" in the matter of justification by faith. Faith, reliance, is the sinful man's "coming in" to accept the sacred amnesty of God in Christ, taking at his Word his benignant King. It is the rebel's coming into right relations with his offended Lord in this great matter of forgiveness and acceptance. It is not a virtue, not a merit, but a proper means.

The Marriage-Bond

"Faith," says Bishop Hopkins of Derry, "is the marriage-bond between Christ and a believer; and therefore all the debts of the believer are chargeable upon Christ, and the righteousness of Christ is instated upon the believer. . . . Indeed this union is a high and inscrutable mystery, yet plain it is that there is such a close, spiritual, and real union between Christ and a believer. . . . So faith is the way and means of our justification. By faith we are united to Christ. By that union we truly have a righteousness. And upon that righteousness the justice as well as mercy of God is engaged to justify and acquit us" [E. Hopkins, *The Doctrine of the Covenants*].

LEANDER WHITCOMB MUNHALL (1843-1934) was a largely self-educated Methodist evangelist who preached the gospel for more than fifty years. He served with distinction during the Civil War, participating in thirty-three battles. He edited *The Methodist*, a weekly publication out of Philadelphia, and served as a representative to denominational conferences. A crusader for biblical orthodoxy, he warned his denomination of liberalism in his book *Breakers! Methodism Adrift* (1913).

41

The Doctrines That Must Be Emphasized in Successful Evangelism

By Evangelist L. W. Munhall, M.A., D.D.
PHILADELPHIA

Revised by Gerald B. Stanton, Th.D.

What constitutes successful evangelism? Some will answer, "Great audiences, eloquent preaching and soul-stirring music." But I reply, "We may have all these and not have real evangelism, and we may have successful evangelism without them."

Others will answer, "Any movement that will add large numbers to the membership of the churches." I reply, "We may have successful evangelism and not many be added to the churches. Also, we may have large numbers added to the churches' membership without successful evangelism."

Yet others will answer, "A work or effort that will bring into the church people who will be steadfast." I reply, "We may have members added to the church who will hold out, yet the work, evangelistically, be unsuccessful. We also may have a highly successful evangelistic work and the accessions to the churches from it not hold out for any great length of time."

No matter how great the multitude, how eloquent the preaching and soul-stirring the singing, if the God-ordained conditions are not fully met, failure is inevitable. While these things are of value, great successes have been achieved without them. The conditions ordained by God are indispensable.

I have known not a few evangelistic campaigns to be successful in a marked degree, with one or more churches identified with it, which received but a few members, or none, from the movement. They united in the movement from wrong motives. They were not prepared for the work; they were formal, worldly and unspiritual, and without faith. Putting nothing of value into the work, they got nothing out of it.

I have known not a few persons who have been faithful members of the church for many years and never been born again. They "had a name to live and were dead." Also, I have known persons who were, without doubt, saved and sincere, to unite with the church as a result of an evangelistic campaign, to run well for a season and then fall away. The falling away was unjustly charged to the campaign, but the real cause of it may have been one or more of the following reasons: *First,* the atmosphere of the church was not congenial, being unspiritual and cold. A proper atmosphere is of vital importance to "babes in Christ." *Second,* in not a few instances the pastors, instead of "feeding the church of God," with "the sincere milk of the word," were like those mentioned in the twenty-third chapter of Jeremiah, or have turned their pulpits into lecture platforms and the members going for bread received a stone. *Third,* the positively bad example set by a large majority of the members of most churches, in that they conspicuously fail to meet their solemn obligations to God and the church, has caused casualties among recent converts. And there are yet other reasons for the falling away of the weak and inexperienced.

The Conditions

But again it is asked, "What constitutes successful evangelism?" I answer, "Preaching the Gospel according to divine conditions and directions." What are the conditions? First, *Discipleship.* Jesus commissioned only such. One must know, experimentally, the power and joy of the Gospel before he is competent to tell it out.

Second, *Power.* The disciples were told: "Tarry ye in the city of Jerusalem until ye be endued with power from on high." Since the apostles and disciples of our Lord, who waited personally upon his wonderful ministry and witnessed his marvelous doings, were not qualified for testimony and service without power from on high, we, most surely, must have divine help, and that by the indwelling Spirit.

Third, *Faith.* God has promised: "My word . . . that goeth forth out of my mouth . . . shall not return unto me void, but it shall accomplish that which I please, and it shall prosper in the thing whereto I sent it." The proclaimer, therefore, need have no misgiving as to the result, knowing full well that "He is faithful that promised."

The Directions

What are the directions? First, *"Go into all the world"* and tell it "to every creature." The field is the wide world; and the good news is for every man.

Second, *It is to be "preached."* The God-sent preacher is a herald. He has no message of his own; it is the King's message he is to proclaim. According to the heraldic law, if the herald substituted so much as a word of his own for the king's, he was beheaded. If this law was enforced in these days a lot of preachers would lose their heads. Indeed, many have lost their heads, judging by the kind of messages they are delivering.

Third, *The preacher is to be brave,* a witness (*martus*—martyr). Practically all the apostles went to martyrdom for faithfully proclaiming the Word of God. As Christ said, "If they have persecuted me, they will also persecute you." Again, "Woe unto you, when all men shall speak well of you, for so did their fathers to the false prophets." Paul said, "If I yet pleased men, I should not be the servant of Christ." The mind of the natural man is enmity against God. Therefore the unsaved demand of the preacher, "Prophesy not unto us right things, speak unto us smooth things, prophesy deceits." A premium is placed upon finesse by many in authority in the church. Because of this, it requires as sublime courage in these days to speak faithfully the Word of God as was shown by Micaiah, when he stood before Ahab, Jehosaphat and the four hundred lying prophets; or Simon Peter when he said to the threatening, wrathful rulers of Israel, "We cannot but speak the things which we have seen and heard." There never was more need of fearlessness on the part of the servant of God as in these days. Brave, true men, who will not receive honors of men or seek their own, are absolutely necessary to successful evangelism.

The Message

Now then, as to the message itself. Timothy was commanded: "Do the work of an evangelist," and, in doing it, to "preach the

Word . . . with all long-suffering and doctrine." Doctrinal preaching is therefore necessary to evangelistic success. But what doctrines? I answer, First, *Sin — its universality, nature and consequences.*

Universality. "As by one man sin entered into the world, and death by sin; and so death passed upon all men, for that all have sinned, . . . by one man's offence death reigned by one, . . . by the offence of one, judgment came upon all men to condemnation, . . . by one man's disobedience many were made sinners" (Rom. 5:12-21, see also Psa. 51:5; 58:3; Ecc. 7:20; Rom. 3:10; I John 1:8, 10, etc.).

Nature. There are numerous words in the Bible rendered "sin." These words mean iniquity, offence, trespass, failure, error, go astray, to cause to sin, and miss the mark. In I John 3:4 we are told that "Sin is the transgression of the law." The word rendered transgression is *anomia,* and means lawlessness. Failure to conform to the law is as certainly sin as to violate the commandments of God. Unbelief also is sin (John 16:9; 3:18).

In Genesis 6:5 we are told, "God saw that the wickedness of man was great in the earth, and that every imagination of the thoughts of his heart was only evil continually," and in Genesis 8:21, "The imagination of man's heart is evil from his youth." The word rendered "imagination" in these passages signifies also the desires and purposes of the individual. Therefore guilt lies in the desires and purposes as certainly as in the act. The common law requires that one shall have committed an overt act of violation before he can be adjudged guilty. But according to the divine law, one is guilty even though he never committed an overt act, since guilt lies in the desires and purposes of the heart (I John 3:15; Matt. 5:28; I Sam. 16:7; Rom. 3:19).

The almighty and sovereign Creator is infinite in holiness. Therefore his "law is holy, and the commandment holy, and just, and good." Sin is ruinous, heinous and damning: the most awful thing in the universe.

Consequences. Sin separates and estranges the sinner from God; and he becomes an enemy of God by wicked works (Rom. 8:7), has no peace (Isa. 57:21), no rest (Isa. 57:20), is polluted

(Eph. 4:17-19), condemned (John 3:18), and without hope (Eph. 2:12). Oh, the curse and ruin of sin!

If unrepenting and unbelieving, the future has for him, first, inexorable and awful judgment (see Matt. 25:30-46; Heb. 9:27; Jude 14, 15; Rev. 20:11-13; 22:11-15). Second, the wrath of God (see Ezra 8:22; Psa. 21:9; John 3:36; Rom. 1:18; 2:5; 4:15; 5:9; 12:19; 13:4; Eph. 2:3; 5:6; Col. 3:6; I Thess. 1:10; Rev. 6:16, 17; 14:10; 16:19; 19:15, etc.). Third, eternal torments (see Psa. 11:6; Isa. 33:14; Dan. 12:2; Matt. 3:12; 22:11-13; 23:33; 25:41, 46; Mark 9:43, 48; Luke 12:5, 16:22-31; John 5:28-29; II Thess. 1:7-9; Heb. 10:28-29; II Peter 3:5-12; Rev. 19:20; 20:14-15; 21:8, etc.).

The preacher who ignores these three awful and inexorable truths preaches an emasculated Gospel, be he ever so faithful in proclaiming other truth. He who preaches the love of God to the exclusion of God's justice and wrath proclaims but idle sentiment. No one will ever truly desire salvation unless he first realizes that there is something to be saved from. "By faith Noah, being warned of God of things not seen as yet, moved with fear, prepared an ark to the saving of his house" (Heb. 11:7); all of which symbolizes the sinner's condition, need, motive and hope. In no way can the love of God be so clearly, beautifully and convincingly set forth as in the fact that God makes plain to the sinner his condition and peril, and then shows him the way of escape, having, in his great mercy, himself provided it at infinite cost. Now, at this point the Gospel comes in as indeed good news, showing God's love for the sinner.

The supreme motive for the atoning work of our Lord was his infinite love for us. The supreme object had in view was to save us from eternal ruin (John 3:16). Our Lord, while among men, had far more to say about the doom of the finally impenitent than about love and heaven. Is it not wise and safe to follow his example who said, "The word which ye hear is not mine, but the Father's which sent me"? How can any minister reasonably expect to have evangelistic success if he fails to imitate the Master in this particular?

Second, *Redemption through Jesus' blood.* The Scriptures are numerous. See especially Isaiah 53:6; Mark 10:45; I Peter 3:18;

II Corinthians 5:21; Romans 10:4; Galatians 3:13; and I Corinthians 6:20; (see also Lev. 17:11; Heb. 9:22; Matt. 20:28; 26:28; John 3:14, 16; Rom. 3:24-26; 5:9; I Cor. 1:30; 10:16; II Cor. 5:14-21; Eph. 1:7; 2:13-17; Col. 1:14, 19-22; I Tim. 2:6; Heb. 9:12-14, 24-26; 10:19; 13:12; I Peter 1:2, 18, 19; 2:24; I John 1:7; Rev. 1:5; 5:9; 12:11). On no other ground than the cross can the sinner be justified and reconciled to God. If the atoning work of our Lord was not vicarious, then the sacrifices, ordinances, types and symbols of the old economy are meaningless and of no value. The moral influence theory of Bushnell is all right for the saint; but the atonement is of no value to the sinner if it is not substitutional.

More than thirty years ago, in Denver, Colorado, I met an aged Congregational minister, who was a pastor in Hartford, Connecticut, during Dr. Horace Bushnell's pastorate in the same city. He told me this: "I spent an hour with Dr. Bushnell the day before he died. He then said to me, 'Doctor, I greatly fear some things I have said and written about the atonement may prove to be misleading and do irreparable harm.' He was lying upon his back with his hands clasped over his breast. He lay there with closed eyes, in silence, for some moments, his face indicating great anxiety. Directly, opening his eyes and raising his hands he said, 'O Lord Jesus, Thou knowest that I hope for mercy alone through Thy shed blood.' "

Third, *Resurrection.* "If Christ be not risen, then is our preaching vain and your faith is also vain. . . . Ye are yet in your sins" and "they also which are fallen asleep in Christ are perished. If in this life only we have hope in Christ, we are of all men most miserable. But now is Christ risen from the dead, and become the firstfruits of them that are sleeping" (I Cor. 15:14-20). Jesus was "declared to be the Son of God with power . . . by the resurrection from the dead" (Rom. 1:4). Therefore the apostles and disciples went everywhere preaching "Jesus and the resurrection" (see Acts 2:24-32; 3:15; 4:2, 10, 33; 5:30; 17:18, 32; 23:6; 24:15, 21; I Cor. 15:3-8; I Peter 1:3-5; Rom. 4:25; I Peter 3:22; Heb. 7:25).

Fourth, *Justification.* Note the following important Scriptures: Romans 3:24-26, Colossians 1:21-22, Romans 8:33, and Romans

8:1-2. Believers are "not under the law but under grace" (Rom. 6:14) and can rejoicingly say, judicially, of course, "As he is, so are we in this world" (I John 4:17).

Fifth, *Regeneration.* The non-Christian is spiritually dead (Rom. 5:12) and must be "born again," or "he cannot see the kingdom of God" (John 3:3). He who receives Jesus as Saviour and Lord, is made a "partaker of the divine nature" (John 1:12, 13; II Peter 1:4). "He is a new creature [creation]: old things are passed away, behold, all things are become new" (II Cor. 5:17).

Sixth, *Repentance.* Repentance means a change of mind; and this change of mind is brought about by the Holy Spirit, through the knowledge of the sinner's condition, needs and peril. The sinner is convicted "of sin, and of righteousness, and of judgment" (John 16:8), and is induced to yield himself wholly, immediately and irrevocably to God (see Matt. 9:13; Mark 6:12; Luke 13:2-5; 24:47; Acts 2:38; 3:16; 17:30; 26:20; Rom. 2:4; II Cor. 7:9, 10; II Tim. 2:25; II Peter 3:9).

Seventh, *Conversion.* Conversion means to turn about, or upon. When the unsaved sinner is convinced of sin and resolves to turn from his transgressions and commit his ways unto the Lord, he has repented; and when he acts upon that resolve, and yields himself to God in absolute self-surrender, he is converted (see Psa. 19:7; 51:13; Matt. 18:3; Acts 3:19; James 5:19, 20).

Eighth, *Faith.* Until the sinner changes his mind with regard to his relation to God, and resolves with all his heart to do it, his faith is a vain thing, he is yet in his sins. But when he sincerely repents and turns to God, and believes the record God has given of his Son, his faith is of the heart and unto righteousness (Rom. 10:9-10. See also Heb. 11:6; Rom. 10:17; Gal. 5:22; Eph. 2:8; Gal. 3:6-12; 2:16-20; Rom. 4:13-16; 3:21-28; Acts 16:30-31; John 6:47).

Ninth, *Obedience.* Faith is a vital principle. "If it hath not works, is dead, being alone" (James 2:17-18). Two things are required of the believer upon his profession of faith in Jesus as Saviour and Lord, namely, verbal confession and water baptism. "With the heart man believeth unto righteousness; and with the mouth confession is made unto salvation" (Rom. 10:10. See also Psa. 107:2; Matt. 10:32-33; Rom. 10:9; I John 4:15, etc.). The believer is not saved because he is baptized; but, baptized because he is saved. We are saved through faith alone, but not the faith that is alone, because "Faith without works is dead, being alone." Water baptism is a divinely ordained ordinance whereby the believer witnesses to the world that he has died with Christ, and is "risen together with him," an habitation of God through the Spirit (see Matt. 28:19, 20; Acts 2:38, 41; 8:12-13, 16, 36, 38; 9:18; 10:47-48; 16:15, 33; 19:5; 22:15-16; Rom. 6:3-4; Col. 2:12; I Peter 3:21; I John 2:3; 3:22).

Tenth, *Assurance.* Salvation from spiritual death by the new birth immediately follows "repentance toward God, and faith toward our Lord Jesus Christ." "For by grace have ye been saved through faith" (Eph. 2:8). "These things have I written unto you, that ye may know that ye have eternal life, even unto you that believe on the name of the Son of God" (I John 5:13). It is here stated that certain things are in God's Word by which the believer is to know he has eternal life. Here are some of them: "He that heareth my word, and believeth on him that sent me, *hath* eternal life, and cometh not into judgment, but *hath* passed out of death into life" (John 5:24). "He that hath the Son *hath* life." "Whosoever believeth that Jesus is the Christ *is* begotten of God" (I John 5:12-13. For confirmation see I John 2:3; 3:14, 24; 4:20-21).

"And by him every one that believeth *is* justified" (Acts 13:39) — an accomplished work. So the Bible uniformly teaches. Believing these words of assurance, one finds peace and joy. It is the business of the preacher to make this matter plain to converts, that they may be surely and safely anchored (Col. 2:2-3).

There are some other doctrines, of a persuading character, such as Love, Heaven, Hope, Rewards, that may be emphasized to advantage in an evangelistic campaign; but, those I have enumerated will most surely be owned of God in the salvation of souls, if proclaimed as they should be.

Life and opportunity are ours. Men are dying, and the whole world lieth in the wicked one, lost in the ruin of sin. Redemption is an accomplished fact, and salvation is possible for all. We have been chosen to tell out the message of life and hope; and are assured of glorious success if faithful; if unfaithful we had better never been born.

HOWARD CROSBY (1826-1891) graduated from New York University and held the chair of Greek there from 1851, and in Rutgers University (named for his great-uncle) from 1859. He became pastor of the Fourth Avenue Presbyterian Church in New York City. His writings include commentaries on Joshua, Nehemiah, and the entire New Testament.

42

Preach the Word

By Howard Crosby
CHANCELLOR, UNIVERSITY OF THE CITY OF NEW YORK

Abridged and edited by Glenn O'Neal, Ph.D.

One of the latest injunctions of the aged Paul, just before his martyrdom, was that to Timothy, which constitutes the text of my address, "Preach the Word." Thirty years of Christian experience, fifteen years of apostolic survey, and the inspiration of the Holy Ghost, all spoke in those words. It was a command from heaven itself, not to Timothy only, but to all who fill the office of evangelists or preachers in the New Testament church. The order, thus succinctly given, is a condensation of all that Paul had said to Timothy or to the church on the subject of preaching.

The sound or healthy doctrine on which he lays so much stress, and the avoidance of fables and the world's wisdom, are both included in this curt command. There has been a tendency from the very beginning to conform the doctrine of Christ to the philosophy of man, to fuse the two together, and to show that all religions have the same divine element at their roots. This was seen in gnosticism, in the Alexandrian school of Clement and Origen, and in a score of heresies that sprang up within the later church.

The distinctive character of Christianity has displeased the philosophic mind, and men have sought to explain away many of its features from the standpoint of the human consciousness and by an appeal to the teachings of nature. These efforts have certain marks in common. They diminish the heinousness of sin, they exaggerate the powers of man, and they suggest a uniformity of destiny. Sin is a defect, perhaps a disease. The defect can be supplied, the disease can be cured by human applications, the divine help being valuable as encouragement to the human effort.

High civilization and moral reform are what man needs, and these can be obtained by the use of general principles common to our race, of which Christianity is only one of the forms.

It is natural and inevitable that, with this teaching, the written Word of God should be neglected, if not ignored. No one can study that Word and then use it for so broad and indiscriminating a purpose. No one can study that Word and then be contented with a superficial polish of society, and a universal brotherhood founded upon such a scheme. Paul saw this tendency in his own day, and he warns the church earnestly against it. "Beware," is his language — "Beware lest any man spoil you through philosophy and vain deceit, after the tradition of men, after the rudiments of the world, and not after Christ" (Col. 2:8). The evil principle is ever at work. Human nature is ever the same. The church is always subject to the same efforts of human nature within itself to remove the foundations of grace and substitute the inventions of pride. Whether it appear in the form of hierarchical assumption, or in the character of rational inquiry and scientific research, the evil principle hides, mutilates, or contradicts the Holy Scripture. The Scriptures, as they are, with their divine claim and their uncompromising teachings, it cannot endure, and the appeal to Scripture it counts as a mark of credulity and an exhibition of ignorance.

One of the saddest sights in the church of Christ is the yielding to this spirit of pride on the part of the ordained preachers of the Word. Many modern Timothys use the pulpit for discourses on art and literature; others take the opportunity for the display of rhetoric and oratory; others proclaim an ethics of expediency; while still others seek only to tickle the ears of an audience that desires to be amused. In all this you look in vain for the Gospel. Plato or Aristotle, and in some cases Lucian, could have said it all. Churches are filled by appealing to carnal desires and aesthetic tastes. Brilliant oratory, scientific music, sensational topics and fashionable pewholders, are the baits to lure people into the churches, and a church is called prosperous as these wretched devices succeed. The preacher delights to get himself into the newspaper and he accommodates his preaching to the newspaper level. Such churches will, of course, have worldly-minded officers and a worldly-minded membership, while godly souls either flee from them, or else mourn in secret, if they are not themselves chilled by the lack of Gospel heat.

It is directly against all this that the holy apostle utters his clarion cry down through the ages, "Preach the Word." What is the Word? It is not man's philosophy nor man's rhetoric. It is the divine revelation. It is called the Word of God, because it is not of man. As God's it has both authority and power — authority to demand attention, and power to convert and save the soul. It is not to be pounded in man's mortar, nor run into man's mould. It is not to be twisted and fitted to man's preconceived ideas. It is not to be filtered through man's strainer, nor mixed with man's conceits. It is God's and as God's let no man dare add to it, or take from it, or alter it in any way. The Lord Jesus stands by his cross, where he offered up the sacrifice for sin, and points backward to the Old Testament, and forward to the New, as alike the Word of God. Of the former he cries, "Search the Scriptures"; of the latter he tells his apostles that the Paraclete would come and teach them all things, and they should bear witness. This Old Testament is one revelation of God — one Bible — one unerring rule of faith. God has not given us a doubtful and deceitful light for our path. He has not given us a bundle of truth and fable tied up together. He has not left us to our weak and discordant reason, and thus made revelation superfluous. He has given his people a "sure word of prophecy" as the only reasonable guide for our reason and our sinful natures; and on this sure Word is his church built. The doctrines of grace have neither human origin nor human support. They are altogether divine, and are received only by the soul that becomes partaker of the divine nature. To go, therefore, to human philosophy or to man's inner consciousness for their confirmation or explanation, is to go to the sentenced criminal to understand the excellences of criminal law. The error of errors is the seeking for the truths of religion from man. It is but the adaptation of religion to the carnal heart. It is the essence of pride and rebellion against God.

It is a favorite charge of the advocates of this looseness that we are worshipping a Book. "Bibliolatry" is the formidable word that they cast at us. But we worship no book. We do worship God who sent the Book, and it is no true worship of God that slights the Book which he gives. If we honor God, we shall honor the Word he has sent, and we shall be jealous for that Word, that not one jot or one tittle of it be disturbed by the vagaries of dreamers or the impious hands of boasting critics. It is the Word of God, and, as such, we shall not allow, for a moment, the speculations, imaginings, and guesses of men, ever so learned, to weigh a feather's weight against it. They have been convicted over and over again of grossest fallacies in their hot endeavor to detract from the influence of the holy Word, and their criticisms have returned upon themselves to their confusion. What gross absurdities have been promulgated by these learned enemies of revelation! Myth, romance, the fiction of poetry, a patchwork of traditions, contradictory records, pious fraud, these are some of the labels that the strutting pride of man has affixed to the books of the Bible, while not one of his sneers has been sustained in the light of honest criticism. No scientific truth has been found opposed, and no historic truth misstated, in all the sacred writings, from Moses to John. The most microscopic investigations have been made by the most eager and learned enemies of the truth in order to find some inaccuracy, but not one has been discovered, except those necessarily resulting from the process of transcription, and those imaginary ones which are perfectly resolvable by ordinary common sense. Apply these tests to the *Vedas*, the *Avesta*, or the *Koran*, and the contrast is overwhelming. These fairly bristle with error and falsehood, but the Bible comes out from the crucible without spot, as the pure Word of God. Men just as learned as the inimical critics, and just as thorough in their investigation, men known and revered in the world of letters, have accepted the Bible, the whole Bible, as the inerrant truth of God. If the verdict of the inimical critics can be thus set aside in an equally learned court, the result shows that their learning goes for nothing in the matter.

But far above all this testimony to the letter is the witness of millions who have found the joy unutterable and the peace which passeth all understanding in the sacred volume, and who are drawn to it as a child is drawn to its father, without question regarding his worth and authority. They never suppose (and the position is a right one) that the fountain that refreshes their soul is defective or corrupt, but they value its every drop as a gift of the divine grace. They go constantly to its blessed waters and always derive strength from the draught. To such the carping critics are as unworthy of regard as those who would argue against the sunshine. Now, it is this holy Word, thus spotless and thus powerful for righteousness and comfort, that the Christian preacher is to preach. The preacher is a proclaimer, a herald, not an originator of theories. He has the Word given him, and that he is to proclaim. He is not to draw from the wells of human philosophy, but from the stream that flows directly from the throne of God. He is to tell the people what God has said. He is to hide himself behind his message, and to receive it equally with those he addresses. Nor is the preacher the mouthpiece of a church to issue ecclesiastical decrees and fulminate ecclesiastical censures. This is as far from preaching the Word as the other. As a herald of Christ, while there is nothing before him but human hearts and consciences to which to appeal, there is nothing behind him but the revealed Word of God to utter and enforce. All church commands laid upon him as to his preaching are as nothing except as they are conformed to that Word. He is responsible as a herald to God and not to the church. He is God's herald and not the church's. The same reason that forbids him from making the people's approbation the guide to his preaching will forbid him from making church authority the guide. He will be happy to please both people and authorities, but he cannot make that pleasing a criterion or standard. His duty is above all that. His allegiance is higher.

In thus limiting himself to the preaching of God's Word, the preacher is not circumscribing his power, but enlarging it. By the jealous use of that Word alone he will accomplish far more for the kingdom of Christ and the salvation of men than by mixing human expedients with the Word. Human expedients are very specious and attractive, and, alas! many preachers employ them. They think they will attract the multitude and fill up the pews; and so they may, but these are not the objects for which the Lord sent out his heralds. Success is not to be reckoned by full houses and popular applause, but by convicted and converted hearts, and by the strengthening of the faith and piety of God's people. A holier life, a more pronounced separation from the world, a stainless integrity in business pursuits, a

Christly devotion to the interests of others, a more thorough knowledge of the Word — these are the true signs of success which the preacher may justly seek. These are the glorious results for which the consecrated soul will pray, and in them he will rejoice with a purer, holier joy than that which comes from numbers, wealth, or popular admiration.

If the preacher preaches the Word only, then he will teach his people to handle the Word — to follow him in his reading and expounding — to study over the Scripture lesson at home, and to pray its blessed truths into their souls. A people will, in this way, become mighty in the Scriptures; and he who is mighty in the Scriptures is a mighty power for Christ and salvation, and in his own soul will have a full experience of the power of divine truth, deriving it directly from its source, and proving how the entrance of God's Word giveth light.

Still again, if the preacher preach the Word only, he will himself be a diligent student of the Word. He will bathe in God's revelation and be permeated by it; and so be proof against all the shafts of ignorance and conceit. He will become familiar with every detail of the sacred history, chronology, ethnology, geography, prophecy, precept, and doctrine, and will take nothing at second hand. He will not go to Pope or Council, nor to Calvin or Arminius, to know what to preach, but his delight will be in the law of the Lord, and in his law will he meditate day and night.

It is a lamentable fact, that in too many of our seminaries where preachers are prepared for their work, the Word of God is not taught, but in its stead the philosophic schemes of so-called "fathers" and great divines are given as the basis of doctrinal belief. It is true, that these schemes are brought to the Scripture for support, and texts are quoted in their defence. It is also true that some of these schemes are consonant with Scripture more or less. But, with these admissions, the mistake still exists, that the Word of God plays a secondary part in the instruction. It is not taught as the authoritative text-book.

Some theological schools might without exaggeration be called "schools for turning believers into doubters." The excuse, that men who are going to be preachers should know all that is said against the credibility, genuineness, and authenticity of the Scriptures, is a flimsy one. If that were the object, these objections would be considered only by way of parenthesis, and the over-whelming evidence of the Scriptures would be the main current of thought; but this is not the way it is done. On the contrary, the objections are magnified, and their authors are commended to the students for their perusal, and the hint is often thrown out that conservative views of the inspiration of God's Word are antiquated, obsolete, and marks of ignorance. We have thus, in the very places where, most of all, we should expect to see the profoundest reverence for God's Word, and its faithful study for the understanding of the divine will, the machinery for un-dermining the doctrine of Scripture inspiration and authority, on which all Christian truth rests, and that, too, in the young minds which are being prepared to become Christ's preachers to a sinful and dying world. It is a most painful thought, and it becomes the church of Jesus Christ to arise to a sense of the evil, and to correct it before the whole church is poisoned by this insidious influence.

We wish our young Timothys to go out to their work with the one controlling desire to put God's Word before the people and to avoid questions and strifes of words which do not minister to godly edifying, knowing that the power to convert and edify is not the wisdom of man, but the power of God.

It is as preachers depart from that Word that their preaching becomes barren and fruitless. The divine Spirit will only accom-pany the divine Word. His mighty power will act only in his own way and by his own means. The Word is supernatural, and woe to the preacher who leaves the supernatural for the natural; who sets aside the sword of the Spirit to use in its stead a blade of his own tempering!

JOHN TIMOTHY STONE (1868-1954) served Chicago's Fourth Presbyterian Church for twenty-one years as pastor and twenty-four years as pastor emeritus. Prior to his outstanding ministry in Chicago, Stone pastored congregations in New York and Maryland; and upon his retirement, he was made president of McCormick Theological Seminary in Chicago. He had a gift for attracting men to the church and enlisting them for Christ's service. He outlined his approach in his book *Recruiting for Christ* (1910). He also published a biography of George Whitefield (1914), a devotional book, *To Start the Day* (1914), and several books of sermons.

43

Pastoral and Personal Evangelism, or Winning Men to Christ One by One

By Rev. *John Timothy Stone, D.D.*
PRESBYTERIAN MINISTER, CHICAGO

Revised and edited by Charles L. Feinberg, Th.D., Ph.D.

The story of evangelism is the specific history of the cross of Christ. Great movements and revivals have made up much of its general history, but slowly and quietly through the centuries the evangel has won, as men and women have led others to repentance, and have by precept and example followed in the footsteps of their Lord.

Christ won most of his followers and chose his apostles one by one. He called men to himself, and they heard and heeded his call. The multitudes sought him and heard him gladly, but he sought individuals, and those individuals sought others and brought them to him. John the Baptist brought Andrew; Andrew found his brother Simon. Christ found Philip who found Nathaniel. The Lord called Matthew from his labors, and so the other apostles. Saul of Tarsus was arrested by the divine call as he persecuted the early Christians.

All through those first decades of the early church, and on through the ages, individual work for individuals has accomplished results. How largely the Gospels, the Acts and the Epistles verify this fact. Even the marvelous work of Philip in Samaria was not the immediate plan of God, but the Spirit sent him past Jerusalem, down into the desert at Gaza, that he might win the Ethiopian eunuch to Christ, and through him no doubt countless hosts of Africa. The missionary journeys and efforts of Paul were filled with personal service. His letters are filled with personal messages.

God has used men mightily in reaching vast multitudes of people, even from the days of his own ministry and the days of Peter and his associates at Pentecost. Even now, more than two hundred years after his unparalleled ministry, we are reminded of George Whitefield, who preached at times to fully thirty thousand people in the open air, and won his thousands and tens of thousands. Vast multitudes were reached by Moody and Sankey; great audiences flocked to hear Spurgeon, week after week, year after year. The strong evangelists of our own generation verify before our eyes God's honor placed on those to whom he gives such signal power. But our thought goes back to the great universal method our Lord himself instituted, of reaching the individual by his fellowman.

The Almighty could have so arranged his divine plan that he himself without human help might arrest and enlist followers as he did with Saul of Tarsus, but this was not his plan. By man he would reach men. Human media of power must do his wondrous work.

The Holy Spirit

The first requisite in winning men to Christ must be the presence and power of the Holy Spirit (John 16:7; Acts 1:8). To live in the power of the Spirit, knowing his leadership, is in itself an assurance of a joyful and successful service. The Spirit will direct us and speak for and through us. Fear and embarrassment will not harass, if we are under the constant influence of God's Spirit. What we say in weakness he will use with power. His Word will not return void (Isa. 55:11). We may always take for granted his preparation, for he does not send but calls us. His word is not "Go," but "Come." Thus we shall always be alert for opportunities to speak the things he would have us, and our words and thoughts will be those he suggests and honors. We shall be nourished constantly by his Word within, and equipped with his sword for sustained protection and aggressive attack. His Spirit will also give us courage and endurance, and we need not fear the unexpected nor the aggressive opponent. The Spirit of God also prepares the one whom we must approach, and is working in his heart as well as with our words.

Prayer is also a real factor in our lives, and we live in his presence by the true conversational method of association. We may pray before and after and as we speak with others, and do it so naturally that we may actually live in the atmosphere of prayer without hypocrisy. Prayer will become more and more a power in our work as we approach individuals from the very presence of the unseen God. Confidence results, and we are agreeably surprised with ourselves to find that our happiness does not depend so much upon the evidence of our success as upon the consciousness of our faithfulness.

We shall also seek to win others to Christ that they too may be used by his Spirit and associated with him, rather than simply to obtain salvation; not what we can do for them, but what God's Spirit can and will do with them.

The Spirit of God will also lead us to gain from others the experiences and methods through which they have gone to learn to do this work for him; hence conferences and testimony will take on new life and gain keener interest. Criticism will give place to appreciation and suggestion to expressions of gratitude. We shall also learn to take the difficult things to God in prayer instead of taking them to men in controversy, and shall be surprised to find how many easily adjust themselves for us.

God's Spirit will also prompt us to spend longer seasons alone and seriously think on life's greatest issues and values. Prayer will be less general and more specific and individual. Souls will mean more, and things less. Lives will become more attractive and fascinating, and books, papers and stories will only control interest when related to lives which can be influenced for him. Others will be won by you as they see in your very face the reflection of Christ, because his Spirit dwells within you.

The Bible

A second most necessary element in winning men to the Lord is a knowledge and proper use of God's Word. We must be workmen who need not be ashamed, who can rightly divide the word of truth. The use of the Bible is the greatest advancing weapon for Christ. The worker who knows his Bible will constantly read it for strength and apply it in dealing with the unconverted. He will not argue with men, nor talk about God's Word, but he will explain it, and repeatedly refer to it. An open Bible before an inquirer almost always means conversion and spiritual growth to follow. When dealing with your subject, ask if he has ever considered what the Bible says on the point under discussion. Pertinent passages will at least arrest his attention, and unconsciously interest him somewhat in reading the Bible himself.

Remember to have an open Bible before your companion as you read. Reading to a man will not help a listener and reading with you will. Let the eye help the ear, and make it personal by letting him follow you as you read. Perhaps sometimes ask him to read an occasional verse that needs emphasis, and then you comment on it, asking him to read on. If a man does not understand how God can love him, do not discuss it, but turn to I Corinthians chapter 13, and read it slowly and thoughtfully. Then read John 3:16. In other words, win a man by the love of God. Do not omit Luke 15 with its parable of the prodigal son, nor I John 3:1, 2. If you have one burdened with a sense of guilt and sin, turn to Isaiah 1:18, then Romans chapter 7 and 8. Many men are reached by these chapters; they are a sort of mirror to most men of their own lives.

Prayer

We do not estimate the place and power prayer has in winning others to Christ, prayer for others in intercession, and prayer with others as we take them individually into the very presence of God. First, there is prayer for them. No matter what your method or lack of method may be, take those for whom you are working, to God in prayer. Pray for them by name; pray that you may approach them correctly and appeal to them with divine wisdom. Pray that you may be patient as well as wise with them. Pray that you may turn to the right Scripture to help them. Pray that you may lead them to Christ instead of talking with them about him. Pray that they may be responsive and willing. Pray that their surroundings may not be a hindrance to them. Pray that you may converse with them on the essentials, and not spend the time on unimportant matters. Pray that you may be fearless, clear and exact. Pray that human sympathy and love may influence you to show your heart and soul to touch and melt their hearts. Pray that just the favorable opening may come to you, and that you may be ready to use it. Pray most of all for the Holy Spirit's power with you.

Then secondly, pray with the individual. After Scripture has had its chance, and decision should be reached, get to your knees, and ask him to decide after you have poured out your heart to God for him and with him. To let one know you love him for Christ's sake breaks many a heart. When thus praying, no matter how cold your heart may have been at first, you will feel three are present, and the third is the Saviour of men.

When you pray with the one for whom you are working, be most specific and plain in your petition. Bring him then and there to a decision if possible, and seal the occasion with prayer again. Pour out your soul to God and labor with Christ for that soul. Sometimes an unforgiving spirit is the cause of delay. There is no place so sure to overcome bitterness or hatred as the place of prayer. Leading the human life into the place of prayer will bring divine power into the work, and conquers where you might fail.

Another form of prayer for the individual may be used by putting down upon a list or card the names of those for whom you are praying. The list is for the individual Christian, a definite prayer for a definite soul. Many of these cards are handed to the pastor, and pastor and people unite in prayer for these souls. It is a real method of binding pastor and people in prayer for individuals. A prayer list which includes all your friends is a most inspiring and useful method. Prayer for individuals also makes one alert when opportunities open to speak to them, and directs aright conversation at such times. Friendship and companionship mean more when we realize that we are meeting each other through Christ at the throne of grace, and individuals are conscious of greater power than human speech when they know that you are praying for them. Prayer, then, is a most effective and powerful agency in winning others.

We ought also to pray more in our public utterances for the immediate and direct result of our preaching; that souls may be converted; that hearts may be arrested in sin and turned to God. When a congregation feels that a preacher actually expects results, they begin to expect and pray for them too. If the soul hungers for souls, then public as well as private prayer will claim them.

Method and Means

The method is, after all, secondary, and if it becomes too set and orderly, it will be self-destructive. As soon as one sees your method, the heart and mind are steeled against it, and there is little or no interest. When God's Spirit leads, we are responsive to all kinds of openings and ways. It is wise and right for us, however, to consider methods and means. Christ himself began his work with reaching individuals and training them to work for others. Christ's method still remains; he sought individuals. Recall the woman of Samaria, Nicodemus, the two disciples on the way to Emmaus, Andrew, Philip, Zaccheus, Matthew, and Saul of Tarsus.

The greatest advantage which the large meeting has is so to interest individuals in the truth, that they will inquire from others who are ready to help them, as to the application of the truth they hear. A valuable series of meetings is only sure in interest and result as individuals invite, seek and lead others to be present, and then follow them by individual effort. God works through men, and individuals must reach other individuals.

One of the most efficient means some have used is that of training men and women to call upon their neighbors and personally invite them to services, not a formal invitation but a friendly one. Many departments in church life do this work, but there should be a more definite personal responsibility put upon the members to reach others in extending them the definite invitation to attend God's house and give their lives to the Lord. The church of Christ universal has an immense force in herself to face the work of winning others to Christ, but we have not used that force. Foreign missionaries have appreciated this fact, and in some places the condition of winning others has been imposed on new members before they are accepted into full fellowship.

Some of our churches have had no new members for several years, and some have very few. On the other hand, here is a great force of hundreds of thousands who are not working in the very line of activity which it is their privilege and duty to pursue. Now, there is no question that a pastor has his definite work of preaching. He must also realize that, no matter how intense and far-reaching that work may be, his preeminent work should be in the pulpit. But it is also his work to shepherd his flock, and a shepherd cannot properly do that work without teaching his flock to follow him. He first must be an inviter and winner of men to Christ, and he must train his people to follow him. The great need of the church today is a work within herself, in which her members may become individual and definite workers for the Lord Jesus Christ, and the winners of others to him.

Another very effective method is by correspondence. So many times when we do not find people at home, or when we are not able to approach them as we desire, if we would sit down and write a direct and personal letter, it would have its weight and influence. It should not be a substitute for a personal interview, but is a splendid addition to it, and where the one is denied the other can be used.

The ways and methods for reaching others are manifold, and they are as diversified as the personalities and training of those who are workers. God has new methods and ways to use constantly, but we must be alert in this great work, and reach out in faith and in earnestness. One of the best means of reaching others is to be able to put oneself directly in the place of another, to feel his temptations, to understand his difficulties, and to be willing to meet him on his own ground and with his own needs. If we can establish this human sympathy, we have gone a long way toward reaching others.

Another most effective way must be through the Sunday School and through the regular channels of active participation. Whatever we can do to bring to others the positive need of settling this question for oneself, communicants' classes, catechetical classes, individual pastor's classes, all such methods should be used. A pastor should get into the public and private schools of the children of his congregation, to know where they live and what their work is and what their problems are. Then he should plan in some way to meet them individually. A pastor should go to the various Sunday School classes in his own church, not regularly or at stated times, but informally or by definite arrangement with the teacher, thus getting in touch with the pupils and meeting them on their own ground. He should also arrange special classes to meet them and talk over their relationship to Christ. All through the church he should have those who are so interested in individuals that they will take to him the special cases and refer them to him.

But after all the greatest method in the world, the greatest means of all in winning others to Christ, is that of persistent, patient, faithful prayer. This activity, followed by action, will be rewarded. Times of revival will spring up. Others will want special services and methods and will suggest them, and our churches will be alive with new material. We shall find men and women are not only crying out, "What must I do to be saved?" but "How may we win others to the Saviour?" We shall all become workmen that need not be ashamed, realizing God's Word never returns to him void. Surely, "He that winneth souls is wise."

CHARLES GALLAUDET TRUMBULL (1872-1941) graduated from Yale in 1893 and joined the staff of *The Sunday School Times*, which was then edited by his father, Henry Clay Trumbull. Ten years later, he became editor. A prolific journalist, he wrote weekly columns on the Sunday school lesson for a number of metropolitan newspapers. In 1910, Trumbull had a profound spiritual experience that erased the intellectual questions he had raised about the inspiration and inerrancy of the Bible. He was active in the "victorious Christian life" movement and served as vice president of the World Christian Fundamental Association. *Taking Men Alive* was perhaps his most popular book. He also wrote *The Life Story of C. I. Scofield.* Trumbull was active in promoting foreign missions and explorations in Palestine.

44

The Sunday School's True Evangelism

By *Charles Gallaudet Trumbull*
EDITOR, *THE SUNDAY SCHOOL TIMES*

Abridged and edited by Glenn O'Neal, Ph.D.

There are more than thirty million persons reported in the enrollment of the Sunday Schools of the world. But if all these persons, and all church members as well, knew what the Sunday School is really for, the enrollment would leap upward millions upon millions.

The Sunday School is often spoken of as the child of the church, or the church of tomorrow, or a branch or department of the church. It is more than any and all of these.

The true Sunday School is the church of Jesus Christ engaged in systematic study and teaching of the Word of God for three great purposes: to bring into the body of Christ those within the membership of the Sunday School who are not yet members of the church or of Christ; to train up those who are in Christ into a full-grown knowledge and appropriation of the riches which are theirs because they are Christ's; and to send out into the world fully equipped, victorious soul-winners who shall be Christ's living epistles to those who do not yet know him.

The whole superb work of the Sunday School centers about its textbook, the Word of God. Bible study in the Sunday School is made the means of the three-fold purpose of the Sunday School. The Sunday School is the great organized movement of the church of God for Bible study which has for its end, salvation, character building, and equipment for evangelism. Or to describe the work of the Sunday School partly in theological terms, the purpose of the Sunday School is Bible study for justification, sanctification and service.

Whoever needs to know what the Bible has to say about next-world freedom from the penalty of our sins, and this-world freedom from the power of our sin, together with the supernatural power of God as the equipment of the full grown man for service, may properly be in the Sunday School. Only those who do not need the fullest possible message of the Bible on these subjects can logically stay outside the Sunday School.

The true Sunday School is the whole church of God engaged in systematic Bible study to ascertain the whole will of God as revealed in his Word for their lives. With the cradle roll at one end of the age limit and the home department at the other end for non-attending members, there is little reason today for any one to remain outside the membership of the Sunday School. It is not necessary to attend the Sunday services of the Sunday School in order to be a member in full and regular standing. Literally the entire church membership can with great profit be enrolled: babies, invalids, shut-ins, traveling men, mothers tied down by home duties, railroad men, telegraph or telephone operators — the Sunday School welcomes the representatives of every walk in life. Cradle roll members do not do much reading or studying for themselves; but when the enthusiastic, tactful, loving cradle roll superintendent hurries around to a home in the neighborhood and asks for the name and enrollment of the baby not yet twenty-four hours old, you may be sure that that household, especially the father and mother, are not offended at this show of interest in the little life which is all the world to them. And stony hearts that may have seemed hopelessly remote from the Gospel have been warmed and won to a wide-open acceptance of the love of Jesus Christ because the littlest member of the family first entered the Sunday School through the cradle roll.

Thus it is that the true Sunday School is a mighty evangelistic agency. If the Sunday School is not evangelistic, it is not the Sunday School. It may bear the name of the Sunday School, but that does not make it one. The true Sunday School of the church of Jesus Christ exists solely to make the whole wonderful reach and splendor of the Good News better known, both to those within and without.

There are many methods of evangelism of which the Sunday School makes blessed use. "Decision Day" when wisely observed has resulted in great blessing. On this day a direct appeal to accept Jesus Christ as Saviour is made from the platform to the school or the department as a whole, and opportunity is given for formal response in the way of signed cards or otherwise. The observance of such a day is most blessed when there has been earnest, faithful preparation for it in prayer, by teachers and officers. It seems better not to have the day announced in advance to the school, but only to teachers and officers, that they may prepare for it in prayer and personal work.

But the all-the-time evangelism of the faithful teacher is the surest and most effective. Most effective, that is, if accompanied by the all-the-time prayer. Prayer meetings of the teachers for the conversion and consecration of the puplis are a secret of the continuously evangelistic Sunday School.

What sort of teaching is done in the Sunday School in which true evangelism is conspicuous?

It is teaching that assumes that the whole Bible is the inspired Word of God; unique, authoritative, infallible. The acceptance of destructive criticism's theories and conclusions can have no place in this teaching.

The evangelistic school knows that all men (and "men" means men, women and children) are lost until saved by the blood of Jesus Christ. The teaching in such a school brings out clearly the lost condition of the entire human race by nature, and recognizes no possibility of salvation by education, character, or any other works of man. It gives full recognition to education as the duty and privilege of the Christian, but it does not substitute education for salvation.

The evangelistic Sunday School holds up the Lord Jesus Christ as the only Saviour of men, accepting the Word of the Holy Spirit that "neither is there any other name under heaven, given among men, whereby we must be saved." And because no man or created being can save another created being that is spiritually lost, the uncreated deity of Jesus as Saviour is recognized and declared. The new birth, accomplished by the Holy Spirit in the one who believes in Jesus Christ as Saviour, marks the passage from death unto life — that is the Gospel of the evangelistic Sunday School.

The workers in such a Sunday School know that no human being can save a soul; they know that no human being, no matter how faithfully and truly he tells the story of salvation and offers the Gospel invitation, can win another soul to Christ or enable that soul to believe on Christ as Saviour. It is recognized that this act of acceptance and belief is not the result of human teaching or telling or persuading or inviting, but is a supernatural work of God. Therefore the evangelistic teacher depends chiefly upon prayer to succeed in the chief mission of the Sunday School. The teacher recognizes that prayer is the great secret, the great essential of effective evangelism. The evangelistic teacher prays souls into salvation before even expecting to be used to that end in teaching or personal conversation.

Not all so-called Sunday Schools are evangelistic. Not all are being supernaturally used of God in the miraculous work of bringing lives into the new birth and the new life in Christ Jesus. There are dangers that threaten the Sunday School of today probably more than in any preceding generation. These dangers not only threaten; they are disastrously and effectively at work in many schools.

The undermining work of the destructive criticism has crept into Sunday School lesson helps. Not only in so-called "independent" courses of Bible study, but in helps on the International Lessons, issued by regular denominational boards, are found lesson comments that assume the error and human authorship of parts of the Bible instead of inerrant, inspired authorship. It has been a distressing thing to many to note this terrible encroachment of the Adversary as he uses the very tools of the church of Christ to lead teachers and pupils away from the hope of eternal life. For, as has been well pointed out, the Adversary's first move is to discredit parts of the Bible, then the atonement of Jesus Christ, then the deity of Christ. And without a Saviour who is God the "evangelism" of the Sunday School is not the Good News.

The Sunday School Times had occasion to investigate a certain "Completely Graded Series" of Sunday School lessons of which the publisher said: "These lessons are already in use in thousands of up-to-date Sunday Schools. The various courses of study have been prepared under the direction of men who are recognized as authorities in this country in religious education, and they therefore embody the results of the latest scholarship." Upon looking into the lesson courses themselves, such statements as the following were found:

"It is easy to see that the age that produced the Gospels would not be anxious for scientific accounts of the deeds of Jesus, but that it would expect of him exactly the acts that are attributed to him. It is possible therefore that some events, like the restoration of the centurion's servant, were simple coincidences; that others, like the apparent walking of Jesus on the water, were natural deeds which the darkness and confusion caused to be misunderstood; that others, like the turning of water into wine, were really parables that became in course of time changed into miracles. As nearly all the miracles not of healing had their prototypes in the Old Testament, many of them at least were attributed to Jesus because men expected such deeds from their Messiah, and finally became convinced that he must have performed them."

The foregoing paragraph was from a help for the Intermediate teacher. In a similar volume for the Junior teacher there appeared the following discussion of the reasonableness of miracles:

"There are some scholars who find traces of this tendency to magnify the marvelous even in the Gospels themselves, which, with all their uniqueness, are human documents, written by flesh and blood human beings. For example, in our story of Jairus' daughter, Mark's comment, as we have seen, leaves us in doubt whether the little girl was really dead, or only in a swoon, or state of coma. In Matthew's later account, however, we find that Jairus says to Jesus, 'My daughter is even now dead.' When they reach the house, flute players, hired for the funeral, are already on the scene. This increases the marvel of the story, but does not seem to add to its moral significance. It is possible that not a few of the accounts of miraculous deeds, attributed to Jesus, are the product of this same tendency. By this is meant the tendency to magnify the marvelous, as seen in apocryphal legends, arising from a 'vulgar craving for signs and wonders.' "

Junior teachers were told, in explanation of the omission of the story of Ananias and Sapphira:

"This fear is explained by the story of Ananias and Sapphira, which precedes this sentence in the complete text of Acts. This story is like a number of other ancient narratives, in that the facts are probably recorded with substantial accuracy; but the author's own interpretation of these facts seems to us, in these days, not altogether satisfactory. There is no reason for doubting the account of the deception practised on the apostles by this unscrupulous couple, Ananias and Sapphira; nor the account of Peter's rebuke; nor the statement that they both died shortly after receiving the rebuke. In that period of the world's history people would inevitably conclude that this death was direct manifestation of the divine wrath invoked by Peter. This interpretation, however, seems inconsistent with the Christian conception of God as a loving and patient Father. On account of the primitive ideas which it reflects, the story has been omitted from the Junior Bible."

As was editorially stated in *The Sunday School Times*, which discussed this series of lessons, it is only too true that: "There are those who have not taught the whole Christ of the New Testament and the Old, but have been busy about the presenting of a different and lesser Person. They have followed and taught Jesus of Nazareth as the ideal teacher and leader, acknowledging him as indeed the most extraordinary development among the noblest sons of God, and the Gospel story of him as usually reliable, but they have not been presenting Jesus unreservedly as the eternal Christ in all that the Scriptures in their uttermost struggling for full expression claim that he is; as all that he was, very Life itself to the disciplined mind and the revolutionized personality of Paul; as all that he is to those who daily testify in word and deed to the liberty from the crushing bondage of sin by his indwelling."

The same editorial discussed the peril of teaching a "modified Christ." It went on to say:

"It is no uncommon thing to find teachers of the Bible who are thus teaching a modified Christ. The cautionary attitude, to say the least, of a type of influential scholarship, on the trustworthiness of the Scriptures, and the encouraging of suspended opinion as to the claims of Christ, are more confusing and insidious in their results on the mind and the life than a flat denial of cherished truth by confessed unbelievers. The New Testament writers, on the one hand, are not wholly able within the range of human vocabularies to find language that will release the streams of inspired truth concerning the Lord Jesus. In their most rapt ecstacy, as in their apologetic, they cannot exalt the Christ as they would, because not he, but language, is inadequate. They simply cannot say enough of him. But, on the other hand, there is a type of modern scholarship not without its influence upon the trained and untrained Bible teacher alike, which is careful not to say too much of Jesus. There is a restraint in its deliverances about him, a cautious and reserved detachment, which would seem to belong as a method rather to the outside observer than to the inner disciple. Ethical and social leadership and supremacy are freely attributed to Jesus, but this type of biblical scholarship does not seem, in dealing with Jesus, to be dealing with the same eternal Christ who was disclosed to John and Peter and Paul and others of like mind and experience. Indeed, the limitless ascriptions of John, the sweeping declarations of Peter, the passionate abandon of Paul, by no means characterizes this kind of scholarship. On the contrary, its Jesus is far less than the New Testament Christ; its New Testament a record quite open to reasonable doubt. Yet the superior advantages of lesson helps embodying the results of this attitude toward Jesus and the record of his life are widely urged upon teachers and pupils in the Sunday School today."

Against all such encroachments upon the Word of God, upon the Gospel of Jesus Christ, and upon a clear vision of men's eternal need of that Gospel, the Sunday School of true evangelism must stand with the firmness of the Rock of Ages. Only the power of Christ can enable us to stand thus firmly in the strength of Christ. He is doing just this, with blessed results, for Sunday Schools that ask him to do so upon his own terms.

The social service program, which includes so many things Christian in spirit, but which in many cases so disastrously puts fruit ahead of root, is a danger against which the Sunday School needs to guard, especially in its adult classes. The salvation of society regardless of the salvation of the individual is a hopeless. task; and the Sunday School of true evangelism will not enter upon it. But the Sunday School that brings the good news of Jesus Christ to the individuals of any community lifts society as the usual social service program can never do.

One last word is necessary. If the Sunday School is really to do its work as an evangelizing agent, the Sunday School must consist of workers whose personal lives are radiant with victory. The Sunday School of true evangelism declares with convincing power the message of the victorious life.

Here is an evangel, a Good News, which is all too new to many a follower of the Lord Jesus Christ who rejoices in the Sunday School as his field of service. But our Lord wants it to be the experienced possession of his every follower.

Evangelism that is limited to the Good News that there is freedom from the penalty of our sins is only a half-way evangelism. It is a crippled, halting evangelism. If we would tell "that sweet story of old," let us tell the whole story.

And the whole story is that our Lord Jesus Christ came, not only to pay the penalty of our sins, but to break the power of our sin. He laid aside his glory and came from heaven to earth, not only that men might be saved from dying the second death, but also that they might live without sinning in this present life. Here is Good News indeed; so good that to many it sounds too good to be true. But, praise God, it is true! When the Holy Spirit says to us, "Sin shall not have dominion over you: for ye are not under law, but under grace," he means it. When Paul declared in the exultant joy of the Spirit, "The law of the Spirit of life in Christ Jesus made me free from the law of sin," he meant it. And the same Spirit of life in Christ Jesus is making men free today from the law of sin, when they are ready to take him at his word. When the beloved Apostle wrote, under the direction of the Holy Spirit, "My little children, these things write I unto you that ye may not sin," he meant just that. When our Lord Jesus himself said, first, "Every one that committeth sin is the bondservant of sin"; and then, instead of leaving us hopelessly there, went on to say: "If therefore the Son shall make you free, ye shall be free indeed," he was trying to tell us what his whole salvation is.

The victorious life is not a life made sinless, but it is a life kept from sinning. It is not, as has well been said, that the sinner is made perfect here in this life, but that the sinner even in this life has a perfect Saviour. And that Saviour is more than equal, while we are still in this life, to overcoming all the power of our sin.

The Keswick convention in England has for many years been blessedly used of God in spreading abroad the Good News of the Gospel of victory over sin. The life that is surrendered unconditionally in the faithfulness of that Saviour Lord to make his promises true, begins to realize the meaning of the unspeakable riches of God's grace.

There are Sunday School teachers who are rejoicing today in the privilege of telling their classes the whole message of true evangelism. May God mightily increase the numbers of those who shall bear witness, by their victorious lives and by their eager glad message, to the whole evangelism of the Word: the saving and the keeping power of our wonderful Lord and Saviour Jesus Christ. Then, "If he shall be manifested, we may have boldness, and not be ashamed before him at his coming."

45

The Place of Prayer in Evangelism

By Rev. R. A. Torrey, D.D.
DEAN OF THE BIBLE INSTITUTE OF LOS ANGELES

Abridged and emended by James H. Christian, Th.D.

The most important human factor in effective evangelism is prayer. There have been great awakenings without much preaching, and there have been great awakenings with absolutely no organization, but there has never been a true awakening without much prayer.

The first great ingathering in human history had its origin, on the human side, in a ten days' prayer meeting. We read of the small company of early disciples: "These all with one accord continued stedfastly in prayer" (Acts 1:14). The result of that ten days' prayer meeting is recorded in the second chapter of the Acts of the Apostles: "They were all filled with the Holy Ghost, and began to speak with other tongues, as the Spirit gave them utterance" (2:4), and "there were added unto them in that day about 3,000 souls" (2:41). That awakening proved real and permanent; those who were gathered in on that greatest day in all Christian history, "continued stedfastly in the apostles' teaching and fellowship, in the breaking of bread, and in prayers" (2:42). "And the Lord added to them day by day those that were being saved" (2:47).

Every great awakening from that day to this has had its earthly origin in prayer. "The Great Awakening" in the eighteenth century, in which Jonathan Edwards was one of the central figures, began with his famous "Call to Prayer." The work of David Brainerd among the North American Indians, one of the most marvelous works in all history, had its origin in the days and nights that Brainerd spent before God in prayer for an enduement of power from on high for this work. In 1830 there was a revival in Rochester, New York, in which Charles G. Finney was the outstanding human agent. This revival spread throughout that region of the state and 100,000 persons were reported as having connected themselves with the churches as the result of this work. Mr. Finney himself attributed his success to the spirit of prayer which prevailed. He says in his autobiography:

"When I was on my way to Rochester, as we passed through a village some thirty miles east of Rochester, a brother minister whom I knew, seeing me on the canal boat, jumped aboard to have a little conversation with me . . . The Lord gave him a powerful spirit of prayer, and his heart was broken. As he and I prayed together, I was struck with his faith in regard to what the Lord was going to do there. I recollect he would say, 'Lord, I do not know how it is; but I seem to know that Thou art going to do a great work in this city.' The spirit of prayer was poured out powerfully, so much so, that some persons stayed away from the public services to pray, being unable to restrain their feelings under preaching.

"And here I must introduce the name of a man, whom I shall have occasion to mention frequently, Mr. Abel Clary. . . . He had been licensed to preach; but his spirit of prayer was such — he was so burdened with the souls of men — that he was not able to preach much, his whole time and strength being given to prayer. The burden of his soul would frequently be so great that he was unable to stand, and he would writhe and groan in agony . . . This Mr. Clary continued in Rochester as long as I did, and did not leave it until after I had left. He never, that I could learn, appeared in public, but gave himself wholly to prayer."

Perhaps the most remarkable awakening ever known in the United States was the great revival of 1857. As far as its human origin can be traced, it began in the prayers of a humble city missionary in New York named Landfear. He not only prayed himself but organized a noon meeting for prayer. At first the attendance was very small; at one meeting there were only three present, at another two, and at one meeting he alone was present. But he and his associates persisted in prayer until a fire was kindled that spread throughout the whole city, until prayer meetings were being held at every hour of the day and night, not only in churches but in theaters. When this had gone on for some time, Dr. Gardner Spring, one of the most eminent Presbyterian ministers in America, said to a company of ministers, "It is evident that a revival has broken out among us, and we must preach." One of the ministers replied, "Well, if there is to be preaching, you must preach the first sermon," and Dr. Gardner Spring consented to preach. But no more people came out to hear him preach than had come out for prayer. So the dependence was put upon prayer and not preaching; the fire spread to Philadelphia, and then all over the land until it is said that there was no part of the country where prayer meetings were not going on, and the whole nation was moved, and there were conversions and accessions to the church everywhere by the hundreds and thousands.

This awakening in America was followed by a similar awakening, though in some respects even more remarkable, in Ireland, Scotland and England, in 1859 and 1860. The most important human factors in the origin of the wonderful work seem to have been four young men who began to meet together in the old schoolhouse in the neighborhood of Kells in the north of Ireland. Here night after night they wrestled with God in prayer. About the spring of 1858 a work of power began to manifest itself. It spread from town to town and from county to county; congregations became too large for any building, meetings were held in the open air, oftentimes attended by many thousands of people. Hundreds of persons were frequently convicted of sin in a single meeting; men were smitten down with conviction of sin while working in the field. In some places the criminal courts and jails were closed because there were no cases to try and no criminals to be incarcerated. The fruits of that wonderful work abide to this day. Many of the leading persons even in the churches of America were converted at that time in the north of Ireland. While men like Dr. Grattan Guinness and Brownlow North were greatly used at that time, the revival spread not so much through preachers as through prayer. The wonderful work of Mr. Moody in England, Scotland and Ireland in 1873, and the years that followed, beyond a question had its origin on the manward side in prayer. His going to England at all was in answer to the importunate prayers of a bed-ridden saint. The first demonstration of God's power through his preaching was in a church in the north of London a year before he went to England for this work. In this meeting 500 people definitely accepted Christ in a single night. This was the direct and immediate outcome of the prayers of this same bed-ridden saint. While the spirit of prayer continued, Mr. Moody went on with power, but as is always the case, in the course of time less and less was made of prayer and his work fell off perceptibly in power.

The great Welsh revival in 1904 and 1905 was unquestionably the outcome of prayer. A year before the writer began his work in Cardiff, it was announced that he was going to Cardiff, and for a year prayer went up from thousands of devoted Christians that there would be not only a revival in Cardiff but throughout Wales. When we reached Cardiff we found that early morning prayer meetings had been held in Penarth, one of the suburbs of Cardiff, for months. Yet at first the work went very slowly. There were great crowds, most enthusiastic singing, but little manifestation of real convicting and regenerating power. A day of fasting and prayer was appointed. This was observed not only in Cardiff but in different parts of Wales. There came an immediate turn of the tide; the power of God fell. For a whole year after our meetings closed in Cardiff, the work went on in that city, meetings every night with a very large number of conversions. All over Wales the work of God continued, largely without human instruments except in the way of prayer with 100,000 conversions reported in a year. It was one of the most remarkable works of God in modern times, and from Wales there went forth a fire from God to the uttermost parts of the earth, and only eternity will reveal the glorious results of that work.

And not only has it been demonstrated over and over again in a large way that widespread revivals are the certain outcome of intelligent and prevailing prayer, but in smaller circles the power of prayer has been demonstrated over and over again. In a very obscure village in the state of Maine, where apparently nothing was being accomplished by the churches, a few earnest Christian men got together and organized a prayer band. They selected apparently the most hopeless case in all the village and centered their prayers upon him, importuning God for his conversion. The man was a drunkard and a wreck. In a short time the man was thoroughly converted. Then the praying band centered its prayers upon another man, the second hardest case in the village, and he was converted; and so the work went on until about two hundred were converted in a single year.

In a little village in the state of Michigan, way off from the railroad, a Presbyterian and a Methodist minister united in an effort to win the unsaved to Christ. They were backed by a faithful praying band. While the Presbyterian preached and the Methodist exhorted, this praying band were in the back room crying to God for his blessing on the work. They would select individuals in the community to pray for. In some instances these men would come into the meeting the very night they were being prayed for and be converted. The work grew to be so remarkable that ministers and multitudes of the people would drive for miles to witness the wonderful work.

The history of foreign missions abounds in illustrations of the importance and power of prayer in worldwide evangelism. All will recall "the haystack" prayer meeting and its results, and the sending out of the 100 by the China Inland Mission in 1887.

Illustrations of this character could easily be multiplied. The history of the church demonstrates beyond a question that the most important human factor in the evangelism of the world is prayer. The great need of the present hour is prayer. In our work at home and abroad we are placing more and more dependence upon men, machinery, and methods, and less and less upon God. Evangelism at home is becoming more and more mechanical, and methods are being resorted to that are more and more revolting to all spiritually minded people; while evangelism abroad is becoming more and more merely educational and sociological. What is needed above everything else today is prayer, true prayer, prayer in the power of the Holy Ghost, and prayer that meets the conditions of prevailing prayer so plainly laid down in the Word of God.

All that is said thus far is more or less general, but if anything practical is to be accomplished we must be specific. In what directions should we put forth prayer, if we would see that effective evangelism for which so many are longing?

First of all, we should pray for individuals. Under God's guidance we should select individuals upon whom we should center our prayers. Every minister and every Christian should have a prayer list, i.e., he should write at the top of a sheet of paper the following words (or words to the same effect): "God helping me, I will pray earnestly and work persistently for the conversion of the following persons." Then he should kneel before God and ask God definitely and in the most thoughtful earnestness and sincerity, to show him whom to put on that prayer list, and as God leads him to put different persons on that prayer list, he should write their names down. Then each day he should go to God in very definite prayer with that prayer list and cry to God in the earnestness of the Holy Spirit for the conversion of these individuals and never cease to pray for them until they are definitely converted. If there were space we could record most marvelous instances of conversion in many lands as the outcome of such prayer lists.

Second, we should pray for the individual church and community. Pray definitely for a spiritual awakening, pray that the members of the church be brought onto a higher plane of Christian living, that the church be purged from its present compromise with the world, that the members of the church be clothed with power from on high and filled with a passion for the salvation of the lost. We should pray that through the church and its membership, many may be converted and that there be a genuine awakening in the church and community. Any church or community that is willing to pay the price can have a true revival. That price is not building a tabernacle and calling some widely-known evangelist and putting large sums of money into advertising and following other modern methods. The price of a revival is honest, earnest prayer in the Holy Spirit, prayer that will not take no for an answer. Let a few people in any church or community get thoroughly right with God themselves, then let them band themselves together and cry to God for a revival until the revival comes, with a determination to pray through, no matter how long it takes. Then let them put themselves at God's disposal for him to use them in personal work, testimony, or anything else, and a genuine revival of God's work in the power of the Holy Ghost is bound to result. The writer has said substantially this around the world; time and again, the advice has been followed, and the result has always been the same, a real, effective, thoroughgoing work of God.

Third, we should pray for the work in foreign lands. The history of foreign missions proves that the most important factor in effective missionary work is prayer. Men, women, and money are needed for foreign missions, but what is needed most of all is prayer. We should pray very definitely for God's guidance upon the secretaries and other officers of our foreign missionary boards. We should pray for definite fields and for the definite thrusting forth of laborers into those fields. We should pray very specifically for the men and women who have gone into the field. One feels when he gets to the foreign field as if the very atmosphere was taken possession of by "the prince of the power of the air." We should pray at all seasons in the Spirit, and watch thereunto in all perseverance, that God would give to these men and women victory in their personal conflict, and power in their efforts to win men from the delusions of the false religions that eternally destroy, to the truth of the Gospel that eternally saves. We should pray too very definitely for the converts on the foreign fields, for their deliverance from error, delusion, and sin, and that they may become intelligent, well-balanced, strong, and useful members of the body of Christ. We should pray for the churches that are formed as the outcome of missionary effort in foreign lands.

Finally, we should pray for the evangelization of the world in the present generation. God has been calling the church as never before to the evangelization of the world, but the church as a whole has slept on and not responded to the call, and it almost seems as if the door was at last being closed and that our Lord was saying to us as he said to the disciples who slept in the Garden of Gethsemane, "Sleep on now, the opportunity I gave you and that you despised is now gone." Let us pray that if he tarry, God will give us one more opportunity and that he will lead his church to improve that opportunity as it is given.

ROBERT ELLIOTT SPEER (1867-1947) was one of America's most effective promoters of foreign missions. A graduate of Princeton University, in 1891 Speer interrupted his course at Princeton Seminary to become Secretary of Foreign Missions for the Presbyterian Board of Foreign Missions. He never returned to complete his seminary course but spent the next fifty-six years traveling and challenging Christians to invest their lives and wealth in the spreading of the gospel. In 1927 he was elected moderator of the Presbyterian Church of the United States, at that time the second layman to hold the position. Edinburgh University granted him an honorary doctorate in 1910. He wrote or edited sixty-seven books, among them *The Principles of Jesus*, *The Man Paul*, *Missions and Politics in Asia*, and *The Finality of Jesus Christ*.

46

Foreign Missions or World-wide Evangelism

By *Robert E. Speer*
Secretary, Presbyterian Board of Foreign Missions
New York

Edited by Arnold D. Ehlert, Th.D.

Argument in behalf of foreign missions is generally either needless or useless. It is needless with believers; with unbelievers it is useless. And yet not wholly so; for often believers and unbelievers alike have taken their opinions at second hand, and an honest first hand study of the facts and principles of the missionary enterprise leads the one group to believe with deeper conviction and a firmer hope, and shakes the skepticism and opposition of the others who have known neither the aims nor the motives which inspire the movement.

Because foreign missions is a religious movement, however, the fundamental argument for it is of necessity a religious argument, and will be conclusive only in proportion as the religious convictions on which it rests are accepted. It rests first of all upon God. If men believe in God they must believe in foreign missions. It is in the very being and character of God that the deepest ground of the missionary enterprise is to be found. We cannot think of God except in terms which necessitate the missionary idea.

He is one. There cannot, therefore, be such different tribal or racial gods as are avowed in the ethnic religions of the East, and assumed in the ethnic politics of the West. Whatever God exists for America exists for all the world, and none other exists. And that cannot be true of God in America which is not true of him also in India. Men are not free to hold contradictory con-

ceptions of the same God. If there be any God at all for me,
he must be every other man's God, too. And God is true. To
say that he is one is merely to say that he is. To say that he is
true is to begin to describe him, and to describe him as alone
he can be. And if he is true he cannot have taught men falsehood. He will have struggled with their ignorance in his education of mankind, but it cannot have been his will (or be his
will now) that some men should have false ideas of him or false
attitudes toward him. A true God must will to be truly known
by all men. And God is holy and pure. Nothing unholy or impure can be of him. Anything unholy or impure must be abhorrent to him, if in religion the more abhorrent because the
more misrepresentative of him, the more revolting to his nature.
If anywhere in the world religion covers what is unclean or unworthy, there the character of God is being assailed. And God is
just and good. No race and no man can have slipped through the
fatherly affection of a loving God. Any inequality or unfairness
or indifference in an offered god would send us seeking for the
real one whom we should know was not yet found. A god who
was idols in China, fate in Arabia, fetiches in Africa, and man
himself with all his sin in India, would be no god anywhere. If
God is one man's father, he is or would be every man's father.
We cannot think of God, I say it reverently, without thinking of
him as a missionary God. Unless we are prepared to accept a
God whose character carries with it the missionary obligation
and idea, we must do without any real God at all.

When men believe in God in Christ the argument for missions
becomes still more clear. It is by Christ that the character of
God is revealed to us. One of his most bold and penetrating
words was his declaration, "The day will come when they shall
slay you, thinking that they do service unto God, and these
things will they do unto you because they have not known the
Father or me." The best people of his day, he declared, were
ignorant of the true character of God. Only those truly knew
it who discovered or recognized it in him. "He that hath seen
me hath seen the Father. No man cometh unto the Father but
by me. No man knoweth the Son save the Father, and no man
knoweth the Father save the Son and he to whomsoever the
Son willeth to reveal him." These are not arbitrary statutes. They

are simple statements of fact. The world's knowledge of the character of God has depended and depends now on its knowledge of God in Christ. A good and worthy, an adequate and satisfying God, i.e., God in truth, is known only where men have been in contact with the message of the historic Christ.

This simple fact involves a sufficient missionary responsibility. Men will only know a good and loving Father as their God, i.e., they will know God, only as they are brought into the knowledge of Christ, who is the only perfect revelation of God. For those who have this knowledge to withhold it from the whole world is to do two things: It is to condemn the world to godlessness, and it is to raise the suspicion that those who think they have the knowledge of God are in reality ignorant of what Christ was and what he came to do. "It is the sincere and deep conviction of my soul," said Phillips Brooks, "when I declare that if the Christian faith does not culminate and complete itself in the effort to make Christ known to all the world, that faith appears to me a thoroughly unreal and insignificant thing, destitute of power for the single life and incapable of being convincingly proved to be true." And I recall a remark of Principal Rainy's to the effect that the measure of our sense of missionary duty was simply the measure of our personal valuation of Christ. If he is God to us, all in all to our minds and souls, we shall realize that he alone can be this to every man, and that he must be offered thus to every other man. The Unitarian view has never produced a mission, save under an inherited momentum or the communicated stimulus of evangelicalism, and it has been incapable of sustaining such missions as it has produced. But when men really believe in God in Christ, and know Christ as God, they must, if they are loyal to themselves or to him, share him with all mankind.

For, child of one race and one time though he was, and that race the most centripetal of all races, Christ thought and wrought in universals. He looked forward over all ages and outward over all nations. The bread which he would give was his flesh, which he would give for the life of the world. He was the light of the whole world. If he should be lifted up he would draw all men unto himself. His disciples were to go into all the world and make disciples of all nations. His sheep were not of a Jewish fold alone. It was not of a race but of a world that the Father had sent him to be the Saviour. He did not regard himself as one of many saviours and his revelation as one of many revealings. He was the only Saviour of men, and his was the only revelation of the Father God. "I have long ago ceased to regard the history of the Hebrew race as unique," writes a well-known Christian leader of our day. "It was well for us in our early days that our studies were directed toward it, and we saw how the Hebrew people found God in every event in their history, but we believe that Assyria and Babylon, Nineveh and Rome, could have similar stories written of God's dealings with them." Now, whether the history of the Hebrew race is unique or not is not a matter of theory. It is a simple question of fact. If it was not unique, then where is its like? What other history produced a vocabulary for a revelation? What other history yielded God to humanity? What other ended in a Saviour? As a simple matter of fact, Christianity, which sprang out of this race and this history, is unlike all other religions in its kind. As such, it never contemplated anything else than a universal claim. If it shrinks into a mere racial cult, it separates itself from its Founder and life, and utterly abandons its essential character.

Not only is the missionary duty inherent in the nature of Christianity and in the Christian conception of God, i.e., in the real character of God, but it is imbedded in the very purpose of the Christian church. There were no missionary organizations in the early church. No effort was made to promote a missionary propaganda, but the religion spread at once and everywhere. The genius of universal extension was in the church. "We may take it as an assured fact," says Harnack, "that the mere existence and persistent activity of the individual Christian communities did more than anything else to bring about the extension of the Christian religion."

Bishop Montgomery in his little book, *Foreign Missions*, recalls Archbishop Benson's definition of four ages of missions, "First, when the whole church acted as one; next, when missions were due to great saints; thirdly, to the action of governments; lastly, the age of missionary societies." The church at the outset was a missionary society. The new Christians were drawn together spontaneously by the uniting power of a common life, and they felt as spontaneously the outward pressure of a world mission. The triumphant prosecution of that mission and the moral fruits of this new and uniting life were their apologetics. They did not sit down within the walls of a formalized and stiffened institution to compose reasoned arguments for Christianity. The new religion would have rotted out from heresy and anemia in two generations if they had done so.

As an old writer of the Church of England has put it: "The way in which the Gospel would seem to be intended to be alike preserved and perpetuated on earth is not by its being jealously guarded by a chosen order and cautiously communicated to a precious few, but by being so widely scattered and so thickly sown that it shall be impossible, from the very extent of its spreading, merely to be rooted up. It was designed to be not as a perpetual fire in the temple, to be tended with jealous assiduity and to be fed only with special oil; but rather as a shining and burning light, to be set up on every hill, which should blaze the broader and the brighter in the breeze, and go on so spreading over the surrounding territory as that nothing of this world should ever be able to extinguish or to conceal it." The sound doctrine of the church was safeguarded by the wholesome hygienic reflex action of service and work and conquest. And its light and life convinced men, because men saw them conquering souls. The church was established to spread Christianity, and to conserve it in the only way in which living things can ever be conserved, by living action. When in any age or in any land the church has forgotten this, she has paid for her disobedience. So long as there are any unreached men in the world or any unreached life, the business of the church is her missionary duty.

The fourth deep ground of missionary duty is the need of humanity. The world needs Christ today as much and as truly as it needed him nineteen centuries ago. If Judaism and the Roman Empire needed what Christ brought then, Hinduism and Asia need it now. If they do not need him now, no more was he needed then. If they can get along without him just as well, the whole world can dispense with him. If there is no missionary duty, the ground falls from under the necessity, and therefore from under the reality of the incarnation. But that world into which he came did need Christ. Men were dead without him. It was he who gave them life, who cleansed their defilement, who taught them purity and service and equality and faith and gave them hope and fellowship. He alone can do this now. The non-Christian world needs now what Christ and Christ alone can do for it.

The world needs the social message and redemption of Christianity. Paul tells us that it met and conquered the inequalities of his time, the chasm between citizen and foreigner, master and slave, man and woman. These are the chasms of the non-Christian world still. It has no ideal of human brotherhood save as it has heard of it through Christianity. Not one of the non-Christian religions or civilizations has given either women or children, especially girl children, their rights. There is human affection. The statement of a recent writer regarding China, that "children are spawned and not born," is surely most untrue save on the basest levels of life. But the proverb of the Arab women of Kesrawan too truly suggests the Asiatic point of view: "The threshold weeps forty days when a girl is born." And between man and man the world knows no deep basis of common humanity, or if it knows, it has no adequate sanction and resources for its realization. Its brotherhood is within the faith or within the caste, not as inclusive as humanity. It wants what all the world wanted until it found it through Christ. "In his little churches, where each person bore his neighbor's burden, Paul's spirit," says Harnack, "already saw the dawning of a new humanity, and in the Epistle to the Ephesians he has voiced this feeling with a thrill of exaltation. Far in the background of these churches, like some unsubstantial semblance, lay the division between Jew and Gentile, Greek and Barbarian, great and small, rich and poor. For a new humanity had now appeared, and the apostle viewed it as Christ's body, in which every member served the rest, and each was indispensable in his own place." The great social idea of Christianity is still only partially realized by us. But we do not have it at all unless we have it for humanity, and it can be made to prevail anywhere only by being made to prevail everywhere.

The world needs, moreover, the moral ideal and the moral power of Christianity. The Christian conceptions of truth and purity and love and holiness and service are original. Every ideal except the Christian ideal is defective. Three other sets of ideals are offered to men. The only other theistic ideals are the Mohammedan and the Jewish. The Mohammedan ideal expressly sanctions polygamy, and the authority of its founder is cited in justification of falsehood. The Jewish ideal is wholly enclosed in and transcended by the Christian. Buddhism and Shintoism and Confucianism offer men atheistic ideals, i.e., ideals which abandon the conception of the absolute and cannot rise above their source in man who made them. Hinduism, with its pantheism, is incapable of the moral distinctions which alone can produce moral ideals, and as a matter of fact owes its worthy moral conceptions today exclusively to the influence of Christianity. But it is not ideals alone — it is power for their realization that the world requires. That power can be found only in life, in the life of God communicated to men. Who offers this or pretends to offer it but Christ? How can it be offered by religions which have no God, or whose God has no character?

Only the Gospel can meet the world's need. Commerce and government, philanthropy and education, deal with it superficially, and in the hands of shallow or evil men only accentuate it. A force is needed which will cut down to the roots, which deals with life in the name and by the power of God, which marches straight upon the soul and reconstructs character, which saves men one by one. Here we are flat upon the issue, and not to evade or confuse it, I will put it unmistakably. It is our duty to carry Christianity to the world because the world needs to be saved, and Christ alone can save it. The world needs to be saved from want and disease and injustice and inequality and impurity and lust and hopelessness and fear, because individual men need to be saved from sin and death, and only Christ can save them. His is the only power which will forgive and regenerate, which will reach down deep enough to transform, and will hold till transformation is fixed.

And Christianity does this by striking down to the individual and saving him. It saves him by the power of God in Christ, working in and upon him. The missionary duty is this duty. "I hold education," says Uchimura, "as essentially personal and individualistic." And he uses the term education in its broad sense. There is more to education than this. Society is something more than the sum-total of individuals, but it begins and ends with individuals, and the need of the world is primarily the need of its individuals, and the salvation of the world in Christ's way can only be the salvation of its soul through the salvation of its souls.

Some years ago we heard a great deal about the need of educating and civilizing the world before we try to change its religion. Dr. George Hamilton advanced this argument in the General Assembly of the Church of Scotland in 1796: "To spread abroad the knowledge of the Gospel among barbarous and heathen nations seems to me to be highly preposterous in as far as it anticipates, nay, as it even reverses the order of nature. Men must be polished and refined in their manners before they can be properly enlightened in religious truths. Philosophy and learning must, in the nature of things, take the precedence. Indeed, it should seem hardly less absurd to make revelation precede civilization in the order of time, than to pretend to unfold to a child the 'Principia' of Newton, ere he is made at all acquainted with the letters of the alphabet. These ideas seem to me alike founded in error; and, therefore, I must consider them both as equally romantic and visionary." We do not hear so much of this view now. Civilization has shown what a vain and empty thing it is, and we know that the sin and passion in human hearts, which it cannot destroy, are as real and dreadful in America and in all the neutral nations as they are in the nations at war. God is man's one need. Man cannot save himself or make anything out of himself. He needs what God and God alone can do for him. If that is true of Europe and America, it is true of all the rest of the world. Jesus Christ is the one Saviour of men and each man in the world needing that Saviour has a right to look to those who know of him to tell of him to all mankind.

Even as a purely religious movement, however, there are some who object to foreign missions on the ground that there are other religions in the world which are true for their followers and which meet their needs as truly as Christianity meets ours. They say that a fair comparison of Christianity with other religions destroys the claim of Christianity and makes foreign missions unnecessary. Is this true? What are the conclusions which such a comparison presents?

1. In the first place it is a significant fact that Christianity is the only religion which is trying to make good its claim to universalism. None of the non-Christian religions is making any real effort to do so. Islam is spreading in Africa and India and even in South America, where it claims thousands, and in Europe, where it boasts of millions, but in North America it has made little progress. The bounds of Confucianism are contracting. Shintoism was dealt a crippling blow by the defeat of Japan in World War II, and while there are many new Shinto sects they do not subscribe allegiance to the state form of it. Zoroastrianism, one of the worthiest of the ancient religions, has almost vanished in the land of its origin, and numbers comparatively few adherents in India. Hinduism is geographically limited, save as a philosophy, by its principle of caste, and Buddhism claims only about 300,000 adherents outside of Asia. But Christianity is moving out over all the earth with steadily increasing power, with ever multiplying agencies, with ever enlarged devotion, and with open and undiscourageable purpose to prepare for Christ's kingship over the world. And not less significant than the fact of Christianity's missionary purpose, is the method of it. With no trust in secular support, in spite of all slanders which charge otherwise, with purely moral agencies and with fair comparison of its treasures with anything that the world can offer, Christianity goes fearlessly forth to deal with all the life and thought of man and to solve his problems and meet his needs in the name and strength of God.

2. At the root of all things is the idea of God. Here all religions meet to be judged. "The truth and the good inherent in all forms of religion is that, in all, man seeks after God. The finality of Christianity lies in the fact that it reveals the God for whom man seeks" (Jevons, *Introduction to the Study of Comparative Religion*, p. 258). The best that can be said of any non-Christian religion is that it is seeking for that which Christianity possesses — the true and perfect God. "The conception of God with which Christianity addresses the world, is the best that man can form or entertain."

If it is asked, "What is that excellence in Christianity by virtue of which it is entitled to be a missionary religion and deserves to be received by all men?" — the answer is:

"Christianity is entitled to be a missionary religion and to displace all other religions, because of its God.

"There are many glories in the religion of Jesus Christ, and it can do many services for men; but its crowning glory, or rather the sum of all its glory, is its God. Christianity has such a conception of God as no other religion has attained; and, what is more, it proclaims and brings to pass such an experience of God as humanity has never elsewhere known. It is in this that we find that superiority which entitles Christianity to offer itself to all mankind.

"It is necessary to tell in few words what this God is who is the glory of Christianity and the ground of its boldness in missionary advances — this God so infinitely excellent that all men may well afford to forget all their own religions, if they may but know him. The God of Christianity is one, the sole source, Lord and end of all. He is holy, having in himself the character that is the worthy standard for all beings. He is love, reaching out to save the world from sin and fill it with his own goodness. He is wise, knowing how to accomplish his heart's desire. He is Father in heart, looking upon his creatures as his own, and seeking their welfare. All this truth concerning himself, he has made known in Jesus Christ the Saviour of the world, in whom his redemptive will has found expression, and his saving love has come forth to mankind."

Set over against this conception of God the views which we have seen that the non-Christian religions take of him, and it does not need to be shown that the religion of the Christian God has supreme rights among men.

"A religion that can proclaim such a God, and proclaim him on the ground of experience, is adapted to all men, and is worthy of all acceptation. Since Christianity is the religion of such a God, Christianity deserves possession of the world. It has the right to offer itself boldly to all men, and to displace all other religions, for no other religion offers what it brings. It is the best that the world contains. Because of its doctrine and experience of the perfect God, it is the best that the world can contain. Its contents can be unfolded and better known, but they cannot be essentially improved upon. At heart, Christianity is simply the revelation of the perfect God, doing the work of perfect love and holiness for his creatures, and transforming them into his own likeness so that they will do the works of love and holiness towards their fellows. Than this nothing can be better. Therefore, Christianity has full right to be a missionary religion, and Christians are called to be a missionary people."

3. From its unique and adequate conception of God, it follows that Christianity has a message to the world which is full of notes which the non-Christian religions do not and cannot possess. Even ideas which some of these religions share with Christianity, such as "belief in an after life, in the difference between right and wrong, and that the latter deserves punishment; in the need of an atonement for sin; in the efficacy of prayer; in the universal presence of spiritual powers of some kind"; belief in the sovereignty of God, in the immanence of God, in the transitoriness and vanity of this earthly life on one hand, and in the infinite significance of this life and the sacredness of the human order on the other — have a relationship and a significance in Christianity, with its perfect God, which makes them totally different from the conceptions of other religions. And beside these, Christianity has a whole world of conceptions of its own — the fatherhood of God, the brotherhood of man, redemption, the incarnation of a personal God, atonement, character, service, fellowship.

4. In its conception of sin, in its provision for sin's forgiveness and defeat, and in its ideals of salvation and the free offer of its salvation to every man, Christianity is unique and satisfying. Christianity sees sin as the supreme evil in the world, it regards it as a want of conformity to the perfect will of God, or as transgression of his perfect law; it teaches that sin is not a matter of act only, but also of thought and desire and will — a taint in the nature; it insists that God is not responsible for it or for any evil; it emphasizes the guilt and horror of it, and the deadly consequences both for time and eternity, and it opens to man a way of full forgiveness and clean victory. In contrast with this view, Mohammedanism teaches that sin is only the willful violation of God's law; sins of ignorance it does not recognize; its doctrine of God's sovereignty fixes the responsibility for sin on God and dissolves the sense of guilt, and it denies the evil taint of sin in human nature. In Hinduism sin as opposition to the will of a

personal God is inconceivable; it is the inevitable result of the acts of a previous state of being; it is evil, because all existence and all action, good as well as bad, are evil, and it is illusion, as all things are illusion. In pure Buddhism there can be no sin in our sense of the word, because there is no God; sin there means "thirst," "desire," and what Buddhism seeks to escape is not the evil of life only, but life itself; and its conception of the sins that impede, while including much that is immoral, does not include all, and does not include much on the other hand that has no immoral character at all. Confucianism makes no mention of man's relation to God, and totally lacks all conception of sin. In one word, Christianity is the only religion in the world which clearly diagnoses the disease of humanity and discovers what it is that needs to be healed and that attempts permanently and radically to deal with it.

And so, also, Christianity alone knows what the salvation is which men require, and makes provision for it. In Christianity salvation is salvation from the power and the presence of sin, as well as from its guilt and shame. Its end is holy character and loving service. It is available for men here and now. In the Mohammedan conception salvation consists in deliverance from punishment, and deliverance not by redemption and the sacrifice of love, but by God's absolute sovereignty. The Hindu idea of salvation is to escape from the sufferings incident to life, to be liberated from personal, conscious existence, and this liberation is to be won by the way of knowledge, knowledge being the recognition of the soul's essential identity with Brahma, the impersonal God, or by the way of devotion, devotion being not faith in a God who works for the soul, but the maintenance by the soul of a saving attitude of mind toward the deity chosen to be worshiped. This is actual Hinduism, not the nobler doctrine of the *Vedas*. In Buddhism salvation is the extinction of existence. Indeed, there is no soul recognized by pure Buddhism. There is only the Karma, or character, which survives, and every man must work out his own Karma unaided. "By one's self," it is written in the Dhammapada, "the evil is done; by one's self one suffers; by one's self evil is left undone; by one's self one is purified. Lo, no man can purify another." The best Northern Buddhism draws nearest to Christianity in its conception of a salvation by faith

in Amitaba Buddha, but even here the salvation is release from
the necessity of continued rebirths, not a creation of new character for human service in divine loyalty. Confucianism has no
doctrine of salvation. The Chinese soul has had to turn, in the
attempt to satisfy its needs, to other teachers. In its ideal and
offer of salvation Christianity stands alone (Kellogg, *Comparative
Religion*, chapters IV, V).

5. Christianity is the only religion which is at once historical,
progressive and spiritually free. Therefore, it is the only religion
which can claim universal dominion. Each religion of the world
has filled a place in history, but Mohammedanism is the only one
whose historical facts are essential to it, and, as Bishop Westcott
says:

"Christianity is historical not simply in the sense in which,
for example, Mohammedanism is historical, because the facts connected with the origin and growth of this religion, with the personality and life of the founder, with the experience and growth
of his doctrine, can be traced in documents which are adequate to
assure belief; but in a far different sense also. It is historical in
its antecedents, in its realization, in itself; it is historical as crowning a long period of religious training which was accomplished
under the influence of divine facts; it is historical as brought out
in all its fullness from age to age in an outward society by the
action of the Spirit of God; but above all, and most characteristically, it is historical because that revelation which it brings is
of life and in life. The history of Christ is the Gospel in its
light and in its power. His teaching is himself, and nothing apart
from himself; what he is and what he does. The earliest creed —
the creed of baptism — is the affirmation of facts which include
all doctrine.

"Dogmatic systems may change, and have changed so far as
they reflect transitory phases of speculative thought, but the
primitive Gospel is unchangeable as it is inexhaustible. There
can be no addition to it. It contains in itself all that will be slowly
wrought out in thought and deed until the consummation.

"In this sense, Christianity is the only historical religion. The
message which it proclaims is wholly unique. Christ said, I am —
not I declare, or I lay open, or point to, but I am — the way, the
truth and the life."

6. The ethical uniqueness of Christianity entitles it to absorb and displace all other religions. It alone makes the moral character of God the central and transcendent thing. Judged by its God, no other gods are really good. It alone presents a perfect ethical ideal for the individual and it alone possesses a social ethic adequate for a true national life and for a world society. It is preeminently the ethical religion. All its values are moral values. All the best life of Christian lands is an effort to embody the Christian ethics in life, and "There is hardly a more trustworthy sign and a safer criterion of the civilization of a people," says the anthropologist Waitz, "than the degree in which the demands of a pure morality are supported by their religion and are interwoven with their religious life." And this is the true test of religions also. Do they supply men with perfect moral ideals? Do they condemn evil and refuse to allow evil to shelter itself under religious sanction? On one or both of these issues every non-Christian religion breaks down. There is much worthy moral teaching in each of the non-Christian religions, but the *Koran* enjoined the enslavement of the women and children of unbelievers conquered in battle, and authorized unlimited concubinage, and its sanction of polygamy cannot be defended as in the interest of morality. "Polygamy," said Dr. Henry H. Jessup, "has not diminished licentiousness among Mohammedans." Even in the *Vedas* there are passages which are morally debarred from publication. "I dare not give and you dare not print," wrote the Rev. S. Williams, "the ipsissima verba of an English version of the original *Yajar Veda Mantras*" (*Indian Evangelical Review*, January, 1891). In the *Bhagavata Purana* the character of the god Krishna is distinguished by licentiousness. And worst of all in the Hindu ethics, even in the *Bhagavadgita*, it is taught that actions in themselves do not defile one, if only they are performed in the state of mind enjoined in the poem. While Buddha and Confucianist ethics are deficient in active benevolence and human service, "Be ye perfect, as your heavenly Father is perfect," is a conception peculiar to Christianity.

7. Christianity is the final and absolute religion, because it contains all the good and truth that can be found in any other religion, and presents it to men in its divine fullness, while other religions have none but partial good; because it is free from the

evils which are found in all other religions, and because it alone can satisfy all the needs of the human heart and of the human race. It is the one true religion. We are glad to find any outreach after the truth in other religions which shows that the hearts of those who hold them are made for that truth and capable of receiving it in its perfect form in Christianity. Christianity is final, because there is no good beyond it and no evil in it, and because it cleanses and crowns all the life and thought of man. It is the end of all men's quest. "I maintain," says Tiele, "that the appearance of Christianity inaugurated an entirely new epoch in the development of religion; that all the streams of the religious life of man, once separate, unite in it; and that religious development will henceforth consist in an ever higher realization of the principles of that religion." And Christianity is absolute as well as final; that is, it fills the field. There can be nothing higher or better. There can be nothing else in the same class. As Bishop Westcott said:

"A perfect religion — a religion which offers a complete satisfaction to the religious wants of man — must be able to meet the religious wants of the individual, the society, the race, in complete course of their development and in the manifold intensity of each separate human faculty.

"This being so, I contend that the faith in Christ, born, crucified, risen, ascended, forms the basis of this perfect religion; that it is able, in virtue of its essential character, to bring peace in view of the problems of life under every variety of circumstance and character — to illuminate, to develop, and to inspire every human faculty. My contention rests upon the recognition of two marks by which Christianity is distinguished from every other religion. It is absolute and it is historical.

"On the one side, Christianity is not confined by any limits of place, or time, or faculty, or object. It reaches to the whole sum of being and to the whole of each separate existence. On the other side, it offers its revelation in facts which are an actual part of human experience, so that the peculiar teaching which it brings as to the nature and relations of God and man and the world is simply the interpretation of events in the life of men and in the life of One who was truly man. It is not a theory, a splendid guess, but a proclamation of facts.

"These, I repeat, are its original, its unalterable claims. Christianity is absolute. It claims, as it was set forth by the apostles, though the grandeur of the claim was soon obscured, to reach all men, all time, all creation; it claims to effect the perfection no less than the redemption of finite being; it claims to bring a perfect unity of humanity without destroying the personality of any one man; it claims to deal with all that is external as well as with all that is internal, with matter as well as with spirit, with the physical universe as well as with the moral universe; it claims to realize a re-creation coextensive with creation; it claims to present him who was the Maker of the world, as the Heir of all things; it claims to complete the cycle of existence, and show how all things come from God and go to God."

As absolute, it must displace all that is partial or false. It must conquer the world. The people who have it must be a missionary people.

This is the solemn duty with which we are charged by our personal experience of the treasure that is in Christ, and this is the solemn duty with which any true comparison of Christianity with the world religions confronts us. Alike from the look within and from the look without we arise with a clear understanding of the missionary character of the religion that bears the name of Christ. The attitude of that religion is "not one of compromise, but one of conflict and of conquest. It proposes to displace the other religions. The claim of Jeremiah is the claim of Christianity: 'The gods that have not made the heavens and the earth, they shall perish from the earth and from under the heavens.' The survival of the Creator, joyfully foreseen, is the ground of its confidence and its endeavor. Christianity thus undertakes a long and laborious campaign, in which it must experience various fortunes and learn patience from trials and delays; but the true state of the case must not be forgotten, namely, that Christianity sets out for victory. The intention to conquer is characteristic of the Gospel. This was the aim of its youth when it went forth among the religions that then surrounded it, and with this aim it must enter any field in which old religions are encumbering the religious nature of man. It can not conquer except in love, but in love it intends to conquer. It means to fill the world." It must do so in order that the nations may have their Desire and the world its Light.

HENRY WESTON FROST (1858-1945) began his working career after graduating from Princeton as an oilman. Yet through the influence of his wife and spurred on by his own vision for evangelistic work, he opted for a life of missionary activity. After being ordained in the Presbyterian church, Frost went on to become a missionary statesman. He began the North American arm of the China Inland Mission. For 40 years, he was the Home Director from his office in Philadelphia. Besides his work with CIM, he was an active worker in the Bible conference movement, he wrote poetry, and he penned numerous books about missions and doctrine.

47

What Missionary Motives Should Prevail?

"The love of Christ constraineth us" (2 Corinthians 5:14)

By Rev. Henry W. Frost
DIRECTOR FOR NORTH AMERICA, CHINA INLAND MISSION

Abridged and edited by Glenn O'Neal, Ph.D.

Various Kinds of Motives

When we contemplate the motives which largely prevail in these days in respect to missionary service, we meet with a surprise. There was a time — within the memory of many — when the motives proclaimed were markedly scriptural and spiritual. More recently the scriptural and spiritual has been giving place either to the selfish or to the simply humanitarian. And this has resulted in a development of weakness, both in the appeal and in its results. It is certainly true, as men say, that non-Christian nations are in a pitiable state, governmentally, educationally, commercially, socially and physically; and it is equally true that nothing but Christianity will alter the conditions which are existing. But such conditions do not constitute the appeal which God makes to his people when he urges them to Christianize the nations. The conditions above named are all "under the sun," and they have to do with the present temporal life. Besides, though a total transformation might be secured in these respects, the peoples so affected — as the present condition of Japan demonstrates — would have been brought no nearer to God than they were before. For, while it is always true that Christianity civilizes, it is never true that civilization Christianizes.

It would appear from the above, if souls are to be reached, if men are to be made inwardly right, if the things which make for eternal security and blessedness are to be obtained, that divine motives, leading to divine methods and results, must prevail. This is the reason why God sets such high motives before the church. He would have Christians look high in order that they may live high; and he would have them live high in order that they may lift others equally high. It is supremely important, therefore, to discover from the Scriptures what the divinely given motives are. Our starting text indicates that Paul felt that these could be expressed in one phrase: "The love of Christ" — that is, Christ's love for us — "constraineth us." But other portions of the word indicate that the Spirit expands the thought so expressed, the one motive including several others. May we anticipate sufficiently to say that these motives appear to be three in number. It is our purpose to consider these, one by one.

A First Motive

During the earlier portion of the ministry of Jesus on earth, that is, between his baptism and crucifixion, he spoke very little about missions; but during the later portion, that is, between his resurrection and ascension, he spoke of nothing else. This last is a striking and impressive fact, especially as there were many other matters, in those last days, about which his disciples might have wished to have him speak and with which he might have desired to occupy himself. It is evident then, during the forty days of his ascension, that one theme was uppermost in his mind and that one burden lay most heavily upon his heart. His redemptive work having been accomplished, he longed to have his disciples proclaim the glad tidings everywhere; and hence he spoke of this, and of this alone.

Moreover, on the several occasions when he discoursed upon the theme of missions, he always spoke as a master would address his disciples, as a captain would address his soldiers, as a king would address his subjects. At other times and in other relationships, he suggested, he exhorted, he urged. But here, without exception and without equivocation, he commanded. Not once did he explain how he could demand what he was requiring; not once did he ask if there were any arguments to be expressed in answer to his proposals; in full knowledge of the terrible cost, without allowing any escape from the obligation imposed, he simply said, "Go!"

In face of such a burning passion and heavily imposed obligation, there is but one conclusion to reach; the Church of Jesus

Christ has no choice as to whether she will or will not do the thing ordered. One who has purchased his people with his own blood, one who owns them in spirit, soul and body, one who is indeed master, captain and king has positively commanded that his gospel shall be preached throughout the world. Of course, the Church, if she chooses, may disobey, as — speaking generally — she is disobeying. But under the conditions prevailing, this on her part is high treason, and it is at her present loss and future peril. The thing which Christ has commanded, in all rightful consideration, is the thing which ought to be fully and immediately undertaken. This, then, is the prime motive which God sets before Christians, individually and collectively, namely, that he who has had a right to comand has done so, and that the command, because of the person, calls for unhesitating, uncompromising and continuous obedience, until the task ordered is fully and finally accomplished.

A Second Motive

There are several passages in the Gospels which speak of Christ as having, or as being moved with, compassion. One is when Jesus saw two blind men and where he gave them sight; another is where he saw a leper and where he touched and healed him; another is where he saw a widow mourning the loss of her dead son and where he raised that son to life; another is where he saw the hungry multitudes and where he fed them; and the last is where he saw multitudes uncared for and where he asked his disciples to offer prayer in their behalf.

Now, all of these passages are interesting, as revealing the heart of Christ, he being the "God of compassion" where "compassions fail not." But the last passage is particularly interesting, as it gives to us a view of present world-conditions and of the thought of God concerning them. For what was true that day in Galilee is still true the world over; and what Christ was he still is. Let us, for a moment, consider the passage.

Jesus had come to his own city of Nazareth, and later he had gone forth from thence throughout the neighboring districts. As a result of his ministrations of healing, he had gathered at last great crowds about him, made up of men, women and children, and now these had no place to turn to for the night and had many physical and spiritual needs still unsupplied. That

Jesus had had compassion upon the people all through the day, his words and acts attest. But now, seeing the multitudes in such a pitiable condition, it is recorded — for this is the implication — that he had peculiar compassion upon them. He saw that they were hungry and weary, just as sheep are at the close of the day when they are unfed and exhausted; and he saw also that they were like a great harvest field, whose past-ripe grain, for lack of hands to gather it into the garner, was rotting on the stalk. Then it was — these physical conditions suggesting the spiritual — that the great heart revealed its longing, and that there came forth the appealing, pathetic cry: "Pray ye therefore the Lord of the harvest, that he will send forth laborers into his harvest."

We would not imply, for a moment, that there was not sufficient cause in the sight of the multitudes that day to thus mightily move the heart of the Son of God. At the same time, we can but think that not a little part of the emotion which Jesus experienced was occasioned by the fact that the multitudes before him were a picture of those other, greater multitudes which went to make up a lost world, and also of those other and still greater multitudes which were yet unborn and which would go to make up the lost world which was yet to be. For Christ ever looked on things with a divinely prophetic eye; and there was everything in that present view to suggest the wider vision. And so the heart bled out its grief; and so the voice plaintively asked the help of man. This same Christ is ever looking down from heaven's throne, the same heart is ever feeling its weight of compassionate woe, and the same voice is ever pleading with his disciples to see as he sees and to feel as he feels. This then is the second motive which God sets before Christians, namely, to enter into Christ's compassion for the lost souls and lives of men, and thus to be moved as he was moved, and to be constrained to do as he did.

A Third Motive

The Gospels, recording the earthly life of Jesus, are full of promises — mostly from the lips of the master — concerning a coming which would be for the purpose of establishing a kingdom. The Epistles, representing the testimony of the risen and glorified Christ, continue this theme, and always give the same order, first the coming and then the kingdom. And at the end of the New Testament, a whole book — Revelation — is taken up with the expansion of the now familiar thought and tells in detail how Christ will come, and what the kingdom will be.

In addition to the above, Gospels, Epistles and Revelation speak of a work to be accomplished, which is preliminary to the coming and kingdom, and which in the divine economy, makes the one and the other possible. As these passages are vital to our subject, we make a selection from them: "The Son of Man is come to seek and to save that which was lost." "Go ye therefore, and teach (disciple) all nations." "Go ye into all the world, and preach the Gospel to every creature." "Ye shall be witnesses unto me both in Jerusalem, and in all Judea, and in Samaria, and unto the uttermost part of the earth." "That by me the preaching might be fully known and that all the Gentiles might hear." As if to remove any possible misunderstanding in regard to the divine plan, the Spirit led to the declaration and preservation of words which tell us what God purposes to do in this present age in preparation for the age to come, and what part the Church is to play in the fulfillment of the purpose so announced. We refer to Acts 15:13-18. There James, quoting Peter, is the spokesman, and the great Apostle confirms his utterance by stating it as a foundation truth that "known unto God are all his works from the beginning of the world." He thus says: "Simeon hath declared how God at the first did visit the Gentiles to take out of them a people for his name; and to this agree the words of the prophets; as it is written, After this I will return and will build again the tabernacle of David, which is fallen down; and I will build again the ruins thereof, and I will set it up; that the residue of men might seek after the Lord, and all the Gentiles upon whom my name is called, saith the Lord, who doeth all these things."

Here then, are a divine utterance and program. And simply speaking, it sets forth the following facts in the following order: first, a present work of grace in which God visits and gathers out, pre-eminently from the Gentiles, a people for his name; second, the return of Christ; third, the restoration and establishment of the Jewish theocratic kingdom with its attendant worship; and fourth, the salvation in the kingdom-age of the "residue" of the Jews, and of "all" the Gentiles upon whom God's name shall be called. And this program, in its first article, makes it clear what share the Church has in its fulfillment. To put it in a single sentence, it is this: God is visiting the nations, and Christians have the high privilege of visiting them with him. He goes forth, in the persons of the missionaries, not to convert all the world — since not all men will accept of him — but to gather out from it a willing people, heavenly in quality and innumerable in quantity, which shall be to the glory of his name throughout time and eternity. And, manifestly, this preparatory work will bring to pass the event which is described as following it, that is, the coming of Christ. This then is the final and consummating motive which God sets before Christians, namely, to go forth everywhere, preaching the good tidings to every creature, in order that the Church may be made complete and that the king and the kingdom may come.

The Effect of Scriptural Motives

It will need only passing consideration to discover that the three motives which have been mentioned, namely, the command, the compassion and the coming of Christ, are like the God who gave them, and are thus worthy of being accepted by the noblest and most devoted of men. And there are two reasons why they are this. First, because they represent spiritual and eternal truths; and second, because they make for the highest glory of God and the greatest good of mankind. As to the last effect, no other motives are so uplifting and purifying to the person who is moved by them, and no other motives are so sure of divine favor and blessing in their exercise. There is enough power in these motives, singly and collectively, to raise the missionary propaganda above everything earthly, selfish and narrow, and to place it, where it ever belongs, upon the plane of the heavenly, the spiritual and the infinite. Moreover there is enough potency here to turn the "forlorn hope" of present-day foreign missions, in which a Gideon's band of men and women are bravely fighting on against overwhelming odds, into an ever victorious army of the Church, where the battle will not only be fought but also be won, and where the end of saving the elect, and thus of bringing back the king and bringing in the kingdom, will be surely and speedily brought to pass. For what foes on earth, or what demons in hell, could stay the onward progress of a people which had determined, in the power of the Holy Spirit, to obey Christ's command, to show forth his compassion, and to press forward with uplifted faces to the rapturous and victorious meeting with him who one day will descend with a shout, with the voice of the archangel, and with the trump of God? Such motives as these are not simply constraining; they are invincible and triumphant.

HENRY WESTON FROST (1858-1945) began his working career after graduating from Princeton as an oilman. Yet through the influence of his wife and spurred on by his own vision for evangelistic work, he opted for a life of missionary activity. After being ordained in the Presbyterian church, Frost went on to become a missionary statesman. He began the North American arm of the China Inland Mission. For 40 years, he was the Home Director from his office in Philadelphia. Besides his work with CIM, he was an active worker in the Bible conference movement, he wrote poetry, and he penned numerous books about missions and doctrine.

48

Consecration

(Exodus 28:40-43)

By Rev. Henry W. Frost
DIRECTOR FOR NORTH AMERICA, CHINA INLAND MISSION

Edited by Arnold D. Ehlert, Th.D.

Some years ago, when I resided in Toronto, I went one Sunday morning to attend service at Knox Church, of which the Rev. Dr. Henry M. Parsons was pastor. I went to the service in a very comfortable state of mind, longing of course, for a new blessing, but without any special sense of the kind of blessing which I needed. God, however, understood my real need, and before the sermon was done that morning my comfort was past and I was in distress of mind and spirit. The sermon had been upon a theme connected with the new life in Christ, and the Lord had made such a personal application of it to me that I felt wholly undone. My situation was similar to that of the bride in Solomon's Song who cried: "Look not upon me, because I am black, because the sun hath looked upon me!" And in that state of heart, I returned to my home.

Immediately after dinner that day, I found a quiet place in our home where I might be alone with myself and God, for I needed to understand myself, and above all, to know God's purpose for me. And so I meditated and prayed, and prayed and meditated. Thus, there was brought to me, at last, the consciousness that I was wrong at the center of my life. Not that I doubted that I was saved, for I knew that I was a Christian; nor that I doubted God's acceptance of me as his servant, for I was being daily blessed and used in my work for him; but that my life was an up and down one, sometimes in fellowship with God, and sometimes out of fellowship with him; sometimes praising him for victory won, and more often confessing sin as a result of deplorable defeat. Thus it was that I saw what I needed was a new consecration.

When I reached this point, I took up my Bible to study the subject of consecration. But not knowing where to turn, I sought the aid of the concordance, with the intention of working out a Bible reading on the subject. Here, however, I met with difficulty. There were few passages which referred to consecration. But I thought to myself that this did not matter, as consecration and sanctification are the same thing, and what I could not obtain under one word I should obtain under the other. But when I looked at the word sanctification, I was in the opposite difficulty, for there were so many passages that I knew not what to do with them. It was in this way that I turned to a passage which I had noticed, which spoke both of consecration and sanctification, namely, Exodus 28:40-43, and it was thus that I shut myself up to it and prayerfully meditated upon it. And I wish to say that God taught me something from this portion of Scripture that Sunday afternoon which has never been unlearned, and which has revolutionized my life. Not that since then I have never known spiritual inequality, and have ever walked blamelessly before God. Alas! my life has often been marred by failure and sin. Nevertheless, I say it to the praise of Christ, that things have been different from what they were, and that I have possessed a blessed secret of living which I had never possessed before. And it is because I have a longing to pass on to you the secret which God gave to me that I am writing thus personally, and that now, I shall beg to lead you in the study of the passage of Scripture referred to.

The first thing that I noticed in my study is, that consecration and sanctification are not one and the same thing. We are dealing, as I believe, with a verbally inspired Scripture, and I observe that the Spirit says, "consecrate and sanctify." This signifies to me that consecration and sanctification — I speak from an experimental standpoint — are separate things. It is clear that they are closely connected, that one precedes the other and leads to the other, and that the other follows the one and results from that one. Indeed, one may truly say that they are inseparable. At the same time, consecration comes first and sanctification comes second. To put it in the form of a picture, consecration is the initial act of going through the outer door of a palace, and the subsequent acts of passing through other doors in the palace in order to occupy the whole and to reach the throne-room of the king; and sanctification is the palace itself, the whole of which is the home of the king, and where the king may be seen face to face. Or, to put it more simply and plainly, consecration is an initial act and many subsequent, similar acts; and sanctification is the consequent and resultant state.

The second thing which I noticed is, that the one who was to be consecrated had to belong to the right family. There were many orders of people in the world at that time. First, there were the great nations without; then, there were the Israelites in an inner circle; then, there were the Levites at large. It was only for Aaron and Aaron's sons, and the only way, therefore, that a person could reach the experience of consecration was by being born into that particular family. This suggests, of course, the idea of exclusiveness. At the same time, it is more inclusive than it appears. For who are the successors of Aaron and Aaron's sons? The answer comes from Rev. 1:5, 6, in John's ascription of praise: "Unto him that loveth us, and loosed us from our sins by his blood, and he made us to be a kingdom, to be priests unto his God and Father." Aaron and his sons were priests. We who believe in Christ are likewise priests. Thus we also may be consecrated.

The third thing which I noticed is, that the person who was to be consecrated had to have the right dress on. Moses, before he came to the act of consecration, was commanded to make linen under and outer garments, and to put these upon Aaron and Aaron's sons. These were called the "garments for glory and for beauty." And notice the order of the words. If Moses, as a mere man, had been writing, he would have said, garments for beauty and for glory; but as a Spirit-inspired man, he said, "garments for glory and for beauty." This is important, for the order of words gives us the clue as to what the garments signify. Man ever seeks to put the beauty before the glory, for he argues that a person must become beautiful in order that he may become glorious. But God, as it were, says no, for it is impossible for a man to become beautiful, and, therefore, it is impossible for him to become glorious, and hence, that he must become glorious in order that he may become beautiful. In other words, God sees only one beauty in this world; it is the glory of his Christ; and, therefore we must be clothed upon with his glory if we are to appear beautiful in his holy presence. These thoughts are amply confirmed by a comparison of Rev. 19:8 and II Cor. 5:21: "And to her [the bride] was granted that she should be arrayed in fine linen, clean and white, for the fine linen is the righteousness of saints." "For he [God] hath made him [Christ] to be sin for us who knew no sin that we might be made the righteousness of God in him." In short, if we have faith in Christ, we are clothed with the priestly garments, and hence, we may be consecrated.

The fourth thing which I noticed is that Aaron and his sons, before they were consecrated, had to be anointed. From the following chapter, the 20th and 21st verses, we learn what this anointing was. First, there was a ram of consecration, which was slain in sacrifice. Then, its blood was put upon the priest's right ear, thumb and toe. And, finally, oil was put upon the blood. Note the emblems and the order. It was not oil, and no blood; it was oil and blood. And it was not oil and then blood; it was first blood and then oil. In other words, there was first the sign of ownership through redemption, and after this there was the sign of acceptance for priestly service and empowering for that service. But once more, the one who believes in Christ has gone through this process. The believer is sprinkled with precious blood, and he is anointed with holy oil, for we have been bought with a price, even with the precious blood of Christ, and we have all been baptized by one Spirit into one body.

Having observed these preliminary conditions, I came at last that Sunday to the thought of consecration itself. And here I met with a great surprise. I had, as I thought, a fairly clear conception of what consecration was. It was going to a consecration meeting and there joining with others in giving one's self to God. Or, if that was not enough, it was shutting one's self into one's room, and there making resolutions and taking vows to put away this and that and to take on this and that and so forever be the servant of God. But I had glanced at the margin of my Bible and had seen opposite the word "consecrate" the three words, "fill their hands," and what filling the hands had to do with consecration I did not know. Thus it was that I read the context of the passage and came to the 29th chapter, the 22nd-24th verses. And thus it was that I learned what true consecration meant, and what it must ever mean. This was what I found. Moses, after clothing and anointing Aaron and Aaron's sons, took the inward parts of the ram and its right shoulder, and also a loaf of bread, a cake of oiled bread, and a wafer out of the basket of unleavened bread, and laid all of these in the hands of Aaron and Aaron's sons. Then Aaron and his sons stood and waved these in the presence of the Lord. And as they did this — nothing more and nothing less — they were consecrated. Do you wonder, when I read this, that I was surprised? How different it was from what I had imagined. And yet how simple it was. But, simple as it is, it is profoundly deep. That ram of consecration symbolized Christ, for those rich inward parts and that strong, right shoulder set forth his eternal deity, and those various portions of bread, made from wheat into fine flour, manifested his matchless humanity. In other words, as those priests stood there holding up these several tokens before God they declared — whether they fully understood it or not — that their only right in holy presence was through the redemption and eternal merit of Another; and that it was in that Person's life and glory that they appeared and dedicated themselves to priestly ministry. And as God looked down from heaven and saw, not them, but the uplifted and interposed symbols of that Other, of the Christ, he accepted Aaron and his sons and consecrated them to holy service. And this is what is necessary now. Anything else is high presumption and sin, for this is the divine way of acceptance, power and glory. In other words, the watchword of every act of consecration is this: "Jesus only!" And do you ask, what is the watchword of sanctification? It is still, "Jesus only!" only this time, it is longer drawn out and it covers the whole of life. Paul put it thus: "For me to live is Christ!" It is for us to put it in the same way.

But I almost hear someone say: This is old-time doctrine, containing old-time ideals; but as for me, I live face to face with new-time conditions, where such doctrines and ideals are not possible of fulfillment. My reader, I will not argue with you. But I beg to suggest to you that you are wrong. For first, our passage says: "It shall be a statute forever unto him, and his seed after him," and, since, as Christians, we are in the priestly line we are also within the privileges of the priestly succession. And also, God never repents of his gifts and callings, and what he has done once and of old he is able and ready to do again and now. Moreover, I have seen lives, in our own day, lived out wholly for Christ, and in the midst of most untoward circumstances, so that I am persuaded that such consecration as has been spoken of is quite possible for any saint of these present days, even amid the undoubtedly difficult conditions which the present times have produced. In closing, then, let me speak of some consecrated lives which I have personally known.

Mr. Hudson Taylor, while once traveling in China, came to a river, and hired a boatman to ferry him across it. Just after he had done this, a Chinese gentleman, in silks and satins, reached the river and not observing Mr. Taylor, asked the boatman to hire the boat to him. This the man refused to do, saying that he had just engaged the boat to the foreigner. At this the Chinese gentleman looked at Mr. Taylor, and without a word, dealt him a heavy blow with his fist between the eyes. Mr. Taylor was stunned and staggered back, but he presently recovered himself, and, looking up saw his assailant standing between himself and the river's brink. In an instant Mr. Taylor raised his hands to give the man a push into the stream. But in an instant more, he dropped his arms at his side. Mr. Taylor then said to the gentleman: "You see I could have pushed you into the stream. But the Jesus whom I serve would not let me do this. You were wrong in striking me, for the boat was mine. And since it is mine, I invite you to share it with me and to go with me across the river." The Chinese gentleman dropped his head in shame, and without a word, he stepped into the boat to accept the hospitality thus graciously offered to him. Mr. Taylor was a man of naturally quick temper, but evidently for him to live was Christ.

The well-known Rev. James Inglis was pastor of a large church in Detroit. He was a graduate of Edinburgh University and Divinity School, was very learned — he was afterwards requested to act with the American New Testament Revision Committee — he was unusually eloquent, and he was having a most successful ministerial career. Indeed, he was the most popular preacher in

Detroit, if not in Michigan, having large audiences on Sundays, with people seated in the aisles and upon the pulpit stairs of his church, and with his listeners hanging upon his words. One week day, at this period, he sat in his study, preparing one of his sermons for the following Sunday, when a voice seemed to say to him: "James Inglis, whom are you preaching?" Mr. Inglis was startled, but he answered: "I am preaching good theology." But the Voice seemed to reply: "I did not ask you what you are preaching, but whom are you preaching?" My uncle answered: "I am preaching the Gospel." But the Voice again replied: "I did not ask you what you are preaching; I asked you whom are you preaching?" Mr. Inglis sat silent and with bowed head for a long time before he again replied. When he did, he raised his head and said: "O God, I am preaching James Inglis!" And then he added: "Henceforth I will preach no one but Christ, and him crucified!" Then my uncle arose, opened the chest in his study which contained his eloquent sermons and deliberately put them one by one into the fire which was burning in his study stove. From that time on he turned his back upon every temptation to be oratorical and popular, preached simply and expositionally, and gave himself in life and words to set forth Jesus Christ before men. Later he became the editor of two widely read religious papers, and the teacher in the Scripture of such men as Dr. Brookes of St. Louis, Dr. Erdman of Philadelphia, Dr. Gordon of Boston, and Mr. Moody of Northfield. He died in 1872, but his name is still held in reverent and grateful remembrance by many of the most spiritual of God's saints in America and Europe. Mr. Inglis was by nature a man of proud and ambitious disposition; but it is manifest that it became true in his life that for him to live was Christ.

A friend of mine — whose name I will not give — was a business man in one of our great American cities. He was an able financier and had become wealthy. Thus it came to pass that he was living in a beautiful brownstone house, situated on a prominent avenue, and in luxury. At the same time he was a Christian, being an elder in a Presbyterian church and generally active in good works. It was thus, when Mr. Hudson Taylor visited his city in 1888, that my friend offered to entertain him. The arrangement was brought to pass, and Mr. Taylor was in his home for about a week. My friend was thus brought into close contact with a man of God, the like of whom he had never before seen. As the days went by he was increasingly impressed by the godliness and winsomeness of the life before him. Finally, after Mr. Taylor had departed to another place, my friend knelt down and said to God: "Lord, if Thou wilt make me something like that little man I will give Thee everything I've got." And the Lord took him at his word. From that time onward his spiritual life visibly deepened and developed. At last one day he said to his wife: "My dear, don't you think we can do with a less expensive house than this, so that we may reduce our living expenses and give more money to the Lord?" He then proposed that they should sell the property, build a cheaper house, and give what might thus be gained to foreign missions. Happily, he had a wife who was a true "helpmeet" to him, and she heartily agreed to the proposal. So the old property was sold, the new house was built, and the sum gained was given to God for his cause abroad. About two years later my friend spoke again to his wife on this wise: "Dear, I feel badly about this house. The architect got me in for more money than I intended to spend on it. What do you say to selling it? I have got a lot on an adjacent street, and we can build there a cheaper house than this, and then we can give the difference to foreign missions." My friend's wife was not a woman who liked changes. However, she loved the Lord, and again she gave a ready assent to the proposal. So the first transaction was repeated, a plainer, cheaper house was built, and all that was made by the change was given to missions. Meanwhile, my friend's general business continued to prosper. Indeed, everything he touched seemed to turn into gold. But his personal and family expenses, by his deliberate choice, were constantly being reduced. He never lived meanly. At the same time he lived more and more simply. Thus he made money, and thus he saved money. Yet all the time he gave and gave to causes at home and abroad. And this continued until his death. At the time of his death he and his wife were supporting some thirteen missionaries, and previously, they had sent to the foreign field, providing for outfits and passages, over one hundred new and older workers. Now my friend, by nature, was a man who loved money. It had a fascination for him, both in the making of it and the selfish spending of it. But it is manifest that such greediness had been taken out of his life. His heart was where his treasure was, and his real treasure was in heaven. In other words, he too was able to say: "For me to live is Christ!"

Dear reader, whoever you are, the consecrated life is possible and practical. It was for the first century; it is also for the twentieth century. It was for early apostles and disciples; it is also for present day missionaries, ministers, lay workers and business men. In truth, it is for anybody and everybody who is the Lord's. As for you, therefore, but one thing is needed. Empty your hands of whatever you have taken up from the world, and then hold up these emptied hands to God. And as surely as he is gracious, he will fill your, even *your,* hands with Christ. And when you find yourself standing thus, holding up Jesus between yourself and God, hiding yourself beneath him, confessing him to be your only merit, glory and power, you too will be consecrated.

THOMAS WILLIAM MEDHURST (c. 1860's) held a productive pastorate from 1862-1869 at the Baptist Church, North Frederick Street in Glasgow, Scotland. During his ministry, the church was involved in extensive church planting, evangelistic, and Christian education activities. They initiated a Sabbath school, a Christian Institute Society (a sort of Y.M.C.A.), a Tract Distribution Society, and a Temperance Society. Under Medhurst's ministry the church doubled in attendance. He is also the author of *Abounding Grace*; *The Christian's Watchword and Encouragement*; *A Voice From Glasgow on Baptism and the Church of England*; and the compiler of *A Collection of Hymns for Public and Private Worship.*

49

Is Romanism Christianity?

By T. W. Medhurst
Glasgow, Scotland

Revised by Gerald B. Stanton, Th.D.

I am aware that, if I undertake to prove that *Romanism is not Christianity,* I must expect to be called "bigoted, harsh, uncharitable." Nevertheless, I am not daunted, for I believe that on a right understanding of this subject depends the salvation of millions.

One reason why Popery has gained so much power in Great Britain, Ireland, and elsewhere, is that many Protestants look on it as a form of true Christianity. They think that, on that account, notwithstanding great errors, it ought to be treated very tenderly. Many suppose it was reformed at the time of the Reformation, and that it is now much nearer the truth than it was before that time. It is still, however, the same; and, if examined, will be found to be so different from, and so hostile to, real Christianity, that it is not, in fact, Christianity at all.

Christianity, as revealed in the Sacred Writings, is based squarely upon the salvation provided by Christ. It sets him before us as at once a perfect man, the everlasting God, the God-man Mediator who, by appointment of the Father, became a substitute for all who were given him. It teaches that by him God's justice was satisfied and his mercy made manifest; that he fulfilled the law, and made available his *complete righteousness,* and that by this alone men can be justified before God. It teaches that his death was a perfect sacrifice and made full satisfaction for their sins, so that God lays no sin to their charge, but gives them a free and full pardon. It teaches that he has ascended to the right hand of God, and has sent the Holy Spirit to be his only vicar and representative on earth. It teaches that Christ is the only Mediator between a righteous God and sinful man; that it is by the Holy Spirit alone that we are convinced of sin and led to trust in Jesus; and that all who trust in him, and obey him with the obedience of faith and love, are saved. Being saved, they are made "kings and priests unto God," and have "eternal life" in him.

This is Christianity, the Christianity which the apostles preached. But side by side with the apostles, Satan went forth also and preached what Paul calls "another gospel." Paul did not mean merely that it was *called* "another gospel," but that as Satan "beguiled Eve through his subtlety" (II Cor. 11:3), so some, while professing to teach the Gospel, were turning men away "from the simplicity that is in Christ." By doing so, they did indeed teach "another gospel." Paul, speaking of those who were thus deceived, said, "I marvel that ye are so soon removed from him that called you into the grace of Christ unto another gospel which is not another; but there be some that trouble you, and would pervert the Gospel of Christ." He means that there can be but *one Gospel*, though something else may be called the gospel. He declares of those who had thus perverted "the Gospel of Christ": "If any one preach any other gospel unto you . . . let him be accursed" (Gal. 1:6-9). He calls those who did so "false apostles, deceitful workers, transforming themselves into the apostles of Christ," and adds, "no marvel; for Satan himself is transformed into an angel of light. Therefore, it is no great thing if his ministers also be transformed as the ministers of righteousness; whose end shall be according to their works" (II Cor. 11:13-15).

Let us consider well the meaning of these passages of Scripture. Paul says that there cannot be "another gospel." The conclusion is evident that such teachers were not teachers of Christianity at all, but of *a Satanic delusion*.

I submit that the teachings of Rome are as different from that of the Sacred Writings as that which Paul calls "another gospel." Therefore, his words authorize us to say that Romanism is not Christianity.

FIRST, *Christianity is founded upon the clear teachings of the New Testament Scriptures.* But Romanism does not profess to be founded on Scripture alone; it claims a right to depart from what is contained in it — a right to add to Scripture what is handed down *by* tradition, and to depart from and add to Scripture by making *new decrees*. It forbids the cup to the people, for instance, in what it calls "the mass," and yet admits that it was not forbidden to them at "the beginning of the Christian religion" (Council of Trent, Session 21, chap. 2). It says that councils and the Pope have been empowered by the Holy Spirit to make decrees by which, in reality, the doctrines delivered by Christ are entirely annulled. To show how extensively this has been done, let the reader endeavor to trace the full effect of what Rome teaches as to baptismal regeneration, transubstantiation, justification by means of sacraments and human works, the invocation of saints — things which are entirely opposed to the teaching of Christ.

The canons of the Council of Trent, which sat at intervals from 1545 to 1563, may be called the Bible of Romanism. They were translated into English as late as 1848 by a Roman Catholic priest, under the sanction of Dr. Wiseman. The Council tells us that one end for which it was called was "the extirpation of heresies." What, then, according to it, is the standard of truth? It tells us that Rome receives "The Sacred Scriptures" and "The Unwritten Traditions . . . preserved in continuous succession in the Catholic Church, with *equal affection of piety and reverence*" (Session 4); also that "no one may dare to interpret the Sacred Scriptures" in a manner contrary to that "Church, *whose it is to judge respecting the true sense and interpretation* of the Sacred Scriptures." Nor may any one interpret them "in a manner contrary to the unanimous consent of the fathers" (Session 4).

Christ commands us to "prove all things" (I Thess. 5:21); to "search the Scriptures" (John 5:39); to ascertain for ourselves, as the Bereans did, whether what we hear agrees with what we read in Scripture (Acts 17:11). He commands us to "hold fast the form of sound words," uttered by himself and his apostles (II Tim. 1:13); to "contend earnestly for the faith *delivered once for all* to the saints" (Jude 3). But Rome says, "Let no one dare to do so" — let all *Christian princes . . . cause men to observe*" our decrees (Session 16), nor "permit" them to be "violated by heretics" (Session 25). The Romanist must not dare to have an opinion of his own; his mind must exist in the state of utter-

prostration and bondage; he must not attempt to understand the Scripture himself. And if others attempt it — if they dare to receive the teaching and do the will of Christ, instead of receiving fictions and obeying commands of men, which wholly subvert and destroy the truth and will of Jesus, Rome commands the civil ruler to restrain them and, by the use of fines, imprisonment, and death, to compel them, if possible, to renounce what God requires them to maintain and follow, even unto death.

"The Bible, the whole Bible, nothing but the Bible," is the standard and rule of Christianity. To know its meaning for ourselves, to receive its teaching, to rely on its promises, to trust in its Redeemer, to obey him from delight of love, and to refuse to follow other teaching, is Christianity itself. But Romanism denies all this; and therefore, Romanism is not Christianity.

SECONDLY, Christ commanded us to show "meekness" towards those who oppose us (II Tim. 2:25). He says, "Love your enemies, bless those who curse you, do good to those who hate you and pray for those who use you despitefully and persecute you" (Matt. 5:44).

But Romanism teaches men *to hate*, and, if they are able, *to persecute to the death all those who will not receive it.* Its deeds have been diabolical and murderous. It is "drunken with the blood of the saints." It has inscribed on the page of history warnings which appeal to the reason and the feelings of all generations. Such a warning is what is told of the 24th of August, 1572. On that day the Protestants of Paris were devoted to slaughter by members of the papal church. For the one offence of being Protestants, thousands were slain. The streets of Paris ran with blood; everywhere cries and groans were mingled with the clangor of bells, the clash of arms, and the oaths of murderers. The king, Charles IX, stood, it is said, at a window, and, every now and then, fired on the fugitives. Every form of guilt, cruelty, and suffering made that fearful night hideous and appalling. Never in any city which has professedly been brought under the influence of Christianity, was there such a revelling in blood and crime. You may say, "Why do you recall the atrocities of a time so remote?" I answer, Because this deed received the sanction of the church of Rome as a meritorious demonstration of fidelity to Romish precepts and doctrines. When the tidings of this wholesale murder were received in Rome, the cannons of St. Angelo were fired, the city was illuminated and Pope Gregory XIII and his cardinals went in procession to all the churches, and offered thanksgivings at the shrine of every saint. The Cardinal of Lorraine, in a letter to Charles IX, full of admiration and applause of the bloody deed, said, "That which you have achieved was so infinitely above my hopes, that I should have never dared to contemplate it; nevertheless, I have always believed that the deeds of your Majesty would augment the glory of God, and tend to immortalize your name."

Some say that Rome has ceased to persecute. But this is not the fact; either as to her acts, or rules of action. *She asserts that she is unchanged, unchangeable; that she is infallible, and cannot alter,* except so far as necessity, or plans for the future, may require. Facts are often occurring which prove that persecution is still approved by her. When Rome has little power, her persecuting spirit is kept in abeyance for a time; but it is still there. When it is free from restraint, it knows no way of dealing with difference of opinion but by the rack, the stake, the thumbscrew, the iron boot, the assassin's dagger, or wholesale massacre. Let all who value their liberty, all who love the truth as it is in Jesus have no fellowship with such deeds of darkness, nor with those who work them.

I agree with Dr. Samuel Waldegrave, when he says that, "The convocation of the English clergy did wisely, when, in the days of Elizabeth, they enacted that every parish church in the land should be furnished with a copy of Foxe's *Book of Martyrs*," and that it would be well if a copy of it were "in every house, yea, in every hand," for "Rome is laboring, with redoubled effort, for the subjugation of Britain," and "the people have forgotten that she is a siren who enchants but to destroy."

THIRDLY, As to *the sacrifice of Christ*, Christianity teaches that he was "offered *once for all*, to bear the sins of many" (Heb. 9:28); that those who are sanctified by his sacrifice are so "by the offering of the body of Jesus Christ *once for all*" (Heb. 10:10); that *"by one offering* he has *perfected forever* those who are sanctified" (Heb. 10:14). These passages declare that the sacrifice of Christ was offered once for all, never to be repeated.

But Rome declares that Christ is sacrificed anew every time that the Lord's Supper, which she calls "the mass," is celebrated; and that those who administer it are *sacrificing priests.*

The Council of Trent (Session 22) says, "Forasmuch as in this divine sacrifice, which is celebrated in the mass, that same Christ is contained, and immolated in an unbloody manner, who once offered himself in a bloody manner, on the altar of the cross, the holy synod teaches that *this sacrifice is truly propitiatory*, and that, *by means thereof*, this is effected — that we obtain mercy and find grace in seasonable aid, if we draw nigh unto God, contrite and penitent, with a sincere heart and upright faith, with fear and reverence. For the Lord, *appeased by the oblation thereof*, and granting the grace and gift of penitence, forgives even heinous crimes and sins. For *the victim is one and the same*, the same offering by the ministry of priests, who then offered himself on the cross, the manner alone of offering being different." The synod commands the use of lights, incense, and the traditional vestments; also that the priests "mix water with the wine."

In chapter 9, canon 1, the synod says, "If any one say that in the mass *a true and proper sacrifice is not offered* to God; or, that *to be offered*, is nothing else but that Christ is given us to eat; let him be anathema."

In canon 3, it decreed that, "If any one say that the sacrifice of the mass is only a sacrifice of praise and thanksgiving; or that it is a *bare commemoration of the sacrifice consummated on the cross, but not a propitiatory sacrifice*; or, that it profits him only who receives; and that it ought not to be offered *for the living and the dead for sins, pains, satisfactions*, and other necessities; let him be anathema."

The Christ of Romanism is one who is sacrificed again and again for the remission of the sins both of the living and the dead, for those alive, and for those in purgatory. *This is not the Christ of Christianity!*

In canon 1 of its 13th session, the synod says, "If any one deny that, in the sacrament of the most holy Eucharist, are contained truly, really and substantially *the body and blood, together with the soul and divinity of our Lord Jesus Christ*, and consequently the whole Christ, but say that he is only therein as in a sign, or in figure, or virtue; let him be anathema."

The Christ of the Bible, and of Christianity, is in heaven "at the right hand of God," where "he ever lives to make intercession for those who come to God through him" (Rom. 8:34; Col. 3:1; Heb. 7:25). Nor will he come in bodily form to earth again until he comes the second time, without sin, unto salvation, to be admired in all those who believe (Heb. 9:28; II Thess. 1:10). But the Christ of Romanism is upon the altars of Rome. He is said to be brought there by the magic spell of her priests, and to be there in the form and shape of a *wafer*. What a fearful blasphemy! The priest pronounces certain words, gives the solemn consecration, and then elevates the wafer. *Taste* it — it is wafer; *touch* it — it is wafer; *look* at it — it is wafer; *smell* it — it is wafer; *analyze* it — it is wafer; but the priest affirms, the Council of Trent affirms, Romanism affirms, the poor victims of delusion affirm, as they bow down before it, *"This is our Christ — our God!"* Here is the climax of this superstition — it exhibits for the person of Christ a morsel of bread. Is that morsel of bread the Christ of the Bible? Is that system which declares it to be so, Christianity?

FOURTHLY, Christianity is in direct opposition to Romanism as to *the mode of a sinner's justification before God*.

What say the Scriptures? "By deeds of law shall no flesh living be justified before God" (Rom. 3:20). "Therefore we conclude that a man is justified by faith, without deeds of law" (Rom. 3:28; cf. 4:6; 5:1; 10:3-4; II Cor. 5:19, 21).

Now, what says Romanism? It says that the righteousness by which men are justified is that which the Holy Spirit, by the grace of God, through Christ, makes them *work out for themselves;* that it is received by means of "the sacrament of baptism . . . without which no one was ever justified"; that it is received "in ourselves" when we are renewed by the Holy Spirit; that is a righteousness "imparted," "infused," "implanted," and not imputed (Session 6, chapter 7). Among the declarations of the Council are these: "If any one say that justifying faith is nothing else but confidence in the divine mercy which remits sin for Christ's sake; or, that this confidence alone is that whereby we are justified; let him be anathema" (Session 6, canon 12). "If any one say that . . . good works are merely the fruits and signs of justification obtained, but not a cause of the increase thereof;

let him be anathema" (canon 24). "If any one say . . . that he who is justified by good works, which are done by him through the grace of God and the merit of Jesus Christ, whose living member he is, does not truly deserve increase of grace, eternal life," etc. . . . "let him be anathema" (canon 32). Thus Romanism anathematizes the preaching of true Christianity!

I will mention but one more proof that Romanism is not Christianity, though there are many others which might be given.

FIFTHLY, Christianity says "there is one mediator between God and men, the man Christ Jesus" (I Tim. 2:5), who is at the right hand of the Father (Eph. 1:20), where he "ever lives to make intercession" for us (Heb. 7:25). Christianity says that there is but *one Mediator*; that we cannot draw near to God except through Jesus.

What says Romanism? I quote from "a book of devotion for every day in the month of May," published by papal authority. "Great is the need you have of Mary in order to be saved! Are you innocent? Still your innocence is, however, under great danger. How many, more innocent than you, have fallen into sin, and been damned? Are you penitent? Still your perseverance is very uncertain. Are you sinners? Oh, what need you have of Mary to convert you! Ah, if there were no Mary, perhaps you would be lost! However, by the devotion of this month, you may obtain her patronage, and your own salvation. Is it possible that a mother so tender can help hearing a Son so devout? For a rosary, for a fast, she has sometimes conferred signal graces upon the greatest of sinners. Think, then, what she will do for you for a whole month dedicated to her service!"

Here you see that Mary is everything; that Jesus Christ is nothing. Romanism teaches also that it is right to ask the intercession of all departed saints (Session 25). How dreadful is it that sinners are thus kept back from Jesus, and are prevented from reaching God through him.

Popery is emphatically *anti-Christian*: it is the adversary of Christ in all the offices which he sustains. It is the enemy of his *prophetic* office; for it chains up that Bible which he inspired. It is the enemy of his *priestly* office; for, by the mass it denies the efficacy of that sacrifice which he offered once for all on

Calvary. It is the enemy of his *kingly* office; for it tears the crown from his head to set it on that of the Pope.

Can that be truly called Christianity, then, which is the reverse of it? Can that be fitly treated as Christianity which hates it, denounces it, and tries to destroy it? Can that be Christianity which forbids liberty of conscience, and the right of private judgment, which commands the Bible to be burned, which teaches the worship of saints and angels, which makes the Virgin Mary command God, which calls her the Mother of God, and the Queen of Heaven? Can that be true which sets aside the mediation of Christ, and puts others in his place, which makes salvation depend on confession to man, and this in a confessional so filthy that Satan himself might well be ashamed of it? Can that be Christianity which condemns the way of salvation through faith as a damnable heresy? Can that be Christianity which, by the bulls of its Popes, and decrees of its councils, requires both princes and people to persecute Christians, which actually swears its bishops and archbishops to persecute them with all their might? Can that be Christianity which has set up, and still maintains the Inquisition — that which has been so cruel, so bloodthirsty, that the number slain by it of the servants of Christ, in about 1,200 years, is estimated at fifty millions, giving an average of 40,000 a year for that long period? No, it cannot be! With the voice of thunder, let Protestants answer, "No!"

To aid such a system is to fight against God. He demands that we "resist the devil" (James 4:7), and have no fellowship with "works of darkness" (Eph. 5:11). *"No peace with Rome,"* must be on our lips, and be in our lives. *"No peace with Rome,"* whether wearing her scarlet undisguised, or using the cloak of a Protestant name.

The voice from heaven: "Come out of her, my people, that ye be not partakers of her sins, and that ye receive not of her plagues" (Rev. 18:4), is proof that there may be true Christians in the Roman body. But it is proof also that even while *in* it, they are not *of* it; and that they will strive to escape from it, so as not to share in its sins.

We are informed by God that this system is the work of Satan; that his ministers are "transformed as the ministers of righteousness, whose end shall be according to their works" (II Cor. 11:15); that it is he who turns men away "from the simplicity which is in Christ" (11:3); that it is he who is the author of that "mystery of iniquity" which was at work even while the apostles were still living, and which was to be further revealed, and to remain, till it should be consumed by Christ, and "destroyed by the brightness of his coming"; a system which is "according to *the working of Satan*, with all power, and signs, and lying wonders, and with all deceivableness of unrighteousness in them that perish; because they received not the love of the truth that they might be saved" (II Thess. 2:7-10).

May those who love God, and yet have some connection with this system, listen to the command, *"Come out of her, my people."* May we in no degree partake of her sins; may we renounce, with a holy loathing, all her symbols; throw off with righteous indignation, all allegiance to her corruptions. May we have nothing of Romanism in our *discipline*. May we be subject, in all matters of religious faith and practice, to *the Word of God*, and to that alone.

Ye who seek salvation, go to Jesus. Him has God exalted to be a Prince and Saviour. He is able to save to the uttermost those who come to God by him. The Father is ready with outstretched arms to clasp the penitent prodigal in his embrace. The Son is ready to give a free, full, complete forgiveness to every redeemed sinner, and to justify all who come unto God by him. The Holy Spirit is ready to sanctify, renew, instruct, and help all who call upon the name of the Lord. The assembly of saved sinners on earth is ready to welcome you to partake of its fellowship and of its joys. Angels are ready with harps attuned, and fingers upon the chords, to give you a triumphant welcome, and to rejoice over you with joy. Come just as you are; come at once. *"Him that cometh to me,"* says Christ, *"I will in no wise cast out"* (John 6:37).

JOHN McGRAW FOSTER (1860-1928) was educated at Harvard, the University of Gottingen, Andover Theological Seminary, Oxford University, and the University of Berlin. He was ordained in the Protestant Episcopal Church and served as a curate of St. Anne's Church in Lowell, Massachusetts; rector of St. John's Church, Bangor, Maine; rector of the Church of the Messiah, Boston, Massachusetts; and also a parish in Washington, D. C.. Foster also held the position of examining chaplain to the bishop of Massachusetts, and president of the standing committee of the diocese of Massachusetts. He was a pulpit orator of wide repute and was called upon to speak throughout the country. He was noted for his scholarship, culture, dignity, tolerance, and cordiality. From his pen came *The White Stone* (1901), *To Know and Believe* (1908), *The Crowded Inn* (1918), and many contributions to theological and other periodicals.

50

Rome, the Antagonist of the Nation

By Rev. J. M. Foster
BOSTON, MASSACHUSETTS

Revised and emended by Arnold D. Ehlert, Th.D.

The Roman Catholic church operates as a politico-ecclesiastical system and is the essential and deadly foe of civil and religious liberty, the hoary-headed antagonist of both church and state. John Milton said, "Popery is a double thing to deal with, and claims a two-fold power, ecclesiastical and political, both usurped, and one supporting the other." Cardinal Manning said, "The Catholic church is either the masterpiece of Satan or the kingdom of the Son of God" (*Lectures on the Four-fold Sovereignty of God,* London, 1871, p. 171). Unquestionably, it is not the latter. Cardinal Newman declared, "Either the Church of Rome is the house of God or the house of Satan; there is no middle ground between them" (*Essays,* 11, p. 116). She is certainly not the former.

I. ROME IS THE ENEMY OF THE STATE

Macaulay summed up in brief the situation when he said, "It is impossible to deny that the polity of the Church of Rome is the very masterpiece of human wisdom. In truth, nothing but such a polity could, against such assaults, have borne up such doctrines. The experience of twelve hundred eventful years, the ingenuity and patient care of forty generations of statesmen have improved that polity to such perfection that among the contrivances which have been devised for controlling mankind, it occupies the highest place" (quoted by Avro Manhattan, *The Vatican in World Politics,* New York, 1949, p. 2). Guy Emery Shipler in the foreword to this book states, "No political event or circumstance can be evaluated without the knowledge of the Vatican's part in it. And no significant world political situation exists in which the Vatican does not play an important explicit or implicit part" (*ibid.*, p. 7). Some of the specific devices employed by the Church of Rome to accomplish its political and social ends should be enumerated.

1. The Roman Catholic church claims a growing membership that is now far larger than that of any Protestant denomination, and is growing rapidly. In the decade from 1948 to 1958 the reported membership in the U. S. grew from 26,000,000 to 34,-500,000. All of Protestantism at the latter date claimed 60,000,-000. The figures become more significant when one remembers that in 200 years the Roman church in America has grown from the smallest denomination to the largest. It is well known, however, that these satistics include infants and nominal Catholics. Names are very reluctantly and seldom dropped from the rolls except in case of death, and not always then. There is a bargaining value in figures, and when the world membership of the Catholic church is used, the figure (1958) of approximately 500,-000,000 is impressive.

2. The Catholic program of development calls for bigness. Impressiveness of architecture, beauty of decoration, and glory of display are inherent in its program. The Catholic church or cathedral is one of the most prominent buildings in any town or city, and often is set on a hill to accentuate this feature, as are also many of their schools. The new University of San Diego, California, is an example. Another common practice is to use the name of the city itself in the name of their universities, as in the one just mentioned, the University of San Francisco, St. Louis University, Boston College, University of Dayton, University of Detroit, Fairfield (Conn.) University, University of Dallas, Seattle University, to name a few.

3. The Catholic church is making a strong bid for educational control in the United States. For a look at Catholic educational policy one should read Pope Pius XI's *Christian Education of Youth*. This document, which is one of the basic sources of Catholic educational policy, takes the position that since the home and the church gave education its initial impetus, the state cannot claim the exclusive right to education. Looked at from the Catho-

lic viewpoint the basic educational philosophy of the Catholic church is sound. The Code of Canon Law urges parents "by a most grave obligation to provide to the best of their ability for the religious and moral, as well as for the physical and civil, education of their children, and for their temporal well-being" (Canon 1113).

Canon 1372 hedges education to the extent that "nothing contrary to faith and morals" is to be taught, and that "religious and moral training takes the chief place." Canon 1374 forbids Catholic children attending non-Catholic schools, except as the local bishop may permit. The Third Plenary Council of Baltimore promulgated a law in 1884 to the effect that a parochial school should be established near every Catholic church where there was not one already, and that all Catholic children should be required to attend these schools, except by permission of a bishop.

In fairness to the Catholic position, it must be admitted that private schools have a right to exist, and it is upon this foundation that the Christian day school movement has developed. In the United States the use of state or federal funds to support denominational schools is prohibited. The Catholics, liberals, and conservatives share the released time provisions for religious instruction in many places.

If this were the sole essence and tendency of the Catholic school system, it would merit little criticism. Just before the close of the first half of the present century criticism of the system came to a strong surge. Cardinal Spellman in 1947 at the Fordham University commencement recognized and replied to this criticism. The campaign to obtain free bus transportation for students to parochial schools was only one element in a trend of events that evoked alarm. Some cities had half their school children in Catholic schools. It is the avowed intention of the Catholic hierarchy to provide as soon as possible, high schools and colleges enough for every Catholic child to be able to get all of his education under the church. This again is the privilege of any group under a democracy,

The thing to be remembered, however, is that even the American Catholic people do not own the Catholic schools. Even though they may furnish the money the title is vested in the administrative clergy — bishop, archbishop, or cardinal — in what is called a corporation sole, that is of one man. This incorporated official is tax-exempt, and can issue notes against the property without consulting the people. The school is operated and administered by the ecclesiastical official over the particular area, with final authority resting in the bishop. The National Catholic Almanac for 1958 says that there were roughly 3,700,000 students in 9,772 elementary schools; 723,000 in 2,835 high schools; and 260,000 in 259 colleges and universities in the United States and its possessions.

Nuns comprise the vast majority of the teaching force of the Catholic elementary schools. Most of them belong to strict orders which enforce poverty and absolute obedience. They have little contact with the outside world. They may be conscientious and work hard, as doubtless many of them do, but they have the handicap of those who are not integrated into society in general. It is easy to see how the entire system can be manipulated and controlled both in general terms and for specific purposes.

4. It is in politics and international relations, however, where the Church of Rome makes its strongest bid and gains its greatest victories. The dual office of the Pope as ecclesiastical head of the Church and political head over the small piece of property known as Vatican City is well known. While it is the smallest sovereign state it boasts the largest palace in the world. It operates as a sovereign state and succeeds astonishingly well in the world scene. Paul Blanshard in his two books, *American Freedom and Catholic Power,* and *Communism, Democracy, and Catholic Power* (Boston 1949 and 1951), and Avro Manhattan in his *The Vatican and World Politics* (New York, 1949), opened the eyes of many to the manipulations of the Vatican in world affairs. The constant struggle of the Washington office of the National Association of Evangelicals with Catholic interests that would seek to gain control of various phases of American and international life cannot be outlined here, but can be studied by consulting these and other books and by reading the reports from time to time of the NAE office in its magazine, *United Evangelical Action.*

In 1958 the Vatican maintained representatives in nearly sixty countries, and forty-seven nations had diplomatic representatives at the Vatican. So far all efforts to get a representative of the United States accredited to the Vatican have failed. The story of the success of the Vatican in the major capitals of the world is graphically told by Manhattan with a chapter devoted to each of the following: Germany, Spain, Italy, Austria, Czechoslovakia, Poland, Belgium, France, Russia, the United States; a final chapter covers Latin America, Japan, and China.

5. In race relations the Catholic church pursues a definite and effective policy. As has often been stated, the Catholic church, particularly its Jesuit division, which determines much of the long-term policy of the church, thinks in terms of centuries, rather than decades. One of the subsidiary plans to the eventual taking over of the United States for Catholicism is the campaign to make the Negroes of America Catholic. The Commission for Catholic Missions Among the Colored People and the Indians leads in this effort. The annual report of this Commission for 1957 shows 490 churches, 748 priests, 345 schools, and 530,702 members among the Negroes. Membership had increased 27,000 over the previous year. Nine new schools for Negro children had been opened. Considerable progress is being made among the Indians, according to the same report, with figures running 415, 230, 57, and 117,281 respectively. Indian membership is reported up five percent for the year.

6. In motion pictures the Catholic church recognizes one of the greatest media of influence in educational and social development. Consequently, there has been no little effort on the part of the church to exert pressure on the motion picture industry, as on the general public, by influencing film production and viewing. Pope Pius XI in 1936 issued an encyclical on it, "Vigilante Cura." The Legion of Decency works to implement the principles set down by this encyclical. A pledge prepared by this organization commits the signer to "condemn indecent and immoral motion pictures, and those which glorify crime or criminals . . . to do all that I can to strengthen public opinion against the production of indecent and immoral films, and to unite with all who protest against them" (*Nat. Cath. Almanac*, 1958, p. 633). A list of films with ratings is published from time to time in Catholic publications. The categories are: Class A, morally unobjectionable for general patronage; Class A, II, morally unobjectionable for adults;

Class B, morally objectionable in part for all; and Class C, condemned.

7. A similar situation obtains with regard to the publication of books. First of all, there is the system of authorizing Catholic readers by means of a statement on the copyright page. This may be "Nihil obstat" (nothing hinders) "Cum permissu superiorum" (with permission of the superiors) or "Imprimatur" (let it be printed). It is pointed out that these permissions and approvals do not mean that the Catholic church officially endorses what is in the book, but that it merely states that there is nothing in the book contrary to Catholic doctrine. Neither does it mean that the Catholic cannot read any book that does not bear this approval; he is under obligaton, however, not to read anything that is contrary to Catholic doctrine. In case of doubt he is supposed to consult his priest. There is the famous "Index Librorum Prohibitorum" which is hundreds of years old, and is revised from time to time, but most of the titles in this index are not English language books. Local and general pressures brought to bear on individual books by Protestant authors that are inimical to Catholic interests, constitute the most effective and general censorship. Catholics who read condemned books are guilty of grave sin.

II. Rome Is the Enemy of Biblical Christianity

There have been many and violent diatribes against the Catholic church by those who have been antagonized by it, excommunicated from it, or merely alarmed about its tendencies. A great deal of this literature, while it is interesting as a body of anti-Catholic polemic, is not the kind of writing that will convince either a Catholic or a non-Catholic unless he is willing to be convinced. (The most lurid title to come to our attention is *The Scarlet Harlot Stripped and Whipped*, a pamphlet in the famous William Andrews Clark Memorial Library in Los Angeles.) The honest soul and mind will be convinced only when the Spirit of God works on the basis of the Word of God to reveal the truth of God in such clarity, that the errors of Rome become shockingly evident. This is the almost universal testimony of those who have come out of Catholicism and into Protestantism.

The main charges brought against the Church of Rome from a doctrinal standpoint are these: (1) She restricts the use of the

Bible, (2) She controls the translation of the Bible, (3) She accepts tradition as of equal authority with the Scriptures, and in effect elevates it above the Scriptures, as may be evidenced in the case of the dogma of the Assumption of Mary (1950), (4) She has seven sacraments, (5) She teaches transubstantiation, (6) She sacrifices the mass, (7) She denies the cup to the laity, and (8) She traffics in masses and indulgences. All of these charges can be found elaborated in the standard polemics against the system, which are too numerous to mention, with the exception of a couple that may be considered classic, George Salmon's *The Infallibility of the Church* (first published 1888, reprinted 1951 by Baker Book House, Grand Rapids) — this because it has stood the test of time as one of the most effective attacks upon the central doctrine of papal infallibility; and ex-priest Emmett McLaughlin's *People's Padre* (Boston, 1954) — this because it is one of the most effective recent exposés of the system by a solidly entrenched Irish priest of a very successful work in Phoenix, Arizona. It is a scholarly and sane autobiography.

The only truly effective weapon against the papal system, as Martin Luther found out, is after all the pure unadulterated Word of God, and it is with some attention to the official Catholic position on the Scriptures that this article will be brought to a close.

One is somewhat astonished to find a book that can be used with equal effectiveness by both Catholic and Protestant to encourage the Catholic himself in, and to give him official Catholic ground for, the personal study of the Bible. This is *Rome and the Study of Scripture*, A Collection of Papal Enactments of the Study of Holy Scripture together with the Decisions of the Biblical Commission (St. Meinrad, Ind., St. Meinrad's Abbey, 5th ed., 1953, 165 pp.). (This book is cataloged by the Library of Congress under the author heading: Catholic Church, Pope; but should be found also by title and subject if properly cataloged.) A number of papal encyclical and apostolic letters, together with seventeen decisions of the highest authority in the church on biblical studies, provide ample material for the purpose mentioned above.

One finds in this book a wholesome attitude toward the Scriptures as inspired and inerrant (one understands, of course, that this in their mind applies also to the apocryphal books, but the

Protestant arguments on that subject are adequate to set the inquirer straight). The statement of the Vatican Council is quite satisfactory: ". . . the Church holds them as sacred and canonical not because, having been composed by human industry, they were afterwards approved by her authority; nor only because they contain revelation without errors, but because, having been written under the inspiration of the Holy Spirit, they have God for their author" (*op. cit.*, p. 24).

An encyclical letter, *Spiritus Paraclitus*, of Pope Benedict XV on the fifteenth centenary of the death of St. Jerome, speaks of Jerome's love of the Scriptures and says, "We confidently hope that his example will fire both clergy and laity with enthusiasm for the study of the Bible" (*ibid.*, p. 71). Likewise, "The same veneration the Bishops should endeavor daily to increase and perfect among the faithful committed to their care, encouraging all those initiatives by which men, filled with apostolic zeal, laudably strive to excite and foster among Catholics a greater knowledge of love for the Sacred Books" (*ibid.*, p. 103). Other encouragements of like kind can be found among these documents. There is one caution, however, that vernacular versions of the Scriptures must be edited with notes by proper Catholic scholars before they may be authorized for personal reading by the laity. While this may be true, the text of the Catholic versions is sufficiently near the original texts to lead any sincere person to faith in Jesus Christ for salvation.

Catholic Biblical Associations have come into being in the United States, Great Britain, Switzerland, and Argentina, and publish some very good material on biblical studies. In Switzerland in particular, which movement came from Austria, family devotions were strongly encouraged with the reading of the Bible as central. In Uruguay some priests with a bent toward Scripture studies used to conduct weekly Bible classes for the laity, and a high degree of spiritual life was attained by some of the attendants.

It must be remembered that the factors just recounted do not represent the actual practice in many parts of the world, but they do rest upon a solid foundation, and any Catholic that wants to read the Bible can appeal to them. The distribution of the Scriptures by Protestants in some parts of the mission field has driven local Catholic authorities to match the effort by a parallel distribution of Catholic gospels and portions, as has happened in Mexico, for instance. Thus the ideal situation developed — the inquirer could compare both versions and discover the striking similarity. May God grant that by any and every means the Scriptures may get into the hands of great numbers of sincere Catholic laymen and thus into their hearts.

JOHN CHARLES RYLE (1816-1900) served as bishop of the Anglican Church and a leader of the evangelicals in that communion. Ordained in 1841, Ryle served several churches; and then in 1880, he was named the first Bishop of Liverpool. He served there with distinction until his death. He wrote many tracts and books that had a wide circulation in England and America, and some of them were translated into foreign languages. He is best known for his multi-volume *Expository Thoughts on the Gospels*.

51

The True Church

By John C. Ryle, D.D.
LORD BISHOP OF LIVERPOOL

Edited by Charles L. Feinberg, Th.D., Ph.D.

Where is the one true church? What is this one true church like? What are the marks by which this one true church may be known? Such questions may well be asked, and here are some answers.

The one true church is composed of all believers in the Lord Jesus. It is made up of all God's elect, all converted men and women, all true Christians. In whomsoever we can discern the election of God the Father, the sprinkling of the blood of God the Son, the sanctifying work of God the Spirit, in that person we see a member of Christ's true church.

It is a church of which all the members have the same marks. They are all born of the Spirit; they all possess "repentance towards God, faith towards our Lord Jesus Christ," and holiness of life and conversation. They all hate sin, and they all love Christ. They worship differently and after various fashions. Some worship with a form of prayer, and some with none; some worship kneeling, and some standing. But they all worship with one heart. They are all led by one Spirit; they all build upon one foundation; they all draw their faith from one single book, the Bible. They are all joined to one great center, Jesus Christ. They all even now can say with one heart, "Hallelujah"; and they can all respond with one heart and voice, "Amen and Amen."

It is a church which is dependent upon no ministers upon earth, however much it values those who preach the Gospel to its members. The life of its members does not depend upon church membership, baptism, and the Lord's Supper, although they highly value these things, when they are to be had. But it has only one great Head, one Shepherd, one chief Bishop, the Lord Jesus Christ. He alone by his Spirit admits the members of this church, though ministers may show the door. Till he opens the door no man on earth can open it, neither bishops, nor presbyters, nor convocations, nor synods. Once let a man repent and believe the Gospel, that moment he becomes a member of this church. Like the penitent thief, he may have no opportunity to be baptized; but he has that which is far better than any water baptism, the baptism of the Spirit. He may not be able to receive the bread and wine in the Lord's Supper; but he eats Christ's body and drinks Christ's blood by faith every day he lives, and no minister on earth can prevent him. He may be excommunicated by ordained men, and cut off from the outward ordinances of the professing church; but all the ordained men in the world cannot shut him out of the true church.

It is a church whose existence does not depend on forms, ceremonies, cathedrals, churches, chapels, pulpits, fonts, baptistries, vestments, organs, endowments, money, kings, governments, magistrates, or any act of favor whatsoever from the hand of man. It has often lived on and continued when all these things have been taken from it; it has often been driven into the wilderness or into dens and caves of the earth, by those who ought to have been its friends. Its existence depends on nothing but the presence of Christ and his Spirit; and they being ever with it, the church cannot die.

This is the church to which the scriptural titles of present honor and privilege, and the promises of future glory, especially belong. This is the body of Christ; this is the flock of Christ. This is the household of faith and the family of God. This is God's building, God's foundation, and the temple of the Holy Spirit. This is the church of the first-born, whose names are written in heaven. This is the royal priesthood, the chosen generation, the peculiar people, the purchased possession, the habitation of God, the light of the world, the salt, and wheat of the earth. This is the "Holy Catholic Church" of the Apostle's Creed; this is the "One Catholic and Apostolic Church" of the Nicene Creed. This is that church to which the Lord Jesus promises, "the gates of hell shall not prevail against it," and to which He says, "I am with you always, even unto the end of the world" (Matt. 16:18; 28:20).

This is the only church which possesses true unity. Its members are entirely agreed on all the weightier matters of the faith, for they are all taught by one Spirit. About God, Christ, the Spirit, sin, their own hearts, faith, repentance, the necessity of holiness, the value of the Bible, the importance of prayer, the resurrection, and the judgment to come — about all these points they are of one mind. Take three or four of them, strangers to one another, from the remotest corners of the earth; examine them separately on these points; and you will find them all of one judgment.

This is the only church which possesses true sanctity. Its members are all holy. They are not merely holy by profession, holy in name, and holy in the judgment of charity; they are all holy in act, deed, reality, life, and truth. They are all more or less conformed to the image of Jesus Christ. No unholy man belongs to this church.

This is the only church which is truly catholic. It is not the church of any one nation or people; its members are to be found in every part of the world where the Gospel is received and believed. It is not confined within the limits of any one country, or pent up within the pale of any particular forms or outward government. In it there is no difference between Jew and Greek, black man and white, Episcopalian and Presbyterian, but faith in Christ is all. Its members will be gathered from north, south, east, and west in the last day, and will be of every name and tongue, but all one in Jesus Christ.

This is the only church which is truly apostolic. It is built on the foundation laid by apostles, and holds the doctrines which they preached. The two grand objects at which its members aim are apostolic faith and apostolic practice. They consider the man who talks of following the apostles without possessing these two things to be no better than sounding brass and tinkling cymbal.

This is the only church which is certain to endure unto the end. Nothing can overthrow and destroy it. Its members may be persecuted, oppressed, imprisoned, beaten, beheaded, burned; but the true church is never altogether extinguished. It rises again from its afflictions; it lives on through fire and water. The Herods, the

Neros, the bloody Marys have labored in vain to put down this church; they slay their thousands, and then pass away to go to their own place. The true church outlives them all and sees them buried each in his turn. It is an anvil that has broken many a hammer in this world, and will break many a hammer still. It is a bush which, often burning, yet is not consumed.

This is the church which does the work of Christ on earth. Its members are a little flock, and few in number compared with the children of the world, one or two here, and two or three there. But these are they who shake the universe; these are they who change the fortunes of kingdoms by their prayers. These are they who are active workers for spreading the knowledge of pure religion and undefiled; these are the life-blood of a country, the shield, the defense, the stay and the support of any nation to which they belong.

This is the church which shall be truly glorious at the end. When all earthly glory is passed away, then shall this church be presented without spot before God the Father's throne. Thrones, principalities, and powers upon earth shall come to nothing; but the church of the first-born shall shine as the stars at the last, and be presented with joy before the Father's throne in the day of Christ's appearing. When the Lord's jewels are made up, and the manifestation of the sons of God takes place, one church only will be named, and that is the church of the elect.

Reader, this is the true church to which a man must belong, if he would be saved. Till you belong to this, you are nothing better than a lost soul. You may have countless outward privileges; you may enjoy great light and knowledge. But if you do not belong to the body of Christ, your light, knowledge, and privileges will not save your soul. Men fancy if they join this church or that church and go through certain forms, all must be right with their souls. All were not Israel who were called Israel, and all are not members of Christ's body who profess themselves Christians. Take notice, you may be a staunch Episcopalian, or Presbyterian, or Independent, or Baptist, or Wesleyan, or Plymouth Brother, and yet not belong to the true church. And if you do not, it will be better at last if you had never been born. "Believe on the Lord Jesus Christ, and thou shalt be saved, thou and thy house" (Acts 16:31).

GEORGE CAMPBELL MORGAN (1863-1945) became a Congregationalist minister after growing up in the home of a Baptist preacher and working on the staff of a Jewish school. A man of wide experience, Morgan taught school, held numerous pastorates in his native England, traveled with D. L. Moody and Ira Stankey, and lectured in Bible conferences in the United States. One of his greatest successes was in taking a dying church, Westminster Chapel, Buckingham Gate, England, and turning it into one of England's most active churches. After leaving that pastorate, he taught at the Bible Institute of Los Angeles (now Biola University) and Gordon College of Theology and Mission. Yet despite all that, he had time to write 60 books of sermons, doctrine, and theology, including *The Crisis of the Christ* (republished in 1989 by Kregel Publications).

52

The Purposes of the Incarnation

By Rev. G. Campbell Morgan, D.D.
PASTOR OF WESTMINSTER CHAPEL, LONDON, ENGLAND

Revised by Gerald B. Stanton, Th.D.

The whole teaching of Holy Scripture places the Incarnation at the center of the methods of God with a sinning race.

Toward that Incarnation everything moved until its accomplishment, finding therein fulfillment and explanation. The messages of the prophets and seers and the songs of the psalmists trembled with more or less certainty toward the final music which announced the coming of Christ. All the results also of these partial and broken messages of the past led toward the Incarnation.

It is equally true that from that Incarnation all subsequent movements have proceeded, depending upon it for direction and dynamic. The Gospel stories are all concerned with the coming of Christ, with his mission and his message. The letters of the New Testament have all to do with the fact of the Incarnation, and its correlated doctrines and duties. The last book of the Bible is a book, the true title of which is *The Unveiling of the Christ.*

Not only the actual messages which have been bound up in this one Divine Library, but all the results issuing from them, are finally results issuing from this self-same coming of Christ. It is surely important, therefore, that we should understand its purposes in the economy of God.

There is a fourfold statement of purpose declared in the New Testament: the purpose to reveal the Father; the purpose to put away sin; the purpose to destroy the works of the devil; and the purpose to establish by another advent the Kingdom of God in the world.

Christ was in conflict with all that was contrary to the purposes of God in individual, social, national, and racial life. There is a sense in which when we have said this we have stated the whole meaning of his coming. His revelation of the Father was toward this end; his putting away of sin was part of this very process; and his second advent will be for the complete and final overthrow of all the works of the devil.

1. To Reveal the Father

"No man hath seen God at any time; the only begotten Son, which is in the bosom of the Father, he hath declared him" (John 1:18). "He that hath seen me hath seen the Father" (John 14:9).

This latter is Christ's own statement of truth in this regard, and is characterized by simplicity and sublimity. Among all the things Jesus said concerning his relationship to the Father, none is more comprehensive, inclusive, exhaustive, than this.

The last hours of Jesus with his disciples were passing away. He was talking to them, and four times over they interrupted him. 'Philip said, "Lord, show us the Father, and it sufficeth us." Philip's interruption was due, in the first place, to a conviction of Christ's relation in some way to the Father. He had been so long with Jesus as to become familiar in some senses with his line of thought. In all probability Philip was asking that there should be repeated to him and the little group of disciples some such wonderful thing as they had read of in the past of their people's history; as when the elders once ascended the mountain and saw God; or when the prophet saw the Lord sitting upon a throne, high and lifted up, and his train filled the temple; or when Ezekiel saw God in fire, and wheels; in majesty and glory.

I cannot read the answer of Jesus to that request without feeling that he divested himself, of set purpose, of anything that approached stateliness of diction, and dropped into the common speech of friend to friend. Looking into the face of Philip, who was voicing, though he little knew it, the great anguish of the human heart, the great hunger of the human soul, he said, "Have I been so long time with you, and dost thou not know me, Philip? He that hath seen me hath seen the Father." That claim has been vindicated in the passing of the centuries.

Revelation to the Race

We will, therefore, consider first what this revelation of God has meant to the race; and secondly, what it has meant to the individual.

First, then, what conception of God had the race before Christ came? Taking the Hebrew thought of God, let me put the whole truth as I see it into one comprehensive statement. Prior to the Incarnation there had been a growing intellectual apprehension of truth concerning God, accompanied by a diminishing moral result. It is impossible to study the Old Testament without seeing that there gradually broke through the mists a clearer light concerning God. The fact of the unity of God; the fact of the might of God; the fact of the holiness of God; the fact of the beneficence of God; these things men had come to see through the process of the ages.

Yet side by side with this growing intellectual apprehension of God there was diminishing moral result, for it is impossible to read the story of the ancient Hebrew people without seeing how they waxed worse and worse in all matters moral. The moral life of Abraham was far purer than life in the time of the kings. Life in the early time of the kings was far purer than the conditions which the prophets ultimately described. In proportion as men grew in their intellectual conception of God, it seemed increasingly unthinkable that he could be interested in their everyday life. Morality became something not of intimate relationship to him, and therefore something that mattered far less.

Think of the great Gentile world, as it then was, and as it still is, save where the message of the Evangel has reached it. We have had such remarkable teachers as Zoroaster, Buddha, Confucius; men speaking many true things, flashing with light, but notwithstanding these things a perpetual failure in morals and a uniform degradation of religion have been universal. The failure has ever been due to a lack of final knowledge concerning God.

At last there came the song of the angels, and the birth of the Son of God, through whose Incarnation and ministry there came to men a new consciousness of God.

He included in his teaching and manifestation all the essential things which men had learned in the long ages of the past.

He did not deny the truth of the unity of God; he re-emphasized it. He did not deny the might of God; he declared it and manifested it in many a gentle touch of infinite power. He did not deny the holiness of God; he insisted upon it in teaching and life, and at last by the mystery of dying. He did not deny the beneficence of God; he changed the cold word beneficence into the word throbbing with the infinite heart of Deity — *Love*. He did more. That which men had imperfectly expressed in song and prophecy he came to state: "He that hath seen me hath seen the Father."

Wherever Christ comes to people who have never had direct revelation, he comes first of all as fulfillment of all that in their thought and scheme is true. He comes, moreover, for the correction of all that in their thought and scheme is false. All the underlying consciousness of humanity concerning God is touched and answered and lifted into the supreme consciousness whenever God is seen in Christ. All the gleams of light which have been flashing across the consciousness of humanity merge into the essential light when he is presented.

Christ comes not to contradict the essential truth of Buddhism, but to fulfill it. He comes not to rob the Chinese of his regard for parents, as taught by Confucius, but to fulfill it, and to lift him upon that regard into regard for the one great Father, God. He comes always to fulfill. Wherever he has come; wherever he has been presented; wherever men low or high in the intellectual scale, have seen God in Christ, their hands have opened and they have dropped their fetishes, and their idols, and have yielded themselves to him. If the world has not come to God through him, it is because the world has not yet seen him; and if the world has not yet seen him, the blame is upon the Christian church.

The wide issues of the manifestation of God in Christ are — the union of intellectual apprehension and moral improvement, and the relation of religion to life. In no system of religion in the world has there come to men the idea of God which unites religion with morals, save in this revelation of God in Jesus Christ.

Revelation to the Individual

Secondly, the effect of the manifestation in relation to the individual. In illustration we cannot do better than by taking Philip, the man to whom Christ spoke. To Philip's request "Show us the Father and it sufficeth us," Jesus said, "Have I been so long time with you, and dost thou not know me, Philip?" The evident sense of the question is, You have seen enough of me, Philip, if you have really seen me, to have found what you are asking for — a vision of God.

What then had Phillip seen? What revelations of Deity had come to this man who thought he had not seen and did not understand? We will adhere to what Scripture tells of what Philip had seen.

All the story is in John. Philip is referred to by Matthew, Mark, and Luke, as being among the number of the apostles, but in no other way. John tells of four occasions when Philip is seen in union with Christ. Philip was the first man Jesus *called* to follow him; not the first man to follow him. There were other two who preceded Philip, going after Christ in consequence of the teaching of John. But Philip was the first man to whom Christ used that great formula of calling men which has become so precious in the passing of the centuries — "Follow me." What happened? "Philip findeth Nathanael, and saith unto him, We have found him, of whom Moses in the law, and the prophets, wrote." That was the first thing that Philip had seen in Christ according to his own confession: One who embodied all the ideals of Moses and the prophets.

We find Philip next in the sixth chapter, when the multitudes were about Christ, and they were hungry. Philip, who considered it impossible to feed the hungry multitude, now sees Someone who in a mysterious way had resource enough to satisfy human hunger. Philip then listened while in matchless discourse Jesus lifted the thought from material hunger to spiritual need and declared, "I am the bread of life." So that the second vision Philip had of Jesus, according to the record, was a vision of him, full of resource and able to satisfy hunger, both material and spiritual.

We next see Philip in the twelfth chapter. The Greeks coming to him said, "Sir, we would see Jesus." Philip found his way with Andrew to Jesus, and asked him to see the Greeks. Philip saw by what then took place that this Man had intimate relation with the Father, and that there was perfect harmony between them, no conflict, no controversy. He saw, moreover, that upon the basis of that communion with his Father, and that perfect harmony, his voice changed from the tones of sorrow to those of triumph: "Now is the judgment of this world: now shall the prince of this world be cast out. And I, if I be lifted up from the earth, will draw all men unto myself." That was Philip's third vision of Jesus. It was the vision of One acting in perfect accord with God, bending to the sorrow that surged upon his soul, in order that through it he might accomplish human redemption.

We now come back to the last scene. Philip said, "Show us the Father and it sufficeth us." Gathering up all the things of the past, Christ looked into the face of Philip and replied, "Have I been so long time with you, and dost thou not know me, Philip?" No, Philip had not seen these things. They were there to be seen, and by and by, the infinite work of Christ being accomplished, and the glory of Pentecost having dawned upon the world, Philip saw it all; saw the meaning of the things he had seen, and had never seen; the things he had looked upon, and had never understood.

He found that having seen Jesus he had actually seen the Father. When he looked upon One who embodied in his own personality all the facts of law and righteousness, who was able to satisfy all the hunger of humanity, who was sent to share the sorrows of humanity in order to draw men to himself and to save them, he had seen God.

This manifestation wins the submission of the reason; appeals to the love of the heart; demands the surrender of the will. Here is the value of the Incarnation as revelation of God.

Let us recall our thoughts for a moment from the particular application in the case of Philip, and think what this means to us. Is it true that this manifestation wins the submission of our reason, appeals to the love of our heart, asks the surrender of our will?

Then to refuse God in Christ is to violate at some essential point our own humanity. To refuse we must violate reason, which is captured by the revelation; or we must crush the emotion, which springs in our heart in the presence of the revelation; or we must decline to submit our will to the demands which the manifestation makes. God grant that we may rather look into his face and say, "My Lord and my God!" So shall we find our rest, and our hearts will be satisfied. It shall suffice, as we see the Father in Christ.

II. To Take Away Sins

"Ye know that he was manifested to take away sins; and in him is no sin" (I John 3:5).

In this text we get nearer to an understanding of the purpose of the Incarnation as it touches our human need. The simple and all-inclusive theme which it suggests is, first, that the purpose of the Incarnation was the taking away of sins; and secondly, that the process of accomplishment is that of the Incarnation.

The Purpose

First, then, we will take the purpose as declared, "He was manifested to take away sins." What is intended by this word "sins"? It is the sum total of all lawless acts. The thought is incomprehensible as to numbers when we think of the race, but let us remember that in the midst of that which overwhelms us in our thinking are our own actual sins.

"Sins" — missing of the mark, whether wilful missings, or missings through ignorance, does not at present matter. The word includes all those thoughts and words and deeds in which we have missed the mark of the divine purpose and the divine ideal.

The phrase "to take away" is a statement of result, not a declaration of process. The Hebrew equivalent of the word "take away" is found in that familiar story of the scapegoat. It was provided that this animal should be driven away to the wilderness "unto a solitary land." This suggested that sins should be lifted from one and placed upon another, and by that one carried away out of experience, out of consciousness. That is the simple signification of this declaration, "He was manifested to bear sins" — to *lift* sins. He was manifested in order that he might come into relationship with human life, and passing underneath the load of human sins, lift them, take them away.

The Process

Secondly, in order that this great purpose of the Incarnation may be more powerfully and better understood, let us reverently turn to the indication of the process which we have in this particular text, "He was manifested to take away sins." Who was the Person? It is perfectly evident that John here, as always, has his eye fixed upon the Man of Nazareth; and yet it is equally evident that he is looking through Jesus of Nazareth to God. That is the meaning of his word "manifested" here. He is the Word made flesh. He is flesh, but he is the Word. He is someone that John had appreciated by the senses, and yet he is someone whom John knew pre-eminently by the Spirit.

Notice, that after he makes the affirmation, "He was manifested to take away sins," he adds this great word, "In him is no sin"; or, "Missing of the mark was not in him." The One in whom there was no missing of the mark was manifested for the express purpose of lifting, bearing away, making not to be, the missings of the mark of others.

I come now to the final thing in this manifestation — the process of the death; for in that solemn and lonely and unapproachable hour of the cross is the final fulfillment of the word of the herald on the banks of the Jordan, "Behold the Lamb of God, that taketh away the sin of the world!" That phrase, "The Lamb of God," could have but one significance in the ears of the men who heard it. This was the voice of a Hebrew prophet speaking to Hebrews. When he spoke of the Lamb taking away sins, they had no alternative other than to think of the long line of symbolical sacrifices which had been offered, and which they had been taught shadowed forth some great mystery of divine purpose whereby sin might be dealt with.

Reverently, let us take a step further. The manifested One was God. If that be once seen, then we shall forevermore look back upon that Man of Nazareth in his birth, his life, as but a manifestation. The cross, like everything else, was manifestation. In the cross of Jesus there was the working out into visibility of eternal things. Love and light were wrought out into visibility by the cross. In the cross I see the sorrow of God, and in the cross I see the joy of God, for "it pleased the Lord to bruise him." In the cross I see the love of God working out through passion and power for the redemption of man. In the cross I see the light of God refusing to make any terms with iniquity and sin and evil. The cross is the historic revelation of the abiding facts within the heart of God. The measure of the cross is God. He who was manifested is God. He can gather into his eternal life all the race as to its sorrow and as to its sin, and bear it.

If it be declared that God might have wrought this self-same deliverance without suffering, our answer is that the man who says so knows nothing about sin. Sin and suffering are co-existent. The moment there is sin, there is suffering. The moment there is sin and suffering in a human being it is in God multiplied. "The Lamb was slain from the foundation of the world." From the moment when man in his sin became a child of sorrow, the sorrow was most keenly felt in heaven.

The man who is burdened with a sense of sin I would ask to contemplate the Person manifested. There is not one of us of whom it is not true that we live and move and have our being in God. God is infinitely more than I am; infinitely more than the whole human race from its first to its last. If infinitely more, then all my life is in him. If in the mystery of Incarnation there became manifest the truth that he, God, lifted sin, then I can trust. If that be the cleaving of the rock, then I can say as never before —

> *Rock of Ages, cleft for me,*
> *Let me hide myself in Thee.*

He was manifested, and by that manifestation I see wrought out the infinite truth of the passion of God which we speak of as the atonement.

III. To Destroy the Works of the Devil

"To this end was the Son of God manifested, that he might destroy the works of the devil" (I John 3:8).

There can be no question as to the One to whom John referred when he said, "the Son of God." In all the writings of John it is evident that his eyes are fixed upon the man Jesus. Occasionally he does not name him, does not even refer to him by a personal pronoun, but indicates him by a word you can only use when you are looking at an object or a person. For instance, "*That* which we have seen with our eyes, *that* which we beheld, and our hands handled. . . ." Upon another occasion he said, "He that saith he abideth in him, ought himself also to walk even as he walked." It is always the method of expression of a man who is looking at a Person. Forevermore the actual human Person of Christ was present to the mind of John as he wrote of him.

The word "manifested" presupposes existence prior to manifestation. In the Man of Nazareth there was manifestation of One who had existed long before the Man of Nazareth.

The enemy is described here as the devil. We read that he is a murderer, a liar, a betrayer; the fountain-head of sin, the lawless one. The work of the murderer is destruction of life. The work of the liar is the extinguishing of light. The work of the betrayer is the violation of love. The work of the arch-sinner is the breaking of the law. These are the works of the devil.

He is a murderer. This consists fundamentally in the destruction of life on its highest level, which is the spiritual. Alienation from God is the devil's work. It is also death on the level of the mental. Vision which fails to include God is practical blindness. On the physical plane, all disease and all pain are ultimately results of sin, and are among the works of the devil. These things all lie within the realm of his work as murderer, destroyer of human life.

He is more. He is the liar, and to him is due the extinguishing of light, so that men blunder along the way. All ignorance, all despair, all wandering over the trackless deserts of life, are due to extinction of spiritual light in the mind of man. All ignorance is the result of the clouding of man's vision of God.

"This is life eternal" — age-abiding life, high life, deep life, broad life, long life, comprehensive life — "that they should know thee the only true God, and him whom thou didst send, even Jesus Christ." The proportion in which man knows God is the proportion in which he sees clearly to the heart of things. By and by, when the redemptive work of Christ has been perfected in man, and in the world, we shall find that all ignorance is banished and man has found his way into light. But the liar, the one who brings darkness, has made his works far spread over the face of humanity, and all ignorance and resultant despair are due to the work of the one whom Jesus designated a liar from the beginning.

Again, the violation of love, as a work of the devil, is seen supremely in the way he entered into the heart of Judas and made him the betrayer. All the avarice you find in the world today, and all the jealousy, and all the cruelty, are the works of the devil.

Finally, he is the supreme sinner. Sin is lawlessness, which does not mean the condition of being without law, but the condition of being against law, breaking law. So that all wrong done to God in his world, all wrong done by man to man, all wrong done by man to himself, are works of the devil.

To summarize then: death, darkness, hatred, find them where you will, are works of the devil.

The Son of God was manifested that he might destroy the works of the devil. If at the beginning we saw him as a soul in conflict with all these things, remember that was an indication of the program and a prophecy of the purpose. The Incarnation was not merely the birth of a little child in whom we were to learn the secret of childhood, and in whom presently we were to see the glories of manhood. All that is true; but it was the happening in the course of human events, of that one thing through which God himself is able to destroy the works of the devil.

What "Destroy" Means

"To destroy." It is a word which means to dissolve, to loosen. It is the very same word as is used in the Apocalypse about loosing us from our sins. It is the word used in the Acts of the Apostles when you read that the ship was broken to pieces; loosed, dissolved, that which had been a consistent whole was broken up and scattered and wrecked.

The word "destroyed" may be perfectly correct, but let us understand it. He was manifested to do a work in human history the result of which should be that the works of the devil should lose their consistency. The cohesive force that makes them appear stable until this moment, he came to loosen and dissolve. He was manifested to destroy death by the gift of life. He was manifested to destroy darkness by the gift of light. He was manifested to destroy hatred by the gift of love. He was manifested to destroy lawlessness by the gift of law. He was manifested to loosen, to break up, to destroy the negatives which spoil, by the bringing of the positive that remakes and uplifts.

Nineteen centuries ago the Son of God was manifested, and during those centuries in the lives of hundreds, thousands, he has destroyed the works of the devil, mastered death by the gift of life; cast darkness out by the incoming light; turned the selfishness of avarice and jealousy into love, joy, peace, long-suffering, kindness, goodness. He has taken hold of lawless men and made them into the willing, glad bond-servants of God. So has he destroyed the works of the devil.

The forces of this Christ have operated, and are operating; and the things that were formerly established are loosened, and are falling to decay. He was manifested to destroy the works of the devil. If you are in the grip of forces of evil; if you realize that in your life his works are the things of strength, then I pray you, turn with full purpose of heart to the One manifested long ago, who in all the power of his gracious victory will destroy in you all the works of the devil and set you free.

IV. To Prepare for a Second Advent

"Christ also, having been once offered to bear the sins of many, shall appear a second time, apart from sin, to them that wait for him, unto salvation" (Heb. 9:28).

We are all conscious that nothing is perfect; that the things which Christ came to do are not yet done; that the works of the devil are not yet finally destroyed; that sins are not yet experimentally taken away; that in the spiritual consciousness of the race, God is not yet perfectly known. "Now we see not yet all things subjected to him." The victory does not seem to be won. It is impossible to read the story of the Incarnation and to believe in it, and to follow the history of the centuries that have followed upon that Incarnation without feeling in one's deepest heart that something more is needed. The Incarnation was essential, but the consummation of its meaning can only be brought about by another coming, as personal, as definite, as positive, as real in human history as was the first.

"Christ . . . shall appear a second time." There is no escape, other than by casuistry, from the simple meaning of those words.

The first idea conveyed by them is that of an actual personal advent of Jesus yet to be. To spiritualize a statement like this and to attempt to make application of it in any other than the way in which a little child would understand it, is to be driven, one is almost inclined to say, to dishonesty with the simplicity of the scriptural declaration. There may be diversities of interpretations as to how he will come, and when he will come; whether he will come to usher in a millennium or to crown it; but the fact of his actual coming is beyond question.

Paul in all his writings is conscious of this truth of the second advent. In some of them he does not dwell upon it at such great length, or with such clarity as in others, for the simple reason that it was not always the specific subject with which he was dealing. In the Thessalonian letters we have most clearly set forth Paul's teaching concerning this matter. In the very center of the first letter we have a passage which declares in unmistakable language that "the Lord himself shall descend from heaven, with a shout, with the voice of the archangel, and with the trump of God: and the dead in Christ shall rise first; then we that are alive, that are left, shall together with them be caught up in the clouds, to meet the Lord in the air: and so shall we ever be with the Lord" (I Thess. 4:16-18).

James, writing to those who were in affliction said, "Be ye also patient; establish your hearts: for the coming of the Lord is at hand."

Peter, with equal clarity, said to the early disciples, "Be sober and set your hope perfectly on the grace that is to be brought unto you at the revelation of Jesus Christ."

John, who leaned upon his Master's bosom, said, "We know that, if he shall be manifested, we shall be like him; for we shall see him even as he is. And every one that hath this hope set on him purifieth himself, even as he is pure."

Jude said to those to whom he wrote, "Ye, beloved, building up yourselves on your most holy faith, praying in the Holy Spirit, keep yourselves in the love of God, looking for the mercy of our Lord Jesus Christ unto eternal life."

Every New Testament writer presents this truth as part of the common Christian faith. Belief in the personal actual second advent of Jesus gave the bloom to primitive Christianity, and constituted the power of the early Christians to laugh in the face of death, and to overcome all forces that were against them. There is nothing more necessary in our day than a new declaration of this vital fact of Christian faith. Think what it would mean if the whole church still lifted her face toward the east and waited for the morning; waited as the Lord would have her wait — with loins girt for service and lamps burning. If the whole Christian church were so waiting, she would cast off her worldliness and infidelity, and all other things which hinder her march to conquest.

Meaning of the Second Advent

The Scriptures do more than affirm the fact of the second advent. In a remarkable way, they declare the meaning thereof. "Christ . . . shall appear a second time, *apart from sin.*" To rightly understand this, we must look upon it as putting the second advent into contrast with the first. That is what the writer most evidently means, for the context declares that he was manifested in the consummation of the ages to bear sins. He now says that "Christ . . . shall appear a second time apart from sin." All the things of the first advent were necessary to the second; but the things of the second will be different from the things of the first.

By his first advent sin was revealed. His own cross was the place where all the deep hatred of the human heart expressed itself most diabolically in view of heaven and earth and hell.

There was also revelation of darkness as contrary to light. "Men loved the darkness rather than the light," was the supreme lament of the heart of Jesus.

In his first advent he not only revealed sin, but bore it. All through his life he was putting himself underneath sin in order to take it away. He bore its limitations throughout the whole of his life. In poverty, in sorrow, in loneliness, he lived: and all these things are limitations resulting from sin. When Jesus Christ entered into the flesh, he entered into the limitations which follow upon sin, and he bore sin in his own consciousness through all the years; not poverty only, but sorrow in all forms, and loneliness. All the sorrows of the human heart were upon his heart until he uttered that unspeakable cry, "My God, my God, why hast thou forsaken me?"

Having finally dealt with sin, and destroyed it at its very root at his first advent, his second advent is to be that of victory. He will come again; not to poverty, but to wealth. He will come again; not to sorrow, but with all joy. He will come again; not in loneliness, but to gather about him all trusting souls who have looked and served and waited. All in his first advent of sorrow and loneliness, of poverty and of sin, will be absent from the second. The first advent was for atonement; the second will be for administration. He came, entering into human nature, and taking hold of it, to deal with sin and put it away. He has taken sin away, and he will come again to set up that kingdom, the foundations of which he laid in his first coming.

He "shall appear a second time, apart from sin . . . unto salvation." To those who have heard the message of the first advent and have believed it, and trusted in his great work, and have found shelter in the mystery of his manifestation and bearing of sin — to such, salvation takes the place of judgment. But to the man who will not shelter beneath that first advent and its atoning value — judgment abides. All the things begun by his first advent will be consummated by the second.

At his second advent there will be complete salvation for the individual—righteousness, sanctification, redemption. We believed, and were saved. We believe, and are being saved. We believe, and we shall be saved. The last movement will come when he comes.

Those who have fallen asleep in Christ are safe with God, and he will bring them with him when he comes. They are not yet perfected, "God having provided some better thing concerning us, that apart from us they should not be made perfect." They are at rest, and consciously at rest. They are "absent from the body . . . at home with the Lord," but they are not yet perfected; they are waiting. We are waiting in the midst of earth's struggle — they in heaven's light and joy, for the second advent. Heaven is waiting for it. Earth is waiting for it. Hell is waiting for it. The universe is waiting for it.

That coming will be to those who wait for him. Who are those who wait for him? "Ye turned unto God from idols, to serve a living and true God, and to wait for his Son from heaven."

The first thing is the turning from idols. Have we done that? Then because we have turned from idols, and are serving him, we are waiting. That is the waiting the New Testament enjoins, and to those who wait, his second advent will mean the consummation of their salvation. "Christ shall appear." Glorious Gospel!

PHILIP MAURO (1859-1952) was a successful lawyer, practicing before the United States Supreme Court, when he was converted after attending meetings at the Gospel Tabernacle in New York City, pastored by A. B. Simpson. That was on May 24, 1903. The next year, he published *From Reason to Revelation*, the first of more than forty books that would come from his pen. One of his most widely circulated books, *Life in the Word*, was published in 1909 and was included in *The Fundamentals* in a condensed version. He continued his law practice while speaking at Christian meetings and writing books and articles. It was Mauro who prepared the legal brief that William Jennings Bryan used at the famous "Scopes Trial" in 1925. In later years, he changed his views of the kingdom and prophecy, but he never strayed from the basic doctrines of the Christian faith.

53

Modern Philosophy

By Philip Mauro
Counsellor-at-Law
New York

Revised and edited by Gerald B. Stanton, Th.D.

"Beware lest any man spoil you *through philosophy* and vain deceit after [according to] the tradition of men, after the rudiments of the world, and not after Christ. For in him dwelleth all the fulness of the Godhead bodily; and ye are *complete in him,* who is the Head of all principality and power" (Col. 2:8-10).

In the foregoing passage occurs the only mention which the Scriptures make of philosophy. Nothing is more highly esteemed among men than philosophy. It is on all hands regarded as the supreme exercise and occupation of the human mind, and is viewed as an occupation for which but very few men have the requisite intellectual equipment. As far back as the tradition of men goes, philosophy has held this high place in human estimation. It is, therefore, a fact of much significance that, in all the Bible, philosophy is but once named.

Even in our day the deference paid to philosophy is such that there are not many teachers of the Bible who would venture to warn their fellow-men of its dangers; for philosophers have managed to maintain in Christendom the same eminence which they occupied in heathendom. Indeed, a course in philosophy is now, and for some generations has been, considered an essential part of the education of a man who is preparing for the Christian ministry. This is not the only one of the "rudiments of the world" which has found its way into our theological seminaries. It is, therefore, not surprising that, in the teaching imparted by these seminary graduates, philosophy holds a very different place from that assigned to it by the Bible.

Not a Human Utterance

We may be very sure that the passage quoted above is not a human utterance. It does not express man's estimate of philosophy — far from it. In pronouncing that warning, Paul is not repeating what he learned while pursuing his course in philosophy at the school of Gamaliel. No *man* would ever have coupled philosophy with vain deceit, or characterized it as a dangerous process against which God's people should be cautioned, lest thereby they should be despoiled of their possessions. No *man* ever defined philosophy as being according to human tradition and the basic principles of this evil world, and not according to Christ. This warning is from God himself; but, alas, like many other of his solemn warnings, it has been despised and utterly disregarded. The thing against which this earnest warning was spoken has been welcomed with open arms, and incorporated into the theological machinery of our ecclesiastical systems. The consequences of this contemptuous disregard of God's warning are such as might have been expected.

This word "beware" (sometimes rendered "take heed" in our version) does not occur very often in the New Testament. There are not many things whereof believers are bidden to "beware." Some of these are "the scribes," "dogs," "evil workers," "the concision," and an "evil heart of unbelief" (Mark 12:38; Phil. 3:2; Acts 13:40; Heb. 3:12). The warning of our text is addressed to believers who have been instructed as to their oneness with Christ in his death (at the hands of the world), his burial, and his resurrection. Additional emphasis is given to the warning by the connection in which it occurs. The word rendered "spoil" signifies literally to make a prey of, as when one falls into the hands of robbers and is stripped by violence of his goods, or into the hands of smooth-tongued and plausible swindlers who gain his confidence, and by means of their arts fleece him of his valuables. It is heavenly treasure that is in contemplation here, even the believer's portion of the unsearchable riches of Christ. Hence empty deceit is contrasted with the fulness of the Godhead which dwells in Christ; and the despoiled condition of one who has been victimized through philosophy is contrasted with the enrichment of those who have apprehended by faith their completeness in him who is the Head of all principality and power.

But why, we may profitably inquire, is philosophy described as an instrument of spoilation in the hands of artful men? And why is it characterized as being after (i. e., according to) the rudiments, or basic principles, of the world? The word rendered "rudiments" occurs four times in Scripture. In Colossians 2:20 it is again rendered "rudiments." In Galatians 4:3 and 9 it is rendered "elements." It seems to convey the idea of basic or foundation principles of the world-system. These elements are described in Galatians 4:9 as "weak and beggarly." They do not strengthen and enrich, but weaken and impoverish those who resort to them.

Philosophy Defined

The reason is perceived in a general way at least when we ascertain what philosophy is, namely, the occupation of attempting to devise, by the exercise of the human reason, an explanation of the universe. It is an interminable occupation for the reason that, if the explanation which philosophy is forever seeking were to be found, that discovery would be the end of philosophy. The occupation of the philosopher would be gone. It is interminable for the stronger reason that the philosopher is bound, by the rules of his profession, to employ in his quest only human wisdom, and it is written that the world, by its wisdom, does not come to the knowledge of God (I Cor. 1:19-21; 2:14). Incidentally, a large part of the time of the philosopher is occupied in criticizing and demonstrating the unreasonableness or absurdity of all philosophical systems except that espoused by himself. This, however, is merely the destructive part of his work, the constructive part being, as has been said, the employment of his reasoning faculties in the task of devising a system which will account, after a fashion, for the existence and origin of, and for the changes which appear to take place in, the visible universe. Having settled upon such a system, the philosopher must thenceforth defend it from the attacks of philosophers of opposing "schools" (who will put forth weighty volumes demonstrating to their entire satisfaction that his philosophical system is a tissue of absurdities), and in replying to their many and varied objections and criticisms.

"Not According to Christ"

We may thus see at a glance that philosophy is, in its essential character, in accordance with human tradition and the fundamental or primary principles of the world-system. It is not according to Christ, who is hated by the world, and who has laid the axe at the root of all its principles. Prominent among the elements of the world and of human tradition is the principle that the world reflects the grandeur of *man,* and that human reason is the highest and mightiest factor in it. In our day it has become a tenet of popular theology that the human reason is the final court of appeal in all matters of doctrine. In man's world human achievement is exalted to the highest place, and no limit is set to what may be accomplished by human ingenuity. "Let *us* build *us* a city and a tower whose top may reach unto heaven, and let *us* make *us* a name" (Gen. 11:4), is the program of humanity, as announced by those who established the basic principles of the world system. In this system, that only is valued and lauded which is attained by the effort of man and redounds to his credit. Philosophy adheres strictly to this tradition and to these principles in that its various explanations, in order to receive recognition as "philosophical," must be purely the products of *human reason* exercised upon the results of *human investigations.*

Philosophy vs. Revelation

It follows of necessity that philosophy and divine revelation are utterly irreconcilable. The very existence of philosophy as an occupation for the human mind depends upon the rigid exclusion of every explanation of the universe which is not reached by a speculative process. If a philosophy admits the existence of a God (as the philosophies just now in favor do), it is a god who either is dumb, or else is not permitted to tell anything about himself, or how he made and sustains the universe. Should the philosopher's god break through these restrictions, there would be straightway an end of his philosophy. For it is not the pursuit of truth that makes one a philosopher. The pursuit of truth, in order to be philosophical, must be conducted in directions in which truth *cannot possibly be found.* For the discovery of what philosophers pretend to be seeking would bring their philosophies to an end, and such a calamity must, of course, be avoided. Therefore, the moment one receives an explanation of the universe *as coming from God* who made it, he can have no further use for philosophy. One who has obtained the truth is no longer a seeker.

The value of philosophy, therefore, lies not in its results, for there are none, but solely in the employment which its unverifiable speculations afford to those whose tastes and intellectual endowments qualify them to engage in it.

Philosophy vs. Christ

Again, philosophy is "not according to Christ" for the simple and sufficient reason that the testimony of Christ puts an end, for all who accept it, to all philosophical speculations concerning the relations of humanity to God and to the universe. Christ set his seal to the truth and divine authority of the Old Testament Scriptures. He, moreover, revealed the Father; and finally, he promised further revelations of truth through his apostles under the immediate teaching of the Holy Spirit. These revelations are not only directly opposed to philosophical speculations, but they cut the ground from under them. The testimony and teaching of Christ were not communicated to men for the purpose of informing them how man and the world came to be what they are — though they do reveal the truth as to that. The purpose of the doctrine of Christ and of his personal mission to the world was to show to men their true condition, as under the dominion of sin and death, and to accomplish eternal redemption for all who believe the good tidings and accept the gift of God's grace. The doctrine of Christ not only instructs men as to the way into the kingdom of God, but also entitles those who accept it to the *immediate* possession and enjoyment of many and valuable rights and privileges which can be acquired in no other way. If, therefore, you are a believer in Christ Jesus, trusting the merit of his sacrifice for your acceptance with God, beware lest any man despoil you of these inestimable rights and privileges through philosophy and vain deceit, according to the principles of the world, and not according to Christ. For in him, and not elsewhere, dwells the fulness of the Godhead; and in him, and not elsewhere, the believer may be filled to his utmost capacity. Philosophy can strip men of part of the inheritance of faith. It has nothing to offer them in exchange.

Fruits of Philosophy

It would be quite possible, for one who had the requisite leisure and curiosity, to trace the main developments of philosophy and to examine the many different "schools" to which it has given rise during a period of several thousand years. Having done so, he would find that philosophy consists in the pursuit of the unattainable, and that, among all the varied fields of human activity there is none which has witnessed such an absolutely futile and barren expenditure of energy as the field of speculative philosophy. A philosopher of repute has declared that "philosophy has been on a *false scent* ever since the days of Socrates and Plato." The following of a false scent for more than two thousand years is surely not a record to boast of; and yet it is true that, so far as *results* are concerned, philosophy has nothing more encouraging than this to offer as an inducement for engaging in it.

We do not, however, propose anything so stupendous (and so unprofitable) as a review of the history of philosophy, but merely a brief statement setting forth the *status* of philosophy at the present day. And this we undertake in order that the non-philosophical reader may be able to ascertain the character of the influence which philosophy is exerting, in these times of change and mental unrest, upon the immediate problems of humanity, and upon what is called "the progress of human thought."

The great majority of men do no thinking beyond the matters which lie within the little circle of their personal interests. This unthinking majority takes its thoughts and opinions from an intellectual and cultured few, or from leaders who manage to gain their confidence. It is important, therefore, to ascertain what ideas are prevalent among those who are in a position to influence the opinions of the mass of mankind. This may easily be done by sampling the current philosophical teaching at the great universities of the English-speaking countries.

Theistic and Atheistic Philosophy

The various schools of philosophy which have flourished through the ages may be divided into two main classes, namely, *theistic* and *atheistic*. The former class embraces all philosophic systems which assume a god of some sort as the originator and sustainer of the universe. It may be remarked in passing that theistic philosophies are more dangerous to humankind than the atheistic class, for the reason that the former are well calculated to ensnare those who, by nature or training, have a repugnance to atheism.

Dualism and Pantheism

Confining our attention, therefore, to theistic philosophies, we find several classes of these, namely, "Dualistic" and "Pantheistic." *Dualism* is the name which philosophers have been pleased to bestow upon those systems which maintain that God (or the "First Cause") created the universe as an act of his will, and has an existence distinct and apart from it. These systems are called "dualistic" because they count God as *one* entity, and the universe or creation as *another* entity, thus making *two* entities. The reader should understand clearly that when a learned professor of philosophy speaks of "dualism" he has Christianity in mind.

Monism and Pluralism

Pantheism, on the other hand, maintains that God and the universe are one being. There are several varieties of pantheism which have followers among philosophers, e. g., *monism* and *pluralism.* Monism is that system which assumes as the basis of reality an "absolute" or "all-knower" — a monstrosity which comprehends in its vast being all things and all their relations and activities. Monism, therefore, asserts that there is but one *entity.* God has no existence apart from the universe, and never had. The latter is, therefore, eternal, and there has been no creation.

The Present Situation

In order to obtain for our consideration a fair and accurate statement of the position of recent philosophy, reference will be made to the Hibbert Lectures of 1909, on "The Present Situation in Philosophy," delivered by Professor William James of Harvard University at Manchester College, Oxford. These lectures have been published in a volume entitled, *A Pluralistic Universe* (Longmans, Green).

Professor James is one of the very few philosophers of note who reject the teaching of monism. He advocates a theory styled "pluralism," of which a sufficient idea may be gained from the quotations to follow. It is of first importance to us to learn from Professor James what is the present status of dualism, since, as we have seen, that class embraces old-fashioned or Bible Christianity. As to this, he says:

"Dualistic theism is professed as firmly as ever at all Catholic seats of learning, whereas it has of late years tended to disappear at our British and American Universities, and be replaced by a monistic pantheism more or less open or disguised" (*op. cit.,* p. 24).

According to this competent authority, the Roman Catholic colleges are the only ones of any consequence wherein the statements of the Bible regarding the creation and government of the universe, the origin of living creatures, including man, the origin of evil, etc., are even "professed." The great universities of England and America, which were founded for the purpose of maintaining the doctrines of Scriptures, and spreading knowledge of them as the revelations of the living God, and as the foundation of all true learning, have been despoiled of all that made them useful for the nurture of young minds, and that made them valuable to the communities wherein they have flourished. This momentous change has been accomplished through the agency of philosophy and vain deceit, according to the ancient tradition of men, according to the rudiments of the world, and not according to Christ.

A *Strange Phenomenon*

Herein, as it seems to the writer, we have an explanation for the strange phenomenon that Romanism is gaining ground rapidly in Protestant England and America, while steadily losing influence in those countries where it has had almost exclusive sway over the consciences of the people. The latter countries have never enjoyed the privilege of the open Bible. They have never had any links attaching them to the living Word of God. All they have had is "the church," and that they are now judging by its fruits.

But in England and America it is far otherwise. For many generations, from father to son, the people have been knit by many strong and tender ties and associations to the Word of the living God. Its influences upon the customs and life of the people have been many and potent. Only those whose minds are blinded will deny the mighty influence which the Bible has exerted as a factor in the national prosperity of the English-speaking countries. The great universities have been their pride, and have been counted among the national bulwarks; and the Bible has been the foun-

dation stone of the universities. But now a change has come —
so swiftly and so stealthily that we can scarcely realize what has
happened. The universities have discarded the teaching of the
Bible, and have repudiated its *authority* as the divinely inspired
teacher. Only at "Catholic seats of learning" is its teaching professed. What wonder, then, in a time of general disintegration
and unrest, that the children of Bible-loving ancestors should be
drawn by the thousand to a system which has the appearance of
stability, where all else is falling to pieces, and which, with all its
errors, does proclaim the infallibility of the Holy Scriptures!
Whoso is wise will consider these things.

A Sudden Change

Professor James, in his lectures at Manchester, treats the teaching of the Bible as being now so utterly discredited and out of
date as to call for only a brief, passing reference in a discussion
purporting to deal with "the present situation in philosophy."
He says:

"I shall leave cynical materialism entirely out of our discussion
as not calling for treatment before this present audience, and I
shall ignore *old-fashioned dualistic theism for the same reason*"
(*op. cit.*, p. 30).

It is important for our purpose to note the suddenness of the
great change which has taken place at our universities, whereby
Christian doctrine has been relegated to a position of obscurity
so profound that it calls for no consideration in a discussion of
this sort. The lecturer, after remarking that he had been told by
Hindoos that "the great obstacle to the spread of Christianity in
their country was the puerility of our dogma of creation," added:
"Assuredly, most members of this audience are ready to side with
Hinduism in this matter." And then he proceeded to say that
"those of us who are sexagenarians" have witnessed such changes
as "make the thought of the past generation seem as foreign to
its successor as if it were the expression of a different race of
men. The theological machinery that spoke so livingly to our ancestors, with its finite age of the world, its creation out of nothing, its juridical morality and eschatology, its treatment of God
as an external contriver, an intelligent and moral governor, *sounds*

as odd to most of us as if it were some outlandish savage religion"
(*op. cit.,* p. 29).

The effect upon the plastic minds of undergraduates of such words as those last quoted can easily be imagined. They artfully convey the suggestion that these young men are, in respect of their philosophical notions, vastly superior to the men of light and learning of past generations, and that it is by the repudiation of Christianity and its living oracles that they furnish convincing proof of their intellectual superiority. There are few minds among men of the age here addressed, or of any age — except they be firmly grounded and established in the truth — which could resist the insidious influence of such an appeal to the innate vanity of men.

Such being then the influences to which the students of our universities are now exposed, is there not urgent need of impressing upon Christian parents the warning of our text, and exhorting them to beware lest their children be despoiled through philosophy and empty deceit?

Buddha or Christ?

It is essential to sound this warning concerning a system of philosophy which, in its several forms, has crowded out of our universities the true doctrine of Christ. We have already stated that this reigning system, now holding almost undisputed sway in "Christian" England and America, is pantheism, which has flourished for thousands of years as the philosophical religious cult of India. We have seen how Professor James defers to the Hindoo estimate of the Bible doctrine of creation, and sides with it. If the test of a doctrine is the way it is regarded by the Hindoos, it is quite logical to go to them for the interpretation of the universe which is to be taught at our schools and colleges.

The philosophers of today have, therefore, nothing to offer to us that our ancestors did not understand as well as they, and that they were not as free to choose as we are. Did our ancestors then prefer the worse thing to the better when they chose, and founded great universities to preserve, the doctrines taught by Jesus Christ and his apostles, rather than (as they might have done) the doctrines associated with the name of Buddha? Our present-day teachers of philosophy appear to say so. But if there remains any judgment at all in the twentieth-century man, he will remember, before lightly acquiescing in the removal of the ancient foundations, that whatever there may be of superiority in the social order of Christianized England and America over that of pantheistic India is due to the choice which our forefathers made when they accepted the teaching of the Gospel of Christ, and to the fact that *every subsequent generation until the present has ratified and adhered firmly to that choice.*

National Responsibility

From the Bible and from secular history we learn that God deals not only with individuals on the ground of privilege and responsibility, but with nations also. Because of the extraordinary privileges granted to the Israelites, a heavier responsibility rested upon them than upon other nations, and they were visited for their unfaithfulness with corresponding severity. And now we are living in that long stretch of centuries known as "the times of the Gentiles," during which the natural branches of the olive tree (Israel) are broken off, and the branches of the wild olive tree are grafted into their place; that is to say, the period wherein the Gentiles are occupying temporarily Israel's place of special privilege and responsibility. The diminishing of them has become the riches of the Gentiles (Rom. 11:11-25).

In dealing with a nation, God looks to its rulers or leaders as responsibile for its actions. The justice of this is specially evident in countries where the people choose their own rulers and governors. In our day *the people* are all-powerful. Rulers are chosen for the express purpose of executing the popular will. Likewise also the time has come when the people not only elect their rulers, but also *heap to themselves teachers,* because they will not endure sound doctrine (II Tim. 4:3, 4). We may be sure, then, that the persons we find in the professional chairs of our colleges are there by the mandate of the people, who have turned away their ears from the truth and give heed to fables which please their itching ears.

By the very constitution of a democratic social order the teach-ers *must* teach what the people like to hear, or else give place to those who will.

God will surely judge the privileged nations for this. The change has been great and sudden. The judgment will be swift and severe. Until our day, whatever may have been the moral state of the masses of people of England and America, governments were established on the foundations of Christian doctrine; kings and other rulers were sworn to defend the faith; the Bible was taught in the schools, and no one was regarded as fit for a position of public responsibility who was not a professed follower of Jesus Christ. As for the teachers in our schools and colleges, not one could have been found who did not hold and teach as the unchanging truth of God the doctrines of Bible Christianity.

A Great Apostasy

Recognizing these facts, which all must admit to be facts, however much they may differ as to the significance of them, it follows that we are living under the dark shadow of *the greatest national apostasy that has ever taken place*. During all the history of mankind there has never been such a wholesale turning away from the Source of national blessings, in order to take up with the gods of the heathen.

Very pertinent are the words of the prophet: "The wise men are ashamed; they are dismayed and taken. Lo, they have rejected the Word of the Lord, and what wisdom is in them?" (Jer. 8:9). For the occupation in which our philosophers are engaged is the impossible task of trying to establish an explanation of the visible universe after having rejected the true account thereof received from its Creator. The god of the ruling philosophy is one who is not permitted to speak or make himself known in any way. Philosophy must needs put these restraints upon him for its own protection; for, should he break through them, the occupation of the philosopher would be gone. So he must remain in impenetrable obscurity, speaking no word, and making no intelligible sign or motion, in order that philosophers may continue their congenial business of making bad guesses at what he is like.

It is not difficult for one who has come to the knowledge of the truth through receiving the Word of God, "not as the word of men, but as it is in truth the Word of God" (I Thess. 2:13), to perceive the folly and futility of all this. But who shall deliver the ignorant, the innocent, and the unwary from being victimized and eternally despoiled by these men who, professing themselves to be wise, have become fools? We can but sound the alarm and give warning, especially to those who are responsible for bringing up children, of the dangers which infect the intellectualistic atmosphere of our universities, colleges, and seminaries.

A Reason for It

In closing we may with profit to our readers point out a profound reason why the enemy of Christ, and of the men whom he seeks to save, should be desirous of impressing upon the minds of the latter the conception of pantheism. That doctrine wholly excludes the idea that man is a sinner, and hence it puts redemption outside the pale of discussion. Under the influence of that doctrine man would never discover his corrupt nature and his need of salvation, and hence, if not delivered from it, he would die in his sins. An enemy of man could devise against him no greater mischief than this.

But the doctrine which the philosophy of our day has imported from India works not only destruction to men, but also dishonor to God. Herein may its satanic character be clearly perceived by all who have eyes to see. Its foundation principle is that God and man are truly one in substance and being, and that the character of God is revealed in the history of humanity. This evil doctrine makes God the partner with man in all the manifold and grievous wickednesses of humankind. It makes God *particeps criminis* in all the monstrous crimes, cruelties, uncleannesses and unnamable abominations, that have stained the record of humanity. It makes him really the prime actor in all sins and wickednesses, since the thought and impulses prompting them originate with him. Thus God is charged with all the evil deeds which the Bible denounces, and against which the wrath of the God of the Bible is declared.

It may be that somewhere in the dark places of this sinful world there lurks a doctrine more monstrously wicked, more characteristically satanic than this, which is now installed in our seats of learning and there openly venerated as the last word of matured human wisdom; but if such there be, the writer of these pages is not aware of its existence. That doctrine is virtually the assurance, given under the seal of those who occupy the eminences of human culture, learning and wisdom, that the pledge of the serpent given to the parents of the race of what would result if they would follow his track, has at last been redeemed. "Ye shall become as God," he declared; and now the leaders of the thought of the day unite in proclaiming that man and God are truly one substance and nature. Beware! Beware! This teaching is, indeed, according to the most ancient of all human traditions. It is according to the basic principles of the world and of the god of this world, and not according to Christ. No greater danger menaces the younger men and women of the present generation than the danger that some man, some smooth-tongued, learned and polished professor, may make a prey of them by means of philosophy and vain deceit.

DAVID JAMES BURRELL (1849-1926) was a Yale-educated pastor who was known for his ability to communicate to young people from the pulpit. His clear-cut, often eloquent style served him well in his work at churches in Chicago, Dubuque, and Minneapolis. But his most notable work was done between 1891 and 1926 at Marble Collegiate Reformed Church in Manhattan, which was the oldest church on this side of the Atlantic, having been founded in 1628. A real activist, Burrell aligned himself with such causes as the Anti-Saloon League of New York, Bennett Female Seminary, the American Tract Society, and the New York Historical Society. His books include such titles as *The Religions of the World, The Wondrous Cross, The Religion of the Future,* and *Why I Believe the Bible.*

54

The Knowledge of God

By Rev. David James Burrell, D.D., LL.D.
MINISTER OF THE MARBLE COLLEGIATE CHURCH, NEW YORK

Revised and edited by Gerald B. Stanton, Th.D.

The man who does not know God has not begun to live. He may eat and drink, make merry, accumulate a fortune or wear a crown; but he has not entered into that better life of high hopes and noble purposes and aspirations which make us worthy of our divine birthright. For "this is life eternal, to know God."

To put ourselves into proper relations with God is literally a matter of life or death. All the "ologies" are worth mastering but THEOLOGY is indispensable. We must know God.

But where is he? "Oh, that I knew where I might find him! . . . Behold I go forward but he is not there, and backward but I cannot perceive him; on the left hand where he doth work, but I cannot behold him; he hideth himself on the right hand so that I cannot see him!" (Job 23:3, 8, 9). The horizons recede as we approach them, and the darkness thickens as we grope like blind men feeling their way along the wall.

There are three roads which are vainly trodden by multitudes who pursue this holy quest. Each of them is marked, "This way to God"; and each of them is a *cul de sac* or blind alley, which leaves the soul still groping and crying, "Oh, that I knew where I might find him!"

The first of these paths is Intuition.

There are no natural atheists. All are born with an indwelling sense of God. In regions of darkest paganism there are traces of two incarnate convictions; namely, the fact of God and a sinful alienation from him. Hence the universal spirit of unrest so pathetically expressed by Augustine: "We came forth from God, and we shall be homesick until we return to him."

No doubt there have been some who, with no light but that which shines along the pathway of Intuition, have made an acquaintance with God; but the vast multitude have simply arrived at idolatry. They have made unto themselves gods "after the similitude of a man"; gods, like the Brocken of the Harz mountains, projected on the skies. An idol is a man-made god. It may be carved out of wood or conjured out of the gray matter of the brain; but all gods, whencesoever they come, are idols, except the one true God.

The second pathway of the God-seekers is Reason. Here we come upon the philosophers and those who travel with them. This path also leads to disappointment, for it is written, "The world by wisdom knew not God."

The golden age of philosophy in Greece followed close upon the decay of the Pantheon. It was when the people had lost confidence in their idols and the cry was heard, "Great Pan is dead!" that the groves and gardens and painted porches arose on the banks of the Ilyssus. The thoughtful men who assumed the name *philosophoi*, that is, "lovers of wisdom," were all seekers after God. The Stoics, Epicureans, Cynics and Peripatetics all hoped to discover him by the light of reason. How vain the quest!

When Simonides was asked for a definition of God, he required some weeks for meditation and then answered, "The more I think of him, the more he is unknown!" The innumerable gods and altars of Athens had been laughed out of court; and the results of philosophic inquiry were recorded on that other altar which succeeded them, "To the Unknown God."

The stock in trade of the philosophers of Athens was precisely that of the philosophers of our time. It consisted substantially of four arguments, namely (1) *The ontological argument,* to the effect that the being of God is involved in the idea of God. This is good as far as it goes, but it falls vastly short of demonstration; and in any case it reaches no conclusion as to the character of God. (2) *The cosmological argument,* which reasons from effect to cause and expresses itself in the epigram *ex nihilo nihil fit*; "out of nothing nothing comes." This is equally inconclusive, since the necessary Someone to which it leads is but the merest shadow of a god. (3) *The teleological argument,* which proceeds from design to a Designer, carrying with it a strong presumption as to infinite wisdom but taking little or no cognizance of the moral nature of God. (4) *The anthropological argument,* which infers the moral nature of God from the moral nature of man. This goes further than the others; nevertheless, it is so far from being final proof in the mathematical sense that one may reasonably question whether any truth-seeker was ever really convinced by it.

These are arguments which have been used by philosophers from time immemorial, and little has been added in the process of the passing years. The result, as a whole, is melancholy failure. The world by its wisdom, that is by the exercise of its unaided reason, has simply reached agnosticism; it has not "found out God."

Not to those who deem themselves wise, but rather to the simple whose hearts are open Godward, comes the great revelation. It is one thing to know *about* God and quite another to *know* him. John Hay knew all about President Lincoln from his boyhood up; little "Tad" had no such information, but he knew his father, knew him through and through. The eyes of faith see further than those of reason. Wherefore Jesus said, "Except ye become as a little child ye shall in no wise enter into the kingdom of God."

The third of the alluring pathways is that of the Five Senses. This is Natural Science, which reaches its conclusions on the evidence of the physical senses.

This rules out faith, which is a "sixth sense" divinely given to men for the apprehension of spiritual truths. To undertake to solve any of the great problems which have to do with our spiritual life by the testimony of the finger tips is to engage in useless labor, for "spiritual things are spiritually discerned." To undertake to grasp a spiritual fact by the physical senses is as preposterous as it would be to insist on seeing with the ears or hearing with the eyes. Faith is not credulity, nor is it unsubstantial, nor is it believing without evidence. On the contrary, it is both substantial and evidential: only it is "the substance of things hoped for, the evidence of things not seen." To refuse to exercise this "sixth sense" or power of spiritual apprehension is to shut one-self out forever from the possibility of apprehending God or any of the great, intangible, but real truths which center in him.

Yet we are constantly hearing, in certain quarters, of the importance of pursuing our theological studies "by the scientific method." With what result? "We have a world of facts," they say, "and from these facts, by the inductive process, we must arrive at our conclusions." It is like an example in algebra. God is the unknown term; let this be expressed by X. The problem, then, is to resolve X into known terms by the use of a multitude of seen and tangible facts. Can it be done? Go on and pursue your researches along the lines of evolution, until back of cosmos you come to chaos, and back of chaos to the nebula, and back of the nebula to the primordial germ; and that last infinitesimal atom will look up at you with the old question on its lips, as loud as ever and involving a problem as deep as when you began, "Whence came I?" What is your answer? God? Call it "God" if you please; in fact, however, it is simply an impersonal, indefinable, inescapable something or other which, for lack of a better term, is designated as a "First Cause," but which is infinitely far from what is meant by a personal God.

Well, then, shall the quest be given up? Is the universal thought of God merely an *ignis fatuus* leading the hopeful traveler into a realm of impenetrable mists and shadows? Or is there still some way of finding out God?

Yes, there is a fourth road by which we approach God. It is an highway cast up by the King himself, and it is called "Revelation."

There is an antecedent presumption in its favor; namely, that if there is a God anywhere in the universe he would not leave us to grope our way hopelessly in the dark toward him, but would somewhere, somehow, unveil himself to us.

Here is a book which claims to be his Revelation. Of all the books in the literature of the ages, it is the only one that claims to have been divinely authorized and "written by holy men as they were moved by the Spirit of God."

It opens with the words, "In the beginning, God"; and proceeds to set forth the two great doctrines of Creation and Providence. It affirms, on the one hand, that everything in the universe has its origin in the creative power of God; and, on the other, that everything is sustained by the providence of God.

In these two doctrines we have the sum and substance of Bible truth. But this is not all. In between the doctrines of Creation and Providence there walks, through all the corridors of Holy Writ, a mysterious Figure who is the foregleam of another revelation further on. At the outset this Figure appears in the protevangel as the "Seed of Woman" who is to come in the fulness of time to "bruise the serpent's head." He appears and reappears, now in kingly guise, again as "a man of sorrows and acquainted with grief," and again with a name written on his vesture, "Emmanuel," which being interpreted is "God with us."

This Book, claiming to be the written Word of God, makes us acquainted with his being, personality and moral attributes; but it does not exhaust the theme. It leads us along a road, lighted by types and prophecies, until it opens into another and clear road, the incarnate Word of God.

This fifth road, the Incarnation, is the way which all truth-seekers must pursue if they would finally arrive at a just and saving knowledge of God.

It is here that we meet Christ, bringing the message from the throne of the Father. He comes into our world with the express purpose of making God known to us. As it is written, "No man hath seen God at any time; the only begotten Son which is in the bosom of the Father, he hath declared him."

He is called the Word because he is the medium of communication between the Infinite and the finite. As it is written, "In the beginning was the Word, and the Word was with God, and the Word was God; and the Word was made flesh and dwelt among us." That is to say, the Incarnation is the articulation of the speech of God. In the Scriptures we have a letter from God; but in the Incarnation, we have the coming down of God to unveil himself before us.

Christ, the Revelation of the Father

If, then, we are ever to learn theology it must be as disciples, sitting in a docile attitude at the feet of Christ. He, as the incarnate Son, is our authoritative Teacher. What, therefore, has he to say about God?

Concerning the moral attributes of God, the teaching of Jesus is indubitably clear. "God is a spirit," he says, "and they that worship him must worship him in spirit and in truth." It need scarcely be said that a spirit, though invisible and impalpable, is a real self-conscious personality. The communion of Jesus with this Spirit is that of one person with another. He does not speak to Law, not to Energy, nor to an indefinable "Something not ourselves that maketh for righteousness," but to One with whom he is on familiar terms. "The only begotten Son which is *in the bosom of the Father*, he hath declared him."

As to divine providence, he speaks in no uncertain tone. The God whom he unveils is in and over all. Out on the hillsides he bids us "Consider the lilies, how they grow," and assures us that our Father, "who careth for them, will much more care for us." In pursuance of this fact he encourages us to pray, saying, "Ask and it shall be given you, seek and ye shall find, knock and it shall be opened unto you." Oh, great heart of the Infinite, quick to respond to our every cry for help! The doctrine of prayer, as taught by Jesus, is simplicity itself. We are to run to God with our longings as children to their parents: "For if ye, being evil, know how to give good gifts unto your children, how much more shall your Father which is in heaven give good things to them that ask him."

As to the moral attributes of God, the teaching of Jesus is not only clear but most emphatic, because at this point it touches vitally our eternal welfare. The divine holiness is presented not so much as an attribute as the condition of God's being. It is the light emanating from his throne, of which Christ is the supreme manifestation. Christ said, "I am the light of the world"; and this light must ever be reflected in the life of his disciples, as he said, "Ye are the light of the world; let your light so shine before men that they may see your good works and glorify God." This holiness is not merely freedom from moral contamination, but such a sensitive aversion to sin as makes it impossible for God to look with complacency upon any creature who is defiled by it. Hence the appeal to the cultivation of a holy life, since "without holiness no man shall see God."

Out of this atmosphere of holiness proceed two attributes which, like opening arms, embrace the world. One of them is Justice, or regard for law. No teacher ever lived, not even Moses, who emphasized as deeply as did Jesus Christ the integrity of the moral law. He defended not only the law itself but the penalties affixed to its violation. The Decalogue is not so severe an arraignment of sin as the Sermon on the Mount, which rings with the inviolability of law.

The other of the outstretched arms is Love. The fulness of divine love is set forth in the words of Jesus: "When ye pray say, 'Our Father'." It was wisely observed by Madame de Stael that if Jesus had never done anything in the world except to teach us "Our Father," he would have conferred an inestimable boon upon all the children of men. God's love is manifest in the unceasing gifts of his providence; but its crowning token is the grace of salvation. "God so loved the world, that he gave his only begotten Son, that whosoever believeth in him should not perish, but have everlasting life."

Now the reconciliation between Love and Justice is found at the Cross. Here "mercy and truth are met together; righteousness and peace have kissed each other." As law is sacred and inviolable, its penalty must be inflicted. It must be inflicted either upon the malefactor or upon some competent substitute who shall volunteer to suffer for him. It is the only begotten Son who volunteers, saying, "Here am I, send me!" The justice of God is shown in the suffering inflicted upon his only begotten Son; and his love is correspondingly shown in the proffer of all the benefits of that vicarious suffering to every one on the sole condition of faith.

It pleased God to vindicate his supreme majesty before his ancient people in the controversy on Carmel. All day the pagan priests assembled at their altar cried, "O Baal, hear us"; but there was no voice nor any that regarded. At evening the lone prophet of Jehovah stood beside his altar and calmly made his prayer, "O God of Israel, let it be known this day that Thou art God!" Was there any that regarded? Lo, yonder in the twilight sky a falling fleece of fire! In awe-struck silence the people saw it descending, lower and lower, until it touched the sacrifice and consumed it. The logic of the argument was irresistible. They cried with one accord, "Jehovah is the God."

The antitype and parallel of that great controversy is at Calvary, where Christ, at once the ministering priest and the sacrifice upon the altar, made his last prayer with hands outstretched upon the cross; and the descending fire consumed him as a whole burnt offering for the world's sin. The logic, here also, is unanswerable. In all the world there is no other gospel which adequately sets forth the divine love. By the power of truth, by the triumph of righteousness, by the logic of events, by the philosophy of history, by the blood of the atonement, let the world answer, "Our God is the God of salvation; and there is none other beside him!"

The failure of other religions and philosophies has been grotesquely pathetic. The irony of Elijah on Carmel is merely an echo of the divine burst of laughter out of heaven in response to those who cry: "Let us break his band asunder and cast away his cords from us!" "He that sitteth in the heavens shall laugh; the Lord shall have them in derision." The pantheons crumble and the priests die; one altar remains, to wit, the cross on Calvary. It is the sole altar and supreme argument of the true God.

But every man must for himself make answer to that argument. Each for himself, must fight his way into the truth. It is like the grapple which Jacob had with an unseen antagonist at the brookside. As the night wore on he came to understand that Omnipotence had laid hold upon him. Then came a sudden wrench and Jacob fell, disabled. God had thrown him! He sank a helpless man, but, clinging still, cried, "I will not let Thee go except Thou bless me!" And thereupon the blessing was given, a blessing which God had waited through the weary years to bestow upon him: "Thy name shall be called no more Jacob, 'the Supplanter,' but Israel; for as a prince hast thou prevailed with God." Then and there he received his guerdon of knighthood and entered into the higher life. At the close of that conflict the light of morning was glowing on the hills of Edom; how significant are the words, "And the sun arose upon him!"

The new life had begun; the long quest was over; Jacob had found God. And he went his way limping on his shrunken thigh, to bear through all the after years the token of that struggle until he came to heaven's gate, at peace with God.

It is thus that every man finds God; in a close grapple that ends in self-surrender, an utter yielding to the beneficent power of God.

So true life begins with knowing God. It begins when a man, oppressed by doubt and uncertainty, hears his voice saying, "Reach hither thy hand and thrust it into my side!" It begins when, standing under the cross, he realizes, as Luther did, "He died for me, for me!" Then the day breaks and the shadows flee away. Love conquers doubt, and the soul, beholding the unveiling of the Infinite in the passion of Christ cries out, "My Lord and My God!"

H. M. SYDENSTRICKER (1858-1914) was born in Lewisburg, West Virginia. He was educated at Washington and Lee University; the College of Wooster, where he received his Ph.D.; and at Union Theological Seminary in Virginia. He had an extensive pastoral ministry in Presbyterian (USA) churches in Missouri, Mississippi, and Texas. This pastor-evangelist-scholar combined this pastoral call with teaching positions at Daniel Baker College in Texas, and at Belvidere College in West Point, Mississippi. From his pen came *The Epic of the Orient* and *Nameless Immortals.*

55

The Science of Conversion

By Rev. H. M. Sydenstricker, Ph.D.*

By Rev. H. M. Sydenstricker, Ph.D.
WEST POINT, MISSISSIPPI

Edited by Arnold D. Ehlert, Th.D.

1. THE CASE STATED

The penetration of scientific investigation into the erstwhile unknown regions of things is one of the wonders of the age. All departments of creation are yielding up their secrets to the searching eye of science.

The causes of things are being sought after, not only in the natural world, but in all realms as well, so that things may be brought more certainly and directly under the human will. The unseen operations by which powerful results are produced are forced to yield and tell their secrets. New powers are discovered in all realms of investigation and subdued as never before to the service of man. Practically everything is reduced to science, and men are learning the how and the wherefore of things physical, mental and spiritual. The better these things are understood, the more completely are we the masters of the world for whose subjection man was commissioned.

Now our inquiry is whether the conversion of the human soul — the divinely wrought new birth — lies within the range of scientific investigation. Can the operations of the divine forces and the divinely appointed means for the conversion of a soul be made to yield to scientific research, so that we can produce results with the same degree of certainty as does the chemist in his laboratory? Do the laws of cause and effect operate in the spiritual realm as in the natural world, and can we apply spiritual means and causes with the same degree of certainty as in physical things? Can we get out of the realm of the uncertain and the vague in working with human souls and operate with absolute assurance of adequate and satisfactory results?

In this greatest of all works, and which is practically committed to man, has God left us to absolute uncertainties as to results? Is it not true that if the divinely ordained means be properly used the results can be obtained with the same scientific certainty as in other things, and results also which are in no sense spurious but the actual effect of efficient and properly applied causes? Are not the promises of God absolute, and do not many incidents in the work and history of the Church demonstrate that the conversion of souls was the direct result of God-appointed and man-applied means thereto, operated by purely scientific methods, although the workers had no thought of science in their work? Are we not bound to obey God's laws in all scientific operations in the physical world, and must we not scientifically obey his laws in the higher realm of his domain?

2. The Case Diagnosed

A careful diagnosis of the case under consideration may help us towards a scientific answer to our investigation. To know the patient, and especially to know precisely the nature of the disease, is of prime importance in the successful treatment of it. Otherwise, all treatment is mere guesswork.

Our subject in this inquiry is a degenerate human soul — degenerate meaning an inherent unrighteousness and an innate corruption that has affected every fiber and faculty of the human soul. This total depravity does not mean that man is actually and practically as mean as he is capable of being, but it means that the total man is depraved in all of his parts, and that he is born in that condition.

This native degeneracy is of a twofold nature: First, it is a legal condemnation descending to every human soul from a justly condemned ancestry who represented and stood for the whole race in the government of God. Second, it is a complete moral corruption of the whole soul, so that all the faculties of the soul are affected in such a way as to make them incapable of right action, so that every imagination of the heart is only evil continually. This morally degenerate man, in the adult stage, is also guilty of manifold actual sins, confirming his condemnation and making his moral nature all the more depraved. In addition to this already depraved condition, this degenerate man has no desire for a better life; his perverted natural taste refuses it, and he is even unwilling to consider anything better. He actually loves his depraved condition and revels in the things that develop still more the baser principles in him. Moreover, his intellect is so blunted that he is incapable of apprehending spiritual truths and his eyes are so stigmatized that he cannot see the light.

Such then is the character of the unconverted man, the subject now under consideration. And it is very evident, that while we may be able with the aid of divine revelation and human observation and experience to diagnose the case correctly, the remedy is found in a higher realm, though it may be applied in part through human agencies.

3. The Divine Proposition

In view of this apparently hopeless case, what is the divine proposition regarding it? What does the divine plan contemplate? It is quite evident that the ultimate goal of the divine proposition is to get rid of sin. But to get rid of the sin we must get rid of the sinner, otherwise sin remains.

In getting rid of the sinner two things are possible, either by judgment to destroy the sinner and with him also the sin, or by divine grace to convert the sinner and thus remove the sin. Both methods are used in the divine government, but conversion is what now concerns us. The divine proposition is not to destroy the sinner, but to save him by making out of him a totally new man — to transform him from a child of sin into a real child of God. Not only a son of God, but an actually born child, so that by birth he becomes an heir of God and a joint-heir with Christ to a heavenly inheritance.

That the divine power is sufficient for such an achievement is not to be questioned for a moment. But does the work fall within the range of scientific investigation and are the methods to be used strictly scientific? Is the divine method in applying complete salvation to this awfully degenerate soul really scientific? Is it supposable that God is less scientific in this the very greatest of all his works than he is in the lesser things in his government?

Does he work by one set of laws in the natural world, and by different laws, or no laws at all, in the higher spiritual realm?

But if God is scientific — if the conversion of the human soul is accomplished by scientific methods — it follows that the work is best done when done by God's methods, if indeed it can be done at all in any other way. And if God's method is scientific, has he adequately revealed to us his method so that it can be certainly and successfully used by us as his workers? And if this revelation is made to us we dare not depart from God's method, whatever other methods may be suggested. For, if we depart from the methods God has given and by which God himself works, our work will be a failure entirely or the results will be inadequate and spurious.

4. The Means Discovered

God's proposition being stated and his methods being scientific, we must next discover the means by which the work is to be accomplished. Let it be remembered that in all things pertaining to man in both temporal and spiritual matters God works by means, and usually through human agencies.

But in the work of converting the human soul it is evident that the means are twofold. First, those means applied directly on the part of God to the soul from within; and second, those means applied from without through the senses by human agencies and instrumentalities. It is a fact, however, that even the means used directly on the part of God are at least in part applied through human agencies; so that the conversion of adult souls, so far as we are able to see, is ordinarily through human instrumentalities.

Hence the means by which the human soul is converted, or born into the family of God, are:

(1) The divine Spirit, which is the sole divine agent, and without which no soul, of infant or adult, can ever pass from spiritual death to spiritual life. This divine Spirit operates how and where he pleases and with or without means and agencies.

(2) The Word of God, which is the sword of the Spirit, reaching and quickening men's souls through the reasoning and emotional faculties. The Word is effectual only as accompanied by the quickening power of the Spirit, while at the same time it may be variously applied externally.

(3) The benign influence of Christians, demonstrating the reality and power and blessedness of the new life in the soul of the converted man.

(4) Real prayer, by which the regenerate soul brings the unregenerate to the very feet of the divine Saviour and insistently implores the divine grace.

(5) An absolute faith on the part of the human agent. This faith is an absolute confidence in the ability of God and in his purpose to accomplish the work through the means then being used, whenever the conditions thereto are complied with. There can be no true faith when the available means are not used and the known conditions not complied with.

5. The Means Applied

Here is where the science of conversion is especially manifest. Everything in nature must be done in God's way, and God's way is always scientific, and all things are best done when we adhere most closely to God's methods. The conversion of the human soul is no exception to this rule. We can convert men most successfully when we adhere strictly to the divine science of the work. Our failures are no doubt largely due to our not complying with God's ways of doing the work.

We adhere strictly to God's laws in growing our crops. The seed is first placed where the dormant life powers are aroused and the seed caused to germinate. Afterwards follow the blade, the stalk and the mature fruit. No human power or wisdom can change this law of germination and growth. So the human soul being spiritually dead is incapable of doing anything towards an awakening to a new life; and being also unable even to will to do such a thing, it is quite evident that the very first thing essential is the direct application of the life-giving power of the divine Spirit to the dormant soul. This life-giving touch prepares the soul for the effectual application of all the other appointed means by which the soul is brought into the realities and fullness of the new life. But ordinarily, if not always, the application of the life-giving Spirit through human agencies is in answer to prayer somehow and somewhere. May it not be true that every soul born into the kingdom of God is in answer to the supplication of some earnest Christian whose heart is as large as humanity and whose prayer touches every lost soul of man?

Hence prayer is scientifically the first means and the prime force to be applied by the true Christian in producing the conversion of a human soul. It is perfectly certain that nothing can be effectively done until the Spirit is applied, and the Spirit is ordinarily given in answer to prayer — that is, the quickening Spirit that arouses the soul and prepares it for the effectual application of other divinely appointed means. We question whether the Spirit is ever given without prayer where prayer is available, as in all other things human agencies are required when available.

Second to the Spirit's work, and along with it, is the application of the Word by which the soul of the hearer is reached through the intellect, the reasoning faculties being aroused, and through them the appeal of the Gospel is forced into the newly awakened conscience. Here all the powers of eloquence and reason and persuasion come into full play and are made effectual in turning the eyes of the awakened soul to the cross.

Next, the awakened soul now becomes co-operative with the divine Spirit, and with the Word and with other external means, and the result is belief in the Word on the part of the aroused soul, and through the receiving of the Word there follows an actual, personal, living faith in the Christ set forth in the Gospel, followed by outward confession, obedience and Christian service.

Hence the scientific order of the application of the means for the conversion of a soul is: The prayer of the Church and the Christian worker for the application of the quickening Spirit on the part of God. The preaching of the Word and the use of other external means. The responsive and co-operative and receptive act of the sinner, now made willing by the Spirit of God. And the wholly personal act of faith in Christ on the part of the sinner by which he actually receives by his own volition the Saviour as set before him, confesses him and becomes obedient to him as his Lord and Master.

6. The Conditions Imposed

In all scientific operations there are conditions that must be complied with, otherwise the results are either spurious or disastrous. This accounts for the vast number of spurious conversions and lapses in the churches. Unscrupulous and ignorant men seeking after a display of numbers use all sorts of devices in all sorts of ways to produce apparent conversions. Just as well might the chemist go into his laboratory and throw together any and all sorts of chemicals and expect correct and scientific results. Correct results might accidentally follow, but the almost inevitable results would be poisons and explosions. Is not the same true in the unscriptural and unscientific methods used by many who pose as expert conversionists in so many of the pseudo-revivals now so much in vogue?

The conditions imposed for the true conversion of souls are both philosophic and scientific, and at the same time supremely gracious and benevolent, ever looking to the highest good of all concerned, both to the soul that is being saved and the worker through whom the results are accomplished.

These conditions are imposed by God himself. Hence he becomes responsible for the results when the conditions are really fulfilled on our part. The results may not always be as we may calculate or desire, but they will always correspond to the means as used.

These conditions are twofold. On the part of the Christian worker they consist in applying God's means for the salvation of men in God's ways. The danger here is in applying all sorts of human means in any way whatever so as to obtain apparent results. Often we blame God directly or indirectly for the poverty and character of the results, when as a matter of fact we have never complied with God's conditions, which are always natural, reasonable and scientific.

Second, on the part of the sinner these conditions apply, because although he is spiritually dead, he is intellectually alive and morally a free agent, and hence responsible for his conduct, including his unbelief and his rejection of Christ as his Saviour. He is responsible for the opportunities placed before him, and consequently he is responsible for the conditions God has imposed for the salvation of his soul. No man, in any Gospel land at least, can truthfully and conscientiously claim that he has fully met God's conditions for his salvation and that God has rejected him, or that the results have not been adequate and scientific. On the other hand, no Christian worker has a right to the God-promised results until he has met the God-imposed conditions. A partial use of means, used in an indifferent way for only a limited time, is not scientific and is not meeting God's conditions. This is true not only in the work of actual soul-saving, but in the Christian life as well.

7. THE RESULTS OBTAINED

The results obtained in the conversion of a human soul are equally scientific with the means used thereto.

The primary result is a new man. Not an old man made over, but a new man, possessed of a new life and endowed with new and enlarged possibilities. A man with a new vision both of this life and of the eternal future. A man inspired with a new hope, the flukes of which are struck into the very throne of God and which is a positive and inalienable title to an inheritance in heaven. A man with a positive personal faith in Christ. A faith that makes Christ his personal possession with all that Christ is and all that he has and all that he has done. A man whose whole life is reversed from the service of sin and self to the kind and willing service of Christ as his new Master.

That such a man is the scientific result of the means that have been applied goes without argument. It is only in harmony with the great laws of God that govern his kingdom from the combination of the most minute chemical atoms to the swing of the spheres in his boundless universe.

First of all, life produces life of its own kind. Hence the life-giving touch of the divine Spirit imparts life of its own kind to the dormant soul and it becomes the living son of God. This result is as manifestly scientific as can be found in all nature. The immortal soul already exists endowed with all the possibilities of a finite being, but the eternal life is the scientific result of the life-giving touch of the Spirit of God. It is in fact impossible that the result be otherwise.

Another result is the effect produced upon the will of the convert. His will is renewed and is now in harmony with the divine will, and this is produced by the action of the divine will upon the will of the sinner. Here again the divine begets its likeness in the changed will of the converted soul, which is a natural and scientific result.

Again, through the enlightening and persuading power of the Gospel the sinner is led to see the error of his way and the condition of his soul, and repentance of sins and faith in Christ are the result. The man is outwardly converted and his whole life and service reversed. These are again the scientific results of the means used according to the divine order of things. That these results do not always follow the preaching of the Word may be largely due to the fact that the means have been used amiss for the mere gratification of the lust of the worker, or that other necessary means have been neglected, especially prayer. And the reason why so many conversions are not genuine is due to the fact that they are merely external conversions, the result of exciting rant called preaching the Gospel, while prayer for the internal work of the Spirit has been totally ignored.

In the whole process of conversion it is a fundamental principle that like begets like, and means produce results according to purely scientific laws, and if the results are not scientific they are spurious, external and temporary. A beautiful and pointed illustration is found in the conversion of the congregation at the house of Cornelius. The means were used — though unwittingly on the part of men — in the scientific order. Prayer, the Holy Spirit, the preached Word; and the results were conversion, confession and Christian service.

56

The Passing of Evolution

By Professor George Frederick Wright, D.D., LL.D.
OBERLIN COLLEGE, OBERLIN, OHIO

Revised and edited by Glenn O'Neal, Ph.D.

The word evolution is in itself innocent enough, and has a large range of legitimate use. The Bible, indeed, teaches a system of evolution. The world was not made in an instant, or even in one day (whatever period day may signify) but in six days. Throughout the whole process there was an orderly progress from lower to higher forms of matter and life. In short, there is an established order in all the Creator's work. Even the Kingdom of Heaven is like a grain of mustard seed which being planted grew from the smallest beginnings to be a tree in which the fowls of heaven could take refuge. So everywhere there is "first the blade, then the ear, then the full corn in the ear."

The word, however, has come into much deserved disrepute by the injection into it of erroneous and harmful theological and philosophical implications. The widely current doctrine of evolution which we are now compelled to combat is one which practically eliminates God from the whole creative process, and relegates mankind to the tender mercies of a mechanical universe, the wheels of whose machinery are left to move on without any immediate divine direction.

This doctrine of evolution received such an impulse from Darwinism and has been so often confounded with it, that it is important at the outset to discriminate the two. Darwinism was not, in the mind of its author, a theory of universal evolution, and Darwin rarely used the word. The title of Darwin's great work was, *The Origin of Species by Means of Natural Selection.* The problem which he set out to solve touched but a small part of the field of evolution. His proposition was simply that species may reasonably be supposed to be nothing more than enlarged or accentuated varieties, which all admit are descendants from a common ancestry. For example, there are a great many varieties of oak trees. But it is supposed by all botanists that these have originated from a common ancestor. Some chestnut trees, however, differ less from some oak trees than the extreme varieties of both do from each other. Nevertheless, the oak and the chestnut are reckoned not as varieties, but as different species. But the dividing line between them is so uncertain that it is impossible to define it in language; hence, some botanists have set up an independent species between the two, which they call "chestnut oak."

What Is a "Species"?

This, however, is but a single illustration of the great difficulty which scientific men have had in determining a satisfactory definition of species. That most generally accepted is "a collection of individual plants and animals which resemble each other so closely that they can reasonably be supposed to have descended from a common ancestor." It is easy to see, however, that this definition begs the whole question at issue. For we have no certain means of knowing how widely the progeny may in some cases differ from the parent; and we do not know but that resemblances may result from the action of other causes than that of parental connection. The definition is far from being one that would be accepted in the exact sciences.

It may be "reasonably supposed" that such small differences as separate species have resulted through variations of individuals descended from a common ancestry, yet it is a long leap to assert that, therefore, it may be reasonably supposed that all the differences between animals or between plants may have arisen in a similar manner.

A characteristic difference between the African elephant and the Indian elephant, for example, is that the African elephant has three toes on his hind feet and the Indian has four. While, therefore, it may not be a great stretch of imagination to suppose that this difference has arisen by a natural process, without any outside intervention, it is an indefinitely larger stretch of the imagination to suppose that all the members of the general family to which they belong have originated in a like manner; for, this family, or order, includes not only the elephant, but the rhinoceros, hippopotamus, tapir, wild boar and horse.

But many of Darwin's followers and expounders have gone to extreme lengths in their assertions, and have announced far more astonishing conclusions than these. Not only do they assert, with a positiveness of which Darwin was never guilty, that species have had a common origin through natural causes, but that all organic beings had been equally independent of supernatural forces. It is a small thing that the two species of elephant should have descended from a common stock. Nothing will satisfy them but to assert that the elephant, the lion, the bear, the mouse, the kangaroo, the whale, the shark, the shad, birds of every description — indeed, all forms of animal life, including the oyster and the snail — have arisen by strictly natural processes from some minute speck of life, which originated in far distant time.

Origin of Life

It need not be said that such conclusions must rest upon very attenuated evidence, such as is not permitted to have weight in the ordinary affairs of life. But even this is only the beginning with thoroughgoing evolutionists. To be consistent they must not only have all species of animals or plants, but all animals and plants descending from a common origin, which they assert to be an almost formless protoplasm, which is supposed to have appeared in the earliest geological ages. Nor does this by any means bring them to their final goal, for to carry out their theory they must leap to the conclusion that life itself has originated, spontaneously, by a natural process, from inorganic matter.

But of this they have confessedly no scientific proof. For, so far as is yet known, life springs only from antecedent life. The first chapter of Genesis, to which reference has already been made, furnishes as perfect a definition of plant life as has ever been given. Plant life, which is the earliest form of living matter, is described "as that which has seed in itself" and "yields seed after his kind." Earlier in the nineteenth century the theory of spontaneous generation had many supporters. It was believed that minute forms of plant life had sprung up from certain conditions of inorganic matter without the intervention of seeds or spores. Bottles of water, which were supposed to have been shut off from all access of living germs, were found, after standing a sufficient length of time, to swarm with minute living organisms.

But experiments showed that germs must have been in the water before it was set aside. For, on subjecting it to a higher degree of temperature, so as apparently to kill the germs, no life was ever developed in it. All positive basis for bridging the chasm between living matter and lifeless matter has thus been removed from the realm of science.

The Mystery of First Beginnings

This brings us to the important conclusion that the origin of life, and we may add of variations, is to finite minds an insoluble problem; and so Darwin regarded it. At the very outset of his speculation, he rested on the supposition that the Creator in the beginning breathed the forces of life into several forms of plants and animals, and at the same time endowed them with the marvelous capacity for variation which we know they possess.

This mysterious capacity for variation lies at the basis of his theory. If anything is to be evolved in an orderly manner from the resident forces of primordial matter it must first have been involved through the creative act of the divine Being. But no one knows what causes variation in plants or animals. Like the wind it comes, but we know not whence it cometh or whither it goeth. Breeders and gardeners do not attempt to produce varieties directly. They simply observe the variations which occur, and select for propagation those which will best serve their purposes. They are well aware that variations which they perpetuate are not only mysterious in their origin, but superficial in their character.

In Darwinism the changing conditions of life, to which every individual is subjected, are made to take the place of the breeder and secure what is called natural selection. In this case, however, the peculiarities selected and preserved must always be positively advantageous to the life of the individuals preserved. But to be of advantage a variation must both be considerable in amount, and correlated to other variations so that they shall not be antagonistic to one another. For example, if a deer were born with the capability of growing antlers so large that they would be a decided advantage to him in his struggle for existence, he must at the same time have a neck strong enough to support its weight, and other portions of his frame capable of bearing the increased strain. Otherwise, his antlers would be the ruin of all his hopes instead of an advantage. It is impossible to conceive of this combination of advantageous variations without bringing in the hand and the designing mind of the Original Creator.

Of this, as of every other variety of evolution, it can be truly said in the words of one of the most distinguished physicists, Clerk Maxwell: "I have examined all that have come within my reach, and have found that every one must have a God to make it work." By no stretch of legitimate reasoning can Darwinism be made to exclude design. Indeed, if it should be proved that species have developed from others of a lower order, as varieties are supposed to have done, it would strengthen rather than weaken the standard argument from design.

But the proof of Darwinism even is by no means altogether convincing, and its votaries are split up into as many warring sects as are the theologians. New schools of evolutionists arise as rapidly as do new schools of biblical critics. Strangely enough the "Neo-Darwinians" go back to the theory of Lamarck that variations are the result of effort and use on the part of the animal; whereas Darwin denied the inheritance of acquired characteristics; while Weissmann goes to the extreme of holding that natural selection must be carried back to the ultimate atoms of primordial matter, where he would set up his competitive struggle for existence. Romanes and Gulick, however, insist that specific variations often occur from "segregation," entirely independent of natural selection.

Nor do the champions of evolution have a very exalted estimate of each other's opinions. In a letter to Sir Joseph Hooker in 1866, referring to Spencer, Darwin wrote: "I feel rather mean when I read him: I could bear and rather enjoy feeling that he was twice as ingenious and clever as myself, but when I feel that he is about a dozen times my superior, even in the master art of wriggling, I feel aggrieved. If he had trained himself to observe more, even at the expense, by a law of balancement, of some loss of thinking power, he would have been a wonderful man" (*Life and Letters*, Vol. ii., p. 239).

To account for heredity, Darwin, in his theory of "pangenesis," suggested that infinitesimal "gemmules" were thrown off from every part of the body or plant, and that they had "a mutual affinity for each other leading to their aggregation either into buds or into the sexual elements." But when he ventured the opinion that these were the same as Spencer's "vitalized molecules" in which dwelt an "intrinsic aptitude to aggregate into the forms" of the species, Spencer came out at once and said that it was no such thing. They were not at all alike. Darwin, in reply, said he was sorry for the mistake. But he had feared that as he did not know exactly what Spencer meant by his "vitalized molecules," a charge of plagiarism might be brought against him if he did not give Spencer due credit. But others seemed to find it as hard to understand what Darwin meant by his "gemmules" with their marvelous mutual "affinity" for each other, as he did what Spencer meant by "vitalized molecules." Bates wrote him that after reading the chapter twice he failed to understand it; and Sir H. Holland set it down as "very tough," while Hooker and Huxley thought the language was mere tautology, and both failed "to gain a distinct idea" from it (*Letters of Darwin*, Vol. ii, p. 262).

Indeed, thoroughgoing evolution has no such universal acceptance as is frequently represented to be the case. Few naturalists are willing to project the theory beyond the narrow limits of their own province. Such naturalists as Asa Gray and Alfred Russel Wallace, who in a general way accepted the main provisions of Darwinism, both insisted that natural selection could attain its ends only as giving effect to the designs of the Creator. Agassiz, Owen, Mivart, Sir William Dawson, and Weissmann either rejected the hypothesis altogether or so modified it that it bore little resemblance to the original. Professor Shaler declared, shortly before his death, "that the Darwinian hypothesis is still unverified." Dr. Etheride of the British Museum said that "in all this great museum there is not a particle of evidence of transmutation of species." Professor Virchow of Berlin declared that "the attempt to find the transition from the animal to man has ended in total failure." The list could be extended indefinitely. Haeckel, indeed, had from his imagination supplied the missing link between man and the apes, calling it Pithecanthropus. While, a few years after, Du Bois discovered in recent volcanic deposits in Java a small incomplete skull in one place, and near by a diseased femur (thigh bone), and not far away two molar teeth. These were hailed as remains of the missing link, and it was forthwith dubbed Pithecanthropus Erectus. The skull was indeed small, being only two-thirds the size of that of the average man. But Professor Cope, one of our most competent comparative anatomists, concluded that as the "femur is that of a man, it is in no sense a connecting link." The erect form carries with it all the anatomical characteristics of a perfect man (*Primary Factors*, 1896, pt. 1, chap. vi.).

But the Darwinians themselves have made their full share of erroneous assumptions of facts, and of illogical conclusions. It will suffice for our present purpose to refer to a few of these.

Darwin himself made two great mistakes which in the eyes of discerning students vitiate his whole theory.

1. As to Geological Time. The establishment of Darwin's theory as he originally proposed it involved the existence of the earth in substantially its present condition for an indefinite, not to say infinite, period of time. In one of his calculations in the first edition of *Origin of Species*, he arrived at the startling conclusion that 306,662,400 years is "a mere trifle" of geological time. It was not long, however, before his son, Sir George H. Darwin, demonstrated to the general satisfaction of physicists and astronomers that life could not have begun on earth more than 100 million years ago, and probably not more than 50 million; while Lord Kelvin would reduce the period to less than 30 million years, which Alfred Russel Wallace affirms is sufficient time for the deposition of all the geological strata. Evolutionists are now fighting hard and against great odds to be allowed 100 million years for the development of the present drama of life upon the earth.

The difference between 306,662,400 years, regarded as "a mere trifle," and 24,000,000, or even 100,000,000 years, as constituting the whole sum, is tremendous. For, it necessitates a rapidity in the development of species which must be regarded as by leaps and bounds, and so would well accord with the theory of creation by special divine intervention.

If a critic of Darwinism had made so egregious an error as this which Darwin introduced into the very foundation of his theory, he would have been the subject of an immense amount of ridicule. The only excuse which Darwin could make was that at the time no one knew any better. But that excuse shows the folly of building such an enormous theory upon an unknown foundation.

2. As to the Minuteness of Beneficial Variations. The unlimited geological time required by Darwin's original theory is closely bound up with his view of the minuteness of the steps through which progress had been made. The words which he constantly uses when speaking of variations are "slight," "small," "extremely gradual," "insensible gradations." But early in the discussion it was shown by Mivart that "minute incipient variations in any special direction" would be valueless; since, to be of advantage in any case, they must be considerable in amount. And furthermore, in order to be of permanent advantage, a variation of one organ must be accompanied with numerous other variations in other parts of the organism.

The absurdity in supposing the acquisition of advantageous qualities by chance variations is shown in the pertinent illustration adduced by Herbert Spencer from the anatomy of the cat. To give the cat power of leaping to any advantageous height, there must be a simultaneous variation in all the bones, sinews, and muscles of the hinder extremities; and, at the same time, to save the cat from disaster when it descends from an elevation, there must be variation of a totally different character in all the bones and tendons and muscles of the fore limbs. To learn the character of these changes, one has but to "contrast the markedly bent hind limbs of a cat with its almost straight fore limbs, or contrast the silence of the upward spring on to the table with the thud which the fore paws make as it jumps off the table." So numerous are the simultaneous changes necessary to secure any advantage here, that the probabilities against their arising fortuitously run up into billions, if not into infinity; so that they are outside of any rational recognition.

The Origin of Man

The failure of evolution to account for man is conspicuous. Early in the Darwinian discussion, Alfred Russel Wallace, Darwin's most distinguished co-worker, instanced various physical peculiarities in man which could not have originated through natural selection alone, but which necessitated the interference of a superior directing power.

Among these are (a) the absence in man of any natural protective covering. The nakedness of man which exposes him to the inclemency of the weather could never in itself have been an advantage to the idea of natural selection. It could have been of use only when his intelligence was so developed that he could construct tools for skinning animals and for weaving and sewing garments. And that practically involves all essential human attributes.

(b) The size of the human brain. Man's brain is out of all proportion to the mental needs of the highest of the animal creation below him. Without man's intelligence such a brain would be an incumbrance rather than an advantage. The weight of the largest brain of a gorilla is considerably less than half that of the average man, and only one third that of the best developed of the human race.

(c) This increase in the size of the brain is connected also with a number of other special adaptations of the bodily frame to the wants of the human mind. For example, the thumb of the hind limb of the ape becomes a big toe in man, which is a most important member for a being which would walk in an upright position, but a disadvantage to one who walks on all fours. The forelimbs of the ape are shortened into the arms of a man, thus adapting them to his upright position and to the various uses which are advantageous in that position. Furthermore, to make it possible to maintain the erect position of man there has to be a special construction of the ball and socket joints in the hip bones and in the adjustment of all the vertebra of the back and neck. All these would be disadvantageous to an ape-like creature devoid of man's intelligence.

(d) Man's intellectual capacity belongs to a different order from that of the lower animals. Naturalists do indeed classify men and apes together in the same genus anatomically. But to denote the human species they add the word "sapiens." That is, they must regard his intelligence as a specific characteristic. The lower animals do indeed have many common instincts with man, and in many cases their instincts are far superior to those of man. But in his reasoning powers man is apparently separated from the lower animals, one and all, by an impassable gulf.

Romanes, after collecting the manifestations of intelligent reasoning from every known species of the lower animals, found that they only equalled, altogether, the intelligence of a child 15 months old. He could find no such boundless outlook of intelligence in the lower animals as there is in man. As any one can see, it would be absurd to try to teach an elephant geology, an eagle astronomy, or a dog theology. Yet there is no race of human beings but has capacity to comprehend these sciences.

Again, man is sometimes, and not improperly, defined as a "tool using animal." No animal ever uses, much less makes, a tool. But the lowest races of men show great ingenuity in making tools, while even the rudest flint inplement bears indubitable evidence of a power to adapt means to ends which places its maker in a category by himself.

Again, man is sometimes, and properly, defined as a "fire-using animal." No animal ever makes a fire. Monkeys do indeed gather round a fire when it is made. But the making of one is utterly beyond their capacity. Man, however, even in his lowest stages knows how to make fire at his will. So great is this accomplishment, that it is no wonder the Greeks looked up to it as a direct gift from heaven.

Again, man may properly be described as a "speaking animal." No other animal uses articulate language. But man not only uses it in speech but in writing. How absurd it would be to try to teach a learned pig to translate and understand the cuneiform inscriptions unearthed from the deserted mounds of Babylonia.

Finally, man may properly be described as a "religious animal," but who would ever think of improving the nature of the lower animals by delivering sermons in their presence or distributing Bibles among them? Yet, the Bible — a Book composed of every species of literature, containing the highest flights of poetry and eloquence ever written, and presenting the sublimest conceptions of God and of the future life ever entertained — has been translated into every language under heaven, and has found in those languages the appropriate figures of speech for effectually presenting its ideas.

The Cumulative Argument

Now, all these peculiarities both in the body and the mind of man, to have been advantageous, must have taken place simultaneously and at the same time have been considerable in amount. To suppose all this to occur without the intervention of the Supreme Designing Mind is to commit logical "hari-kari." Such chance combinations are beyond all possibility of rational belief.

It is fair to add, however, that Darwin never supposed that man was descended from any species of existing apes; but he always spoke of our supposed ancestor as "ape-like," a form, from which the apes were supposed to have varied in one direction as far as man had in another. All efforts, however, to find traces of such connecting links as this theory supposes have failed. The Neanderthal skull was, according to Huxley, capacious enough to hold the brain of a philosopher. The Pithecanthropus Erectus of Du Bois had, as already remarked, the erect form of a man; in fact, was a man. The skeletons of prehistoric man so far as yet unearthed, differ no more from present races of men than existing races and individuals differ from each other.

In short, everything points to the unity of the human race, and to the fact that, while built on the general pattern of the higher animals associated with him in the later geological ages, he differs from them in so many all-important particulars, that it is necessary to suppose that he came into existence as the Bible represents, by the special creation of a single pair, from whom all the varieties of the race have sprung.

It is important to observe, furthermore, in this connection, that the progress of the human race has not been uniformly upward. In fact, the degeneration of races has been more conspicuous than their advancement; while the advancement has chiefly been through the influence of outside forces. The early art of Babylonia and Egypt was better than the later. The religious conceptions of the first dynasties of Egypt were higher than those of the last. All the later forms of civilization shine principally by borrowed light. Our own age excels, indeed, in material advancement. But for art and literature we fall far below the past, and for our best religion we still go back to the psalm singers and prophets of Judea, and to the words of him who spoke "as never man spake." Democracy has no guides whom it dares trust implicitly. We have much reason to fear that those we are following are blind guides leading on to an end which it is not pleasant to contemplate, and from which we can be delivered only by the coming of the Son of Man.

Conclusion

The title of this paper is perhaps a misnomer. For, doubtless, the passing of the present phase of evolution is not final. Theories of evolution have chased each other off the field in rapid succession for thousands of years. Evolution is not a new thing in philosophy, and such is the frailty of human nature that it is not likely to disappear suddenly from among men. The craze of the last half century is little more than the recrudesence of a philosophy which has divided the opinion of men from the earliest ages. In both the Egyptian and the East Indian mythology, the world and all things in it were evolved from an egg; and so in the Polynesian myths. But the Polynesians had to have a bird to lay the egg, and the Egyptians and the Brahmans had to have some sort of a deity to create theirs. The Greek philosophers struggled with the problem without coming to any more satisfactory conclusion. Aniximander, like Professor Huxley, traced everything back to an "infinity" which gradually worked itself into a sort of pristine "mud" (something like Huxley's exploded "bathybius"), out of which everything else evolved; while Thales of Miletus tried to think of water as the mother of everything, and Aneximenes practically deified the air. Diogenes imagined a "mind stuff" (something like Weissmann's "biophores," Darwin's "gemmules possessed with affinity for each other," and Spencer's "vitalized molecules") which acted as if it had intelligence; while Heraclitus thought that fire was the only element pure enough to produce the soul of men. These speculations culminated in the great poem of Lucretius entitled, *De Rerum Natura*, written shortly before the beginning of the Christian era. His atomic theory was something like that which prevails at the present time among physicists. Amid the unceasing motion of these atoms there somehow appeared, according to him, the orderly forms and the living processes of nature.

Modern evolutionary speculations have not made much real progress over those of the ancients. As already remarked, they are, in their bolder forms atheistic; while in their milder forms they are "deistic" — admitting, indeed, the agency of God at the beginning, but nowhere else. The attempt, however, to give the doctrine standing through Darwin's theory of *the Origin of Species by Means of Natural Selection* has not been successful; for at best, the theory can enlarge but little our comprehension of the adequacy of resident forces to produce and conserve variations of species, and cannot in the least degree banish the idea of design from the process.

It is, therefore, impossible to get any such proof of evolution as shall seriously modify our conception of Christianity. The mechanism of the universe is so complicated that no man can say that it is closed to divine interference. Especially is this seen to be the case since we know that the free will of man does pierce the joints of nature's harness and interfere with its order to a limited extent. Man, by cultivation, makes fruits and flowers grow where otherwise weeds would cover the ground. Man makes ten thousand combinations of natural forces which would not occur without his agency. The regular course of nature is interfered with every time a savage shapes a flint implement or builds a canoe, or by friction makes a fire. We cannot banish God from the universe without first stultifying ourselves and reducing man's free will to the level of a mere mechanical force. But man is more than that; and this everyone knows.

The field is now free as it has ever been to those who are content to act upon such positive evidence of the truth of Christianity as the Creator had been pleased to afford them. The evidence for evolution, even in its milder form, does not begin to be as strong as that for the revelation of God in the Bible.

EDWARD JOHN STOBO (1867-1922) was the son of a Scottish Baptist pastor who emigrated to Canada in 1872. The younger Stobo received degrees from McMaster University (B.Th.; B.D.), from Western University (B.A), and from Temple University (D.S.T.). After his ordination as a Baptist minister, he stood behind the pulpit in churches in Ontario and Manitoba. *The Glory of His Robe* was published in 1922, the year its author died.

57

The Apologetic Value of Paul's Epistles

By Rev. E. J. Stobo, Jr., B.A., S.T.D.
SMITH'S FALLS, ONTARIO, CANADA

Abridged and emended by James H. Christian, Th.D.

In this paper we shall deal only with four epistles which are acknowledged by biblical critics of all schools as undoubtedly genuine; viz., Galatians, I and II Corinthians and Romans. The four epistles in question have the advantage of being more or less controversial in their nature. Debate leads to clearness of statement, and we have the advantage of hearing the words of Paul as well as of understanding the views of those against whom he contends. The controversy in these epistles concerns the nature and destination of Christianity, and consequently we may expect to learn what Paul deemed central and essential in the Christian faith. There is enough Christology in these epistles to show us what Paul thought concerning the Great Founder of Christianity. Moreover there are, in these writings, references to the solemn crisis-experience in his spiritual history, and these of necessity have a bearing upon Luke's letters to Theophilus, which are popularly known as the Gospel of Luke and the Acts of the Apostles. With such clues to follow we are able to argue for the credibility of the New Testament documents, and also for the accuracy of the portrait painted of its central figure, the Lord Jesus Christ.

Our first argument has to do with the apologetic value of the references, in Paul's epistles, to his Christian experience.

His theology is an outgrowth of his experience. In such words as law, righteousness, justification, adoption, flesh, spirit, there is undying interest, if we remember the intense, tragic, moral struggle behind Paul's theology.

The passages in these four epistles, which exhibit most conspicuously the autobiographical character, occur in the first chapter of the Epistle to the Galatians and the seventh chapter of the Epistle to the Romans. From the former we learn that he belonged to a class which was thoroughly antagonistic to Jesus. His religion was Judaism. He was an enthusiastic in it. He says: "I advanced in the Jew's religion beyond many of mine own age among my countrymen, being more exceedingly zealous for the traditions of my fathers." In other words, he was a Pharisee of the most extreme type. His great aim in life was to become legally righteous, and thus all his prejudices were most strongly opposed to the new teaching. In the seventh chapter of Romans we learn that Paul in time made a great discovery. One of the commandments, the tenth, forbids coveting; and so he learned that a mere feeling, a state of the heart, is condemned as sin. In that hour his Pharisaism was doomed. "When the commandment came sin revived and I died." He discovered a world of sin within of which he had not dreamed, and legal righteousness seemed unattainable. He had been trying to satisfy the hunger of his soul with legal ordinances; he found them chaff, not wheat, and so he sought for true nourishment. Eventually he became a convert to Christianity.

Paul's conversion is one of the hard problems for those who undertake to give a purely naturalistic solution of the origins of Christianity. All attempts to explain it without recognizing the hand of God in it must be futile. He himself says devoutly concerning it: "It was the good pleasure of God . . . to reveal his Son in me." This argues that Christianity is a supernatural religion.

When a religious crisis comes to a man of Paul's type it possesses deep significance. For him to become a Christian meant everything. He saw that all was over with Judaism and its legal righteousness, all over with the law itself as a way of salvation. He realized that salvation must come to man through the grace of God, and that it might come through that channel to all men alike on equal terms, and that therefore the Jewish prerogative was at an end. These consequences are all borne out in the biographical notice in the first chapters of Galatians.

It can easily be seen that if the accounts of Paul's conversion in the epistles be accepted, they lend support and give value to the accounts in the Acts of the Apostles. The consequences of that conversion as previously indicated are in entire harmony with the teaching of the latter part of the Acts, and so we must come to the conclusion that the contents of that book are trustworthy whether Luke be the author or not. And since Acts of the Apostles purports to be a continuation of the Gospel of Luke, we are led to conclude that the Gospel must be trustworthy also, and that all the Synoptists set forth real facts. Such a conclusion involves the historicity of Jesus Christ.

Our second argument is concerned with the apologetic value of the references in Paul's epistles to the person of Christ.

The conversion of Paul leads back by degrees to the fact of Christ. But what sort of a Christ? The reader will be struck with the fact that, in these epistles, the earthly life of the Christ is represented as singularly free from the miraculous. He is born of a woman, born under the law (Gal. 4:4). He springs from Israel, and is, according to the flesh, from the tribe of Judah and the seed of David (Rom. 9:5; 1:3). He is unknown to the princes of this world (I Cor. 2:8). He is poor, hated, persecuted, crucified (II Cor. 8:9; Gal. 6:14; I Cor. 1:23-25; 2:2). He is betrayed at night just after he has instituted the supper (I Cor. 15:23). He dies on the cross, to which he had been fastened with nails, and is buried (1 Cor. 15:3, 4). This account it will be seen is at one with that of the Synoptists, with the exception that we do not hear of a supernatural birth, nor is there any emphasis placed upon supernatural works. In its main outlines the portrait of the man Jesus agrees perfectly with that of the Synoptic Gospels, and lends credence to their history.

On the other hand, Christ is represented as a being of ideal majesty. The doctrine of Christ's person as found in these four great epistles is no mere theological speculation. It is the outgrowth of religious experience. Jesus was, for Paul, the Lord because he was the Saviour. Four leading truths with reference to Christ are brought into prominence in his writings:

1. *Relation to time.* He is God's Son who was "born of the seed of David according to the flesh." On the side of his humanity our Lord "was born" (Rom. 1:2). That nature begins only then. He is possessed of another nature that dates back long before the incarnation. He is in a peculiar sense God's "own Son"

(Rom. 8:32). His eternal existence is stated in II Cor. 8:9: "Ye know the grace of our Lord Jesus Christ, that though he was rich, yet for your sakes he became poor," and finds full expression in the Epistle to the Philippians (2:5-9). The straggling hints we have in the four great epistles confirm the teaching of the letter to the Philippians, and above all the classic statement of the Fourth Gospel: "In the beginning was the Word."

2. *Relation to man.* Paul says Christ was "made of a woman" (Gal. 4:4), and that he was sent into the world "in the likeness of sinful flesh" (Rom. 8:3); that is, he came into the world by birth and bore to the eye the aspect of any ordinary man. But though Christ came in the likeness of sinful flesh, he was not a sinner. He "knew no sin" (II Cor. 5:21). The mind that was in him before he came ruled his life after he came. However, Paul regards the resurrection as constituting an important crisis in the experience of Christ. Thereby he was declared to be the Son of God with power (Rom. 1:4), "the man from heaven" (I Cor. 15:47). Yet to Paul, Jesus is a real man, a Jew with Hebrew blood in his veins, a descendant of David. The portrait thus painted agrees perfectly with that of the Evangelists who depict him as a real man, but, in some strange fashion, different from other men.

The Son of David was, for Paul, moreover, "The second man" (I Cor. 15:47). This title points out Christ as one who has, for his vocation, to undo the mischief wrought by the transgression of the first man. Hence he is called in sharp contrast to the first man Adam, "a quickening spirit" (I Cor. 15:45). As the one brought death into the world, so the other brings life (I Cor. 15:22). This teaching agrees with the declaration of the Synoptists: "The Son of Man is come to seek and to save that which was lost," and "Thou shalt call his name Jesus, for he shall save his people from their sins."

3. *Relation to the universe.* He is represented in the Epistle to the Colossians as the first-born of all creation, as the originator of creation as well as its final cause, all things in heaven and on earth visible and invisible, angels included, being made by him and for him (Col. 1:15-16). This goes beyond anything found in the four great epistles, yet we may find rudiments of a cosmic

doctrine even in these letters. For Paul it was an axiom that the universe has its final aim in Christ its King (see I Cor. 8:6).

4. *Relation to God.* Paul applies two titles to Christ, "the son of God" and "the Lord." The most convincing proof of the divinity of Christ Paul found in the resurrection. He is "declared to be the Son of God with power, according to the spirit of holiness, by the resurrection of the dead" (Rom. 1:4). Writing to the Corinthians he says: "If Christ hath not been raised then is our preaching vain—your faith is vain, ye are yet in your sins" (I Cor. 15:14-17). He submits to them the proof of his apostleship in the fact that he has seen "Jesus our Lord" (I Cor. 9:1). He tells the Galatians that his Gospel came "through revelation of Jesus Christ" (Gal. 1:12). The Gospel, according to I Cor. 15:3-8, contains five elementary facts: (1) Christ died for our sins; (2) he was buried; (3) he rose on the third day; (4) he appeared to many disciples, and (5) he appeared to Paul himself. These are the things that are vital in Paul's preaching. When we remember that, as a Pharisee, his prejudices were all against the Gospel, we must come to the conclusion that Paul's testimony argues most strongly for the historicity of the resurrection and the truths involved therein.

It may not be out of place to reiterate what has already been stated regarding Paul's use of the expression, "his own Son," in Rom. 8:3. This passage deals with the brotherhood of sons. Jesus, amid the multitudes having the right to call themselves sons of God, is an unique figure, towering above them all. In II Cor. 4:4 it is stated that Christ is the image of God, and in Rom. 8:29 it is said that the destiny of believers is to be conformed to the image of God's Son. The ideal for Christians is to bear the image of Christ. For Christ himself is reserved the distinction of being the image of God. This throws a side light upon Paul's idea of Christ's sonship.

He is represented as the one Lord through whom are all things (I Cor. 8:6). Jesus the Creator of all things. This agrees with John's Gospel when it teaches the creatorship of the Word (John 1:3).

In I Cor. 8:5, 6, the term "Lord" gains equal significance to that of "Son." In view of pagan polytheism, the apostle sets one real God over against the many called gods by paganism, and one real Lord over against its many lords. This inscription indicates that the apostle equated Christ with God. The famous benediction at the close of the Second Epistle to the Corinthians, moreover, implies a very high conception of Christ's person and position. One could scarcely believe that Paul would use such a collocation of phrases as the grace of the Lord Jesus, the love of God and the fellowship of the Holy Spirit, unless he believed Christ to be God. Now all this simply adds force to John's prologue: "In the beginning was the Word, and the Word was with God, and the Word was God."

The four great Pauline epistles agree, in the most important details, with the portraiture given us of Jesus in the Gospels. The conception of the person of Christ, as we have already shown, was not natural to Paul. He was a bitter opponent of Christianity. It was not the result of gradually changing convictions regarding the claims of Jesus Christ; all the testimony which bears upon the subject implies the contrary. It was not due to extreme mysticism, for Paul's writings impress us as being remarkably sane and logical. No endeavor to account for it upon merely natural grounds is satisfactory, and so we must accept his own statement of the case. The truth of the Messiahship of Jesus was a matter of revelation in the experience of his conversion, and if we accept that, we must necessarily accept all that it involves. The Gospels and Epistles do not contradict, but only supplement this portraiture. They add lines of beauty to the rugged outline painted by Paul, and are inextricably connected with the four great epistles. Accepting these letters as genuine and Paul's explanation of his doctrine as true, we must accept the whole of the New Testament documents as credible, and the portraiture of the Christ as that of a real person — Son of man and Son of God, the God-Man.

ARTHUR TAPPAN PIERSON (1837-1911) had the unenviable task of following C.H. Spurgeon in the pulpit of London's Metropolitan Tabernacle when Spurgeon became ill. Before succeeding Spurgeon, Pierson had served Congregational and Presbyterian churches in New York and Pennsylvania from 1860-1911. He was an editor of the *Scofield Reference Bible*. Notable among his books are *Crisis of Missions, The Coming of the Lord*, and *Miracle of Missions*. Besides his theological work, Pierson founded the First Penny Saving Bank of Philadelphia.

58

Divine Efficacy of Prayer

By Arthur T. Pierson, D.D.
PASTOR, SPURGEON'S TABERNACLE, LONDON

All the greatest needs, both of the church and of the world, may be included in one: the need of a higher standard of godliness; and the all-embracing secret of a truly godly life is close and constant contact with the unseen God; that contact is learned and practised, as nowhere else, in the secret place of supplication and intercession.

Our Lord's first lesson in the school of prayer was, and still is: *"enter into thy closet"* (Matt 6:6). The "closet" is the closed place, where we are shut in alone with God, where the human spirit waits upon an unseen Presence, learns to recognize him who is a Spirit, and cultivates his acquaintance, fellowship, and friendship.

Everything else, therefore, *depends upon prayer.* To the praying soul there becomes possible the faith which is the grasp of the human spirit upon the realities and verities of the unseen world. To the praying soul there becomes possible and natural the obedience which is the daily walk of the disciple with the unseen God. To the praying soul there becomes possible the patience, which is the habit of waiting for results yet unseen and hopes yet unrealized. To the praying soul there becomes possible the love that, like a celestial flood, drowns out evil tempers and hateful dispositions, and introduces us to a new world of gentle and generous frames. To the praying soul there becomes possible and increasingly real the holiness which is personal conformity to an unseen divine image and ideal, and the innermost secret of a heavenly bliss.

Those who yearn for revivals naturally lay much stress on preaching. But what is preaching without praying? Sermons are but pulpit performances, learned essays, rhetorical orations, popular lectures, or it may be political harangues, until God gives, in answer to earnest prayer, the preparation of the heart, and the answer of the tongue. It is only he who prays that can truly preach. Many a sermon that has shown no intellectual genius and has violated all homiletic rules and standards has had dynamic spiritual force. Somehow it has moved men, melted them, moulded them. The man whose lips are touched by God's living coal from off the altar may even stammer, but his hearers soon find out that he is on fire with one consuming passion to save souls.

We need saints in the pew as well as in the pulpit, and saint-ship everywhere is fed and nourished on prayer. The man of business who prays, learns to abide in his calling with God; his secular affairs and transactions become sacred by being brought into the searchlight of God's presence. His own business becomes his Father's business. He does not trample on God's commands in order to make money, nor does he drive his trade and traffic through the sacred limits of the Lord's Day, or defraud his cus-tomers, "breaking God's law for a dividend."

Praying souls become prevailing saints. Those who get farthest on in the school of prayer and learn most of its hidden secrets often develop a sort of *prescience* which comes nearest to the prophetic spirit, the Holy Spirit showing them "things to come." They seem, like Savonarola, to know something of the purpose of God, to anticipate his plans, and to forecast the history of their own times. The great supplicators have been also the seers.

There is no higher virtue in a church than that it should be a praying church, for it is *prayer that makes eternal realities both prominent and dominant.* A church and a pastor may have any one of the current, popular types of "religious" life, and souls may not be saved; but, as the late Dr. Skinner of New York, used to say: "If the peculiar type of piety is that which is in-spired by a sense of the powers of the world to come, sinners will be saved and saints edified." Even the world that now is will feel the power of such piety.

Praying feeds missions at home and abroad. It promotes giving. Parsimony is stifled in the atmosphere of God's presence. Gifts are multiplied and magnified when the giver is consecrated. When disciples begin to pray for souls they begin to yearn over them and to be willing to make sacrifices for their salvation. The key that can unlock the treasury of God's promises has marvelous power also to unlock the treasures of hoarded wealth, and makes even the abundance of deep poverty to abound into the riches of liberality till the widow's mites drop into the Lord's hands even more frequently than the millions of merchant princes. No man can breathe freely in the atmosphere of prayer while he stifles benevolent impulses. The giving of money prepares for the giving of self, and thus prayer makes missionary workers as well as missionary givers and supporters.

Few, even amongst the most devout, have ever fully felt how far workers in "the mine of heathendom" depend on those who "hold the ropes." James Gilmour, whose rare and radiant spirit so impressed the rude Mongolians, said that, unprayed for, he would feel like a diver in the river bottom with no air to breathe, or like a fireman on a blazing building with no water in his empty hose.

Prayer is not to be thought the less of because we are so often driven to the throne of grace as a last resort. It is part of the philosophy of prayer that it shall reveal its full efficacy only when and where all beside fails us. Here, as in all else, it is only at the end of self with all its inventions, that we find the beginning of God with all his interpositions.

A praying heart is the one thing that the devil cannot easily counterfeit. It is easy enough to imitate praying lips, so that hypocrites and Pharisees feign devoutness. But only God can open in the heart's depths those springs of supplication that often find no channel in language, but flow out in groanings which cannot be uttered.

It is not worthwhile to waste much time in defending or advocating prayer. Experiment makes argument needless. This is not so much a science to be mastered by study as an art to be learned by practice. Like the Bible, prayer is self-evidencing. It is a mysterious union of divine and human elements not easy of explanation; but to him who prays and puts God to the test along the lines of his own precepts and promises, God proves how real a force prayer is in his moral universe. The best way to prop up prayer is to practice it.

The pivot of piety, therefore, is prayer. A pivot is of double use, it acts as a fastener and as a center; it holds other parts in place, and it is the axis of revolution. Prayer likewise, keeps one steadfast in faith and helps to all holy activity. Hence, as surely as God is lifting his people to a higher level of spirituality, and moving them to a more unselfish and self-denying service, there will be new emphasis laid by them upon supplication, and especially upon intercession.

The revival of the praying-spirit is not only first in order of development, but it is first in order of importance, for without it there is no advance. Generally, if not uniformly, prayer is both starting-point and goal to every movement in which are the elements of permanent progress. Whenever the church's sluggishness is aroused and the world's wickedness arrested, somebody has been praying. If the secret history of all true spiritual advance could be written and read, there would be found some intercessors who, like Job, Samuel, Daniel, Elijah, Paul and James; like Jonathan Edwards, William Carey, George Müller, and Hudson Taylor, have been led to shut themselves in the secret place with God, and have labored fervently in prayer. And as the starting-point is thus found in supplication and intercession, so the final outcome must be that God's people shall have learned to pray; otherwise there will be rapid reaction and disastrous relapse from the better conditions secured.

Prayer Puts Men in Touch with God

There is a divine philosophy behind this fact. The greatest need is to keep in *close touch with God;* the greatest risk is the loss of the sense of the divine. In a world where every appeal is to the physical senses and through them, reality is in direct proportion to the power and freedom of contact. What we see, hear, taste, touch or smell — what is material and sensible — we can not doubt. The present and material absorbs attention and appears real, solid, substantial; but the future, the immaterial, the invisible, the spiritual, seem vague, distant, illusive. imaginary. Practically the unseen has little or no reality and influence with the vast majority of mankind. Even the unseen God himself is to most men less a verity than the commonest object of vision; to many he, the highest verity, is really vanity, while the world's vanities are practically the highest verities.

God's great corrective for this most disastrous inversion and perversion of the true relation of things is prayer. "Enter into thy closet." There all is silence, secrecy, solitude, seclusion. Within that holy of holies the disciple is left alone — all others shut out, that the suppliant may be shut in — *with God.* The silence is in order to the hearing of the still, small voice that is drowned in worldly clamor, and which even a human voice may cause to be unheard or indistinct. The secrecy is in order to a meeting with him who seeth in secret and is best seen in secret. The solitude is for the purpose of being alone with One who can fully impress with his presence only when there is no other presence to divert thought. The place of seclusion with God is the one school where we learn that he is, and is the rewarder of those that diligently seek him. The closet is "not only the oratory, it is the *observatory,*" not for prayer only, but for prospect — the wide-reaching, clear-seeing, outlook upon the eternal! The decline of prayer is therefore the decay of piety; and, for prayer to cease altogether, would be spiritual death, for it is to every child of God the breath of life.

We cannot too strongly emphasize this fact, that *to keep in close touch with God in the secret chamber of his presence is the great fundamental underlying purpose of prayer.* To speak with God is a priceless privilege; but what shall be said of having and hearing him speak with us! We can tell him nothing he does not know; but he can tell us what we do not know, no imagination has ever conceived, no research ever unveiled. The highest of all possible attainments is the knowledge of God, and this is the practical mode of his revelation of himself. Even his holy Word needs to be read in the light of his own presence if it is to be understood. The praying soul hears God speak. "And when Moses was gone into the tabernacle of the congregation to speak with him, then *he heard the voice of One speaking unto him* from off the mercy seat that *was* upon the ark of testimony — from between the two cherubim, and he spake unto him" (Num. 7:89).

Where there is this close touch with God, and this clear insight into his name which is his nature, and into his Word which is his will made known, there will be a new power to walk with him in holiness, and work with him in service. "He made known his *ways* unto Moses, his *acts* unto the children of Israel." The mass of the people stood afar off and saw his deeds, such as the over-throwing of Pharaoh's hosts in the Red Sea; but Moses drew near into the thick darkness where God was, and in that thick darkness he found a light such as never shone elsewhere, and in that light he read God's secret plans and purposes and interpreted his won-drous ways of working.

All practical power over sin and over men depends on main-taining this secret communion. Elijah was bidden, first, "go, *hide* thyself," and then, "go *shew thyself.*" Those who abide in the secret place with God come forth to show themselves mighty to conquer evil, and strong to work and to wait for God. They are permitted to read the secrets of his covenant; they know his will; they are the meek whom he guides in judgment and teaches his way. They are his prophets, who speak for him to others; be-cause they watch the signs of the times, discern his tokens, and read his signals. We sometimes count as mystics those who, like Savonarola and Catherine of Sienna, claim to have communica-tions from God; to have revelations of a definite plan of God for his church, or for themselves as individuals, like the reformer of Erfurt, the founder of the Bristol orphanages, or the leader of the China Inland Mission. But may it not be that if we stumble at these experiences it is because we do not have them ourselves? Have not many of these men and women afterward proved by their lives that they were not mistaken, and that God has led them by a way that no other eye could trace?

Prayer Imparts God's Power

In favor of close contact with the living God in prayer, there is another reason that rises perhaps to a still higher level. Prayer not only puts us in touch with God, and gives knowledge of him and his ways, but it imparts to us his power. It is the touch which brings virtue out of him. It is the hand upon the pole of a celestial battery, which charges us with his secret life, energy, efficiency. Things which are impossible with man are possible with God, and with a man in whom God is. Prayer is the secret of imparted power from God, and nothing else can take its place. Absolute weakness follows the neglect of secret communion with

God — and the weakness is the more deplorable, because it is often unconscious and unsuspected, especially when one has never yet known what true power is.

We see men of prayer quietly achieving results of the most surprising character. They have the calm of God, no hurry, or worry, or flurry; no anxiety, or care, no excitement or hustle or bustle — they do great things for God, and, like John the Baptist, are great in his eyes, yet they are little in their own eyes; they carry great loads, and yet are not weary nor faint; they face great crises, and yet are not troubled. And those who know not what treasures of wisdom and strength and courage and power are hidden in God's pavilion wonder how it is. They try to account for all this by something in the man — his talent, or tact, original methods, or favoring circumstances. Perhaps they try to imitate such a career by securing the patronage of the rich and mighty, or by dependence on organization, or fleshly energy — or what men call "determination to succeed" — they bustle about, labor incessantly, appeal for money and cooperation, and work out an apparent success, but there is none of that power of God in it which cannot be imitated. They compass themselves about with sparks, but there is no fire of God; they build up a great structure, but it is wood, hay, stubble; they make a great noise, but God is not in the clamor.

Nothing is at once so indisputable and so over-awing as the way in which a few men of God have lived in him and he in them. The fact is, that in the disciple's life the fundamental law is, "Not I, but Christ in me." In a grandly true sense there is but one *Worker*, one Agent, and he divine; and all other so-called "workers" are instruments, and instruments only, in his hands. The first quality of a true instrument is *passivity*. An *active* instrument would defeat its own purpose; all its activity must be dependent upon the man who uses it. Sometimes a machine becomes uncontrollable, and then it not only becomes useless, but it becomes dangerous, and works damage and disaster. What would a man do with a plane, a knife, an axe, a saw, a bow, that had any will of its own and moved of itself? Does it mean nothing when, in the Word of God, we meet so frequently the symbols of passive service — the rod, the staff, the saw, the hammer, the sword, the spear, the threshing instrument, the flail; and, in the

New Testament, the vessel? Does it mean that in proportion as a man is *wilful* God can not use him; that the first condition of service is that the human will is to be lost in God's so that it presents no resistance to his, no persistence beyond or apart from his, and even ventures to offer no *assistance* to his? George Müller well taught that we are to wait to know whether a certain work is *God's;* then whether it is *ours,* as being committed to us; but, even then, we need to wait for God's *way* and God's *time* to do his own work, otherwise we rush precipitately into that which he means us to do, but only at his signal; or else, perhaps, we go on doing when he calls a halt. Many a true servant of God has, like Moses, begun before his Master was ready, or kept on working when his Master's time was past.

Intercession

There is one aspect of prayer to which particular attention needs to be called, because it is strongly emphasized in the Word, and because it is least used in our daily life, namely, *intercession.*

This word, with what underlies it, has a very unique use and meaning in Scripture. It differs from supplication, first in this, that supplication has mainly reference to the suppliant and his own supply; and again, because intercession not only *concerns others,* but largely implies the need of *direct divine interposition.* There are many prayers that, in their answer, allow our cooperation and imply our activity. When we pray, "Give us this day our daily bread," we go to work to *earn* the bread for which we *pray.* That is God's law. When we ask God to deliver us from the evil one, we expect to be sober and vigilant, and resist the adversary. This is right; but our activity in many other matters hinders the full display of God's power, and hence also our impression of his working. The deepest convictions of God's prayer-answering are therefore wrought in cases where, in the nature of things, we are precluded from all activity in promoting the result.

The Word of God teaches us that intercession with God is most necessary in cases where man is most powerless. Elijah is held before us as a great intercessor, and the one example given is his prayer for rain. Yet in this case he could *only pray;* there was nothing else he could do to unlock the heavens after three years and a half of drought. And is there not a touch of divine poetry in the form in which the answer came? The rising cloud took the shape of "a man's hand," as though to assure the prophet how God saw and heeded the suppliant hand raised to him in prayer! Daniel was powerless to move the king or reverse his decree; all he could do was to "desire mercies of the God of heaven concerning this secret"; and it was because he could do nothing else, could not even *guess* at the interpretation, inasmuch as he knew not even the dream — that it became absolutely sure, when both the dream and its meaning were made known, that *God* had interposed, and so even the heathen king himself saw, felt and confessed.

All through history certain crises have arisen when the help of man was utterly vain. To the formal Christian, the carnal disciple, the unbelieving soul, this fact, that there is nothing that man could do, makes prayer seem almost a folly, perhaps a farce, a waste of breath. But to those who best know God, man's extremity is God's opportunity, and human helplessness becomes not a reason for the silence of despair, but the argument for praying in faith. Invariably those whose faith in prayer is supernaturally strong are those who have most proved that *God* has wrought, by their conscious compulsory cessation of all their own efforts as vain and hopeless.

George Müller set out to prove to a half-believing church and an unbelieving world that God does directly answer prayer; and to do this he purposely abstained from all the ordinary and otherwise legitimate methods of appeal, or of active effort to secure the housing, clothing and feeding of thousands of orphans. Hudson Taylor undertook to put missionaries into inland China by dependence solely upon God, asking no collections and even refusing them in connection with public meetings, lest such meetings should be construed as appeals for help. He and his co-workers accustomed themselves to lay all wants before the Lord, and to expect the answer, and answer always came and still comes. The study of missionary history reveals the fact that, at the very times when, in utter despair of any help but God's there has been believing prayer, the interposition of God has been most conspicuously seen — how could it be most conspicuous except amid such conditions?

Every church ought to be a prayer circle; but this will not be so long as we wait for the whole church, as a body, to move together. The mass of professing Christians have too little hold on God to enter heartily into such holy agreement. To all who yearn for a revival of the prayer spirit we suggest that *in every congregation a prayer circle be formed, without regard to numbers.* Let any pastor unite with himself any man or woman in whom he discerns marks of peculiar spiritual life and power, and without publicity or any direct effort to enlarge the little company, begin with such to lay before God any matter demanding special divine guidance and help. Without any public invitation which might draw unprepared people into a formal association — it will be found that the Holy Spirit will enlarge the circle as he fits others, or finds others fit, to enter it — and thus, quietly and without observation, the little company of praying souls will grow as fast as God means it shall. Let a record be kept of every definite petition laid before God — for such a prayer circle should be only with reference to very definite matters — and as God interposes and answers follow let the record of his interposition be carefully kept, that it may become a new inspiration both to praise and to believing prayer. Such a resort to united intercession we have ourselves known to transform a whole church, remove dissensions, rectify errors, secure harmony and unity, and promote Holy Spirit administration and spiritual life and growth beyond all other possible devices. If in any church the pastor is unhappily not a man who could or would lead in such a movement, let two or three disciples who feel the need and have the faith meet and begin, perhaps, by praying for *him.* In this matter there should be no waiting for *anybody else;* if there be but *one* believer who has power with God let such a one begin intercessory prayer. God will bring to the side of such an intercessor, in his own time and way, others whom he has made ready to act as supplicators.

Not long since, in a church in Scotland, a minister suddenly began to preach with unprecedented power. The whole congregation was aroused and sinners marvelously saved. He himself did not understand the new enduement. In a dream of the night it was strangely suggested to him that the whole blessing was traceable to one poor old woman who was *stone deaf,* but who came regularly to church, and being unable to hear a word, *spent all the time in prayer* for the preacher and individual hearers. In the biography of Charles G. Finney similar facts are recorded of "Father Nash," Abel Cleary, and others.

Examples might be multiplied indefinitely. But the one thing we would make prominent is this: God is summoning his people to prayer. He wills that "men pray everywhere, lifting up holy hands without wrath and doubting"; that, *first of all,* supplication, prayers, intercessions, and giving of thanks be made for all men (I Tim. 2:8). If this be done first of all, every other most blessed result will follow. *God waits to be asked.* In him are the fountains of blessing and he puts at the disposal of his praying saints all their abundance; they are, however, sealed fountains to the ungodly and the unbelieving. There is one key that always unlocks even heaven's gates; one secret that puts connecting channels between those eternal fountains and ourselves. That key, that secret, is prevailing prayer.

God has no greater controversy with his people today than this, that with boundless promises to believing prayer there are so few who actually give themselves unto intercession. This is represented as being a matter even of divine wonderment:

"And there is none that calleth upon Thy name,

That stirreth up himself to take hold of Thee" (Isa. 64:7).

The very fact that so many disciples, and in so many parts of the world, are forming prayer circles or unions is itself a great incentive to increased and united prayer.

True Prayer

Our Lord taught a great lesson in Matthew 18:19. He said: "If two of you shall agree [symphonize] on earth as touching anything that they shall ask, it shall be done for them of my Father which is in heaven." The agreement referred to is not that of a mere human covenant, nor even sympathy; it is *symphony.* Symphony is agreement of sounds in a musical chord, and depends upon fixed laws of harmony. It cannot be secured by any arbitrary arrangement. One cannot lay his finger accidently or carelessly upon the keys of a musical instrument and produce symphony of sounds. Such touch may evoke only intolerable discord, unless regulated by a knowledge of the principles of harmony. Nay, there is even a deeper necessity, namely, that the keys touched shall themselves be *in tune the whole instrument.* Two conditions, then, are needful; first, that a skilful hand shall put the whole instrument in tune; and then an equally skilfull hand shall touch keys which are capable of producing what is called a "true chord."

This language evinces divine design. He is teaching a great lesson on the mystery of prayer, which likewise demands two great conditions; first, that the praying soul shall be in harmony with God himself; and then that those who unite in prayer shall, because of such unity with him, be in harmony with each other. There must be, therefore, back of all prevailing supplication and intercession One who, with infinite skill, tunes the keys into accord with his own ear; and then touches them, like a master musician, so that they respond together to his will and give forth the chord which is in his mind.

No true philosophy of prayer can ever be framed which does not include these conditions. Many have false conceptions of what prayer is. To them it is merely asking for what one wants. But this may be so far from God's standard as to lack the first essentials of prayer. It may be asking something to consume it upon our own lusts. We are to ask *"in the name"* of Christ. But that is not simply *using his name* in prayer. The *name* is the *nature;* it expresses the character, and is equivalent to the person. To ask in Christ's name is to come to God, as *identified with the very person of Christ.* A wife makes a purchase in her husband's name. She says, "I am Mrs. A————," which means, "I am his wife, identified with his personality, character, wealth, commercial credit, and business standing." To go to God in Christ's name is to claim identity with Christ as a member of his body, one with him before the Father, and having in him a right to the Father's gifts, a right to draw on the Father's infinite resources.

Again, we are told that, if we ask anything *"according to his will,"* he heareth us. But what is asking according to *his* will but ceasing to ask according to our own self-will? Here the impulse is not human, but essentially divine. It implies a knowledge of his will, an insight into his own mind, and a sympathy with his purpose. Now is this possible unless by the Holy Spirit we are brought into such fellowship with God as that he can guide us in judgment and yearning, and teach us his way? He is indeed "able to do exceeding abundantly above all that we ask or think," but it is "according to his power which worketh in us." If that power work not *in* us first, how can it work *for* us, in answered prayer?

In order to gain higher results, wrought for the church or the world, in answer to supplication, there must first be deeper results wrought in the believer by the Holy Spirit. In other words, *there must be a higher type of personal holiness if there is to be a higher measure of power in prayer.* The carnal mind does not fall into harmony with God, does not even see and perceive his mind, and hence the carnally-minded disciple can not discern the will of God in prayer, but is continually hindered and hampered by mistaking self-impelled petitions for divinely inspired prayers, confounding what self-will craves with what is spiritually needful and scripturally warranted.

God is calling his people to a revival of *faith in the divine efficacy of prayer.*

Our Lord teaches us that the prayer of faith has the power of a *fiat* or a divine decree. God said sublimely, "Let light be!" and light was. The Lord Jesus Christ says: "If ye have faith as a grain of mustard seed" — in which, however small, is the possibility and potency of *life* — "ye shall say to this mountain, Be thou removed; or to this sycamore tree, Be thou plucked up by the root, and it shall obey you." This is the language not of petition, but of decree. It is, in some sort, a laying hold on Omnipotence, so that nothing is impossible to the praying soul.

When we reach such heights of teaching and compare them with the low level of our life we are struck dumb with amazement, first at the astounding possibilities of faith, as put before us, and then at the equally astounding impossibilities which unbelief substitutes for the offered omnipotence of supplication. When we think of the possible heights of intercession we seem again to hear the saintly McCheyne crying out: "Do everything in earnest! If it is worth doing, then do it with all your might. Above all, keep much in the presence of God; never see the face of man till you have seen his face." That is the preparation of prayer, prevailing first with God to enable us to prevail with man. Jacobi must have been thinking along these lines when he said: "My watchword, and that of my reason, is not I, but One who is more and better than I; One who is entirely different from what I am — I mean God. I neither am, nor care to be, if he is not!" It is prayer that makes God real — the highest reality and verity; and that sends us back into the world with the conviction and consciousness that he is, and is in us, mighty to work in us, and through us, as instruments, so that nothing shall be impossible to the instrument, because of the Workman back of it who holds and wields the weapon.

The power of such prayer defies all competition or imitation by the most perfect forms of liturgy. Who can copy or canvass the imprisoned flame of a priceless gem with mere brush and pigments! Or counterfeit the photosphere of the sun with yellow chalk! There is a flame of God which prayer lights within; there is a glow and light and heat in the life which can be kindled only by a coal from the golden altar which is before the throne. It is only the few who find their way thither and know the enkindling power; but to those few the church and the world owe mighty upheavals and outpourings (Rev. 8).

Chemical galvanism possesses this peculiarity, that an increase of its powers cannot be gained by increasing the dimensions of the cells of the battery, but can be by increasing their number. We need *more* intercessors if we are to have greatly increased power. The number of cells must be increased. More of God's people must learn to pray. The foes are too many for a few to cope with them, however empowered of God. The variety of human want and woe, the scattered millions of the unsaved, the wide territory to be covered with intercession—all these and other like considerations demand multiplied forces. Each human being has only a very limited knowledge of human need. Our individual circle of acquaintance is so comparatively narrow that even the most prayerful spirit cannot survey the whole field. But when in all parts of the destitute territory supplicators multiply, even these narrow circles, placed side by side and largely overlapping, cover the whole broad field of need. Our own personal and limited knowledge and range of intelligent sympathy meet and touch similar and sympathetic souls, so that what we do not see or feel or pray for, appeals to others of our fellow disciples; and so, in proportion as the intercessors multiply, every interest of mankind finds its representatives in the secret place and at the throne.

We cannot make up for lack of praying by excess of working. In fact working without praying is a sort of practical atheism, for it leaves out God. It is the prayer that prepares for work, that arms us for the warfare, that furnishes us for the activity. It behooves us, studying intently the promises to prayer, to say unto the Lord: "This being Thy word, I will henceforth live as a man of prayer and claim my privilege and use my power as an intercessor."

Here is the highest identification with the Son of God. It is almost being admitted to a sort of fellowship in his mediatorial work! During this dispensation his work is mainly intercession. He calls us to take a subordinate part in the holy office, standing, like Phinehas, between the living and the dead to stay the plague; like Elijah, between heaven and earth to unlock heaven's floodgates of blessing and command the fire and flood of God! Is this true? Then what can be more awful and august than such dignity and majesty of privilege! Ignatius welcomes the Numidian lion in the arena, saying: "I am grain of God; I must be ground between the teeth of lions to make bread for God's people." He felt in the hour of martyrdom the privilege of joining his dying Lord in a sacrifice that Bushnell would call "vicarious."

Who will join the risen Lord in a service of intercession? The greatest difficulty in the way of practical conversion of men may not be in God's eyes so much a barrier of ungodliness among the heathen as a barrier of unbelief among his own disciples!

The sixteenth century was great in painters, the seventeenth in philosophers, the eighteenth in writers, the nineteenth in preachers and inventors; God grant that the twentieth may be forever historically memorable as the century of intercessors.

ARTHUR TAPPAN PIERSON (1837-1911) had the unenviable task of following C.H. Spurgeon in the pulpit of London's Metropolitan Tabernacle when Spurgeon became ill. Before succeeding Spurgeon, Pierson had served Congregational and Presbyterian churches in New York and Pennsylvania from 1860-1911. He was an editor of the *Scofield Reference Bible*. Notable among his books are *Crisis of Missions, The Coming of the Lord,* and *Miracle of Missions*. Besides his theological work, Pierson founded the First Penny Saving Bank of Philadelphia.

59

Our Lord's Teachings About Money

By Arthur T. Pierson, D.D.
Pastor, Spurgeon's Tabernacle, London

Abridged by Arnold D. Ehlert, Th.D.

Our Lord's teachings as to money gifts, if obeyed, would forever banish all limitations on church work and all concern about supplies. These teachings are radical and revolutionary. So far are they from practical acceptance that, although perfectly explicit, they seem more like a dead language that has passed out of use than like a living tongue that millions know and speak. Yet, when these principles and precepts of our Lord on giving are collated and compared, they are found to contain the materials of a complete ethical system on the subject of money, its true nature, value, relation and use. Should these sublime and unique teachings be translated into living, the effect not only upon benevolent work, but upon our whole spiritual character, would be incalculable. Brevity compels us to be content with a simple outline of this body of teaching, scattered through the four Gospel narratives, but gathered up and methodically presented by Paul in that exhaustive discussion of Christian giving in II Corinthians 8 and 9.

I. The Principle of Stewardship

The basis of Christ's teaching about money is the fundamental conception of stewardship (Luke 12:42; 16:1-8). Not only money, but every gift of God, is received in trust for his use. Man is not an owner, but a trustee, managing another's goods and estates, God being the one original and inalienable Owner of all. The two things required of stewards are that they be "faithful and wise," that they study to employ God's gifts with fidelity and sagacity — fidelity so that God's entrustments be not perverted to self-indulgence; sagacity, so that they be converted into as large gains as possible.

This is a perfectly plain and simple basal principle, yet it is not the accepted foundation of our money-making and using. The vast majority, even of disciples, practically leave God out of their thoughts when they engage in finance. Men consider themselves owners; they "make money" by their industry, economy, shrewdness, application; it is theirs to do as they will with it. There is little or no sense of stewardship or of its implied obligation. If they give, it is an act, not of duty, but of generosity; it ranks, not under law, but under grace. Hence there is no inconsistency felt in hoarding or spending vast sums for worldly ends and appropriating an insignificant fraction to benevolent purposes. Such methods and notions would be utterly turned upside down could men but think of themselves as stewards, accountable to the one Master for having wasted his goods. The great day of account will bring an awful reckoning, not only to wasters, but to hoarders; for even the unfaithful servants brought back to their lord the talent and the pound at last, but without profit, and the condemnation was for not having used so as to increase the entrusted goods.

II. The Principle of Investment

In our Lord's teachings we find this kindred principle of investment: "Thou oughtest to have put my money to the exchangers" (Matt. 25:27). Money-changing and investing is an old business. The "exchangers," as Luke renders, are the bankers, the ancient Trapezitae, who received money on deposit and paid interest for its use, like modern savings institutions. The argument of our Lord refutes the unfaithful servant on his own plea, which his course showed to be not an excuse, but a pretext. It was true that he dared not risk trading on his own account; why not, without such risk, get a moderate interest for his Master by lending to professional traders? It was not fear but sloth that lay behind his unfaithfulness and unprofitableness.

Thus indirectly is taught the valuable lesson that timid souls, unfitted for bold and independent service in behalf of the kingdom, may link their incapacity to the capacity and sagacity of others who will make their gifts and possessions of use to the Master and his church.

James Watt, in 1773, formed a partnership with Matthew Boulton, of Soho, for the manufacture of steam engines — Watt, to furnish brains, and Boulton, hard cash. This illustrates our Lord's teaching. The steward has money, or it may be other gifts, that can be made of use, but he lacks faith and foresight, practical energy and wisdom. The Lord's "exchangers" can show him how to gain for the Master. The church boards are God's bankers. They are composed of practical men, who study how and where to put money for the best results and largest returns, and when they are what they ought to be, they multiply money many-fold in glorious results. The church partly exists that the strength of one member may help the weakness of another, and that by cooperation of all, the power of the least and weakest may be increased.

III. The Subordination of Money

Another most important principle is the subordination of money, as emphatically taught and illustrated in the rich young ruler (Matt. 19:16-26). This narrative, rightly regarded, presents no enigma. With all his attractive traits, this man was a slave. Money was not his servant, but his master; and because God alone is to be supreme, our Lord had no alternative. He must demolish this man's idol, and when he dealt a blow at his money, the idolatry became apparent, and the slave of greed went away sorrowful, clinging to his idol. It was not the man's having great possessions that was wrong, but that his possessions had the man; they possessed him and controlled him. He was so far the slave of money that he could not and would not accept freedom by the breaking of its fetters. His "trust" was in riches — how could it be in God? Behind all disguises of respectability and refinement, God sees many a man to be an abject slave, a victim held in bonds by love of money; but covetousness is idolatry, and no idolator can enter the kingdom of God.

IV. The Law of Recompense

We ascend a step higher, and consider our Lord's teaching as to the law of recompense. "Give, and it shall be given unto you" (Luke 6:38). We are taught that getting is in order to giving, and consequently that giving is the real road to getting. God is an economist. He entrusts larger gifts to those who use the smaller well. Perhaps one reason of our poverty is that we are so far slaves of parsimony. The future may reveal that God has been withholding from us because we have been withholding from him.

It can scarcely be said by any careful student of the New Testament that our Lord encourages his disciples to look or ask for earthly wealth. Yet it is equally certain that hundreds of devout souls who have chosen voluntary poverty for his sake have been entrusted with immense sums for his work. George Müller conducted for over sixty years enterprises requiring at least some hundred and twenty-five thousand dollars a year. Note also the experiences of William Quarrier and Hudson Taylor, and D. L. Moody and Dr. Barnardo. Such servants of God, holding all as God's, spending little or nothing for self, were permitted to receive and use millions for God, and in some cases, like Müller's, without any appeal to men, looking solely to God. This great saint of Bristol found, in a life that nearly rounded out a century, that it was safe to give to God's purposes the last penny at any moment, with the perfect assurance that more would come in before another need should arise. And there was never one failure for seventy years!

V. Superior Blessedness

Kindred to this law of recompense is the law of superior blessedness. "It is more blessed to give than to receive" (Acts 20:35). Paul quotes this as a saying of our Lord, but it is not to be found in any of the Gospel narratives. Whether he meant only to indicate what is substantially our Lord's teaching, or was preserving some precious words of our Great Teacher, otherwise unrecorded, is not important. It is enough that this saying has the authority of Christ. Whatever the blessedness of receiving, that of giving belongs to a higher plane. Whatever I get, and whatever good it brings to me, I only am benefited; but what I give brings good to others — to the many, not the one. But, by a singular decree of God, what I thus surrender for myself for the sake of others comes back even to me in larger blessing. It is like the moisture which the spring gives out in streams and evaporation, returning in showers to supply the very channels which filled the spring itself.

VI. Computation By Comparison

We rise a step higher in considering God's law of computation. How does he reckon gifts? Our Lord teaches us that it is by comparison. No one narrative is more telling on this theme than that of the poor widow who dropped into the treasury her two mites. The Lord Jesus, standing near, watched the offerings cast into the treasury. There were rich givers that gave large amounts. There was one poor woman, a widow, who threw in two mites, and he declared her offering to be more than any of all the rest, because, while they gave out of a superfluity she gave out of a deficiency — they of their abundance, she of her poverty. She who cast her two mites into the sacred treasury, by so doing became rich in good works and in the praise of God. Had she kept them she had been still only the same poor widow.

He tells us here how he estimates money gifts — not by what we give, but by what we keep — not by the amount of our contributions, but by their cost in self-denial. This widow's whole offering counted financially for but a farthing or two-fifths of a cent. What could be much more insignificant? But the two mites constituted her whole means of subsistence. The others reserved what they needed or wanted for themselves, and then gave out of their superabundance. The contrast is emphatic; she "out of her deficiency," they "out of their supersufficiency."

Not all giving — so-called — has rich reward. In many cases the keeping hides the giving, in the sight of God. Self-indulgent hoarding and spending spread a banquet; the crumbs fall from the table, to be gathered up and labeled "charity." But when the one possession that is dearest, the last trusted resource, is surrendered to God, then comes the vision of the treasure laid up in heaven.

VII. Unselfishness in Giving

We ascend still higher to the law of unselfishness in giving. "Do good and lend, hoping for nothing again" (Luke 6:35). Much giving is not giving at all, but only lending or exchanging. He who gives to another of whom he expects to receive as much again, is trading. He is seeking gain, and is selfish. What he is after is not another's profit, but his own advantage. To invite to one's table those who will invite him again, is simply as if a kindness were done to a business acquaintance as a basis for boldness in asking a similar favor when needed. This is reciprocity, and may be even mean and calculating.

True giving has another's good solely in view, and hence bestows upon those who cannot and will not repay, who are too destitute to pay back, and too degraded, perhaps, to appreciate what is done for them. That is like God's giving to the evil and unthankful. That is the giving prompted by love.

To ask therefore, "Will it pay?" betrays the selfish spirit. He is the noblest, truest giver who thinks only of the blessing he can bring to another's body and soul. He casts his bread-seed beside all waters. He hears the cry of want and woe, and is concerned only to supply the want and assuage the woe. This sort of giving shows God-likeness, and by it we grow into the perfection of benevolence.

VIII. Sanctified Giving

Our Lord announces also a law of santification. "The altar sanctifieth the gift" — association gives dignity to an offering (Matt. 23:19). If the cause to which we contribute is exalted, it ennobles and exalts the offering to its own plane. No two objects can or ought to appeal to us with equal force unless they are equal in moral worth and dignity, and a discerning giver will respond most to what is worthiest. God's altar was to the Jew the central focus of all gifts; it was associated with his worship, and the whole calendar of fasts and feasts moved round it. The gift laid upon it acquired a new dignity by so being deposited upon it. Some objects which appeal for gifts we are at liberty to set aside because they are not sacred. We may give or not as we judge best, for they depend on man's enterprises and schemes, which we may not altogether approve. But some causes have divine sanction, and that hallows them; giving becomes an act of worship when it has to do with the altar.

IX. Transmutation

Another law of true giving is that of transmutation. "Make to yourselves friends of the mammon of unrighteousness; that, when ye fail, they may receive you into everlasting habitations" (Luke 16:9). This, though considered by many an obscure parable, contains one of the greatest hints on money gifts that our Lord ever dropped.

Mammon here stands as the equivalent for money, practically worshipped. It reminds us of the golden calf that was made out of the earrings and jewels of the crowd. Now our Lord refers to a second transmutation. The golden calf may in turn be melted down and coined into Bibles, churches, books, tracts, and even souls of men. Thus what was material and temporal becomes immaterial and spiritual, and eternal. Here is a man who has a hundred dollars. He may spend it all on a banquet, or an evening party, in which case the next day there is nothing to show for it. It has secured a temporary gratification of appetite — that is all. On the other hand, he invests in Bibles at ten cents each, and it buys a thousand copies of the Word of God. These he judiciously sows as seed of the Kingdom, and that seed springs up a harvest, not of Bibles, but of souls. Out of the unrighteous mammon he has made immortal friends, who, when he fails, receive him into everlasting habitations. May this not be what is meant by the true riches — the treasure laid up in heaven in imperishable good?

Never will the work of missions, or any other form of service to God and man, receive the help it ought until there is a new conscience and a new consecration in the matter of money. The influence of the world and the worldly spirit is deadening to unselfish giving. It exalts self-indulgence, whether in gross or refined form. It leads to covetous hoarding or wasteful spending. It blinds us to the fact of obligation, and devises flimsy pretexts for diverting the Lord's money to carnal ends. The few who learn to live scriptural principles learn also to love to give. These gifts become abundant and systematic and self-denying. The stream of beneficence flows perpetually — there is no period of drought.

Once it was necessary to proclaim to the people of God that what they had brought "was more than enough," and to "restrain them from bringing" (Ex. 36:6). So far as known, this is the one and only historic instance of such excess of generosity. But should not that always be the case? Is it not a shame and disgrace that there ever should be a lack of "meat in God's house"? When his work appeals for aid, should there ever be a reluctance to respond or a doling out of a mere pittance? Surely his unspeakable gift should make all giving to him a spontaneous offering of love that, like Mary's, should bring its precious flask of spikenard and lavish its treasures on his feet, and fill the house with the odor of self-sacrifice!

AMZI CLARENCE DIXON (1854-1925) worked alongside R.A. Torrey in editing *The Fundamentals*. Dixon was born in North Carolina and received his higher education at Wake Forest College and at Southern Baptist Theological Seminary. During his years as pastor, he ministered at two very important churches: Moody Church in Chicago (1906-11) and Metropolitan Tabernacle in London (1911-19). Here is a partial list of books Dixon wrote: *Destructive Criticism vs. Christianity* (1912) and *The Birth of Christ: The Incarnation of God* (1919).

60

"The Scriptures"

By Rev. A. C. Dixon, D.D.

PASTOR, METROPOLITAN TABERNACLE CHURCH, LONDON

Revised and edited by Gerald B. Stanton, Th.D.

When our Lord said, "Search the Scriptures," every Jew to whom he spoke knew what he meant. There were other writings in Hebrew, Greek and Latin, but the Scriptures were a body of writings marked off from all others by their sacredness and authority as the Word of God. Their history can be traced from the time of Moses to Christ. In Exodus 17:14 we read: "And the Lord said unto Moses, Write this for a memorial in a book, and rehearse it in the ears of Joshua." As to the writing material Moses used we do not know, but we do know that in Egypt papyrus plant, linen and cotton cloth, the skins of animals and stone were used in making books of various kinds. The Ten Commandments were written on tables of stone, and with Egyptian mummies we have preserved even to this day cotton and linen cloth such as was frequently used for writing.

In Deuteronomy 31:9 we have the historic record of the fact that Moses obeyed the command of God: "And Moses wrote this law and delivered it unto the priests, the sons of Levi, which bare the Ark of the Covenant of the Lord." And in verse 24: "It came to pass when Moses had made an end of writing the words of this law in a book, until they were finished, that Moses commanded the Levites which bare the Ark of the Covenant of the Lord, saying, Take this book of the law and put it in the side of the Ark of the Covenant of the Lord your God." The book was finished and placed by the side of the Ark for safe keeping.

In Joshua 1:8 we read: "This book of the law shall not depart out of thy mouth, but thou shalt meditate therein day and night, that thou mayest observe to do according to all that is written therein; for then thou shalt make thy way prosperous, and then thou shalt have good success." Now that the pillar of fire by night and of cloud by day has departed, the book is to be the guide of Israel and their religion is to be to a large extent a book religion. God is speaking to them out of the "Book of the Law."

It is probable that the book which Joshua read was the identical manuscript which Moses wrote in the wilderness. There may have been copies made of it, but we have no record of the fact. Frequent mention of it is made through the books of the Bible. The same book, or a copy of it, appears again a thousand years afterward under the reign of Josiah, as we learn from II Kings 22:8: "And Hilkiah the high priest said unto Shaphan the scribe, I have found the book of the law in the house of the Lord. And Hilkiah gave the book to Shaphan and he read it."

In Ezra we find it again in the hands of the prophet on the pulpit of wood in the open air, reading it and making its meaning plain unto the people. From these and other Scriptures three inferences may be fairly drawn:

1. *The Bible is literature written by the command of God.* He certainly commanded Moses to write the book of the law. To John on the Isle of Patmos a great voice as of a trumpet said, "What thou seest write in a book, and send it unto the seven churches." And before the vision vanished he was commanded: "Write the things which thou hast seen, and the things which are, and the things which shall be hereafter." He was to write history, current events and predictions; and much of "the Scriptures" may be classified under these three headings.

2. The Bible is literature written by the command of God, and *under the guidance of God.* In II Peter 1:21 we read: "No prophecy ever came by the will of man, but man spake from God, being moved by the Holy Spirit." The superintendency of the Spirit is clearly taught.

3. The Bible is literature written by the command of God, under the guidance of God, and *preserved by the providential care of God.* Moses commanded that the book of the law should be placed by the side of the Ark. No safer place could have been found, and the more I study the history of the Bible the more profoundly am I convinced that God has kept his book by the

side of some ark all through the ages. As the church has been under his care and protection, so has the Book.

It is not difficult to believe that the manuscript which Hilkiah found in the Temple was the identical book which Moses wrote in the wilderness, and that this very manuscript was in the hands of Ezra on the pulpit of wood as he preached in the open air. It is only one thousand years from Joshua to Josiah and only one hundred and seventy-five years from Josiah to Ezra. There are now in our libraries scores of manuscripts which we know to be over a thousand years old, two or three which have certainly been preserved more than fourteen hundred years, and others for even longer periods. With the kindly oriental climate and the care which the Jewish reverence for the book would naturally lead them to have, it is not at all improbable that the manuscript of Moses should have been preserved for more than a thousand years. And the history of the Bible from the time of Christ to the present confirms the proposition that it has been preserved by the providential care of God.

Let us now look at "the Scriptures" in their own light. In John 5:39 Jesus said: "Search the Scriptures, for in them ye think ye have eternal life, and they are they which testify of me." In II Timothy 3:16 we read, "All Scripture is God-breathed, and is profitable for doctrine, for reproof, for correction, for instruction in righteousness, that the man of God may be complete, thoroughly furnished unto all good works." In these Scriptures are four things:

I. A BIBLICAL DEFINITION OF THE BIBLE

The phrase, "the Scriptures," suggests a synthetic definition of the Bible. There were other writings, but these were *the* writings. They had them in the Hebrew tongue, and also a translation into the Greek, known as the "Septuagint," made nearly three hundred years before Christ. But it takes our second Scripture to complete this definition of the Bible — "Every Scripture is God-breathed." A noted scholar has taken the pains to collate the texts in the New Testament where this Greek idiom occurs, and he declares that the King James version, and not the Revised, is the correct translation, and several eminent scholars on the Committee of Revision agreed with him. "All Scripture is God-breathed" is evidently what the Holy Spirit meant to write. Of course, the writers wrote under the direct influence of the Spirit. "The Holy Ghost spake by the mouth of David" (Acts 1:16). "The word of the Lord came expressly unto Ezekiel" (Ezek. 1:3). But the writings rather than the writers were inspired, because "all Scripture is "God-breathed." God, who "breathed into man the breath of life and he became a living soul," has also breathed into his book the breath of life, so that it is "the Word of God which liveth and abideth forever."

There are many writers, but one Author. These writers were not automata. Each one shows his own style and personality which the Holy Spirit uses.

II. A Biblical Use of the Bible

It is fourfold: "Profitable for doctrine, for reproof, for correction, for instruction in righteousness." "Doctrine" is the teaching, not of the *man* as he may express his opinion in social converse, but of the ambassador who carries with him the weight of his government's authority. In the Bible we find *God's official proclamation* of love, pardon, cleansing, righteousness and peace.

The word "reproof" comes after doctrine, because it has to do with the character which doctrine makes. The Bible is profitable not only for the doctrine which we get out of it, but it is the standard by which we try our doctrines. It proves and reproves. It is the plumb-line that we drop by the wall to see if it is straight. It is the yard-stick by which we measure every creed.

The word "correction" means *restoration,* and gives a thought in advance of doctrine and reproof. It has in it the thought of making right what we have found to be wrong. The plumb-line may show that the wall leans, but it cannot straighten it. The yard-stick may reveal that the cloth is too short, but it cannot lengthen it. The Bible, however, not only shows us wherein we are wrong, but it can right us. When Canova saw the piece of marble which, at great expense, had been secured for a celebrated statue, his practiced eye discovered a little piece of black running through it, and he rejected it. He could discover the black, but he could not make the black white. The Bible discovers the black *and* makes it white.

The fourth word, "instruction," means literally "child-culture," and has in it all that the parent needs for the growth, development and maturing of the child. The Bible is a training school in *righteousness*. Other books give training in music, rhetoric, oratory, but the specialty of the Bible is training in righteousness.

III. A BIBLICAL METHOD OF BIBLE STUDY

It is suggested by the two words "search" and "profitable." Whatever is profitable is apt to cost labor. The worthless we can get without effort. Hence the strength of the phrase, "Search the Scriptures." It means to "look through and through." It is the word used in the Scripture, "The Spirit searcheth all things, yea, the deep things of God." As God searches our hearts so let us search the Bible.

The Bible unsearched is a mine unworked, the difference between the Klondyke years ago and the Klondyke enriching its industrious owners today. To learn the Word of God requires diligent and persistent searching. A man who died in an English almshouse several years ago gave to his relatives an unproductive piece of land, so worthless that he did not have to pay taxes on it. The relatives searched it, and as a result they are today millionaires. The pauper was rich without knowing it, and he was ignorant of the fact because he did not search his possessions.

Every Christian with the Bible in hand is rich whether he knows it or not. Let him search and find hidden treasures. This search implies sight and light. There is need of spiritual discernment. "The natural man discerneth not the things of God." And hence there is the need of inspiration which comes from trusting the Holy Spirit as the revealer of truth. When Galileo turned his little telescope to the heavens, he found that he really had a new pair of eyes. He could now see the mountains of the moon, the satellites of Neptune, and the ring around Saturn. So we read the Bible in the light of the Bible, and as more light comes, better sight is imparted; while, on the other hand, as better sight is imparted, more light is revealed.

A Christian with spiritual discernment can afford to "search the Scriptures" with the Holy Spirit alone as his guide. Commentaries are good, but not good as substitutes for independent search. When Alexander the Great stood before Diogenes as he sat by his tub, the general asked the philosopher what he could do for him. The rather grim reply was. "Simply get out of my light." And any searcher has a right to say "Get out of my light" to every one whose shadow comes between him and the truth.

Any method of searching is good, though some may be better than others. The "grasshopper method" by which we take a word or subject and jump from one place to another, collating the texts which have the word or subject in them, is not to be despised. God shook the world through Dwight L. Moody, who was fond of this method. I have learned to love what, for lack of a better word, I call the sectional method, by which one begins at a certain place and goes through paragraph, chapter or book, gathering and classifying every thought. It reminds one of Mr. Spurgeon's saying suggested by the worm-eaten Bible which he found on the table of a Scottish wayside inn. Holding it up to the light, he noticed only one hole through which the light shone. One worm, it seems, had begun at Genesis and eaten through to Revelation, and Spurgeon prayed, "Lord, make me a bookworm like that." Such a bookworm never turns into an earthworm. It will have wings by and by.

But whatever be your method, do not fail to read the Bible by books. Read Genesis at a sitting. You can do it in less than three hours. Then take Exodus; then Leviticus, and so on through the whole library of sixty-six volumes. The astronomer should look at the heavens as a whole before he takes to his telescope. The botanist should look at the fields and gardens before he takes to his microscope. If you have not read the Scriptures, a book at a sitting, you may take it for granted that you do not know your Bible.

A study of words yields a rich harvest of knowledge and blessing.

Luther said that he studied the Bible as he gathered apples. First, he shook the whole tree, that the ripest might fall. Then he climbed the tree and shook each limb, and when he had shaken each limb, he shook each branch, and after each branch every twig, and then looked under each leaf. Let us search the Bible as a whole; shake the whole tree; read it as rapidly as you would any other book; then shake every limb, studying book after book.

Then shake every branch, giving attention to the chapters when they do not break the sense. Then shake every twig by careful study of the paragraphs and sentences, and you will be rewarded, if you will look under every leaf, by searching the meaning of words.

IV. Biblical Motives for Bible Study

There is a two-fold motive:

1. That we may have right thinking about eternal life. "In them ye think ye have eternal life." In Christ we have eternal life, but in the Scriptures is our thinking about it. We have the blessedness of the man whose "delight is in the law of the Lord, and in his law doth he meditate day and night." My arch of salvation rests upon two pillars. The first pillar is what Christ did for me, and that is always the same length. Time was when the second pillar was assurance of salvation through my feelings. If I felt well and happy, that pillar was of the right length, and seemed solid enough, but when depressed feelings came, the pillar seemed shorter and threatened the arch. One day, however, I read I John 5:13: "These things have I written unto you that believe on the name of the Son of God, that ye may know that ye have eternal life." And I saw that I was expected to trust the Scriptures and not my feelings for assurance. From that day the pillar of assurance has been all the time of the same length, for God's Word never changes. Feelings may come and go, but "I keep on believing" the promise. I know I have eternal life, not because I feel so and so, but because God says so. Now the pillar of Christ's merit and the pillar of his promise are of the same length, and the arch of salvation is no longer threatened by changing feelings.

2. That we may learn of Jesus. "They are they which testify of me." Few things are more interesting and none more profitable than tracing the Messianic idea through the Bible. It begins with the curse upon the serpent in Genesis, and closes with "the Lamb as it had been slain in the midst of the throne" in Revelation. In Christian character the image of Christ is marred by imperfections, but in the Scriptures the portrait is perfect. A friend described to me a painting which hung on the wall of his boyhood home. When you first saw it, it was a beautiful landscape with trees, streams, houses and people, but, while gazing upon it, all

these beautiful things began to form into a human face. On a closer inspection you perceived that the whole picture was intended to give the face of Christ. The devout student of the Scriptures is constantly having experiences like this. He sees in the Bible trees of faithfulness, streams of truth, landscapes of loveliness in deed and character, but they are all so arranged in their relation to Christ as to bring out the features of his character. While we thus see him as he is, we become more and more like him, until by and by we shall see his unveiled face and be completely transformed into his likeness. "Search the Scriptures" for a vision of the Lord Jesus Christ.

GEORGE FREDERICK PENTECOST (1842-1920) was a Presbyterian clergyman who served as chaplain during the Civil War and then pastored churches in Indiana, Kentucky, New York, Massachusetts, Pennsylvania, and London, England. He conducted successful evangelistic meetings in Scotland, working with D. L. Moody, and also in India. He visited mission works in China, Japan and Korea as an official representative of the American Board of Commissioners for Foreign Missions. He authored many books, including ten volumes of Bible studies.

61

What the Bible Contains for the Believer

By Rev. George F. Pentecost, D.D.
DARIEN, CONNECTICUT

Edited by Charles L. Feinberg, Th.D., Ph.D.

I. *The Bible is the only book that can make us wise unto salvation.*

The Bible is not a book to be studied as we study geology and astronomy, merely to find out about the earth's formation and the structure of the universe; but it is a book revealing truth, designed to bring us into living union with God. We may study the physical sciences and get a fair knowledge of the facts and phenomena of the material universe. But what difference does it make to us, as spiritual beings, whether the Copernican theory of the universe is true, or that of Ptolemy? On the other hand, the eternal things of God's Word do so concern us. Scientific knowledge, and the words in which that knowledge is conveyed, have no power to change our characters, to make us better, or give us a living hope of a blessed immortality. But the Word of God has in it a vital power; it is "quick and powerful" — living and full of divine energy (Heb. 4:12) — and when received with meekness into our understanding and heart is able to save our souls (Jas. 1:18, 21). It is the instrument of the Holy Spirit wherewith he accomplishes in us regeneration of character. The Word of God is a living seed containing within itself God's own life, which, when it is received into our hearts, springs up within us and "brings forth fruit after its kind"; for Jesus Christ, the eternal Word of God, is the living germ hidden in his written Word. Therefore it is written, "The words that I speak unto you, they are spirit and they are life" (John 6:63), and so it is that "he that heareth my words — that is, receiveth them into good and honest hearts — that heareth the Word and understandeth it, "hath everlasting life" (John 5:24). Of no other book could such things as these be said. Hence we say, the Word of God is the instrument in his hand to work in us and for us regeneration and salvation (Jas. 1:18, 21).

This leads us to say that we are related to God and the eternal verities revealed in this book, not through intellectual apprehension and demonstration, but by faith. Not by reasoning, but by simple faith, do we lay hold on these verities, resting our faith in God, who is under and in every saving fact in the book. (See I Pet. 1:21.) It seems to me, therefore, to be the supreme folly for men to be always speculating about these spiritual and revealed things; and yet we meet constantly even good people who are thus dealing with God's Word. First of all, they treat the revelation as though it were only an opinion expressed concerning the things revealed, and so they feel free to dissent from or receive it with modification, and deal with it as they would with the generalizations and conclusions, more or less accurate, of the scientists, and the theories, more or less true, of the philosophers. If the Word commends itself to their judgment they accept it; thus making their judgment the criterion of truth, instead of submitting their opinions to the infallible Word of God. It is not seldom that we hear a person say he believes the Word of God to be true; and then the very next instant, when pressed by some statement or declaration of that Word, say, "Ah! but then I believe so and so" — something entirely different from what God has declared. Then again, many people who profess to believe God's Word seem never to think of putting themselves into practical and saving relation to it. They believe that Jesus Christ is the Saviour of the world, but they never believe on him or in him; in other words, that he is Saviour to them.

God's book is full of doctrines and promises. We declare them, and some one says, "You must prove that doctrine or that promise to be true." The only way to prove a doctrine to be true is by a personal experience of it through faith in Jesus Christ. Jesus Christ says, "Ye must be born again." Should you attempt to master the meaning and power of that doctrine by mere speculation, you would presently land just where Nicodemus did, and say, "How can these things be?" Instead of doing so, suppose you attend further to what is said, namely, "Whosoever believeth is born of God" (I John 5:1; John 1:12, 13). In obedience to this divine teaching, not knowing how it is to be done in us, we take that Word and yield ourselves to Jesus Christ; and lo! there dawns upon us an experience that throws light upon all that which before was a mystery. We have experienced no physical shock, but a great change is wrought in us, especially in our relation to God (II Cor. 5:17). Thus we come into an experimental understanding of the doctrine of the new birth. So every other doctrine pertaining to the spiritual life is by God's grace transmuted into experience. For just as a word stands for an idea or thought, so the doctrines of God stand for experiences; but the doctrine must be received before the experience can be had. And, moreover, we are to receive all doctrines, all truth, through faith in him, for Christ and his Word are inseparable, just as a man's note is only current and valuable because the man is good.

But there are some things revealed in the Word of God which we believe without experience. For instance, we believe that this "vile body" (Phil. 3:21), dishonored by sin and upon the neck of which death will soon put his foot, will in the day of his appearing and kingdom (II Tim. 4:1; I Thess. 4:15) be raised, changed and fashioned like unto his glorious body (Phil. 3:21). Do you know how we can so surely believe these things? We answer, because God has proved to us so much of his word, that when he announces something yet to be made true, on the basis of past experience we reach out and accept as true the promise of the future things. Indeed, he already makes it true in our hearts, for "faith is the substance of things hoped for" (Heb. 11:1). For even here we have a present spiritual experience which is as an earnest to us of the culmination yet future; for we are already risen with Christ (Col. 2:13; 3:1; Eph. 2:5, 6; Rom. 8:11).

2. *The Bible contains in itself the absolute guarantee of our inheritance in Christ.*

Suppose we should come to you some day and call in question your ownership of your house, and demand that you give it up, a homestead bequeathed to you by your father. Pushed to the wall, you take us with you down to the courthouse, and show us your father's will, duly written, signed, sealed and recorded. This may serve to illustrate the point. A great many Christians are at a loss where and how to ground their title. It is not in the fact that you are a descendant of a saintly father, a child of believing parents, for, as old Matthew Henry says, "Grace does not run in the blood"; nor is it that you have membership in the visible church of Christ; nor is it to be found in delightful frames and feelings — in a word, not even a genuine Christian experience constitutes your title-deed. Where then are we to base our hope? Why, just in the naked Word of God (John 5:24). Straight to the record do we appeal for a final test as to our possession in God (I John 5:11, 12). Our faith lays hold on the Son of God, in whom we have redemption (Eph. 1:7) by means of and through the recorded Word of promise, for this record was "written, that ye might believe that Jesus is the Christ, the Son of God; and that believing ye might have life through his name" (John 20:31). The Scriptures are the covenants, old and new, in which God has guaranteed to us, by word and oath (Heb. 6:17, 18), sealed with the blood of Jesus Christ (Matt. 26:28), an inheritance among the saints. We do not emphasize this point in any wise to underrate Christian experience (for it is most blessed and true), or undervalue the blessing of believing parents, or the Church and her ordinances, but only draw your attention to the more sure word of prophecy (II Pet. 1:19), which is better to us for confirmation than visions and voices, frames and feelings, parental benedictions, and church sacraments.

3. *The Word of God is the means appointed for the culture of our Christian life.*

James tells us (1:18) that the word of truth is the instrument of our regeneration, and Jesus tells us that the truth not only makes us free, but prays the Father that we may be sanctified through the truth (John 6:32-36; 17:17-19). And Paul tells us, in words which the Holy Spirit teacheth, that "Christ loved the church, and gave himself for it, that he might sanctify and cleanse it with the washing of water by the Word" (Eph. 5:25, 27). "This is the will of God, even your sanctification" (I Thess. 4:3), for God hath not called us to uncleanness, but unto holiness (I Thess. 4:7). After regeneration, nothing can be more important than this. We are told in the Bible and we believe it, that by and by we shall be in another state of existence, in heaven in the presence of the loving and glorified Jesus; that we shall see his face, and his name shall be on our foreheads (Rev. 22:4), that we shall be with the angels, an innumerable company, and with the spirits of just men made perfect, the saints of all ages (Heb. 12:23), that we shall know them and be in their society (Matt. 17:3; I Cor. 13:12), that we shall be absolutely untainted with sin, as glorious as the uncreated light of God. (Rev. 21:4, 27; Matt. 13:45.) This being the place and the company toward which we are being borne along so rapidly, we want to be prepared for both place and society.

You are anxious to be cultured for this world and its best society, in its knowledge, in its customs, and in its manners. Yes, you lavish time and money upon yourself and your children, in order that they may be furnished with the accomplishments and culture of this world. You say when you appear in good society you want to be at ease, to be a peer among the most accomplished, and you wish the same for your children. Were you invited to go six months hence to take up your abode at the Court of St. James, as the guest of England's royalty, you would ransack all the books at your command that treated of court etiquette and manners; you would brush up in English history, so that you might not be taken unawares either in your knowledge of the affairs of the country, or in court ceremonial. But in a little while we are going to the court of the King immortal, eternal, in the kingdom of glory. We know not the day nor the hour when the Lord will come, or call us hence; and we want to be ready, both as to purity of character and the courtly culture of the heavenly city. We wish to be familiar with the history of redemption, and with the mysteries of the kingdom. We should not want to appear as an awkward stranger in our Father's house of light. We can only get this sanctification of character and culture of life and manner by constant familiarity and communion with God and the saints through the word.

Men of the world are anxious that they and their children should appear well in the society of this world. To this end they devote themselves and them to the schools of the world and fashion. Believers, too, are anxious that their children should be cultured and accomplished in every way worthy of being the King's sons or daughters, as by grace they are. But they should not think of seeking for them the entree of what is called in this world the best society in order to such end. If they may have their hearts filled with the dear, great love of God, and the sweet grace of Christ; if they hang on the chamber walls of their souls as pictures, "Whatsoever things are honest, just, pure, lovely and of good report, and think on these things" (Phil. 4:8); if they journey through this world in companionship with him; if the Holy Spirit guides them through the Word and shows them wonderful and beautiful things out of his law; if the fruit of the Spirit, which "is love, joy, peace, long-suffering, gentleness, goodness, faith, meekness, and temperance" (Gal. 5:22, 23), adorns their lives and characters — Christians are not then afraid that their children will be a whit behind the foremost society people in the land in culture of mind and heart, and grace of manner. There is a heavenly culture and a divine grace of manner that far transcend anything found in the schools of this world. Only a Christian could think of saying with Paul, standing before his judge, "except these bonds" (Acts 26:29).

John Bunyan, locked up for twelve years in Bedford Jail, with his Bible and concordance for his constant companions, produced and sent forth to the world his immortal dream, written with such beauty of style and in such chaste and simple manner, as to make it classic in English literature. So matchless was the intellectual and spiritual culture of this unlearned tinker of Elstow, that the scholarly John Owen testified before the King, "Your Majesty, if I could write as does that tinker in Bedford Jail I would gladly lay down all my learning." Where did John Bunyan get his culture? In glorious fellowship with Moses in the Law, with David in the Psalms, with Isaiah and the prophets and holy men of God, who wrote as they were moved by the Holy Spirit; with Matthew, Mark, Luke and John; with Paul, Peter and all the rest who wrote and spoke not the thoughts, nor in the words, of man's wisdom, but God's thoughts, and in words which the Holy Spirit giveth. Read Homer and Milton, Shakespeare and Dante; read Bacon, Macaulay, Addison and Carlyle; go through all the best literature of all ages, and it will fall infinitely short of the purity, beauty and grandeur of thought and expression found in God's Word.

Goethe, who said he was not Christian, has declared of the canonical Gospels: "The human mind, no matter how much it may advance in intellectual culture, and in the extent and depth of the knowledge of nature, will never transcend the high moral culture of Christianity as it shines and glows in the canonical Gospels." Renan, the French infidel author, concludes his life of Jesus with these remarkable words: "Whatever may be the surprises of the future, Jesus will never be surpassed; his worship will grow young without ceasing; his legend will call forth tears without end; his suffering will melt the noblest hearts; all ages will proclaim that among the sons of men there is none born greater than Jesus." And Strauss, the rationalistic German author of the *Life of Jesus,* says: "Jesus presents within the sphere of religion the culminating point, beyond which posterity can never go; yea, which it cannot even equal. He remains the highest model of religion within the reach of our thought, and no perfect piety is possible without his presence in the heart." Thus the power of the book and the Person for the highest culture of the highest nature of man, is affirmed by those who do not admit the divine origin of the Scriptures, or the deity of him of whom they are from first to last the witness. If, then, you want to know how to serve God and do his will on the earth, and be thoroughly prepared and cultured for heaven hereafter, take his Word, and make it the rule and companion of your life.

4. *The Bible is the Christian's armory.*

The Christian's calling in the world is that of a soldier. He must fight the good fight of faith (I Tim. 6:12; II Tim. 4:7). Sinners are to be won from the power of the devil to God. Their intelligence, their wills, and their affections, are to be stormed and carried for him; they are to be turned from the power of darkness to light. Their prison-houses of sin are to be broken into; their chains knocked off and the captives set free (Acts 26:16-18). We also, in our own Christian life and pilgrimage, are set upon by the powers of darkness, by the fiery darts of the devil. Doubts, infidelity, temptations, evil imaginations, unclean, unholy, and vain thoughts assail us, poured in upon our souls by Satan, the lusts of the flesh being thus set on fire of hell, if by this means the child of God may be overtaken in a fault or overcome by sin. But this warfare is not carnal, or after the manner of the flesh (II Cor. 10:3-5). Just as Joshua went up against Jericho, and took its strongholds and high towers, and cast them down and made captive the city, not with carnal weapons, but with trumpets of rams' horns (Josh. 6), so we, proceeding against the strongholds, imaginations, and infidel arguments of men, are to take the Gospel trump. The sword we are to wield is the Word of God, the sword of the Spirit (Eph. 6:17) which makes him who wields it invincible. The Bible itself must be brought out, not only as the best defense against all the assaults of infidelity from the lofty towers of human reasonings, but also as the mighty weapon to overcome and bring the enemies of God into captivity to Christ (Rev. 12:11; Eph. 6:13-17). We have only to recall how our Saviour overcame the devil with the all-prevailing weapon, "It is written," in order that we may be furnished with the secret of successful warfare for him.

Very often Christians, young and old, come to us in the inquiry room and say, "Won't you come and talk with this friend of mine?" "Why don't you talk with him (or her) yourself?" we reply. "Because I don't know what to say to him, and, besides, you know more of the Bible." "Well, why don't you know more of the Bible?" To this, various answers are given. At any rate we meet here one grave mistake. An ignorance of the Bible, which not only furnishes us with our spiritual weapons, but "thoroughly furnishes us unto all good works" (II Tim. 3:17), leads many earnest Christians to the doubtful use of their own argumention in dealing with their own and others' souls. It is a hopeless task to pull down the strongholds of the unregenerate mind and heart with anything less than these divine weapons. But all may equip themselves from this great armory. The Bible contains ideas which no philosophy or human theory can furnish, and therefore, puts us in possession of weapons which the enemy cannot withstand when hard pushed by them, re-enforced as they are by the mighty presence of the Holy Spirit, and which renders us impregnable to the assaults of the adversary. Of this mighty power of the Word and Spirit of God we have a splendid example in the case of Stephen, and other early disciples, whose words drawn from the Scripture the Jews could not withstand. We have never yet met an infidel or atheist whose arguments we could not turn aside when depending simply on the Word of God. Nay, more, we have never yet met one in the inquiry rooms who has been able to withstand God's Word and the mighty facts of the Bible, when in humble dependence upon God we have set them in array before him. If you know God's thoughts and seek to be guided by the Holy Spirit, he will say out of your mouth the right word at the right time, both to ward off an assault and to strike a telling blow for the truth. And amidst all this warfare, the light and love and gentleness of Jesus Christ will so shine out in your bearing and manner that they will be convinced of your sincerity, and God will give you the victory.

5. *The Bible is a perfect map and chart to the Christian on pilgrimage through the world.*

With God's Word in hand and heart you may tread your way with perfect safety and confidence through all the labyrinths of this world. The straight and narrow way is so clearly and sharply marked that he who runs may read. It is a highway in which a wayfaring man, though a fool, need not err (Isa. 35:8), for it is everywhere marked by his commandments. More than that, we have an unseen Guide, even the Spirit of truth, who leads us, and says to us, in places of doubt or uncertainty, "This is the way, walk ye in it" (Isa. 30:21). Thus, a pilgrim and a stranger, you may keep your onward way to the city of God in safety and confidence, following in the light of the Word, which is "a lamp to your feet, and a light unto your path" (Psa. 119:105), the path that no one knoweth save he that leadeth thee. Yea, and you will find that the way, over hills and through valleys, shines more and more unto the perfect day (Prov. 4:18). The Word of God is a chart that marks all the rocks and reefs in the sea of life; if we heed, and sail our frail bark by it, we shall come safely into the haven of rest at last. But if we are heedless and proud, and self-sufficient in our own conceits, we shall make shipwreck of our faith. Many a Christian suffers shipwreck through unheeding conceit or neglect of his infallible chart. May the Holy Spirit incline us to study diligently our divine chart, and sail closely by it!

6. *The Bible reveals things to come.*

It contains not only the history of the past, of God's dealings with nations, but it also contains much unfulfilled prophecy. Revelation is a book devoted to things that must shortly come to pass. Prophecy has been called unacted history, and history is but fulfilled prophecy. It is a mistake to suppose that God's hand in history has been limited to those nations mentioned in the Bible.

Could we have the story of God in history, it would be seen that his providence has been in and over all the great and small events of all nations. Daniel in his great prophecy has given a rapid and graphic sketch of the course of history from the golden-headed Babylonian Empire down to the end of time (Dan. 2:44; 7:13-27). Meantime God among nations will be overturning, overturning, and overturning until he comes whose right it is (Ezek. 21:27). The Book of Revelation is a detailed exposition of the second and seventh chapters of Daniel, and the two books should be read together.

Rulers are rapidly bringing to pass things that God has marked out in prophecy ages ago. But they know not what they do (Luke 21:25-27). Of the day and hour when the flaming heavens shall reveal the appearing and Kingdom of our Lord Jesus Christ (II Tim. 4:1), no man knoweth; but men are bidden to wait and be ready, lest they be surprised by the great and notable day of the Lord. To this end the Scriptures are also written, that the loving student of them may live in advance of history, and be overtaken by no untoward event. If his prophetic Word dwell richly in our hearts and minds, there will be no great surprise for us as time goes on. We shall discern through the prophetic telescope, dimly it may be, the approaches of those things out of which history is made. We know that there is a disposition on the part of many Christians to make light of all prophetic study; but our risen Lord, in his last revelation to John concerning things to come, caused him to write differently (Rev. 22:6, 7).

May the Spirit of God give us a mind to study his Word reverently and believingly with a prepared heart, as did Ezra (7:10), in the light and under the guidance of the Holy Spirit. Then will he show us things to come (John 16:13).

JOHN McNICOL (1869-1956) had his dreams of foreign mission work dashed when he was turned down for overseas service. Yet his influence in the field of missions—as well as his impact on students he taught—more than made up for that disappointment. McNicol was educated at the University of Toronto where he received his B.A. with honors in Classics. Later, he earned a B.D. degree from Knox College. In 1896, McNicol became the minister of the Presbyterian church in Aylmer, Quebec. Soon, however, he returned to education as a teacher at Toronto Bible Training School (later Tornoto Bible College). He was named principal of the school in 1906, a position he held until 1946. During those years he also served on the councils of the China Inland Mission and the Sudan Interior Mission—thus fulfilling his early desire to contribute to mission work. His commentary on Luke became part of the *New Bible Commentary*, but his most notable literary achievement was *Thinking Through the Bible*, republished in 1976 as *McNichol's Bible Survey* by Kregel Publications.

62

The Hope of the Church

By Rev. John McNicol, B.A., B.D.
PRINCIPAL OF THE TORONTO BIBLE TRAINING SCHOOL

Edited by Charles L. Feinberg, Th.D., Ph.D.

There are many indications of a revival of interest in the study of eschatology. The latest attack upon the Christian faith is being directed against the eschatalogical teaching of the New Testament. The Christian church was founded upon the promise of a speedy return of Christ to establish his Kingdom in the world, but its history has taken an entirely different course. The expectation of the early Christians was not fulfilled. The teaching of the apostles has been falsified. Such is the argument that is used in some quarters to discredit the founders of Christianity. This has compelled Christian scholars to give renewed attention to the teaching of the New Testament about the Lord's second coming, and will doubtless lead to more earnest and thorough examination of the whole outlook of Christ and his apostles upon the future.

It is acknowledged that the eschatology of the New Testament is not the eschatology of the church today. The hope of the early Christians is not the hope of the average Christian now. It has become our habit to think of the change which comes at death, at our entrance into heaven, as the crowning point in the believer's life, and the proper object of our hope. Yet the apostles never speak of death as something which the Christian should look forward to or prepare for. They do not ignore death altogether, nor do they cast a halo about it. It is always an enemy, the last enemy that is to be destroyed. But they do not take account of it at all in the scheme of things with which we have now to reckon.

Nor is heaven set forth as the Christian's hope. The New Testament represents the church as in heaven already. We have been raised up with Christ and to sit with him in the heavenly places (Eph. 2:6). Our warfare is carried on against spiritual hosts of wickedness in the heavenly places (Eph. 6:12). Our citizenship is there (Phil. 3:20). Neither death nor heaven, then can be the church's hope, for, in their essential relation to the Christian life, death lies in the past and heaven in the present.

The conversion of the world is not the object of the church's hope. It is quite true that this glorious consummation lies in the future, for "the earth shall be filled with the knowledge of the Lord as the waters cover the sea," but the task of bringing this about was not committed to the church. On the contrary, the New Testament descriptions of the last days of the church upon earth preclude the thought. They are depicted in dark colors (II Tim. 3:1-5; II Pet. 3:1-4). The history of the preaching of the Gospel in the world should be enough to show that this cannot be the object set before us, for, while whole nations have been evangelized, not a single community has ever been completely converted. It is a striking fact that the apostles had nothing to say about the conversion of the world. While they were busy preaching the Gospel in the world they gave no indication that they expected this work to result at length in the transformation of the world. They were not looking for a change in the world, but for the personal presence of their Lord. Jesus Christ himself was their hope, and his appearing they intensely loved and longed for.

The attitude of the New Testament church is represented by the Apostle John in the closing words of the Apocalypse. Visions of heavenly glory and millennial peace have passed before him. He has seen the new heaven and the new earth wherein dwelleth righteousness. But, at the end of it all, the longing of the aged apostle is not for these things to come. Greater than all these glories, dearer than all these dear things, is the Master himself, and the prayer that rises from his heart as he closes his wondrous book is simply, "Come, Lord Jesus."

The hope of the church, then, is the personal return of her Lord. Let us see how this hope lies upon the pages of the New Testament revelation, and how it influenced the life of the New Testament church.

1. Christ taught his disciples to expect his return. This was the last of the stages through which his teaching about himself

advanced. In the early part of his ministry he seems to have kept his personality in the background; he forbade those whom he healed to tell about him. Then there came a time when he asked the disciples, "Who do men say that I am?" and led them to think of his divine origin. After that he began to instruct them about his approaching death and resurrection (Luke 9:31). In the last days of his ministry his return to the world largely occupied his own thoughts, and he kept it prominently before the minds of his disciples. During his last journey to Jerusalem he foreshadowed his own history in the parable of the nobleman going into a far country to receive a kingdom and return, who left his servants behind with the command, "Occupy till I come" (Luke 19:12, 13). One evening during the last week he sat on the Mount of Olives, looking down no doubt upon the massive buildings of the temple, the total destruction of which he had just foretold. The disciples gathered about him with the request: "Tell us, when shall these things be? and what shall be the sign of thy coming and of the end of the world?" (Matt. 24:3). It is evident from the form of this question that his coming was no new thought to them. It was occupying their minds already. They knew that he was coming again, and they wished to know how to recognize the approach of that event. In answer to the question, the Lord unfolded a panorama of intervening history, and emphasized the need of watchfulness, because the time of his coming would be uncertain. He enforced this teaching with two striking illustrations of the twofold kind of preparation needed on the part of the disciples, the inward preparation of spiritual life set forth in the parable of the virgins, and the outward preparation of diligent service in that of the talents. Then he closed his discourse with a graphic picture of the changed conditions in which he would appear when he came the second time as the Son of Man sitting upon the throne of his glory.

Through the sad and dark hours of the very last night his thoughts were occupied with his return. In the upper room, when the faithful little band were grouped about him in sorrow for the parting which all vaguely felt was near, he began his farewell words to them with comforting assurance (John 14:1-3). A few hours afterwards he was in the midst of the shameful scenes of his trial. Mark his answer to the high priest, when he calmly acknowledged the claim to be the Christ, the Son of God (Matt. 24:64). He did not look like the Messiah at that moment as he stood there with bound hands before his accusers. His appearance seemed to belie his words. But the time would come when they would see that his claim was true. This was what was in his thoughts. Through all the shame of those awful hours, the vision of his return in glory to the world that was rejecting him now shone like a beacon upon his soul (Heb. 12:1-2).

At his ascension the same truth was brought again to the minds of the disciples. As they stood gazing in wonder towards the place where the Lord had disappeared from their view, the two angels were sent to remind them of his return (Acts 1:11). It was this thought that sent the disciples back to Jerusalem with the joy which Luke describes in the closing verses of his Gospel. It is very clear, therefore, that when Jesus departed from this world after his first coming, he left his disciples radiant with the joyful assurance of his coming again.

2. The apostles taught their converts to wait for the coming of the Lord. All the New Testament churches have the expectant attitude. No matter in what part of the world or in what stage of development they are found, they have this characteristic in common. The conversion of the Thessalonians is described as "turning to God from idols to serve the living and true God, and to wait for his Son from heaven" (I Thess. 1:9-10). The Corinthians "come behind in no gift, waiting for the revelation of our Lord Jesus Christ" (I Cor. 1:7). To the Galatians Paul writes, "We through the Spirit by faith wait for the hope of righteousness" (Gal. 5:5); and to the Philippians, "Our citizenship is in heaven, whence also we wait for a Saviour, the Lord Jesus Christ" (Phil. 3:20). In the Epistle to the Hebrews the same attitude is disclosed (Heb. 9:28). It is evident that the early Christians not only looked back to a Saviour who had died for them, but forward to a Saviour who was to come. There were two poles in their conversion. Their faith was anchored in the past in the facts of the death and resurrection of the Lord, and also in the future in the assured hope of his return. It is manifest, therefore, that the second coming of the Saviour occupied a most important place in the Gospel which the apostles preached, and which these Christians received.

3. The whole life and work of the New Testament church has the coming of the Lord in view. All the lines of her activity and experience lead to this event. The sanctification of the disciple is a preparation for the coming of the Lord (I Thess. 5:23; I John 2:28). Christian service gets its encouragement in the same inspiring issue (I Tim. 6:14; I Pet. 5:2, 4). The patience of the early Christians in suffering and trial is bounded by the same event (Jas. 5:7, 8; Phil. 4:5). Their life of fellowship and brotherly love reaches its holy consummation at the Lord's return (I Thess. 3:12-13). Their acts of worship, as for example, their observance of the Lord's Supper, have the same end in view (I Cor. 11:26). Thus, whatever aspect of the church's life and work we consider, we find it to be a stream which moves on towards one glorious future. The appearing of the Lord Jesus himself fills the whole horizon.

4. The New Testament grace of hope rests upon the coming of the Lord. This word is emptied today of much of the meaning it had among the early Christians. It has come to be a vague and misty thing, the general habit of expecting things somehow to turn out well. Their hope was no such shallow optimism. It was the light that shone from that one glad coming event, casting its sacred glow over all their lives. Paul sums up the true Christian attitude (Titus 2:11-13).

The word "hope" was often upon the lips of the apostles. It is used more than a score of times in the epistles in direct connection with the coming of the Lord. It is not unlikely that, even when it is used alone without any qualifying phrase, as in the expressions, "We are saved by hope," "rejoicing in hope," it has the same specific reference. The Epistle to the Hebrews makes frequent use of the word in this way. There was a special reason for this. The Hebrew Christians were a small and despised community, living under the continual influence of that majestic ritual which was still going on in the temple at Jerusalem. The return of Christ was delayed, and there was a strong tendency to slip back into the old ceremonial system. Their patience and hope had need of every encouragement. The writer of the epistle turns their eyes again and again from the shadows of the past to the realities that lay before them. Their Messiah had indeed come to put away sin by the sacrifice of himself, but he would come a second time, in glory, with a final and complete salvation. This was the hope set before them to which they had fled for refuge (Heb. 6:18). Let them hold fast their boldness and the glorying of their hope firm unto the end (Heb. 3:6).

In a beautiful passage in his first epistle, the Apostle John points out the practical value of this Christian grace in its essential relation to the coming of the Lord as a purifying hope (I John 3:2, 3).

5. Redemption is not complete until the second coming of the Lord. The apostles think of salvation in three different ways; sometimes with reference to the past, as a fact already assured at the moment of belief in the Lord Jesus Christ; sometimes with reference to the present, as a process still going on; and sometimes with reference to the future, as an act yet to be accomplished. In this last sense Paul uses the word in Romans 13:11; and Peter also, in I Peter 1:5. Our Lord refers to the same thing when, after telling the disciples about the signs of his coming, he exhorts them to look up for the expected redemption (Luke 21:28).

Think of what this crowning act of redemption will mean for the Redeemer himself, when, attended with heavenly glory, he prepares to descend to the very world that witnessed his suffering, sorrow, and shame. What will it mean to him when the multitudes of the redeemed gather about him, and at last he sees of the travail of his soul and is satisfied? Is it not reasonable that there should be such a manifestation of the Redeemer to the world? Is it reasonable that the despised Man of Nazareth should be the only view the world should have of him who is to be the heir of all things? Is it likely that God would allow his Son's retirement from the world in apparent defeat without any subsequent vindication? If the prophetic vision of the suffering Servant had an actual personal fulfillment, surely the prophetic vision of the conquering King will also have a personal fulfillment. As the world was astonished at him when he came the first time, so it will be astonished when he comes a second time (Isa. 63:1).

And what will it mean for the redeemed? There will be, of course, the happy reunion of all the saints when the dead are raised and the living are changed, for, when the Lord descends from heaven with a shout, "the dead in Christ shall rise first, and we that are alive and remain shall be caught up together with them in the clouds to meet the Lord in the air." But glorious as these things are, they are only preliminary steps to a higher and holier bliss. The climax of redemption will be the manifested union of the Church with her Lord in the marriage of the Lamb. For then the Bridegroom shall come to claim his Bride, and take her to share his glory and his throne. Then the church that Christ loved and purchased shall be presented to him a glorious church, not having spot or wrinkle or any such thing. Then the astonished world, beholding her transformation, shall cry, "Who is this that cometh up from the wilderness leaning on her beloved?" Think of what it will mean when, after sharing his humiliation in the midst of a scoffing and unbelieving world, the redeemed church is exalted to his side, and, as the consort of the King of kings and Lord of lords, stands "all rapture through and through in God's most holy sight." Nothing less than this is the destiny that awaits the church of Jesus Christ.

If the Lord committed to his disciples the promise of his personal return, and if it occupied so large a place in the lives of the early Christians, surely it is unfair to banish it from the church today. It is unfair to the world, for this truth is part of the Gospel which should be delivered to the world. It is unfair to the church, for it deprives the people of Christ of one of the most powerful motives for spiritual life and service. It is unfair to Christ himself, for it obscures the reality of his personal presence within the heavenly veil and substitutes for it the thin air of a mere spiritual influence.

The hope of the second coming of our Lord has an important bearing upon Christian life and doctrine. It has a vital relation especially to some points of our faith which are being attacked or obscured by the subtle tendencies of modern thought.

1. It is bound up with belief in the supreme and infallible authority of the Holy Scriptures. It would never be adopted on rationalistic grounds. Those who receive it rest their belief wholly on the authority of Scripture, believing that therein God has spoken in a way that can be trusted. They accept the Bible as the record of God's revelation to man, and believe that in prophecy he has disclosed his purpose concerning the future of the

world. It is a protest against the tendency within the Church to exalt the human reason above the Word of God, and to reduce inspired prophecy to the level of merely human foresight.

2. It bears testimony to the presence of God in human history. The tendency of our times is to explain away the supernatural element in history whether in the past, the present, or the future. To this tendency those who accept the doctrine of the second coming refuse to yield. The history of the world is controlled by God; his hand is on the affairs of men. In the person of Jesus Christ he has already supernaturally intervened in the course of human history. It is believed, on the authority of his Word, that he will supernaturally intervene again. The first coming of Christ was a descent of God into the life of the human race. The Scriptures teach us to expect another divine descent, not to bring history to a close, but to introduce new forces and to inaugurate a new dispensation.

3. It exalts the divine person and work of the incarnate Son of God. It is in direct opposition to the Unitarian tendencies which pervade so large a part of modern religious thought. It holds the truth of the Lord's continued existence in a glorified body, and regards this fact as of primary importance and of prophetic signifiance. The personal existence of the risen Son of Man is not to be dissolved away into a mere general spiritual presence. The risen and ascended Redeemer exists today in heaven in the true reality of his glorified humanity; and this same Jesus shall be revealed one day in his glorious personality from behind the unseen veil, to carry on the redemption of the world to its full completion.

4. It takes due account of the fall of the human race. The tendency today is greatly to exalt man and to ignore the fact of the fall. The great advance that is being made in every department of human knowledge and activity predisposes men to form the highest conceptions of the possibilities of the race. The theory of evolution, which dominates modern thinking, leads men to expect a gradual perfecting of the race under the laws of its own being, which will issue at last, with the beneficent aid of Christianity, in a perfect state of human society and the redemption of the race as a whole. But human sin is too deep-rooted and too widespread for the attainment of this end in the present order of

things, even with the aid of existing spiritual agencies. It is acknowledged to be the teaching of Scripture that, even with the aid of divine grace, the triumph of the kingdom of God in the individual is not complete in the present order, but only at his translation to a higher order at the resurrection. It would seem that the analogy should hold as regards the race, and that the triumph of the Kingdom in the race as an organic unity will be brought about only by a supernatural intervention of divine power and the introduction of humanity into a new order of things.

5. It presents a sublime view of God's great purpose in his creation. It places the redemption of the whole world, the restoration of all things, in the very forefront of the divine purpose regarding fallen man. Everything has been arranged and foreordained by God to this end. This is the divine event to which the whole creation moves. He who has this hope has a large vision, a vision not limited to the present day and its affairs. He sees the will of God moving on through the history of the ages. The present age is but preparatory. A grander age is to be ushered in by the advent of the victorious Redeemer, an age in which man shall come to his own at last, and creation shall be restored to its harmony, under its true head, the glorified Son of Man.

6. It provides the most inspiring motive for Christian life and service. It is a supremely practical hope. The repeated instructions of the Lord and his apostles to be ready for his return indicate the force this doctrine had as a motive in the lives of the early Christians. The great leaders who have left their impress on the history of the church did not discard this doctrine, but made it a real hope in their own lives. Martin Luther, in the midst of the throes of the Reformation, wrote, "I ardently hope that, amidst these internal dissensions on the earth, Jesus Christ will hasten the day of his coming." The acute and learned Calvin saw that this was the church's true hope. "We must hunger after Christ," he said, "till the dawning of that great day when our Lord will fully manifest the glory of his Kingdom. The whole family of the faithful will keep in view that day." The intrepid soul of John Knox was nerved by this hope. In a letter to his friends in England he wrote: "Has not the Lord Jesus, in despite of Satan's malice, carried up our flesh into heaven? And shall

he not return? We know that he shall return, and that with expedition." John Wesley believed this same truth, as is shown by his comment on the closing verses of Revelation: "The spirit of adoption in the bride in the heart of every true believer says, with earnest desire and expectation, 'Come and accomplish all the words of this prophecy.'" It formed the burden of Milton's sublime supplication: "Come forth out of Thy royal chambers, O Prince of all the kings of the earth; put on the visible robes of Thy imperial majesty; take up that unlimited scepter which Thy Almighty Father hath bequeathed Thee. For now the voice of Thy bride calls Thee, and all creatures sigh to be renewed." It was the ardent longing of the seraphic Rutherford: "Oh, that Christ would remove the covering, draw aside the curtains of time, and come down. Oh, that the shadows and the night were gone." It was the prayer of Richard Baxter in the *Saints' Everlasting Rest:* "Hasten, O my Saviour, the time of Thy return. Send forth Thine angels and let that dreadful, joyful trumpet sound. Thy desolate Bride saith come. The whole creation saith come. Even so, come, Lord Jesus." And if we would follow in the steps of these men, we will return to the simple, unmistakable New Testament type of experience, and with faces uplifted towards the veil within which the Lord of glory waits, and with hearts all aglow with a personal love for him, we will carry on through all our life and service the same apostolic prayer.

CHARLES ROSENBURY ERDMAN (1866-1960) graduated from Princeton Theological Seminary before being ordained in 1891. After holding pastorates in Pennsylvania between 1890 and 1905, he returned to Princeton to teach practical theology at the seminary. At the same time, he pastored First Presbyterian Church in Princeton. Erdman was the author of 35 books, many of which were translated into other languages, and was a popular expository preacher in the Bible conference movement.

63

The Coming of Christ

By Professor Charles R. Erdman, D.D.
Princeton Theological Seminary

Revised and edited by Gerald B. Stanton, Th.D.

The return of Christ is a *fundamental doctrine* of the Christian faith. It is embodied in hymns of hope; it forms the climax of the creeds; it is the sublime motive for evangelistic and missionary activity; and daily it is voiced in the inspired prayer: "Even so, come, Lord Jesus."

It is a peculiarly *a scriptural doctrine*. It is not, on the one hand, a dream of ignorant fanatics, nor, on the other, a creation of speculative theologians; but it is a truth divinely revealed, and recorded in the Bible with marked clearness, emphasis and prominence.

Like the other great truths of revelation, it is *a controverted doctrine*. The essential fact is held universally by all who admit the authority of Scripture; but as to certain incidental, although important, elements of the teaching, there is difference of opinion among even the most careful and reverent students. Any consideration of the theme demands, therefore, modesty, humility and abundant charity. According to the familiar view outlined in this paper, the Bible describes the "second coming of Christ" as *personal, glorious, and imminent*.

I. His Coming Will Be Personal

By *personal* is meant all that is suggested by the words visible, bodily, local; and all that may be contrasted with that which is spiritual, providential, figurative. Of course, the spiritual presence of Christ is a blessed reality. One of the most comforting and inspiring truths is the teaching that Christ does come to each believer, by his Holy Spirit, and dwells within and empowers for service and suffering and growth in grace. But this is to be held in harmony with the other blessed truth that Christ will some day literally appear again in bodily form, and "we shall see him" and shall then "be like him," when "we see him as he is."

Nor yet did that special manifestation of the Holy Spirit at *Pentecost* fulfill the promise of Christ's return. Subsequent to Pentecost, Peter urged the Jews to repent in order that Jesus, whom for a time "the heavens had received," might be "sent back again." He wrote his epistles of comfort based upon the hope of a returning Lord, while Paul and the other apostles, long after Pentecost, emphasized the coming of Christ as the highest incentive for life and service.

According to the interpretation of others, Christ is said "to come" in various *providential events of history,* as notably in the destruction of Jerusalem. This tragedy of history is supposed by many to fulfill the prophecies spoken by Christ in his great discourse on the Mount of Olives, recorded in Matthew 24, Mark 13, and Luke 21. When one combines these predictions, it becomes evident that the capture of the holy city by Titus was a real but only a partial fulfillment of the words of Christ. As in the case of so many Old Testament prophecies, the nearer event furnished the colors in which were depicted scenes and occurrences which belonged to a distant future, and in this case to "the end of the age." When Jerusalem fell, the people of God were not delivered nor the enemies of God punished, nor did "the sign of the Son of Man" appear in the heavens, as was predicted of the time when he comes again. Moreover, long after the fall of the city, John wrote in Gospel and in Apocalypse of the coming of the King.

Nor is the coming of Christ to be confused with *death.* It is true that this dark messenger ushers us into an experience which is, for the believer, one of great blessedness. To depart is "to be with Christ, which is far better," and "to be absent from the body" is "to be at home with the Lord." But death is for us inseparable from pain and loss and sorrow and tears and anguish; and even those who are now with their Lord, in heavenly joy, are waiting for their bodies of glory and for the rewards and reunions which will be theirs at the appearing of Christ.

More marvelous than the scenes at Pentecost, more startling than the fall of Jerusalem, more blessed than the indwelling of the

Spirit or the departure to be with the Lord, will be the literal, visible, bodily return of Christ. No event may seem less probable to unaided human reason; no event is more certain in the light of inspired Scripture. "This same Jesus which is taken up from you into heaven shall so come *in like manner* as ye have seen him go into heaven." "Behold, he cometh with clouds; and *every eye shall see him*" (Acts 1:11; Rev. 1:7).

II. His Coming Will Be Glorious

This coming of Christ is to be *glorious,* not only in its attendant circumstances, but also in its effects upon the church and the world. Our Lord predicted that he would return "in his own glory, and the glory of his Father, and of the holy angels" (Luke 9:26). He will then be revealed in his divine majesty. Once during his earthly ministry, on the mount of transfiguration, there was given to his followers a glimpse of the royal splendor he had for a time laid aside, and in which he will again appear.

As on the great day of atonement the high priest put off his usual robes "for glory and for beauty" and appeared in spotless white, when he offered the sacrifices for sin and went into the holy place to intercede for the waiting people, so our Great High Priest laid aside the robes of his imperial majesty when stooping from heaven he assumed his garb of sinless flesh. He then offered himself as the perfect sacrifice and entered the holy places not made with hands to appear in the presence of God for us. But as the high priest again assumed his garments of scarlet and blue and purple and gold when he came forth to complete his work in the presence of the people, so Christ, when he returns to bless and to receive the homage of the world, will be manifest in his divine glory (Heb. 9:24-28). As he appeared to Isaiah in his vision, to the disciples on the holy mount, to Saul on his way to Damascus, to John on Patmos, so will the Son of Man appear when, as he promised. he is seen "sitting at the right hand of power, and coming on the clouds of heaven" (Matt. 26:64).

Nothing could be more natural than such a triumphant return of the risen, ascended Lord. What a pathetic picture Christ would present in the history of the race, if, after all his claims and promises, the world should see him, last of all, hanging on a cross as a malefactor, or laid lifeless in a tomb! "He was despised and rejected of men," but he is to return again "with power and great glory," attended by thousands of the heavenly host. As the Epistle to the Hebrews strikingly says: "When he again bringeth in the first born into the inhabited earth he saith, And let all the angels of God worship him" (Heb. 1:6).

> *Thou art coming, O my Saviour,*
> *Thou art coming, O my King,*
> *In Thy beauty all resplendent;*
> *In Thy glory all transcendent;*
> *Well may we rejoice and sing:*
> *Coming! in the opening East*
> *Herald brightness slowly swells;*
> *Coming! O my glorious Priest,*
> *Hear we not Thy golden bells.*

Then will Christ *reign in glory* over all the world. It is true that now "all power" has been given to him "in heaven and on earth," but that power has not been fully manifest; "we see not yet all things put under him." He has "sat down on the right hand of God," but he is "henceforth expecting till his enemies be made the footstool of his feet." He is now reigning, seated on the Father's throne; but this world is still in reality a revolted province, and Christ is yet to sit upon his own throne. Then "before him every knee will bow, and every tongue confess that he is Lord" (Heb. 10:12, 13; Phil. 2:10, 11).

These expressions need not be interpreted so as to insist that Christ will rule visibly in some one earthly locality, "establishing in Jerusalem an oriental court." But they mean at very least that the coming of Christ will be followed by the universal reign of Christ. "When the Son of Man shall come in his glory, and all the angels with him, then shall he sit on the throne of his glory" (Matt. 25:31). He will determine who may enter and who must be excluded from his kingdom. He will then say: "Come ye blessed of my Father, inherit the kingdom prepared for you from the foundation of the world." Then will be fulfilled his prediction: "Not every one that saith unto me, Lord, Lord, shall enter into the kingdom of heaven, but he that doeth the will of my Father who is in heaven. Many *will say to me* in that day, Lord, Lord, . . . and then *will I* profess unto them, I never knew you, depart from me, ye that work iniquity" (Matt. 7:21-23). He will be the supreme Judge, but he will also be manifest as the universal Ruler in his perfected kingdom. Then the voices will be heard proclaiming: "The kingdom of the world is become the kingdom of our Lord, and of his Christ; and he shall reign forever and ever" (Rev. 11:15).

In this glory of Christ his followers are to share. *The resurrection of the dead* will take place when he returns; "For as in Adam all die, so also in Christ shall all be made alive. But each in his own order: Christ the first fruits; then they that are Christ's at his coming." The *body* of the believer is thus to be raised in *glory.* "It is sown in corruption; it is raised in incorruption: it is sown in dishonor; it is raised in glory." As to how the spirits now with Christ are to be united with their resurrection bodies, the Bible is absolutely silent; but we know that this will be at the coming of the Lord (I Cor. 15:22-23, 42-43).

Then, too, the bodies of *living believers* will be glorified, and made deathless and immortal like the body of their divine Lord. "For our citizenship is in heaven; whence also we wait for a Saviour, the Lord Jesus Christ: who shall fashion anew the body of our humiliation, that it may be conformed to the body of his glory" (Phil. 3:20, 21). Sometimes it is carelessly said that "nothing is so sure as death." One thing is more sure; it is this: some Christians will never die. One generation of believers will be living when Christ returns, and they will be translated without the experience of death. What "is mortal will be swallowed up of life." They never will be "unclothed," but "clothed upon" with the glory of immortality (I Cor. 15:51-52; II Cor. 5:4).

Then, also, will be the blessed *reunion in glory* of the risen and the transfigured followers of Christ. "For this we say unto you by the word of the Lord, that we that are alive, that are left unto the coming of the Lord, shall in no wise precede them that are fallen asleep. For the Lord himself shall descend from heaven, with a shout, with the voice of the arch-angel, and with the trump of God: and the dead in Christ shall rise first; then we that are alive, that are left, shall together with them be caught up in the clouds to meet the Lord in the air: and so shall we ever be with the Lord" (I Thess. 4:13-18).

> *Some from earth, from glory some,*
> *Severed only 'Till He Come.'*

The time of the return of the Lord will be, furthermore, the time of *the reward* of his servants. The Son of Man is likened to a nobleman who has gone "into a far country to receive for himself a kingdom, and to return." He has entrusted various talents to his servants with the command to use them wisely, until his return. When he has "come back again, having received the kingdom," *then* he "maketh a reckoning with them." It is popularly said, and in a sense it is true, that when our loved ones go to be with Christ "they have gone to their reward"; but more strictly speaking, the full reward of the blessed awaits the coming of Christ. Whatever may be meant by being "set over many things," or having "authority over ten cities," the complete recompense of the faithful is "at the resurrection of the just" (Matt. 25:14-23; Luke 19:11-27; Luke 14:14).

That the real coronation day of the Christian is not at death but at "the appearing of Christ" was strikingly suggested by Paul when, realizing that he was to die before the Lord returned, he gave to Timothy his triumphant farewell: "I have fought the good fight, I have finished the course, I have kept the faith: henceforth there is laid up for me the crown of righteousness, which the Lord the righteous Judge shall give to me *at that day:* and not to me only, but also to all them that have loved *His appearing*" (II Tim. 4:7, 8). So Peter encourages pastors to be faithful, by the familiar promise: "And when the chief Shepherd *shall be manifested,* ye shall receive the crown of glory that fadeth not away" (I Peter 5:1-4). In large measure this reward will consist in being changed into a moral likeness to Christ. This is far more marvelous than the transfiguration of our bodies, but no less real. "Beloved, now are we the children of God, and it is not yet made manifest what we shall be. We know that if he shall be manifested, we shall be like him; for we shall see him even as he is" (I John 3:1-3).

The rule of Christ and of his people who reign with him must secure unparalleled blessedness for the world. "The end of the world" does not mean, in prophecy, the end of the earth and the destruction of its inhabitants, but the end of the "present age," which is to be followed by *an age of glory.* Nature itself will become more beautiful and joyous. "The whole creation which is groaning and travailing in pain together until now will be delivered from the bondage of corruption unto the liberty of the glory of the children of God" (Rom. 8:21). In spite of the sin and failures of man, we are not to look for the destruction of this globe, but for an era when true full life of humanity will be realized, when all shall know the Lord from the least unto the greatest, when all art and science and social institutions shall be Christian, when "nation shall not lift up sword against nation, neither shall they learn war any more" (Isa. 2:1-4). Such an age, of which poets have sung and philosophers have dreamed, such an era as psalmists, and prophets, and apostles have promised, will dawn at the coming of the King.

III. His Coming Is Imminent

The Bible further describes the coming of Christ as *imminent*. It is an event which may occur in any lifetime. Whatever difficulties the fact involves, there is no doubt that all the Biblical writers and their fellow Christians believed that Christ might return in their generation. This has been the normal attitude of the church ever since. Paul describes believers as men "who have turned to God from idols" and who "wait for his Son from heaven." Christians are further described as "those that wait for him," and as "those that love his appearing." They are everywhere in the New Testament exhorted to "watch," and to be ready for the return of their Lord. His coming is their constant encouragement and inspiration and hope (I Thess. 4:10; II Peter 4:8; Matt. 24:42; Mark 13:35, 37; Luke 21:36; Phil. 4:5).

However, "imminent" does *not* mean "*immediate*." Confusion of these ideas has led some writers to assert that "Paul and the early Christians were mistaken in their views as to the Lord's return." But, when Paul used such a phrase as "*we that are alive and remain unto the coming of the Lord*," he meant simply to identify himself with his fellow Christians, and to suggest that, if he lived until Christ came, their blessed experience would also be his. He could not have said, "*ye that are alive and remain*"; that would have indicated that Paul was to die first. This he did not then know. He believed that the Lord *might* return in his lifetime; he never asserted that he *would*.

"Imminence" as related to our Lord's return indicates *uncertainty* as to time, but *possibility* of nearness. "Take ye heed, watch, for ye know not when the time is" (Mark 13:33). Such statements rebuke those who have brought the doctrine into disrepute by announcing dates for "the end of the world," and by setting times for the coming of Christ. So, too, they suggest caution to those who assert that the age is *now* drawing to its close; it *may* be, but of this there is no certainty.

These scriptural exhortations to watch seem to contradict, also, those who teach that a "millennium," a thousand years or a protracted period of righteousness, must intervene between the present time and the advent of Christ. Those who hold this last view are commonly called "Post-Millennialists" to distinguish them from "Pre-Millennialists," who hold the return of Christ will precede and usher in such an age of universal blessedness.

There are several positive statements of Scripture which intimate that *the millennium* follows the coming of Christ.

According to Daniel, it is *after* the Son of Man comes with the clouds of heaven that he is given "dominion and glory and a kingdom, that all peoples, nations and languages should serve him" (Dan. 7:13, 14, 27). According to the Psalms, the appearing of the Lord, in flaming fire upon his adversaries, prepares the way for the establishment of his glorious kingdom, as "he comes to rule the world with righteousness and the peoples with equity" (Psa. 96-98, etc.). According to Paul (in II Thess. 1 and 2) the advent described by Daniel is not to an earth which is enjoying millennial peace, but it is "in flaming fire" to destroy an existing "Man of Sin" whose career is the culmination of the lawlessness already manifest and to continue until the personal coming of Christ. According to our Lord himself his return is to bring "the regeneration," not the destruction of the world (Matt. 19:28; Luke 22:28-30). But this rule of blessedness is preceded by judgments that come "as a snare on all the earth" (Luke 21:29-36). According to Peter, "seasons of refreshing" and "the restitution of all things," not annihilation of the globe, will come with the return of Christ (Acts 3:19-21). According to John, the coming of Christ (Rev. 19) *precedes* the millennium (Rev. 20).

However great the divergence of views among students of prophecy may seem to be, and in spite of the many varieties of opinion among the representatives of the two schools which have been mentioned in passing, the points of agreement are far more important. The main difference is as to the order, rather than as to the reality of events.

The great body of believers are united in expecting both an age of glory and a personal return of Christ. As to many related events they differ; but as to the one great precedent condition of that coming age or that promised return of the Lord there is absolute harmony of conviction: *the Gospel must first be preached to all nations* (Matt. 24:14). The church must continue to "make disciples of all the nations . . . even unto the end of the age" (Matt. 28:19-20).

This is therefore a time, not for unkindly criticism of fellow Christians, but for friendly conference; not for disputing over divergent views, but for united action; not for dogmatic assertion of prophetic programs, but for the humble acknowledgment that "we know in part"; not for idle dreaming, but for the immediate task of evangelizing a lost world.

For such effort, no one truth is more inspiring than that of the return of Christ. None other can make us sit more lightly by the things of time, none other is more familiar as a Scriptural motive to purity, holiness, patience, vigilance, love. Strengthened by this blessed hope let us press forward with passionate zeal to the task that awaits us:

> *Till o'er our ransomed nature*
> *The Lamb for sinners slain,*
> *Redeemer, King, Creator,*
> *In bliss returns to reign!*

EDGAR YOUNG MULLINS (1860-1928) was president of the Southern Baptist Convention from 1921 to 1924. The road to the top began with a varied educational career that included time at Texas A & M, Southern Baptist Theological Seminary, and Johns Hopkins University. Because of poor health, Mullins had to set aside his dream of being a foreign missionary. Instead, he pastored churches in Kentucky, Massachusetts, and Maryland. In 1899, he returned to Southern Baptist Seminary as a professor, and soon, its president. Theologically conservative, Mullins enjoyed apologetics the most. Some of his books include *Why Is Christianity True?*, *A New Interpretation of the Baptist Faith*, and *The Life of Christ*.

64

The Testimony of Christian Experience

By President E. Y. Mullins, D.D., LL.D.
LOUISVILLE, KENTUCKY

Abridged and emended by James H. Christian, Th.D.

Human experience is the one datum of all philosophy and all science. The experience of the individual and of the race is the grist which is poured into all the scientific and philosophic mills. Hence Christian experience as a distinct form of human experience ought to receive more attention than it has ever received before.

Christian experience, the experience of regeneration and conversion, of moral transformation through Christian agencies, has evidential value in several directions.

I. EXPERIENCE AND PHILOSOPHY

Christian experience is the supplemental link to complete philosophy. Philosophy is man reaching up towards God. Christian experience is the effect of God reaching down to man.

Philosophy seems always on the point of discovering the secret of the universe, but it never succeeds in doing it. Now why is it that philosophy seems to expend so much labor for naught? To me it is clear that the reason why it seems to labor so long without satisfactory results is that it refuses to consider all human experience, including the religious. It splits experience up into little bits and hunts among the bits for some single abstract principle which will explain all the rest. It is very much as if one were going to attempt to explain the ocean, its contents, its variety and marvelous abundance of life, by taking a single fish scale and on that scale as a foundation build up his theory of the ocean and its contents. How accurate do you suppose his account would be? Yet this is analogous to what philosophers have done. Spinoza scaled off from the world of experience and being the idea of substance, and built a pantheistic system on that scale. Hegel scaled off the conception of reason or the idea and reared a vast idealistic system on that. Schopenhauer scaled off the conception of will and reared his pessimistic system of philosophy on that. Haeckel scaled off the conception of matter and built his materialistic system on that.

The result of the process is that the philosophers get clear away from human life and experience. They fix their gaze on the photograph of a dim and far away image of reality and become absorbed in excessive star-gazing, metaphysical cliff-climbing and transcendental soap-bubble-blowing. They are like the Indian juggler who hung his ladder on thin air without touching the ground below, sprang upon it, climbed out of sight, pulled the ladder after him, and disappeared in the clouds.

All this ought not to discredit philosophy but teach it a lesson. Men fail to find the secret of the world until God and God's dealing with men are considered. Dr. Ashmore tells of some men on a raft floating down the Mississippi River who stopped for supper one night. However, their float went on and returned after awhile to the same place. They did this several times until they discovered that they were caught in an eddy of vast dimensions and were being swept in a circle back again repeatedly to the starting point. So has philosophy moved in a circle. There are way stations along the route, but it has never been able to escape from the circular movement of human thought. There is one way for philosophy to escape from its situation and find the current on the bosom of the river of thought which will carry it on to its destination. That current is religious experience wherein man's upward soaring thought is met by God's descending revelation and love. When this current of thought is once reached, a new day will dawn for philosophy, and ere long the philosophers will see the gleam on the gates of pearl and the sparkle of the jasper walls of the city of God, whither they would find the way.

Christian experience takes all the abstractions of philosophy and recombines them and gives us the conception of the Fatherhood of God. The one substance of monism comes back as the one person behind the world. The one idea of Hegel comes back as the thought and plan of eternal love. The one energy of those who glorify force and change comes back as the beneficent will of the holy and loving Father. The plan and progress of nature and the moral ongoing of the world come back as the infinite and eternal design of the Holy and Loving. Thus when in our hearts we can say, "Abba, Father," and know what we mean, we hold in our hands the clue to all the philosophies which remain in a state of unstable equilibrium until we find this key. All philosophy is thus summed up as in the words of Dr. Fairbairn: "God is the Father, everlasting in his love. Love was the end for which he made the world, for which he made every human soul. His glory is to diffuse happiness, to fill up the silent places of the universe with voices that speak out of glad hearts. Because he made man for love he cannot bear man to be lost. Rather than see the loss, he will suffer sacrifice. In the place we call hell, love as really is as in the place we call heaven, though in the one place it is the complacency of pleasure in the holy and the happy which seems like the brightness of everlasting sunshine or the glad music of waves that break in perennial laughter; but in the other it is the compassion of pity for the bad and the miserable which seems like a face shaded with everlasting regret or the muffled weeping of a sorrow too deep to be heard. That grand thought of a God who is eternal Father, all the more regal and sovereign that He is absolutely Father, can never fail to touch the heart of the man who understands it, be he savage or sage." Moreover, we may add, it cannot fail to become the one generalization large enough and broad enough to include the data of life, history, science, and philosophy.

II. Unique Claims of Christianity

In the second place, Christian experience sheds light on all the unique claims of Christianity.

Scientific observers concede that religious experience is a witness to the supernatural. They refuse, however, to admit that Christ is the author of it and do not concede the other unique Christian claims. The attempt is to find a common denominator, so to speak, between Christianity and other religions, and show that all are essentially alike and that the distinctive Christian ideas are over-beliefs. But these men have not thought through the problem of Christian experience. In particular they are shy of facing the actual claim of Christ and his relation to it all. However, Christ's place in Christian experience is the supreme matter. All other Christian claims go with this.

Now the spiritually regenerated and morally transformed man proves the deity of Christ and proves his presence in religious experience for the following reasons:

a. First, no man has moral resources to transform himself. The law of moral gravitation in a man's life no more reverses itself suddenly than the law of physical gravitation. You cannot juggle the immoral elements of a sinner's nature into the moral elements of a saint any more than you can combine the acid of an unripe lemon and an unripe apple and unripe grapefruit and get the taste of a caramel.

b. Second, the morally transformed life proves the deity of Christ also because when the sinner turns to Christ he gets the response. Christ invites him and he responds. He calls and Christ answers. He calls to Mohammed and Mohammed does not come; he calls to Confucius and Confusius does not come; he calls to Buddha and Buddha does not come; he calls to Christ and Christ comes. The whole process is as simple as that. In his outward life also a new force begins to work a new design, a new labor working to an end. But especially within is there Another, one with whom there is fellowship, to whom he becomes passionately devoted, whose presence is happiness and whose absence is sorrow, who can sing with full meaning, "How tedious and tasteless the hours, when Jesus no longer I see," etc.

The spiritually regenerated man discovers that intellectual difficulties die in the light of this experience. The mysteries are not all solved. But the difficulties cease to be relevant. Miracles do not trouble him now, because he has a sample of the miracle working power in his own soul. Hume's argument that miracles cannot be true because contrary to experience, is exactly reversed and the Christian says miracles are true because they accord precisely with his experience.

In particular he has moral reinforcement. This is the final test of any religion, what can it do with a bad man? None of them can compete with Christ in this respect. Look at Peter, Saul of Tarsus, Augustine, and John Bunyan, and thousands of others.

A sense of moral power comes with Christian experience. There is not a grace or virtue that Christ cannot and has not produced in human character, not all at the same time or in the same person, but all have been produced.

In this way Christ becomes final for the man, final for his reason, final for his conscience, final for his will, final for his intellect and most of all, final for his faith, his hope and his love, his aspiration.

He now understands why all the creeds of Christendom have Christ as their center. He becomes a judge and critic of other religious systems than the Christian discerning that their unworkableness is due to their lack of Christ. He understands the perennial and remarkable power of the Scriptures over the human heart as Christ's power. Ten thousand other witnesses and confessors around him and a long line of them running back to Christ confirm his experience and thus create a spiritual community the parts of which mutually support each other.

III. CHRISTIAN PRAGMATISM

In the third place, Christian experience transfers the whole problem of Christian evidences to the sphere of practical life.

Now the Christian method throughout is the practical method of answering the question, "What must I do to be saved?" Its answer is in Christian experience. It says to every man, You can test the reality and power of Christ practically. It says to every man, You have a "seeing spot" in your soul which God gives and which will recognize Christ, if you submit to him, just as philosophy tells us we all have a blind spot, and that if focused right we cannot see a black mark on a white card with our eyes open, and the card in front of us. Christianity does not say renounce reason but only waive your speculative difficulties in the interest of your moral welfare.

The Gospel is practical in its methods. The man born blind did not have to accept any theory of Christ, God or the universe, neither monism or idealism, nor any special form of theism. One thing only was required. Says Christ, "Let me anoint your eyes with clay and you go wash in the pool of Siloam." This he did. His faith worked. It grew by exercise. They plied him with questions and he said, "A man named Jesus healed me." Later,

"He was a good man." Later, "He is a prophet." And finally, "he worshipped him." He rose from faith to faith under the guidance and inspiration of Christ and this is the experience of all who put their trust in him.

Index

Arno C. Gaebelein

The Prophet Daniel

A chapter-by-chapter commentary which explains simply the historical events and details of prophecy contained in the Book of Daniel.

ISBN 0-8254-2701-0 218 pp. paper

James M. Gray

Home Bible Study Commentary

(Foreword by William Culbertson.) A unique commentary which provides stimulating expositions of the entire Bible. Each section is followed by helpful comments and pertinent questions to reinforce the material. Not only an excellent work in family devotions and in group Bible studies, but also a valuable source of background material in the preparation of expository messages.

ISBN 0-8254-2727-4 447 pp. paper

G. Campbell Morgan

The Crises of the Christ: The Seven Greatest Events in His Life

(Foreword by Vernon C. Grounds.) A unique examination of Christ's person and work as seen through the seven great events of His life—His incarnation, baptism, temptation, transfiguration, crucifixion, resurrection and ascension. "... The greatest single volume which Morgan has ever produced ... no one volume has ever had as much influence on my thinking as this volume has."— Wilbur M. Smith

ISBN 0-8254-3258-8 352 pp. paper

H. C. G. Moule

"Popular Commentary" Series

One of the greatest expositors of all time, Moule ministered effectively as one of Keswick's most valued and admired speakers. In these commentaries, Dr. Moule provides a doctrinal study of the Christian life in *Studies in Ephesians*, magnifies the message of

Philippians, gives a rewarding in-depth study of practical Christianity in *Studies in Colossians and Philemon*, offers a devotional study of *2 Timothy*, and records thirteen extensive, yet concise topical messages from *Hebrews*. An excellent series for personal or group study!

Studies in Ephesians
ISBN 0-8254-3218-9   176 pp.   kivar

Studies in Philippians
ISBN 0-8254-3216-2   136 pp.   kivar

Studies in Colossians and Philemon
ISBN 0-8254-3217-0   196 pp.   kivar

Studies in Second Timothy
ISBN 0-8254-3219-7   180 pp.   kivar

Studies in Hebrews
ISBN 0-8254-3223-5   120 pp.   kivar

The Epistle to the Romans
A true classic. "One of the finest and most helpful expositions available today. Deeply devotional, based upon a very careful exegesis of the text, and abounding in practical truths." — *The Minister's Library*
ISBN 0-8254-5195-7   437 pp.   hardcover

Colossians and Philemon Studies
Dr. Moule penned this delightful devotional classic in which he carefully integrated the apostle's teaching with the life and spiritual growth of the child of God. Moule's writings represent the cream of evangelical scholarship, and no Bible student should be without his excellent works!
ISBN 0-8254-5196-5   328 pp.   hardcover

James Orr

The Christian View of God and the World
(Foreword by Vernon C. Grounds.) An extensive description and defense of the Theistic world view centering in the incarnation of Jesus Christ. Offers the most critical thinker a reasonable presentation of the perfect plan of a loving and wise Creator.
ISBN 0-8254-3370-3   504 pp.   paper

W. H. Griffith Thomas

Christianity Is Christ

(Introduction by Charles C. Ryrie.) Thomas, a co-founder of Dallas Theological Seminary, asks the question in this book, "What makes Christianity unique?" This careful study on the person and work of Jesus Christ demonstrates that Christ is the focus of the Christian faith— historically, theologically, and personally.

ISBN 0-8254-5323-2   169 pp.   paper

Genesis: A Devotional Commentary

A pictorial panorama of God's dealings with the human race from creation to the death of Joseph. Here we have the foundation, explanation, and preface, as well as the key to the rest of the Word of God.

ISBN 0-8254-3817-9   507 pp.   paper

The Pentateuch: Chapter by Chapter

A valuable collection of notes on the first five books of the Bible. Each section begins with a helpful introduction followed by a chapter-by-chapter study of the text. A special section on how to approach the study of the Bible will provide additional insight.

ISBN 0-8254-3833-0   192 pp.   paper

Outline Studies in Matthew

(Foreword by Donald R. Campbell and Introduction by Warren W. Wiersbe.) Sixty outline studies with practical applications on the truths of Matthew's Gospel. The outlines also refer to related passages elsewhere in the Bible and are useful for pastors, teachers, and all general readers.

ISBN 0-8254-3831-4   476 pp.   paper

Outline Studies in Luke

(Foreword by J.I. Packer and Introduction by Warren W. Wiersbe.) A collection of sermon outlines developed from the author's devotional life which originally appeared as addresses or articles as the occasion arose. A section-by-section outline, particularly geared at drawing out the central concepts of Luke's Gospel.

ISBN 0-8254-3821-7   406 pp.   paper

The Apostle John: His Life and Writings

(Foreword by Arthur L. Farstad and Introduction by Warren W. Wiersbe.) Written especially to help those "who are called to preach and teach," Griffith Thomas' material is presented in systematic, organized fashion. Rich with homiletical outlines.

ISBN 0-8254-3822-5   376 pp.   paper

Studies in Colossians and Philemon

Recognized as a Bible teacher perhaps without peer, W. H. Griffith Thomas excelled in spiritual depth, practicality, and simplicity of expression that make the most profound truths come alive with excitement. "One of the best expositions available, not only for the advanced student, but also for the average believer who wants to gain a working knowledge of this important Epistle." —Warren W. Wiersbe

ISBN 0-8254-3834-9   192 pp.   paper

The Apostle Peter: His Life and Writings

(Foreword by John F. Walvoord and Introduction by Warren W. Wiersbe.) The author's main purpose was "to offer Christians help and guidance in their personal meditation on the Scriptures. . . ." Anyone who will trace these outlines through Scripture will develop deep insights and new applications for preaching or teaching.

ISBN 0-8254-3823-3   304 pp.   paper

The Holy Spirit

This extensive work has gained the respect of many for its survey of the works on the Spirit, its historical interpretation, theological formulation, and modern application. A classic work which is the basis for much of the newer writing on the Holy Spirit. Offers greater understanding of this key doctrine for the encouragement of believers today.

ISBN 0-8254-3835-7   304 pp.   paper

Sermon Outlines on Christian Living

Thirty-seven clear, concise outlines which provide the backbone for great expository messages on the Christian life. These biblical studies are easy-to-use, yet very complete. A great collection from one of the greatest Bible teachers, this volume is sure to be an indispensible friend in the great work of sermon preparation.

ISBN 0-8254-3830-6   128 pp.   paper